AF425097

DANIEL

THE PROPHET.

NINE LECTURES,

DELIVERED IN

THE DIVINITY SCHOOL

OF

THE UNIVERSITY OF OXFORD,

WITH COPIOUS NOTES.

BY THE

REV. E. B. PUSEY, D.D.

REGIUS PROFESSOR OF HEBREW, AND CANON OF CHRIST CHURCH.

SECOND THOUSAND.

SOLD BY

JOHN HENRY AND JAMES PARKER, OXFORD,

AND 337, STRAND, LONDON;

RIVINGTONS, WATERLOO PLACE, LONDON,

AND 41, HIGH STREET, OXFORD.

1864.

PLYMOUTH:

PRINTED AT THE PRINTING-PRESS OF THE DEVONPORT SOCIETY.

1864.

PREFACE.

The following lectures were planned, as my contribution against that tide of scepticism, which the publication of the " Essays and Reviews " let loose upon
the young and uninstructed. Not that those Essays
contained anything formidable in themselves. Human inventiveness in things spiritual or unspiritual
is very limited. It would be difficult probably to invent a new heresy. Objectors of old were as acute
or more acute than those now ; so that the ground was
well-nigh exhausted. The unbelieving school of
Geologians had done their worst. Chronology had
been pressed to the utmost long ago. The differences
of human form and of language lay on the surface.
The Jews had tried what pseudo-criticism could do
against the prophecies as to our Lord and His Church.
German rationalism had been deterred from no theory
in regard to Holy Scripture, either by its untenableness or its irreverence. The Essays contained nothing
to which the older of us had not been inured for some
forty years. Their writers asserted little distinctly,
attempted to prove less, but threw doubts on every
thing. They took for granted that the ancient faith
had been overthrown ; and their Essays were mostly
a long trumpet-note of victories, won (they assumed,)
without any cost to *them*, over the faith in Germany.
They ignored the fact, that every deeper tendency of

thought or each more solid learning had, at least, done away with something shallow, something more adverse to faith. They practically ignored all criticism which was not subservient to unbelief. Yet the Essayists, Clergymen (with one exception), staked their characters, although not their positions, on the issue, that the old faith was no longer tenable; that it was dead and buried and the stone on the grave's mouth fast sealed. Their teaching was said to be "bold." Too "bold" alas! it was towards Almighty God; but, from whatever cause, its authors shrank, for the most part, from stating explicitly as their own, the unbelief which they suggested to others. They undermined men's faith, without denying it themselves in such definite terms as would materially risk their offices or positions. This, however escaped notice; and the shock was given, not by the things which were said, (for the same had been said more clearly in publications avowedly infidel,) but that the faith was attacked by those, who, from their position, were expected to be its defenders. Regarded as, (what the Essays were, after a time, understood to be,) a challenge to the Church of England to admit their misbelief as allowable denial of truth, it has not befallen me to read another book so cowardly. Had the writers ventured, in plain terms*, to deny half the truths, as

***

* "First then to ascertain the real meaning of the passages extracted, and I must say that this is no easy task. *If the author had studied to express his sentiments with ambiguity, I doubt if he could have been more successful.*" Dr. Lushington on Dr. Williams, Judgment, p. 18. "I turn to Mr. Wilson's own words. It is indeed to be regretted that Mr. Wilson in his Essay has *frequently* expressed himself in language so ambiguous as to admit of opposite constructions." Dr. Lushington, Ib. p. 33. "This sentence is

to the Bible or the Faith, which they suggested to

open to diverse interpretations, and some of its terms are self-contradictory." Ib. p. 34. "Mr. W's use of these contradictory terms, 'supernaturally communicated speculation,' together with his imputing blame to those of the Clergy who would base the Church of Christ, as a society, upon the possession of this 'supernaturally communicated speculation,' rather than upon 'the manifestation of the divine life in man' might leave upon some readers the impression that Mr. W. *doubted whether the Holy Scriptures had been supernaturally communicated,* and that he doubted whether the doctrines, as distinguished from the moral teaching of Chrsitianity, were the necessary basis of the Church. Without saying this impression of this passage is false, I cannot say that is *necessarily* the true, especially considering this is a criminal case.—*As a criminal charge,* this Article cannot be supported." p. 34, 5. "The drift of all the reasoning contained in these passages is to prove that subscription to the xxxix Articles does not impose on the Clergy *the obligation of honestly believing them* to be true and binding on their consciences." Ib. 38.

"What is meant by *'passing by* the side of the first five Articles, and 'as to the humanifying of the Divine word and the Divine personalities, without directly contradicting impugning or refusing assent to them?' The Clergy are bound by the King's declaration to take the Articles in their literal and grammatical sense; the first five Articles are the most important of all. Is it consistent with their literal and grammatical sense to 'pass by' them? I think not. Is it consistent with the declaration that 'they are agreeable to the Word of God?' If so, why pass by? Is it consistent with the declaration 'I do willingly and ex animo subscribe, &c?' I think not. And yet, according to Mr. W., the clerk is to 'pass by' these articles ' without *directly* contradicting, impugning or refusing assent to them.' In my opinion, this is not possible. I think that the substance of what Mr. W. has written is this; to suggest modes, by which the Articles subscribed may be evaded, contrary to the King's declaration and the terms of subscription." Ib. p. 39, 40. Of the other writers, the Rev. Prof. Powell was soon removed from human judgment to the Judgment-seat of God. Mr. Pattison contented himself with shewing the weakness of Evidence-writers of the last century, without hinting on what grounds men's faith in

others to deny, they would have aroused the indignation of the whole believing people of England against them, that they denied such truths and remained ministers of the Church of England.

Others, who wrote in defence of the faith, engaged in larger subjects; I took, for my province, one more confined but definite issue. I selected the book of Daniel, because unbelieving critics considered their attacks upon it to be one of their greatest triumphs. The exposure of the weakness of some ill-alleged point of evidence has often thrown suspicion on a whole faith. The exposure of the weakness of criticism, where it thought itself most triumphant, would, I hoped, shake the confidence of the young in their would-be misleaders. True! Disbelief of Daniel had become an axiom in the unbelieving critical school[b]. Only, they mistook the result of unbelief for the victory of criticism. They overlooked the historical fact that the disbelief had been antecedent to the criticism. Disbelief had been the parent, not the offspring of their criticism; their starting-point, not the winning-post of their course.

In other books of Holy Scripture, disbelief could

Jesus and His Gospel rests. He did not mention doctrine, except to say that the command to destroy the Canaanites and the eternity of future punishment are "questioned," (he does not say "denied,") by "natural conscience." Continued study of Professor Jowett's Essay makes one think sadly, "What does there remain of Christianity, which the writer can believe?"

[b] "Auberlen indeed defends [Daniel] but says, 'Die Unächtheit Daniel's ist in der modernen Theologie zum Axiom geworden.'" Dr. Williams in Essays, p. 76. "It is one of the highest triumphs and most saving facts of the more recent criticism, to have proved that the book of Daniel belongs to the time of Antiochus Epiphanes." A well known writer, now dead.

and did sever what, if true, (as it is,) was necessarily Divine, from what admitted of being represented as human. Rejecting what, if they accepted, they must own to be from God, they assigned to man the humanised residuum. They laid down, to their own satisfaction, that the miracles, related in any historical book of Holy Scripture, were magnified representations of the real truth[c], or that insulated prophecies were inserted after the event[d]; or that a long-lived

[c] e. g. Davidson, Introd. "The narratives of the Pentateuch are usually trustworthy, though partly mythical and legendary. The miracles recorded were the exaggerations of a later age." i. 131. "It is only neccessary to examine the history as it lies before us, to find in it a mythological, traditional, and exaggerated element, forbidding the literal acceptation of the whole.—The ten miraculous plagues, which spared the Israelites, while they fell upon the Egyptians—the crowd of extraordinary interpositions of Jehovah in behalf of the people as they journeyed through the wilderness, shew the influence of later traditions on the narrative, in dressing it out with fabulous traits. *The laws of nature are unchangeable.* God does not *directly* and *suddenly* interfere with them on behalf of his creatures; neither does he so palpably or constantly intermeddle with men's little concerns." Ib. 103. "The Almighty does not violently interfere with the eternal laws of nature which he established at first." Ib. 221. "In regard to the miraculous element connected with these plagues, it appears that the national traditions account for all that appears as miraculous. We resolve what is miraculous in the plagues into a traditional element," &c. Ib. 225. "The narrative of the passage of the Red Sea must not be viewed as literal history. Later traditions exaggerated the event, surrounding it with wonder, &c." Ib. p. 430. "The traditional and mythical (in the passage of the Jordan) are perceptible. A miracle is made out of a natural event." add p. 470, 1. ii. 41, 2. 450. iii. 32. 279, 80. 347.

[d] "It [Jacob's prophecy] has the form of a prediction; but it is a *vaticinium post eventum*." (Dav. i. 198.) i. e. a falsehood, professing to be "a prophecy," but written "after the event." So i. 338, of Balaam's prophecy; i. 428, of the prophecy of the judg-

prophet lived to recast his prophecies, and gave to his prophecies of nearer events a definiteness which, (they stated as confidently as if they had lived and had heard them,) they had not when he uttered them[e], or, if the events prophesied were too remote to be so accounted for, that the prediction must have been given close upon the events, when human sagacity could, (they held,) foresee them[f], and then, without prejudice to their unbelief, they could afford to admire what they claimed to be man's own. The old prophets, (they tacitly assumed,) were inferior to themselves; still, for their own times, they were, "[g] amid frailty and national contractedness," above their age.

The book of Daniel admitted of no such compromises. Its historical portions are no history; for the people, as such, had, in the period of their Captivity, no history. The period was like one of those in the book of Judges, whether of oppression or of rest, in which their whole condition exemplified God's Providence and dealings with them, and no marked change occurred. Jeremiah had bidden them, in God's name, live as peaceable denizens in the land of their captivity. "[h] Build ye houses, and dwell; and plant gardens and eat the fruit of them; take ye wives, and beget sons and daughters; and take wives for your sons

ment on the rebuilder of Jericho; ii. 452, of predictions in the Judges; ii. 450, of others in Samuel; iii. 32, of those of Isaiah as to Sennacherib and Hezekiah; iii. 99, 100, as to some of Jeremiah.

[e] Davids. iii. 146, 7. and 150, of Ezekiel.

[f] Dav. i. 383, of the predictions in Deuteronomy; iii. 15, of Is. xxi; iii. 19, of Is. xxiii; iii. 98, of Jeremiah's prophecy of the 70 years' captivity of Judah.

[g] Dav. ii. 456. Comp. Dr. Stanley, as quoted below, p. 257.

[h] Jer. xxix. 5-7.

and give your daughters to husbands, that they may
bear sons and daughters; that ye may be increased
there and not diminished. And seek the peace of the
city whither I have caused you to be carried away
captives, and pray unto the Lord for it; for in the
peace thereof ye shall have peace." Their habits in
their subsequent dispersions make it, in itself, probable, that they followed the advice. The Psalms of
the captivity describe them as waiting for God. But
a dissolved people, individuals scattered amid an overwhelming population, with no unity save that of their
faith, has no history, unless it rebel. For history is
of changes. These had no power to change. The
history then in Daniel relates not to his people; nor
was it Daniel's office to record the history of his own
administration in the position to which, for the protection of his people, he had been raised. The book
of Daniel then has nothing of the nature of secular
history; it records only certain events whereby God
acted upon the Heathen Monarchs in whose keeping
His people, the depositories of His revelation to man,
for the time were. And these events were mostly supernatural. The prophecies also are one connected
whole; they admit of no dislocation; they speak definitely of a long period far beyond Daniel's time.
To the nearer future there was nothing to add. The
restoration from the captivity, the date of that restoration, the name of the conqueror who was to grant
it, had been foretold already. In this respect, there
was nothing left but to await the flowing-by of the
seventy years[i]. The temporal prophecies in Daniel
join on with those of Isaiah and Jeremiah.

[i] Davidson says, "Deliverance from Babylon is not predicted.

The former prophets had predicted the destruction of Babylon by the Medes and Persians, and the restoration of Israel. The visions in Daniel shew the succession of world-empires, beginning with the description of the Babylonian world-empire and its displacement by the Medo-Persian. Thenceforward, there is no break. They are outlines, shaded here and there, and at times more strongly, which embrace the whole space from Nebuchadnezzar to (as every one admits) Antiochus Epiphanes. Many a cleft is purposely left out of the picture; as the years of Nebuchadnezzar's worthless successors; or the century and a half of the miserable kings of Persia from the gathering of the storm against Greece by Xerxes until it rolled back under Alexander; or lesser intervals in the yet later period. Whatever details are given, the prophecies are neither chronology nor history. But since there *is* prophecy from the time of the Babylonian empire, there is no date between that empire and the reign of Antiochus Epiphanes, where men could place the writer. For, by placing him at any intervening point,

That event, which might be considered of greatest importance in the eye of a Hebrew seer living in Babylon whither he had been carried captive, is unnoticed." (iii. 174.) The prophets, who foretold the judgment of the Captivity, were also themselves consoled by the prediction of the close of that judgment, (e. g. Ezek. xi. 13-20.) or God foretold by them that close, as He ever, in this life, mitigates judgment by hope. Davidson assumes the spuriousness of Jeremiah's prophecy of the restoration after the 70 years, the later date of prophecies of Isaiah which predict the destruction of Babylon and the restoration of Judah from it, and then, since, *on those and the like assumptions*, that deliverance would not have been prophesied before, and would have been predicted *then*, he argues that Daniel too, had he lived then, must *also* have prophesied those same events, had he prophesied at all.

they would have invented to themselves a prophet, who should speak of things past as if he were prophesying them, and yet prophesy, with equal distinctness, those yet to come; half-forger, half-prophet. Men had then no choice between believing all and disbelieving all, compressing into the time before Antiochus Epiphanes, as best they could, whatever they could not evaporate into a mere ideal, and, as in the ancient fable, laying the amputated and disjointed limbs of the old prophet, piece by piece, into the cauldron whence was to issue the renovated form of the Daniel of the 19th century.

One prophecy only, which fills up outlines of the earlier prophecy, stops with the Old Testament Anti-Christ, Antiochus Epiphanes; the others exhibit in the distant vista, the final establishment of the Gospel, the second Coming of Christ, the Resurrection. There being then no choice but to believe all or disbelieve all, a school to whom it was a postulate, that Almighty God did not reveal Himself to His creatures except through their human reason, and that He did not interfere in His own creation, must make its choice to disbelieve all.

This being the real root of the objections to the book of Daniel, I felt that any answer, which should only consider critical or historical objections, must fail of its end, because these are mere outworks, thrown up to keep men off from the real issue, as to prophecy or miracle. I therefore set myself primarily to shew, 1) that let men place the book where they would, there is in it definite unmistakeable prophecy; 2) that such definite prophecy as the minuter prophecies in Daniel, the foreground of more distant and larger prophecy, is in harmony with the whole system of prophecy, as well in the Old Testament as in the prophecies of our Lord. In the notes, I have set myself to answer, more in detail than an oral lecture admitted, the criticisms, which have been raised as pleas for an unbelief which was antecedent to criticism. This I did, in order to meet the pseudo-criticism on its own grounds, for the sake of those who *would* see; well knowing that the grace of God alone could touch those who now *wish* not to see. I have also, here and there, pointed out how the pseudo-critical argument recoils.

In the sketch of the gradual gathering of the Canon, my argument was concerned with its close, not with its beginning. For the main point, in which its history bore on the book of Daniel, is, that it was closed before the date, where unbelievers place, and must place, their pseudo-Daniel. Since the wildest criticism now places but very few of the older books later than the Captivity, the different theories, devised to remove them from the date when they were written, affected not *this* argument. But I have pointed out tokens of a gradual formation of the Canon[k], because the rationalist school assumes as a convenient starting-point, that the books of Holy Scripture were first collected into one whole after the captivity. In regard to its close, I have entered into the grounds alleged to bring

---

[k] The genuineness of the Pentateuch occupies two 8vo. volumes of Hengstenberg. Obviously, the argument could not be condensed. Forty years of study have only shewn me the more, both from language and the subsequent books of the Old Testament, the evidence of its genuineness, which I already believed on the authority of our Lord. In examining for my class the first volume of Dr. Colenso, I could only be amazed that any mind could be shaken by such arguments. Faith, of course, could not.

down the date of Ecclesiastes, Ezra, Nehemiah, and
the Chronicles, both in disproof of the later closing of
the Canon, and in illustration of the sort of criticism,
which is used to prop up foregone conclusions.

But nothing is gained by a mere answer to objections, so long as the original prejudice, "there cannot
be supernatural prophecy," remains. Be the objections ever so completely removed, unbelief remains
unshaken, because these objections are put forward to
delude others, scarcely to blind itself; for they who
believe not, know well that the ground of their unbelief rests on their conceptions of God and of His relation to man, not on history. And therefore, while I
have conscientiously read every thing which has been
written against the book of Daniel[1], and have met

---

[1] The 3rd part of Dr. Davidson's Introduction to the O.T., which
contains what he has written against the book of Daniel, had not
appeared, until the four first lectures were printed. But his work
is only a reproduction of the rationalist German works which he
either epitomises or translates. I have not met with any new
argument or even an old argument more forcibly put in it. The
Hebrew criticisms are transferred from the German writers, sometimes in a way which implies ignorance of the elements of Hebrew.
Thus, Stähelin (Einl. §. 36.) alleged in proof of the lateness of the
books of Kings, "the aramaising suffixes 2 Kgs. iv. 2, 3, 7." Dr.
Davidson (ii. p. 37,) gives this, "לְכִי for לָךְ 2 Kgs. iv. 2. לָךְ for לָךְ
2 Kgs. iv. 7." The first, "לְכִי for לָךְ" may mean; "לְכִי is for לָךְ which
the Masorethes pointed לָךְ, but which they ought to have pointed
לָךְ, although לָךְ not לָךְ is their uniform punctuation." But in 2 Kgs.
iv. 7. Dr. D. overlooked נָשַׁיכִי, בָּנַיכִי, which Stähelin meant, although
they are marked by the Kri, and lighted upon לְכִי, the regular feminine Imperative, "go," which he supposed ought to be לָךְ, although לָךְ, as being masculine, would have been a "false concord." Again, Stähelin had said of the title of Proverbs xxxi.
דִּבְרֵי לְמוּאֵל מֶלֶךְ מַשָּׂא אֲשֶׁר יִסְּרַתּוּ אִמּוֹ, "The words of king Lemuel; the utterance which his mother taught him," "Hitzig and Bertheau

every argument in those writings, my own conviction is, that the point really at issue remains, when they are answered. For the real objection is, that God should reveal Himself to His creature man, in any other way than by the operation of man's natural reason, or that He should tell man any thing, "beyond the grasp of eye or hand."

It is mere dust in people's eyes, that some speak of the present conflict, as a question of reconciling phy-

maintain, that מלך cannot thus, without the Article, be united with Lemuel, that therefore it must stand in the stat. constr. with משא 'king of Massa.'" p. 414. Dr. Davidson (ii. 338.) says, "The word Massa is not a proper name, because למואל מלך משא 'Lemuel king of Massa,' is *not* Hebrew. To make it good Hebrew, מלך should have the article prefixed." Were there even any such place as 'Massa,' any one knows that what Dr. D. says is *not* Hebrew, is Hebrew; and that what he says would "make it good Hebrew" is not Hebrew. As matter of history, Dr. D. tells us, " It is incorrect to say, as Hengstenberg and many others have done, that the series of opponents to the authenticity of the book of Daniel was opened by Porphyry in the third century. *Porphyry was not the first impugner of Daniel.* Hippolytus, a Roman bishop and orthodox Christian writer, also referred the work to the Maccabæan period and Antiochus Epiphanes, as we know from his explanations of his book, partly Greek and partly Syriac." And for this he refers us to Ewald in the Gött. gel. Anz. 1859. p. 270, 1. St. Hippolytus an "impugner of Daniel!" Ewald says nothing of this; but only alleges a certain amount of agreement of exposition as to the Seleucidæ and Ptolemies. Yet S. Hippolytus believed that the prophecy of the 70 weeks related to Jesus and ended in Him; that the 4th empire was the Roman, that it would last to the end, that Anti-Christ was yet to come. I see not what point of contact there is between his expositions and Porphyry's, save those which are common to Porphyry with all Christians, all but the unbelief that they were " vaticinia post eventum." In Dr. Davidson's " series of opponents to the authenticity of the book of Daniel" there is a cleft, from Porphyry the Heathen to Collins the Deist, of 1400 years.

sical science and theology[m].   Men can hardly be so
wilfully blind as to think it.   The contest runs along

[m] I deeply regret to see that Bp. Tait, in minimising or apologising for the opinion, expressed by the Judicial Committee upon
the inspiration of Holy Scripture, inadvertently aids this delusion.
He says, "It is satisfactory to feel assured that no Clergyman of
the Church of England can be called upon to maintain the unwarranted position that the Bible is an infallible guide *in questions of
physical science*." (Preface to Five Discourses on the Word of God,
p. viii, &c.) The like words are ascribed to him in a speech in
Convocation. "He did not think that the Church was in danger, because the highest Court of Appeal had said, that a Clergyman was not legally liable, because he held that statements with
regard *to physical science* in the Bible were not the inspired Word
of God." The Court of Appeal did not limit their opinion to
"physical science." To imply that it did, would be to deceive
ourselves and others. This was not the issue raised by Dr. Williams or Mr. Wilson. In regard to Dr. Williams they put indeed
a non-natural construction on his words, which no honest man
could accept. The misbelief of Dr. Williams on the inspiration of
Holy Scripture was virtually condemned by the very terms in
which he himself was acquitted, as the heresy of Pelagius was
condemned at the Synod of Diospolis, which reversed the judgment of S. Augustine and the African Synod as to himself. In
regard to Mr. Wilson the issue on the one passage before them was
definite. Mr. Wilson stated, "the word of God is contained in
Scripture, whence it does not follow that it is coextensive with
it." (Essays, p. 176.) The Committee, in their opinion, laid down,
as Bp. Tait quotes them, that "it is not a contradiction to the law
of the Church—to affirm that *any part of the Canonical Scriptures*
of the Old and New Testaments, *however unconnected with religious faith or moral duties*, was not written under the inspiration of the Holy Spirit." It justified Mr. Wilson's statement in a
way condemned by the two Primates. (The ABp. of Canterbury's Pastoral, p. 10, 11. ABp. of York's Pastoral, p. 10-13.)
But there is nothing to limit the Committee's opinion to "physical science." Probably it would cover any denial of the historical truth of any history in Holy Scripture, as when Mr. Wilson,
(although the passages were not before the Court,) denied "the

the whole range of God's Revelation and of man's thought. What should be one universal harmony jars with one discord of rebellion. The fact of God's Revelation, and the tokens which He gives of His revealing Himself; His Being in Himself, and the mode of His Being, His Character, His Attributes, His relation to us His creatures, His rights over us, His care and Providence towards us, what it is befitting for Him to Be or to reveal, how He shall reveal what He does reveal, what condescension towards us we shall allow Him to use, in consideration of His high Epicurean dignity, what aweful Justice we may admit Him to possess, consistently with our "moral sense" of what His Attributes should be—every thing is alike disputed : only men use courteous language towards Him, as to a dethroned Monarch, Who is to be treated with respect and the semblance of royalty, provided that He transgress not the bounds which His creatures assign to Him. Alas that, while they are laying down the laws upon which it beseems their Maker to act, they forget that He *is* their Maker, that these brave words of their's are but like the speeches in the mouth of a player; that the great reality, now veiled, is at hand; and that

thorough reliableness " of almost all the history in Holy Scripture, to "the time of the divided kingdom," (i. e. nearly half of the Old Testament, Essays, p. 170.) or implied the existence of an " admixture of legendary matter or embellishment in" the Gospels, (Ib. p. 161.) and the want of "exactness" in that of St. John. (Ib.) He spoke of "the dark patches of human passion and error, which," he said, "form a partial crust upon" Holy Scripture. (Ib. p. 177.) People only blind themselves and others, when, with such books or those of Dr. Colenso's before them, they speak of the relation of physical science to Holy Scripture as the leading question of this day.

their God, Who bears so long with our presumptions,
will shew indeed, as He has said, "whose word shall
stand, Mine or their's. [n] "

Physical science is made a battle-field, because it
is the favorite study of the day; the mistake made
about Galileo is a convenient Io Pæan over theologians. Theologians used wrong inferences from Holy
Scripture once; therefore we are to mistrust—what ?—
the inferences of Theologians? No, but the Bible itself. And yet not we, in common life, but scientific
men, use the same language as before Galileo, "the
sun rises, the sun sets," the self-same language as the
Bible uses. The mistake was not in the language
of the Bible, but that men argued from language,
adapted, (as language relating to visible phænomena
must be,) to the phænomena whereof it speaks, as
though it necessarily contained scientific truth. The
claims of geology do not even touch upon theology.
The belief that creation, at least, dated backward for
countless ages, was current in the Church some 1400
years before Geology. "Six thousand years of our
world," says St. Jerome[o], "are not yet fulfilled; and
what eternities, what times, what originals of ages,
must we not think there were before, in which Angels, Thrones, Dominions, and the other Powers served
God, and, apart from the vicissitudes and measures of
times, subsisted, at the command of God!" "Almost
all the teachers of the Church throughout the world,"
says a later Greek writer [p], " teach that the whole spiritual and angelic being existed before this world out

[n] Jer. xliv. 28.   [o] in Tit. c. i. quoted by Petav. de Angel.
i. 15. Opp. iii. 38.   [p] Græc. Script. MS. ib. n. 22. See S. Basil
in Hexaem. Hom. i. S. Greg. Naz., S. Chrys. and others. ibid.

of nothing." Holy Scripture expressly speaks of the stellar system, as existing before the foundation of the earth. "[q] Where wast thou, when I founded the earth? declare, if thou knowest understanding. Who laid the measures thereof, for thou knowest! or Who stretched out the line upon it? Whereon are the foundations thereof sunken? or who laid the corner-stone thereof? When all the morning stars jubilated together, and all the sons of God shouted for joy?" And this agrees with the remarkable parenthetic mention of "the stars" in Genesis, when, in the detailed account of the creation of the sun and moon and of their offices for our earth, there are appended the simple words, "and the stars," as though it was intended only to guard against the error, that they might otherwise be thought to be uncreated. Then, there is nothing to connect the time spoken of in Gen. i. 2. with that of the first great declaration of the creation of all things *in the beginning*. "In the beginning God created the heaven and the earth." Rather, of the forms of speech, which could have been chosen, to express past time, *that* has been chosen, which least connects the state, when the earth was one vast waste, with the time when God created it. Both were in past time; but there is nothing to connect those times together[r]. First, we have, as far back as thought can

[q] Job xxxviii. 4-7.

[r] The substantive verb not being used in Hebrew as a mere copula, had Moses intended to say that the earth was " waste and desolate " when God created it, the idiom for this would have been וְהָאָרֶץ תֹהוּ וָבֹהוּ, (omitting the verb,) just as there actually follows, וְחֹשֶׁךְ עַל פְּנֵי תְהוֹם, "and darkness on the face of the deep." The insertion of the past verb, הָיְתָה, has no force at all, unless it be used to express what was the condition of the earth in a past time, pre-

reach, creation, *in the beginning*, of all those heavens of heavens through those all-but-boundless realms of space, and of our earth. Then, detached from this, a past condition of the earth,—how far separated from it, is not said,—but not a condition in which God, Who made all things very good, ever made any thing[e].

vious to the rest of the narrative, but in no connection at all with what preceded. Such connection in Hebrew might have been expressed by וַיְהִי הָאָרֶץ, "and the earth became" or "was," &c. or by the omission of the verb. Moses was directed to choose just that idiom, which expresses a past time, anterior to what follows, but in no connection of time whatever with what precedes. Yet, on the other hand the "and," by which v. 2. is united with v. 1, shews that v. 1. does not stand as a mere summary of what follows. The revelation, "In the beginning God created the heaven and the earth," declares a fact by itself. To this is added that other fact, "*And* the earth *was* (in the past, but at some unexplained time) "void and waste." The explanations, given to get rid of this simple statement, illustrate its force. 1) The statement that v. 2. is a mere summary, is precluded by the "and." 2) The explanation "In the beginning, when God created the heaven and the earth, the earth was, &c." besides being unnaturally artificial, is ungrammatical. It must have been וַיְהִי הָאָרֶץ. 3) That of Ewald from Rashi, "In the beginning, when God created the heaven and the earth, (and the earth was then a chaos,) God said, Let there be light," is yet more unnaturally artificial, and has the simple sense of mankind against it. So would no Hebrew have written; so could no reader understand it, except he wished it. Human will can persuade itself of any thing.

[e] The words *tohoo va-bohoo*, (obviously forming one idea, from the alliteration,) are, in the two other places in Holy Scripture where they occur together, used of desolation. Jeremiah (lv. 23.) predicts a future desolation, in pointed reference to the former condition of the earth. The sentence, "I saw the *earth* and lo, *tohoo va-bohoo*," is as near being a quotation of Gen. i. 2, "And *the earth* was *tohoo va-bohoo*," as any words could be, which did not preserve the precise grammatical structure. The addition, "*and to the heavens, and their light was not*," exhibits the heavens as they were when the earth was *tohoo va-bohoo*, and before the light was creat-

What follows *is* connected with this state.   First, we have a contemporary condition, (as it is expressed in Hebrew,) "and darkness upon the face of the deep;" then a contemporaneous action, of more or less duration, "and the Spirit of God brood*ing* upon the face of the waters;" then successive action, (as this too is expressed in Hebrew,) "And God said;" which is continued on through the rest of the history of the Creation.   It seems then that God has told us, in the two first sentences, just what concerned us to know, first, that He created all which is; then, how He brought into order this our habitation which He has given us.   What intervened between that creation "in the beginning" and that re-modelling for our habitation, does not concern us; and on this God is silent.   He tells us the first and the last, that He created all things, and that He prepared this our beautiful earth for us, and created all things in it and ourselves.   In the interval there is room for all the workings of God, which Geology speaks of, if it speaks truly.   The history of the Creation in Genesis falls in naturally with it, in that it *does* say that this our mysterious habitation, which God has made the scene of such wondrous love, was created "in the beginning," i. e. before the time of which it proceeds to speak.   Another period of undefined duration is implied by the words, "And the Spirit of God was brood*ing* upon the face of the deep."   For action, of course, implies time, in which the action takes place.   And this action was previous

ed, on the first day. Isaiah xxxiii. 11, " He shall stretch out over it the line of *tohoo* and the stones of *bohoo*," i. e. He shall, as it were, measure it out, not to be built by line but to be destroyed, also relates to an utter desolation of what had once been beautiful. .

to that of the first "day" of the creation, which begins, like the rest, with the words, "And God said."

Geology, then, may pursue its course, with belief, not unbelief, for its condition; only let it not be credulous, (as the way has too often been,) of any thing which tends to unbelief, eager to find grounds to disbelieve Scripture, averse only to believe it[t].

In like way, as to the flood. Scripture is in harmony, when it speaks of the water having, before God created man on the earth, covered the whole earth, and of its having again covered it at the flood. The assumption of a *partial* deluge, in any sense which would not contradict Scripture, would meet no

[t] "Between the first and second, and between the second and third, verses of the Biblical history of the creation, revelation leaves two great white pages, on which human science may write what it will, in order to fill up the blanks of natural history, which revelation omitted itself to supply, as not being its office.

"Of each of these 'cartes blanches' revelation has only given a superscription, a summary table of contents. The first runs, ' In the beginning God created the heaven and the earth.' How this was, how long it lasted, what followed thereon, what evolutions and revolutions took place, down to that state of things which v. 2. describes, it says nothing. Let human science fill up the void, if it can.

"The 2nd 'carte blanche' has the summary inscription, 'the earth was void and waste, and the Spirit of God was brooding on the face of the waters.' What influences the Spirit of God, Which brooded over the waters, had upon them, what operations and formations It called forth in them, revelation says not.—

"Revelation has, in the superscription of the two 'cartes blanches,' laid an ever-firm and immoveable foundation, which leaves none for Atheism or Pantheism. Experience, combination, and speculation, investigation, and philosophy of nature or of religion, and Theology may try to build further on this foundation. But no other foundation shall any one lay than that which is here laid." Kurtz, Bibel u. Astronomie, 1853. p. 433.

difficulty of science. A flood, which would cover Mount Ararat, would cover the globe. This objection is mere anthropomorphism, as if any miracle were "hard" for God. The difficulty as to the animals found, each in their several habitats, in Australia, New Zealand, &c, is properly no *scientific* difficulty. It lies on the surface. But it presupposes, that the "rest" of God, spoken of in Genesis, implies that He created nothing afterwards; which is contrary to our Lord's words, "My Father worketh hitherto and I work," and to the fact that He is daily and hourly creating those myriads of human souls which He infuses into the bodies prepared by His Providence. Science has, on the other hand, to account for the fact, that the known population of the world is much what it would be, according to recognised rules of the increase of our race, dating from the received Chronology of Noah, and starting with six persons [u].

[u] See a remarkable article by Moigno in Les mondes, 1863. T. i. p. 516, 17. (Prof. Price kindly pointed it out to me.) It includes a calculation by "Mr Faå de Bruns, one of the most distinguished scholars of Cauchy, now Professor at Turin," that, starting from the received Chronology of the Flood " B.C. 2348, and taking as the annual increase $\frac{1}{227}$, a number not far from that which represents the annual increase of the population of France, you would light on the net number of the population of the earth 1400,000,000.

Europe	275,000,000.
Asia	755,000,000.
Africa	200,000,000.
America	60,000,000.
Australasia	3,000,000.

1293,000,000."

M. Faå de Bruns has included Noah alone with his 3 sons and their wives, which is obviously wrong, according to the Bible and the multiplication of the human race; but at the close of 4200, (the

Rough as such calculations must needs be, they wholly exclude the fabulous unbroken antiquity which some claim for the human race.

In this thickening strife with unbelief, it is of much moment for the Church and for individuals, that we do not allow unbelievers to choose for us our battle-fields. Rationalism, in its assaults, ever chooses what is obscure, avoids what is clear; it chooses what is minute, it avoids what is comprehensive; it chooses what is negative, it avoids what is positive; it chooses what is at a distance from the centre of the faith, it avoids the central truth, or would fain hide it in the cloud of dust raised in the subordinate controversy. " Most," said Claudius [v] of the German paraphrasts of St. John's Gospel in the 18th century, "frizzle at the evening cloud which floats over the surface of the full moon; but the full moon behind is left in its still repose." Science, at one time, ridiculed the history of the Creation, because Moses spoke of light as existing independently of and before the sun. Science now owns that Moses was right in distinguishing light from the luminary [w]. Yet, untaught by experience, men still press inferences from a science, not as yet a century old, against that same history, forgetful or ignorant, that that same chapter which they impugn, first of Holy Writ declared that truth, which Heathen philosophy never dreamed of, against which it struggled and still struggles, but which the hun-

number of the years from the Flood) the increase is so rapid that the substitution of the real number, 6, does not make a difference (Prof. Price tells me) of more than thirty five years and 25 days.

[v] See Claudius' Wercke (1774,) T. i. p. 9. " Paraphrases Evangelii Johannis," &c.　　　　[w] אוֹר Gen. i. 3-5. מָאוֹר Ib. 14-16.

dreds of millions of Christians and of the heresy of
Mohammed, and they themselves mostly, acknowledge,—absolute creation at the will of God. Heathenism conceived only of an eternity of matter developing
into life, or of a deity, in its weary loneliness, evolv-
ing worlds out of itself and embodying itself in them,
in order to be no longer alone, itself not the author
of life, but the life itself, such as it exists, insensate,
irrational, or sinning, in the various gradations of existence in the world.   The cosmogonies of the ancients
were pantheistic, atheistic, or, at best, developement
of præexistent matter.   Over against all these, Moses enunciated, as simple, undemonstrated truth, "In
the beginning God created the heaven and the earth."
Men ask us to account for those thousands of years,
which Geology claims, as if our faith were to depend
upon *our* knowing the answer.   Faith asks them in
return, how they account for the fact, that, through
Moses, that truth of the creation was made known,
which human reason cannot explain, which even now
it relegates as far back as it can, in order to prevent
the dread reality of its Personal Creator from pressing
so closely upon it, while yet it is constrained to acknowledge the fact of the Creation.   God speaks still
through His words, "In the beginning God created
the heaven and the earth," and the soul, which lis-
tens, is sure that the truth spoken so simply, so surely, so unmistakeably, so alone, so different from all
speculations of philosophy, is from Him.   In the
possession of that truth, which God first taught the
world through Moses, faith, yea, and God-enlightened
reason too, is sure that there is some solution for the
claims of Geology, be they what they may.

This has been, for some thirty years, a deep conviction of my soul, that no book can be written in behalf of the Bible like the Bible itself. Man's defences are man's word; they may help to beat off attacks, they may draw out some portion of its meaning. The Bible is God's Word, and through it God the Holy Ghost, Who spake it, speaks to the soul which closes not itself against it.

But if defences are weak, except as far as God enables us to build them, or Himself "builds the house" through man, defences, not built as He would have them, will not only fall, but will crush those who trust them. The faith can receive no real injury except from its defenders. Against its assailants, those who wish to be safe, God protects. If the faith shall be (God forbid!) destroyed in England, it will be not by open assailants, (such as the writers in the Westminster Review, &c.) but by those who think that they defend it, while they have themselves lost it. So it was in Germany. Rationalism was the product, not of the attacks on the Gospel but of its weak defenders. Each generation, in its controversies with unbelief, conceded more of the faith, until at last it was difficult to see what difference there was between assailants and defenders ᵂ. Theology

---

ᵂ I stated this in my "Collegiate and Professorial teaching," p. 53 sqq. and explained some things which, at 27, I purposely left unexplained in my early book on Germany. Many things in it were crudely said; I was also over-sanguine about the restoration of faith, then beginning in Germany. But my sympathies were solely with that revival of faith; my strictures were solely directed against the "human system" built up in Lutheranism. Nothing which I wrote had any bearing on the English Articles, whose positive teaching I ever valued, or any part of the Catholic faith, in

was one great grave-yard; and men were disputing over a corpse, as if it had life. The salt had "lost its savour." The life was fled.

A writer[x], who seems to think exclusive adherence which, (as I acquainted myself with Rationalism as a duty,) God ever, in His goodness, preserved me, without any temptation to part with any of it. I say this, because some are fond of quoting an early work of mine, the remaining copies of which I withdrew some 30 years ago.

[x] It seems to be almost a principle with Dean Stanley, to hold *that* to be uncertain which is assailed. Conviction, amid contradictions of truth, seems to him undue dogmatism. His mind has been remarkably characterised, as one which, "having a poetical faculty of seeing resemblances, lacks the philosophical power of seeing differences." In his lectures on the Jewish Church, worthless heathen or Jewish tradition (some of it entitled Mohammedan, as drawn by Mohammed from his apostate Jewish teacher,) is mixed up with Scripture truth, wherever it adds a poetic feature to the history. But the impression is given, that most is alike tradition; of which some being patently absurd and untrue, an atmosphere of haze is thrown over the whole. Hints are given, as occasion suggests, of the uncertainty of the date of this or that portion of prophecy, against which German Rationalism has declared, as if it were of no account. He does not seem to be conscious, what he is parting with. He speaks, e. g. of "innocent questions about the date of the book of Daniel," (J. Ch. p. 467. comp. p. 423) when the question is, "Is that book Divine? or human, claiming to be Divine?" One who teaches on these subjects, ought to have made up his mind upon them. And so, of course, would Dean Stanley, had he thought it of any account. Meanwhile, truth and doubt are mixed up together; and to censure denial of truth, is to secure his sympathy with the denial. The truth of the Old Testament history, in its details, is apparently presupposed throughout his work; at the close (p. 521,) Dr Colenso's attacks on the Pentateuch are endorsed, and we are told to reckon the "errors and defects of the Old Testament" "amongst its safeguards." p. 522. The same habit of indefiniteness extends to doctrine also, even as to the doctrine of the Atonement. Indeed, he seems unable to grasp or to state any doctrine definitely.

to definite truth the great antagonist to the mind of Christ, would have us to agree to differ in every particle of faith, yet to hold ourselves to be one in one "common Christianity." Like the Pantheon of old Rome, every thing is to be inshrined in one common Temple of Concord, not of faith or minds or wills, but of despair of truth. Nothing, in this new school, is to be exclusively true, nothing is to be false. No words are to have any exclusive meaning. Every one is to decypher the old inscriptions as he likes, so that he do not obtrude that meaning upon others, as *the* sole meaning. "Everlasting" is to one to mean "lasting for ever," to another, for what seems to be "an age," as men say; "atonement" is, to one, to mean *only* "being at one" with God somehow, by imitation, or admiration of the "[y] greatest moral act ever done in this world;" to another, if he likes, it is to be that Act of God's aweful Holiness, which human thought cannot reach; to one the Bible is to be, if he wills, "the word of God," so that he allow his neighbour to have an equal chance of being right, who holds that it "contains" somewhere "the word of God," i. e. a revelation, of no one knows what, made, no one knows how, (it may be through man's natural faculties, or his own thoughts or mind,) and lying no one knows where, except that it is to be somewhere between Genesis and Revelations, but probably, according to the neo-Christianity, to the exclusion of both. We are to recognise together, that God the Holy Ghost "spake by the prophets," yet not so as to exclude their being fallible in matters of every day-morality. The authority of Jesus is to be respected;

[y] Prof. Jowett on St. Paul, ii. 591.

yet not so far but that modern critics may be held to know more then He, our God. These things (as far as they have been yet applied,) are, of course, the beginning, not the end. On the same ground that "everlasting," in the mouth of Jesus, is to be an ambiguous word, so, and much more may we be called upon to hold that "grace," "faith," nay, "God," are ambiguous words, and to harmonize with those who hold, like the Pelagians of old, that "grace" is God's gracious help through man's natural powers, and only so far the help of God, in that man received those powers from God; or that "faith" is faithfulness; or that "god" may (as the Arians taught) designate a secondary god, and that the Mohammedans may perchance hold the right faith, since the Socinians declared themselves their "nearest fellow-champions for the faith of one supreme God without personalities or pluralities[1]."

The servants are less than their Lord, from whom they have their authority. In compass the misbelief is larger, in essence it is less to misbelieve, that "grace" is the working of man's natural faculties, or "inspiration" their quickened exercise; it were all one to say that "revelation" is man's own thought, as to say that Jesus, the Fountain of truth and the Truth, used one ambiguous or (God forgive it!) ignorant word in matter of truth.

It seemed, to one[a], the extreme of Theological hos-

[1] "Epistle Dedicatory to Ameth Ben Ameth Embassador of the mighty Emperor of Fez and Morocco to Charles II. King of Great Britain," re-printed by Leslie, Works, i. 207-11. fol. see p. 209. and Leslie's letter, Ib. p. 217. The Socinians never attempted to deny the genuineness of the document.   [a] Rev. H. B. Wilson in the Daily News. Mr Maurice admits the fact, but blasphemes God,

tility, that I said, that they who deny eternal punishment, *as inconsistent with the attributes of God*, do not really believe in the same God. This, to any mind which reflects ever so little, is self-evident. For it is God Himself, Who is revealed in His attributes. They then, who hold that what Jesus revealed as to God, is inconsistent with the attributes of God as they themselves believe of God, do not believe in God Whom Jesus revealed. To speak the truth, as I did, thus plainly, (mournful as that truth is,) is alone real faithfulness to God and true charity to man. It is Jesus Who said, "[b] He that believeth not, shall be damned." Who those shall be, He Alone is the Judge. Of this we are sure, that they will be those only, who, through fault of their own, reject Divine truth. But, since the rejection of truth, as well as unholiness of life, will have to do with the final doom of man, then, not to state the truth as explicitly as we can, to allow truth and falsehood to be jumbled together in one evershifting kaleidoscope of opinions, to allow that all may have an equal chance of being right, and so, (since they are contradictories,) that all have an equal chance of being false, is treason to the God of truth, and cruelty to the souls of man. We have been blamed already, that we do not "[c] consent to be *taught*, even by an enemy, and accept the *faith* however imperfect, the *adoration* however inconsistent, offered to Him, Who most assuredly would never have broken that bruised reed or quenched that smoking flax." This is but an instance of that variegated use of terms, which de-

Whose aweful Justice Christians adore. Letter to the Bp. of London.
[b] S. Mark xvi. 16. [c] Dr Stanley's Farewell Sermon, p. 18, 19.

stroys all definiteness of meaning. It is not the
one or other "harsh or revolting expression," in
M. Renan's "Life of Jesus," which has so shocked
Christian Europe. It is the intense and entire unbelief which underlies the whole of that patronising
novel, in which the supercilious insolence of superiority, which makes allowance for its God, is more
sickening even than its hinted blasphemy. Of course,
there can be no vestige of "faith" or "adoration"
in that dreary picture, which describes a young
enthusiast, who had once "the germs of a true fanaticism[d]," at one time "[e]*probably* not involving himself in *innocent(!)* frauds, whereby people tried to secure to him the title of son of David," which, however, "he accepted[e]," but who finally became a "won-
der-worker[f]" against his will, conniving at fraud in
the resurrection of Lazarus, falling short of "[g]the
delicacies of the critical spirit [of the 19th century]
whereby good faith and imposture are irreconcileable terms." Jesus was born a Jew, and "[g]material
truth has little value for an Eastern. He sees all
through his ideas, his interests, his passions." I cannot bring myself to translate or accumulate the blasphemies. They are essential to M. Renan's conception of Him Whom he once believed in as his God,
for whose "decline and fall" he now apologises, as
the faults of his age and nation, to which he "bent[h],"
sooner than "[i]renounce his mission." "Faith," of
course there cannot be, in one who would explain as
human, what our Lord declared to be Divine. The
"adoration" of one, who, by force of circumstances,

[d] Renan, Vie de Jesus, p. 326.   [e] Ib. p. 237.   [f] p. 257 sqq.
[g] Ib. p. 252, 3.   [h] Ib. p. 239.   [i] Ib. p. 264-9.

is to have fallen short of the morality of the 19th century, would be the hideous mockery of those who bowed the knee before Him, and mocked Him, saying, "Hail, king of the Jews." M. Renan believed once; now he only thinks that his former belief makes him the better judge of his Judge Whom he has rejected. Dr Stanley bids us "[1]think of our controversies, as they will appear, when we *shall be forced* to sit down at the feast with those whom we have known only as opponents here, but whom we must recognise as companions there." Would God, it may be so! Joyous, besides its joy in God, will be that reunion of His redeemed, when those who have been severed for awhile, through no wilful rejection of the truth, shall, in the sight of the Everblessed and Adorable Trinity, together see and adore the perfect Truth. Yet in order that it may be so, they who, through no merits of their own but through the mercy of our God, have that one truth which He has revealed, are bound the more not, through any fear of man, or faint-heartedness, or sloth, or dread of repelling an already alienated world, to soften or pare down the truth with which we are entrusted. Rather, let the world say what it will, or the more because it proposes this deadly peace, in which we are to unite in one apathy of despair of God-given truth, we must bear about with us the Apostle's words; *Brethren, if any of you do err from the truth, and one convert him, let him know, that he which converteth the sinner from the error of his way shall save a soul from death and shall hide a multitude of sins.*

[1] The Bible, its Form and Substance, p. 92.

S. Mark's Day. 1864.

CONTENTS.

LECTURE I.

LECTURE II.

of the third; terribleness and permanent subdual, of the fourth. Periods distinguished in the fourth Empire in Daniel's vision. The ten "horns" or kingdoms belong to a later period, yet are simultaneous. Contrast of Roman Empire with those before it in Dionysius. The kingdom of God the chief subject of Nebuchadnezzar's dream and Daniel's vision. The title, "the kingdom of God" taken from Daniel and part of the popular belief before Christ came. Belief in the Messiah, as Man but more than man, also rested on his prophecy before our Lord, as shewn in the book of Enoch. Title, "Son of Man," as used by our Lord, taken from Daniel. Daniel prophesied the worship of the Son of Man. iii. Symbols in Daniel's second vision, which are explained, in Daniel, to represent Persia and Greece, correspond respectively with those of the 2nd and 3rd Empires, and disagree with those of the 3rd and 4th. Antiochus Epiphanes does not correspond to the Anti-Christ either of the viith or xith chapter of Daniel. Contrast of his character with that of the Anti-Christ in Daniel ch. xi. Rationalists miss the special character of this Anti-Christ and pervert the prophecy of his death. It is in conformity with nature, that there should be types of Anti-Christ. Eastern tradition of the 4th Empire and of the Messiah derived from Daniel. . . . . p. 58—99.

LECTURE III.

Attempts to make out four Empires, (subtracting the Roman,) which should end with Antiochus. Four different experiments tried. The advocates of each solution agree in holding the other three to be untenable. i. Ewald's. The 1st Empire, the Assyrian, and Daniel an adaptation of an earlier Assyrian Daniel, who is to have prophesied the overthrow of the Assyrian empire. Ezekiel's mention of Daniel, in each place, suits Daniel himself. Grounds of the selection of Daniel with Noah and Job as examples of righteousness, and of the order in which Ezekiel names them. No explanation of Daniel's being named in Ezekiel, unless he was the prophet. No ground for Ewald's imaginary Daniel. Daniel's vision on the Hiddekel. Rivers, places of prayer among the Jews. The human-headed winged-lion of Nineveh was an essentially different symbol from the eagle-winged lion of Daniel; probably it, as well as the human-headed bull, was a religious symbol, certainly not a symbol of Assyrian *empire*. The lion or eagle were symbols of Babylon, as well as of Assyria. ii. Babylonian Empire under Nebuchadnezzar not a distinct empire from that of his successors. Greatness of the Babylonian empire, under him, both in conquest and internal policy. Medo-Persian inferior to Babylonian. Fainéant character of Nebuchadnezzar's successors; in no sense a separate empire. iii. Medo-Persian empire owned never to have existed as two. Its unity presupposed in Scriptures which Rationalists allege the writer of the book of Daniel to know, and in Daniel himself. The authority of Darius stated in Daniel to have been delegated. Xenophon's account likely, confirmed in part against Herodotus by Inscriptions. Policy of placing Median Vice-King

LECTURE IV.

unnatural expositions.   Re-casting of old theories in opposition to Hengstenberg.   Wieseler's unnatural expedients and admissions.   Lengerke's fantastic theory incontrovertible in his own eyes.   Ewald's two attempts to take the numbers in their natural order; arbitrary dates assumed by him, and arbitrary expedients to get rid of the superfluous years.   Mutual exchange of theories.   Assumption that the fault as to the chronology was Daniel's, not their's, contrary to their own assumption that the writer knew the history; the charge recoils, since the years are too many for their theory, not too few.   Naturalness of the interpretation that Jesus was the Messiah said to " cut off," owned by Hitzig.   Rationalist agreement, in pulling down only ; their disagreement in constructing.   Table of their variations as to the 70 weeks.   Their failure as to the last week, the supposed agreement of which was to be the basis of the whole.   Dates in the reign of Epiphanes.   Events at its close ; his death no relief to the Jews ; the 2300 days probably had a double fulfilment.   Events of the last 7 years agree with no 7 years of Epiphanes ; aggravations of the failure ; unmeaningness of the meanings imported by rationalists into the prophecy.   Contrast of the whole prophecy with the rationalist expositions of it.   The Messiah was not expected, when, according to Daniel, He was not to come ; when, according to Daniel, He was to come, He was expected.   .   .   .   p. 162—231.

LECTURE V.

The minuteness of a portion of Daniel's prophecies is in harmony with the whole system of Old Testament prophecy, in that, throughout, God gave a nearer foreground of prophecy, whose completion should, to each age, accredit the more distant and as yet unfulfilled prophecy.

Argument of rationalists and the Essays against the prophecies of Daniel involves the denial of all supernatural prophecy.   Prophecy, and prediction, which the Rationalists distinguish from it, are alike human, according to them.   Indications of minute prophecy, throughout the Old Testament.   1) Test given to distinguish the true prophet from the false, Deut. xviii. 20, 21. 2) Struggle between the false prophets and the true.   3) Urim and Thummim.   4) " Enquiring of God."   5) " The Seer."   Old Testament prophecy related to a nearer or a more distant future of temporal judgment and mercy, and the Redeemer.   Predictions to the Patriarchs.   Continuous fulfilment of the blessings of Jacob and Moses, a continuous witness of God's foreknowledge and Providence.   " Until Shiloh come ; " no temporal fulfilment can be made out.   Series of individual prophecies.   Prophecies to the ten tribes.   Minute temporal prophecies to Israel end in larger.   Succession of prophets in Judah.   Prophecies of the Christ, connected with Jerusalem, imply that it would continue in being ; prophecies against Sennacherib and Babylon ; prophecies of exact dates ; ends of cities foretold, minute but varied ; Jeremiah's distinct unvarying prophecy of the destruction of Jerusalem, and lesser intervening prophecies.   Jeremiah and Ezekiel foretell details of the cap-

LECTURE VI.

On the proof of the genuineness of the book of Daniel, furnished by the date of the closing of the Canon of the Old Testament, and by the direct reference to it in the Canonical Scriptures, and in other books before or of the Maccabee period.

Josephus' statement of the closing of the Canon, and of the ground, why it was closed about 400 B. C.   The intervening period before our Lord, one of much mental activity.   Date of the Wisdom of the son of Sirach fixed by the mention of Simon son of Onias and Euergetes in his grandson's preface, early in the 3rd cent. B. C.   His grandson attests that the Canon was closed when his grandfather wrote.   The lowest date of the son of Sirach, and the existence of his book out of the Jewish Canon, prove the early date of Daniel. The son of Sirach alludes to the Canon.   Tradition, insisted upon by rationalists, as to Nehemiah's collecting the scattered books of the Canon, relates, not to an original collection, but to the gathering of books already in the Canon, which had been dispersed.   Gradual formation of the Canon. The Pentateuch laid up from the first ; gradual accessions implied in Scripture itself.   The Pentateuch an authority before Jeroboam's schism.   Each later prophet presupposes the earlier prophets.   Gradual accessions of the historical books.   Probable date of Joshua, Judges, Samuel, Ruth ; the Books of Kings before the close of the Captivity.   Prophetic documents probably embodied in the Books of Kings.   Gradual formation of the Psalter ; the first book wholly David's ; the 5th book alone implies times after the Captivity ; no one Psalm contains any indication of the Maccabee period ; those selected as such belong to the Captivity.   The Psalter probably translated by the LXX before the Maccabee times.   The accession of Proverbs of Solomon, in Hezekiah's time, to the collection already existing, shews

LECTURE VII.

On the "historical inaccuracies" falsely imputed to the book of Daniel, and the "improbabilities" alleged. i. Agreement of dates in Daniel together, and

DANIEL THE PROPHET.

LECTURE I.

THE book of Daniel is especially fitted to be a battle field between faith and unbelief. It admits of no half-measures. It is either Divine or an imposture. To write any book under the name of another, and to give it out to be his, is, in any case, a forgery, dishonest in itself, and destructive of all trustworthiness. But the case as to the book of Daniel, if it were not his, would go far beyond even this. The writer, were he not Daniel, must have lied, on a most frightful scale, ascribing to God prophecies which were never uttered, and miracles which are assumed never to have been wrought. In a word, the whole book would be one lie in the Name of God. The more God, as we shall see, is the centre of the whole, the more directly would the falsehood come into relation to God. The book truly ascribes to God, that *He* gave wisdom to Daniel to interpret the visions of Nebuchadnezzar and Belshazzar; that *He* delivered the children from the burning fiery furnace and Daniel from the den of lions; that *He* revealed to Daniel things to come, the largest and the least, comprising successions of Empires and Christ's Kingdom, with some exact dates and minute details. The miracles it implies, the prophecies it avers, to have been recorded by Daniel a contemporary. Either then we have true miracles and true prophecy, or we should have nothing but untruth. An apology for the supposed forger, such as those put out by some Germans [1], and lately in England [2], is utterly untenable and immoral. "The truth seems," says one [2], "that starting, like many a patriot bard of our own, from a name traditionally sacred, the writer used it with no deceptive intention, as a dramatic form which dignified his encouragement of his countrymen in their great struggle against Antiochus." Doubtless the book of Daniel was, and was meant to be, an encouragement in all that desolate period after prophecy had ceased, to mitigate their trials, and especially that one, which wrecked the faith of so many, the persecution of Antiochus. For it shewed them visibly before their eyes, that God, in Whose Hands all things are, knew the whole course of events and overruled them. But it was no encouragement at all, except on the belief of its truth. Yet a writer could not more distinctly claim, that the prophecies which he delivers were revealed to himself. It is idle to deny a "deceptive intention," when the writer, had he not been Daniel, would have deceived first his own people, and then the whole Christian world, until now. Strange, that some who deny the "deceptive intention" of the writer, adduce the declarations made to or by Daniel, that the prophecies were true, as a proof that they were false. Yet wherein differs this from our Blessed Lord's own assertion that His words were true [3], that He is the Truth [4]? St. John avers his own truth [5], St. Paul [6] also, and Jeremiah [7]. The assertion in Daniel is not more frequent than in St. Paul. Once only it is made in Daniel's own person: else it is made to assure the first recipient of the revelation. Daniel impresses

[1] De Wette speaks of it as "the intelligent act of a patriot," Einl. § 257. Zunz, an 'enlightened' Jew, (Gottesdienstl. Vortr. d. Juden, p. 318 sqq. 405 sqq.,) and Lengerke, (§ 15.) excuse it from habits of the times. Bleek does not seem to think such fraud needs excuse. (Schleiermacher, &c. Zeitschrift, iii. 250 sqq. § 23.) It was "necessary for his end, prophecy having ceased in the time of the Maccabees." (1 Macc. ix. 27. iv. 46. xiv. 41.) Einl. p. 593.

[2] Essays and Rev. p. 76.   [3] S. John v. 31, 2. vii. 18. viii. 14, 17, 18, 40, 45. xviii. 37.   [4] Ib. xiv. 6.   [5] Ib. xix. 35. xxi. 24.   [6] Acts xxvi. 25. 2 Cor. vi. 8. 1 Tim. i. 12, 15. iv. 9. 2 Tim. ii. 11. Tit. iii. 8.   [7] xxvi. 15.

on Nebuchadnezzar, *the dream is certain and the interpretation thereof sure* [8]*;* Gabriel gives the like assurance to Daniel [9]; Daniel repeats it [10]. In some way, this is to betray in the writer's mind an uncomfortable feeling that on good grounds he would not be believed [11]; although the like assurance implies no such fear in St. John, St. Paul, and Jeremiah : and yet while thus accrediting himself, as being what he is not to be, a prophet of the future, he is to have no "deceptive intention." The assertion of the truth of his prophecy or interpretation is to be intended to guarantee their truth, being (as these say) false; and yet he is to have had no "intent to deceive." More consistent is Hitzig's [12] undisguised statement; "when the books Coheleth and Wisdom claim to be Solomon's, we see in this disguise simply that the author has chosen a certain vehicle : the case of the book of Daniel, if it is assigned to any other, is different. Then it becomes a forged writing, and the intention was to deceive his immediate readers, though for their good." A deceit which would fall under the sentence of God against those who say, [13]*Let us do evil, that good may come ; whose damnation is just.*

The moral law, written in the hearts of the heathen, strongly condemned forgery [14] even when not ungodly. It

---

[8] ii. 45. [9] viii. 26. x. 21. xi. 2. [10] x. 1.

[11] "On the other side, the author betrays his mask through the repeated assurances that his prophecies contained truth." Lengerke, Einl. § 13. n. 11. p. lxxiii. "With the words, *and the dream is certain,* &c. Daniel is to be designated as a true genuine prophet and interpreter of visions : for the later Jews called the older prophets, πιστοὶ ὁράσεως or πιστοὶ ἐν ὁράσει, *and the later prophets* often appeal to their faithfulness and reliableness." Id. on Dan. ii. 45. p. 87. "*It is true.* True, even Jeremiah remarks with emphasis (xxvi. 15. comp. 12. xxviii. 9.) that he speaks *truth,* as also the Apostles (1 Tim. i. 15. iv. 9.)—but here (as in x. 1..comp. xi. 2.) the addition is made, to guarantee the age of the book." Id. Ib. viii. 26. p. 404. [12] Vorbemerkungen z. Daniel, § 6. Rosenmuller speaks out, imputing the direction to *seal the book* (as he thinks, viii. 26. x. 4. 9.) and the change of language from Hebrew to Chaldee, to fraud, in order to give to the work the appearance of having been written in the captivity. Procem. p. 28, 30, 1. [13] Rom. iii. 8.

[14] Hävernick (neue Untersuch. üb. d. B. Daniel, p. 10.) instances the banishment of Onomacritus by Hipparchus to whom he had rendered great ser-

was reserved for persons within Christianity to apologise for it [1].

It is well to have so clear an issue before us. Porphyry, in the well-known attack upon Daniel in his work "against the Christians," saw how direct the issue was between him and Christians. "Daniel," says S. Jerome [2], "not only, as do the other prophets, writes that Christ should come, but also teaches at what time He should come, and arranges the kings in order, and numbers the years, and announces the most evident signs. Porphyry then, seeing all these things to have been fulfilled, and unable to deny that they had taken place, had recourse to this calumny. On the ground of a partial resemblance, he contended that those things which Daniel foretold as to Anti-Christ at the end of the world had been fulfilled under Antiochus Epiphanes : whose assault is a testimony to the truth. For such was the accuracy of the Prophet's words, that to unbelieving men he seemed not to have foretold the future, but to relate the past." A modern school, which has disbelieved with Porphyry, has echoed Porphyry. Out of some remaining respect for Holy Scripture or for Christian belief, it evaded the question of the truth or falsehood of Scripture where it could, consistently with the maintenance of its unbelief. If it could generalise a prophecy, so that it should not seem to be a prophecy, it did so. It adopted non-natural interpretations of prophecy, and so admitted the books which contained it. It objected not to admit the author, if it need not admit the prophet. Hence arose all those modern interpretations of prophecy, as relating to Hezekiah, Zerubbabel and the

vices, for falsifying Musæus; (Herod. vii. 6.) the blame attached, not only to Cynæthus, (Scholl. on Pindar Isthm. iii. 55. Eustath. Scholl. on Hom. i. 1.) but to Solon for forging a verse of Homer on Salamis. (Plutarch, Solon, c. 15. Diog. Laert. i. 48) [This, however, if true, had political consequences.] "Herodotus scruples not to lay bare dishonesty which stained the sanctuary, and to disgrace the memory of a bribed Pythia, whom he mentions by name." vi. 66. Dahlmann, Forschungen, ii. 103.   [1] Lengerke apologises for Heathen forgeries and the book of Daniel with them. (§ 15.) He could see no moral wrong in untruth, unless it had a malicious intent.   [2] Præf. in Daniel.

like. If a prophecy, like those more definite prophecies of Daniel, admitted of no wresting, there was no choice left, except to acknowledge prophecy, or to deny the genuineness of the book. Of course, other grounds must be found to veil the nakedness of unbelief; but it is manifest from the writers themselves, that the central argument is this; "Almighty God does not or cannot work miracles, or reveal the future to His creatures. Therefore, since miracles or prophecy are impossible, a book which contains an account of miracles must be written long after the alleged miracles are related to have been worked; a book containing predictions beyond the unaided sagacity of man must have been written after the events which are predicted." This is laid down broadly by that class of writers; it underlies every so-called critical argument used by them; it crops out continually where it does not, as with avowed unbelievers, stand in the forefront. Four or five idioms are found, a poetical form, which happens also to be Aramaic, and then follows some such statement as, "Besides, had Isaiah written this, it would imply a knowledge of the future." And it is obvious, all the while, that the real ground lies, not in those half-dozen idioms, to which no one who has any idiomatic knowledge of Hebrew would attach any weight, but in the fact that the chapter of the prophet contains, if his, undeniable prophecy. It has even been laid down as a test of the date of the books of Holy Scripture [3]; "Wherever, in the Hebrew Scriptures, there are numerous myths and legends, [miracles] as in the history of the patriarchs, of Moses, Balaam, Samson, Elijah, there we have uniformly relations, not committed to writing until long after the events. Where, contrariwise, the facts appear natural, as in the books of Ezra, Nehemiah and the Maccabees, there the relation, although not always, is contemporaneous with, or shortly subsequent to, the events. This is an historical canon of unquestionable validity. Hence it follows that

---

[3] Knobel, Prophetismus d. Hebräer, ii. 401. quoted by De Wette, Einl. § 255e. ed. 7.

not Daniel, but only a writer long subsequent, can be the author of our relation, and so of our book."

The same writer says [1], "To maintain the genuineness of Isaiah ch. 23, and yet to refer it to a siege of Tyre by Nebuchadnezzar more than a century later, as Jerome, &c. do, is impossible, in that, in Isaiah's time, *there could be* no anticipation of it, much less a confident and definite announcement of it. If any would refer the prophecy to that event, he must at least, with Eichhorn, Rosenmuller, Hitzig, hold it to be spurious."

More broadly yet [2], " *The main argument* for the later date of our Gospels is, after all, this; that they, one by one and still more collectively, exhibit so much out of the life of Jesus in a way which is *impossible*, " [i. e. miraculous.]

A recent unbelieving writer, speaking of a late German answer to the objections against the book of Daniel, says [3], "As to the visions and prophecies of the later part of the book, the Author describes the clearness with which the events are described in ch. 8, 10, 11, up to the time of Antiochus Epiphanes, which is, in fact, to give up the whole argument for the book concerning prophecies properly so called."

Such statements, however often they occur in books of unbelieving criticism, plainly have nothing to do with criticism or historical enquiry. They assume, in each case, the whole question about which criticism can be engaged. If any of us, on our side, say; " our Lord, being God and having a Divine knowledge, pronounced Daniel to be a prophet and quoted words of his as prophetic and as still to be fulfilled," we *do* thereby mean to close up the question of criticism. We, on grounds extrinsic to the book of Daniel, believe critical enquiry to be superseded by Divine authority. We feel satisfied, of course, that

---

[1] on Is. p. 160 sqq. [2] Baur, Crit. Untersuchung. üb. d. Evang. 1847. p. 530. [3] Westminster Review, N. 40. p. 544. A German reviewer puts the issue more nakedly; " Unless, with Auberlen and others, one will abide by the pure miracle of *supernatural inspiration*, the book Daniel is incomprehensible, except as the expression of the first Maccabee rising, embodied in writing." The same is implied in Essays and R. p. 76.

there can be no real grounds of criticism, contradictory to that Divine authority; and, in fact, the deeper any critical knowledge is, the more subservient it is to that authority. But we do not pretend that this antecedent certainty of our's belongs to the province of criticism. As little, plainly, does the opposite denial of the abstract possibility of prophecy. Those who use the argument call themselves "unprejudiced," simply because they are free from what they call *our* prejudices. But of course one who lays down, that such a book cannot have been written at a given time, *because*, in that case, it would contain definite predictions of the future, as much prejudges the question on the ground of his antecedent anti-doctrinal prejudices, as he can allege of us, that we decide it on our doctrinal prejudices, i. e. on our previous belief. His major premiss is, " Since there cannot be either prophecy or miracle, a book claiming to contain definite prophecies or a contemporary account of unmistakeable miracles cannot belong to the period to which it is ascribed :" his minor is, " The book of Daniel does make such claims." Our major is, " Whatever Jesus has said, is true;" our minor is, " He has said that Daniel is a prophet." This whole ground, on either side, is antecedent to criticism. *Their* denial of the possibility of miracles and prophecy denies, in fact, to our Creator powers which we possess ourselves, of regulating our own work, or communicating to others beforehand our own designs. It has its source in an utter ignorance of God, and is to be remedied by a knowledge of Him and of ourselves, our Creator and His creatures.

But, although the belief as to the prophecies of Daniel must be part of my religious being, since it is inseparable from my belief that Jesus is God, this in no way interferes with the examination of these prophecies in themselves.

I cannot indeed examine them, as one who doubts. No one who believes in Christ, can or ought to assume that to be doubtful, upon which Christ has set His seal. So it is as to the whole substance of the faith and each detail of it.   Our own knowledge is certain, and we shall never win others to our certainty of faith and knowledge by assuming the character of persons who have themselves to arrive at faith.   Even in matters of certain human knowledge, men do not ignore their own knowledge, in order to impart it to others or to remove their objections to it.   Nor can I make-believe, as to what I do not believe, that these objections to the book of Daniel have any special plausibility.   I select them out of the flood of pseudo-criticism with which we have been inundated, because the school which propagates them has given out its achievements here to be "[1] one of the greatest triumphs of modern criticism."   "Crimine ab uno disce omnes."

Since none of those petty questions, which people set in the foreground, are their real central grounds of objection, but rather the fact that the book of Daniel does contain unmistakeable prophecies, I will apply myself to these points; 1) to shew that even if, per impossibile, the book of Daniel had been written at the latest date at which these men venture to place it, there would still remain clear and unquestionable prophecies; 2) That those definite prophecies which were earlier fulfilled are not out of, but in harmony with, the rest of the Old Testament; 3) That even apart from the authority of our Lord, the history of the closing of the Canon, as also the citation of Daniel in books prior to, or contemporary with Antiochus, establish the fact that the book was anterior to the date of Antiochus Epiphanes, and so, that those definite prophecies are, according to this external authority, not history related in the form of prophecy, but actual predictions of things then future.   And then, I will answer every objection alleged against the book, whether as to matters of doctrine or history, which shall not have received its answer in the course of the other enquiries.

But first, it may be best to mention some points, which were questioned in the last decennia of the last century, but which are conceded on all hands now.

<hr>

[1] Bunsen, Gott in d. Geschichte, i. 302.

1. No one doubts now that the book of Daniel is one whole[2]. That hacking school of criticism, which hewed out the books of Holy Scripture into as many fragments as it willed, survives only in a few expiring representatives. It reigned with an Oriental despotism in Germany for a time, but is now deposed even there. Bertholdt, (followed by Augusti,) who so dissected the book of Daniel and ascribed it to nine different authors of somewhat different dates, was constrained to admit that the authors of each accession to the book were acquainted with the fore-existing portions; that they were, in fact, successively continuators of the portions which previously existed, each of the later writers imitating the style and language of those who preceded him. A tacit admission, of course, of the unity of style and language which pervades the whole, while the assumption of such a close imitation betrayed the arbitrariness of the theory. It admitted identity of style and manner, and denied the identity of the author.

But no less is that other theory of Eichhorn now rejected by all, that the Chaldee and Hebrew portions of the book are by different authors. Besides the general proofs of the unity of the whole, the division of the languages does not coincide with any obvious division of the book. There are in the book two chronological series; the one containing the six first chapters; the second, the six last. The first is chiefly historical, in which the chief persons acting are the kings reigning in Babylon, Nebuchadnezzar, Belshazzar, or Darius; while Daniel or his companions are instruments in the hand of God, passive or subordinate. The revelation is conveyed to Nebuchadnezzar in his dreams, or to Belshazzar by the handwriting; Daniel is but the interpreter of what has been conveyed to the king. In the last six chapters, the revelations are made directly to Daniel alone. In one chapter (the IXth) there is some personal history of Daniel, his study of Jeremiah's prophecy, his self-humiliation and

---

[2] De Wette, Bleek, Von Lengerke, Gesenius, even Hitzig, Ewald and Stähelin, admit the unity of the book just as fully as those who believe its divinity.

prayer, upon which God unfolded to him that brief much-containing series of prophecy from the restoration of Jerusalem to the Death of the Messiah and its destruction. But here he himself is the recipient of the revelation. Yet both in the order of time and in the language, the two divisions (so to speak) overlap one another. Both series are chronological in themselves; but the first extends beyond the date when the second begins. The first series consists of six narratives, selected with one object, four of the six from the reign of Nebuchadnezzar, the fifth from that of Belshazzar; the last from that of Darius the Mede. The second series, the visions or revelations to Daniel, are also dated, like the ancient prophecies, and that, at four successive times; in the first and third years of Belshazzar, in the first year of Darius son of Ahasuerus, and in the 3rd year of Cyrus. So that after having, in the histories, gone on to the reign of Darius, we go back again, at the beginning of the second series, to a date a little earlier, the first year of Belshazzar.

But these two series are not distinguished by language, nor can the Chaldee portion of Daniel make a whole. Daniel, after having related in Hebrew the early history of himself and his companions, passes naturally into Chaldee in the answer which the Magi made to the king, when he required them to tell him his forgotten dream. But the Chaldee does not cease with that portion of the book which is connected with the history or the public events of the empire. The first of Daniel's visions is also in Chaldee. This is not what we should have expected; perhaps it has at some time puzzled some of us, its reason not being obvious. The connection is in the subject. The vision of the VIIth chapter is a supplement to the revelation in Nebuchadnezzar's dream. It too relates to the four great empires of the world. It expands that first disclosure to Nebuchadnezzar, fills it up, continues it. The prophecies which follow relate more especially to Israel. Those events, then, or prophecies, which belonged to the revelation of God to the heathen, were written in

the language of the then great heathen empire. They
were for the world, and were written in the language
common to the people of God and to the world, a language understood through all that then populous tract
from the Persian Gulf to Damascus, the seat, in early
times, of so many Christian Churches. The prophecies
which bore especially upon Israel or the time of our Lord's
first Coming, were written in the language of the ancient
Prophets. As a slight instance of the same ground of
varying languages, Jeremiah wrote in Chaldee a single
verse which he gave to the Jews as an answer to the Heathen among whom they were[1], *Thus shall ye say unto them,*

The gods who heaven and earth made not,

Perish from earth and from under heaven shall they.

These intersecting lines of arrangement and this hidden ground of order in the book of Daniel, in themselves,
imply the oneness of the author's hand. The book is arranged upon a real plan; its languages are chosen upon a
distinct principle. Yet neither the ground of its arrangement nor the principle of the variation of the languages
are explained in the book itself; nor are they obvious at
first sight. Amid apparent want of unity on the surface
of the book, there is a real unity in the whole, resting on
the unity of the plan of the writer.

Besides this, it has been noticed how the first part of
the book prepares for what follows; how the subsequent
parts look back to the first. The account of Daniel's three
years' education in the wisdom of the Chaldees accounts
for his falling under the king's decree, that all the wise
men should be slain; the mention of his three companions
and their qualifications in ch. i. is introductory to their
elevation in ch. ii.; and both, to their accusation in ch. iii[2].
The mention of the carrying away of the sacred vessels ch.
i. is preparatory to the account of the desecration of them
by Belshazzar, ch. v. The narrative of Belshazzar's im-

---

[1] Jer. x. 11.   [2] ii. 49. is alluded to in iii. 12. as an aggravation of the alleged
disobedience. Their accusers represent it as the greater ingratitude, that *certain Jews,* (i. 3.) elevated so high by the king, yet refused obedience to him.

pious feast alludes throughout to points scattered over the whole previous history; Daniel's having been brought captive by Nebuchadnezzar from Judæa; his wisdom, as acknowledged by Nebuchadnezzar, and as ascribed to *the spirit of the gods in* [1] him; his being placed at the head of the Magi; Nebuchadnezzar's exceeding greatness, his subsequent insanity as the punishment of his pride, and his restoration, upon his acknowledgment of the supremacy of God. The emphasis on the titles, "Belshazzar the king *of the Chaldeans* was slain and Darius *the Mede* received the kingdom [2]," alludes to the vision of the succession of empires, earlier and later in the book [3]. The chapter closes with the statement of the succession of Darius the Mede, which prepares for the independant history in ch. vi. The vision in ch. vii. is an expansion of Nebuchadnezzar's dream. In the short authentication of the vision of the kings of Media and Persia and the king of Greece in ch. viii. Daniel expressly refers to the former vision [4]. The revelation as to the 70 weeks is related to have been communicated to him by Gabriel, *whom*, Daniel says, *I had seen in the vision at the beginning* [5], i.e. in ch. viii. as related.

The contents of the prophecies are also progressive. The revelation in ch. vii. (as before said) is expansive of that of ch. ii. Ch. viii. developes still more fully one part of that revelation, viz. the relation of the 2nd and 3rd of those kingdoms, and most especially that point of deepest interest, warning, instruction to the Jews, the way in which the third kingdom, that of Greece, would, in Antiochus Epiphanes, try their faith for a time, and be brought to nought [6]. Ch. ix. in the prophecy of the 70 weeks, gives a summary of the trial-time before the Coming of the Messiah, fixed their expectations so that they should not look for it as near nor yet at an undefined distance, describes it as a time of mingled mercy and judgment, of mercy to the many with whom the covenant should be

---

[1] v. 11, 14. comp. iv. 8, 9, 18. [5,6, 15. Ch.]   [2] v. 30, 1. [v. 31, vi. 1. Ch.]
[3] ii. 39. vii. 5.   [4] viii. 1.   [5] ix. 21.   [6] viii. 9-12. 23-26

confirmed; of judgment, on Jerusalem. The xith chapter developes with great fulness certain prominent events in the relations of two kingdoms of Alexander's successors, selecting those which most affected the Jewish people.

The histories are also in like way selected with one object, the way in which the true God was glorified amid the captivity of His people in a heathen Empire. The relations in the first 6 chapters, differing as they do in kind, have this one end. God it is, Who gives knowledge and skill to the four youths above all the magicians and astrologers in the realm [7]. God, from Whom Daniel obtains knowledge of Nebuchadnezzar's dream [8]. He it is *Who giveth wisdom to the wise and knowledge to them that know understanding* [9]. Before Nebuchadnezzar Daniel depreciates himself; *this secret is not revealed to me for any wisdom that I have, more than any living* [10]; he ascribes it wholly to the *God in heaven that revealeth secrets* [11]. Nebuchadnezzar, at the end, acknowledges the God of Daniel, as [12] *God of gods and Lord of kings, and a revealer of secrets.* The delation of Shadrach Meshach and Abednego, as far as relates to themselves, ends simply in their restoration [13]; its main issue is the decree, that none in the whole empire should *speak any thing amiss against* their *God, because no other god can deliver after this sort* [14]. In Nebuchadnezzar's edict upon his restoration to reason, mention is made incidentally only of Daniel, and that, in the king's appeal to him to explain the dream, not for any wisdom of his own, but *because the spirit of the holy gods is in thee* [15]. With this the king begins and ends. The end of the relation is, that the king praises and honors *the King of heaven* and owns the justice of His ways [16]. The whole history of Belshazzar is God's vindication of His honour against the insolence of the sensual prince.

God it is, in sum, Who *changes times and seasons* [17], Who *removeth kings and setteth up kings,* Whose *are wisdom and might ;* He it is Who giveth either to any who have either,

[7] i. 17-20.   [8] ii. 17-23.   [9] Ib. 21.   [10] Ib. 30.   [11] 22, 28, 45.   [12] 47.
[13] iii. 30.   [14] Ib. 28, 29.   [15] iv. 9, 18.   [16] Ib. 2, 3, 37.   [17] ii. 20-22.

whether it be His own servants or the Heathen king [1]. He delivereth those who trust in Him [2]; His dominion is for ever; His kingdom on earth, not like the kingdoms of men, indissoluble [3]. The same is the manifest object of all the temporal revelations in the following chapters.

In all those histories, moreover, the human agent is brought in without his will; he speaks, but it is not by his own wisdom; or he is delivered, but it is not by his own strength; and then he retires from sight. Daniel's exposition of Nebuchadnezzar's first dream is occasioned by his being involved in the decree, which doomed all those, educated as he was, to die [4]; in the second, he comes in obedience to the king's edict [5]; in the third, he is called for through the intervention of the Queen-mother [6]. To Daniel the historian it is all one, through *whom* God was glorified. Every thoughtful child has probably, on hearing the history of Shadrach Meshach and Abednego, asked, "where was Daniel ?" The history suggests but does not state the answer. Those only were punished, who were accused. Daniel's three companions had been promoted at the request of Daniel, not for any services of their own. With these the accusers began [7]; they did not venture upon Daniel yet. It is no uncommon art of human policy to begin by attacking the inferior, in order to prepare the way for the real object, the destruction of one who stands in higher favor. The first attack is a test of the probable success of the later, and may be made with less risk. So then the glory came to God through the three youths, and Daniel, in noble self-forgetfulness, left unstated the grounds of his non-participation in their steadfastness. In the time of Darius, the attack upon

---

[1] ii. 37, 8. iv. 25, 35, 36. v. 21, 26, 28.   [2] ii. 28, 9. vi. 16, 20, 22, 3, 27.
[3] ii. 44. iv. 3, 34. vi. 26.   [4] ii. 14 sqq.   [5] iv. 8.   [6] v. 10-12.
[7] iii. 8, 12. It is probable that the command was purposely not extended to those in the position of Daniel. For in iii. 27. mention is again made of the three first classes named in iii. 3. " the satraps, sagans, pechahs ;" but besides these, we hear there, for the first time, of ministers of a higher rank than the satraps, and who stood in direct relation to the king, the "haddabere malca," "the king's councillors." Daniel was one of these (ii. 49.) and, as

Daniel seemed to be the safer, because his services had been to another dynasty. With this withdrawal of self coincides the character of the great revelations, of which he became the channel. The first most comprehensive revelation is given not to himself, but to the Heathen king. Of this, he is but the expositor; of the rest, he is only the receiver; these too he does not understand, until they are explained to him. As to what is not explained to him, he is a vehicle to others of revelations, which are hidden from himself[8]. He returns from his revelations, in which God had shown him somewhat of the fate of empires, *to do the king's business in the king's palace;* but he mentions even this, only because he had intermitted it, when sick by reason of the awefulness of the revelations[9].

The character of Daniel himself runs one and the same through the book, majestic in its noble simplicity. As a revealer of God in a Heathen Court, and as raised to high dignity in God's Providence for the sake of his brethren, he occupies, in this temporary dissolution of the political existence of his people, a place somewhat corresponding to that of Moses at the beginning. Like Moses, he was educated in the highest wisdom of a people famed for its wisdom. Even this likeness has its unlikeness. In Moses God manifested not His wisdom but His power. Yet, as the wise of the Egyptians were put to shame by the power of God wherewith He clothed Moses the shepherd, so He paled the reputation of the wisdom of the Babylonian Magi by His Spirit which He placed in the captive boy Daniel. But the resemblance lies only in the common principles of God's Providence, whereby He, at extraordinary times, raises up, singly for the most part, extraordinary instruments of His own, to effect His Will. Man has but two great gifts of God to direct against Himself, wisdom and power. The conflict must ever lie in these. In Joseph the slave, and Daniel the captive, God put to

such, certainly he was not included in the letter of the edict. Probably the "councillors" were intentionally excepted.   [8] xii. 8, 9.   [9] viii. 27.

shame Egyptian and Babylonian wisdom, in that through them He taught their monarchs what their own wise men could not teach them.   But therewith the likeness ended. Neither Joseph nor Moses are originals from which Daniel could (as men have said,) be a copy[1].

The book of Daniel gives but a slight hint, that Daniel was formed amid suffering and privation, in that, in his person, the prophecy of Isaiah to Hezekiah was fulfilled[2], *of thy sons which shall come from thee shall they take away, and they shall be eunuchs in the palace of the king of Babylon.*   Thither, with several other Jewish youths, he, himself of royal blood, was taken while yet a boy, and placed in the care of the chief of the eunuchs. His name was changed as well as those of his three chief companions ; a badge of servitude[3], destined to obliterate the memory of their early home, and, in the case of these Jewish children, of their God.   All of them had, before, borne names commemorative of their God.   "[4]God is my Judge." "[5]The Lord gave graciously." "[6]Who is like God?"   "[7]The Lord helpeth."   Two of these, where the meaning of the new name can be ascertained, were changed into idol-names.   "Bel is the Prince."   " Servant of Nego."   Nebuchadnezzar himself alludes to the signification and object of Daniel's new name, [8]*Daniel, whose name is Belteshazzar, after the name of my god.*   He was probably now about 14.   For Plato relates of the Persians, "[9]After twice 7 years have passed, those whom they call royal instructors receive the boy" to educate.   The

---

[1] As Lengerke imagined.   [2] Is. xxxix. 7.   It appears from their being put in charge of the *master of the king's eunuchs.* (Dan. i. 3.) Josephus relates it simply as a fact. Ant. x. 10. 1.   [3] i. 3. "This is deemed by some a right of ownership ; for, when they buy slaves, they change their names, that, even in the change of name, they might recognise their servitude." Theod. "The master, having bought a slave, then, wishing to show him that he *is* master, changes his name."—"That the imposition of names is a symbol of mastership, is plain from what we too do," &c. S. Chrys. Serm. 12. in loc. N. T. Opp. iii. 121.   See such changes among the Egyptians, (2 Kings xxiii. 34.) Babylonians, (Ib. xxiv. 17.) Persians, (Ezr. v. 14. Esth. ii. 7.)

[4] דָּנִיֵּאל   [5] חֲנַנְיָה   [6] מִישָׁאֵל   [7] עֲזַרְיָה   [8] iv. 5. Ch. 8. Eng.   [9] Alcib. i. 37. Häv. p. 21.

three years, during which he was to be taught *the learning and tongue of the Chaldæans* [10], would bring him to 17; but according to Xenophon [11], 16 or 17 was the age of the adults, at which they entered upon the king's service. As he was taken captive in the third year of Jehoiakim, when Nebuchadnezzar was at the head of his father Nabopolassar's army and was not as yet king, some time in the second year of Nebuchadnezzar coincided with the time when he was *to stand before the king*, entering upon his service. It was then in boyish faithfulness to the law of his God, that he, about 14, refused the king's meats [12], which, (as being connected with idol-sacrifices, and the animal food thereof being killed with the blood,) were forbidden to him by the law [13]. Hosea's prophecy [14], *they shall eat unclean things in Assyria*, shews how difficult it was to avoid them. God says by Ezekiel [15], *the children of Israel shall eat their defiled bread among the Gentiles whither I will drive them;* and Ezekiel protests to God, *Ah! Lord God; my soul hath not been polluted.* It was part of that simplicity of boyish faith, which is the herald of future greatness, that, in uncompromising obedience to the law of his God, he, the soul of the action of his three companions, trusted that God would uphold his health and strength, as well through the pulse as through the forbidden food. He tells us that it was so, as a simple fact. Even now too God protects religious abstinence. "I have remarked," Chardin relates [16], "that

[10] Not what we call Chaldee, which is Aramaic, אֲרָמִית, in Daniel ii. 4. Ezr. iv. 7. but the Medo-Persian which the Magi brought with them.

[11] Cyrop. i. 2. 8.   [12] פַּתְבַּג from the Persian. See further note A. at the end. It is clear from Dan. v. 2-4. that the royal banquets were liable to be mixed up with idolatry. Libations of wine and offerings of a first portion (comp. ἀπαρχή, ἀπάρχεσθαι) to the gods were held far and wide to consecrate the meal, and so, being idolatrous, did to the Jews desecrate them. Häv. quotes Strabo (xvi.3, 26.) alleging that the Nabatæans [Babylonians by origin, see on Obad. p. 242, 3.] offered libations of wine to the sun. The כַּוָּנִים, cakes offered to the "Queen of heaven" in Jer. vii. 18. xliv. 19. were probably Babylonian. "Judging it to be a defilement to partake of such things, since they, serving their idols, received for good cheer the portion set apart thence for them." Polychr.

[13] Idol-sacrifices, Ex. xxxiv. 15. eating with the blood, Lev. xix. 26, &c.

[14] ix. 3.   [15] iv. 13, 14.   [16] MS. Notes in Harmer, Obs. 59. ii. 110.

the countenances of the Kechicks (kashishin, monks) are in fact more rosy and smooth than those of others, and that those who fast much, I mean the Armenians and Greeks, are notwithstanding very beautiful, sparkling with health, with a clear and lively countenance."

But whether God did unusually bless that meagre sustenance or no, boys do not foresee, that, amid abstinence from the vices which surround them, God gives power of mind and body, which others, through sinful self-indulgence[1], destroy in themselves. The faith was the same, in whatever way God answered it. In that same strong faith, he, with his companions, obtained from God that knowledge of Nebuchadnezzar's dream and its meaning, which saved him from death. In that same simple faith, in his advanced age, he continued, like the Psalmist[2], to pray three times in the day, openly, when the penalty was the den of lions.

Yet with this uncompromising duty to his God, he shews, where he may, a subject's deference. What respectful tenderness there is in that explanation of the dream, whereby Nebuchadnezzar's impending insanity was foreshewn to the king[3]. *He sat astonied for one hour, and his thoughts troubled him.* The king had to encourage him to speak ; so amazed was he at such a reverse to such greatness. We almost hear the accents of tenderness and sympathy with which he spake. With what gentle words does he exhort him to those acts of mercy and righteousness, whereby the chastisement might yet be averted, [4] *Let my counsel be acceptable unto thee—if it may be a lengthening of thy tranquillity.* He longs that God may yet reverse the doom, which he had to announce, [3] *The dream be to them that hate thee,* if, by mercy to man, the king would but place himself within reach of the Mercy of God ! To the impious Belshazzar he had to announce the imminent judgment of God ; yet then too with what longing remembrance does he look back to the days of Nebuchad-

---

[1] Rycaut gives a horrible account of the pages at the Ottoman court.
[2] Ps. lv. 17.   [3] iv 19.   [4] Ib. 27.

nezzar, his greatness, glory, honour, humiliation, repentance[5].   Human greatness is, when unabused, a majestic
sight; for [6] *the powers that be, are ordained of God.*   They
are reflections of His Supremacy.   The greatness of Nebuchadnezzar was probably the more elevated, as being
the first who changed the robber-tyrant-domination of
Assyrian or Babylonian might into organised rule.   Daniel's admiration of that greatness, (uniformly as the gift
of God,) shews itself alike in the explanation of his dream
of that majestic statue which depicted his glory; in that
of the hewn tree which betokened his extreme humiliation; and in the description of it to Belshazzar, when
Nebuchadnezzar was with the dead, and his empire was
within a few hours of its dissolution.   The memory dwells
in the mind of the aged seer, as of a glorious sight which
had faded.   Even of the weak king, who had let himself
be entrapped into a law which constrained the condemnation of Daniel, he dwells on all the good side, his reluctance to execute the decree, (which perhaps with safety
to his throne he could not recall,) his sorrow at it, his ineffectual desire to evade it, his one night's repentance.
They are few words of his own which he has preserved;
but they are in the same gentle respectful tone ; [7] *Before
thee also, O king have I done no hurt.*   Yet the love of his
home and of the country which God had chosen for His
people, lived through all those years of a lifelong absence
and greatness.   We see it in the aged man of fourscore
and three years, streaming back on that life of 69 years
of exile.   It is told us incidentally.   But for the decree of
Darius we should not have known it.   "[8]When Daniel
knew that the writing was signed, he went into his house,
and his window being open in his chamber *towards Jerusalem,* he kneeled upon his knees three times a day and
prayed and gave thanks before his God, *as he did aforetime.*"   What a yearning for the dust of the city of his God
does there lie in those two words, *towards Jerusalem;* what
a life of longing prayer in those closing words, *as he did*

[5] v. 18-21.   [6] Rom. xiii. 1.   [7] vi. 22.   [8] Ib. 10.

c 2

aforetime. Yet he prayed *toward Jerusalem,* not simply as his native land, but in memory of the prayer at the dedication of the temple; "[1] *If they shall bethink themselves in the land whither they have been carried captives, and repent and return unto Thee with all their heart—and pray unto Thee toward their land which Thou gavest unto their fathers, the city which Thou hast chosen and the house which I have built for Thy name, then hear Thou their prayer, and forgive Thy people.*

That same earnest longing we see developed in that full and deep outpouring of his soul[2], when, in the first year of Darius, the 70 years of the captivity were all but accomplished; we see the intensity of his love for the city of his God, which with his bodily eyes he was no more to see. We hear it in words, which now too express the yearnings of the soul, longing for the restoration of one's country or of the Church. One who could doubt their truth, knows nothing of prayer or of the voice of the soul. It were a psychological contradiction. We see that same longing again a little later, in the third year of Cyrus, in those unexplained words, [3]*In those days I Daniel was mourning three wecks of days.* The cause of the mourning is hinted in the subsequent vision, where Gabriel says,[4] *The prince of the kingdom of Persia withstood me one and twenty days.* It is related by Ezra[5]; *The people of the land hired counsellors against them to frustrate their purpose all the days of Cyrus king of Persia.*

This love survived an unbroken political greatness of 70 years. The stripling of 17 *sat in the king's gate* ("in the Porte," as we say, retaining the Oriental term,) President over all the Colleges of the *wise men*[6], and of the whole province of Babylon. [7]*Daniel continued even unto the first year of king Cyrus,* are the simple words; but

---

[1] 1 Kgs. viii. 47-50.   [2] ix. 4-19.   [3] x. 2.   [4] x. 13.   [5] iv. 4, 5.

[6] Dan. ii. 48. רב-סגנין על כל-חכימי בבל lit. "chief of the sagans [prefects] over all the wise men of Babylon." Each college or division of the Magi had its own head, and Daniel had the supervision of all.   [7] i. 21.

what a volume of tried faithfulness is unrolled by them!
Amid all the intrigues, indigenous, at all times, in dynasties of Oriental despotism, where intrigue too rolls round
so surely and so suddenly on its author's head; amid all
the envy towards a foreign captive in high office as a
king's councillor; amid all the trouble, incidental to the
insanity of the king or to the murder of two of his successors, in that whole critical period for his people Daniel
continued. We should not have had any statement of his
faithfulness, but for the conspiracy against his life under
the new Median dynasty which knew not those past years.
[8] *The president and Satraps sought* in vain *to find any occasion against him concerning the kingdom; forasmuch as
he was faithful, neither was any error or fault found in
him.* The picture is the greater, because the lines which
mark it are so few. They arc a few simple touches of
truth. It is the fact, which is so eloquent. It is not
the language of panegyric to say, *Daniel continued, even
unto the first year of king Cyrus; Daniel* was *in the gate
of the king; this Daniel prospered in the reign of Darius
and in the reign of Cyrus the Persian* [9]. The force of the
words is not drawn out; but, as perseverance is the one
final touchstone of man, so these scattered notices combine in a grand outline of one, an alien, a captive, of that
misused class who are proverbially the intriguers, favor-
ites, pests of Oriental courts, who revenge on man their
illtreatment at the hands of man [10]; yet, himself, in uni-

---

[8] vi. 4.   [9] i. 21. ii. 49. vi. 28.

[10] Ctesias gives most fully the lists of Eunuchs, who had "influence with" the
different Persian kings, from Cyrus ("with whom the Eunuch Petisakas had
great influence," Pers. n. 5.) downwards. Ib. n. 11. 13. 20. 27. 29. 30. 39. 45.
49. 53. He mentions also some of their intrigues and assassinations. Of their
character in Christian times, Gibbon does not speak more strongly than S. Atha-
nasius, who calls them "a pleasure-loving race, that has no serious concern;"
"scarcely entrusted with household service." "The law forbade them to be admitted into any Ecclesiastical Council." Yet they were always causing evil
by their intrigues. In the Arian persecutions under Constantius, "it was the
Eunuchs who instigated the proceedings against all." (S. Ath. Arian Hist.
§ 38. Hist. Tracts p. 251, 2. Oxf. Tr. see also Ib. p. 287.) So Chrysaphius the
Eunuch, the friend of Eutyches, was the author of the Eutychian troubles.

form integrity, outliving envy, jealousy, dynasties; surviving in untarnished uncorrupting greatness the 70 years of the Captivity; honoured during the 43 years of Nebuchadnezzar's reign; *doing the king's business*[1] under the insolent and sensual boy Belshazzar; owned by the conquering Medo-Persians; the stay doubtless and human protector of his people during those long years of exile; probably commissioned to write the decree of Cyrus which gave leave for that long-longed-for restoration of his people, whose re-entrance into their land, like Moses of old, he was not to share. Deeds are more eloquent than words. Such undeviating integrity, beyond the ordinary life of man, in a worshipper of the One God, in the most dissolute and degraded of the merchant-cities of old, first minister in the first of the world-monarchies, was in itself a great fulfilment of the purpose of God in converting the chastisement of His people into the riches of the Gentiles.

A self-laudatory school has spoken much of the laudation, as they call it, of Daniel, as being unnatural, on our belief that he was the author of the book. To me certainly much more striking is his reserve about himself. A chief statesman in the first Empire of the world, he has not recorded a single voluntary act of his own. Conceive any mere human writer, occupying such a position as Daniel had, a chief adviser of a great monarch, and a great protector doubtless of his people, saying not one word of all the toils, plans, counsels of those 70 years, nothing of the good which he furthered, or the evil which he hindered! And, amid this self-abnegating silence, what is the self-laudation? Literally this, that God gave him

---

through his influence with Theodosius, and of the horrors of the latrocinium of Ephesus. (see Petav. de Incarn. i. 13.) The heathen Lampridius speaks of them, as the " sole destroyers of princes ;" (Vit. Sev. c. 66.) Gibbon sums up, " If we examine the general history of Persia, India, and China, we shall find that the power of the Eunuchs has uniformly marked the decline and fall of every dynasty." (c. 19. n. 7.) Gibbon speaks of the pernicious influence of the Eunuchs "under the third Gordian," (c. 7.) their evil ascendancy over Constantius, (c. 19. beg.) Honorius, (c. 31.) Arcadius, (c. 32. at length) and Theodosius the younger. (c. 34.)   [1] viii. 27.

and his companions wisdom above the rest of the youths;
that this was proved on their examination; that Daniel
relates, in all simplicity, the Queen-mother's account
of the skill given to him by God in interpreting difficulties, which moved Belshazzar to send for him; that the
envious Presidents could find no crime whereof to accuse
him; that the angel Gabriel thrice spake to him, as
greatly beloved[2]. If not fact, this were blasphemy; otherwise, how differs it from that touching title by which St.
John loves to call himself, *the disciple whom Jesus loved*?

Whatever mention, however, Daniel makes of himself
(although not self-praise,) it is one and the same through
the book; and so, even opponents have acknowledged
herein an evidence of its oneness. It is, in fact, unity
amid diversity.

There is another characteristic of true history, visible
throughout the book, statements which need but can receive explanation. Daniel was not writing continuous
history, but recording facts in which God's glory was
manifested. As a contemporary writer, he presupposes
that things would be understood, which then were notorious. He does not guard his relations; he does not
explain more than is needed for his immediate end.
Those for whom he immediately wrote understood him.
To those of a later age those allusions, even if not understood, presented no difficulties; for the truth of the prophecies guaranteed *their* truth. These I will consider
hereafter. Now, I will only say, that that free unembar-
rassed style which troubles not itself about making clear
its own truth, is visible throughout Daniel.

It is equally conceded, that the language and style both
in the Chaldee and Hebrew portions of the book are such
as belong to one writer. Even De Wette ranks this uniformity among the proofs of its unity. "[3] The similarity
of style binds together the Chaldee and Hebrew portions, not only in themselves but with each other."

ii. It is now conceded, that there are neither Greek

<hr>

[2] ix. 23. x. 11, 19.　　　　　[3] Einl. n. 256.

words, nor Græcisms [1], beyond the names of two or three
musical instruments. In the ignorance of general philology at the close of the last century, words whose Semitic
origin was not obvious, or which belonged to the Indo-
European family, nay, some whose Aramaic origin is obvious, were assumed to be Greek. *Kerads* [2], an indigenous Aramaic root, common to Syriac Chaldee Samaritan,
was assumed not only to be from a common root with
κηρύσσω, but to be the very word; *kerods* [3] was to be the
same as κήρυξ; *partemim* [4] was to be πρότιμοι (which is,
of course, not even Greek [5],) *pattish* [6] to be πέτασος; *ne-
bidsbah* [7] to be νόμισμα; *pithgam* [8] to be φθέγμα (none of
which last Greek words would suit the meaning of the
passages.) Then, among the names of musical instruments employed in Nebuchadnezzar's solemn dedication,
mashrokhitha was to be σύριγξ; *sabka* was not to be, (what
it was) the original Semitic name which the Greeks,
adopting the instrument, pronounced σαμβύκη, but was,
despite of the Greeks themselves, to be the Greek word;
soomphonia was more naturally thought to be συμφωνία;
khitharos was probably κίθαρις, our "guitar;" and *pesanterin,* ψαλτήριον. Of these 9 or 10 alleged Greek words,
(two are from the same root) improved philology swept
away at once all which are not names of musical instruments; three roots belonging to the Aryan family, two
probably being genuine Chaldee. Of the four musical instruments, *mashrokitha* has probably a common Sanskrit
root with σύριγξ, but is a genuine Aramaic word; *sabka* [9]
is the Aramaic name of the instrument which the Greeks

---

[1] This was an imagination of Bertholdt, e. g. p. 248, 752,3. wherein he neglected Greek idiom as well as Chaldee.   [2] קרא v. 29. also Syriac and Sam.;
in Sanscr. *krus*, (whence Gr. κηρύσσω, κρίζω, κράζω;) Germ. kreischen. Ges.
The Arabic use is borrowed probably from the Aramaic, yet is not exclusively
Christian.   [3] קרד iii. 4. also in Syr. and Arm.

[4] פרתמים Dan. i. 3. also of Persian nobles, Esth. i. 3. vi. 10. see Note A. at the
end.   [5] It should be ἔντιμοι.   [6] פטיש ktib or פטש kri iii. 21. also in Syriac.
πέτασος is "a broad brimmed hat."   [7] נבזבה probably from בזבן see Ges.

[8] פתגם iii. 16. iv. 14. Ezr. iv. 17. v. 7, 14. see Note A.

[9] סבכא a "harp," from Semitic סבך, שבך. comp. Shabaka Ar. Melit. Zab. "intertwined;" שבכה, "net;" *shabaka* Ar. *Shibke* Melit. Id.

called σαμβύκη, inserting the m, as the Zabians and Maltese [10] did in the Syriac *aboobo*, " reed, pipe," an insertion familiar to us in Horace's " ambubaia [11]," "female fluteplayer."   But the Greeks themselves say that the σαμβύκη was " [12] a Syriac invention," as indeed it has a Syriac, but no Greek, etymology.   Now, whether there remain two or three musical instruments, this would be nothing more remarkable, than the corresponding fact, that Greeks imported Syriac or Hebrew names of instruments, together with the instrument themselves, as κινύρα, νάβλα [13].   We know that the Babylonians loved foreign music also, and that they saddened their Hebrew captives by bidding them, [14] *sing* to their harps some *of the songs of Zion.*   Isaiah, foretelling the destruction of Babylon, says, [15] *Thy pomp is brought down to the grave, the noise of thy viols.* (nebaleica.)   Babylon was *a city of merchants* [16] *;* she *exulted in her ships* [17].   Her manufactures found their way to Palestine in the days of Joshua [18].   The Euphrates connected Babylon downwards with India, and above even with Armenia [19] and the line of Tyrian commerce, and, through Tyre, with Greece.   Nebuchadnezzar had, himself, at enormous expense, connected it with the Persian Gulf, by a gigantic navigable canal [20].   We know the rival lines of commerce, that from Sardis by land across to Armenia [21] and, beyond, to Susa; and that from Petra to Babylon [22], a transit both from Egypt [22] and Tyre. Tyre again had its own Northern line, through Tadmor (Palmyra) to Tiphsach (Thapsacus) and thence Southward to Babylon [23].   [24] Thapsacus was the North-Eastern

---

[10] *amboob*, Zabian ; *lenboob* for *el enboob*, Melit. Ges. v. אביב.

[11] Hor. Sat. i. 2. 1.   [12] Juba, Hist. Theatr. iv. in Athenæus, iv. 77. p. 391. Dind.   [13] from קנר, נבל. " Sopater says that the νάβλα too was a Phœnician invention." (Ib. p. 390.) Strabo says, " some musical instruments have Barbarian names, Nablas and Sambuke and Barbitos and Magadis and many others." x. 3. 17. αθλος is probably from חלל, " perforated," " pipe or flute."

[14] Ps. cxxxvii. 2.   [15] xiv. 11.   [16] Ezek. xvii. 4.   [17] Is. xliii. 14.

[18] vii. 21.   [19] Herod. i. 194.   [20] Rawl. Herod. Ess. 8. i. 512. The canal is shewn on Spruner's map.   [21] Herod. v. 52.   [22] Strab. xiv. 4, 2. see on Joel iv. 10. p. 144.   [23] See Heeren, Ideen, ii. 127. iii. 402, 3.

[24] 1 Kgs. iv. 24. [v. 4. Heb.]

extremity of the kingdom of Solomon; and the line of commerce, for which doubtless he built or rebuilt Tadmor [1], was, at least, more than four centuries anterior to this date. The intercourse of Greece with Tyre, in Ante-Homeric times, is evidenced by the use of a Phœnician or Hebrew word to designate "gold [2]." Asia, from the Tigris Westward, was systematically intersected with lines of commerce. Sardis and Babylon were proverbially luxurious. It were rather a marvel, if *the golden* music-loving *city* [3] had not gathered to itself foreign musical instruments of all sorts, or if, in a religious inauguration at Babylon, all the variety of music which it could command had not been united, to grace the festival and bear along the minds and imaginations of the people. The Greek names are but another instance of the old recognised fact, that the name of an import travels with the thing. When we speak of tea, sugar, coffee, chocolate, cocoa, cassia, cinnamon, tobacco, myrrh, citrons, rice, potatoes, cotton, chintz, shawls, we do not stop to think that we are using Chinese, Malay, Arabic, Mexican, Hebrew, Malabar, S. American, Bengalee [4], Persian words, and we shall continue to use them, even though they were originally misapplied, and we know that the word tobacco was the name, not of the plant but of the vessel out of which the natives smoked it. When Solomon's ships brought him the peacocks, apes, ivory, almug or algum-wood, they brought with them also the Sanskrit and Malabar names of the ape, (which passed thence into Greek and our European languages) and of the Algum wood; the Tamul name of the peacock, and the Sanskrit of the elephant [5]. There is nothing stranger in our find-

---

[1] Ib. ix. 18.   [2] χρύσος from חָרוּץ, add ἅρπη, scymetar, from חֶרֶב; μνᾶ from מָנֶה.   [3] Is. xiv. 4.   [4] The authority, except for the Hebrew Arabic Persian words, is Adelung.

[5] see in Ges. v. קוֹף, אֳנִי, שֶׁנְהַבִּים. Prof. Max Müller approves of these etymologies and adds for the algum wood (which had hitherto baffled Philologists) the Malabar and Sanskrit "valguka." Science of Language, p. 203. The pronunciation in the Chronicles, (2 Chr. ii. 8. ix. 10, 11.) "algum," is then nearer the original than that in the Kings, "almug." 1 Kgs. x. 11, 12.

ing Greek instruments of music in Nebuchadnezzar's time at Babylon, than in the Indian names of Indian animals and of an Indian tree having reached Jerusalem under Solomon. Perhaps there is a trace of the trade in female slaves, for which Phœnicia was early infamous, 900 years before Nebuchadnezzar, in the Pentateuch, there being no etymology for the Hebrew word "concubine," "pilegesh," or "pillegesh," in any Semitic or other Eastern language, while it does correspond with the Greek πάλλαξ, " maiden."

The Greek names of musical instruments being then only evidence of indirect commerce between Babylon and Greece, the evidence was to be eked out by calling them "[6] Macedonian instruments." In regard to pesanterin, this was to be proved, in that the Alexandrians, like the Dorians of old, are supposed to have changed the λ into ν ; and so "pesanterin" *might be* a Doric or Alexandrian pronunciation of ψαλτήριον. Only, in fact, 1) although the word ψαλτήριον occurs in the LXX. and other Greek translations of Holy Scripture[7], and sometimes in classic authors[8], the form ψαντήριον never does occur. The Greek translators of Daniel render Pesanterin by ψαλτήριον. 2) If it *had* occurred, being a Doric form, it would have been obviously the Doric name for the instrument, Doric music being ancient and celebrated, whereas any special Macedonian music is unheard of. Nor is it likely that there ever was such, since we are here on later historic times, and we know, in detail, of Æolic, Doric, Ionian, Lydian, Phrygian music, and have no hint of Macedonian. The Dorians were, of old, established in Crete, with which both Assyria and Tyre were in proximate intercourse. A change of consonants which the Macedonians, (if it had been so) would have retained from the Doric, could have been no proof that a word, had it existed, was not Doric but Macedonian. We might as well say, that any word which we retain in use

---

[6] Essays and Rev. p. 76. from Ges. v. פִּילֶגֶשׁ.

[7] See Tromm or Schleusner, sub v.   [8] See Scott and Liddell, sub v.

from old French or Saxon, "oyez" or "yclept," was a proof that any older writing in which it may occur belongs to the 19th century, not to the period from which it is retained.   In truth, the n being pronounced against the palate like l, only somewhat harder and lower, l and n are notoriously interchanged, not in Greek dialects only, but in all languages.   It is one of the acknowledged changes in the Semitic dialects, both in themselves and with each other [1], as it is between ourselves and the Germans [2].   But 3) there is no proof whatever, that the Macedonians ever did substitute the n for the l [3].   So then, as relates to "pesanterin," we have an imaginary dialectic variation to account for an imaginary Greek word, whereas the change is according to the recognised principles of all languages.

[1] Gesenius, who v. פְּסַנְתֵּרִין accounts for the word in that "l was changed into n after the manner of the Macedonian dialect, which (dialect) was from the time of Alexander received among the Syrians and Alexandrians," accounts for it rightly under ל; "l is not seldom hardened into n, as עֲלַם Ar. zanam, and in popular Arab. zanzala for zalzala, earthquake; sansala for salsala, a chain : *frequently in foreign words*, as פְּסַנְתֵּרִין from ψαλτήριον; margonitho (Syr.) margelitha (Ch.) from μαργαρίτης; Isrâin and Isrâil; Michâin and Michâil. Zab. Enshebeth, for Elizabeth."   In Heb. we have נָטַע, לָטַע; נָצַן, לָצַן; נִשְׁבָּה, לִשְׁבָּה; נָטַשׁ, לָטַשׁ; and also נָגַן, (whence Dan. נְגִינָה,) Targ. לְחֵן; Bochart adds, (Phaleg p. 520.) נָכַב Ar. lakaba ; lympha, νύμφη ; lutra, ἔνυδρις ; pulmo, πνεύμων. Ges. refers to Scheid in Diss. Lugd. p. 953. for instances within the Arabic itself.

[2] ermel ermine ; kummel cummin ; himmel heaven ; orgel organ.

[3] "There seems to be no trace of any such word as ψαλτήριον.   The change of λ into ν is not exemplified in any of the words known to be, or by Grammarians said to be, Macedonian.   Of the words in which it is exemplified in profane writers, φίνταται is pure Doric ; (Epicharmus fr.) γέντο is Homeric ; ἐνθεῖν, βέντιστος are Theocritean ; φίντις (which Ahrens questions) is in Pindar ; δέντα is said to be Doric by Grammarians.   There remains, *possibly* to countenance the Macedonian theory, ἐλιφενά ; אֱלִיפְלֵהוּ in LXX. 1 Chr. xv. 16. But this, as you say, could only indicate a Doric or Æolic affinity in the Macedonian dialect."   Letter of Rev. J. Riddell, Fell. of Ball.   The reading ἐλειφενά is an accidental variation of the Vatican MS. of the LXX.   The *Alexandrian* MS. has 'Ελιφαλδ ; 15 others and the Comp. have λ ; in v. 21. conversely the Vat. MS. has alone 'Ενφαναίας, 4 MSS. have 'Ελιφαναίας, ; the Alex. Ald. xi. and 3 others have 'Ελιφαλαίας ; 10 others have also the two λ.   Contrariwise, for the Hebrew *Mikneahu* the Vat. has Μακελλεία ; another, Κελλία, v. 18. but all have the Hebrew n in v. 21.   Such changes probably arose in copying from dictation and indistinct hearing.

In the "Macedonian word, symphonia," we have, further, an imaginary meaning[4] attached to an ordinary Greek word, and, because Antiochus Epiphanes is related to have danced in a wild way under the stirring of the *symphony,* "concert," of music, it is assumed that the "symphonia" was some one instrument, and that, Ma-

[4] Gesenius alleges two places of Polybius, as authority for a Greek instrument, συμφωνία. In the one, it is manifestly "concert" (quoted by Athenæus x. 52. p. 439. Cas.) "The concert stimulating him, the king [Antiochus Epiphanes] jumping up danced and jested with the actors, so that all were ashamed." The other is equally clear, with Athenæus' reading; "If he heard of any young men feasting any where, he came in with a jar [of wine] and music, so that most, for the strangeness, rose and fled." There is no other place where συμφωνία even *seems* to be a single instrument; and indeed the name contradicts that idea. In Latin S. Jerome corrects those who so misinterpreted the word in S. Luke xv. "Some Latins think wrongly that the symphonia is a sort of organ, whereas the concordant harmony in the praises of God is signified by this word. For συμφωνία is expressed in Latin by *consonantia.*" (Ep. 21. ad Dam. n. 29.) S. Augustine in Ps. 41. ed. Bened. has symphoniaci, "a band of music," not, as was of old read faultily, symphoniam. (Du Cange s. v.) Others explain the word of some one instrument, shewing by their contradictions that they had no certain knowledge. Isidore (Orig. ii. 21.) and Ugutio (Du C.) describe it as a drum; Glosses on Prudentius (A. D. 405,) sistrum or trumpet; Mamotrectus, "lyres;" others, "pipe." Ven. Fortunatus (A.D. 530,) uses it in poetry for a powerful wind-instrument. Later, "sweet" is its epithet. (Nic. de Braya and Joh. Molinet in Du Cange.) Du Cange supposes the "chifonia" of old French poetry to be derived from it, (an instrument hung on the neck of itinerant minstrels.) ib. Others identify the Italian sambogna. Menage (whom Gesenius quotes for this) says, "It is beyond question that sambogna is derived from Sambucina, diminutive of Sambuca; sambucina, sambucna, sampogna." (le orig. della ling. Ital.) In whatever way later writers may have understood the word, there is no evidence of any actual instrument called "symphonia," until times when it would be altogether a new instrument. Many repeat from Ges. as a fact, that "in Syria and Asia Minor it is called sambogna." This could only be true of itinerant musicians; but is without authority and probably a mistake. In the passage of Polybius, I have supplied the only meaning which κεραμίου *can* have, and which, in the Greek of Polybius, it *may* perhaps have. There is, however, no instance in which κεράμιον, without the addition of οἰνηρόν, οἴνου, is used of a jar of wine. It may, however, have been intelligible from the context, that the king brought it as his contribution to the feast. The κεράτιον however of Diodorus (Exc. ii. 577.) is still more unintelligible. κεράτιον is used of the hornlets of a prickly crab; of a slight projection of the uterus; but not as a diminutive of κέρας, either as a drinking horn or as a wind-instrument. Hemsterhuis (on Lucian D. Dial. xii. p. 233, 4.) referred to by Wess. on Diod. does not even name it.

cedonian. In the absence of all evidence that the Greek word *symphonia* was ever used of any single instrument, German critics of the most opposite schools have found for the Chaldee instrument a not improbable etymology in Aramaic [1].

Criticism then, as it became more accurate, retreated, point by point, from all which, in its rashness, it had asserted. First, it gave up the so-called Græcisms; then that there were any Greek words in Daniel except three of the musical instruments; then, that there was any thing incredible in some Greek musical instruments being used at Nebuchadnezzar's solemn religious festival: lastly, this crotchet, that two of the musical instruments were Macedonian words, must give way likewise. Yet at each stage these pseudo-criticisms did their work. Those who disbelieved Daniel believed the authority of the critics. "[2] To fix the time in which this chapter (i) was written we have a date in the Greek [not Greek but Aryan] word ' partemim,' according to which we can hardly go further back than the time of Artaxerxes Longimanus." "[3] The use of the Greek [Aramaic] word ' nebidsba ' leaves no doubt that this chapter (ii) must have been composed in the times after Xerxes." And so on.

I have treated this question of the mention of Greek instruments, on what I believe to be the only philosophical

---

[1] Meyer and Hävernick prefer the etymology from סָפ "a reed;" "thence" says Meyer, "סוּף (like מִסְוָן from מִן) and then an adj. stat. emphat. סָפְיָא (the form of the word in Dan. iii. 10. Keth.)   This is confirmed by the Copt. ϭⲏⲃⲓ arundo, [perhaps the original of σίφων, siphon, tube, which has no satisfactory Greek etymology] tibia; and tibia itself is perhaps Semitic, as rohr (reed) rohrbein (thigh-bone) röhrpfeife, a reed-pipe, also used of some organ-pipes. סַנְפְיָא would be formed from this by the insertion of the n. See above p. 25. Fürst, in like way, says of סַנְפְיָא, "since the Greeks themselves did not so name the instrument, it is perhaps Semitic." He mentions the same etymology, as also another given by Meier, סָפַן cover (coll. Ar. tsofno or tsofono, a leathern vessel for washing or drawing water: tsafno, tsofono, tsafna, a scrip or leathern tablecloth; tsafano, scrip;) then a Hebrew intensive adj. form סַפְנִי resolved into סַפְנְיָ. stat. emph. סַפְנְיָא.   Meier himself rightly regards this as improbable, although the Arabic meanings, being unconnected with the others of the root, are probably derived from some other dialect.

[2] Bertholdt, Dan. § 6. p. 98.   [3] Ib. § 7. p. 61.

ground, the fact of an old and extensive commerce between Babylon and the West. "The name travelled with the thing," is an acknowledged principle of philology. It needed not that a single Greek should have been at Babylon. Tyrian merchants took with them the names of the wares which they sold, just as our English merchants transmitted the names of our East Indian imports with them into Germany, or the Spaniards brought us back the American names of the products of the new world, or at this day, I am told, some of our Manchester goods are known by the name of their eminent manufacturer in Tartary, where the face of an Englishman has probably been scarcely seen. Yet the actual intercourse of the Greeks with the East is now known to have been far greater than was formerly imagined. Brandis thus opens his book "on the historical gain from the decyphering of the Assyrian inscriptions;"

"'Long before the Greeks began to write History, they had, as friends and foes, come into manifold contact with the empire of the Assyrians. That Assyria took part in the Trojan war, as Ctesias and others[5] related, no one would give out for an historical fact; but the battle and victory of Sennacherib in the 8th century B.C. over a Greek army which had penetrated into Cilicia is fully attested by a relation out of the Babylonian history of Berosus[6]. On the other hand, the extensive commerce of Greek colonies must not unfrequently have led Greek merchants into Assyrian territory. Did they not penetrate even to the inhospitable steppes of Russia on the Dnieper and the Don[7]? The most important however must have been the intercourse with the Assyrian provinces of Asia Minor, especially with the countries bordering on the Black Sea and the Mediterranean, and certainly with Lydia also; which, as appears, for above 500 years until near the end of the 8th century B.C., was de-

<hr>

[4] Histor. Gewinn aus d. Entziff. d. Ass. Inschrift. p. 1, 2.   [5] Diod. ii. 22.
[6] Fragm. Hist. Gr. ed. Müller. ii. 534.   [7] Heeren's Ideen. i. 920 sqq.
[from Herod. iv. 24. (see Rawl. on Her. iv. 17. T. iii. p. 14, 16.) coll. Strab. xi. 2. 16.]

pendant upon Assyria [1]. In Cyprus too, where the Greeks traded and the Assyrians had established themselves even in earlier times, these nations must have come into manifold contact. That Greeks came to Assyria itself as merchants, must remain conjecture only; but certainly Esarhaddon who, first of the Assyrian rulers, had a paid army, was accompanied by Greek soldiers also on his marches through Asia [2]. Be this as it may, Anaximander's map of the world [3] (he was born about 610, B. C.) implies an accurate acquaintance with the East. That the Westerns generally took more part in the revolutions of the East than we should have thought, appears from the fragment of a poetical address of Alcæus to his brother Antimenides, who had won glory and reward under the banner of Nebuchadnezzar [4]." The name of Javan or Greece occurs in the inscriptions of Sargon among those from whom he received tribute [5]. We know that articles of luxury formed part of the tribute to Assyria [6]. Sargon's statue found at Idalium commemorates his expedition against Cyprus [7]. More recently, Labynetus I. of Babylon had been present at the great invasion of the Lydians by Cyaxares [7]. It was no great matter for monarchs who transported a monolith obelisk from Armenia [8], and moved those colossal bulls [9], and brought cedars from Lebanon [10], to import a few Greek musical instruments. Either way then, whether as spoils of war or articles of commerce, Greek instruments of music might easily have found their way to Babylon. In the monuments even of Sennacherib, "the Assyrian Generals,"

[1] Niebuhr, Vorlesung. üb. alt. Gesch. i. 405.

[2] Abydenus in Euseb. Chron. Arm. i. 53.　　[3] i. e. the fact that he could construct a map of the world. "Anaximander the Milesian, hearer of Thales, first ventured to depict the world in a map." Agathemerus, Compend. Geogr. in Hudson's Geogr. V. Scriptt. T. ii. "He first described the circumference of earth and sea." Diog. Laert. ii. 1.　　[4] Strabo, xiii. 3. 2.　　[5] Rawl. Herod. Essay vii. T. i. 474.　　[6] Ib. 465. Fox Talbot's annals of Essarhaddon in Journal of Sacr. Lit. N. 17. p. 72, 3. Layard, N. and Bab. p. 356.

[7] Her. i. 74.　　[8] Diod. ii. 11.　　[9] See the description from the bas relief in Layard, N. and Bab. c. 5. p. 104-114. or the bas-relief itself in the British Museum.　　[10] Ib. p. 118. 357. 644. Rawl. Her. i. 475.

says Layard[11], are represented as " welcomed by bands of men and women, dancing, singing and playing upon instruments of music.—We find from various passages in the Scriptures, that the instruments of music chiefly used on such triumphant occasions were the harp, one with ten strings, (rendered viol or lyre in some versions, but probably a kind of dulcimer) the tabor and the pipe; precisely those represented in the bas-reliefs. First came five men; three carried harps of many strings, which they struck with both hands;—a fourth played on the double pipes, such as are seen on the monuments of Egypt, and were used by the Greeks and Romans. They were blown at the end like the flutes of the modern Yezidis, which they probably resembled in tone and form. The fifth musician carried an instrument not unlike the modern Santour of the East, consisting of a number of strings stretched over a hollow case or sounding-board." "The Santour of the East " was recognised by Gesenius as the Pesanterin[12] of Daniel. Even the two ways of spelling[13], which occur in Daniel, recur in the modern Arabic instrument[14]. The Psaltery, as described by S. Augustine[15], corresponds with the " Santour", as recognised by Layard on the bas-reliefs of Babylon.

Bertholdt, who invented Græcisms for the book of Daniel, discovered also Rabbinisms, as he thought, but none which he could allege. It had been nothing surprising, if the Hebrew which Daniel spoke or wrote had been less pure than belonged to his age. First minister at a foreign court, using probably Aramaic as his ordinary language, diligently instructed in the Aryan language of the Magi, he knew Hebrew probably only from the remi-

---

[11] Nin. and Bab. c. 20. p. 454. [12] "the *p* being cast aside at the beginning (as *talma* for Ptolemy,) and *in* or *i* from the end." v. פסנתרין.

[13] with the ס iii. 7. and the ת Ib. 5. 10. 15. (varying in the MSS.)

[14] It is written in Arabic with slight variations, מסנר, צנתור, מסניר, מסנר, סנתר.

[15] in Ps. 32. n. 5. "That hollow-wood, like a tabor, on which the strings rest in such wise that when they are touched, being from it set in a tremulous motion and from that cavity gathering sound, they are made more sonorous; this wood the cithara has in the lower part, the psaltery in the upper."

niscences of boyhood, and from the study of the law and
of the prophets who had been before him. The use of
Syriac or Median words belongs to his situation; they
fit in with it. Bertholdt conceded thus much. "An
acute enquirer of our time[1]," he says[2], "thinks it very
conceivable that the language of Daniel, taught as he
was in the language and learning of the Chaldæans,
living under several Babylonian kings, under Cyaxares
the Mede and under Cyrus the Persian, at court and in
high office, might take precisely such a colour, as to become unlike all other remains of Hebrew antiquity, and
sink below the Hebrew of Ezra, Nehemiah and the book
of Esther, although far older than it.   But if Daniel's intercourse with Chaldæans, Medians, Persians in succession
occasioned certain peculiarities in his diction, then the
Hebrew style which we should expect would be one con-
forming to the language of the Chaldees, Medes and Persians.   Chaldaisms, Medisms, Persisms could, accordingly, be nothing strange in the Hebrew portion of his book;
the approximations of his expressions to Rabbinism must
remain the mark whereby the later date of this book is
quite clearly to be recognized."   A definite issue! But
where is the proof?   Bertholdt offered none.   In his fuller introduction, he rejected the obvious remark of Staüdlin which he had before admitted, dropped the imputation
of Rabbinisms, but appealed to his own critical tact, that
the Hebrew of Daniel must be two centuries later than
Ezekiel, Jeremiah, or such Psalms as were written during
or soon after the captivity.   He himself, he says[3], "could
not support this by proof in that place, without taking
up the room required for other more necessary investigations."   An "accurate critical history of Hebrew and
of its developement would," he thought, "supersede the
necessity of appealing to his own philological feeling, and
would make it plain to sight, that the author of the last
five chapters of Daniel must have lived a considerable time

<hr>

[1] Staüdlin, Neue Beyträge, p. 115.
[2] Bertholdt, Dan. Einl. p. 28, 9.   [3] Einl. ins. A. u. N. T. § 388. iv. 1537.

after Haggai, Zechariah, and Malachi." A commencement of such a history of Hebrew appeared two years later
from one who shared all Bertholdt's doctrinal prejudices ;
but Gesenius [4] simply classed Daniel in the " silver age "
of Hebrew, with Ezra, Nehemiah, the Chronicles, Esther,
and some older books. The words, which he selects as
characteristic of that age, occur chiefly in those historical books and in Ecclesiastes, some in Job; and but
few in Daniel. Bleek, and De Wette, after a careful examination of the Hebrew portion of Daniel with a view
to the question [5], for the time distinctly renounced Bertholdt's notion of the lateness of the style of Daniel ; and
Bleek seemed to think it a gain if any how the style should
prove nothing one way or the other [6]. Even Ewald has
no thought except of three marked periods of Hebrew writers [7]; that before David; that before the Captivity; and
the decline, upon and through the Captivity. He classes
together the language of Ecclesiastes, the Chronicles,
Daniel.

It were an easy, but unsatisfactory, way, simply to
shew that the words alleged by Von Lengerke [8], and
transferred thence to the Introduction of De Wette [9], as far
as they prove any thing, coincide with the age and circumstances of Daniel. This however would only have been
an answer to the individual. I have therefore examined

[4] Gesch. d. Hebr. Sprache u. Schrift. Leipz. 1815.

[5] " Bertholdt and others maintained that the Hebrew of Daniel fell far below
that of the very latest book of the O. T. ; but Bleek has given up the ground,
since we have no standard for the gradual decay of the language after the
Captivity. I confess that a fresh comparison of the Hebrew style of the book,
with a view to the present work, *yielded few or rather no results*. The style
is sometimes careless and unclear (as ix. 26. לֹ יֵאָן xi. 6. קְהָל) and has harsh-
nesses (as xi. 7. עַם for עַל עַם ;) the idiom is also sometimes strange (as מֵישָׁר
for ' peace' xi. 6 ;) else there is but little deviation ; especially if one takes into
account that the style is prophetic, to which belongs the use of the apoc. future, as [וְיִשְׁם] מָגַן לֵיַזֵב xi. 10." Hall. Encyc. 1813. Daniel, p. 10.)

[6] Schleiermacher, &c. Theol. Zeitschr. iii. p. 596. 212, 3. In his posthumous
Einleitung, he insists on the Greek musical instruments, but drops the subject
of the style.   [7] Ausf. Lehrb. d. Hebr. Sprache 1855. p. 22, 3.   [8] D. Buch
Daniel, 1835. p. lx. lxi.   [9] They do not occur in his Einleitung ins. A. T.
ed. iv. 1833. and are in the posthumous edition, 1852., probably in that of 1844.

expressly for this object every notable word and idiom used in the Hebrew of Daniel, and have set down under four heads, 1) what is peculiar to Daniel; 2) what he has in common with the middle period of language, i. e. words or idioms, not occurring in the Pentateuch, but received in books free from the influence of Aramaic; 3) what Daniel has in common with the later writers, i. e. words or idioms which, in our remaining Hebrew, do not occur before the times bordering on the Captivity, as Jeremiah; 4) what, like other of the sacred writers of the same date, he has revived out of the Hebrew of the Pentateuch. The enquiry was simply historical, *where* any words or idioms employed by Daniel occurred in previous or contemporary Hebrew [1]. There is, for the most part, little characteristic in any of this language. In very many words or idioms, which do not occur at an earlier date, there is no reason from the nature of the language, why they should not. The unchanging East has not our variations of language. The inhabitants of Mecca still speak, in its purity, precisely that same Arabic in which the Coran was written 12 centuries ago [2]. What *is* characteristic, however, falls in with the time of Daniel.

1. It is manifest from that number of words or idioms peculiar to the book of Daniel, that, like every other Hebrew writer, he moulded the language in which he wrote, freely for himself. It is not the language of one, who writes after received models in a dead language. Like all the other sacred writers, he uses the language of those who went before him [3]. When describing a vision like one of Ezekiel, he uses language of Ezekiel. But he does not, in the least, copy the style of Ezekiel, and, in fact, his Hebrew is freer from unusual grammatical

---

[1] See Note B. at the end. I have not noticed idioms which, occurring throughout all periods of Hebrew, belonged to the unchanging store of the language.

[2] The late Professor Freytag (author of the Arabic Lexicon) told me this on the authority of an Arab, who, being too late for the solemnities of the Haj, remained at Mecca till the following year.   [3] See Introduction to Hosea, p. 6. Joel, p. 94. Obadiah, p. 228, 230, 1. Jonah, p. 252. and on iv. 2. p. 284. Introd. to Micah, p. 289.

forms than that of Ezekiel. It could not have been formed upon it.

2. It should be observed, how the style of Daniel varies with his subjects. One may say that there are four distinct styles in Daniel. a) the simple narrative, (as of ch. i. and elsewhere.) b) The impassioned language of his prayer (ch. ix.) with which his short thanksgiving in the Chaldee portion remarkably corresponds. Of the 4 verses of that thanksgiving, two are, for cadence and language, as remarkable as any in Hebrew [4]. c) The purely prophetic style of the prophecy of the 70 weeks. d) The condensed descriptive prophecy of ch. xi., in which every phrase characterises an event or a course of events, yet so that while we can now, with the light of history, identify the events, no one could, beforehand, make a history from them. The simplicity of the narrative, the pathos of the prayer, the solemn stateliness of the prophetic style, and the vivid condensation of this historical prophecy, combined in one, are no slight evidence of the grasp which the writer had of the language wherein he wrote in styles so varied [5].

3. The Aryan or other foreign words occur almost exclusively in the Chaldee of Daniel, and, with one exception, they occur solely in his narrative. That one exception is, that the technical word for the " royal meats," "pathbag," to which Daniel had been accustomed, is once repeated in the same exact sense in the prophetic portion of the book [6]; but it is a word altogether naturalised in Syriac, and so probably in the Aramaic of Daniel's time, although unknown to the later Chaldee. Of all these foreign words it may be said, that they do not enter into

---

[4] Dan. ii. 21, 22. vehoo mĕhashnĕ 'iddĕnayyă vĕzimnayyă, mĕha'dĕh malkeen ûmĕhakeem malkeen ; yăhĕb chochmĕthă lĕchakkeemeen, ûmande'ă lĕyădĕ'ei beenah. hoo gălĕ 'Ameekăthă ûmĕsattĕrăthă, yăda' măh băchăshŏkă, oonĕhiră immĕh shĕră.   [5] Hitzig, with his wonted arrogance towards the prophets, says, " The bare fact that the author meant to write Hebrew, throws off this garb on the first occasion, and writes Aramaic for 6 chapters together, without any ground, beyond the historical portion, proves that the Aramaic style suited him best, the Hebrew was burdensome to him." Heidelb. Jahrb. 1832. p. 119. followed by Leng. p. xxxi. On the grounds of the variation of the languages see ab. p. 9, 10.   [6] xi. 26.

the prophet's ordinary style, nor do they in any way influence it.   All of them are technical names[1], relating to
foreign offices, dress, food, musical instruments, which
Daniel had occasion to speak of, and without which he
could not describe what he has to describe.   He uses foreign names of foreign offices, just as we have received
into English the Arabic names, Caliph, Sultan, Vizier,
Emir, Cadhi, &c. or the Persian Pasha.   Up to the time of
the captivity there were in Hebrew two foreign names
of offices only, one as old as Solomon, the etymology
of which is lost, (Pechah [2]) the other from the time of Isaiah [3].   To these, Daniel, from his situation in the Babylonian Court, adds eight more, two of which only are mentioned elsewhere in Holy Scripture; "Satrap" in Ezra and
Esther; "treasurer" in Ezra only, and with a different
pronunciation.   Daniel's word, *gedabar*, could not have
been taken, (as some theorised) from Ezra; for in Ezra,
as in Syriac, it is *gidsbar*.   They are probably dialectic
differences.   Another Aryan word of the same class,
partemim, *nobles*, occurs in directions given by Nebuchadnezzar, and is probably employed as having been so
used [4].   It is twice used in the book of Esther of Persian
nobles, but was unknown in Syriac, and occurs once only
in Chaldee, being retained out of the Hebrew in one of
the two passages of Esther.   Names of dress are more

---

[1] *Officers*, Hammelzar, (Dan. i. 11, 16.) achashdarpenin, (Dan. iii. 2, 3, 27. vi.
2, 3, 4, 7, 8. in Heb. Ezr. viii. 36. Esth. iii. 12. viii. 9. ix. 3.) gedabar, (in Ezra, gidsbar, i. 8. Heb. vii. 21. Ch.) dethabar, (Dan. iii. 2, 3.) sarca, (Dan. vi. 3, 4,
5, 7, 8.) Aryan. Tiphtayya, prob. from a root now only in Arab. (Dan. iii. 2.)
haddaberin, (Dan. iii. 24. 25. iv. 33. vi. 8.) adargadserin, (Dan. iii. 2, 3.) Aramaic.
Dress, Sarbal, (Dan. iii. 21, 27.) pattish, (Dan. iii. 21.) hamnuk, (Dan. v. 7, 6,
29.) Aryan : carbal, (Dan. iii. 21.) probably Aramaic.   *Food*, pathbag, Aryan.
(Dan. i. 5, 8, 13, 15. xi. 26.) *Musical instruments*, karna, mashrokitha, sabka
(iii. 5, 7, 10, 15.) and probably sifonia (iii. 10.) or soomfonia, (Dan. iii. 5, 15.)
Aramaic ; kitharos and pesanterin, (iii. 5, 7, 10, 15.) Greek.   I have not counted
the word *pithgam*, " word," in the Chaldee of Daniel, because, although Aryan
originally, it was naturalised in all Aramaic, and is one of its most common
words.   It occurs in the Chaldee of Daniel, not in his Hebrew, as it does in that
even of Ecclesiastes (viii. 11.) and Esther (i. 20.)   [2] see Note A at the end.
  [3] Is. xli. 25. prophesying of Cyrus.   [4] Dan. i. 3. In Esther i. 3. vi. 9.
it is used of Persian nobles.

likely to survive; and so two out of the three Aryan terms
in Daniel lived on in ordinary Syriac[5]; the 3rd is retained out of the Chaldee in the Syriac translation of
Daniel, but disappeared out of the language; a fourth
name of dress, probably Aramaic, was lost.   The Chaldee
as well as the Syriac retained the name of the Greek instrument *kathros;* else the Chaldee retains even fewer
of these terms than the Syriac.   It has been noticed how
this use of Aryan words exactly corresponds with the situation of Daniel[6].   Those who invent a later date for
the book of Daniel can attempt no real explanation how
a Jew who, according to their hypothesis, lived in Palestine about 163, B.C., should be acquainted with Aryan
words, which related to offices which had long ceased to
exist, or to dress which no one wore, words which were
mostly obliterated from Aramaic, which (as far they survived) were inherited only from Daniel's text; and several
of them were misunderstood or not understood by Aramaic translators, or by Jews who, on the unbelieving theory, were almost his contemporaries, and yet these words
have been verified to us by the opening acquaintance with
the Aryan languages.

I will add here, how four Syriac words which have been
singled out by the opponents of Daniel as being in some
way, marks against his Hebrew, fall in with his situation.   1) *Aphadno,* " his palace."   The word survived in
heathen[7] and Christian[8] Syriac as well as in the translation of the Scripture[9], and was also, in a slightly varied
form[10], probably introduced into Arabic from the Syriac.
It must have been known in Mesopotamia, since it became the name of a place, Apadnas[11], near Amida on the
Tigris.   But it was wholly lost in Chaldee[12], was unintel-

[5] see Note C.   [6] Delitzsch, in Herzog's Real-Encyclop. v. Daniel, p. 274.
[7] Chron. Edess. in Ass. B. O. i. 390, 1. See note of Ass. p. 391. Ges.
[8] Assem. Acta Mart. i. 166. S. Ephr. ii. 393. iii. 220, in a quotation as if
from Holy Scr. (Bernstein Coll.)   [9] In 1 Chr. xv. 1. S. Eccl. xxi. 5. for οἶκος
ὑπερηφάνου. Ges.   [10] *phadano,* "a palace built aloft," *phaddana,*" built such a
palace." (a denom.)   [11] Procop. de ædif. Justinian. ii. 4. Reland, p. 571.   [12] It
remains only in one proverb, and a doubtful reading, Jer. xliii. 10. Buxt. p. 181.

ligible to all the Greek translators[1], and, was rendered in the Syriac translation not according to the meaning of the actual Syriac word, but according to the common meaning of padan[2], which forms part of the name Padan-Aram.   2) *Ashaph*, which occurs in the Chaldee[3], as well as the Hebrew[4] of Daniel, occurs in no other Hebrew or Chaldee.   Many as are the Hebrew names of those who, in different ways, used divination, this name occurs no where in Holy Scripture, except in Daniel.   It is a common Syriac term, and probably represents some character of Aramaic divination, with which Daniel became acquainted in Babylon.   3) *Rasham*, (we know from the Chaldee of Daniel) was the official term used of the king's signature[5], which, when it was affixed, was, according to the Medo-Persian law, unchangeable.   Daniel uses it alike in his Chaldee and Hebrew of that which was written irreversibly[6].   4) *Palmoni*, "a certain one, " is remarkable as, apart from one passage of Daniel, only occurring as a very rare Syriac word.   It was formed out of two Hebrew words which survive only in conversations recorded in the Old Testament[7].   In Syriac also, as Theodoret attests, it still, in the 4th century, survived in the spoken language[8].   Else, except in one passage, it was lost from the written language and disappeared from the native Dictionaries.   It was then doubtless part of the Aramaic, as spoken in the time of Daniel.

The modern opponents of the book of Daniel have been constrained to admit that the Chaldee of Daniel is nearly

---

[1] The LXX. omit it altogether; Theod. has Apadano or Ephadano; Aq. Aphadano; Symm. ἱπποστασίου αὐτοῦ, "his stable;" S. Jer. (in Greek) "his throne."   [2] "a smooth place." Pesh. Dan. xi. 45.   [3] Dan. ii. 10, 27, 11. iv. 4. v. 7, 15.   [4] i. 20. ii. 2.   [5] Dan. vi. 9, 10, 11, 13, 14.   [6] Of the writing on the wall, Dan. v. 24, 25. Ch. of that "written in the Scripture of truth," Dan. x. 21. Heb.   [7] Ruth iv. i. 2 Sam. xxi. 3. 2 Kgs. vi. 8.

[8] Theodoret, explaining the word φελμωνί, as retained by Theod[n]. (as also by the LXX. and Aq.) τόν τινα, "such an one," adds, "The Syrian language, which is akin to the Hebrew, attests this." Barhebræus too (about A. D. 1270.) still used the word, which he wrote as in Daniel, (in his Scholia on 2 Kgs. vi. 8.) for the common Syriac word "phelon." (Bernstein from Vat. MS.) But the Peshito does not use it for the Hebrew phrase, and in Daniel the ortho-

identical with that of Ezra, and is as distinct as his from
that of the earliest Targums. The Aramaic of Ezra consists chiefly of documents from 536, B. C. the 1st year of
Cyrus to the 7th year of Artaxerxes Longimanus, B. C.
458. The documents are, a decree of Cyrus embodied
in one of Darius Hystaspes [9]; two letters of Persian Offi-
cials to the kings [10]; rescripts of Pseudo-Smerdis [11], Darius
Hystaspes [12], and Artaxerxes [13]. The first series is knit together by a short historical account in Aramaic by a contemporary [14]. Of the documents, the rescripts were probably *written* in Aramaic, it being the custom of the Persian kings to have the letters written to each people in
his own language [15]. If, moreover, they were translations
at all, they would probably have been translated into
Hebrew, the language of the rest of the book of Ezra.
This Aramaic then is any how the Aramaic of the first half
of the 5th century before our Lord; most of it probably
is original Aramaic of persons, not Jews. Some of Daniel's Aramaic is stated in his book to have been written
in the first year of Belshazzar [16], about 542, B. C., 6 years
before the earliest of the documents in Ezra, and some 64
years before the latest. The great similarity between the
Aramaic of these writings is such as one should expect
from their nearness; at the same time there is variation
enough utterly to exclude any theory that the Chaldee
of Daniel could have been copied from that of Ezra.

On the other hand doubtless the practice of delivering
orally translations of the Scriptures read in the Syna-
gogues, began in the time of Ezra [17]. It is certain, moreover, that these were not left to the arbitrary or extempore
efforts of each officer in each synagogue. The Turgeman
was not to be under 50 [18]; his was one of the most honourable offices in the Synagogue [19]. The paraphrase was learn-

graphy is corrupted into "phelumene," (transposing the u) as would happen
in a word not belonging to the written language. The Arabic has folo, folano
(span. fulano,) folaniyyo. Freyt. Lex. iii. 372. [9] Ezr. vi. 3-5. [10] iv. 11-16.
v. 7-17. [11] iv. 17. [12] vi. 6-12. [13] vii. 12-26. [14] Ezr. v. 4. [15] Esth.
iii. 12. viii. 9. [16] vii. 1. [17] Neh. viii. 8. Buxt. Tiber. c. vii. p. 34. [18] Juchasin,
f. 44. 2. Buxt. Lex. p. 2644. [19] Zunz, Gottesd. Vortr. d. Juden, p. 332.

ed by heart[1]. The instances of the paraphrast's expanding the text, while he translated it, are obviously exceptional[2]. The Talmud speaks of the Targum as an authority, without which this or that passage could not be understood[3]; which, of course, implies an old and, in their opinion, certain tradition from times nearer the living language. In reference to the Paraphrases of Onkelos and Jonathan, they explicitly say, that they received them from those before them[4]. Jonathan lived a little before our Lord[5]; Onkelos was a pupil of Gamaliel[6], and so lived about the same time. The Chaldee which they represent was certainly anterior, probably long anterior, to themselves. For the Chaldee Paraphrases had doubtless taken a definite form, before the Greek translation was ventured upon. Any how, it is probably prior to the time of Antiochus Epiphanes, who died 163, B. C., certainly not much later than his date. The question then, which any opponent of Daniel has to solve, is this, "whence this marked agreement between the Aramaic of Daniel and Ezra, and this marked difference of the Aramaic of both from that of the Targums of Onkelos and Jonathan?" Men are dishonest to themselves and to others, when they try to escape from this broad question under cover of the dust of other counter-questions. Such questions as, "[7]why was not the Aramaic of Daniel more pure, if his, seeing that

[1] Zunz, p. 8. quoting Mishna Megilla, c. 4. § 5. 10. Tosefta, ib. c. 3. j. Megilla, 4. 1. Megilla, f. 24. a. Sota, f. 39. b.

[2] "The Targumist, or interpreter, *sometimes* used a license of expatiating: instances of this are Hier. Bicc. f. 65. 4. Sanh. f. 20. 3. Bab. Berach. f. 28. 1." Lightfoot, Horæ Hebr. ad Matt. iv. 23. add ad Luc. iv. 16.   [3] Hott. Thes. phil. p. 256.

[4] " R. Jeremiah, or, as others, R. Chaiiah B. Abba, says, 'The Targum of the Law Onkelos the proselyte spake it from the mouth of R. Elieser and R. Joshua; the Targum of the prophets Jonathan B. Uziel spake it [ultimately] from the mouth of Haggai, Zachariah and Malachi.'" Megilla, c. 1. f. 3. 1. Wolf, de nom. et orig. Targ. B. H. ii. 1138.   [5] " Our Rabbins taught; ' Hillel the elder had 80 disciples, of whom 30 were meet that the Shechinah should rest upon them, as on Moses.—The greatest of all of them was Jonathan B. Uziel.' " Bava Bathra, c. viii. p. 134. Succa, f. 28. in Wolf, ii. 1159. Hillel taught about 32, B. C. Id.   [6] Wolf, ii. 1148.   [7] Bleek, in Schleierm. ZS. Th. iii. p. 214. In his (posthumous) Einleitung, Bleek had ignored the whole argument from language. p. 557 sqq.

he was taught it in a king's court?"   "[8]Why does not the Aramaic of Daniel and Ezra vary more, seeing that it is a Jewish patois which was formed at Babylon, and that it is the character of all patois to vary?" "[9]Why does the Aramaic of Daniel and Ezra vary at all?" ought to receive and can receive their answer; but they do not touch the real question.   The answers in brief are, 1) Daniel was taught *the learning and tongue of the Chaldæans*[10], i. e. an Aryan dialect and an Aryan literature, which the Chaldees brought with them, not Aramaic, which Daniel himself distinguishes from it[11].   2) The assertion, that the Biblical Aramaic is a patois, is simply an assertion.   It does not follow that the Hebrew of Daniel and Ezra is less pure than that of Onkelos and Jonathan, because it is different.   The Aramaic of Daniel and Ezra is the Aramaic of Babylonia; that of Jonathan and Onkelos, the Aramaic which developed itself in Palestine.   A certain number of definite Hebrew inflections *(if such)* would not make a patois.   3) The slight variations between the Aramaic of Daniel and Ezra are in conformity with their slight difference of age.   But these are petty surface-questions.   The question as to the book of Daniel, (it must always be borne in mind,) lies only between the real date of the old age of Daniel, about the middle of the 6th century, B.C., and the death of Antiochus Epiphanes, 164, B.C.; a distance of 370 years.   No one pretends that any intermediate date is possible.   His prophecies are as detailed in the latter as in the earlier part.   Either all must be prophecy, or all must be fiction, the relation of the past in the form of prophecy.   All petty questions then, "[13]how long the language, as we find it in Ezra,

---

[8] De Wette, Einl. 1833. p. 322. In his Einl., 1852 ed. 7. De Wette condensed his statement into the two words, " grounds of spuriousness lie in the corrupt Hebrew *and Chaldee*," without alleging an instance of the corruptness of the Chaldee, p. 346.

[9] Hitzig, Heidelb. Jahrb. 1832. ii. p. 119. Lengerke (p. xxxi. ii.) sets, side by side, the two contradictory arguments of Hitzig and De Wette.   [10] Dan. i. 4. What *we* call Chaldee, the Jews in Hezekiah's time, (Is. xxxvi. 11.) Daniel, Ezra (iv. 7.) call Aramæan.   [11] ii. 4.   [12] Bertholdt, Einl. p. 1527.

lasted," are but dust in people's eyes ; for no one imagines that it lasted to the 2nd century, B. C.   If the Aramaic of Daniel had been an imitation of Ezra, it must have been like Ezra ; whereas the resemblance is in principles, not in details ; the variations are such as never could have occurred, if the one had imitated the other.   It is absurd e. g. to suppose that one, meaning to copy the style of another in order to make his work seem to belong to the age of the writer whom he copied, half-copied an idiom of that other, which lay before him.   The slight variations in a phrase, when both are correct according to the principles of the language, imply that each writer had an independent knowledge of the language, and wrote independently.

In the earlier stage of the controversy, it was assumed, on both sides, that those nice shades in certain forms of speech, which separate Biblical Aramaic from the Aramaic of the Targums, were Hebraisms.   All which was said about " impure," " corrupt," Chaldee, " patois," &c. presupposed this.   Some of those forms might be Hebraisms.   It has been recently pointed out, in a very careful analysis [1], that this was a superficial solution, since some of the principal variations are forms which do not, or scarcely, occur in Hebrew.   There must then be some wider solution, which shall take in the non-Hebrew variations.   The diligent and accurate author of that Essay pointed out that they could be accounted for on no other ground than that such was the Aramaic of the period. He noticed also, that some of these variations are to be found in West Aramaic or Syriac, indicating that, in the time of Daniel and Ezra, the Western and Eastern Aramaic were not so much separated, as they were subsequently.   With this it agrees, that many of these peculiarities of Biblical Chaldee occur in Samaritan also, which, although the extant memorials are not earlier

---

[1] In a condensed essay on "The Chaldee of Daniel and Ezra" in the Journal for Sacred Literature, Jan. 1861. p. 373-91. by J. Mc. G. (I am permitted to say, the Rev. J. Mc. Gill.)

than the Targums, still, on account of the severance of
the Samaritans from the Jews, must be pretty nearly the
Chaldee which they brought with them from Eastern
Mesopotamia, some dialect of Aramaic.

I can here but give (as I am permitted to give) an epitome of those condensed observations, referring to the
treatise itself for details, as also for the proof that these
variations are not Hebraisms; adding only, which of
these variations are found also in Samaritan.

The differences of the Biblical, from the later Aramaic,
belong, in the main, to an earlier stage of language.

1) In the Chaldee of Daniel and Ezra, the stronger as-
pirate *h*, is used, where, in the Chaldee of the Targums,
it is nearly effaced. This occurs so manifoldly, as evidently to involve a principle of language. It is found in
the characteristic letter of three conjugations [2]; in verbs,
whose last letter it is [3]; in infinitives of derived conjuga-

---

[2] 1) *Hafel, Afel;* " in 96 cases, (80 in Daniel, 16 in Ezra,) whereas there are,
of *Afel,* only 2 cases in Daniel, 1 in Ezra." " In 35 other cases, this ה is retained after the preformants of the future and participle, while in 25 it is dropped." " In Hebrew, there are but six words, in which the ה of *Hifil* is retained after the preformative; and of these, 5 are in ע." "In the Targums, there
is no instance in which the ה is retained in the regular verb," although " in
verbs ע it is very frequently employed in the present, and retained in the future and participles. This is occasionally the case also in verbs נ, and with some
verbs אפ." Ib. 382, 3. In Samaritan, Hafel is frequent. "In no conjugation
did the Samaritans come nearer to the Hebrew forms, than in this *(Afel;)* and
first, the instances of the ה are most frequent; not only in words beginning with
ע, where the weakness of the letter might seem to occasion the change, but in
many others also." Uhlemann, Gram. Samar. § 23. The word חקם is adopted as a whole in Syr. and Arab. The Samaritans have both אקם Uhl. Gr. § 27.
and חקם Id. Lex. p. 5.

2) "*Hithpeal* and " 3) "*Hithpaal* occur 18 times in Daniel 4 times in Ezra.
On the other hand, *eth* is used 6 times in Daniel ii. 45. iii. 19. iv. 16. vi. 8. vii.
8, 15. In 4 of the 6 cases in Daniel, the punctuation is אֵת as in Syriac." "The
same word occurs with את ii. 45. תו ii. 34. In iii. 19. both the forms occur in
different verbs, התקטל and אשׁתני." Ib. p. 384, 5. In Samaritan both forms are
common. " Since the Samaritans often interchange א and ה, forms result like
the Hebrew Hithpael. But although in some words these forms are to be accounted as Ethpael, yet in others, where there is no trace of Pael in Samaritan
or of the corresponding Hebrew form, they must rather be considered as belonging to Ethpeel, as, אשׁתבע *swear.* Gen. xxv. 33." Uhl. § 20.   [3] see p. 47, 8.

tions [1] ; " in the feminine of participles always in Daniel, in adjectives usually [2] ", in the emphatic form, which in Chaldee represents the Article [3]; in the pronoun I [4] ; and three particles [5].   All these peculiarities occur in Ezra as well as Daniel, and with the remarkable agreement in both, that, although in a lesser degree, they do use the later forms also.   The language, then, was apparently still in an unfixed state.   They are not Hebraisms, because many of the forms do not belong to Hebrew; all occur in Samaritan.   It is a law of all language, that gutturals weaken, as time goes on.

2) Two conjugations, which still existed in the time of

[1] " In Daniel 20 times, in Ezra 4 times; with א once only in Daniel, ii. 24. in a word written with ה, Ib. 12. vii. 16. twice in Ezra." Ib. 386.   In Samaritan, the infinitives of all the derived conjugations end in ה.

[2] Id. ib. " In the Targums ה is only used after א; in Biblical Chald. there are, in substantives, adjectives, participles, 58 instances in Daniel, 7 in Ezra.   Three nouns are written both ways in Dan. ; (vii. 12. and iv. 24 ; vii. 5, 7. and iv. 13. ii. 40. and 42.) one in Ezra, (iv. 10, 15.) Other variations are, שַׁפִּיר adv. Dan. 6 times, שַׁפִּירָא adj. Dan. v. 12. and the numerals תְּרֵין adv. Dan. 3 times, Ezra twice ; תְּרֵין adj. Dan. twice, Ezr. once ; מִלָּה Dan. 5 times, Ezr. vi. 15. מִלְּתָא Ezr. vi. 4." Ib. 386.   In Samaritan, " the feminine ending, in far the most cases, is ה, especially such feminines as are formed from Masculines ; not a few end in ו or י. [for ה, ית.]   Uhl. § 41.   א is not a Samaritan feminine ending at all.

[3] "א is the most usual ending, but ה occurs 11 times in Daniel, 11 times also in Ezra." Ib. 385.   "The two forms occur even in different words in the same verse, and in the same word in the same writer.   In fact, only 4 words have ה only, and three of these occur but once each, Ezr. vi. 2. vii. 17. Dan. ii. 38; the fourth twice only, Dan. vii. 7, 19." Ib. 385. where the several variations are given.   In Samaritan the Status Emphaticus always ends in ה.   " In the singular Masc., ה, pronounced with the vowel *a*, is added, so that it does not differ from the Fem. sing. abs. ; so also in adjectives, which stand in the status Emph., when the substantive does.   So also nouns ending in י end in יה ; the ending יא becomes אה.   In the Plur. Masc. ין or ים become יה (Ch. אַיָּא)   In the Fem. sing. ה becomes תה, which is added to feminines ending in י or ו ; in the Fem. Plur. ן and ין are changed into תה and אתה (Ch. אתָא) this last is far the most frequent."   Uhl. p. 113-15.

[4] " אֲנָה occurs frequently [13 times] in Dan. and Ezr. ; אֲנָא Dan. ii. 8. Ezr. vi. 12. the plur. is אֲנַחְנָה Ez. iv. 16. אֲנַחְנָא Ezr. v. 11. Dan. iii. 16, 17." Ib. p. 388. In Sam. also אנה is more frequent than אנא.

[5] i) מָה "what," Dan. ii. 22. Ezr. vi. 9. "what?" Dan. iv. 32. עַל מָה "why?" ii. 15. מָא "how!" iii. 33. מָה דִי, "what," Dan. ii. 28, 9. 45. Ezr. vii. 18. לְמָה "why?" Ezr. iv. 22. דִי לְמָה "lest," Ezr. vii. 23. but לְמָא דִי "as to what." Ezr. vi. 8. Sam. מה, במה, כמה, למה, ממה. Uhl. Lex. p. 40.

Daniel and Ezra, were, the one mostly [6], the other wholly [7] effaced; and a conjugation [8] was formed, unknown to Biblical Chaldee.

3) A fuller orthography, implying a more prolonged pronunciation of vowels, (Daveed for David,) has long been recognized as belonging to the later Hebrew of the O. T.   The same difference, though more extensive, is observed between the Biblical Chaldee and the Targums [9].

4) There are forms in Biblical Chaldee, common with Syriac, which shew that, at the time when it was written, the dialects of Assyria and Syria, East and West Aramaic, were not so much separated as in the time of the Targums. It is like the fusion of dialects in Homer.   Here too the Eastern Aramaic became softer in the time of the Targums [10].

ii) כַּחֲדָה "together," lit. "as one," Dan. ii. 35. Sam. (Uhl. Lex. p. 32) ; with א Syr., Targg.   iii) לָה for לֹא, "not," occurs once in Daniel, iv. 32. as לֹה does also once in Hebrew. Deut. iii. 11.   The Masoretes corrected both.

[6] Hofal.   "It occurs in Dan. 11 times ; ii. 10. iii. 13. iv. 33. (twice) v. 13, 15, 16, 20. vi. 24, 18. vii. 11. Ezr. iv. 15." Ib. see Winer, Gr. Chald. § 12. 5. p. 41. הָקִימַת (Dan. vii. 4.) seems to be an anomalous Hofal form ; הֵיתָיִת is still more anomalous, but must be a sort of Hofal. Dan. vi. 48.

[7] The inflection of the passive participle by the afformatives of the preterite, Dan. v. 27, 8. viii. 4. (twice) 11. (twice) 12, 27. Ezr. v. 14. The participle is used for the 3rd person masc. without inflection. Dan. v. 30. vi. 4. vii. 6. Winer, § 13. 2. p. 42. Mc G. p. 384.   [8] Ittafal, instead of Hofal.

[9] " *Yod* is inserted in the *Afel* forms without suffixes in the Targums," (p. 377.) whereas, in Daniel, it nowhere occurs except in verbs ע (as טָחֵיב Dan. ii. 14. forms of הָקִים 13 times, קָיְמִין Dan. vii. 2.) and in the *Shafel* שֵׁיזִב Dan. iii. 17, 28. vi. 28. but שֵׁיזִב Dan. vi. 28.   "It is used also generally in such forms as וַעֲיֵק, סָלִיקוּ in the Targums ; " (Ib.) whereas Daniel nowhere inserts the vowel-letter, and uses the form 16 times without it.   (The cases are, סָלְקוּ Dan. ii. 29. Ezr. iv. 12. מָאר Dan. ii. 46. קָרְבוּ Dan. iii. 8. vi. 13. זְקַף Dan. iv. 8, 17. וְזַן Dan. vi. 21. שְׁלֵו Dan. vi. 25. יְתֵב Dan. vii. 9, 10.   Even the pass. part. is so written in יְתֵב Dan. vii. 14, 22. יְתֵב Dan. vii. 26.   Also the form תְּשַׁבְּקוּן Dan. ii. 44. הִתְרֲמַת Dan. iii. 28. יִתְיְהִב Dan. iv. 13. In Targg. mostly אִתְקֵטַל or אִתְקְטִיל)   "The same difference is seen in nouns e. g. עֲנַן Dan. iii. 2, 3. Ezr. vi. 16, 17. but in Targg. ן, even though followed by Dagesh forte.   In Bibl. Ch. דֵּן, fem. דָּן ; but in Targg. דֵּין, fem. דָּאן.   Very frequently such words as חָכְמָה Dan. v. 11. Ezr. vii. 25. שְׁלָם Dan. vii. 14. קְלָם Ezr. vii. 19. occur in the Targg. with ו after the first radical." Ib. So, for קְדָם Dan. ii. 11. you have קֳדָם in the Targg.

[10] The א, however slight its pronunciation, could not have been so soft as the י.   1) " In Syriac, as in Biblical Chaldee, the א of words אב is mostly retained after preformants in the inf. and fut. peal ; even if dropped, י is not substituted ;

5. This correspondence of the Biblical Chaldee with the Syriac best explains a form of the substantive verb, found only in Biblical Chaldee, alike in Daniel and Ezra, yet insulated from all other Semitic forms, and one of the most remarkable phænomena of Biblical Chaldee [1].

in the Targums it is always substituted." (Inf. with א Dan. ii. 9. fut. Dan. ii. 7, 36. iii. 29. iv. 30, 32. vii. 23. Jer. x. 11. א twice dropped, inf. Dan. iii. 2. 19. Ezr. v. 11. מאמר (noun) Dan. iv. 14. Ezr. vi. 9. מימר Targg.

2) "In verbs לא, א remains throughout the future. Afel fut. does not insert י (as the Heb.) but agrees with the Syriac." p. 378. "There are 19 such cases in all; fut. Dan. 6, Ezr. 6; partic. Dan. 5, Ezr. 2. Daniel has the contracted form מטא, and 4 ending in ה; and, in the same verse with ה, he has once י. v. 12. (Ib. 381.) The Targums have always י." (Ib.) "The derived conjugations, in the 3rd sing. present, end in י, as in Syriac, not as in Hebrew, and so are not Hebraisms." (p. 378.) "In Daniel, there are 5 such forms; in Ezra, 3." (p. 381.) "The 3rd present Peal has ה 11 times in Dan., twice in Ezr.; א 7 times in Dan., once in Ezra; in Targg. י is the most frequent ending even of the present Peal." [In Samaritan, the 3rd sing. pres. Peal ends in א or ה; the derived conjug. only in י, but there are exceptions with לו; very rare with לא." Uhl. p. 71, 2.] "Even in the words written לה in *the present and fut. Peal,* א remains in the other conjugations." "The *act. part. Peal* ends 41 times in ה; מטה 13; עטה 22; and 6 other cases, 3 of which end in א also: 6 in א only." No case of י. "Ezra has a passive part. בנה v. 11.; Dan. has ה 3 times; מטא, v. 25, 26; י twice." "Some of these occur in the Targg." (Ib. p. 378, 9.) "In the *Inf. and Part. Peal.* א and י are equally [?] frequent" [in the Targg.] Winer, Ch. Gr. § 23, 1. "In the *Inf. construct,* א always remains; (Dan. 7 times, Ezra 8 times.) the Targums always have י." (p. 380.) The Sam. Inf. is או—. In the *fut Peal*, Bibl. Ch. and Syr. have א [Dan. 17 times, Ezr. 3.] Daniel has 7 times ה. (with א, however, elsewhere in the same 3 words) Targg. always י."

3) In verbs עע, the particle plur. masc. has א (עללין &c.) when the Targg. have י. The form with א occurs 9 times in Dan., in Ezra once; (as in the Syr. masc. abs.) (Ib. 382.) In 9 out of the 10 cases, the Kri would conform it to the Targum orthography with י, so strange was it to those accustomed to the later Chaldee.

4) The form קריא (the emphatic plur. of nouns in י- in the Bibl. Chald. and Syriac) is in like way corrected by the Kri into קריי. The old form must have sounded fuller.

The punctuation אבי Dan. v. 2. is Syriac. (C. B. Mich. lum. Syr. § 13. Ges. Thes. s. v.) "The Targg. have uniformly אבא, "*the* father," for "*my* father." (Ib. 389.)

[1] The use of ל instead of the י in the future, להוא (Dan. 7 times, Ezra 6 times.) להוה (Dan. iv. 22.) להון 3 m. pl. (Dan. 4 times, Ezr. 2.) להן 3 f. pl. (Dan. v. 17.) In these three forms 3 m. sing. 3 m. and f. pl., the West-Aramaic or Syriac has נ as a preformant, (which was itself questioned as anomalous. See Hofmann, Gr. Syr. § 56. p. 175.) But the ל and נ continually interchanged. See on the form at length Beer, Inscrr. Sem. in Æg. repert. i. 18. inserted by Maurer in his Commentary, ii. 84-7.

6. Daniel and Ezra use unabridged, and so, older forms[2].

7. The Biblical Chaldee has pronominal forms nearer the original Semitic pronoun, and Daniel the older form of the two[3].

8. Other pronouns or particles are used in a form which ceased to be used in the Targums[4].

9. "In regard to the use of *n*, in the Biblical Chaldee the older uncontracted forms prevail; in the Targums the later contracted forms; but there is considerable variety[5]." In part, the Biblical agrees with the Samaritan Chaldee.

---

[2] 1) דִי, as the sign of the genitive, a relative, and conjunction. It occurs 254 times in Daniel, 89 times in Ezra; (see Fürst, Conc.) דִי מֶן i. q. כִּי אִם Dan. ii. 9, The antiquity of the form is evidenced by the proper name דִי זָהָב "of gold," i. e. a place abounding in it. Deut. i. 1.

2) אִיתַי "there is;" לָא אִיתַי "there is not." אִיתַי occurs 7 times in Daniel, לָא אִיתַי 6 times, besides the form לָא אִיתֵיהּ, "it is not," Dan. ii. 11. which presupposes אִיתַי. In Ezra each occurs once. (Fürst, Conc.) There are traces of a regular inflection with the pronouns, (as in אַיִן in Hebrew) 4 such instances occurring in Daniel. (see Fürst, Conc. p. 58.) In Samaritan and Syriac this inflection with the pronoun is complete. In both, the absolute form is אִית, לִית. In Samaritan this form remains, even when the words are so inflected. (Uhl. § 36. p. 90, 1.) In Syriac, when so inflected, the ' occurs before the pronouns. (Hofmann, § 146. p. 377.) The ' is wanting also in the Arabic אִשׁ, לִשׁ, although, in Arabic, the אִשׁ only remains in one idiom, as the counterpart of לִשׁ. In Hebrew, the form occurs in the proper name, אִיתִיאֵל, "God is." Pr. xxx. 1. "The Targums have always the shorter form אִית and לִית," or לֵית.

[3] 1) הִמּוֹן Dan. 3 times; and הִמּוֹ Ezra 9 times; for אִנּוּן or הִנּוּן of the Targums.

2) Daniel has always (13 times) the primitive form אַנְתָּה i. e. the primitive Sanscr. Semitic, תה i. q. tu, and the demonstrative אַ. This is contracted even in Hebrew into אַתָּה; corrected always in Daniel by the Kri into the אַנְתְּ of the Targg.

[4] 1) אִלֵּן, "they;" Dan. iii. 12, 13, 21, 22, 23, 27. vi. 6, 12, 16, 25. Ezr. iv. 21. v. 9. vi. 8. (twice); not in Targg. 2.) דְּנָה emph. demonstr.; Jer. x. 11. Dan. 16 times; Ezr. 14 times: as part of compound כְּדֶרְכָה דְּנָה Ezr. v. 23. adverb, אֲמַר דְּנָה Dan. twice; כְּאמַר דְּנָה Dan. twice; עַל דְּנָה, Dan. iii. 16. Ezr. 6 times; כָּל קֳבֵל דְּנָה, Dan. 6 times, Ezr. vii. 17; כִּן קַרְכָּה דְּנָה, Dan. vi. 11.; כְּדְנָה Jer. x. 11. Dan. twice; Ezr. v. 7. (see Fürst, v. דֵּן.) The Maltese has *dan, dana,* (masc.) *din, dina,* fem. (Vassalli, Gr. Melit. p. 147. Ges.) The Sam. has דן. The Targg. have mostly the lengthened form דֵּין, (דֵן Eccl. xi. 6.) הָדֵין, מִידֵין, אִידֵין, הְּדֵין, אִבְּדֵין, כֵּין, דֵן, כְּדֵין. Buxt. p. 556. i. e. they have forms which the Biblical Chald. never has, and none have the form of the Bibl. Chaldee. 3.) דָּא. 4) דְּן 5) אֲזַי see below, p. 54. 6) אֵי, אֵלִי, (see below, Note D.)

[5] Ib. p. 390. On the same principle that Daniel writes אַנְתָּה not אַתָּה, ן is retained in Hofal, הָנְחַת Dan. v. 20. [omitted in Ezr. v. 15. vi. 15. and Targg. in

10. In one word, *haddabar*, " councillor," there is probably a trace of the Article in its Hebrew form. For the word has no Aryan, but has an obvious Semitic etymology. In Sam. Chaldee also, the same Article is prefixed as a demonstrative to pronouns, nouns, participles [1].

11. The Hebrew plural ending, *im* for *in*, occurs in two words in Daniel [2], and in a third in Ezra [3]. The two terminations are used in Samar. Chaldee, and that indifferently, even when two words are closely united together, as two nouns joined by the copula, or the substantive and adjective [4].

12. According to the punctuation, there was a dual at the time of the Bibl. Chaldee [5], which existed also in the Samaritan Chaldee [6], but was lost in the time of the Targums.

13. There is a correspondence in other vowels between the Biblical Chaldee and the Hebrew [7], as distinct from the Targums, inexplicable except on the ground of a real, accurate tradition [8].

14. A letter seems to have, at least, become less used,

Afel] in the inf. Hafel of פסק Dan. vi. 24. [omitted in Hafel present, iii. 22.] in Hafel present, Dan. v. 2. 3. Ezr. v. 14. vi. 5. (not in Targg.) in נתן Peal after preform. (fut. Dan. ii. 16. Ezr. iv. 13. inf. Ezr. vii. 20.) never in Targg. " In Samaritan, in the future, the instances are not rare, in which the נ is retained." Uhl. Sam. Gr. 26. 3. Ann.

יִדַּע, 3 fut. Peal for יֵדַע, occurs 6 times in Dan., once in Ezra, and is the only form used by either. Buxtorf noticed one instance only in Targg. (Ps. ix. 21.) among many of יַע, as also ינדע, ינדע. Hengst. has noticed another, Ruth iv. 4. The noun מנדע is frequent in the Targg. (see Buxt.) probably taken from Daniel.

[1] Uhlem. p. 116-8.   [2] iv. 14. vii. 10.   [3] Ezr. iv. 13.
[4] Uhlem. p. 104.   [5] There are five duals in Daniel, ii. 34. 45. vii. 47. (ii) one in Ezr. vi. 17. There was no temptation, any how, to make קרן dual, (when Daniel speaks of " ten horns,") except a traditional knowledge that it was so.   [6] Uhlem. § 42. iii. p. 108, 9.

[7] " There are only 6 Heb. segolates, אֶבֶן, חיל, חֶלֶם, קֶרֶן, שֵׁם, עֶלֶם, of which אֶבֶן frequently, קֶרֶן occasionally occurs in the Targg.; שֵׁם is written שֻׁם 8 times in Dan. [not שֵׁם at all] 17 times in Ezra; and אֵל, 3 times in Dan. אֵל [אֵל 5 times, אֵלָא emph. 8 times] On the other hand, 20 Chaldee nouns are pointed as segolates in Dan., some pretty frequently; and 11 such nouns in Ezra, some also pretty frequently." Mc. G. p. 377. note. Besides this, is the corresponding feminine ending ָ ֶ in מְחָאָה Dan. ii. 34. אֲמָרָה Ib. 45.

[8] The whole system of Hebrew and Chaldee punctuation implies a minute

between the times of Biblical Chaldee and the Targums[9].

It may be added, that even in the space of those six chapters of Daniel, there are a certain number of words, which do not occur in the Targums or Gemara; quite as many or more, probably, than would be found in any six chapters of any of the Hebrew historical Scriptures. They are not technical words, which there might not be occasion to use elsewhere, (as offices or dress or instruments, the names of which were disused with the things;) but ordinary words of the language. Some of these, which are lost in the later Jewish Aramaic, survive in Syriac[10].

And now you will be able to see, how utterly superficial it was, when an unbelieving German critic[11] picked out two plural pronouns, in the form in which they are united with other words, as a proof that the Aramaic of Daniel was later than that of Ezra, or what is the character of such a sentence as this. "[12]Not only Macedonian words, such as *symphonia* and *psanterion*" [which are not Macedonian] "but the texture of the Chaldee, with such late forms as לכון, כן and אתה, the pronominal ם and ה having passed into ן, and not only minute description of Antiochus's reign, but the stoppage of such description

knowledge of the spoken language, whose pronunciation is fixed so carefully. An artificial system, invented subsequently, would not have had its anomalies or its minuteness. The punctuations, which seem anomalous at first sight, are still found to proceed on a principle. The old tradition, which ascribed them in the main to times, when the language was ceasing to be spoken, those of Ezra and the great Synagogue, seems to me the most probable.

[9] The ב. For שגא, "increase," Dan. iii. 31. vi. 26. Ezr. iv. 22. the Targg. have always סגא; for שגיא, "great, greatly," (Dan. 12 times, Ezr. once) the Targg. have סגי pl. סגיאין. In like way as for שהדותא, "witness," Gen. xxxi. 47. the Targg. have סהדותא. חכּימין, "wise," Dan. vii. 8. אשכלתם Dan. v. 11, 12, 14. In Targg. mostly סכל. Buxt. שנא, hate, Dan. iv. 19. mostly סנא, rarely with ב. Buxt. שער Dan. iii. 27. vii. 9. mostly סער. [10] See Note B at the end.

[11] Hitzig, Heidelb. Jahrb. 1832. p. 119, 20. "We observe on our side, for the time and only as an example, that in Ezra the form nearest to the original להם, להם *always* stands, Ezr. v. 3, 4, 8, 9. vi. 9. Contrariwise in Daniel always the להן, which originated in the effacing of the ם; notwithstanding this, Dr. Hengstenberg will have it, that the book of Daniel is genuine, on the ground of the character of its language also, i. e. that it was composed before the book of Ezra." [12] Ess. and Rev. p. 76.

at the precise date 169, B.C., remove all philological and critical doubt as to the age of the book." The history is as bad as the philology; but of this, hereafter. Why these three forms should have been selected, it is difficult to say. They ought to be three wondrously characteristic forms, to determine the age of a book; whereas they are three of the most ordinary. But the assertion involved must be this. " It can be proved that, in the time of Daniel, the plural pronoun of the 2nd person in Chaldee was written with the *m*, and not with the *n;* and that the ending *n* was not at that time added to other pronouns which, in Hebrew, end in *eh*." The supposed proof must be that the forms in Daniel are not found in Ezra. For there is no other Aramaic to serve as a standard, in comparison with which these are to be pronounced to be "late forms." Both statements are plainly false. Of course, it was on one principle of pronunciation, that the pronominal forms, *hom* " them," *com* "you," were written with the *m*, as in Hebrew or Arabic, or the *n*, as in Syriac and Samaritan. The two forms always go together. The Hebrews and Arabians used the *m* exclusively; the Syrians and Samaritans used the *n* exclusively. But there is no language in which *m* was used for the one pronoun, *n* for the other. Of both pronouns, Daniel has only the form of the Western and the Samaritan Aramaic. Ezra has both forms; as, indeed, the more Hebrew form lingered on in the Chaldee of the Targums. Of the third person, Ezra uses most frequently the same form as Daniel; the more Hebrew form occurs almost exclusively in the context of one conversation which was reported to the King. The 2nd person occurs only 6 times altogether in Ezra; 5 times in the more Hebrew form, once in that used by Daniel[1]. The criticism breaks down, then, both in principle and in fact. In *principle*, because 1) the form

---

[1] Ezra uses the form הן, 15 times; הם, 10 times; he uses כם, 5 times; כן once, (the only time that it is joined with a verb.) He uses הן with three prepositions, הם with two of them. • "Their God" is twice expressed with the הם; "your God" twice with the כם; "their companions" is expressed 6 times with the הן. Else the הם is used with three, הן with 4 ordinary words. Both forms

in Daniel is the most usual Aramaic form ; 2) the corresponding form, *hon,* is the most common in Ezra ; 3) both these forms *hom, com,* which are to be characteristic of the earlier Aramaic, occur in the Targums also.   In *fact,* because the actual form, *con,* the existence of which in Daniel is to prove the late date of Daniel, occurs in Ezra also, and so can, on the hypothesis, be no "late form."

The second case is more marvellous.   *Den,* in Chaldee and Samaritan as also in Maltese, corresponds to the Hebrew demonstrative, *tseh.*   Daniel and Ezra *alike* use, not *den,* but the emphatic form, *denah,* while the Targums do not use the *denah* of Biblical Aramaic, nor *den,* but *dein,* according to the principle of the later language, to employ the more lengthened form.   So then in later Aramaic a form is used, which is *not* found in Biblical Aramaic ; and the Biblical Aramaic does *not* use the form of later Aramaic.   The Biblical form became obsolete in the time of the Targums ; the age of the Targumists revived a form not used by Daniel and Ezra.

But the broader allegation of the Essayist is, that, in the Aramaic of Daniel, " the *h* had passed into the *n*" in both *den, this,* and *illeen, these,* and that this change is an evidence of later language.   The major premiss must be, that " it is known that, in Daniel's time, they had not so passed."   The *h* does not "pass into the *n*" at all : *n* is not one of the letters into which *h* ever passes.   The facts are

are used in the same verse, as v. 3.   So that I see no explanation of the variation, except that both forms were alike in use in Ezra's time.   The several instances are ;

לְהֹם v. 3, 4. repeated v. 9, 10. עֲלֵיהֹם vii. 24.

אֱלָהֲהֹם v. 5. vii. 16. בְּהֹם v. 9.

שְׂמָתֵהֹם v. 10.

בַּאדַיִן הֹם v. 10.

לְהֹם v. 3. repeated v. 9. vii. 24.

אֱלָהֲהֹם vii. 17, 18.

לְהֹן iv. 20. v. 3. עֲלֵיהֹן v. 1, 2. עֲשֵׂהֹן v. 2.

בְּהֹן iv. 9, 7, 23. v. 3. vi. 6, 13. בְּמַלְכוּתְהֹן vi. 18.

בְּמַלְכוּתְהֹן Ib. וְאַנְפֹּהֹן מִנְהֹן vii. 17.

לְהַצָּלוּתְהֹן vii. 21.

these. The primitive forms of the two words are *da*[1], *this*, as found in Daniel; *el*, *these*. *Da*, as a demonstrative, is, in fact, a different pronunciation of the Hebrew *dseh*, and is connected with a large range of demonstrative pronouns in the Semitic dialects[2]. This shorter form is lengthened in various ways in Semitic languages by additions at the beginning[3] and the end[4]. One of the additions, made probably in the infancy of the language, was that of the 2nd person, which occurs in Biblical Aramaic and in Arabic, not in Syriac or Samaritan, nor, in this pure form, in the Aramaic of the Targums. It strengthened the demonstrative in a way which we can scarcely express, " hoc tibi." In this way, we have the *illec* of Daniel and Ezra[5], and the *deec*, and *dac* of Ezra[6]. Another Aramaic ending, applied more manifoldly, and in more dialects of Aramaic, is *en*. It is used in the ordinary pronoun, *they ;* in the demonstrative, *these;* and, by Daniel and Ezra, in the particle of time, *then*. Thence we have in Daniel alone, a form lengthened from the *deec* in Ezra, *dicceen*[7]. From it, we have, in Daniel and Ezra only, the particle of time, *edain*[8]; from it the form *den* was made, which, in Daniel and Ezra, exists only in the emphatic form, *denah*[9]; from it we have the *holein* or *ailein* of Syriac[10]; the *illein* of Samaritan Aramaic[11], used in five places in Daniel.

We cannot suppose an ending, so widely spread and so rooted in the language, to be a " later form." It is an

---

[1] דא four times. Dan. iv. 27. vii. 8. and in the phrases דא לדא "the one against the other " v. 6. דא מן דא " one from the other." vii. 3.

[2] *dsu*, Arab. *dsa*, Æth. *da* Malt. Nasor. In Syriac and Samaritan it occurs only in lengthened forms.   [3] הדא Syr. probably corresponding to the Heb. סהד ; hâdsâ, hadsâ. Arab.   [4] הדן, for Heb. הללה Sam. Uhlem. § 14. p. 31.

[5] Dan. 10 times ; Ezra, 4 times. see above, p. 49.

[6] דך masc. דך fem., each 6 times. They correspond with the Arab. *dsaca dsaleca*, and the Malt. *daka*.   [7] Dan. ii. 31. vii. 20, 1.

[8] אדין (i. q. Heb. אז with ן added) Dan. 20 times ; Ezra 8 times. באדין Dan. 23 times ; Ezr. 3 times. (Fürst, p. 10[b] 11.)   [9] see above, p. 49.

[10] *holein* is the common Syriac form ; *ailein* is rarer, perhaps older. see Hofmann, Syr. Gr. § 45. p. 161.

[11] They use אל, האיל as the Heb. האלה,) Uhl. p. 31.

integral part of the language, as much as *ov* or *um* in Greek and Latin. As far as the evidence goes, it would shew in this case also, that the language, in the time of Daniel and Ezra, was in the same unfixed state, as other idioms imply it to have been. There was, then, no one word, appropriated to signify "these." Jeremiah has once *eeleh*[12]; Ezra has it once also[13]. These *are* instances of the Hebrew form of the pronouns occurring in Aramaic. But it was not the prevailing form in Ezra's time. Ezra four times used another form, *illeec*, which occurs yet oftener in Daniel [14], a form obsolete in the time of the Targums. Daniel employs this which, not occurring in Syriac or Samaritan, was probably the more antique form, ten times [14], whereas he uses five times [15] only the form *illein*, which is the Samaritan form, and the Syriac ending.

In sum, then, these endings, which are to be so characteristic as to establish the later date of the Aramaic of Daniel, are endings belonging to all Aramaic. The other forms are exceptional archaisms apparently in the language both of Daniel and Ezra. The variations as to the use of two of the three words supply a part of the larger evidence, (if it were needed) of the independence of Daniel and Ezra; the third furnishes part of the proof of the difference of their language from that of the Targums. Criticism, which should have made endings, which are an integral part of the language, which occur not in one dialect of it only but in three, not in one case, but in several, characteristic of a later date of a book in which they occur, could not have been even imagined in any well-known language. It would have carried on its face its own refutation.

In fine, then, the Hebrew of Daniel is exactly that which you would expect in a writer of his age and under his circumstances. It has not one single idiom, unsuited to that time. The few Aryan or Syriac words remarkably belong to it. The Chaldee marks itself out as such,

---

[12] Jer. x. 11.　　[13] Ezra v. 15. The Kri corrects אֵל.　　[14] See above, p. 49.
[15] ii. 40, 44. vi. 3, 7. vii. 17.

as could not have been written at the time when, if it had not been a Divine and prophetic book, it must have been written.

No opponent has ever ventured to look steadily at the facts of the correspondence of the language of Daniel and Ezra, and their difference from the language of the earliest Targums.

It is, plainly, cumulative evidence, when both portions so written are united in one book. Over and above, the fact, that the book is written in both languages, suits the times of Daniel, and is inexplicable by those, who would have it written in the time of the Maccabees. No other book, or portion of a book, of the Canon, approximates to that date. The last book, Nehemiah, was finished 2½ centuries before, viz. about B.C. 410.

The theory of Maccabee Psalms lived too long, but is now numbered with the dead[1]. Only one or two, here and

[1] "The existence of Maccabee Psalms, to which Bertholdt appealed, as one of the surest proofs of the later closing of the Canon, is contested not only by *Bleek* (Schleierm. ZS. p. 203.) and Hassler (de Ps. Maccab. Ulm. 1827.) but even by *De Wette*, (Comm. z. d. Ps. ed. 2. 3.) and *Gesenius* (Vorr. zu Gramberg's Religionsid. p. xii.) and it is granted that, in the whole Psalter, there is no Psalm later than the times of Ezra and Nehemiah." (Hengst. Auth. d. Dan. p. 238. note.) Even *Ewald* and *Dillmann* have since granted the same. "All the later Psalms, whose contents admit of or require a historical explanation, can be fully explained out of the circumstances of Israel down to Nehemiah, and are explained out of them alone. To refer them to later relations does not hold, as matter of interpretation." Dillmann (üb. d. Bildung d. A. T. in Dorner, Jahrb. iii. 460.) Ewald even contends, 1) that the Psalms were collected into one whole, before the writing of the Chronicles ; and that 2) a considerable interval must have elapsed between the completion of the titles, the latest part of the whole, and the LXX. ; in that it misunderstands or alters arbitrarily much contained in them, while it agrees in the main with the Masorethic text of the Psalms themselves. (Poet. Büch. i. 205, 6. add his Jahrbücher, vi. 20-32.) It was one of the paradoxes of Hitzig to place Ps. i. ii. and the last three books (Ps. lxxiii.—cl.) in Maccabee times, and even as low as 85, B. C. "through very rash exegesis and precarious combinations ; me, at least, his grounds only convinced as to Ps. 74. 79. 80. and 83," says even Grimm (Kurzg. Exeg. Hdb. Einl. z. 1 Macc. § 9. p. xxvii.) No one could find in these, Maccabee Psalms, who did not wish to find them ; Ps. 79. is quoted as Scripture in 1 Macc. vii. 6. Dillmann considers these Psalms in detail. Ib. 460-8. *Hupfeld*, too, with whom it is a ruling passion to contradict Hengstenberg, assents that there are no Maccabee Psalms.

there, who believe little besides, believe in this phantom of a past century. But, even if such Hebrew, and (which is utterly inconceivable) such Aramaic, *could* have been written in the times of the Maccabees, it would still have been inexplicable that both should be written.

If the object of the writer be supposed to have been, to write as should be mostly readily understood, this would account for the Aramaic; but then one, who wrote with that object, would not have written in Hebrew what was of most interest to the people, what was most especially written for those times. If his object had been, (as was that of Haggai, Zechariah, Malachi) to write in the language of the ancient prophets, then he would not have written in Aramaic at all. The prophecies in the Chaldee portion of Daniel are even more comprehensive for the most part than those of the Hebrew. Had such been the object, one should have rather expected that, with the exception of the prophecy of the 70 weeks, the languages should have been reversed. For the Aramaic portions confessedly speak most of the kingdom of the Messiah.

The use then of the two languages, and the mode in which the prophet writes in both, correspond perfectly with his real date; they are, severally and together, utterly inexplicable according to the theory which would make the book a product of Maccabee times. The language then is one mark of genuineness, set by God on the book. Rationalism must rebel, as it has rebelled; but it dare not now, with any moderate honesty, abuse philology to cover its rebellion.

LECTURE II.

*The Prophecies of the Four Empires, Babylonian, Me-
do-Persian, Greek, Roman, and of the establishment
of the Kingdom of Christ during the Fourth Empire.*

Two great subjects of prophecy in Daniel, plainly and
on their surface, extend into a future beyond the sight of
one who lived even in the time of Antiochus Epiphanes;
1) the prophecies of the fourth Empire; 2) that of the 70
weeks and the Death of the Redeemer.

Before entering on the first, let us advert to the ancient
prophecy of Balaam, in which the conquest of the East
by the West, and the subsequent perishing of the Western
Empire in its turn, are predicted in the plainest terms.
They are the words with which Balaam's prophecy closes.
They are without a figure, and relate to things (he himself says) far distant. [1] *He beheld the Kenite, and took
up his parable and said, Strong is thy dwelling place and
place in the rock thy nest ; for the Kenite shall be for a prey,
until Asshur shall carry thee,* (Israel,) *away captive. And
he took up his parable and said, Alas ! who shall live when
God doeth this? And ships shall come from the side of
Chittim*[2], i. e. (as is well known) Cyprus, *and shall afflict
Asshur and shall afflict Eber,* (i. e. the country beyond
the river,) *and he too* (who should so afflict them) *shall
perish for ever.* Balaam foretold the quarter whence
they should come, not the people who should come.
For as yet they were no people. But Cyprus was a

---

[1] Num. xxiv. 21—24.   [2] צִים כִּתִּים

great link of East and West by sea. Tyre early subdued it, and held it subdued, as a station for its commerce [3]. It would contrariwise be the last station, when the West should invade the East. Unbelieving criticism avers that Balaam's words "[4] refer to an incursion of Greeks into Cilicia in the time of Sennacherib, and are a prophecy derived from the event." In plain words, these writers assert that this prophecy, which stands in the Pentateuch as contemporary with Moses, was in fact, the relation of an event, 750 years subsequent to Moses, by some writer who falsely alleged it to have been foretold. The explanation, upon which they have ventured, may serve for a foil to the truth. They from the West, both Alexander and the Romans, *did* afflict the great Empires beyond the river; we know how Alexander and his empire in turn perished; how the Roman empire was broken, although it still lives on, because it was not to be destroyed until the end. That inroad on Cilicia, related by Polyhistor [5], was in itself of no account, no joint or systematic effort. For Greece did nothing in common between the Trojan and Persian wars [6]. There was no commencement of centralisation or common endeavour, until B.C. 560, 140 years after the time of Sennacherib. The Greek marauders did *not* march against Sennacherib, but Sennacherib against them; he defeated them, although with considerable loss, "and set up his own image in the place as a monument of his victory, and had his prowess and valour engraven in Chaldee, as a memorial for the time to come." Can any one seriously assert that he honestly thinks that this description of the afflicting of Asshur and Eber, and the utter perishing of him who so afflicted them, relates to one battle, far from Assyria, in which a marauding party was defeated?

Such an outline of prophecy as to the world's Empires

[3] Hengst. de reb. Tyrior, p. 55, 6.

[4] Von Lengerke, p. lxxx. from Hitzig, Begr. d. Kritik, p. 55. v. Bohlen, Einl. z. Gen. § 17.   [5] in Eus. Chron. Arm. T. i. p. 43.   [6] Thuc. i. 12. 17. Grote, Greece, c. 28.

probably lingered on in Mesopotamia, Balaam's home, when this new flood of light burst upon the Heathen world. Nebuchadnezzar, now in the second year of his reign, was already a conqueror. He had succeeded to a parent who was a conqueror. According to Berosus, "[1] his father Nabopolassar, hearing that the Satrap, appointed in Egypt and the parts about Cœle-Syria and Phœnicia, had revolted, and being himself no longer equal to fatigue, committed to his son Nebuchadnezzar, who was yet in the prime of life, some parts of the army, and sent him against the rebels. Nebuchadnezzar defeated him in pitched battle and brought the country again under his rule. At this time his father fell sick at Babylon and died. Nebuchadnezzar, hearing of his death not long afterwards, set in order the affairs in Egypt and the rest of the country, and, having commissioned some of his friends to transport to Babylonia the prisoners of the Jews, Phœnicians, Syrians, and the nations in Egypt, together with the heaviest part of the army, himself with few attendants went across the desert to Babylon." There "he received the government which had been administered by the Chaldæans, and the kingdom which had been kept for him by the chief of them, and ruled over all his father's empire."

The young monarch, who had already shown himself so energetic and victorious, had in his mind, not only his subsequent career of conquest, but, (which, in any mind of large grasp, ever follows close upon those thoughts,) what would be the end of all. It is a striking picture of the young conqueror, that, not content with the vista of future greatness before him, he was looking on beyond our little span of life, which in youth so fills the mind, to a future, when his own earthly life should be closed. *O king*, says Daniel[2], *thy thoughts came up upon thy bed, what should come to pass hereafter.* To him God revealed, how empire should succeed empire, each great in its day, each misusing its greatness, until, at last, a king-

[1] In Jos. c. Ap. l. 19. more correctly in some things that in his Ant. x. 11. 1.

[2] ii. 29.

dom should come, not founded by human means, and so not by human means destructible, which should absorb all empires into itself, and should itself endure for ever. It is remarkable that this vicissitude of human things, this marked outline of the succession of Empires till our Lord should come, is laid open, not to the believing Hebrew, but to the Heathen monarch. The king is the organ and first depository of the revelation ; Daniel is but its expositor. This change in the organ of prophecy is in remarkable harmony with those former revelations through the Prophets. To them the foreground is the kingdom of God, as already existing among them. Apart from their office of moral and religious teachers, the developement of that kingdom was the subject of their prophecies. From this foreground they looked out on the powers of the world, as they bore upon His people, and as they should hereafter be absorbed into it or be punished for their misdeeds against it and against God in it. To Nebuchadnezzar, at the then centre of earthly greatness, God exhibits, as *his* foreground, the Empire of the world as it should develope in its different stages, until it should be confronted at last by the Kingdom of God, and universal obedience should be claimed, not by any one Empire of this world, but by God in His Kingdom. The form exhibited to Nebuchadnezzar is one ideal form, man in colossal majesty. The separate world-monarchies are but successive parts of one whole. The human commanding figure stands, [3]*its brightness excellent and the form thereof terrible,* until the end. Human power, consolidated by human wisdom, has a majesty, lent to it by God, even while it abuses the God-entrusted gift. Three of these world-monarchies were to be displaced by the succeeding; the fourth by one, wholly unlike the four, *not made with hands.*

Of the last of these Empires, (strange enough) no one has been found to doubt that it is the Kingdom of Christ.

-----

[3] ii. 31.

The greatest of all miracles is conceded; the less is questioned. It is owned by those who set these prophecies at the very latest, that, nearly two centuries before our Lord's ministry began, it was foreshewn that the kingdom of God should be established without human aid, to replace all other kingdoms and to be replaced by none; to stand for ever, and to fill the earth. Above 18 centuries have verified the prediction of the permanency of that kingdom, founded, as it was, by no human means, endowed with unextinguishable life, ever conquering and to conquer in the four quarters of the world; a kingdom one and alone, since the world has been; embracing all times and climes, and still expanding; unworn by that destroyer of all things human, time; strong amid the decay of empires; the freshness and elasticity of youth written on the brow which has outlived eighteen centuries. This truth, so gigantic, so inconceivable beforehand, so inexplicable now except by the grace of God, was, (it is granted,) foreseen, foreshewn. Nay more, it is granted, that, the Prophet believed that He, the King of this new kingdom, was to be more than man! The question then is; " Did the soul which grasped this truth, err (for it comes to this) as to some 150 years?" Porphyry was consistent; for he denied both. Having apparently rejected Christianity, as too hard for him, he wrote against Daniel as a part of a whole. In his times men had witnessed, for $2\frac{1}{2}$ centuries only, the inherent vitality of the Gospel. They predicted the date of its expiry[1]. But in men who call themselves Christians, and who believe in some sense that the Gospel is *the power of God*, it *is* strange to grant or maintain so much, and yet to dispute what, if they believe what they say, is comparatively so little. When Infinity has been granted, the endless Kingdom of the Infinite God; it seems strange to dispute about an atom, some 150 years of our narrow time. Yet

[1] S. Aug. de Civ. D. xviii. 53, 4. in Ps. 40. § 1. Ps. 70. § 4. Baronius, A. 304. viii. gives two inscriptions of Diocletian in Spain, " nomine Christianorum deleto:" "superstitione Christi ubique deleta, cultu Deorum propagato."

so it is.　The question is this, " Granted that the author of our book was right in predicting the founding of a kingdom of God, which should not pass away, was the fourth kingdom in which he foretold that it should arise, that of Alexander's successors, and did he himself, living (according to different rationalist hypotheses) during or shortly after the reign of Antiochus Epiphanes, wrongly look that the kingdom of God should be founded soon after the death of that Old Testament Anti-Christ, B.C. 164? or did he expect that kingdom to come, when it did come, in the time of the Roman Empire, as almost all have believed from our Lord's time until now?"　For if the 4th Empire was the Roman Empire, then we have a temporal prediction too, beyond the sight of one who lived even in the reign of Antiochus Epiphanes.

It is allowed on all hands, that the four beasts in Daniel's vision in the first year of Belshazzar correspond exactly to the four empires represented in the image exhibited to Nebuchadnezzar.　To the king God chiefly revealed that which most concerned him to know, the beginning and the end, the greatness of the power given and to be given to him by the King of heaven, and the nothingness of the mightiest human power, compared and in collision with the Kingdom of God.　To this end, after briefly saying, that the second kingdom should be inferior to his own power, and that the third should rule over the whole earth, he dwells at length on the fourth kingdom, as symbolised by the strong, all-subduing, all-crushing iron, yet itself, with all which went before it, the whole fabric of human power, as being, before the Kingdom of God, *like the chaff of the summer-threshing-floor which the wind carrieth away, and there is no place found for them.*　The intense nothingness and transitoriness of man's might in its highest estate, and so of his own also, and the might of God's kingdom, apart from all human strength, are the chief subjects of this vision as explained to Nebuchadnezzar.

Yet although thus much only was explained to the king, the symbol represented much more. The image, as one, represented the one principle of human Empire; in its manifold parts, it pourtrayed not only a manifoldness, but a variety in the successive Empires. The symbols which *are* explained shew that there is a meaning in the corresponding symbols, which are not explained. In regard to the first and the fourth empires, those represented by the *head* and the *legs*, both the parts of the human figure and the metal of which, in the statue, they consist, are explained in their symbolic meaning. Then, doubtless, the parts of the human figure and the metals have, both of them, their symbolical significance, in regard to the second and third empires also. The head of gold has an unity, a magnificence, an insight of its own. It is not only the first empire in time; the conception of the whole idea of world-empire lay in it, and in him whom chiefly it represented[1]. And so again, at the other extremity, in the fourth Empire, not only is the iron substance of the legs alluded to, as symbolical of heavy iron might, but the human form too, in that he speaks of its *subduing all* things, trampling them under foot, (as is said more fully in the next vision.) The inferiority of the 2nd empire to the first, then, doubtless is symbolised by the pale silver, as compared with the gold, inferior not in value only but in solidity and power of resistance, more liable to impression from without. The form moreover in the human figure is two-fold; nor only so, but the right is stronger than the left. The kingdom then, which was to succeed Nebuchadnezzar's, was not only to be inferior to it, but was to be compounded of two parts, the one stronger than the other[2]. The symbol already suggests the Medo-Persian

[1] Hofmann, Weissag. u. i. Erfüll. i. 278, 9.

[2] Ib. 279. "The chest is twofold and unequal; the heart, the centre of the circulation of the blood, belongs to one side only. Then the arms hang on both sides of the chest: *they* especially have activity; the chest, firmness. Medes and Persians are the two sides of the chest, the arms stretch out from the chest, yet are not severed from it; so Phœnicia and Egypt stretched out on the

Empire. The third Empire, in its dark lowering colour, is to us even at first sight remarkably combined, "the belly and thighs." Yet the lower part of the human figure singularly combines the greatest activity and strength with the dullest, most inactive, proverbial sluggishness. Just so were the two parts of Alexander's empire contrasted. The old fierce energy of Egypt and the Mesopotamian powers was gone. "[3]The loins of Greece held together the belly of Asia, yet could not impart to it its own activity. As the most active part of the body, the centre of its strength, motion, power of turning, is in closest nearness with that, which will simply be carried, so, in the kingdom of Alexander, was the then most stirring and self-adapting people with the mere passive East." It reminds us involuntarily of the contrast, which impressed itself on Aristotle[4], of " the thoughtful and contriving but spiritless character " of the Asiatics, and "the spirited and thoughtful" genius of the Greeks, which would enable them to "rule the world, if" concentrated by "one government." The third Empire, one at first, is then represented in the thighs, as two great portions; not closely united together as the two sides of the chest, but one only by their common connection with the upper part, or in them continued. Nothing could more exactly represent those two subdivisions of Alexander's empire, the account of which is expanded to Daniel in ch. xi, those by which his people were most affected.

The kingdoms of the Seleucidæ and the Ptolemies, ever

one side, the territory of the Lydian empire with the Greeks of Asia Minor on the other, controlled from the centre of the empire, yet ever inclined to make themselves independant, and often successful. Alexander, before he attacked the centre of the kingdom, mastered the two arms which the Persian king had once stretched out, so full of peril to Greece."   [3] Ib. 280.

[4] In his well known passage (Pol. vii. 7.) speaking of his own (Alexander's) time, " The nations in the cold countries and those around Europe are full of spirit, but are rather wanting in thought and contrivance; wherefore they retain their freedom, but have no fixed polity and cannot govern their neighbours. Those of Asia are thoughtful and contriving, but spiritless, wherefore they abide in subjection and servitude. But the Greek race, as it occupies the mid-space between them, so it partakes of both; for it is both spirited and

at variance with one another, had no unity, they were in no sense a kingdom, except as they were connected with the great Empire-plan of Alexander. They were continuations of Greek predominance over the nations of Oriental character in Asia Minor, Egypt, Syria, Assyria. They carried out that interpenetration of the Greek and Oriental nations, which Alexander must have contemplated; they Hellenised Egypt and Western Asia, and unknowingly prepared the way for the Gospel by diffusing, through means of their Greek cities, the language in which it was to be given.

In the fourth Empire we have again strength, ending in division; strength yet greater than in the third Empire, ending in greater division; yet, even in its division, retaining to the end, in its several portions, its original iron might. Its chief characteristic is its strength. It is likened to the metal proverbially strong; *it is strong as iron*[1]; and it crushes all successively. *Forasmuch as iron breaketh in pieces and subdueth all things; and as iron that breaketh all these, it shall crush and break.* It is an annihilating power, which leaves to that which it conquers, no trace of its existence, but itself replaces it. Twofold in its form, as the Roman power, itself one, came to be divided into East and West, it ends in yet further division into ten kingdoms; and the iron commingles itself with a material as plastic, as itself is unyielding, *potter's clay.* This, as Daniel interprets it, expresses partly the mingled strength and weakness of the later condition of the empire, strong, as before, in some parts, yet side by side with weakness, partly the union of this fourth empire with that which was foreign from itself, through intermarriages, *the seed of men*[2], whereby however the two powers do not cohere. History down to Antiochus Epiphanes exhibits nothing of this sort. There was no such subdivision into ten; no three which were

thoughtful; whence it abides free and with excellent polities, and is able to rule the world, if it should come to have one government."

[1] ii. 40.   [2] Ib. 42.

uprooted. An union moreover between the Seleucidæ and Ptolemies by intermarriages would have been an union of like, not of unlike, materials. It would have been a cementing of the kingdom within itself, iron with iron, not iron with clay. There were also (as we shall see) only two such alliances between the two houses, and even those on no one policy. The ancient explanation corresponds best with the symbol, that the Eastern and Western Empire subdivided still further. "[3] When Germans and Slaves advanced partly into Roman ground, anyhow into the historical position of the Roman Empire, their princes intermarried with Roman families. Charlemagne was descended from a Roman house; almost at the same time the German Emperor Otho II.[4] and the Russian Grand-Prince Vladimir[5] intermarried with daughters of the East-Roman Emperor. This was characteristic for the relation of the immigrating nations to Rome; they did not found a new kingdom, but continued the Roman. And so it continues to the end of all earthly power, until its final ramification into 10 kingdoms. To attempt now to mark out these would be as misplaced, as to fix the Coming of Christ, [with which they stand connected] tomorrow or the next day."

Even an opponent has said; "[6] It is in favor of this interpretation [of the 4th empire as the Roman] that the two feet of iron can be referred to the Eastern and Western Empire."

This dream of Nebuchadnezzar is confessed on all hands to be expanded in the first vision of Daniel. Nebuchadnezzar's dream had represented human empire in its intelligent, well-proportioned might. It was man's power as formed, in some measure, in the image of God. The substance, the strength, the character, of the several empires were different; the form was one. Daniel's vision exhibits them on another side. The four winds of hea-

---

[3] Hofmann, p. 281.

[4] see l'Art de vérifier les Dates, ii. 2. p. 103.   [5] A. D. 989. Ib. 250.

[6] De Wette, Hall. Encycl. art. Daniel. He adds that, in his opinion, the

ven are driving at once upon the great sea, that representative, throughout Holy Scripture, of our troubled world [1], and out of it there arise four forms of more than human strength. The terrific and wasting power of the world-empires is exhibited under the image of brute force, *four great beasts* [2], *diverse one from the other.* A sort of unity is given to them, in that they are all exhibited at first to the prophet's eye at once. God shews them to him first, as He Himself sees all things, at once [3]; then, as they arose in fact, succeeding one another. Nor did they arise of their own power. "[4] Not without being acted on by the winds of heaven, does the sea send forth those beasts; not without being set in motion by the powers above, does the heathen world form itself into those great empires."

The intervals in the vision are marked very distinctly by the words, [5] *I continued gazing, till—After this I gazed on, and lo,—After this, I gazed on in the night visions and lo,—I continued considering the horns and lo,— I went on gazing till the thrones were set—I went on gazing because of the great words—I gazed on, till the beast was slain;—I gazed on in the night visions, and behold, one like a Son of man came in the clouds of heaven.* The

European kingdoms " can only in a very figurative way be looked upon as a continuation of the Roman Monarchy, and that the number 10 cannot be verified in them ; yet it has its difficulty to make out the ten kings according to the other explanations." See further in Lect. 3. I only cite him, as an instance how that interpretation, so far, commended itself to one on the extreme opposite side. [1] see Is. xvii. 12. Babylon is "the dragon by the sea." Ib. xxvii. 1. Pharaoh, Ezek. xxix. 3. add xxxii. 2. comp. Rev. xiii. 1. xvii. 1, 5. xxi. 1. "The sea is the world." S. Ephr.

[2] as Ps. lxviii. 30. lxxiv. 13, 4. Is. and Ez. n. 1. Jer. li. 34.   [3] vii. 3. As in Rev. viii. 2. the "seven trumpets" are given at once, sounded successively.

[4] Hofm. 283.   [5] הֲוֵית חָזֵה vii. 4, 6, 7, 9, 11, 13. מִשְׂתַּכַּל הֲוֵית vii. 8. lit. "I was (one) considering," much as people say in idiomatic English, "I was a' considering." The substantive verb with the participle never means in Hebrew or Chaldee *mere* relative time, but always marks an abiding and continued condition. See Ew. krit. Gramm. § 282. p. 537. Winer, Gr. Chald. § 47. The idiom occurs in Daniel ii. 31, 34. iv. 7, 10. and in this ch. vii. 2, 21. and in his Heb. viii. 5. הָיִיתִי מֵבִין. On the like use of the participle as a Hebraism in the N. T. see Buttmann, Gramm. d. N. T. Particip. n. 26. p. 266. 7.

idiom in all these cases expresses an abiding condition, a period during which the objects displayed to Daniel remained before his sight, and he gazed upon each, until the next came. The continuance of the sight before him in the vision implies a duration of that which is exhibited. Once only, in the course of the vision, is the idiom omitted; and that, in remarkable correspondence with the circumstances. Daniel saw this vision *in the first year of Belshazzar;* just at the close, then, of the Babylonian Empire, and just before the beginning of the Medo-Persian. As to the Medo-Persian Empire alone, which was to come at furthest in a very few years, he does not use the idiom. After closing the account of the Babylonian, *a man's heart was given to it,* he proceeds, *and behold another beast;* as describing an event which was immediately to follow.

In the first year of Belshazzar, when Daniel saw this vision, the sun of the Babylonian Empire was now setting. It was setting, (as it seems,) in its grandeur, like the tropic sun, with no twilight. It continued in its integrity, until, through the weakness of its rulers, it sank at once. Daniel sees it in its former nobility. As it had been exhibited to Nebuchadnezzar under the symbol of the richest metal, *gold,* so now to Daniel, as combining qualities ordinarily incompatible, *a lion with eagle's wings.* It had the solid strength of the king of beasts of prey, with the swiftness of the royal bird, the eagle. Jeremiah had likened Nebuchadnezzar both to the lion [6] and the eagle [7]. Ezekiel [8] had compared the king, Habakkuk [9] and Jeremiah [10], his armies, for the rapidity of his conquests, to the *eagle.* So he beheld it for some time [11], as it had long been. Then he saw its decay. *Its* eagle-*wings* were *plucked*; its rapidity of conquest was stopped; itself was *raised from the earth* and set erect; its wild savage strength was taken away; *it was made to stand on the feet of a man.* " [12] In lieu of quickness of motion, like eagle's wings, is

<hr>

[6] iv. 7. xlix. 19. l. 17, 44.   [7] xlix. 22.   [8] xvii. 3, 12.   [9] i. 8.
[10] iv. 13. Lam. iv. 19.   [11] חֲזֵה הֲוֵית עַד דִּי vii. 4. see n. 5.   [12] Ibn Yech.

the slowness of human feet." *And the heart of mortal man*[1] *was given to it.* It was weakened and humanised. It looks as if the history of its great founder was alluded to in the history of his empire. As *he* was chastened, weakened, subdued to know his inherent weakness, so should they. The *beast's heart was given* to him, then withdrawn, and he ended with praising God. His empire, from having the attributes of the noblest of beasts yet still of a wild beast, is humanised. "[2]The last empire ends in God-opposed blasphemy and perishes by the direct judgment of God."

The second beast, the bear, corresponds with the solid, heavy chest of Nebuchadnezzar's statue. The two-fold division and the relative strength of the two sides, the one stronger than the other, recur in this symbol also, in that the bear *is raised up on one side*[3], ready to use the arm in which its chief strength lies[4]. It lifts itself up heavily, in contrast with the winged rapidity of the Chaldæan or Babylonian conquests. The *three ribs in its mouth* correspond accurately to the three kingdoms which the Medo-Persian empire swallowed up, the Lydian, Babylonian, Egyptian[5]. It is bidden, *Arise, devour much flesh,* in conformity with the greedy, "all-eating[6]," character of the animal. Waste of human life was a characteristic of the Persian Empire in its heavy aggressiveness. Heaviness was, after Cyrus, the characteristic of its wars.

It never moved, except in ponderous masses, avalanches, precipitated upon its enemy, sufficient to overwhelm him, if they could have been discharged at once, or had there been any one commanding mind to direct them.

[1] שׁנא, with the idea of weakness, as in אָנַשׁ.

[2] Hofmann, 284.   [3] according to the pointing, הֳקִמַת ; or, if הֲקִמַת, "lifts up one side."   [4] see Rev. xiii. 2. Oppian singles out "the right hand," Cyneg. iv. near the end, quoted Boch. Hieroz. iii. 9. ii. 132. Leipz.

[5] "Cyrus, the first king of Persia, subdued the whole East to the Hellespont; Cambyses his son, Egypt and Æthiopia; Darius Hystaspes, the Scythian Nomads in the North." Theod. Rather, "Thrace." But it is questionable whether he permanently subdued more than the sea-coast. comp. Her. v. 2. and 10.   [6] πάμφαγον. Aristot. H. A. viii. 5. see others in Boch. l. c. p. 143.

Like Attila or Timour, they wielded vast masses of human strength on their enemies; their armies varied from 300,000 on slighter expeditions to a million. Darius' army, with which he marched through the desolate regions of Scythia, was counted at 700,000, exclusive of his fleet of 600 ships[7], which would add a naval force of 120,000 men[8]. Xerxes' expedition against Greece resembled more the emigration of vast hordes, than an army; they were calculated at above two million and a half of fighting men[9]. Artaxerxes Longimanus, his successor, gathered two armies, each, it is said, exceeding 300,000 men, to subdue the single province of Egypt[10]. The first was defeated chiefly through 200 Athenian ships[10]. It is noticed how Artaxerxes gathered his army from all quarters to resist his brother Cyrus the younger[11]. Xenophon tells us that deserters and prisoners counted it 1200,000, and that it was actually 900,000, a contingent of 300,000 not having arrived in time[12]. Even its last unwarlike king brought an army of 500,000[13], or 600,000[14] to the battle of Issus; and, two years after its defeat, he gathered 1000,000[15], in splendid array[15], to cover the plain of Gaugamela, a multitudinous host from all the nations yet left under his sway, to be mostly but the spectators of his disgrace.

"When the Persians first became a conquering people,"

[7] Her. iv. 87.   [8] At 200 to each trireme. vii. 184.

[9] Her. vii. 185. The Greeks believed that 3 millions were gathered against them at Thermopylæ. Her. vii. 228.   Xenophon calls it " a countless army." Anab. iii. 2. 13.   [10] Diod. xi. 74, 75.

[11] Diod. xiv. 22.   Their gathering place was Egbatana.   " But when those from India and some other nations, were behindhand on account of the distance," &c.   He gives its numbers from Ephorus at " not less than 400,000."

[12] Anab. i. 7. 10.   [13] Diod. xvii. 31. Arrian says, on the authority of Ptolemy Lagi, that 110,000 were slain. ii. 11.   [14] Arrian, ii. 8. 12.

[15] " 1000,000 foot, 40,000 horse, 200 scythed chariots." Arr. iii. 8. 8. Arrian mentions Indians near Bactria, Bactrians, Sogdians, Sacian allies, Arachoti, and the mountaineer Indians, Arians, Parthians, Hyrcanians, Tapyrians, Medes, Cardusians, Albanians, Tacesinæ, those on the Red Sea, Uxii, Susians, Babylonians, with transplanted Carians, and Sitaceni, Armenians, Cappadocians, Cæle-Syrians, Mesopotamians.   Diodorus states the foot at 800,000, the horse at 200,000, the chariots at 200. xvii. 53.

says Heeren [1], "it was their uniform practice to strengthen their armies by means of the conquered nations,
who were forced to accompany them on their further
advances. But when they had founded and organised
their Empire, and were lords of all Asia from the Indus
to the Mediterranean, it would have involved endless difficulties to collect troops out of lands so distant. To do
this on all little occasions, such as internal disturbances
or easy wars, would have been as unmeaning as impossible. Still it continued to be their practice, that, on all
great national undertakings, whether directed to the enlargement of the empire in distant lands or to meet
mighty aggressions from without, such musters were
made of all the subject nations, as is shewn by the great
arrays under Darius Hystaspes, Xerxes, and even under
the last Darius.

"Even the preliminary preparations were of immense
extent. The king's command issued to all nations of the
empire, directing what each was to contribute, in men,
horses, ships or provisions [2]. The commotion occasioned
thereby throughout Asia lasted, before the expedition of
Xerxes, for four full years [3]. Time was required, before
the contingents out of the distant countries could be
brought together.

"For all in common there was one rendezvous; in Xerxes' expedition, this was in Cappadocia. Here all those
contingents out of all provinces of the empire met together, each led by its Satrap. In the war itself these retained no command, the officers were taken from the Persians. This was a privilege of the conquering nation,
just as it was among the Moguls and Tatars. The subject nations were treated as property, and were called
slaves, in contrast with the Persians [4] who on their side
were called Freemen. Such was the relation of the nations to each other; towards the king the Persians were
as little free as the others.

"The order of march in their own territories was mar-

[1] Ideen, i. 513-18.   [2] Her. iv. 88. vii. 21.   [3] Her. vii. 20.   [4] Her. vii. 9.

vellous; rather there was scarce any order. The men
were not even separated according to nations [5], but formed an immense chaos. In the midst was the king with
the Persians; the baggage went before. As they advanced, the inhabitants of the countries through which they
passed were driven on and had to swell the multitude [6].
So the mass grew continually;—the baggage must have
become incalculable [7]. The most inconceivable thing is
the provisioning. In the countries through which they
passed, corn had to be laid up long before; other was
brought by ships. Else the hordes had to provide for
themselves. Meals were ordered for the king and his attendants; but were given at such an expenditure, that
this alone exhausted the cities [8]. The king and his gran-
dees had their tents, the rest encamped under the open
heaven [9], which must have unavoidably entailed a number
of diseases.

"On approaching the enemy's country, the army was
divided according to nations. This was connected with
a muster which the king commonly made. Hence the
document in which Herodotus has preserved to us an accurate list of the nations in Xerxes' army [10]. The muster
took place in Europe. Little instructive as the scene may
be for military men, there could scarce be one more in-
teresting to the observer of nations. The history of the
world gives no instance, in which such a multitude and
variety of nations was compressed into one spot of the
earth, as appeared, each in his peculiar costume and arms,
on the plain of Doriscus. Herodotus counts and describes 56 nations, which served by land, horse and foot,
or part in the fleet [11]. There were Indians in their cotton

---

[5] Her. vii. 40.   [6] As, e. g. the Thracians. Her. vii. 110.

[7] "The number of women-bakers, concubines, eunuchs, baggage-horses and
other beasts of burthen, and of dogs, Herodotus says, was countless."   vii. 187.

[8] Her. vii. 118.   '[9] Ib. 119.   [10] vii. 59-100.

[11] "Herodotus says that all the nations were horsemen, but that the Persians
employed some only as such. (vii. 84.) They were limited by the means of sub-
sistence. The whole number of fighting men he fixes at rather more than 2½

dress, and Æthiopians from beyond Egypt, clad in skins of lions; the black Walruchs from Gedrosia and the No-mad tribes from the steppes of Mongolia and the great Buchary; wild hunting tribes, like the Sagartians, who, without weapon of bronze or steel, caught their enemies, like the animals they hunted, in leathern lassoes, and Medes and Bactrians in rich array; Libyans with 4 horse chariots [1], and Arabs upon camels; Phœnician mariners with numerous squadrons, and Asiatic Greeks compelled to fight against their countrymen. Never did despotism exhibit a spectacle, which began so splendidly, to end so pitiably."

Every lineament then of the description agrees with the Medo-Persian empire; the heavy fierceness and the de-structiveness of the animal; the prominence given to the one side; the three ribs, which can receive no explanation as to any other empire.

Of the third Empire, the characteristics are swiftness and insatiableness of conquest, and four-fold division. The panther [2], an animal, insatiable above every other beast of prey, gifted with a swiftness which scarce any

million. We, in our days, have seen France alone, by a like conscription, send towards a million of fighting men into the field. In itself then, it is nothing strange, if out of the vast Asia and no small portion of Europe and Africa one and a half as many again could be brought together. (Her. vii. 185.) The counting by 10,000s was a Persian custom in such expeditions. Witness Darius in his Scythian expedition; the sum told was engraven on columns. (Her. iv. 87.) This counting then is certainly no fable, nor the sum any exaggeration of Herodotus. Whether it was misstated in the Persian documents, we have now no means of judging."   [1] Her. iv. 170. 189.

[2] "Most naturalists have arrived at the conclusion that the Leopard and Panther are one and the same animal." Museum of Nat. Hist. p. 113. "It is about a third less than the tiger." "The size varies, and independantly of this, there occur varieties from dark brown to black. The size of the spots and the arrangement of the rows vary without any variation in the essential cha-racters." Giebel die Sauge-Thiere, p. 875. Dr. Rolleston. I have substituted the word "Panther," for the "Leopard" of the E. V. because at present the name "leopard" is popularly used of a smaller animal; of old, it was used to designate the larger animal, which was supposed, on account of its size, to be a cross betwen the lion and the pard. (Bochart.) The Panther is next in size to the Tiger, whose habitat is more Eastward. Dr. Rolleston tells me, "The extreme point of the Tiger's westward distribution seems to be the Southern

prey can escape[3], is represented yet further with four wings. The subdivision of the Empire is indicated by its four heads. Its colour in the animal corresponds to the brass of the image; its swiftness to the activity of the loins and thighs in the image. Probably moreover, the multiplication of the heads means more than the subdivision of rule. The human head was, in the dream of Nebuchadnezzar, a symbol of human intelligence. Probably these heads, like the four-headed creatures in Ezekiel's vision[4], looked all ways, E. W. N. S. Their so looking was in itself a symbol of circumspection, of manifold versatile intelligence. This remains further to be developed in the next vision.

But, again, the chief object of interest in the vision, as in Nebuchadnezzar's dream, is the 4th Empire. For the living creature which represents this, there is no name. No one creature can express its terribleness, not even if the attributes of different creatures, (as in the symbol of the lion with eagle's wings) were combined to picture it. Only, words expressive of terror and might are heaped, the one

slopes of the Caucasus, which was the Eastern boundary of the Leopard's distribution, its western boundary being the Atlantic, as the Tiger's Eastern is the Pacific ocean."

[3] " It is borne," says S. Cyril, " with swiftest course against what it wills, and runs with feet so swift, that no track is seen nor any imprint left on the ground." on Hos. xiii. 7. The Abbe Poiret (in his Voyage en Barbarie, 1789. i. 224.) gives this account of the Panther; " The Arabs have assured me that they fear the Panther more than the lion, both for themselves and for their flocks. It is of the nature of the tiger. Its rage is to drink its fill of blood, and, when satisfied with it, to see it flow and, as it were, to bathe in it. Its fury is never slaked; but seems even to gain fresh nourishment, the more victims it destroys. If it precipitate itself in the midst of a large flock, unless chased away, it leaves nothing alive. It breathes only blood, carnage, death. It attacks all animals except the lion, and conquers all. Extremely light in its course, it is fleeter than any ; its motions are so subtle, so prompt, that it is difficult to escape it. Thickets, ditches, even small rivers cannot arrest it in its course. It lightly clears them all, and if the creature which it pursues, escape into a tree, the Panther, notwithstanding the bulk of its body, is there as soon. Thus it declares war against the inhabitants of earth and air. The bird, too young to leave its nest, although placed at the summit of the tallest tree, becomes its prey. The thirst of blood is seen in its look : its eye is always sparkling with anger and rage."   [4] Ezek. i. 10.

upon the other, to characterise it. We have the *terribleness* which was ascribed to the aspect of the image, as a whole; and the *strong might*, which was the property of the fourth kingdom in it, and that, *exceedingly*; and Daniel framed apparently a new word, to enforce the conception of its strength. He calls it [1]*terrible and mightful*[2] *and strong exceedingly, diverse from all the beasts before it*, with *great iron teeth* and *nails of brass*, which should not only *devour*, like the bear, *but should stamp the residue with its feet.* "In the former beasts," says S. Jerome, "there are single tokens of terribleness; in this there are all." The beast of the Revelations, which was framed after this description of Daniel, is combined of the first three of Daniel. [3]*The beast which I saw was like unto a leopard, and his feet as the feet of a bear, and his mouth as the mouth of a lion.*

Of the last Empire, like the first, Daniel sees not only certain characteristics, but a history. Intervals of its history are marked. It embraces a long period[4]. The beast appears at first with the ten horns at once, as the third beast with its four heads. Its characteristic is stupendous strength, as that of the third is manifold intelligence. But although, in order to manifest its unity, it appears as one whole, the explanation shews that the ten horns belong to a subsequent stage of its existence. For first its characteristic crushing power and its use of that power are dwelt upon; [5]*The fourth beast shall be the fourth kingdom upon the earth, which shall be diverse from all kingdoms, and shall devour the whole earth and shall tread it down and break it in pieces.* Then, *after this*, the ten horns are explained to be kings or kingdoms which should issue *out of it.* [6]*And the ten horns out of* (i. e. going forth from) *this kingdom* are *ten kings* that *shall arise.* Throughout

---

[1] vii. 7.   [2] אֲסִירָא. The root exists only in Arabic in this sense, whence in Heb. מָתְנַיִם, "loins," as the seat of human strength. In the extant Aramaic, the root has only the meaning "wished for, lingered." No other was found either by Quatremère or Bernstein.   [3] Rev. xiii. 2.

[4] see ab. p. 68, 9.   [5] vii. 23.   [6] 24.

these prophecies the king represents the kingdom, and the kingdom is concentrated in its king. *The kings* then or *kingdoms* which should *arise out of* this kingdom, must, from the force of the term as well as from the context, be *kings* or *kingdoms* which should arise at some later stage of its existence, not those first kings without which it could not be a kingdom at all. For these do not arise out of it, but are a part of it. *We* could speak of the United States, or (should we erect these into independent states hereafter) of India, the Canadas, the Australasian Colonies, as arising, springing out of the kingdom of Britain. We could not speak of our own line of sovereigns, as kings who came forth from the kingdom of Britain; for they were all along an integral part of it. The kingdom never existed without them.

These 10 horns or kingdoms are also to be contemporaneous. They are all prior in time to the little horn which is to arise out of them. *Another*, he says, *shall arise after them*, and *it diverse from the rest ;* as the whole kingdom should be diverse from those kingdoms which were before it. Yet the ten horns or kingdoms are to continue on together, until after the eleventh shall have risen up; for it is to rise up *among* them and to destroy three of them. The description, in itself, implies, that the ten horns symbolise ten kingdoms, not ten kings only. For in this way only could the two traits be compatible, that the eleventh was to *come up among them* and yet *after them*. One could say of the new kingdom of Italy, that it came up *after* the other kingdoms of Europe, and yet *among them*. But one could not say of the king of Sardinia, that he arose up *among* the kings his predecessors, who were of necessity dead before he arose. To *arise up after*, and yet *among*, are incompatible, except when those former things abide.

So then, within the period of the fourth empire, there are these distinct periods, 1) the time until it is divided into the ten portions symbolized by the ten horns, as, before, it was represented as *ending* in the ten toes;

2) the period of those ten horns. 3) That in which the eleventh, diverse from the rest, held its sway. This also is marked to be no brief time, both from the events in it, and from the wondering lengthened contemplation of the Prophet : [1]*I continued narrowly observing these horns; and, behold, there came up among them another little horn, before whom three of the first horns were uprooted ; and behold, in this horn were eyes like the eyes of a man, and a mouth speaking great things—[2]I continued gazing then because of the voice of the great words which the horn spake ; I gazed on even till the beast was slain,—[3]I gazed on, and the same horn made war with the saints, and prevailed against them.* 4) The period after the destruction of that power and of the whole fourth kingdom which is to perish with him, indicated by the words; *And the rest of the beasts*, the other kingdoms, *their dominion was taken away, yet their lives were prolonged on to a season and time,* [4]i. e. on to the time appointed by God. The sentence seems most naturally to relate to a time after the destruction of the 4th empire; for it continues the description. It does not seem to be simply an account of what God *had*[5] done afore-time to those former empires, viz. that when He took away their world-rule, He left them in being as nations, but of something which should be after the destruction of the fourth. This however will be made clear when the time comes.

The latter part of this, being still future, we cannot explain certainly. Prophecy is not given to enable us to prophesy, but as a witness to God when the time comes. This prophecy reaches on to the end of time. Much of it is confessedly expanded in the Revelations, as still to come. It would then be as inconsistent in us to attempt

---

[1] vii. 8.   [2] 11.   [3] 21.

[4] עִדָּן וְעִדָּנִין עַד. עִדָּן (i. q. Heb. מוֹעֵד) is a definite time, as in the phrase בְּעִדָּן iii. 28. iv. 33. Ezr. v. 3. See also vii. 25. and in Heb. Eccl. iii. l. Neh. ii. 6. and in the N. T. ὁ καιρὸς S. Luke xxi. 8. χρόνους ἢ καιροὺς Acts l. 7. 1 Thess. v. 1.

[5] v. 12. depends apparently on v. 11. " I gazed on until the beast was killed and his body destroyed—and the rest of the beasts, their dominion," &c.

to explain it, as it would be in the school of Porphyry, not to explain it. For, according to them, it relates to past facts. They assume the book to have been written in the times of Antiochus Epiphanes, to relate to his times, and to be intended to influence his times. *Then*, they are bound by their own hypothesis to explain it, if they *can*, with reference to those times. For, according to them, it represents past facts. The impossibility of pointing out these has, since Porphyry's time, been one chief rock, on which those theories have been wrecked.

Christians *can* point out the correspondence of the fourth Empire, as far is incumbent on them, viz. in its beginning. Crushing power was the characteristic of the fourth beast. Permanent subdual distinguished the Roman Empire. Other Empires swept over like a tornado. They ravaged, extorted submission, received tribute. But their connection with the states whom they subdued, was loose and disjointed. The title "king of kings," which Assyrian[6], Babylonian[7], Persian[8], assumed in succession, was a boast which confessed weakness. They had not the power of consolidating into one the disjointed materials of their greatness. The plans of Nebuchadnezzar, Cyrus, Alexander, the previous founders of world-Empires, failed in the hands of unworthy successors. Rome kept in dependence on itself all which it acquired, inferior yet still integral members of its polity. Dionysius, comparing it to the empires before it, especially the Assyrian, Persian, Alexander's, says[9], "If any one, considering the governments of which we have any account in the past, apart and as compared with one another, would judge which had the largest rule, and wrought the brightest deeds in peace and war, he will find the Roman far to surpass all before it, not only in the greatness

<hr>

[6] Hos. viii. 10. Is. x. 8. and Merodach-baladan's title, Is. xxxix. 1.

[7] Ezek. xxvi. 7. Dan. ii. 37. comp. Is. xlvii. 5.

[8] Ezr. vii. 12. Strab. xv. 3. 7. Amm. Mar. xix. 2. 16. Persepol. Cuneif. Inscr. in Grotefend; Pehlevi coins in De Sac. Mem. s. diverses Antiq. de Perse, p. 87, 8. Ges. on Is. x. 8.

[9] Antiq. Rom. l. 2-4. see Newton on the Prophecies.

of its empire and the splendour of its deeds but in its duration until now.   For the Assyrian Empire, of fabulous antiquity, held but a small part of Asia. The Median, which destroyed the Assyrian and gained a wider rule, lasted no long time, but was overthrown in its 4th generation. The Persians, who subdued the Medes, mastered at last wellnigh all Asia; but, invading Europe also, they brought over to them not many nations, and their empire continued not much more than two centuries. The Macedonian Dynasty, which destroyed the Persian Empire, surpassed in extent of empire all before it : yet neither did it flourish long, but on Alexander's death began to decline.   For being rent asunder straightway by his successors (Diadochi) into many governments, and having strength to last out to the second or third generation after them, it was internally weak, and at last was effaced by the Romans. Nor did it either subdue all land and sea. For it did not conquer that wide Africa except about Egypt, nor all Europe, but advanced only Northwards as far as Thrace and westward to the Adriatic."

" Such was the acmé and might which the most illustrious Empires, recorded in history, attained, and they decayed. But the city of Rome rules over the whole habitable and inhabited earth, and the sea, not only within the columns of Hercules, but the ocean too, as far as ships may venture. It, first and alone of all in all recorded time, made East and West bounds of its sway; and the period of its might is not brief, but such as no other city or kingdom ever had.—Since it subdued Macedonia, which at that time seemed the most mighty on earth, it has now, for 7 generations, ruled without rival, barbarian or Greek. No nation, so to speak, disputes her supremacy or declines to obey her."

Abating what is the language of panegyric, Rome had consolidated a dominion different in character from any before her and wider in extent.

Such was the aspect of the successive kingdoms, such their outline. But the chief object of interest, that

chiefly expanded, as in Nebuchadnezzar's dream, is that
in which they should end, the kingdom of God victorious
over the evil of the world.   One verse is assigned to each
of the first three kingdoms; one verse contains the explanation of them all; the rest of the vision and the explanation is occupied with that great conflict.   We see,
on earth, [1] *the little horn with eyes like the eyes of a man,*
man's intellectual acuteness, *and the mouth speaking great
things,* setting himself *over against God* [2], destroying the
saints of the most High, *essaying to change* worship [3] *and
law ;* and all is, for the allotted time, given into his hand.
On the other side heaven is opened to us; we see the
Throne of God, and the Eternal God, and the judgment
set, and the books opened, the records of man's deeds and
misdeeds; and *one like a Son of Man* in Heaven ; like man,
but not a mere man ; Man, but more than man ; in the
clouds of heaven, to Whom, as Man, *is given power and glory and kingdom ; all peoples* should *serve Him, and His dominion* should last for ever.   It is a sublime picture ; man,
with his keen intellect, a look more stout than his fellows,
overthrowing kings, doing his own will, speaking against
God, placing himself over against Him as His antagonist,
having, for a set time, all things in his hand; and above,
out of his sight, God, enthroned in the serenity of His
Majesty, surrounded by the 1000s of 1000s of heavenly
beings who serve Him; and, near Him, One in human
form, born of a human birth, yet, like God, above in the
clouds of heaven, the darkness shrouding Him from human eye, but reigning and to reign for ever, His kingdom neither to *pass away* by decay nor to be *destroyed* by

---

[1] vii. 8.

[2] לְצַד עִלָּאָה vii. 25. לְצַד ἅπ. λεγ. lit. ad latus, is probably i. q. "לְנֶגֶד over against,"
"opposed to," like לְנֶגֶד Dan. x. 13. comp. *adversus.*

[3] זִמְנִין "set times," i. e. probably "the times" of the set feasts, (as we speak
of sacred "seasons,") and so the worship of those times. In Onk. it stands for
מֹעֲדִים Gen. i. 14. and Jon. puts זִמְנֵי סְעַד for מֹעֵד Zeph. iii. 18. and וּמִן סְעַד Lam.
i. 4. Pseud. Jon. paraphrases מֹעֲדֵי יְהֹוָה "feasts" by וּמִן סְדֵרִי מֹעֲדַיָּא Lev. xxiii. 2. 37.
by זְמַן Ib. 4. 44. Else זְמַן is used of the place of sacred assembly, Num. i. 1. Is.
xxxiii. 20. but מֹעֵד is retained of the festival, Lev. l. c. Lam. i. 4. Hos. ix. 5.

violence. "[1] God is patient because He is eternal."   Below, all is tumult; above, all is tranquillity; the heavenly King over against the earthly potentate, until the last blasphemy draws down the lightning upon him; the voice of his great words ascends, the judgment of God descends. *Because of the voice of the great words which the horn spake, I beheld till the beast was slain, and his body destroyed and given to the burning flame.*

The vision, in all its parts, corresponds to Nebuchadnezzar's dream; only, whereas *that* mentions the beginning of this kingdom of God, as well as the annihilation of all human power by it, this exhibits mainly the last rebellion of man and its subdual. Its fulfilment we cannot, of course, point out, because *the end is not yet* [2], but we can, at least, own its harmony and oneness with the Gospel. At the same time we shall see the impression which the prophecies of Daniel made on those to whom they were given.

1) No one hesitated about S. John Baptist's meaning[3], *Repent ye, for the kingdom of Heaven is at hand.* [4]*All men mused whether he were the Christ or no.* It was a known class among the Jews, who *waited for the kingdom of God* [5]; the same, of whom it is said, that they [6]*waited for the consolation of Israel,* [7]*looked for redemption in Jerusalem.* The Pharisees demanded of Jesus[8], *when the kingdom of God should come?* They understood His answer, [9]*The kingdom of God cometh not with observation. The kingdom of God is within you. The kingdom of God, the kingdom of heaven,* occur in the Gospels, as names, as well known to the whole people of the Jews as faith, hope, charity, worship, or any other religious term. They are not explained, but are assumed to be understood. Our Lord embodied the title in His prayer which He gave us, *Thy kingdom come.* The *kingdom of Heaven* occurs exclusively, *the kingdom,* almost exclu-

---

[1] " Patiens quia æternus."   [2] S. Matt. xxiv. 6. S. Mark xiii. 7. S. Luke xxi. 9.   [3] S. Matt. iii. 2.   [4] S. Luke iii. 15.   [5] S. Mark xv. 43. S. Luke xxiii. 51.   [6] S. Luke ii. 25.   [7] Ib. 38.   [8] Ib. xvii. 20.   [9] Ib. 20, 1.

sively, in S. Matthew's Gospel, as being written especially
for Jewish converts ; but he has also that other term more
frequent in S. Luke, *the kingdom of God*[10].   Of these equivalent terms, *the kingdom of heaven* is especially suggested
by Daniel's words [11], *the God of heaven shall set up a kingdom which shall never be destroyed*, as also by the contrast with those kingdoms of man, which should arise
from the earth[12].   *The kingdom* is the word of Daniel[13].

2) The King of this kingdom was to be of human birth[14],
like a son of mortal man, and therefore not a mere man ;
accompanied by angels to the Throne of God, in that Majesty which had, before Daniel in this place, been spoken
of God only, *coming with the clouds of Heaven.*

As God manifested Himself in the cloud in the Exo-
dus[15], the wilderness [16], the tabernacle[17], or the temple[18],
as the clouds hide from us what is beyond them, so they
are spoken of as the visible hiding-place of the Invisible
Presence of God.   To ascribe then to any created being a
place there, was to associate him with the prerogative of
God.   Holy Scripture says of God, [19]*He maketh the clouds
His chariot ;* [20]*clouds and darkness are round about Him ;*
[21]*His pavilion round about Him were dark waters and thick
clouds of the sky:* [22]*the clouds are the dust of His Feet :* [23]*behold the Lord rideth upon a swift cloud, and shall come into*

[10] *The kingdom of Heaven*, occurs 32 times in S. Matt. (see Schmid, Conc.
v. οὐρανός ;) *the kingdom*, 6 times ; S. Matt. iv. 23. viii. 12. ix. 35. xiii. 19.
38. xxiv. 14. *the kingdom of God*, 5 times.   In S. Luke *the kingdom of God*
occurs 33 times ; in S. Mark 15 times ; S. John iii. 3-5. ; Acts, 7 times ; S. Paul,
11 times ; Rev. once. (Schmid, v. βασιλεία) *the kingdom*, S. Luke xii. 32.

[11] Dan. ii. 44.   [12] Ib. vii. 17.   [13] vii. 18, 22.

[14] אֱנָשׁ כְּבַר. Ib. 13. The כַּ "son" expresses descent, as בֶּן in אֱנוֹשׁ בֶּן in Heb.   When
in Syriac, a compound word, *barnosho*, had been formed, the etymology was
forgotten, and the compound word came to signify " man," so that it could be
used even of Adam ; not so, while they remained two words, (as in Ch.)   The
book of Enoch speaks of the Messiah, not only, in reference to Daniel, as the
Son of Man, but (from Gen. iii. 15.) as " the Son of woman, sitting upon the
throne of His glory ; " lxi. 9. Oxon. lxii. 5. Dillm.

[15] Ex. xiii. 21, 22. xiv. 24.   [16] Ex. xvi. 10. xix. 9. xxiv. 15, 16, 18.
xxxiv. 5. Deut. iv. 11. Judg. v. 4.   [17] Ex. xl. 34. Lev. xvi. 2. Num. ix. 19.
x. 34. xi. 25.   [18] 1 Kgs. viii. 10. 2 Chr. v. 13. Ezek. x. 4.   [19] Ps. civ. 3.
[20] Ib. xcvii. 2.   [21] Ib. xviii. 11.   [22] Nah. i. 3.   [23] Is. xix. 1.

Egypt. It says, [1] *one like a Son of man came with the clouds of heaven.* It says the like of no other, save in prophecy of that evil being who said, [2] *I will ascend above the heights of the clouds; I will be like the most High.*

Even before our Lord came, the description was recognised as relating to the Messiah. The passage was cited in the book of Enoch [3], when affirming the pre-existence of the Messiah "before the creation of the world and for ever [4]," that He was the Revealer to man [3], the Object of prayer [5], and would be, to all nations [6], the stay, the light of nations [7]; the hope of the troubled [8]; the righteous Judge [9], with Whom the saints should dwell for ever [10]. 'Anani, 'He of the clouds', continued to be a name of the Messiah [11]; and the Jews, unable to distinguish beforehand His first and His second Coming, reconciled the account of His humiliation and His glory by the well-known solution; "[12] It is written of king Messiah, *and see, with the clouds of heaven One like a son of man* came; and it is written, *meek and riding upon an ass.* Be they [Israel] worthy, *with the clouds of heaven;* be they not worthy, *meek and riding upon an ass.*" Caiaphas understood it and all which it claimed for Him, his Judge, Who was arraigned before him, and Whom he had *adjured by the living God,* to say whether He were *the Christ, the Son of God.* [13] *Thou*

---

[1] Dan. vii. 13.   [2] Is. xiv. 14.

[3] ch. xlvi. 1-3. "Then I beheld the Ancient of days, Whose head was like white wool, and with Him Another, Whose countenance resembled that of man. His countenance was full of grace, like one of the holy Angels. Then I enquired of one of the angels who went with me, and who shewed me every secret thing, concerning this Son of man ; who He was ; whence He was; and why He accompanied the Ancient of days. He answered and said to me ; This is the Son of man to Whom righteousness belongs ; with Whom righteousness has dwelt, [dwelleth, Dillm.] and Who will reveal [revealeth D.] all the treasures of that which is concealed," &c. Abp. Laur. transl.   [4] xlviii. 3. 5. lxi. 10.   [5] "In that hour was this Son of Man invoked before the Lord of spirits, and His name in the presence of the Ancient of days," xlviii. 2. Dillmann renders "was named."

[6] xlviii. 4.   [7] xlviii. 3.   [8] Ib. 4.   [9] lxi. 5. lxviii. 39.

[10] lxi. 17.   [11] Tanchuma, 13. 2. Ver. quoted by Beck, Targ. Chron. p. 54, 5. Breshith, R. on Gen. xxviii. 10. in the time of Mart. Pug. Fid. P. iii. lii. 9. 6. p. 769. ed. Carpz.   [12] Sanhedr. Chelek, f. 98. 1. Mart. p. 344. Schöttg. i. 1151.   [13] S. Matt. xxvi. 63, 4.

hast said; Nevertheless I say unto you, Hereafter ye shall see the Son of Man sitting on the Right Hand of Power and coming in the clouds of Heaven. Caiaphas understood, and thereon condemned Him for blasphemy. Once more our Lord applied the words of Daniel to Himself, [14]*All power is given unto Me in heaven and in earth.* The title, *the Son of Man* [15], as employed by our Lord, is the more remarkable, in that He always uses it of Himself as to His work for us on earth; no one ventures to use it of Him, except that S. Stephen points to the commenced fulfilment of His prophecy to Caiaphas, [16]*I see the heavens opened and the Son of Man standing at the Right Hand of God.* Our Lord called Himself "*the* Son of Man," i. e. He Who was foretold under that Name in Daniel.

3) Daniel foretold, not a kingdom in Israel only, not a conversion of the Heathen only, but that He Who sat above, in a form like a son of man, should be *worshipped*[17] *by all peoples nations and languages*, and that this His kingdom should not pass away. And to Whom have peoples nations and languages throughout the world, millions on millions, and hundred millions on hundred millions in successive generations, looked to and worshipped as their King, hereafter to come to be their Judge; Whom have they confessed in their Creeds all these centuries since any questioned it, as Him "Whose kingdom shall have no end," save Him Who came in the form of a servant, like a Son of man, in Judæa?

iii. These two visions of the four empires both ended with the end of time, with the destruction of all human

---

[14] Ib. xxviii. 18. from Dan. vii. 13, 14.

[15] It occurs 34 times in S. Matth.; 14 times in S. Mark; 26 times in S. Luke; 10 times in S. John. (See Schmid, Conc. v. *υἱός.*) It is not used after the Resurrection, except when the Angels repeat our Lord's words before His Death, (S. Luke xxiv. 7.) and by S. Stephen in reference to His prophecy.

[16] Acts vii. 56.   [17] vii. 14, 27. It is the same word, under which the three youths had refused the worship to Nebuchadnezzar's image; (Dan. iii. 12, 14, 17, 18, 28.) it is used of Daniel's worship of God; (Dan. vi. 17, 21. Ch. 16, 20. Eng.) Artaxerxes uses the verb of those who serve God in His temple, (Ezr. vii. 24.) and the noun, of Divine Service. (Ib. 19.) [all.]

power, the everlasting kingdom of Christ.   The next vision, which developes a part of Daniel's former vision, stands in remarkable contrast with it, in its limited extent. It developes the account of two of the four kingdoms, just those two which had been touched on most slightly before; but has nothing of the kingdom of God, of the Coming of Christ, or of the end of the world.   It is one detailed picture of an intermediate portion of the history; of events which meantime much affected God's people, but which were comprised in their history.   The vision is of the more moment in the interpretation of the rest, because its symbols are authoritatively interpreted in the Prophet himself.

The two empires represented to Daniel are, that of Persia under the symbol of the ram, that of Greece, in the person of its first monarch, under that of the he-goat. Daniel, in his vision, is himself in Susa in Elam, the seat of the future Persian Empire.   He sees the Medo-Persian world-empire forming itself, (as then, in the 3rd year of Belshazzar, it actually was,) *and the higher*, he says, *was shooting up* (lit. *ascending*[1]) *at the last*.   The empire united in itself the strength of two kingdoms, the later of which was the mightiest; as, in fact, Persia, which before was the chief dependency on Media, by a revolution rather than by a conquest, absorbed Media into itself. The ram, its symbol, butted West and North and South; for itself came from the East.   Westward, it conquered Babylonia, Syria, Asia Minor; Northward, Colchis, Armenia; Southward, part of Arabia, Egypt, Æthiopia.   It did according to its will[2], great, proud, mighty things[3]. *No beasts* (i. e. no power,) *could stand before it, neither*

---

[1] i. e. as he was gazing.   The Part. עֹלָה is of relative time.

[2] See Her. iii. 31.   [3] תַּגְדִּיל viii. 4. see on Joel ii. 20. p. 124.   There is no special allusion to *Persian* pride, of which Greeks (Herod. i. 89. 184.) and Latins (Amm. M. xxiii. 6. 80.) speak.   Daniel says, just afterwards, of Alexander, that *he waxed very great*, or *did exceeding greatly*, הִגְדִּיל עַד מְאֹד, viii. 8.   Pride is, of course, inseparable from the greatness and success of unregenerate man. Alexander was as much intoxicated with it as the Persians.   Both *did great things*, and *acted as great*, i. e. proudly.

could any deliver out of its hand.　Scripture joins together the meridian and the sunset.　The power arose, ascended to its zenith, fell.　The fall is the issue of all human greatness, which man, whether exercising it or suffering under it, loses out of sight; and so God brings it home to him.　The he-goat, as described in an image which has been admired in classic poetry [4], speeds from the West over the whole earth without touching the ground, slays the ram and tramples upon it.　In its turn, the Persian Empire has no internal power to resist, and none to deliver it [5].　The he-goat is represented (according to the well-known symbol of Persepolis,) with its *one beautiful horn between its eyes;* wonderful symbol of strength and intelligence.　*As it became strong, its horn was broken.*　In the midst of designs, the vastest and most multiform probably, which intelligent ambition ever conceived, when not yet 33, Alexander perished.　But for the marsh-fever of Babylon, aggravated by intemperance, they might have been fulfilled.　Then grew up the *four beautiful horns in its stead towards the four winds of heaven,* i. e. as it is explained, *four kingdoms from that* same *nation, but not in his power.*　No one has been found to doubt that by these are intended Alexander's four successors, the Diadochi, who collectively held whatever survived of his Asiatic conquests and his own dominions, subject to the rule of Greece.　The network of Greek intelligence still lay spread over the whole compass of territory, which Alexander had laid open.　The power of mind continued, although the might of strength was broken. The vision again, as to this empire too, hastens to the end, *the latter time of this kingdom* [6].　Then all the evils, which the people of God had had to endure, were concentrated and intensified.　The office of Alexander's empire was to prepare the way for the Gospel, by spreading Greek intelligence and the Greek language over Asia West of the Indus.　We are familiar with the language, "to Hellenise Asia."　Antiochus Epiphanes mistook his

[4] Æn. vii. 806-10.　　　[5] viii. 7.　　　[6] viii. 23.

office, directed against God what was to be subservient to God, and, in his mad self-will, profaned the temple, stopped the daily sacrifice, and would have trampled out the worship of God. The vision closes with the extinction of this Anti-Christ of the Old Testament; [1]*he shall be broken without* [human] *hand; the sanctuary shall be cleansed.*

To which empires, then, of the four do these two correspond? The Persian Empire is symbolised by a strong but heavy animal, the ram, corresponding to the bear of the preceding vision; the threefold direction of its conquests answer to the three ribs in the bear's mouth; the pre-eminence of the one of the two horns, to the greater power of striking attributed to the one side. So also as to the Greek Empire. The characteristics of the Grecian Empire, as given here, are exceeding swiftness and four-fold division. But these are precisely the characteristics of the 3rd Empire in the dream and the vision. Only in this later symbol it is explained in addition, that this four-fold division should not exist from the first. No one symbol could represent the whole without being unnatural. The oneness was represented in the four-headed, four-winged panther, fierce and destructive, as all human conquests are, yet sagacious and beautiful, as the panther is above other beasts of prey, carrying in its four-headed empire, acute intelligence. The successiveness was symbolised by the horns. The one horn could be represented as replaced by the four horns. Such a change did not destroy the oneness of the living symbol. The one head could not have been exhibited as replaced by four, without interruption of its oneness by death.

Either of these identifications, the he-goat with four horns with the four-headed panther, or the ram with the bear, involves the other. For the symbol relates to two consecutive empires. It is cumulative evidence, when each has a visible agreement with the corresponding symbol in the previous vision. Conversely, it is an

[1] viii. 25. 14.

aggravated disagreement with the previous symbols, when, in order to make out the fourth empire to be the Greek, the two symbols of the 8th chapter are fitted to two in the 7th, with which they severally disagree. The four-horned he-goat, i. e. an empire, as it is explained, divided into four kingdoms, cannot agree with the 4th Empire, whose division into ten is marked by the ten horns of the terrible beast, and the ten toes of the image. Nor can the heavy ram, with its two horns, be identified with the superhuman swiftness of the four-headed leopard. The correspondence of the two symbols, each to each, in the one case, and their disagreement each from each, in the other, leave no question but that the third empire is the Grecian. But the third Empire being the Macedonian, there remains for the fourth empire, only the Roman.

Nor is it any objection to this, that, in this way, opposition to God and anti-religious persecution occur both in the 3rd and 4th empire under the symbol of a little horn, yet with a visible difference even in this symbol. For in the Grecian empire the little horn issues, not from the empire itself, but from one of its fourfold divisions. *Out of one of them* [the *four beautiful horns*] *came forth a little horn.* Antiochus Epiphanes came out of one of the four kingdoms of Alexander's successors, and that kingdom existed in him, as the fourth horn issued in the little horn. But in the fourth empire, the horn proceeds, not out of any one horn but, out of the body of the empire itself. It *came up among them*, [the horns,] wholly distinct from them, and destroyed three of them. Such a marked difference in a symbol, otherwise so like, must be intended to involve a difference in the fact represented.

And why should there not be, under the fourth empire, an antagonism to the true God, concentrated in and directed by one individual, as it was in and by Antiochus in the third? Human nature repeats itself. What man has done, man will do. We, Christians, look for an Anti-Christ yet to come. Our Lord forewarned of him and his deceivableness [1].   S. Paul describes such an one as Daniel speaks of [2].   Isaiah had before foretold of him and his destruction [3].   This is *now*, thus far, a question of interpretation only.   Why should we not suppose Daniel to have meant what our Lord and His Apostles meant?   Certainly Daniel himself makes a difference between the God-opposed power symbolised in the little horn of the 8th chapter and that in the 7th.   For the opposition to God in the eighth is manifestly the persecution by Antiochus Epiphanes, and ends simply in the death of the individual and the cleansing of the visible sanctuary. In speaking of the great God-opposed power, in which the Fourth Empire should centre, he speaks of a shaking of the world's powers, such as the world has not yet seen. What he speaks of in plain reference to Antiochus Epiphanes, had its exact fulfilment in him.   Had he meant that other description for him, it would have accorded also.   The opponents of Daniel can find no escape from this, through assertions that the prophecy did not correspond with the event.   For their hypothesis is, that Daniel is describing *past* events.   Their other assumption, then, that the writer described the same event, in the one case, so exactly, in the other case, in a way so radically different, they leave unexplained and inexplicable.

But it is said, that Antiochus Epiphanes is again spoken of in ch. xi. and, that, after his destruction, the resurrection of the dead is foretold.   This, if so, would prove nothing.   It would only be that same foreshortening, which we find throughout Holy Scripture, and in our Lord's own prediction, first of the destruction of Jerusalem, and then of His 2nd Coming to judge the world.

But although Antiochus Epiphanes, the great sifter of the faith before our Lord came, is again in part described in the xith chapter, there are traits, which have nothing to correspond to them in Antiochus, which are even the exact contradictory of the character of Antiochus, but which do reappear in St. Paul's account of the Anti-

<hr>

[1] S. Matt. xxiv. 24.   [2] 2 Thess. ii. 3, 4.   [3] Isaiah xiv. 13, 14.

Christ to come. The image of the Anti-Christ of the Old Testament melts into the lineaments of the Anti-Christ himself. Antiochus was a propagator of false religions, a would-be-destroyer of the true. He opposed God, but he worshipped and was zealous for his false gods. " In two great and right things," say two heathen historians [4], " his was a truly royal mind, in gifts to cities and worship of the gods." "[5]In the sacrifices [sent] to the cities and in the honour to the gods, he surpassed all who had reigned before him. This one may judge from the temple of Jupiter Olympius at Athens and the statues around the altar at Delos." In his great show at Antioch, in which he wished to outdo the Roman games, "[7]The number of statues was past telling. For the images of all gods or dæmons, yea and of heroes also, which are named or accounted of among men, were borne in procession, some gilded, some arrayed with cloth of gold, and to all there were appended the corresponding myths, according to the transmitted stories, in costly array." And this culture of Heathen worship continued to his death. "[8]At Antioch too, having promised a magnificent temple of the Capitoline Jupiter, not with a gilded ceiling only, but its whole walls covered with gold-plating, and many other things in other places, he did not complete them, because his reign was very short." One trait only of the anti-religious character of Anti-Christ was true of Antiochus also; *he shall speak marvellous things against the God of gods.* Blasphemy against God is an essential feature of any God-opposed power or individual. It belongs to Voltaire as much as to Antiochus. All besides has no place in him. [9]*He shall exalt himself and magnify himself above every god ; and he shall not regard the God of his fathers, nor regard the desire of women nor any god ; for he shall magnify himself above all. But in his estate he shall honour the god of forces, and a god whom his fathers knew not shall*

[4] Liv. xli. 20. from Polybius.

[5] Polyb. in Ath. v. 21. p. 94.a. Cas. with Livy.   [7] Pol. Ib. 23. p. 195. a.   [6] θυσίαις. Gron. corrects δωρεαῖς   [8] Liv. Ib.   [9] xi. 36-39.

*he honour with gold and silver and with precious stones
and pleasant things.   Thus shall he do in the most strong
holds with a strange god whom he shall acknowledge and
increase with glory.*   Not only is all this alien from the
character of Antiochus, but, in its essential traits, it belongs to an apostate from the truth, not to one who, like
a heathen, should exchange one error for another.   It
would be no blame to a heathen, *not* to *regard the gods of
his fathers*, nor *to honour gods whom his fathers knew not.*
The characteristics of this infidel king are (1) self–exalt-
ation above every god; *he shall magnify himself above
every god;*   (2) contempt of all religion; (3) blasphemy
against the true God; (4) apostacy from the God of his fathers; (5) disregarding " the desire of women; " (6) the ho-
nouring of a god whom his fathers knew not.   Of all these
six marks, one only, in the least, agrees with Antiochus.
Even if we translate the words, *the gods of his fathers*[1] *shall
he not regard*, this, as is attested by Polybius and Livy,
was the very opposite of his character.   For he was more
zealous in their worship, than any of the kings before him.
He was even a propagator of it.   Like the Imperial persecutors of the Gospel afterwards, he thought, we are told
by the author of the first book of Maccabees, to hold
his kingdom in one by oneness of worship.   "[2] King Antiochus wrote to his whole kingdom, that all should be one
people, and every one should leave his own laws; so all
the heathen agreed according to the commandment of
the king."   What Antiochus forbade, was exclusiveness.
People might worship what they liked, so that they did
not refuse worship to the state-gods.   Non-Greek Heathen could fulfil the king's commandment by the worship
of the Greek gods, without abandoning their own.   To
the Jews such worship involved the abandonment of
God, who had forbidden it.   On the same principle as

[1] Bertholdt, Lengerke, &c. interpret " Syrian gods."   But the Syrians were
one, and one only of the nations, held in subjection by the Greek kingdom.
They were in no sense *the fathers* of the Seleucidæ.

[2] 1 Macc. i. 41, 42.   Josephus alludes to this decree in his summary of the
speech of Mattathias which alludes to it. Antt. xii. 6. 2. from 1 Macc. ii. 19.

Hadrian afterwards, Antiochus called the temple at Jerusalem "the temple of Zeus Olympius," the Pan-Hellenic god; and that on Gerizim, "of Zeus Xenios[3]," or, as Josephus says[4], at the request of the Samaritans also, of Zeus Hellenios.

The spoiling of temples which is related of Antiochus was an irreligious act, according to their light, yet it was not so uncommon[5] as to form the groundwork and occasion of the picture of anti-Theism. Daniel relates the capture of even the sacred vessels of the temple of God, as one of the ordinary events of captivity. Nebuchadnezzar is, notwithstanding, described as the "Servant of God," as having his kingdom and his glory given to him by God. No punishment came upon him for this. It was the direct and purposed insult to God, in the licentious and sensual desecration of those vessels, the idolatrous triumph over God, which brought down the judgment on Belshazzar. Seleucus Philopator had attempted, through Heliodorus, to plunder the temple at Jerusalem. The act, in itself, is no more than has been done by the Catholic sovereigns of Spain and Portugal, and lately in Italy, in employing to secular purposes what had been given to God.

Since it was suggested that *the desire of women* might be the Syrian goddess, Mylitta[6], the Germans have commonly adopted the explanation. Yet there is nothing in the revolting and also unnatural worship of Mylitta,

[3] 2 Macc. vi. 3.   [4] Jos. Ant. xii. 5. 5. gives the letter of the Samaritans and the rescript of Antiochus to Nicanor.

[5] Xerxes attempted to plunder Delphi; (Her. viii. 35-9.) the sacred war was occasioned by its actual plunder. The Ætolians destroyed the temple of Dodona; (Polyb. iv. 67.) Antiochus the Great had lost his life in attempting to plunder a temple of Bel in Elymais. (Strabo xvi. 1. 18. p. 744. Cas.) A Parthian king succeeded in spoiling temples of Athene and Artemis there. (Ib.) Valerius Max. justifies the Roman Senate for a decree to "melt the golden and silver ornaments of the temples to pay the soldiers," in the civil wars of Marius and Sylla. (vii. 6. 4.) Sylla, to the same end, spoiled three temples, Delphi, that of Æsculapius at Epidaurus, and of Jupiter at Olympia. (Diod. Exc. ii. 614.) Diodorus remarks on the wealth of that of Olympia, as having been unspoiled. That of Delphi, the Amphictyons gave up to Sylla. Dio Fragm. 122, 3.

[6] This was devised by I. D. Mich.; then adopted by Ges. v. אדה.

which should entitle that degrading worship to be called *the desire of women.*   Nor can I bring myself to think that Daniel, in a picture of the sin of Antiochus, would mention the abstinence from such a worship as a portion of that sin.   And that the more, when Antiochus, in a degree frightful in his shamelessness even to Heathen, wallowed in the degradations which desecrated that worship. Nanæa, whose temple Antiochus attempted to plunder, was very probably worshipped with Heathen abominations.   But there was nothing characteristic in this attempt, that it should be singled out as exhausting the three descriptions, *Neither shall he regard the gods of his fathers ; nor the desire of women, nor any god shall he regard.*

But, further, these insulated attempts at explanations miss entirely the fact, that the whole of the character centres in the one point, that intensity of pride and competition with God, which we know of only in Satan and in the Anti-Christ to come.   This is the recurring trait ; [1] *he shall exalt and magnify himself above every god ; he shall not regard the God of* his fathers ; nor the desire of women nor any God shall he regard ; for he shall magnify himself above all.*"   The character is a blank denial of God, not a forgetfulness, nor a practical impiety, nor insolent spoliation ; but a self-idolatry, a self-deifying, which shall compete with the true God, and look down on all besides, as being himself greater than they.   Even his god is of his own creation ; [2] *a strange god whom he shall acknowledge and increase with glory.*   It is not *strange gods*, but one strange, unknown-of, god whom he shall recognise, and, by recognising, shall magnify.   The prophecy remarkably corresponds with that which, in the Revelations, is still future, where [3] *the second beast causeth the earth and all that dwell therein to worship the first beast,* giving to them a god whom they should adore.

And yet, according to the school of Porphyry, he who

[1] Navaîa 2 Macc. i. 13, 14. "Nani," according to Sergius in Bar Bahlul, is "the planet Venus." Ges. on Is. ii. 33.   [2] xi. 39.   [3] Rev. xiii. 11, 12.

so described Antiochus, knew him and his history perfectly, and truly pictured his deceits, flatteries, treacheries,
successes, disgraces, anger, corruptions of God's people.
Whence then this utter deviation in describing acts which
must have been still more public and notorious ?　In the
8th chapter, where Daniel did pourtray Antiochus, every
trait corresponds ; we are at a loss for nothing ; not a word
is without meaning.　What then is the inference as to
this description, of which only one line is in common with
Antiochus, and that *one* line, belonging to every sort of
blasphemer ?　What can be the inference, but that Antiochus is not intended ?　If you have two portraits by one
hand, the one resembling its original, the other wholly
unlike, you doubt not that it represents some other man.
Again as to his end.　The end of Antiochus was briefly and
strikingly characterised in the 8th chapter, a sudden yet
not violent death, amid a life of war and plunder.　The
end of *this* Anti-Christ is also clearly marked.　*He shall
place the tabernacles of his palace between the seas in the
glorious holy mountain, yet he shall come to his end and none
shall help him.*　Like Sennacherib of old, he is in the Holy
Land, between its two boundaries, the Dead Sea and the
Western Sea [4], (the Mediterranean,) shaking his hand
against *the holy Mountain,* mount Zion ; and he perishes.
The writer of the book, on the unbelieving hypothesis,
knew of the end of Antiochus.　He died of grief at Tabes,
a town of Persia.　" In what glorious holy mountain
he encamped," S. Jerome justly says [5], " he [Porphyry]
cannot say, nor can he prove that he encamped between
two seas, and it is absurd [as Porphyry did] to interpret
the two seas to be two rivers of Mesopotamia."

There is, then, no place for this Anti-Christ in the
times of Antiochus Epiphanes.　Yet the supposed identity
of this Anti-Christ with him who is spoken of in the former vision, is the only plea for confounding the 3rd and 4th
Empires.　Even the Jews in S. Jerome's time looked
upon this prophecy as having still to receive its fulfil-

<hr>

[4] see on Joel ii. 20. p. 123.　　　[5] on Dan. xi. 44, 5.

ment. "[1] From this place onwards, the Jews think that
Anti-Christ is spoken of, that, after the *little help* of Julian, a king shall arise who shall do according to his own
will, and lift himself up against all which is called god,
and speak great things against the God of gods, so that
he shall sit in the temple of God, and make himself god,
and his will be performed, until the wrath of God be fulfilled; for in him shall the end be.   Which we too understand
of Anti-Christ."   The shadow was projected before.   "As
the Saviour," says S. Jerome, "had Solomon and the
other saints as types of His Coming, so we may rightly
believe that Anti-Christ had as a type of himself that most
evil king Antiochus, who persecuted the saints and profaned the temple."   Good and evil have grown together
all through this world's history: all good foreshadowing
and concentrating in Him Who alone was good; all evil
having its diverse counterparts in those more signal manifestations of evil, and culminating at last in the highest
antagonism to good and God.   Even apart from revelation, it is, in itself, in conformity with human nature, that
as good is intensified, so is evil.

Such is the natural meaning of these great series of
prophecy, as developed from themselves.   It is an interpretation older than the Gospel.   For Josephus, shews,
beyond all question, that he believed the fourth Empire
to be the Roman [3].   The belief still lingers on, but slightly

---

[1] S. Jer. on Dan. xi. 36.   [2] on Dan. xi. 21, 2.

[3] "These things (Dan. viii. 9-14.) it befel our nation to suffer under Antiochus Epiphanes, as Daniel saw, and, many years before, wrote down what
should come to pass.   In like manner Daniel wrote also concerning the empire of the Romans and that it shall be made desolate by them."   Ant. x. 11.
fin.   The well-known reserve in speaking of the stone which should break in
pieces the 4th empire had no ground but his fear of his Roman masters.   He
speaks of it, as yet to come.   He paraphrases Daniel's explanation to Nebuchadnezzar.   "The *golden* head designates thee [Neb.] and the Babylonian
kings before thee; but the two hands and shoulders shew that your rule will
be destroyed by two kings [Medo-Persian] : and their's another will destroy,
clothed with *brass* [Macedonian] and this another will cause to cease, being like
iron in might, and will subdue altogether, on account of the nature of iron ;
this being stronger than that of gold and silver and brass.   Daniel also explained to the king about the stone.   But I do not think good to relate this, my

disguised in the East. The Parsees still have a tradition which speaks of the four Empires from one root, after which the Saviour is to come. "[4] As is evident from the Çtûtgar, Zertusht requested of Ormusd immortality. Then shewed Ormusd, the all-knowing Wisdom, to Zertusht; he saw a tree with such a root that four trees sprang from it, a golden, a silver, a steel, and an iron. Then said Zertusht, 'Ruler, Greatest of all in heaven and earth, I have seen the roots of a tree, from which four trees have sprung.' Ormusd spake to the holy Zertusht; Of this one the root which thou seest (is the world) and these four trees are the four times which are coming: this golden, when I and thou are speaking, and Kotaçpshah receives the law, and the body of the Dēws is broken and they hide themselves; this silver is the rule of the royal Artashir; the steel is the rule of Anoshêrevân-khosru, son of Kobat; that formed of iron is the evil reign of the Dēws," &c. "[5]After this kingdom of the Dēws, [the fourth kingdom] comes, according to the Persian doctrine, Sosiosh the Saviour." These are broken fragments, petrified remains, as it were, of an ancient belief, which, in its day, when living, prepared doubtless for the Gospel. We have the result attested in the times of the Gospel, in the well-known passages of Suetonius and Tacitus. Suetonius mentions the extent of the belief; Tacitus, its source. Suetonius says[6], " an ancient and settled opinion had become very prevalent in the whole East, that, it was in the fates, that, at that time, persons going forth from Judæa should obtain the empire of the world. This, which, (as the event subsequently showed) was predicted of the Roman Emperor, the Jews, drawing to themselves, rebelled." Tacitus [7]; "most [of the Jews] had an implanted conviction, that it was contained in the ancient

task being to write the past and present, not the future. But if any one, eager for the truth, does not shrink from curious search, wishing to learn, (if it may be) about things uncertain, let him be at pains to read the book of Daniel; he will find it in the sacred writings." Ant. x. 10. 4.   [4] Bahman Yesht. MS. of Prof. Spiegel, imparted by him to Delitsch. Hall. Enc. Art. Daniel, p. 276. note.   [5] Delitsch, ib.   [6] Vespas. c. 4.   [7] Hist. v. 13.

writings of the priests, that at that very time the East should prevail, and persons going forth out of Judæa should obtain the empire of the world, which ambiguities had predicted Vespasian and Titus. But the common people, according to the wont of human cupidity, interpreting in their own favour this exceeding fated greatness, were not turned to the truth even by adversity."

Whether or no they believed their own interpretations, the two Roman historians are witnesses to the fact, that this new kingdom was to be founded *then*. It was not a vague expectation, that the East should prevail, but that it should prevail *then*. Both agree, that the new king was not to come forth from the East any where or any how, but from the despised Judæa. Both agree that this persuasion was of old; "it was an ancient and settled opinion[1]," says Suetonius; "it was in the ancient writings of the priests," says Tacitus. The kingdom of Christ had been foretold by Solomon[2] and Isaiah[3]. The time had been defined only by Daniel. Yet, according to the Porphyry school, these writings, which Tacitus thought so ancient, were not older than their own Terence.

But we have yet nearer witness. We have seen that Daniel's prophecy was handed down in a disguised form among the Persians. The firstfruits of the Heathen were from that very order, of which Daniel was made the head. Over and above the natural meaning of those gifts which the Magi brought in their hands, they came with the certain conviction, that one was there born king of the Jews, and that the Child so born was the Object of Divine worship. They knew Whom they sought, why they sought Him. The star fixed the immediate time, which seemingly they had long looked for. They ask only the precise spot where He was to be found. Unbelievers may deny the being of Daniel or the Gospel of S. Matthew. The agreement of the two histories they cannot deny. It is not brought out on the surface; it lives in

---

[1] Percrebruerat Oriente toto vetus et constans opinio.

[2] Ps. lxxii.   [3] ix. 6, 7. xxxii.

the facts. Nebuchadnezzar, it was recorded, on the interpretation of his dream, *made Daniel chief of the governors over all the wise men,* or magi *of Babylon*[4]. It is foretold in the book of Daniel, (no one disputes this,) that a kingdom should be founded in the 4th empire, the King of which should be *like a Son of man, Whom all people, nations and languages should worship*[5]. The first worshippers of Him, Whom now many millions out of all peoples, nations, and languages worship, were from that same school, over which Daniel is related to have been set. [6]*Behold, there came wise men, (magoi,) from the East to Jerusalem, saying, Where is He that is born King of the Jews? For we have seen His star in the East and are come to worship Him.*—[7]*When they came to the house, they saw the young Child with Mary His mother, and fell down and worshipped Him.* Truth brings out the hidden harmony, when unbelief can only, with a dull dogmatism, deny. While we give account of the lesser points, they are these larger agreements, on which one who wishes to know the truth should dwell. "Granted," sums up S. Jerome, "that these things are said of Antiochus, how injureth it our faith? was anything said of Antichrist in the former vision [the 8th chapter] when the prophecy was completed in Antiochus? Let him [Porphyry] dismiss doubtful points, and hold fast to what is plain. Let him say, Who that stone is, which was cut out of the mountain without hands, grew into a great mountain, filled the world, and brake in pieces the four-formed image; Who is that Son of man, Who should come in the clouds, and stand before the Ancient of days, and to Whom a kingdom should be given, which should have no end, and all people and nations and languages should serve Him."

Lesser questions easily receive their light, or, without injury to the faith, remain for the time obscure, when the eye has once seen the central truth.

⁴ Dan. ii. 48.   ⁵ Ib. vii. 13, 14.   ⁶ S. Matt. ii. 12.   ⁷ Ib. 11.

H 2

LECTURE III.

Modern attempts to make out four Empires, which should end with Antiochus Epiphanes.

IT is assumed in rationalist interpretation, that the Fourth Empire is no empire later than the Macedonian, to which Antiochus Epiphanes belonged. For else there would be prophecy. And since it is an axiom or postulate of the school of Porphyry, that there should be no prophecy, facts must in some way be made to square with this first principle. There is to be no allusion to the Roman Empire; for, in the time of Antiochus, human foresight could not yet discern that it would become an Empire of the world.

But if the Greek Empire is to be the fourth Empire, which are the other three? The sum must be made up, though one of the items is withdrawn. 1, 1, 1, and 0 have somehow to be made 4. The result is accounted to be infallibly certain: else God must be admitted to have revealed to His creatures a future which they could not foresee; which, it is assumed, is impossible. Yet no one can dispute that there are four empires. How then is the subtracted fourth to be replaced? The process has been tried upon all the remaining three. Two halves are somehow to become two wholes. Only, agreed as this school is as to the result, they have been nothing less than agreed as to the process whereby it is to be arrived at. Every possible combination has been tried.

1) Nebuchadnezzar alone was made the first Empire; the weak descendants of his house, the second.

2) The Medo-Persian Empire was divided, so that the Median should become the second Empire, the Persian should be the third.

3) Leaving both these in their integrity, the Macedonian Empire was divided, Alexander alone being made to constitute the third Empire; his successors, amid the weakness of their perpetual divisions, the fourth. This was Porphyry's expedient [1].

4) Lastly, all three Empires were left entire, and the Empire, which was subtracted at the end, was replaced by one added at the beginning. Ewald was rightly dissatisfied with all those former solutions; yet, with the contempt for the necessity of any evidence, which so often characterises German theory, he assumed, that Daniel lived, not at Babylon but at Nineveh ; that "[2]the winged lion traditionally meant the Assyrian Empire." "The bear" then became "the Babylonian symbol; the leopard that of the Medes and Persians, while the 4th beast represented, as is not uncommonly held," says Dr. Williams [2], "the sway of Alexander."

Now of these theories, (as happens so often) each concedes by turns so much of the truth as it can afford. Out of the four theories, the adherents of three concede or contend that the Babylonian Empire in its integrity is one entire Empire; three maintain the same as to the Medo-Persian ; three, as to Alexander and his successors. So that the traditional interpretation of, I may say, both the Jewish and the Christian Church, nay, of the Heathen world before Christ, has, in each case, the support of three out of the four parties, which oppose it. No one for a moment hesitates to admit whatever, in order to make out his case, he is not constrained to deny. Each in turn opposes the other, just as much as the old established explanation. Then, in regard to their disagreement among themselves, the one makes that rapid re-

<hr>

[1] S. Jer. on Dan. vi. 7.   [2] Essays and Rev. p. 76.

sistless conqueror, Nebuchadnezzar, to be the sluggish bear; two make the Medes and Persians the swift Leopard; one makes Alexander's successors, who fell, one by one, an easy prey, into the Roman empire, the all-crushing iron, or that beast, which was more terrible, mightful, world-trampling, than all which preceded it.

But apart from this, each is, on the first view, untenable and baseless.   I will take them in order.   1) The grounds alleged for assuming an Assyrian empire to have been the first of the four, are these; that the Daniel, mentioned by Ezekiel, must have been older than the Babylonian captivity; that the lion *may* have been a symbol of the Assyrian empire; that, in the last vision recorded in the book of Daniel, the vision in the third year of Cyrus, Daniel is spoken of, as being by the river Hiddekel or Tigris, on which Nineveh lay, whereas Babylon lay on the Euphrates.   The first of these arguments implies the falsehood of the book of Daniel; the last assumes its minute accuracy, and traditional knowledge of slight facts as to Daniel's person.

In regard to the first, it has been remarked long ago, that Ezekiel names as characteristics of Daniel, qualities which appear in him in early life.   *In the eleventh year* [1], (i. e. as Ezekiel dates, of Jehoiachin's captivity [2], B.C. 588,) Ezekiel, in his prophecies to the prince of Tyre, says in irony; [3] *Behold thou* art *wiser than Daniel ; there is no secret that they can hide from thee.*   Of the manifold varieties of human wisdom, Ezekiel selected that form, for which Daniel was celebrated [4] in the 2nd year of Nebuchadnezzar, i. e. the 5th of Jehoiakim, B.C. 606, eighteen years before this date.   It is that for which the king praises the God of Daniel, that He is *a revealer of secrets, seeing thou couldest reveal this secret* [5].   In asking

---

[1] Ezek. xxvi. 1.   [2] Ib. i. 2.   [3] Ib. xxviii. 2.

[4] Dan. i. 17, 20. *As for these four youths, God gave them knowledge and skill in all learning and wisdom: and Daniel had understanding in all visions and dreams. In all matters of wisdom of understanding, that the king enquired of them, he found them ten times better than all the magicians and astrologers that were in his realm.*   [5] Ib. ii. 47.

him to explain his own later dream as to himself, the king says to him, [6]*no secret troubleth thee.* The Queen-mother spake of him to Belshazzar, [7]*shewing of hard sentences and dissolving of doubts were found in the same Daniel.* One who had his wisdom from God, but was placed by a heathen king as head over those far-famed wise-men, the Magi, might well stand as an eminent pattern of Divine wisdom in man. Tyre and its prince boasted themselves against the people of God in its overthrow, and plumed themselves on their human wisdom and sagacity. It is an anti-Theistic boast. Human wisdom would be wiser than Divine. The prince of Tyre claimed, by his wisdom to have created all this wealth for himself[8]. He despised Hebrew wisdom and the wisdom of God in it, because it was oppressed. The event, Ezekiel says, should shew. Plainly, unless Ezekiel had meant to speak of a contemporary, over against the contemporary prince of Tyre, the wisdom of Solomon had been the more obvious instance to select.

In the other place in Ezekiel[9], God says, that, when the time of His judgment upon the land was come, whether it were *famine, or noisome beasts, or the sword, or the pestilence,* no righteousness of any individuals in it should avert His then irrevocable sentence; and, as pre-eminent instances of righteousness, He gives Noah, Daniel and Job. It is objected, "How came Ezekiel to mention Daniel his contemporary ? and, if he did, how came he to place him between those two ancient patriarchs, Noah and Job ?"

The objection tacitly assumes the thing to be proved, the non-Divinity of prophecy. It assumes that Ezekiel spoke with a mere human judgment. Human judgment dares not pronounce even as to the holiness of those of greatest promise, until perseverance unto the end shall have sealed up their life. Ezekiel says in the name of God, that *God* so pronounced. *Then* there is nothing more remarkable in this, than in other cases in which God pro-

[6] iv. 9.　　　[7] v. 12.　　　[8] Ez. xxviii. 4, 5.　　　[9] Ib. xiv. 13-21.

nounced as to men, yet living and not as yet fully tried. Such was Noah himself[1], and Job[2], and Abraham[3], and David[4], Jeremiah and S. Paul.   Saul was but just converted, when, in answer to the demurring of Ananias, God said of him, *he is a chosen vessel unto Me*[5].   Jeremiah was yet a youth, when God said to him ; [6]*Before I formed thee in the belly, I knew thee ; and before thou camest forth out of the womb, I sanctified thee, I ordained thee a prophet unto the nations.*   The same was said of S. John Baptist; [7]*He shall be great in the sight of the Lord ; he shall be filled with the Holy Ghost, even from his mother's womb.*   Any how, then, Holy Scripture is in keeping with itself.   No one can consistently deny that Ezekiel's words could relate to a living contemporary, unless he deny also that Samuel could have spoken those words of David, nay and deny every other judgment pronounced in Holy Scripture as to the living.   Daniel now, in the 6th year[8] of the captivity of Jehoiachin, had, according to his book, passed through some twelve years of greatness, trying above others to men, for its novelty and his youth.   There is then, at least, nothing inharmonious in the selection of Daniel, to be united with Noah and Job.   Rather it has a special force, that God joined with those two great departed patriarchs, a living saint.   The Jews, as they trusted afterwards because Abraham was their father[9], so now they hoped that, amid their own unholiness, they should be spared for the righteousness or intercession of others.   To cut at the root of this hope, God singles out the great living example of righteous life, and pronounces him, in this early life, one of His chief saints, and says, that, though not he only, but two also of the greatest before him, were among them, their holiness should be unavailing except for themselves.   The eyes of all the Jews must have been the more fixed upon Daniel, the more marvellous his rise,

---

[1] Gen. vii. 1.   [2] Job i. 8. ii. 3.   [3] Gen. xviii. 17-22.
[4] 1 Sam. xiii. 14.   [5] Acts ix. 15.   [6] Jer. i. 5.   [7] S. Luke i. 15.
[8] Ezekiel so dates ch. viii. 1. *in the sixth year, in the sixth month.* He dates ch. xx. *in the seventh year, in the fifth month.*   [9] S. Matt. iii. 9. S. Luke iii. 8. S. John viii. 33, 39.

at that early age, from being a captive boy, though of royal blood, to be *ruler over the whole province of Baby-lon, and chief over the governors of all the Magi of Baby-lon.* The more depressed their lot, the more they must have looked to *him*, whom God, in His Providence, had so raised up to be a bright star in the night of their captivity, a protection to themselves, declaring the glory of their God.

In this case, also, had not the selection of a contemporary had an especial force, we should have looked rather for one of the names of the righteous men of old, who interceded with God, as Abraham.   But Noah, Daniel, and Job, do all agree in these things; 1) that all had had especial praise of God, over against the world.   Noah was the unlistened-to preacher of righteousness during those 120 years in which the flood was delayed.   God singles out Job, in answer to Satan who had been [10]*going to and fro in the earth and walking up and down in it,* as his domain and his kingdom.   " [11] How greatly Daniel's piety and prayer weighed in that scale, wherein Belshazzar was too light, the fact may attest, that he, like David and Abraham, and afterwards, the Virgin at Nazareth [12], was marked out as one *greatly beloved* [13], whereas the word of God comes to the contemporary prophet, *son of man.*"

2) All the three stood too, as representatives of a distinct relation of God to the world; Noah at the head " of the newly cleansed and as it were reborn world; " Job, as a worshipper of God in purity among the heathen world; Daniel, as the revealer, to the heathen world, of that kingdom, which was hereafter to supersede and absorb the kingdoms of the world [14].

The order in which the three saints stand is explained by the application which Ezekiel makes of their history. All were holy, all interceded; but Job was heard, for the time, least of all.   It is a climax of seeming failure [15].   To Noah, his wife and his three sons and their wives were

---

[10] Job ii. 2. See Zündel, Daniel, p. 264. [11] Ib. p. 266, 7. [12] S. Luke i. 27, 8. [13] Dan. ix. 23. x. 11. [14] Zündel, p. 267. [15] Hävern. on Ezek. xiv. 14. p. 207.

given; Daniel delivered his three friends by his prayer to God; Job was for the time bared of all. He [1]*sanctified [his sons and daughters] and rose up early in the morning, and offered burnt offerings, according to the number of them all, for Job said, It may be that my sons have sinned;* and he saved neither son nor daughter. In Job especially was that fulfilled, which Ezekiel gives as the result of the whole, "[2] though these three men were in it, *they shall deliver neither sons nor daughters,* they only shall be delivered."

The mention of Daniel, then, by Ezekiel, in both cases, has the more force from the fact that he was a contemporary; both correspond with his actual character, as stated in his book. Granted the historical truth of Daniel, no one would doubt that Ezekiel did refer to Daniel, as described in his book. But then the objection is only the usual begging of the question. "Ezekiel is not likely to have referred to Daniel, a contemporary, unless he was distinguished by extraordinary gifts or graces." "But his book not being genuine, there is no proof that he was so distinguished." "Therefore," &c.

Scripture is in harmony with itself. Ezekiel is the first witness to the book of Daniel. The book of Daniel explains the allusions of Ezekiel. No other explanation can be given of Ezekiel's words. Ezekiel manifestly refers to one, well known to those to whom he spoke; one, as well known as the great Patriarchs, Noah and Job. Such was Daniel, under whose shadow they of the captivity lived. But, apart from him, where is this man, renowned for his wisdom, holy as the holiest whose memory had survived from the foundation of the world; whom the Jews would recognise at once, as they would Noah and Job? "He does but name him," says an opponent rightly[3], "because he could presuppose that he was already sufficiently known by all as a pattern of righteousness and wisdom." Three answers have been attempted. 1) The usual resource of perplexity; "The verse of

---

[1] Job i. 5.   [2] xiv. 16, 18.   [3] Bleek, p. 284.

Ezekiel was interpolated [4]." No one holds this now [5]. 2) Ezekiel was supposed to have referred to some well-known person of remote antiquity [6]. But where was such an one? It is a paradox to pass by the historical person, and to assume that there was one, who for antiquity could be placed with Noah and Job, of whom the memory was familiar to the contemporaries of Ezekiel, preserved by tradition through all those centuries, yet of whom not a trace survives. This school is fond of the argument "ex silentio." They all (though, as we shall see, wrongly,) use it as a palmary proof of the non-existence of the book of Daniel in the time of the son of Sirach, that he does not name Daniel among the prophets. Yet, in the same breath, they assume the existence of one, whom no one but themselves ever thought of, in order to disprove the existence of him who is known to history. They assume that Ezekiel and his people knew of one *like* Daniel for wisdom and holiness, whom in all those centuries no one mentions, in order to deny or question the existence of Daniel himself, whom Ezekiel's words pourtray, just as he stands in his book. Truly they give us a shadow for the substance. This theory too has probably died with its author [7], having lived its 36 years.

3) Ewald so far modified the theory, that he invented a Daniel, who was to have lived at Nineveh shortly before its destruction, prophesied there, and was in a manner the type of Daniel himself. Ewald allows that it is

[4] Bernstein in Tzschirner's Analekten, i. 3. p. 11.

[5] "Interpolation in the above passages of Ezekiel cannot be assumed without the greatest arbitrariness." Bleek, ib. 285.

[6] Bleek, ib. 284, 5. "In both places, one should *much rather* conjecture, that he thought of a celebrated man in antiquity, than of a contemporary who lived with him in exile," &c. "a person of antiquity well known of yore," repeated, Einl. p. 607-9. De Wette followed him for a time, e. g. Einl. § 253. ed. 4. Lengerke, § 18. p. xciv. Knobel, Prophet. ii. 397.   [7] Bleek said, Einl. 607. (1860) "Most of those scholars, who set the composition of the book at a later date, and do not receive its details as historical, accept this, viz. that Daniel and his 3 companions were historical persons, Jewish exiles, distinguished in Babylon for piety and wisdom, who attained to favour and good repute, even with the rulers of the land." Even Eichhorn held this as certain,

clear from Ezekiel, "[1]that, at least in the beginning of the 6th century (B.C.,) Daniel was the historical type of that rare union of the same two virtues, in which he shines in the present, much later, book, viz. moral purity and wisdom." He infers that, because Ezekiel "[3]speaks of Noah and Job after the well-known books [Genesis and Job] so he did of Daniel; this book, which Ezekiel presupposes his readers long to have known, must be different from the present; Ezekiel contemplates Daniel, as a hero of antiquity who was perfected and long since had disappeared from sight, as much as Noah and Job; according to the historical horizon of Ezekiel's contemporaries Daniel must at latest have lived in the Assyrian exile more than a century before: there, as an Israelite, *perhaps* at the court of Nineveh, he became distinguished for those great virtues; there, *perhaps* he became the subject of a book, which *may* have been early known to Ezekiel's contemporaries in that same country."

It is no uncommon resource of unbelieving criticism, to raise a difficulty, which itself cannot solve, and, having employed it against the belief, which it wishes to uproot, to assume that all was proved, which had to be proved, ignoring the fact that it has itself no explanation to give of the supposed difficulty which it has urged against the truth. Ewald's "perhaps's" leave the fact of the mention of Daniel between Noah and Job, just where it was. The series, Noah, Daniel, Job, is plainly not chronological. No theories as to the date of the book of Job could make it so; for Ezekiel speaks, not of the book, but of the blameless man. The disparity of above 1700 years between Noah and Daniel is not materially lessened by the subtraction of one or two centuries. Take any secular instance. Were one to join the name of Wellington with Alfred and Cœur de Lion it would not mend the disparity of date, to substitute Marlborough for Wellington;

Einl. § 612, 13. and Rosenm. in Dan. § 1. De Wette, Einl. 1852, floated between Bleek, Ewald, and history. § 325.   [1] Propheten, ii. 560.
      [3] abridged from Ewald, Propheten, ii. 560.

or if one were to join Bp. Wilson with St. Augustine and
St. Cyprian, the substitution of Andrewes would not bring
the modern Divine perceptibly nearer to the early Father.
We should feel equally that time did not enter into the
grounds of their being brought together. There is a
meaning in associating a contemporary with the great
departed. Saints of all ages are one glorious company
before God. Time is no element in estimating those who
shine for ever in the glory of God. We classify stars according to their several magnitudes, wherever in our material heavens they may shed their lustre. This unity
of glory formed the oneness of those whom Ezekiel exhibits in one constellation, Noah, Daniel, Job: Job he mentioned last, since his outward lot was most akin to that
which he had to predict. Both the blending of them in
one, and the outward order used by Ezekiel, correspond
with the actual facts in Scripture. The invention of that
phantom-Daniel at Nineveh explains nothing; but concedes the point, that the disparity of time is of no account, since it admits that disparity into its own theory.

It was strikingly said, " a good book might be written
on the credulity of the incredulous [3]." If Scripture had
required us to disbelieve the existence of one in historical
times, and to believe the existence of an ideal person corresponding to him, with a whole history about him which
no one recorded; that God, e. g. had raised up a prophet
in Nineveh to foretell its impending overthrow, and he
had prophesied it truly; that the memory of this prophecy
and the outlines of the prophet's marked combination of
excellencies lived on for centuries, although not the faintest trace of his existence appears in history, it would
have been thought a hard requirement. Yet this is but
what the critical school announces to us as a certain fact,
and would have us receive it thankfully in exchange for
our Divine belief. " Ewald is right," said Bunsen [4], "that
Daniel was led captive in the first Assyrian invasion, and
lived and prophesied in Nineveh, not in Babylon."—" If

[3] Sur l'Incrédulité des Incrédules.   [4] Gott in d. Gesch. l. 515, 6.

we assume that the old real Daniel was carried captive by the Pul of Scripture, and so, probably, by the Sardanapalus of the Assyrian monuments, some 21 years before the overthrow of the old Dynasty and the conquest of Nineveh by the founder of the new, many points are explained, in regard to which the critical school has not as yet been in condition to give an answer. It is intelligible, that the holy and gifted man, who prophesied in Nineveh and announced its destruction, appears two centuries afterwards as the seer and prophet in and of Babylon, &c." and, in his summary, Bunsen relates, as facts,

"[1] Daniel was a noble pious man, a saint and a seer from the middle of the 8th century (B. C.) reverenced by his fellow captives, the Jews in Nineveh. Traditions and popular songs were early full of his sayings and prophecies, as also of his wonderful distresses, sufferings, deliverances. In all is an unity of the personality unmistakeable; the personality of a man who united exalted wisdom and righteousness with the eye of a seer."

For all this confident statement, there is not one shred of evidence.

But 2) "[2]We still see Daniel on the Hiddekel, or Tigris, the river of Assyria, but which is here called the great river, Babylon's river, the Euphrates." "If the scene," it is subjoined, "had been Babylon under Darius, the river must have been the Euphrates."

Daniel, just at the close of his life, when his secular offices, apparently, were ended, received his last vision, when on the bank of the Tigris[3]. Rivers, in later times, were often the places of devotion. "On the sabbath," S. Luke says[4], "we went out of the city by a river's side, where prayer was wont to be made." A decree of the Halicarnassians gives leave, "[5]that those of the Jews

---

[1] Gott in d. G. 536.

[2] Ib. and Essays, p. 76.   [3] Dan. x. 2-4.   [4] Acts xvi. 13.

[5] in Gronov. Decret. Rom. et Asiat. pro Judæis, p .22. Wolf, Curæ in Actt. l. c. p. 1236. Vitringa (Synag. Vet. 1. 2. p. 218) quotes two more instances. Wolf also quotes Aristeas, Hist. lxx. Intt. p. 33. and refers to Zorn, Diss. de Scholis quas ant. Judæi prope a lac. et fluv. ripis, &c. exstruxisse perhibentur.

who willed, men and women, should keep the sabbaths, and perform their rites according to the Jewish laws, and make oratories by the sea, according to their country's wont." It is commonly thought that they resorted there for the facility of making their customary ablutions before prayer. A time of prayer is, any how, a time in which God is likely to vouchsafe visions to those to whom He does give them. Daniel was come to the close of 3 weeks in fasting and prayer. In like way, Ezekiel received his first vision[6], *as* he *was among the captives by the river of Chebar;* and in a former vision, Daniel was in his vision[7] *by the river of Ulai.* What led Daniel, in that third year of Cyrus, to the banks of the Tigris, he has not told us; but since Babylon on the Euphrates was only 40 Roman miles from the Tigris, it was not so far removed from it as Gloucester on the Severn from Oxford on the Isis. Strange ground of questioning a person's identity, that, in the course of a book, he mentions his having been in two places, 40 miles apart!

But 3) we are reminded[8] that winged lions have been disinterred from the mounds which cover the temples and palaces of Nineveh. It is argued then, that the winged lion was *the* emblem of the Assyrian Empire, and, it is quietly assumed, "*not*, of the Babylonian;" and so, since in the book of Daniel it is the symbol of the Babylonian, this could only have arisen in the misapplication of the ancient Symbol. The lion with eagle-wings in Daniel is then itself to be a proof of the existence of some ancient tradition of four empires, of which the Assyrian was the first.

Now, 1) considering the close connection of Assyria and Babylonia, in worship, in language, in writing, in art, nothing could be less certain than that Babylon and Nineveh would not have had the same symbol of their empire, if either had had any known symbol at all. Both the lion and the eagle, as the kings of birds and beasts of prey, were too obvious symbols to be characteristic of any one

---

[6] Ezek. i. 1.   [7] Dan. viii. 2.   [8] Bunsen, Gott in d. G. i. 540.

power.   Twelve lions supported the arms of the throne of
Solomon on its six steps[1].   Both eagle and lion are used
by Ezekiel as symbols of Babylon[2].   The eagle was the
standard of the Parthians, and Persians; it was adopted by
Alexander on his coins, and inherited by the Ptolemies;
was used by the Romans after Marius[3]; the two-headed
eagle became the symbol of the Roman Empire of the
East; it was assumed by the German Empire; the black
eagle is the standard of Prussia; the lion is emblazoned
on the arms of England.

2) The human-headed lion of the Assyrian monuments is
not the eagle-winged lion of Daniel.   For just that which
is most characteristic of the Assyrian figure, the human
head, is designedly omitted from the symbol in Daniel.
The symbols of the beasts, in Daniel, in themselves, express brute might, the fierceness of conquering empire.
If intelligence is intended to be expressed, the idea is
conveyed by a separate symbol.   The eagle-winged lion
of Daniel received no symbol, characteristic of humanity,
until it ceased to be eagle-winged.   [4] *I beheld*, Daniel says,
*till the wings thereof were plucked, and it was lifted up
from the earth, and made to stand upon the feet as a man,
and a man's heart was given it.*   A man's heart is also a
different symbol from a man's head.   The symbol in
Daniel expresses superhuman strength which was lost,
when it was humanised.   In the Assyrian symbols, on
the other hand, the animating characteristic is the human
countenance, serene, majestic, intelligent, penetrating,
benevolent[5].   Superhuman strength, is there, but in entire repose.   The majestic form, as beheld in front, is represented as motionless, its broad chest resting on its
solid legs, side by side.   The wings are pourtrayed as
closely folded on its back, traced slightly upon it.   All is

[1] 1 Kgs. x. 19, 20.   [2] see above p. 69.
[3] see e. g. in Hofmann, Lex. v. Aquila, and coins of the Ptolemies in
Smith's Biogr. Dict.   [4] Dan. vii. 4.
[5] "The expression was calm yet majestic."   Layard, Nin. i. 65.   Those now
in the British Museum seem to me unmistakeably to express those other attributes also.

subordinated to the human head; it seems almost to speak. The eye, by a bold design, stands forth from the head, as if even the cold stone could gaze; the benevolence of the rounded cheeks is heightened by the almost smile of the lips, the chin enveloped in the grave solid beard. The rest of the massive figure gives one idea, strength in perfect repose; the countenance, in its varied expression, is the soul of the whole. This is the more evident, because the expression in the human-headed lions and bulls is precisely the same. The animal-symbol must have been altogether subordinate, because it varies, without varying in the least that expression of mind, which arrests the gazer. When brute force is meant to be represented, it is figured in all its fierceness, as in the colossal lion with vast wide-open jaws, found in one of the temples at Nimrud[6]. It expresses devouring fierceness and rage, and these alone. Instead of that calm human head, are the vast jaws outstretched, as if ready to devour, and purposely disproportioned for magnitude to the rest of the colossal figure[7], because the object was to express terrible fierceness.

[6] British Museum Catalogue of Antiq. p. 81. Bunsen overlooked all this in his statement; " It was a lion with eagle's wings, and a human heart, vii. 4. [not together] and so doubtless with a human countenance [this is in no way implied.] Certainly it is also said, ' it stood on feet like a man,' which is to be interpreted doubtless of the king of that empire, emblematically, not in the visible figure." Gott, &c. i. 540. Thus, to produce the resemblance, two symbols are omitted, the stripping off of the eagle's wings and the standing erect; one is added, the human head. The Assyrian symbols were yet further varied. " I ascertained," says Layard, " the existence of a 2nd pair of winged human-headed lions, differing from those previously discovered in form, the human shape being continued to the waist and furnished with arms. In one hand each figure carried a goat or stag, and in the other, which hung down by the side, a branch with three flowers." Layard, i. 68.

[7] The length of the whole figure, (12 feet 3¼ inches,) is twice that of the average length of the animal (6 feet;) whereas the upper lip (from the centre to the angle of junction) is ⅙ of the whole, 2 feet 1 inch; the lower lip, 1 foot 5 inches; in the living animal it is 5 inches, not ¹⁄₁₄ of the whole length. The gape from the lower lip to the upper immediately below the nose, in the Nimrud lion, is 15½ inches; in the living it would be about 5. The measurements of the Nimrud lion were kindly supplied me by W. H. Coxe Esq. British Museum; those of the actual animal by Dr. Rolleston.

3) It is clear, then, that the human-headed lion was not *the* symbol of Assyrian Empire. For the lion-element of the symbol was wholly subordinate, and identical in meaning with that of the bull. No one can study those wondrous forms, the human-headed lion and bulls of Nineveh, and fail to see that they are both one symbol. Both are simply symbolic of strength; not of victorious strength, like a conquering empire's; not of strength put forth, but simply of strength possessed. Both figures stood indiscriminately or together at the entrance of the Assyrian temples or palaces [1]. We have no right to select the one of two figures, which suits us, as *the* symbol of Assyrian power; and we have no statement whatever, that either of them was so accounted. It was plainly no symbol at all of Assyrian power; for the lion as well as the bull is represented as defeated. "[2]The winged human-headed lions and bulls, those magnificent forms which guarded the portals of the Assyrian temples— are not only found as separate sculptures, but, like the eagle-headed figures, are constantly introduced into the groups embroidered on the robes. It is worthy of observation, that, whenever they are represented, either in contest with the man, or with the eagle-headed figure, they appear to be vanquished. Such is also the case on cylinders. Frequently a human figure is seen suspending them in the air by the hind legs, or striking them with a mace. I have already ventured to suggest the idea which these

[1] Layard found both together at Arban on the Khabur in Northern Mesopotamia, Layard, Nin. and B. 275-8. So also at Koyunjik, (Nin. and B. 229, 30.) at Nimrud, (Nin. T. i. 47 App. p. 374. *i k* 376. 10. *a b c* 378. 381. 383. 384. 386. 390.) " I saw at once that the head must belong to a winged lion or bull, similar to those of Khorsabad and Persepolis." Ib. i. 65. See Porter's Travels, Plate xxxi. T. i. 585. xxxii. p. 591. xxxv. p. 598. Lassen in the Allg. Encycl. art. Persepolis, p. 361, 2. " Chairs, tables, and couches, are adorned with the heads and feet of the bull, the lion and the ram, all sacred animals." Ib. 474. add 300. 302. see also n. 4.

[2] Layard, Nineveh, ii. 460. add 458. At Bavian, "the Assyrian Hercules" is represented, "strangling the lion between two winged human-headed bulls back to back, as at the giant entrances of the palaces of Kouyunjik and Khorsabad." Nin. and B. 214.

singular forms were intended to convey, the union of the highest intellectual and physical powers; but certainly their position with reference to other symbolical figures would point to an inferiority in the heavenly hierarchy. Although the Andro-sphinx of the Egyptians was the type of the monarch, we can scarcely believe it to have been so amongst the Assyrians; for, in the sculptures, we find even the eagle-headed figure, the vanquisher of the human-headed lion and bull, ministering to the king."

4) Very probably both the human-headed lions and bulls, and perhaps conversely, the lion-headed men[3] were religious[4], not political symbols at all. Lions, bulls and cherubim were on the bases in the court of Solomon's temple[5]. Ezekiel saw, in his vision by the river Chebar, four-faced creatures, each with the face of the lion, the bull, the eagle, the man, fulfilling God's bidding, going *whither the spirit was to go, turning not when they went*[6]. It seems most probable, that the symbols of the powers of nature, including man's intelligence, which he saw around him, as entering into the heathen worship, he saw in his vision, subordinated to and fulfilling the will of God.

I have dwelt longer on this theory, than it deserved, because it has been emphatically recommended to you. Strange that such a superstructure could be built on the three facts, that Ezekiel mentions Job after Daniel, that Daniel saw a vision on the Tigris, that there were eagle-winged human-headed lions at Nineveh. A compeer of the author's dismissed it more summarily. "[7]Ewald's conjectures have something very improbable and unfounded— By such assumptions the explanation of the origin of the book is no way facilitated; rather it is embarrassed." It is a strange phænomenon of the human mind, that men could

---

[3] Nin. ii. 461. "lion-headed, eagle-footed, human figure." N. and B. 462.

[4] So Layard conjectures, i. 70. "The winged bull with the human head is evidently a pure Assyrian type. Its position in the religious system seems to be identical with that of the Androsphynx; and, in the mythic groups as in the architecture, they both occupy the same place. Power was probably typified indiscriminately by the body of the lion and the bull." Ib. ii. 461.

[5] 1 Kgs. vii. 29.   [6] i. 10-12.   [7] Bleek, Einl. p. 610.

so lose their perception of the nature of evidence. Yet unbelief cannot altogether part with a theory which it acknowledges to be baseless. It serves at least, like clay to the American savages, to stop craving after truth. It affords something to say, something to bribe the conscience with, even amid the consciousness that it is base metal. "Any how," says a recent writer[1], "this assumption makes it conceivable up to a certain point, how this sphere of working was assigned to Daniel; *only one must wish their hypothesis a securer historical basis!*"

ii. The 2nd theory, that Nebuchadnezzar personally was the first empire, his successors the second[2], was rested on Daniel's words to the king, *thou art this head of gold,* and on his statement, that the second kingdom should be inferior to him; which, it is assumed, the Medo-Persian Empire was not. But, plainly, this cannot be the meaning of the text, since, nine times in the context, the symbols are said to represent, not mere kings but kingdoms[3]; *the God of heaven hath given thee a kingdom; after thee shall arise another kingdom inferior to thee, and another kingdom of brass, and the fourth kingdom shall be strong as iron; the kingdom shall be divided; the kingdom shall be partly strong;* and over against all these, it is said, *the God of heaven shall set up a kingdom;* and *the kingdom shall not be left to other people, but it shall consume those kingdoms.*

The words then *shall be inferior to thee,* must signify "inferior to thee in thy kingdom;" in other words, "inferior to thy kingdom as it exists in thee."

In Nebuchadnezzar, the Babylonian monarchy reached its meridian. It had risen in the 20[4] years of his father Nabopolassar; its greatness culminated in his own 43

---

[1] Stähelin, Einl. p. 357. [2] Hitzig (Jahrb. 1832. 2. p. 131.) Redepenning (Theol. Stud. u. Krit. 1833. p. 863.) who follows him, says only, "It hath every thing for it, according to the words, *Thou art this head of gold,* to consider Nebuchadnezzar and his Dynasty as separate, and so to find in this chapter four rulers not 4 Empires, as was the wont according to the old interpretation." [3] ii. 37, 39, 40, 41, 42, 44. [4] Berosus in Jos. c. Ap. i. 19. Alex. Pol. in Eus. Chr. Arm. i. 44., or 21 years, in Jos. Ant. x. 6.

years[5]. God recognised *him* by Jeremiah as, [6] *My servant, Nebuchadnezzar.* Of him He foretold to those who were concerting with Zedekiah to rebel against him, [7] Edom, Moab, Ammon, Tyre, Zidon, that it was in vain. He had *given all their lands into the hands of Nebuchadnezzar king of Babylon, My servant, and all nations shall serve him, and his son, and his son's son.* Jeremiah speaks directly of those nations to which Judah could specially look for help, including Egypt [8]; but the recesses of Arabia, Kedar, and Hazor [9], would not lie too deep to be reached by his armies. Two writers on Indian history [10] and "Diocles in the 2nd book of his Persian history [11]," Josephus says, "make mention of him." "Megasthenes," he says, "through the 4th book of his Indian history, tries to shew that he surpassed Hercules in valour and in the greatness of his deeds. For he says that he subdued the greater part of Libya and Iberia," "[12] and settled colonies of them on the right of the Pontus." The mention of Nebuchadnezzar in Persian and Indian histories implies some vast extent of conquest; the more so, since Megasthenes, whose history, as such, is highly spoken of [13], wrote of Nebuchadnezzar throughout one book [14]. And when Ezekiel pronounces the destruction of Egypt by Nebuchadnezzar, and foretells [15] that Pharaoh shall meet in the grave *Asshur and all her company; Elam and all her multitude; Meshech, Tubal and all her multitude; Edom, her kings and all her princes; the princes of the north, all of them; and all the Zidonians, fallen by the sword;* certainly the most natural interpretation is, that they

[5] Beros. in Jos. c. Ap. i. 20. Alex. Pol. l. c. Can. Ptol.

[6] Jer. xxv. 9. xxvii. 6. xliii. 10.   [7] Jer. xxvii. 3, 6, 7.   [8] xliii. 8-10. xlvi.
[9] xlix. 28-33.   [10] Philostratus and Megasthenes in Jos. Ant. x. 11. 1.
[11] Ib.   [12] Id. in Eus. Præp. ix. 41.   [13] "Megasthenes, and Eratosthenes, approved men." Arr. Alex. v. 5.   [14] Josephus, both in his Ant. and c. Ap., uses the expression, "Megasthenes, in the fourth book of his Indica, *through which* (δι' ἧς) he tries to shew that this king surpassed," &c. Cocc. would, in the Ant., correct, δι' ὧν. Megasthenes denied that any made any conquest *in* India, except Dionysus, Hercules and Alexander. Accordingly he denied that Nebuchadnezzar did. Strabo, xv. 1. 6. p. 687. Cas.   [15] Ezek. xxxii. 31, 32, 18, 22, 24, 26, 29, 30.

too were conquered by Nebuchadnezzar. We know this
of the first and the last, Asshur, Edom, Zidon; and so
doubtless it was true of the intermediate, Elymais, the
Tibaren and Moschi, and whomsoever besides he includes
among the princes of the north, such as Gomer and Togarmah [1]. Ezekiel speaks of these defeats and slaughters
as having actually taken place; and he speaks of them in
connection with the victories of Nebuchadnezzar.

The colonies of Tyre in Africa and Spain are likely to
have submitted to him, after the subdual of the mother-
country. There is then no ground to charge Philostratus with exaggeration, when he says that Nebuchadnezzar "[2] advanced to the columns of Hercules." "Berosus
related much besides of the great king;" and Josephus
adds [3] that much was contained in the Archives of the
Phœnicians, agreeing with what was said by Berosus
concerning the king of Babylon, that he subdued Syria
too and the whole of Phœnicia." Megasthenes added [4],
that he subdued Egypt also. It has been thought, not
improbably, that the Egyptians disguised their defeat by
Nebuchadnezzar in their account of the dethronement of
Apries by Amasis, and that Amasis was, in truth, a tributary king, placed on the throne, according to the policy
of those times, by Nebuchadnezzar [5]. Josephus relates [6],
that Nebuchadnezzar "invaded Egypt with the view of
subduing it, slew the then king and set up another." The

---

[1] *The house of Togarmah, of the north quarters and all his bands.* Ezek.
xxxviii. 6.   [2] In Strabo, l. c. This combination is suggested by Tholuck,
Die Propheten, p. 130.   [3] c. Ap. i. 20.   [4] in Syncellus, p. 221. D. Fragm.
Hist. Gr. ii. 416.   [5] Sir G. Wilkinson, in Rawl. Herod. ii. 386, 7. Tholuck
suggests the same, referring to the statement of Herodotus, (iii. 16.) that the
Egyptians put a good appearance ($\sigma\epsilon\mu\nu\upsilon\tilde{\upsilon}\nu$) on the indignities offered to the corpse
of Amasis; in fact, falsified the history, Die Proph. p. 128.

[6] Ant. x. 9. 7. Josephus places the commencement of the expedition in the
5th year after the destruction of Jerusalem, and so in the course of 584, B.C.
and in Nebuchadnezzar's 23rd year, but says that it was directed against Cæle-
Syria (first) and that, after he had got possession of it, he warred against the
Ammonites and Moabites, and so marched against Egypt. This would naturally presuppose that the siege of Tyre took place then; only, it must have begun earlier.

death of Apries or Pharaoh Hophra, (571, 570, or 569 [7],)
was a few years after the fall of Tyre [8], upon which followed an expedition of Nebuchadnezzar against Egypt [9].

But conquest was the least part of the glory of Nebuchadnezzar. He must have had the command of well-
nigh unlimited human strength to accomplish his works,
and this doubtless he gained by conquest. The works
themselves were partly of magnificence and luxury; but
they also indicate a mind, religious [10], as a polytheist, and
concerned about the internal prosperity of his Empire.
His capital was guarded by those stupendous walls, whose
giant height, enclosing a space of above 130 square miles [11],
secured the provisioning, as well as the defence of the
city; embankments on the Persian gulf against the irrup-
tion of the sea [12]; a reservoir for irrigation, 40 farsangs
(about 138 miles) in circumference and about 20 fathom
deep; navigable canals, one of which, the Nahr Malka
[king's river,] still retains its name [13]; (others are attributed
to him [14];) enormous embankments along the Euphrates, of

[7] Brugsch (Hist. d' Eg. p. 256.) places the death of Apries, 571, B.C. Sir
G. Wilkinson, 569, B.C. (Rawl. Herod. ii. 387.) Movers says "The reign of
Apries is fixed on all sides, on the mean, for the years, 588 or 89—570, as are
few dates in ancient history." ii. 1. 457. (Tholuck, D. Proph. p. 130. note.)

[8] According to the number of years, assigned by Phœnician historians (in Jos.
c. Ap. i. 21.) to the rulers of Tyre after Nebuchadnezzar's 13 years' siege, the
end of that siege fell in B.C. 574. For the whole sum to Cyrus' capture of Babylon B.C. 538, was about 36 years, thus; "Baal reigned 10 years; Ecnibal,
Judge, (i. e. Sufet,) 2 m.; Cheleb, Judge, 10 m.; Abbar, high-priest, 3 m.;
Muthgon and Gerastrat, Judges, 6 years, Balator reigning 1 year between;
Merbal, from Babylon, 4 y.; Hirom, his brother, also from Babylon, was in the
14th year of his reign, when Cyrus took Babylon," in all, 35 years + 3 months,
+ x months of Hirom's 14th year. But 538 + 36 = 574. The beginning of the
siege would be 587, B.C., the year after the capture of Jerusalem.

[9] The last prophecy of Ezekiel against Pharaoh Hophra (xxix. 17-20) is dated
in the 27th year of Jehoiachin's Captivity, i. e. 572.

[10] See the account of his rebuilding of the temple of Borsippa in the Inscr. of
Borsippa translated by Sir H. Rawl. Journ. As. Soc. T. xvii.   [11] Rawl.
Herod. Essay viii. n. 13. p. 511. from Strabo, xvi. 1. 5.   [12] Abydenus in
Eus. Præp. Ev. ix. 41.   [13] The Armakalis in Euseb. from Abydenus.
הר-מכלא for נהר מלכא. Abydenus also mentions the Acracanos as his work.

[14] "One portion of the extensive Nahrawán, eastward of the Tigris." (Ches-
ney, Exped. ii. 160.) "It is believed that the Pallacopas was cut by him." (Ib.)

which that at Bagdad exists to this day[1]; besides the re-building of almost all the cities of Upper Babylonia, "[2]upon the bricks of which scarcely any other name is found," attest the practical concern of the great conqueror for the well-being of his realm. Deep as is the reverence in the East for those afflicted by insanity, and well-ordered as may have been the provisions, at least in the case of the decease of a monarch[3], yet it indicates an affecting respect for the great monarch, that his nobles waited patiently those 7 years in which he was afflicted, and then returned to him[4], and his glory was greater than before.

After his decease, the Babylonian empire only awaited its fall. His son, Evilmerodach, was slain after a vicious reign of two years[5]. Nebuchadnezzar's line was still continued in his son-in-law and his son's murderer Neriglissar, who, if he was the Nergalshareser, one of Nebuchadnezzar's princes present at the capture of Jerusalem[6], B.C. 578, must have been in advanced age. Yet his son, on his decease, about 3 years afterwards, was but a lad[7]. Things, then, must have been very disorganised, that he, "[8]shewing many signs of a bad disposition, was beaten to death by his friends," after a reign of 9 months. Then succeeded Nabonid, or Nabunahit, the Labynetus of Herodotus, whose son Belshazzar was entrusted with the government of Babylon, his father having associated him in his throne[9]. Of Nergalshareser nothing

---

[1] Rawl. p. 513. The embankment of Bagdad was identified by Sir H. Rawl. Ass. Comm. p. 77. note Ib.   [2] Rawl. p. 512.

[3] Upon his father's death, the kingdom was held for him by "the chief of the Chaldeans" (Magi) until he could return. Berosus. see ab. p. 60.

[4] Dan. iv. 36.   [5] Berosus in Jos. c. Ap. i. 20. Berosus says, that he "governed carelessly and dissolutely."

[6] Jer. xxxix. 3, 13. Rab-mag, "chief of the Magi," (ib.) *might* be added as a title to distinguish the one Nergalshareser from the other; and this would agree with the title "Rubu-emga" given to Nergalshareser in the Inscriptions. (Sir H. Rawl. in Rawl. p. 518.) But Rab-saris (chief Eunuch) is not an appellative; (ib.) for it follows on the name Sarsechim, v. 3 and on Nabushasban, v. 13. This makes it doubtful, whether Rab-mag either is an appellative.

[7] μειράκιον, about 14.   [8] Beros. ib.   [9] See Lect. vii.

is recorded, and no memorials remain, except some traces of a palace[10]. Of Labynetus, in a reign of 17 years, history only records an unfulfilled alliance with Crœsus, in union with Egypt, against the rising power of Cyrus[11], some defensive works of baked brick on the Euphrates, and the defeat, after which he shut himself in Borsippa, and was sent into honourable exile in Carmania [12]. With such successors, the glory of the Babylonian empire could only be spoken of, as now concentrated in Nebuchadnezzar.   Only as the Empire was seen in him, not in his degenerate successors, could it be said that the following world-empire should " be inferior."   The dynasty lived on, as that of the Bourbons was prolonged after Louis XIV. but its glory expired before itself.

I have given this lengthened explanation of the words, *Thou art this head of gold,* because it illustrates Holy Scripture.   It was not needed to point out the weakness of the theory, which would erect the fainéant successors of Nebuchadnezzar into a distinct world-empire; and which would represent these kings, who murdered their predecessors only to sink into inactivity or passiveness, to be the much-devouring bear, with the three kingdoms between its teeth.   This theory is as marked by its dulness as the first by its wild contempt of evidence.

iii. The third theory, which divides the Medo-Persian Empire into two, a Median and a Persian, is admitted by its supporters to be contrary to the fact.   They assert it truly to be an error ; they could not but see, that some places at least in Daniel were distinctly opposed to it. Yet they scrupled not to impute the error to Daniel, simply on the ground of that one statement, that, on the death of Belshazzar, king of the Chaldæans, [13]*Darius the Median received the kingdom, being about threescore and five years old.* Now if there is one theory, in which this critical school is agreed, it is the acquaintance of the Author of the book of Daniel with the previous books of

<hr>

[10] Rawl. p. 518.   [11] Her. i. 77.
[12] Megasth. in Arm. Chr. p. 60, 1.   [13] Dan. v. 31. Eng. vi. 1. Ch.

Holy Scripture. They urge against it, that he uses language of Ezekiel, (as he does adopt a few expressions[1],) that he speaks of the sacred writings which he studied, as "Scriptures," and implies thereby that there was, when he wrote, a collection of sacred books; they allege, even untruly, that he copied the prayer of Nehemiah, and formed his Chaldee on the study of that of Ezra. This theory of copying does not solve the fact of their resemblance, but it is essential to the unbelieving hypothesis. Then it is absurd to suppose, that one so acquainted with the book of Ezra and with the prophets before him should not have known, that Ezra records that the prophecy of Jeremiah, which he relates that he studied, was fulfilled through Cyrus, or that Ezra inserts in his book the proclamation of Cyrus, *the Lord God of heaven hath given me all the kingdoms of the earth*, or that Cyrus was foretold by name, as the deliverer of Israel from Babylon, in the prophecies of Isaiah. It is absurd to suppose, even on the unbelieving theory, that the writer of the book of Daniel would frame a history contradictory to what he knew to be the statements of the books which he studied.

But the theory directly contradicts the book of Daniel itself. For Daniel speaks of Darius himself, as having a delegated royalty; and in this same chapter, as well as every where else, he speaks of the kingdoms of Media and Persia, as one.

His two statements as to the authority of Darius are, 1) that he *received*[2] the kingdom, 2) that he *was made king*[3]. Both statements imply a delegated authority. To be "made king" implies that he had the authority, not of his own right, but, from some other authority which made him king. God[4], the people[5], a superior power[6],

---

[1] See note B at the end.   [2] vi. 1. Ch. v. 31. Eng.   [3] ix. 1.

[4] 1 Sam. xv. 11, 35. 1 Kgs. iii. 7. 1 Chr. xxviii. 4. 2 Chr. i. 8, 9, 11. Samuel in God's name, 1 Sam. viii. 22. xii. 1.   [5] Judg. ix. 6, 16, 18. 1 Sam. xi. 15. 1 Kgs. xii. 1, 20. xvi. 16, 21. 2 Kgs. viii. 20. (the great men, x. 5.) xi. 12. xiv. 21. xvii. 21. xxi. 24. xxiii. 30. (mighty men, 1 Chr. xi. 10.) 1 Chr. xii. 31, 38. (ii.) xxix. 22. 2 Chr. x. 1. xxi. 8. xxii. 1. xxiii. 11. xxvi. 1. xxxiii. 25. xxxvi. 1.

[6] Abner, Ishbosheth; 2 Sam. ii. 9. David, Solomon; 1 Kgs. i. 43. 1 Chr.

are, in different places of Holy Scripture, said to "make" a person, "king." The corresponding expression, "made a person king," was used of the acts of Pharaoh Necho and Nebuchadnezzar in setting kings over Israel[6], and of the purpose of Syria and Ephraim towards Judah. It is even remarkable that the idiom is so little used in regard to God. It is never used of God's ordinary providence, but only of the first appointment of a king in Israel, or by David and Solomon when speaking to God, and in God's answer to Solomon[4]. It is then contrary to the idiom, when men, to avoid the inference, say, that the words, *was made king over the land of the Chaldæans*, mean, that he was so made by God[7]. 2) So again the word, "received," in Chaldee[8] as well as in Hebrew[9], always means "received from another, giving or offering." It never means "took" as a right, at his own will; (this would have been expressed by another word[10];) it always means, "received what came to him from another."

Who Darius the Mede was, is a matter for secular history. The name Daryawesh is confessedly an appella-

---

xxiii. 1. Rehoboam, Abijah ; 2 Chr. xi. 22. Pharaoh Necho, Jehoiakim ; 2 Kgs. xxiii. 34. 2 Chr. xxxvi. 4. Nebuchadnezzar, Zedekiah ; 2 Kgs. xxiv. 17. 2 Chr. xxxvi. 10. Jer. xxxvii. 1. Ezek. xvii. 16. Syria, Ephraim and the son of Remaliah, in Judah if conquered, the son of Tabeal ; Is. vii. 6. Ahasuerus, Vashti, queen ; Esth. ii. 17. [all the cases in which הִמְלִיךְ is used, viz. 48.]

[7] Lengerke's expedient. De Wette and Bertholdt render ungrammatically, "was become king ; " Maurer avoids it ; Rosenmüller, "was made king by the Medes and Persians ; " but a conqueror is not said to be made king of the people whom he conquers, by his army. *He* conquers with them. Hitzig ; "The choice of the passive is to indicate that he did not become king according to the ordinary course of things. He did not *become* king of Babylon, as a matter of course in his own time by succession, but had first to be *made* king by human agency, viz. through the army led by Cyrus. It is scarcely the writer's meaning that, he was so made by God." (iv. 14.) "Darius the Mede was set as king over the Chaldæan kingdom, (probably by Cyrus,") says even Paullus, üb. d. 3 erst. Ev. iii. 418.

[8] Gifts from the king, Dan. ii. 6 ; the kingdom (from God,) Ib. vii. 18.

[9] Persons offering themselves, 1 Chr. xii. 18 ; offerings, Ez. viii. 30 ; a gift, Esth. iv. 4 ; a choice offered, 1 Chr. xxi. 11 ; God's appointments, Job. ii. 10 ; [ii.] instruction, Prov. xix. 20 ; an observance, Esth. ix. 23, 27 ; the things brought by the priests out of God's house, 2 Chr. xxix. 16 ; the blood of the animals sacrificed, Ib. 22. [10] לָקַח or נָשָׂא.

tive [1], and so, it is consistent with his being known in secular history by some other name.   There is a probability, that there was a king of Babylon at this date, known in secular history too by the name of Darius.   It is possible that the Darius, who, (as Megasthenes relates[2],) expelled for a time from Carmania Nabonedoch, the last king of Babylon, to whom Cyrus had committed the government of that province, may have been Darius Hystaspes.   But as Nabonedus was probably not young at the time of his accession, being selected by his fellow-conspirators for the throne[3], and he reigned 17 years in Babylon, and was again restored [4] by this Darius who removed him, it is probable that this Darius was a contemporary of Cyrus, not one who came to the throne 15 years later.   For if this Nabonedus was 40 at his accession to the throne of Babylon, he would have been 72 in the first year of Darius Hystaspes, and of a very advanced age to be restored to the government of a province subsequently.

The Daric is said also to have been named not from Darius Hystaspes, but "[5] from an older king."

Be this as it may, it is a question of secular not of Biblical history, whether Cyrus placed on the throne the Cyaxares II. of Xenophon, or Astyages, or neither, but a Median, a descendant of their celebrated sovereign Achashwerosh [6], (Cyaxares.)   Xenophon, although writing a historical novel, may very possibly, (like great modern writers of " the historical novel,") have, in great points,

---

[1] from *dara* Pers. (the end *esh* being a Persian termination [see Ges. s. v. p. 350.] as in דריוש.)   *Dhari* Sanscr. signifies ' hold,' ' rule,' which falls in with the interpretation of Herodotus, ἑρξείης. (vi. 98.)   This agrees with the cuneiform inscriptions, Darheus or Darieush, (Grotefend in Heeren. T. xi. p. 347.) Dareioush, Dareiouoush (S. Martin, Journ. As. Fev. 1823. Ges.) or DARaYaWUS. (Ib. App. 83.)   [2] Chron. Arm. i. p. 61.

[3] Berosus in Jos. l. c.   [4] " depulit aliquantulum," Lat. transl. of Arm. Chron. which, I am told, is accurate.   [5] Harpocration, sub v. Schol. ad Aristoph. Eccl. 545.

[6] In like way, Frawartish, in Media, claimed the Median throne, and Sitrantachmes, a Sagartian, that of Sagartia, as descended from Cyaxares.   " I am Xathrites, of the race of Cyaxares." " I am king of Sagartia, of the race of Cyaxares." Behist. Inscr. col. ii. par. 5. 14. in Rawl. Her. ii. 598. 602.

known the historical truth and adhered to it.   Certainly
as to the fact that Cyrus himself was of royal birth[7], he
is borne out by the inscriptions[8] against Herodotus.   Xenophon also, in another case, speaks of the family of Cyrus, as one who meant to write history.   He sets his own,
as an historical statement, against their's[9].   But when almost all Herodotus' account of Cyrus is embellishment,
and the evident object of Xenophon is to adorn his hero,
they have no authoritative weight for any statement, unless they are supported from without.   Probably those who
quote Herodotus so freely against Holy Scripture would
be surprised, if they made clear to themselves, what an
almost nothing they themselves believe of the account
which they so employ.   He needs to be confirmed by
Holy Scripture, not Holy Scripture by him.   But, in fact,
there is not the shadow of contradiction.   There would
have been contradiction, had Daniel said, that Darius the
Mede reigned in his own right; but he says exactly the
contrary.   Daniel tells us more than Herodotus; but that
"more" is in conformity both with other Scripture and
external authority.

Isaiah, in that wonderful prophecy of the destruction
of Babylon, ch. xxi, a prophecy acknowledged even by unbelievers[10] to have been prior to the event, assigns to Persia the first place, but to Media, the second[11]; *Go up, O
Elam; besiege, O Media.*   In another prophecy, he speaks
of the Medes alone as fierce instruments of its destruc-

---

[7] Cyrop. i. 2. 1.   [8] "the son of Cambyses, the powerful king." "Brick at
Senkeereh in Lower Chaldæa."   Sir H. Rawl. in Rawl. Herod. i. 250. note.
264. note.   [9] "When he came to Media, he, with the good will of his father
and mother, marries the daughter of Cyaxares, whose exceeding beauty is still
spoken of.   But *some of the historians say*, that he married his mother's sister.
That maiden would have been altogether an old woman." Cyrop. viii. 5. end.
Cyaxares' daughter was his first cousin, granddaughter of Astyages; but if, as
Herodotus said, (i. 109.) Astyages had had no son, she would have been, *not*
the granddaughter, but the daughter of Astyages and his mother's sister.

[10] "Is. xxi. a prophecy which, as is now recognised, is to be placed before
the actual fall of Babylon." Lengerke, p. 209.   So also Ges. Is. p. 648—50.
Ewald (Proph. ii. 394.) supposes it, in his way, to have been spoken during the
approach of Cyrus.   [11] xxi. 2.

tion[1]. Jeremiah foretells, that God would bring against Babylon[2] *an assembly of great nations from the North country;* [3]*a people, a great nation, and many kings from the coasts of the earth;* and then he specifies by name[4], *the Lord hath raised up the spirit of the kings of the Medes.* Neology is constrained by its hypothesis to suppose the prophecy to have been spoken close on the event; but then, in consistency with itself, it is constrained to grant that it is accurate. The Medes then, under Cyrus, had a prominent place in the siege and destruction of Babylon; and that, according to the custom of the East, under their own subordinate kings. Just this same subordinate relation is contained in the well-known Chaldæan tradition, preserved by Megasthenes. "[5]It is said by the Chaldæans, that, going up upon the palace, he [Nebuchadnezzar] was overmastered by some god and thus spake,'I, that Nebucodrosor, foretell to you, O Babylonians, the calamity which will overtake you, which Bel, my forefather, and the queen Beltis are alike unable to persuade the fates to turn aside. A Persian mule will come, aided by your gods, and will bring slavery upon you. Whose accomplice shall be a Mede, the boast of Assyria.'" Josephus uses the same language, saying that "[6]the city was taken, Cyrus, king of the Persians, having brought an army against it;" and then speaking of "Darius who, with Cyrus his kinsman, destroyed the Babylonian Empire." What marvel then, that, bound up as Media was with Persia, a large portion of its power, Cyrus, in whose career of victory Babylon was but a part, should commit its government to one in whom he could confide, while he himself was engaged in foreign conquests? The policy of placing a Vice-king at Babylon is in accordance with the previous history of Babylon for a long time under the Assyrian Empire, and with the actual relation of the Medes to the Persians. The Median Empire had been destroyed, more, probably, through the personal defects of its sove-

---

[1] xiii. 17.   [2] l. 9.   [3] l. 41.
[4] li. 11. 28.   [5] in Eus. Præp. Ev. ix. 41. p. 456. 7.   [6] Ant. x. 11. 41.

reign, than through any decay in the nation.   Their formidable rebellion against Darius Hystaspes, in conjunction probably with the neighbouring Armenians, in which the whole army quartered in Media joined, and which was finally repressed by Darius in person, shews that they were still unbroken[7].   They had energy for a new revolt against Darius Nothus[8], some 116 years later, B. C. 409. The Babylonians, in like way, by their repeated rebellions, (the first of which was carefully arranged, as soon as the confusion from the usurpation of Pseudo-Smerdis made room for it[9],) shewed that, though betrayed by their security and by the weakness of their kings, they were more easily conquered than retained.   Their resistance, in the first revolt against Darius, was more courageous than that against Cyrus.   Only after two pitched battles they shut themselves up in their walls[10]; and the traditions of their desperate expedient to prolong the siege[11], and of the stra-

---

[7] In the Behistun Inscription translated by Sir H. Rawlinson, (As. Soc. T. x. p. 195 sqq. revised in Rawl. Herod. ii. 590 sqq.) Darius mentions nine countries which revolted from him, " Persia, Susiana, Media, Assyria, Armenia, Parthia, Margiana, Sattagydia, Susiana." Media and Armenia alone offered a determined resistance.   Darius first sent Hydarnes, one of the seven, against Media ; then Dadarses, an Armenian, against Armenia, who thrice defeated them ; then Vomises a Persian, who twice defeated them ; then, all three armies having waited for Darius, he moved from Babylon and defeated Phraortes, who met him in Media. (Beh. Inscr. col. ii. Par. 6-13.) There is nothing to connect their revolt with the Median, except the neighbourhood and the fact, that their five defeats fell between the first and last of Fravartaish. But Parthia and Hyrcania are said to have " declared for Fravartaish ;" (Ib. 16. and col. iii. 1.) so he may very possibly have been the centre of the whole, and all may have been one movement (as Sir H. Rawlinson conjectures,) under a representative of the old Median monarchy to throw off the Persian yoke. Monarchs do not record their reverses, so we have only an account of one side. Prof. Rawlinson conjectures not improbably, that the successes against the Persians, attributed by Herodotus to Phraortes, father of Cyaxares, (i. 102.) really belonged to this Fravartaish, i. p. 409.   [8] Xen. Cyrop. i. 2. end.

[9] " During all the time that the Magian ruled, and the seven conspired, in all this time and the confusion they prepared for the siege ; and somehow they escaped notice."   Her. iii. 150. Darius places this first revolt early in his reign, soon after he had gained the sceptre, the Susianians rebelling at the same time. (Behist. Inscr. col. 1. par.16.)

[10] Beh. Inscr. col. 2. 18-20. They first disputed the passage of the Tigris ; then fought near Babylon.   [11] Her. iii. 150.

tagem of Zopyrus [1], involving self-sacrifice especially abhorrent to Persians and the sacrifice of 7000 Persians, imply the memory of no easy conquest.   Two revolts against one king, and a third against his successor [2]; were evidences of a strong surviving energy.   Babylon then, probably, could not be safely left to itself; and it was a wise policy to attach the Medes by placing over it, out of their royal line, as Vice-king, one who, by reason of his age and apparent softness of character, would have no temptation to revolt, and who would find, in Babylon, no old associations or support.   To transplant the Babylonian king to Carmania, and to place a Median over Babylon, was a policy correlative to that of removing disaffected populations.   An account, as credible as any, mentions a continuance of this policy, that Cyrus placed his second son as Satrap of the Medes, Armenians, and Cadusia [3].

That same distinction of the Medes continued.   Medes, it has been remarked [4], alone of all conquered nations, were employed in offices of confidence in the Persian Empire.   Cyrus employed Mazares, a Mede, to quell the revolt of Sardis [5]; on his death, he appointed another Mede, Harpagus [6], to continue the war, and subdue Ionia, Caria, Caunus, Lycia, the government of which last appears to have remained in his family [7].   A Mede, Intaphres, subdued Babylon on its first revolt [8].   In Darius' account of

---

[1] Ib. 153 sqq. It was part of the alleged stratagem, that 7000 Persians should be given up to be slain.   Herodotus does not mention the battles, nor Darius the stratagem, but he only relates the results, and what was to his glory.

[2] The 2nd revolt was, when Darius was "absent in Persia and Media." Beh. Inscr. Col. iii. P. 23. 14. Ctesias relates the revolt against Xerxes, when engaged in his Greek expedition, and says that they slew his general. (Pers. § 22. p. 69. ed. Bähr.) Plutarch alludes to a revolt against Xerxes; (Apoph. Regg. p. 688. Wytt.) Herodotus speaks of his spoiling the temple of Bel; (i. 183.) Arrian (vii. 17.) and Strabo (xvi. 1. 5.) of his destroying the temple, Arrian says, after his return rom Greece.   [3] Xen. Cyrop. viii. 7. 11. Ctesias makes Cyrus assign to him three Eastern Provinces, Bactria, Parthia, Carmania. Pers. 8. Herodous (iii. 30.) is contradicted by the Behist. Inscr., in that he places Cambyses' murder of his brother when in Egypt.

[4] Rawl. Herod. T. i. Essay iii. on the Median Empire, p. 402. n. 7.

[5] Herod. i. 356, 7.   [6] Ib. 162-176.   [7] Rawl. on Herod. i. p. 312. n. 2.

[8] Behist. Inscr. col. iii. par. 14. Ib. Prof. Rawlinson also instances Datis at

his quelling the great revolts against him, Persians and Medes are, in various ways, named as especially united [9].

Media was allied to Persia by its common Aryan descent [10] and by nearness of language [11]. Media "capta ferum victorem cepit." Persia had then too that pliancy and plastic character [12], which distinguishes it now. Composed of separate tribes [13] up to the time of the revolt of Cyrus, (if the account of Herodotus be true [14],) or of his war with Media, Persia adopted apparently the institutions of its more civilised conquest. It appears to have joined on its history to that of Media [15], to have adopted its laws, as it did, subsequently, its religion. Even such an external change as that of the adoption of its dress [16] is significant. It was the adoption of the more elegant and luxurious attire for its own simple hardy dress. Persia continued to rank Media next to itself.

But, on whatever ground Cyrus placed Darius the Mede as Vice-king over Babylon, there is not a plea for thinking that Daniel speaks of a Median Empire distinct from Persia. The account of Daniel, throughout, expresses the contrary. The first mention of *Darius the Mede* occurs, as the fulfilment of the writing on the wall, explain-

Marathon, (Her. vi. 94.) his sons, commanders of Xerxes' cavalry, (Ib. vii. 88.) Tachamaspates, employed to bring Sagartia into subjection. (Behist. Inscr. col. ii. par. 14.) Ib.   [9] "Persia, Media, and the other provinces," col. i. § 11, 12, 14; "the army of Persians and Medians that was with me," ii. 6. iii. "I sent an army of Persians and Medes," "no man, neither Persian nor Mede, who would dispossess him," i. 13.   [10] See Rawl. Essay iii. p. 401.

[11] Ib. n. 8.   [12] Herod. i. 135.   [13] Ib. 125.

[14] If Prof. Rawlinson's conjecture (p. 128. n. 9.) be right, we have no account of any conquest of the Persians by the Medes.

[15] In the book of Esther, mention is made of *the book of the chronicles of the kings of Media and Persia*, (x. 2.) Media being placed first, as the history of the kings of Media necessarily preceded that of the kings of Persia; whereas, speaking of the present time, the writer places the Persians first; *the power of Persia and Media*, (i. 3.) *the seven princes of Persia and Media*, (i. 14.) *the ladies of Persia and Media*, (i. 18.) *the laws of the Persians and the Medes*. (i. 19.) The state documents, which were originally deposited in the Record-office at Babylon, were afterwards transferred to Egbatana in Media, (Ezr. vi. 1, 2.) probably as the ancient depository of documents.   [16] Her. i. 135. vii. 63. See the woodcuts in Rawl. Herod. i. p. 276.

K

ed to Belshazzar by Daniel.   In that writing, *Mene, Mene, Tekel, Upharsin,* the Persians are referred to, and that prominently.   All the words of that writing contain, not an ambiguous but a twofold and so a fuller and more pregnant meaning[1], as explained by the Prophet himself. [2] *Mene* signifies at once, "numbered" and "ended;" [3] *Tekel,* "weighed" and "light" on the weights; [4] *Peres,* "divided" and "Persian."   A word, subsequently, at least, rare[5], is purposely chosen[6] to bring out the "Persians" prominently.   The two nations conjointly were to have the world-empire, which was now in the hands of the Chaldees; but the pre-eminence of the Persians is expressed in the word foretelling it.   The word "*and they are parting,*" also means "and Persians."   There is also the direct explanation, *and is given to the Medes and Persians.*   He does not say, "is given first to the Medes and then to the Persians," given, as these would say, first to Darius, then to Cyrus.   A thing is not *divided,* which is given to two persons successively.   It is given whole to each.   He says, "*is* given."   It was the last doomed night of Belshazzar and of the Chaldæan Empire.   It was already night.   For the hand-writing had been seen some time before, written where the light of the chandelier fell on it[7].   The Medes and Persians must have been already in motion.   The city, buried in its revelry, was virtually

[1] So far Lengerke too agrees.   [2] מנא is "counted" and "counted to the end," whence in Arabic it signifies "defined," and the noun, "the term defined, death."   [3] תקל with allusion to קלל, "light," "is weighed."

[4] ופרסין "and (they are) dividing," 2) "and Persians."

[5] Buxtorf, (whom Gesenius follows,) noticed only one instance in which the verb פרס is used in this sense in the Targums, 1 Sam. ix. 13. פרס קרצא "breaking and distributing food." Caspari (Zeitschr. f. Luth. Theol. 1841. 4. p. 130) adds another, 2 Kgs. iv. 39. where it is for the Heb. פלח "shred," (orig. "split.") Its common meaning both in Syr. and the Targg. is, "spread," i.q. Heb. פרש. Here it is the same as the Heb. פרס.

[6] Lengerke says, "the ground is, that there was no suitable word wherewith to allude to the name, Mede." p. 265.   1) This is not true.   The root מד, "measure," existed in Chaldee then, as appears from מדה Ezr. iv. 20. מנדה Ezr. iv. 13. vii. 24.   This would have furnished a verbal allusion.   2) The verbal allusion is chosen to give greater emphasis to the meaning, to impress it.   Of course, the meaning would not be sacrificed to the emphasis.   [7] v. 5.

already in their hands. They were all-but-marching along the half-dried bed of the Euphrates, to take possession of what God had given into their hands. *It was given.* Two sentences relate the fulfilment of the words in the close of the first empire and the commencement of the second. [8]*In that night was Belshazzar, king of the Chaldæans, slain. And Darius, the Median,* (in contrast to the *Chaldæan,*) *received the kingdom.* The word, *received,* in itself, implies one from whom it was *received.* But, apart from this, it would have been no fulfilment of the words, had Darius *succeeded* independently. Half of the prophecy would have failed, which the statement is made to prove. The law also, which was in force, (it is thrice said) was *the law of the Medes and Persians*[9], i. e. a law which had been originally the *law of the* more cultivated *Medes;* but which, since its adoption by the Persians, was become *the law of the Medes and Persians.* The term belongs to the recent times of Persian conquest, when the memory of the Median origin of the law was fresh; and much of law could not have been added by the Persians. Perhaps it was used by the councillors of the Median Vice-king out of national feeling. Yet the term was the most accurate which could have been used. Had it been a mere Median empire, the law must have been "the law of the Medes" only.

The titles, "Mede," "Persian," are strictly personal. The empire was Medo-Persian : (as under the name Britain, we think chiefly of the three or four nations first combined in its kingdom, not of the dominions which have accrued to it.) Cyrus, strictly speaking, was Perso-Median, his mother having been a Mede. Darius was a Mede. Their personal nationalities, *Darius the Mede, Cyrus the Persian,* do not imply that the empire was Median or Persian, and not rather Medo-Persian.

The fact, that there was only one Medo-Persian empire, is stated in the precisest terms in the vision which foretells its destruction. A living symbol cannot, without be-

---

[8] v. 30, 31. Eng. vi. 1. Ch.   [9] vi. 9, 13, 16. Ch. 8, 12, 15. Eng.

coming unnatural, correspond in all details to the thing symbolised. Change had to be represented in such wise that the symbol itself should not be destroyed. The symbol of the ram having been chosen for the Medo-Persian empire, the shifting relation of its two parts could not be pictured, without offensiveness and untruth, in the body of the animal. It is represented in the horns. As in the dream as to himself, Nebuchadnezzar saw the tree, which represented his fortunes, *growing* [1] and cut down, so Daniel sees the Medo-Persian empire from its first formation. The body of the ram represents the aggregate of tribes, Median and Persian, which were united throughout its existence. Each was an aggregate of tribes in itself, the Median, of six, the Persian, of ten, tribes. Both were joined together, as England and Scotland. The body remained numerically the same, neither increased nor diminished, whichever was dominant. This could not have been more vividly represented than by the oneness of the animal, while the horns, the symbol of power, varied. The vision gives briefly its rise, its prosperity, its fall. The angel explains it to represent the *kings of Media and Persia,* not of Media and Persia successively, but together; for it remained to the end what it was at the beginning; it was the ram with two horns, the king or kingdom of Medo-Persia, when its horns were broken, and it was trampled under foot.

In regard to the other objection, that the second Empire is said to be inferior to Nebuchadnezzar in his greatness, it is not improbable that the Persian *was* inferior, even in extent, to the empire under Nebuchadnezzar. But neither extent nor numbers constitute the superiority of an empire. Else the Chinese would be, for its numbers, far the first of modern empires; and, in extent, Russia. The Turkish empire would be far superior to any European; and the British empire, as nothing but for its East-Indian dominions. But, in every thing which *does* constitute the greatness of an empire, the Persian was very far

[1] iv. 8. Ch. 11. Eng.

inferior to Nebuchadnezzar's. Cyrus himself *was* a great instrument of God, not only, like all great conquerors, as the scourge of sin, but towards His own people. The edict in behalf of the Jews is one of the most remarkable events in the history of the world; one, fullest of consequences. Personal character too, as a heathen, he must have had, since Isaiah describes him as one, whom *righteousness called to her foot*[2], as its disciple. God *gave the nations before him and made him rule over kings.* He inverted the relations of the Medes and Persians; two great empires, the Lydian and the Babylonian, fell before him. But his plan of universal empire left him no time to consolidate his work, and, while his plans were stretching out to India and to Egypt, perhaps even to Europe[3], he fell, in conflict with some wild nation[4], (it is not known which,) who defeated and slew one, who was lord of nations from the confines of India to the encircling sea which bounded Asia, the Mediterranean, Ægean, Black Sea. But, of all his imperial greatness, his tomb at Pasargadæ is his only memorial. The conqueror had seemingly neither the special genius nor leisure for internal organization. He left none of the works for the good of his people, which distinguished the reign of Nebuchadnezzar. Even in his own reign, we have that sure token of bad government, public measures undone through corrupt influences around the sovereign. Cyrus allowed his own edict to be in great measure neutralised, and his policy towards the Jews changed, because his councillors were bribed. *The people of the land weakened the hands of the people of Judah and troubled them in building, and hired counsellors against them to frustrate their purpose all the days of Cyrus king of Persia even until the reign of Darius king of*

---

[2] Is. xli. 2. [3] Cambyses in Egypt, and Darius Northwards, seem to have been carrying out his plans. According to Ctesias, (c. 6.) the Indians supported the Derbices against him, doubtless as holding themselves to be menaced. [4] The Massagetæ according to Herodotus (i. 214 ;) the Derbices, according to Ctesias. (Exc. 6-8.) Xenophon's account, that he died in his bed, seems only devised to give room for a philosophic discourse. (Cyrop. viii. 7.) In Herodotus' time, there were "many accounts" of his death. (i. 214.)

Persia [1].   An epitome of Persian misrule!   It was, in a prince who had felt the power of God, the self-same principle of mis-government, which led the sensual Xerxes to sell to Haman for 10,000 talents of silver the lives of all the Jews in his dominions, as an alien, uncongenial, race, scattered through all his provinces, and then to squander on his favorite the price of their blood [2].   The successors of Cyrus the Great degenerated at once.   The mad Cambyses, whom even the Persians are said to have designated as "[3]despotic," the "[4]tradesman" Darius, were succeeded by Xerxes, who, uniting the vices of both to a sensualising voluptuousness, prepared for the downfall of Persia by his stupendous but impotent aggression on Greece.   The expedition of Alexander was (as it stands so pointedly in Daniel[5],) the natural and legitimate result of the exhibition of inherent weakness in the multitudinous force of Persia.   That vast wave, in which the accumulated hosts of Asia seemed ready to submerge the tiny republics of Greece, dashed itself upon them, was broken, and recoiled.   The failure of Darius at Marathon was but the mistake of one who, after the tide of victory over the Ionian Greeks, superciliously despised his foe[6].   Xer-

[1] Ezr. iv. 4, 5.

[2] Esth. iii. 8-15.   [3] δεσπότης Her. iii. 99.   [4] κάπηλος Ib. iii. 89. 117.

[5] xi. 2. 3. Bertholdt and Lengerke, acknowledging this connection, think it above " the Jewish writer," and accuse their Pseudo-Daniel of supposing that there were only four kings of Persia, whereas Ezra mentions Artaxerxes. 8. Jerome says well ; "Idly does one write, ' Darius, who was conquered by Alexander, was the 4th king,' who was not the 4th, but the 14th after Cyrus.   Observe that, having enumerated four after Cyrus, he passed over 9, and passed on to Alexander.   For the prophetic spirit cared not to follow the order of history, but to touch on the marked points."   The Epistle, however, of Alexander to Darius after the battle of Issus, so often quoted, has no bearing on this, since he is referring to wrongs in his father's time and his own. (in Arr. Exp. ii. 14. 7-9.)   The whole of the Persian history was future in the time of Daniel, the omission was the usual prophetic fore-shortening, of which St. Jerome speaks.

[6] Only 6400 men fell on the side of the Persians ; (Her. vi. 117.) and the 10,000 heavy-armed Greeks formed a front as long as the Medo-Persian, weakening their centre only ; " both the wings were deep." (Ib. 111.)   The triremes, in which the Persians were embarked, 600 according to Herodotus, (vi. 95.) 300 according to Plato, (Menex. p. 190. Tauchn.) would (according to Herodotus' calculation, vii. 184.) convey 138,000, or 69,000 men.   They had

xes evidently meant to overawe, gathered for four years the varied hordes of his vast empire, and failed. The vast bulk of the Persian empire was ever crumbling through intestine disorganisation. The internal arrangements which were made, had a view rather to the better collecting of tribute in preparation for those expensive wars, than to the good government of the people.

The defeat of Xerxes closed the 60 years of its seeming prosperity: for 150 years more [7] it held together, because Greece was divided. But it did nothing for mankind; it left no memorial of itself. There is not a trait in its history upon which the human mind can dwell with interest, save the one scene of the kindness of Artaxerxes to Nehemiah, scarce any, from which human nature does not turn away [8]. Its heterogeneous elements were not more assimilated after two centuries, than at the first. Its connection with its provinces consisted in the appointments of satraps with the state of kings, military governors, and governors of the garrisons which kept them in check ; and the contribution, on the part of the provinces, of fixed tribute, of contingents of troops when required, or, in times also pressed Greeks on their way, (Her. vi. 99.) and had cavalry, but these not numerous ; (10,000. Nepos Milt. c. 4.) " The aggregate crews of all their ships must have been between 150,000 and 200,000 men ; but what proportion of these were fighting men, or how many actually did fight at Marathon, we have no means of determining." (Grote, Greece, T. iv. 468.) Darius is said to have led against Thrace 700,000 men, apart from the fleet of 8600 ships. (v. 87.)

[7] Platæa, 480. B.C. Arbela, Sept. 331.

[8] " Through those unhappy undertakings against Greece in the last six years of his reign, Darius saw the splendours of all his former glorious undertakings darkened. From that moment Persian history exhibits to us only the monotonous account of cabals, internal disturbances and expeditions against the Greeks, which occasioned on their part and justified maraudings and wars against the great king. The Greeks [in Xerxes' time] could use their victories unhindered, in that Xerxes was involved in most distressing relations in his own family, and left war-concerns wholly to his satraps. Under Darius, the Empire sank wholly ; for the Satraps became almost independent princes ; the king was governed by a woman, Parysatis, and 3 Eunuchs ; and Greek mercenaries formed the core of the royal army, as well as those in the several satrapies. The horrible savageness, treacheries, murders, maimings, we cannot relate in a general history of mankind, since the Persian courtiers are only of account to those like them : for mankind they are an abhorrence." Schlösser, Weltgesch. p. 269.

of peace, of eunuchs and replenishers of the Persian harems. Government by favorite, often revengeful, Queens, or by eunuchs, was the order of its policy; fratricide, a path to the throne, or a condition of its tenure. The jealousies or even mutual wars of its satraps, in that they kept each other in check, were thought to be the safety of its government. Its external history, in every instance, shewed its internal weakness. Its provinces rebelled and re-rebelled; some succeeded in detaching themselves. Even in its more prosperous times, the petty prince of Salamis in Cyprus held the Persian power at bay for 10 years[1], and was at last acknowledged by them as a tributary king. Egypt had three brief dynasties of native princes[2], during the period of Persian rule. Its employment of Greek mercenaries, and its intrigues with the Greeks of Europe, attest its sense of its inherent weakness. Its chief wars were to quell the revolts of its own satraps. Like a volcanic country, the internal, unsubdued force, which periodically shook it, was felt in the earthquake, now here, now there, but underlay the whole empire. At the battle of Arbela, in which the Empire fell, its million of men were drawn out of twenty only of the 46 provinces, which had supplied the armament of Xerxes.

The inferiority then of the 2nd Empire to the first under Nebuchadnezzar is no ground why the second should not be the Medo-Persian. For it *was* inferior in everything which constitutes an Empire. Nor could the symbol be adapted to the Median empire alone. A world-empire, which lasted two years, would in itself be an absurdity, which it would be insolent to fasten on the book of Daniel. But no explanation whatever could be given of the *three ribs* in his mouth, or of the command to *devour much flesh*. Again it would be a strange incongruity, that the third Empire should be represented by symbols implying activity, in the 2nd and 7th chapter, and, if it was to be the Persian, by the heavy animal in

---

[1] See Grote, Hist. of Greece, c. 76. T. ix. p. 27-32.

[2] Dyn. xxviii. xxix. xxx. Brugsch, Hist. d' Eg. c. 17. p. 279-285.

the 8th; or that the four heads in the 7th chapter should *not* symbolise the same as the 4 horns in the 8th, but should relate to a different empire.   But, over and above this, the four heads have no possible explanation as to the Persian Empire.   They exist simultaneously.   Even rationalist interpreters explain the four horns in the 8th chapter as representing four contemporary kingdoms, those of the four successors of Alexander.   Much more must the four heads be powers existing together.   And not only so, but, even waiving this, not even in succession can four kings of Persia be pointed out, to answer to the four heads.   For in the xith chapter to which these writers appeal, five are probably spoken of[3], and prophecy breaks off with Xerxes, because his invasion and failure were the far distant causes of the expedition of Alexander, the earnest of its success.   The explanation of the four heads by those four kings is inconsistent alike with the believing or unbelieving hypothesis.   With the believing, because, although prophecy foretells the truth in part only, it does not foretell what is untrue, and it is untrue that the Persian Empire was four-headed.   On the unbelieving, because it is absurd to make mere silence an argument of ignorance, when yet a 6th king, Artaxerxes Longimanus, is mentioned in the book of Ezra, with which, on the rationalist hypothesis, the writer of the book of Daniel was well acquainted[4].

iv) There remains yet the paradox, that, seeing that the first empire must be the Babylonian and the 2nd the Medo-Persian, (for so far the maintainers of this paradox see clearly,) the number is to be filled up by making Alexander himself the 3rd empire, his successors the fourth.

---

[3] *" There are yet three kings,"* (xi. 2.) naturally means, three *after* Cyrus, viz. Cambyses, Pseudo-Smerdis, Darius Hystaspes; and then "and the fourth," means the fourth who was *yet* to be, viz. Xerxes.

[4] The argument was dishonest in those writers, because they well knew that, in the xith chapter, kings both of the Ptolemies and the Seleucidæ are not alluded to, whom the writer, had he lived after the event, must have known of.   But what was no argument of ignorance in the one case, could not, of course, have been so in the other.

To this it would seem to be answer enough, " then the empire of the successors of Alexander was to be stronger than that of Alexander itself."   Terribleness, crushing might and deed, permanent dominion, are the characteristics of the 4th empire.   But in the vision, which is expressly explained of the Greek Empire, it is said, "*four kingdoms* shall stand up out of the nation, *but not in his power*,[1]" [the power of the first king;] and again, "[2] when he [Alexander] shall stand up, his kingdom shall be broken and shall be divided toward the four winds; and not to his posterity, *nor according to his dominion which he ruled*."   There could not be two pictures more opposite to one another.   In both visions, those in the 2nd and the 7th chapter, the exceeding strength of the fourth empire, in contrast with those before it, is dwelt upon; *the fourth kingdom shall be strong as iron, forasmuch as iron breaketh in pieces and subdueth all things; as iron that breaketh all these, shall it break in pieces and bruise : a fourth beast dreadful and forceful and strong exceedingly, and it had great iron teeth; it devoured and brake in pieces and stamped the residue with the feet of it, and it was diverse from all beasts that were before it*[3].

An empire, stronger than all before it, cannot be meant to be the same as that, of which it is emphatically said, that it should be weaker than that before it.

Again as to the facts, cast your eyes on the picture of the two chief of Alexander's successors, the Seleucidæ and the Ptolemies, in Daniel himself.   Two dynasties equally balanced against each other; at one time the king of the South superior, at another, the king of the North; multitudes given into his hands; *casting down ten thousands but not strengthened* by it; *unable to stand !*   See the tide of war reeling, ebbing, flowing, from North to South, and from South to North.   One king of the South (Ptolemy Euergetes) prevailing and carrying away captives[4]; the king of the North [Seleucus Callinicus] fail-

---

[1] viii. 22.   [2] xi. 4.   [3] ii. 40. vii. 7.   [4] xi. 8.

ing in his invasion of Egypt[5]; Antiochus the Great invading Egypt, and defeated by the wretched Ptolemy Philopator, yet he too, casting down many ten thousands, but not strengthened by it[6]; then Antiochus victorious and Egypt powerless, but the victor checked by the Romans and perishing[7]; then *a raiser of taxes*[8] (Seleucus Philopator;) then[9] *a vile person* (Antiochus Epiphanes) working deceitfully, *strong with a small people*, his fraudulent victories checked at last by Roman power. Where, in all this division, is the surpassing, iron strength of the 4th kingdom or the terribleness of the 4th creature for which no name could be found? If this, as is said, was the decay of the fourth kingdom, that decay began from the very existence of those separate kingdoms as described by Daniel. Its strength was no where but in Alexander himself. Two intermarriages alone are alluded to in Daniel[10], or took place between the Seleucidæ and the Ptolemies; and these two, on no common principle. The marriage of Antiochus Theos with Berenice, daughter of Ptolemy Philadelphus, was not, like those in Teutonic empires, to cement two nations against others whose strength was dreaded. It was simply a way of ending a war, of which Ptolemy was weary[11]. It was the policy of Antiochus the Great alone, to unite Egypt with him against Rome. One intermarriage is not characteristic of the policy of an empire. Again, it is said that 'the attempt to cement their strength by intermarriages' is a characteristic of Alexander's successors. These intermarriages belong to the decay of the fourth empire in Daniel, when the iron strength, symbolised in the iron legs of the image, was gone, and there had succeeded to it the

---

[5] Ib. 9. It should be rendered; *And he* [i. e. the king of the North] *shall come against the kingdom of the king of the South, and shall return to his own land.*   [6] 10-12.   [7] 13-19.   [8] 20.   [9] 21-23.

[10] Dan. xi. 5, 17.   [11] "Ptolemy Philadelphus, wishing, after many years, to end a troublesome struggle, gave his daughter Berenice to Antiochus to wife, and conducted her as far as Pelusium, and gave countless thousands of gold and silver under the name of dowry. Whence she was called φερνόφορος, dowry-bringer." S. Jer. on Dan. xi. 6.

mixed strength and weakness in the toes, the iron mingled with the miry clay. But of those two marriages, the one took place in the 2nd generation of the Seleucidæ; the other, in that of Antiochus the Great, who broke the strength of the Syrian kingdom against the Romans. When then was the time of strength, if this was its decay?

The successors of Alexander were not, in any sense, one kingdom, except as the fragments of his empire; as the parts are equal to a whole. They had no unity. They themselves claimed to hold their kingdoms as *his* successors. Four kingdoms could not be one, except as representing that one from whom they descended. Daniel too leaves the two out of sight altogether, and speaks of those only whose history touched the people of God. But these were throughout their history in perpetual conflict.

They were one, doubtless, in the Providence of God. It matters little, how much lay in the mind of Alexander, whether his Greek cities were to be links of commerce, or means of blending East and West into one, or bands of his dominions, or centres of civilisation, any or all of these. Certainly his enquiry of Aristotle, as to the best mode of colonising[1], shews how deep the plan lay in his mind. His instantaneous perception of the value of the site of Alexandria, and his choice of a situation whose value the circumnavigation of Africa has not lessened, and the experience of 2000 years have confirmed, imply no ordinary scheme. "He founded," Plutarch says[2], "above

---

[1] Aristotle's work was entitled "Alexander, or concerning colonies." Diog. Laert. v. 22. Ammonius says, " or what, being asked by Alexander the Macedonian, he wrote concerning the kingdom, and how colonies should be made." Stahr, Arist. ii. 63. Droysen, Hellenism. ii. 589.

[2] Plutarch de fort. Alex. i. 5. Wytt. He relates as facts; "He taught the Hyrcanians to marry, and the Arachosii to till the ground, the Sogdiani to cherish, not to slay their fathers; the Persians to reverence, not to marry their mothers. The Indians (Bactrians and Caucasians) worship Greek gods; the Scythians bury, and do not eat, their dead." "Asia being civilised, Homer was their study, and the sons of Persians, Susians and Gedrosii sang the tragedies of Euripides and Sophocles. Myriads received and *receive* the laws of Alexander.—They would not have been civilised, had they not been subdued,—Egypt would not have had Alexandria, nor Mesopotamia Seleucia, nor the Sogdians

70 cities among the barbarous people, and sowed Asia with Greek troops[3]." Apart from garrisons, towards 70 cities, founded by him or by his generals at his command[4], have been traced in Asia Minor, Syria, Egypt, Mesopotamia, Media, Hyrcania, Parthia, Aria, Margiana, Drangiana, Arachosia, Paropamisus, Bactria, Sogdiana, India on the Hydaspes, Acesines, Indus ; in modern terms, in the whole of Turkey in Asia, Egypt, all habitable Persia, North, East, and South, and beyond it, in Beloochistan, the Deccan, Cabool, Afghanistan, the Punjaub, and yet Northward, in Khorassan and Khondooz to Bokhara and Turkestan. The main characteristic of this colonization is the evident purpose to establish Greek cities along all the lines of communication by land or water. It is marvellous to follow the march of that wonderful genius, and to observe him seizing each important spot, alike in Egypt, in the long civilised countries of the Euphrates and the Tigris, and in lands but lately known to European energy or curiosity ; conquering, not to desolate but to settle with fixed populations. "[5]Media was girt round by Greek cities." At the pass of the Caspian Gates, in the rich valley of the Herat, at the confluence of the Indus and the Chenab, or in the valley of the Jelum, or the mouth of the Indus, or on the Persian gulf, Alexander, with intuitive intelligence, seized the points which became bands of the intercourse of nations. "[6] Merv, Herat, Kandahar,

Prophthasia, nor India Bucephalia, nor would Caucasus have been encircled by Greek cities, whereby savageness was checked and extinguished."

[3] τέλεσι. The troops unfit for active service, (Arr. iv. 3. fin. 22, 6. Ell.) or the Greek mercenaries who so wished. Diod. xvii. 83. (Droysen, Hellen. ii. 614, 616, 622.) He *purposed* so to settle in Persia " the Greek mercenaries who had served Darius and Satraps." Paus. i. 25. 5.

[4] Droysen, ii. Anhang. Die Grundungen Alexanders. 587-651. [5] Polyb. x. 27.

[6] Droysen, ii. 649. "The colonies were thickest, when it was the question of occupying the road, which leads out of India to the narrow pass of the Cabool, and of protecting it, Southward around the Paropamisos, and Northward over the height of the Caucasus down to the Oxus. Three lowlands with their double streams lay beneath the towering mountains of Iran. On colonising these especially Alexander employed the utmost diligence. The country of the Euphrates and the Tigris, being so much nearer to Europe, was more accessible

attest to this day, how surely Alexander chose the most important points, while Propthasia [it is thought, Furrah] protected the connection with the S. W. towards the Kermanian Alexandria [Kerman.] They are the knots in the great net of this natural line of intercourse, which intersect Iran, and, at the same time, in a military aspect, the most important points."

But it would have been little in comparison, to have guarded that intercourse by Greek stations. Over and above, Greek and Barbarian were blended [1], and the Greek element, from its greater force of character, would have ultimately prevailed, and outwardly leavened the whole. This union of Greek and Barbarian in the colonies on equal terms, cemented by his celebrated intermarriages, when above ten thousand Macedonians, urged by him, followed his example in taking Persian wives [2], prepared the way for the predominance of Greek mind, far otherwise than a military occupation could have done. The same purpose shewed itself in his different blendings of choice native and Macedonian troops, both in the phalanx and in the cavalry [3], in his proposed education of the children of Macedonian soldiers from Persian mothers [4], and in that large plan, found in his papers, " [5] of the joint colonisation of cities, and removal of persons from Asia to Europe and conversely, in order to bring those greatest continents into mutual harmony and the love of kindred

to colonisation : the king bestowed double pains on the country of the Oxus and Jaxartes, the Indus and Hesydrius. [the Sutlej.]"

[1] See ab. p. 141. n. 3.   [2] Arr. vii. 4, 5-end. 6. 3. in Phot. cod. 91.

[3] The different measures were; 1) Training 30,000 youths from the newly founded cities, with Macedonian arms and tactics. Diod. xvii. 108. Arr. vii. 6. 2) The admission of Sogdian, Arachosian, Drangian, Aryan, Parthian, Sacian, horsemen, in the ranks of the Companions, and that, so as to form ¼ of the whole, a 5th squadron being added on their accession, not of the Asiatics apart, but Macedonians and Asiatics being blended in each squadron. Arr. ib.   3) In the remodelled phalanx, the posts of honour and the Macedonian arms were reserved to Macedonians, but, in number, the Persians were 3 to 1 ; the three first soldiers, in the file 16 deep, and the last, being Macedonians, the twelve intermediate being Persians. Arr. vii. 23.

[4] Arr. vii. 12, 3. being 10,000. Diod. xvii. 110.   [5] Diod. xviii. 4.

by intermarriages and intimacies." A grand conception
of union, to be realised only by Christianity.

Yet this extension and infusion of Greek intelligence
and energy is just the one token of unity between his
kingdom and those of his successors. Seleucus Nicator
is related to have founded above 60 cities, "along the
length of his whole empire," "whence," Appian says [6],
"many Greek and Macedonian names of cities still exist
in Syria and among the Barbarians above it." He specifies 5 in Parthia, one in India, Scythia, and Armenia.
This was in our 2nd century. (140, A.D.) The cities
founded by Alexander's successors have been traced [7] in
each well-known province of Asia Minor, Bithynia, Pontus, Paphlagonia, Cappadocia, Phrygia, Lycaonia, Lydia,
Pergamus, Troas, Caria, Lycia, Pisidia, Pamphylia, Cilicia; in Syria, Mesopotamia, Babylonia, Susiana; on the
Tigris; in Armenia, Persia, Media, Parthia; on the Jaxartes, the Indus, and even East of the Indus, near the
Ganges; in Arabia also, on the Red Sea, in Egypt and
Cyrene.

Nor did the followers of Alexander imitate him only
in colonising. The blending of races was continued; and
very remarkably in part, through the position given to
the Jews on the ground of their faithfulness to their sovereigns. The early Ptolemies and Seleucidæ multiplied,
as they thought, faithful subjects, and prepared a seed-
plot for the Gospel. We are told expressly that the two
founders of the two lines, Ptolemy Lagi in Alexandria [8],
Seleucus Nicator in the then third [9] city of the known
world, Antioch, and in the other cities of his vast portion

----

[6] Syr. 57.   [7] Droysen, Hellen. ii. 651-747.

[8] Ptolemy Lagi, "understanding that those from Jerusalem were most reli-
able as to their oaths and fealty, (from the answer which they gave to the embassy of Alexander after he had conquered Darius,) having located many of
them in the garrisons and given them equal rights of citizenship with the Macedonians in Alexandria, took an oath of them that they would keep fealty to
the descendants of him who gave them this charge. And no few of the other
Jews came of their own accord into Egypt, invited both by the goodness of the
soil and the liberality of Ptolemy." Jos. Ant. xii. 1.   [9] Jos. B. J. iii. 3, 4.

of the Empire of Alexander [1], gave to the Jews equal rights with Macedonians. In religion only they were Jews; as members of a polity they had sometimes special privileges bearing on their law and religion, else they were Alexandrians, Antiochenes, Ephesians [2]. It is stated, on the authority of extant documents, that *this* union of races, too (as well as that between the Persian and Macedonian,) was begun by Alexander [3], carried on by his successors. This moreover took place to such extent

[1] "They [the Jews] obtained the honor from the kings of Asia also, having served in the army with them. For Seleucus Nicator, in the cities which he founded in Asia and in lower Syria, and in the metropolis itself, Antioch, conferred on them citizenship, and made them rank with the Macedonians and Greeks who were settled therein, so that this citizenship remains even now also." Ant. xii. 3.

[2] "His [Apion's] marvelling, how, being Jews, they were called Alexandrians, betrays the same ignorance. For all who are invited into a given colony, much as they may differ in race, take their name from its founders. Those of us, who dwell at Antioch, are called Antiochenes. For Seleucus, the founder, gave them citizenship. And so too in Ephesus, and the rest of Ionia, they bear the same name with the natives, the Successors [of Alexander] having given it to them." Jos. c. Ap. ii. 4.

[3] "Alexander gave them [the Jews] a place to dwell in, and they obtained equal rank with the Macedonians. I know not what Apion would have said, had they been settled near the Necropolis and not near the Palace, and were not their race now too called ' Macedonians.' If then he [Apion] has read the Epistles of Alexander the king, and has met with the rescripts of Ptolemy Lagi and the kings after him, and has lighted on the column which stands in Alexandria and contains the rights, given by the great Cæsar to the Jews; if, I say, he knows these things, and, knowing them, has dared to write the contrary, he is unprincipled; if he knew nothing of them, he is ill-instructed." "Alexander collected some of our people there, not for want of such as should colonise the city which he founded with great earnestness. But carefully proving all as to good faith and probity, he gave this distinction to our people. For he honoured our nation, as Hecatæus too says of us, that, for the probity and good faith which the Jews evinced towards him, he gave them in addition the territory of Samaria, to hold free from tribute. And Ptolemy Lagi too was like-minded with Alexander as to those who dwell in Alexandria." Jos. Ib. This early equalising of the Jews with Alexandrians is recognised in the edict of Claudius; "Having learnt that the Jews in Alexandria were from the first called Alexandrians, having been settled there together with the Alexandrians straightway at the earliest period, and having received from the kings equal citizenship, as appeared plain both from their letters and from the ordinances," &c. (in Jos. Ant. xix. 5, 2.)

that ⅓ of the population of Egypt consisted of Jews[4]. "[5]Ptolemy Lagi— when he wished to have strong hold of Cyrene[6] and of the other cities in Libya sent Jews to settle there." "This people," says Strabo[7], "hath now found its way into every city, and it is not easy to find a spot in the world, which hath not received this race, and which is not overpowered by them. Many other places have imitated Egypt and Cyrene— in this too, that they support especially bodies of Jews, and are enlarged together, using the hereditary laws of the Jews. In Egypt at least a settlement has been assigned them apart, and great part of Alexandria has been set aside for this nation. And they have an Ethnarch of their own, who administers the affairs of this nation, hears causes, takes charge of contracts and ordinances, as if he were the ruler of an independent polity. In Egypt then the nation gained great power." Nor was this intermingling only in large places. Josephus[8] mentions decrees in favor of Jews, not only at Ephesus, Laodicea, Miletus, Pergamus, Philadelphia, but in Delos[9] also.

In this case Greece was the recipient. Actively, it concentrated its energy of colonisation chiefly on the "[10]lands around or within the Tigris and Euphrates;" "40 new cities can still be counted in Upper Syria between Mount Taurus, Lebanon, and the Euphrates." And these were undoubtedly only a portion[11]. The Ptolemies "[12]colonised southward on the coast of Abyssinia, and that

[4] "The Governor, [Flaccus,] knowing that the city and all Egypt have two sorts of inhabitants, us and these, and that there are not fewer than 1,000,000 Jews dwelling in Alexandria and the country from the steep slope towards Libya to the confines of Æthiopia," &c. Philo, Cont. Flacc. ii. 533. Mang. Diodorus sets the whole population at 3,000,000 only. See on Joel iii. 19. p. 143.

[5] Jos. c. Ap. ii. 4.   [6] "In the city of the Cyrenians there were four [classes ;] the citizens ; the agriculturists ; the resident aliens; and fourthly the Jews." Strabo in Jos. Ant. xiv. 7. 2.   [7] l. c.   [8] Ant. xiv. 10.   [9] Ib. § 8. and 14.   [10] Droys. Hell. ii. 748.

[11] "The traditions still extant in no way inform us of the whole extent of Greek colonies, founded in the first century especially of Hellenism. How many cities do we find only named once ; of how many is the notice only accidental." Id. ib.   [12] Ib. 748-51.

so solidly, that, far into Christian times, the Greek maintained itself together with the native element, rivalling too the advancing Arab."

In both Asia and Egypt, Alexander laid the foundations; in both his successors built on, towards an end in God's Providence which they knew not. But even man's "rough-hewing his ends," which God so "shaped," was no chance work. Letters were the hereditary province of even degenerate Ptolemies. The Septuagint, the dialect which, uniting the depth of Hebrew with the intellectual precision of the Greek language, was to be the vehicle of the revelation of the Gospel, the Greek of Alexandria modified by the Old Testament, were productions of the peculiar character of the third Empire in Alexander and his successors. Alexandria and Antioch, early conquests of Christianity, chief sees and schools of thought, were their joint production. Nisibis and Edessa, where Eastern tone of thought prevailed, the great schools of the Christian East [1], had felt the intellectual influence of the Greek mind. This and much more, which was in the purpose of God, was first developed in distant centuries; but it illustrates the oneness of the empire of Alexander and his successors, that these worked out, in an inferior degree, yet remarkably, the characteristic conception of the great intellectual conqueror, the largest-minded probably, whom the earth ever saw.

These colonisations were the great and lasting influence of the Greek empire. They involved, of necessity, a mixture of races, in which the energy of Greek character and mind must needs predominate over the weaker Persian. Its influence continued. "[2] It was no new idea in Alexander, to complete the military occupation of the subject countries through colonies; but the character of his foundations shews, that military objects were by no means his sole motives. His immediate and more

---

[1] See Assem. de Scriptt. Syr. in Bibl. Or. T. l. prol. and 270, 204, 351. n. 2. 353. [2] Droysen, Gesch. d. Hell. ii. 589.

distant successors[3] carried on his work more or less in his spirit; the result, in most countries, was the lasting foundation of Hellenism. Even the barbarian occupations of the Parthians or Sacæ could not at once extinguish it. The Arsacidæ, to the latest times, call themselves on their coins, '[4] friends of Greece:' the Parthians despised king Vonones, because he had estranged himself from Persian ways, and was encircled by Greeks[5]. Seneca still says[6], ' What mean Greek cities in the midst of barbarian countries? what means the language of Macedonians among Indians and Persians?' Even the Barbarians, who penetrated to India, had, as it seems, for above a century, Greek letters and words on their coins. In truth, the language in which the Apostles preached was a language of the world."

There is no tenable way, then, in which the Empires of Alexander and his successors, either together or apart, can be made into the fourth Empire. Not together; for, counted together, they make the 3rd not the 4th Empire; not Alexander's successors alone, both because they are, in no sense, by themselves one empire; and the theory patently contradicts the symbol in both visions, which it ought to explain. There is no possible explanation moreover, either way, of the tenfold division of the fourth empire, expressed alike in the toes of the image and the horns of the fourth beast, nor any solution, how, if the little horn (the 11th) were Antiochus Epiphanes, he overthrew three of those ten. The theory fails doubly in that which is to be its mainstay. The little horn of the 7th chapter is to be Antiochus Epiphanes; in truth, lest there should be prophecy; ostensibly, because it is so in the 8th. But granted to these interpreters, for the time, all which they ask; that the ten horns are individual kings, not kingdoms; supposing too, for the time, (what contradicts the text,) that 7 out of the ten kings need not be contemporaneous with the 11th who is to overthrow three of them; still

---

[3] Diadochoi and Epigonoi, see Diod. i. 3. Strabo xv. end. [4] Philhellenes. [5] Tac. Ann. ii. 2. [6] Consol. ad Helvid. 6. T. iii. 363. ed. Frisk.

the interpreters cannot make out either the ten kings or
the three, specified in the vision. Porphyry's expedient
of making up ten kings out of those in any kingdom "who
were most cruel[1]" [i. e. to Israel] failed both in principle and in fact. In principle, because there is no indication of this limitation in Daniel; in fact, because no such
ten kings could be found. It is doubtful whether Porphyry specified any. Later writers have enumerated the
10 any how[2]; some kings, with whom Israel was in no
way concerned; some who were its benefactors[3]; three,

[1] "From Alexander to Antiochus he [Porphyry] enumerates ten kings who
were most cruel ; and these kings he sets down, not of one kingdom, e. g. of
Macedonia, Syria, Asia, Egypt, but he makes a succession of kings out of different kingdoms, in order that what is written of *a mouth speaking great
things* may be understood, not of Antichrist but of Antiochus." S. Jerome on
Dan. vii. 7.

[2] Junius, Piscator, Polanus, Grotius and Collins (following Grotius) did not
trouble themselves to make out more than 10, counting Antiochus Epiphanes
twice, as the last of the ten horns, and as the "*other* little horn," which "came
up among them :" (contrary to language and sense.) Junius, Piscator, Polanus, count them, Seleucus Nicator, Antiochus Soter, Ant. Theos, Sel. Callinicus, Ptolemy Euergetes, Sel. Ceraunus, Ant. Magnus, Ptol. Philopator,
Seleucus Philopator, Ant. Epiphanes. Grotius, out of 14 or 15 kings alluded
to in ch. xi, selected 9, adding an apocryphal king, Ptolemy Eupator. The real
kings were, Ptolemy Lagi, Sel. Nicator, Ptol. Euergetes, Sel. Callinicus, Antiochus M., Ptol. Philopator, Ptol. Epiphanes, Sel. Philopator, Ant. Epiphanes.
Collins adopted this. (Scheme of Lit. Proph. p. 162.) Rosenmüller (or whomever
he followed) adopted a third enumeration, adding Antigonus and Demetrius
Poliorcetes before the division of the four kingdoms, taking 6 Ptolemies, Lagi,
Philadelphus, Euergetes I., Philopator, Epiphanes, Philometor, and the two last
of the Syrian line before Epiphanes, viz. his father and brother. Since there
were eight Seleucidæ, (including Ant. Epiph.) and seven Ptolemies down to
this date, 1365 different combinations of 11 might be made out of these 15,
each as good as the other, i. e. all equally bad, since there is no ground for
selecting one rather than another. There would be a fixed principle in selecting either house, the Ptolemies or the Seleucidæ ; but either house furnishes
less than ten, both together more than ten. If any begin earlier with Rosenmüller, the possible changes would be still more absurdly manifold. Yet Hitzig begins with Alexander, and is followed by Hilgenfeld, l. c.

[3] 1) Seleucus Nicator, the author of privileges to the Jews which lasted till
the times of Josephus. (Jos. Ant. xii. 3.) 2) Ptolemy Lagi, who took Jerusalem indeed by fraud, yet bestowed afterwards such privileges on the Jews,
ranking them with Macedonians, that many Jews migrated into Egypt. (Ib.
c. 1.) 3) Ptolemy Philadelphus. (Ib. c. 2.) 4) Ptolemy Euergetes. (Jos. c. Ap.
ii. 5.) 5) Ptolemy Philometor and Cleopatra. 6) Antiochus the Great. (Ant.

who began with harshness and repented[4].   But if the ten
horns were to represent kings at all, there must plainly
be some unity, some common ground, for which they were
to be selected out of the many successors of Alexander
who were called kings; some one relation to the fourth
empire as a whole. . Of late, then, they have been sought
in the Syrian kingdom, to which Antiochus Epiphanes belonged.   These however were not 10, but 7[5].   Nor were
there any three of them, nor indeed any three at all, whom
Antiochus Epiphanes overthrew.   And yet there have
been no lack of guesses, *who* might be meant by those
three, who, on the unbelieving hypothesis, were contemporary with the writer, and whose signal fall he is to have
witnessed.   Three kings of Syria have been chosen, three
of Egypt, the assassin of Seleucus Philopator, and a king
of Armenia[6].   Of these, the Ptolemies would be excluded
by the fact, that the three kings are of the number of the
10, and that it is senseless to bring the Ptolemies into the

xii. 3.) And, generally, Josephus appeals to, as exstant and accessible in his time,
"rescripts of the kings of Egypt after Ptolemy Lagi." (c. Ap. ii. 4.) 7) Even
Seleucus Philopator, for a time at least, bore the expenses of the sacrifices at
Jerusalem. (2 Macc. iii. 3.)

[4] Ptolemy Lagi, (Ant. xii. 1.) Antiochus M., and even Ptolemy Philopator,
(3 Macc.) or Physcon, according to the Latin of Jos. c. Ap. ii. 5.

[5] 1) Seleucus Nicator, 2) Antiochus Soter, 3) Ant. Theos, 4) Seleucus Cal-
inicus, 5) Sel. Ceraunus, 6) Antiochus the Great, (whom Appian calls "6th
from Seleucus, who, after Alexander, reigned over Asia about the Euphrates,"
Syr. init.) 7) Seleucus Philopator.

[6] *Artaxias* was chosen by Porphyry, Harenberg, Rosenmüller, Herzfeld.
(Gesch. d. V. Isr. i. 424.)

Antiochus the Great, by Junius, Polanus, Piscator.

Seleucus Philopator, by Junius, Polanus, Piscator, Broughton, (Works,
p. 190.) Calmet, l'Empereur, Grotius, (Collins) Hitzig.

Heliodorus, by Calmet, Harenb., Bertholdt, Maurer, Hitzig, Leng. Hilgenfeld; (Apok. p. 26.) "will do at a pinch,"("passt auch noch zur noth.") Herzf.

Demetrius, by Brought. l' Emp. Calm. Grot. Berth. Maur. Hitz. Leng.
Hilg.; "will not do in any case." Herzf.

Ptolemy Philopator, by Junius, Polanus, Piscator, l'Emp. Grot.

Ptolemy Philometor, by Porph. Brought. Harenb. Berth. Ros. Maur.
Leng. Hilg.; "will do, but is one of the 'former horns,' only if Ptolemies belonged to them." Herzf.

Ptolemy Physcon, by Porphyry, Rosenmüller.

line of Syrian kings[1]. One wonders too, what place
1) Artaxias, the first of his line, could have here, who in
no way belonged to the successors of Alexander.   Once a
general, then a Satrap under Antiochus, then, by aid of
the Romans, an independent king[2], he was defeated and
perhaps taken[3] by Antiochus, and had to fulfil certain

[1] In order to connect Ptolemy Philometor with Syria, Bertholdt, Lengerke,
Davidson (Horne, Introd. ii. 909.) have a fable, that "his mother and guardian
Cleopatra wished to place him on the throne of Syria."   Of this there is not
a vestige in history.   On the contrary, Cleopatra maintained friendly relations with her brother Ant. Epiphanes until her death.   Even then his guardians, Eulæus an eunuch, and Lenæus a Cæle-Syrian slave, declared war, not
for Syria, but for the old cause of strife, Cælesyria. (Diodorus in Mai Scriptt.
Vett. p. 75. S. Jerome on Dan. xi. 22. Polyb. xxviii. 19.)   A Syrian, perhaps
a Cæle-Syrian, party held aloof from Epiphanes at first, but even they took no
active measures.   They were Syrians, whom Antiochus won by pretending to
pardon.   S. Jerome says, "Antiochus Epiphanes, to whom the dignity of king
was not at first given by those who *in Syria* favoured Ptolemy; but afterwards,
by simulating clemency, he obtained the kingdom of Syria."   Bertholdt argues
that "since Philometor obtained the kingdom of Syria at the end, (1 Macc.
xi. 13. Polyb. xl. 12.) there is no doubt that his mother destined him for it at
the beginning."   In 1 Macc. it is only said, "at Antioch, he set two crowns
upon his head, the crown of Asia and of Egypt."   Josephus supplies the fact,
that he did this unwillingly, and proceeded, both out of natural moderation
and for fear of the Romans, to decline the kingdom of Syria, and persuaded
them to accept Demetrius Nicator, the great nephew of Epiphanes. (Ant. 13.
4. 7.)   This account of his unambitious mild temperament coincides with all
his conduct to his brother, and the judgment of Polybius. (Hist. fin.) Diodorus
moreover, says that he "did *not* desire the kingdom, but wished to acquire
Cæle Syria, and agreed with Demetrius upon common action, that Ptolemy
should have *Cæle Syria* as his own, and Demetrius *his paternal kingdom*."
in Müller, Fragm. Hist. ii. p. xvi.

[2] Strabo's account is, "The Persians and Macedonians gained possession of
Armenia; then those who held Syria and Media; lastly Orontes, descended
from Hydarnes, one of the 7 Persians, was its viceroy; then it was divided in
two by the generals of Antiochus the Great, who warred with the Romans,
Artaxias and Zariadris; and these ruled it, the king entrusting them: when
he was defeated, they, joining themselves to the Romans, were made independent, and were entitled kings." (xi. 14. 15. p. 532. Cas.)

[3] App. Syr. 45, 6. 66. Diodorus says nothing of his capture.   C. Müller doubts
Appian's accuracy in this.   S. Jerome says, "We *know* that Antiochus fought
against Artaxias, but that he [Artaxias] continued in his ancient kingdom."
Appian's statement, as a proof of the prowess of Antiochus, that he *took* Artaxias, even if true, implies that Artaxias was not slain, and, if so, his restoration, on the sudden death of Antiochus and the confusion consequent on it,
would have followed as a matter of course.

conditions imposed upon him [4]. This, of course, implies that he was set at liberty, else he could not have executed them; he was not *uprooted*, for he transmitted his throne to his own descendants [5]. Not less marvellous are the rest, whether Ptolemies or Seleucidæ. 2) Antiochus the Great, father of Epiphanes, perished in the attempt to plunder a Persian temple, while Epiphanes was a hostage at Rome. 3) Seleucus Philopator was poisoned by Heliodorus his treasurer, who wished to seize the crown for himself, while Antiochus was returning from Rome, yet not further than Athens [6]. 4) Heliodorus, while "forcing his way to the throne [7]," (not as yet reigning) was "cast out," not by Epiphanes, but by Attalus and Eumenes, who set Epiphanes on the throne, "courting his favor" against the Romans. 5) Demetrius was sent as a hostage to Rome by Seleucus Philopator, his father, to replace Epiphanes [8]; he was not dethroned by Epiphanes, but lived to succeed him, murdering his son Antiochus Eupator [9]. 6) Ptolemy Philopator defeated the father of Epiphanes, and died while Epiphanes was yet a boy [10]. 7) Ptolemy Philometor. His guardians were defeated by his uncle

[4] [Antiochus] "having conquered him, compelled him to do what was enjoined." Diod. Fragm. in Müller, Fragm. Hist. Gr. ii. p. 10. The fragment comes in order, after the mention of the joint reign of the two Ptolemies, Philometor and Physcon, B.C. 170-165, and so at the end, not (as Herzfeld) at the beginning of his reign.

[5] Tigranes, (the son-in-law of Mithridates) was his descendant. (Strabo ib.) His line continued until about A. D. 20-30.

[6] App. Syr. 45. Bertholdt and Lengerke say that Porphyry ascribed the murder of his brother to Epiphanes; Porphyry says nothing of *Antiochus Ep.* but that "*Ptolemy* Epiphanes was plotting [war, not assassination] against Seleucus, (quod Seleuco sit molitus insidias) and therefore was himself poisoned by his captains;" on occasion of a speech, implying that they were his "walking treasure," to defray the expenses of the war. Diod. in Mai Scriptt. Vett. ii. 71. 8. Jerome.   [7] *ἐς τὴν ἀρχὴν βιαζόμενον.* App. Ib.

[8] "Seleucus freed his brother Antiochus from being hostage to the Romans, giving in exchange his own son Demetrius." App. Ib. The change of hostages, after a time, was part of the treaty with Rome.   [9] App. Syr. 47.

[10] Ptolemy died B.C. 205. But the eldest son of Antiochus was born B.C. 221. (See Clinton, Fasti H. ii. 316. n. s.) Epiphanes, who was his 5th son, could not have been born before B.C. 217. or have been above 12 at the death of Ptolemy.

Epiphanes; but it was the policy of Epiphanes to reign, if he could, over Egypt through his nephew, Philometor. He kept him therefore prisoner for a short time, "under the guise of friendship [1]," "pretending to provide for the boy's interests [2]." The Alexandrians, however, at once made his brother king, and expelled Antiochus. "[3] Epiphanes profited nothing, for he could not hold the kingdom, being rejected by the soldiers of Ptolemy, who restored Philometor to liberty." A boy-king, who falls into an uncle's hands, is treated by him with show of friendship, and is restored at once, within the year, by his own people, is neither *subdued* nor *uprooted.* All know how Popilius protected Egypt against Epiphanes. Philometor survived Antiochus 18 years; his brother and successor, 8) Euergetes II. or Physcon, survived him 47 years. Instead of being uprooted by him, even Philometor lived to see the line of Epiphanes extinct and his brother's grandson dependent upon him for restoration to the throne of Syria, and to restore him.

The words of the vision are, *before whom three of the first horns were plucked up by the roots.* In the explanation it is said, *he shall be diverse from the first, and he shall subdue three kings.* Antiochus, degraded as he was by his sensuality, had no ordinary talents [4]. He was a thorough dissembler, able to hide his purpose and skilful to

[1] Parcens puero et amicitiam simulans. S. Jer. on Dan. xi. 21.

[2] Pueri rebus se providere simulans. Ib. "He, [Antiochus] cutting short the [Rhodian] embassador, while yet speaking, said, 'there was no need of many words; *for the kingdom did belong to the elder Ptolemy;* that he had moreover long been reconciled with him; that they were friends; and now, if those in the city [Alexandria] wished to bring him back, he, Antiochus, was no obstacle.' And so he did." Polyb. xxviii. end.   [3] S. Jer. xi. 27. from Porph. "When Antiochus had warred against Egypt and taken his crown, the Alexandrians committed affairs to the younger, and, having chased Antiochus, they rescued Philometor, and it was called the 12th year of Philometor, the first of Euergetes." Porph. in Eus. Ann. i. 239. see further Polyb. xxvii. 17. xxviii. 1. 16. 17. esp. 19. xxix. 8-11. Jos. Ant. xii. 5. 2. Diod. l. c. Prideaux, Conn. B. 3. A. 173, 171. 109, 8. and Clinton, Fasti Hell. iii. 318-21. 386-8.

[4] "He was both energetic ($\pi\rho\alpha\kappa\tau\iota\kappa\acute{o}\varsigma$) and worthy of the name of king, save the stratagems as to Pelusium." (Polyb. xxvii. end.) "Antiochus, who held

execute it; he was engaged, throughout his reign, in war and was successful; and yet, as a note against these misinterpretations, he *uprooted* no one king.

Schemes, so various and so contradictory, could not leave an easy conscience. So Rationalism, like a restless sleeper, turned round on the other side, and took, so far, the true interpretation, that the ten horns were, not kings but kingdoms, and that three of those ten were overthrown. "I agree," Bleek said[5], "with Auberlen, that the ten horns of the fourth Empire *cannot be meant* of ten successive Syrian kings, (as Bertholdt, v. Lengerke, Maurer, Hitzig, Delitzsch, think) nor of kings, some Syrian some Egyptian, (as Rosenmüller, &c. and Porphyry of old) but rather of the single portions into which the kingdom was divided. The mention of the little horn, as arising *amidst* the ten horns, constrains us to conceive of ten kings, or rather kingdoms, existing contemporaneously, arising out of the fourth kingdom. I will not deny that this occasions a degree of difficulty as to the reference to the successors of Alexander, in that ch. 8. speaks of *four* monarchies as arising out of that of Alexander after his death. However, the portions of his kingdom, which were formed into independent *kingdoms, may* have been counted in different ways, and so, as ten, according to the generals, who, in the partition 323, B. C., obtained the chief

that acquisition by war was the strongest and noblest title." (Id. xxxvii. 1.) "He governed Syria and the neighbouring nations with vigour, having Timarchus as Satrap in Babylon—he warred against Artaxias, king of Armenia, and, having taken him, died, leaving a nine-years-old boy, Antiochus, to whom the Syrians gave the name Eupator, on account of his father's valour. The senate was pleased, that Antiochus shewed himself brave in a little space, and speedily died." (App. Syr. 45. 6.) Of his dissimulation Polybius gives a vivid picture, after the decisive act of Popilius. "The games just over, Tiberius [Gracchus] came as embassador, in truth to see how things lay. Him Antiochus received so dextrously and friendlily, that Tiberius could not suspect any designs, or any appearance of soreness on account of what had happened at Alexandria, but even condemned those who said aught of the kind: and this, on the ground of the exceeding courtesy of his reception. For besides other acts, he gave up his palace, nay almost his crown, to the embassadors, whereas inwardly he was most hostilely disposed to the Romans." xxxi. 5.

[5] Jahrb. f. Deutsch. Theol. v. p. 60, 1.

provinces." So then he selected ten out of the Satrapies allotted to Alexander's officers.

This abandonment of ground, taken up by former impugners of the prophecy, is a confession of its untenableness. But the new position is as patently untenable as the old. For 1) the division B. C. 323, modified B. C. 321, was not of kingdoms at all, but of satrapies in and under a nominal kingdom. The memory of Alexander was still respected. His weak brother Aridæus was made king, "[1] on condition that the Alexander, whom Roxana was about to bear of Alexander, should, when born, reign with him, which also took place as soon as the boy saw the light." Perdiccas was made guardian; the Satraps were appointed by him, under the crown, just as there had been Satraps under Alexander himself[2]. The object of the appointments was, not to increase but to lessen the power of those appointed, removing them to a safe distance[3], and separating them. Some of the more distant satrapies were continued to the self-same persons. "[4]No one at this moment talked of dividing the empire. Perdiccas, profiting by the weakness of Aridæus, had determined to leave to him nothing more than the imperial name, and to engross for himself the real authority. Still, however, in his disputes with the other chiefs, he represented the imperial family and the integrity of the empire, contending against severalty and local independence." So again at the re-arrangement, B.C. 321, at Triparadisus in Syria. It was still done in the names of the kings. "[5]Antipater made a second distribution of the Satrapies of the empire, somewhat modified, but coinciding in the main with that which had been drawn up shortly after the death of Alexander." Perdiccas, Antipater, Polysperchon, were successively guardians of the weak or infant representatives of Alexander. They held nominally the

---

[1] Arrian, in Phot. cod. 92. p. 69. Bek. Dexippus, in Phot. cod. 82. p. 64.

[2] See Grote, Greece, xii. 321-3.   [3] "He proclaimed as Satraps those whom he suspected." Arr. l. c.   [4] Grote, xii. 431.   [5] Ib. p. 454, 5,

one empire, until the murder of Alexander Ægus, B.C. 310.
The remaining years until the battle of Issus, B.C. 301,
were spent in a struggle, whether any general of Alexander should succeed to his universal empire.   The struggle was not between satrapies but between talented generals.

2) Even of these satrapies there was no division into ten.
Justin, representing præ-Christian authority [6], mentions
twenty eight [7]; all, who speak of that division, agree in the
great outlines.

[6] Trogus Pompeius was about 20, B. C. (see Smith, Biogr. Dict. v. Justinus.)
Diodorus probably soon after B. C. 8. (see Ib. v. Diodorus.)

[7] The distribution of the Satrapies, according to *Justin*, (xiii. 4.) *Diodorus*,
(xviii. 3, 4.) *Arrian*, (in Phot. Cod. 92. p. 69. Bek.) *Q. Curtius*, (x. 30. end of
his work,) *Dexippus*, (in Phot. cod. 82. p. 64. who, Photius says, here as elsewhere mostly agrees with Arrian,) was, as follows,

1 *Macedonia and Greece*, Antipater. (Justin.) *The parts beyond Thrace, to
the Illyrians, Triballi and Agriani, Macedonia, Epirus, and all the Greeks.*
Craterus and Antipater. (Arrian.)

2 *Egypt, part of Africa and of Arabia;* (J. Diod.) *Egypt and Libya and
parts of Arabia, bordering on Egypt;* (Arr.) *Egypt and the nations of Africa
in its domain;* (Curt.) *Egypt and Libya and the parts beyond, bordering on
Egypt;* (Dex.) Ptolemy Lagi. all.

3 *Syria*, Laomedon. J. Di. A. De. with Phœnicia, C.

4 *Cilicia*, Philotas. all.

4 *Illyrii*, Philo. J.

5 *Media greater*, Atropatus. J. Di.   *Media*, Python. Di. A. C. De.

6 *Media lesser*, father in law of Perdiccas. J.

7 *Susiana*, Scynus. J.

8 *Phrygia greater*, Antigonus. J.; with 9, Di. A. C. De.

9 *Syria and Pamphylia*, Nearchus. J.

10 *Caria*, Cassander, J. A. C. Asandros. Di. De.

11 *Lydia*, Menander, J. A. C. De. Meleager. Di.

12 *Phrygia lesser (on the Hellespont*, Di. A. C. De.) Leonatus. all.

13 *Thrace and countries on Euxine*, Lysimachus. J. Di. A.

14 *Cappadocia, Paphlagonia*, (J.) *and all the adjoining countries* (Di.)
and all bordering on the Euxine to Trapezus, (A. De.) *and to subdue all to
Trapezus*, (C) Eumenes. all.

15, 16, 17. *Bactria the farther, and countries of India*, their former prefects
retained. J.

15 *Paropamisii and borders of Mount Caucasus*, [Indian,] Oxyartes (king of
Bactria Di.) J. Di. De.

16 *Lands between Hydaspes and Indus*, Taxiles. J. Porus. De.

17 *The rest of India, his own kingdom*, Taxiles. De. Porus. Di.

18 *Colonies founded among Indi*, Pithon. J. De.

3) In the arbitrary selection of *ten*, not the "chief provinces" but chief individuals of Alexander's generals have been chosen. Of the countries which Alexander ruled, and which were held by Satraps in that first distribution, this selection of ten includes Macedonia, Greece, Thrace, lesser Phrygia on the Hellespont, Greater Phrygia (and as some say, Pamphylia and Syria) Caria, Lydia, Cappadocia, Paphlagonia, Syria, Palestine, Media, Egypt. It omits, any how, the Eastern portion of the Empire, Mesopotamia, Babylonia, Persia, Susiana, Parthia, Sogdiana, Carmania, Hyrcania, Aria, Drangiana, Arachosia, Gedrosia, Bactria, Paropamisus, and the countries under the Caucasus, India; and even Cilicia, perhaps Illyria; held, as these were, under 15 or 16 Satraps. Yet of these, Babylonia was the centre, whence the kingdom of the Seleucidæ took its rise.

In utter hopelessness then, one of the last of these critics declares "ten" to be a "[1] round number" "for the many larger and lesser kingdoms which were formed out of what Alexander left behind him." Only, no such kingdoms were formed; and *ten kingdoms* would be a strange "round number" for *twenty eight satrapies*. On this theory Daniel, when he speaks of "four kingdoms" into which Alexander's empire was to be divided, is to mean what he says, the "four kingdoms" of his successors; but

19 *Arachosii and Gedrosi*, Sibyrtius. J. Di. De.

20 *Drancæ and Arians*, Stasanor. J. Di. De.

21 *Bactrians*, Amyntas. J.

22 *Sogdiani*, Philip. J. De. with 23 Di. Dexippus, (in Photius' text,) assigns them a 2nd time, to Scopas.

23 *Parthians*, Stagnor. J.

24 *Hyrcanians*, Phrataphernes, J. together with 26, Di. Radaphernes. De.

25 *Carmanians*, Tleptolemus, J. Tlepolemus, Di. Neoptolemus. De.

26 *Persians*, Peucestes. J. Di. De.

27 *Babylonia*, Archon, J. Di. Seleucus. De.

28 *Mesopotamia*, Arcesilaus, J. Di. Archelaus. De.

"Many also remained undistributed [i. e. to Greek Generals] under their native rulers, as they were appointed by Alexander." A. "Those who were over India, the Bactri, and Sogdiani, and the other inhabitants either of the Ocean or Red Sea, were to retain the right of rule in the bounds which each had." C.   [1] Herzfeld, Gesch. Isr. i. 425.

when he speaks of the "ten kingdoms" of the 4th empire,
he is to mean, not "ten kingdoms" but, 28 Satrapies; and
when he says, that three of the ten kingdoms are to be uprooted, he is to mean, not kingdoms or satrapies, but three
kings[2]. As to these three kings, who are to have been
uprooted by Antiochus, the later rationalist criticism has
concentrated itself upon four, out of which to select them,
although not more than three persons are found to agree
as to the same three. They are, Seleucus Philopator,
poisoned while Antiochus was returning from Rome;
Heliodorus, who never reigned; Demetrius, who was never dispossessed, but who did reign afterwards; and Ptolemy Philometor, who never ceased to reign and who
survived Antiochus and his house. And this is to be
consistent harmonious literal interpretation of Holy
Scripture! Such interpreters can hardly believe themselves.

The negative evidence then, that no scheme can be
made out, whereby the four Empires, pourtrayed to Daniel, can be brought within the limits of the times before
Antiochus Epiphanes, coincides with the previous direct
evidence that the fourth empire is the Roman. For the

[2] Herzfeld, i. 424. Bleek, (p. 68. note) yet more marvellously, makes the "little horn" to be at once Seleucus Nicator, the most powerful of Alexander's generals and the founder of the kingdom of the Seleucidæ; "and also Antiochus
Epiphanes who, according to the horizon of the vision and of the book generally, appears as the last ruler of the Seleucidæ." And yet, since Bleek's Daniel was to have survived Epiph., he would have lived under his son Eupator at
least. The "horizon of *prophecy*" might, of course, be at any distance, without implying that such was the end of the Empire, any more than the visible horizon is of the world. It is the utmost point of vision, given supernaturally to
the prophet. But it is absurd to represent a contemporary as speaking of one
as the last of his line, of whom he knew, that he was not the last of his line.
Bleek also maintained, that the little horn of ch. 8. and ch. 7. was to be the
same, and yet he was to be two individuals, separated by 105 years, one of whom
was to overthrow three kingdoms (which he did not,) and the rest of the character was to be filled up by the other. And the three horns, which the "little
horn" uprooted at the last, are to be Antigonus, (whom Nicator defeated, not
alone, but in alliance with Ptolemy Lagi and Lysimachus,) and then Ptolemy
and Lysimachus, the Diadochi, with whom he united in parting Alexander's
empire. Ptolemy restored Seleucus to his satrapy, but was never even at war
with him, and survived him.

Roman was the next world-empire which succeeded the Greek in Alexander and his successors.

Men will hardly turn round and say, that, in the times of Antiochus Epiphanes, it could have been foreseen that the Roman commonwealth, with its annually changing Consuls, would become a kingdom, and that, a kingdom of the world. Men's consciences will surely hardly allow them. All these various strivings by Porphyry and his recent followers, to make the four empires end with Alexander's successors, bear witness to their conviction, that it was beyond human sagacity, within any time which could be assigned to the book of Daniel, to predict the Roman Empire. Else they would not have invented so many farfetched and contradictory ways of excluding it.

But look at its state, 164, B.C. the year when Antiochus Epiphanes died. A generation only (37 years) had passed since the close of the 2nd Punic war, when the war had been carried to its own gates; Carthage, its rival, still stood over against it. It was felt by Romans to be a formidable foe. Witness the "delenda est Carthago," and the unscrupulous policy adopted in encouraging the aggressions of Masinissa. Enriched by the commerce of the West, Carthage was recovering its resources, and fell through its intestine divisions. Egypt and Antiochus had lately mustered powerful armies : Perseus, king of Macedonia, had been but recently defeated, and might have repelled the Romans, but for his timidity and avarice. They had defeated Antiochus the Great, and, by their enormous fine for the expenses of the war, had crippled him. But, true to their policy of dividing and conquering, supporting the weak whom they feared not against the strong whom they feared, they had diminished the empires, which were their rivals, by giving a portion of their possessions to the weaker, to be taken at their own will hereafter. Who should foresee that all these nations should remain blinded by their avarice; that common fear should never bind them in one ; that they should never see, until their own turn came, that Rome used her instruments successively, and flung each aside, and found some excuse of quarrel against each, as soon as she had gained her end? The absence of any such fear on any side shews how little human wisdom could then foresee the world-empire, which as yet existed only in the embryo; and which the nations, whom Rome in the end subdued, were, in God's Providence, the unwilling, unconscious, blinded, instruments of forming. To us it seems inconceivable that no experience should have opened men's eyes, until it was too late. Each helped in turn to roll round the wheel, which crushed himself.

Rome had at that time (B. C. 164.) no territory East or, except Sicily, South of Italy. Masinissa held the throne of Numidia; Rome had not a foot of ground in Africa. In Spain, she only held so much as had before been in the power of Carthage, the Western and Southern Provinces, now Catalonia, Valencia, Murcia, Andalusia, Grenada: two centuries almost elapsed before it was finally reduced. Gaul and Germany were almost unknown countries. Even Cis-Alpine Gaul had not been formally made a Roman Province; Venetia was friendly; Carniola unsubdued; Istria recently subdued; (B. C. 177.) Illyricum had been divided into three, yet left nominally free. The Battle of Pydna had destroyed the kingdom of Macedon four years before, (B. C. 168.) but it seemed as if Rome knew not how to appropriate territory. It took nothing which it could not at once consolidate. Macedonia was only divided into four independent Republics. The territory which it required Antiochus to cede, it gave to Eumenes: Lycia and Caria, which it took from the Rhodians, it made independent.

Such was the impenetrable mask which it wore; everywhere professing to uphold the weak and maintain justice; every where unjust, as soon as the time came; setting free in order to enslave; aiding, in order to oppress.

But we have two Jewish documents, the one probably a little after the death of Antiochus Epiphanes, the other not later than the death of John Hyrcanus, (B.C. 105.)

which shew two very different aspects of the Jewish mind toward the Romans, the one in Alexandria, the other in Palestine.   Yet in neither is there the slightest apprehension of Roman greatness.

The 3rd Sibylline book is now generally held to be the work of a Jew in the time of Antiochus Epiphanes [1].   It threatens unhesitatingly, that all the evils which had been done by the Romans to Asia should be requited with usury upon them.

" [2] What wealth soe'er Rome hath received from tributary Asia, Asia shall again receive thrice-told from Rome, and shall requite to her her baleful insolence.   And how many soe'er from Asia have waited in the houses of Italians, twenty-fold as many Italians shall be serfs in Asia, and shall incur payment ten thousand fold.

"O delicate, o'er-wealthy, virgin daughter of Latin Rome, often intoxicated by thy much-wooed bridals, a servant thou, thou shall not be espoused in the world.   Oft shall thy mistress shear thy delicate locks, and, executing vengeance, shall cast things from heaven to earth, and from earth again shall lift them up to heaven, because mortals were entangled in a wicked and unjust life.   And Rome shall be *rume*, (a street.)"

The first book of the Maccabees, on the other hand, relates the simple unsuspecting trust, which Judas Maccabæus had in the Romans in the reign of Demetrius, son of Antiochus Epiphanes, as if they were wholly unambitious, conquering only, when assailed.   " [3] Now Judas had heard of the fame of the Romans, that they were mighty and valiant men and such as would lovingly accept all that joined themselves unto them, and made a league of amity with all that came to them; and that they were men of great valour.—Besides, how they destroyed and brought under their dominion all other kingdoms and isles that at any time resisted them ; but with their friends and such as relied upon them they kept amity, and that

---

[1] See Lect. vi.   [2] Orac. Sibyll. iii. § 3. v. 350- 64. T. 1. p. 123, 4. ed. Alex.
[3] 1 Macc. viii. 1, 2, 11, 12, 14-16.

they had conquered kingdoms both far and nigh, insomuch as all who heard of their name were afraid of them—yet for all this none of them wore a crown or was clothed with purple to be magnified thereby ; moreover, how they had made for themselves a senate-house, wherein 320 men sat in council daily consulting alway for the people, to the end they might be well-ordered, and that they committed their government to one man every year, who ruled over all their country, and that all were obedient to that one, and that there was neither envy nor emulation among them."

The immediate result of Judas' application to the Romans was a mere defensive alliance between the Romans and their confederates on the one side, and the Jews on the other, couched in terms of studied equality[4]; and a message to the Jews, that the Romans had written to Demetrius; "[5] Why hast thou made thy yoke heavy upon our friends and confederates the Jews ?   If therefore they complain any more against thee, we will do them justice, and fight with thee by sea and by land."

The writer of the book of Maccabees had as yet had no reason to think this simple kind-hearted judgment of Judas wrong.   Rome, although powerful, had, as yet, given no grounds to apprehend its ambition.   The facts coincide with the instinct of Porphyry and his followers, that no one could have anticipated, in the days of Antiochus, that Rome would become the empress of the world.   He then who foretold it must have had, on this ground also, a Divine foreknowledge.

[4] Ib. 22-30.   [5] Ib. 31, 2.

LECTURE IV.

The prophecy of the 70 weeks and of the Death of the Messiah, and the attempts to make the 70 weeks end with Antiochus Epiphanes.

In the first year of Darius, the term of the Captivity was, according to the prophecy of Jeremiah, all but come. Babylon was conquered; the captors of God's people were captives; but their own bonds were not broken. For the term, although all but come, was not ended. It was one of those seasons of breathless expectation, by which God teaches to man intense dependence upon Himself. Deliverance was at the door; the deliverer was come, but there was no token of deliverance. God had revealed the future through, or to, Daniel. But what was within the reach of man's powers, He left to the exercise of those powers. So Daniel sought to learn the term of the Captivity, where God had revealed it, in the prophecy of Jeremiah. *I understood*, he says [1], *by the Scriptures the number of the years, which the word of the Lord was to Jeremiah the Prophet to fulfil as to the desolations of Jerusalem, seventy years.* And he set himself to do that which Jeremiah foretold that they should then do. [2]*After seventy years shall be accomplished at Babylon, I will visit you, and perform My good word toward you, in causing you to return to this place.—Then shall ye call upon Me and shall go and pray unto Me, and I will hearken unto you.* On that deep

---

[1] ix. 2. in reference, in the words too, to Jer. xxv. 11, 12.
[2] Jer. xxix. 10, 12.

fervid prayer, in which Daniel, adoring God's judgment
and mercy, confessing his own sins and the sins of his people, besieged God, as it were, to have mercy upon His holy
city, His people, His sanctuary which was desolate, God
anew uplifted the veil which lay upon futurity.

The prophecy of the 70 weeks defined much more closely the period of the Coming of the Messiah, of which the
two visions of the four empires had already given an outline. Daniel had himself survived the first Empire, and
seen the dawn of the second. In the fourth, He, *like a
Son of man*, was promised. But would those 2nd and
3rd Empires be as brief as the first ? Would two successive lives, long as his own, see the rising of that fourth
empire, in which He was to come? Would He, a Prince
of peace, as Isaiah had prophesied, come to be a shelter
amid the terrific power of the fourth Empire, which, in
the end, He was to break in pieces? Such thoughts
could not but occupy the mind of Daniel at that crisis of
the fortunes of his people, and the passing away of the
first of the three world-empires interposed before the establishment of that, in which the Redeemer was to come.
The answer embraces those thoughts, but goes beyond
them. Daniel had prayed for his people and his holy city.
In harmony with that revelation of a world-embracing
kingdom, but not of this world, contained in the visions
of the four empires, Daniel's mind is carried beyond his
own people, his holy city and the visible sanctuary. The
temporary restoration of the city is promised, but *in strait
of times ;* the restoration of the temple and of sacrifice
are implied, since they were anew to cease and to be destroyed. But the prophecy went beyond all things visible, both in what it promised and in what it took away.
It promised forgiveness of sins, everlasting righteousness,
a Messiah, who was to be cut off and yet to confirm a
covenant. It took away all things visible, on which, as
images of that which was to come, they had hitherto rested. It took away all which was local and visible ; for He,
the Messiah, was to make all sacrifice to cease and city

and temple were to be an abiding desolation.   A definite period, counted by sevens of years, is assigned, within which this purpose of God was to be accomplished.

The period, which should elapse before the Coming of Christ, is fixed as nearly, we suppose, as it could be, without destroying man's free-agency.   Man was still to be on his trial, whether he would reject God.   God, in revealing the future, still preserves unimpaired His own great law of His creatures' free-agency.   Our redemption was to be wrought by the death of our Redeemer at His creatures' hands.   He was [1] *the Lamb slain from the foundation of the world.*   All sacrifice foreshewed His Death; David [2] and Isaiah [3] had foretold it; and now it was again to be foretold through Daniel.   Perhaps it would have been impossible for man to have fulfilled this, which lay in the counsels of God, had he known what he was doing; or, if he had, the sin would have been irremediable.   Jesus pleads it, as a ground of forgiveness, that His executioners knew not what they did [4].   We are told of those who stirred up their passions [5], *had they known it, they would not have crucified the Lord of glory.*   It may be, that, on these grounds, He did not declare, so that it should be certainly known beforehand, the precise year when the Messiah should come and should be cut off. But He intimated that time with sufficient nearness, to create the expectation which did arise, to awaken men's minds, to predispose them to listen and to obey.   What He does, He does not unprepared.

The interval, which God assigned, had an evident reference to the 70 years of the captivity.   That number had a bearing on the broken sabbaths, in punishment of which Moses had foretold that *the land* should *enjoy her sabbaths* [6] in the captivity of his people.   Seventy years were the term of their captivity; seven times seventy years was to be the main sum of their new period of probation, in the possession of their land and of their restored city.

[1] Rev. xiii. 8.   [2] Ps. xl.
[3] Is. liii.   [4] S. Luke xxiii. 34.   [5] 1 Cor. ii. 8.   [6] Lev. xxvi. 34.

The date, whence those 490 years began, is described, not absolutely laid down. But it is described in words which leave no large or uncertain margin, [7] *from the going forth of a commandment to restore and rebuild Jerusalem unto Messiah the Prince.* Above three thousand years had flowed by before; above two thousand years have flowed away since. The event, which was to change and regenerate millions upon millions, was fixed beforehand, within some surplus upon 490 years. The choice of the form of prophecy was itself prophetic. Greek and Latin philosophers too, (probably from some real mysterious connection of the number with the developement of man's frame,) have known of "weeks of years [8]." To the Hebrew, the 7 times 7 spoke of that recurring Jubilee year, when all debts were released, slavery was ended, every one was restored to all the inheritance which had, during the half-century, been forfeited; slight, joyous, ever-recurring picture of the restoration, for which all creation yearned and groaned. There could not be any ambiguity to the people's mind. The period could not be "70 weeks of days," i. e. a year and about 4 months. The events are

[7] Dan. ix. 25.

[8] "Which some of the poets have said, who measure age ταῖς ἑβδομάσι, by the sevenfolds." Aristotle (quoted Liddell and Scott. v. ἑβδ.) " Heraclitus and the Stoics say, that man's perfection begins about the second 7th." Plut. de Plac. Phil. v. 23. (ib.) Censorinus mentions the opinions of many who so counted ; " Solon makes ten parts of human life, so that each age should have seven years. To these 10 hebdomades of Solon, Staseas the Peripatetic added two, and said that the space of a full life was 84 years. Varro mentions that in the Etruscan books of the Fates the age of man is described by 12 hebdomades, in that it could be protracted to 12 times 7 years, by deprecating the fated period through sacred rites.—Of all these, they seem to have come nearest to nature, who have measured human life by hebdomades. For that, almost after every seventh year, there is some new developement. As you may see in Solon's elegy. For he says that in the first seven the teeth are shed; in the second, &c. In the 2nd hebdomas however, or at the beginning of the 3rd, the voice becomes thicker and unequal.—Physicians too, and philosophers have written much as to these hebdomades.—Some say that those years are most to be observed which are made up of 3 hebdomades, i. e. the 21st, 42nd, and 63rd. The 63rd is made of 9 hebdomades, or 7 enneads." [de Die Nat. c. 4.] " Varro adds, that he too had entered the 12th hebdomada of life, and, up to that day, had written 70 hebdomadas of books." Gell. Noct. Att. iii. 10.

too full for it. Seven weeks, (to go no further,) was no period in which to rebuild the city. It remained then to understand it, according to a key which God had given[1], of a sevenfold period of years.

The decree spoken of was doubtless meant of a decree of God, but to be made known through His instrument, man, who was to effectuate it. The *commandment went forth*[2] from God, like that, at which, Gabriel had just said, using the same idiom, he himself came forth to Daniel. But as the one was fulfilled through Gabriel, so the other remained to be fulfilled through the Persian monarch, in whose hands God had left, for the time, the outward disposal of His people. In themselves, the will and decrees of God are in all eternity; but His immutable decree seems then to *go forth*, when He, in Whose hands are all things, so disposes men's wills, that it comes into effect. But, since there was no decree at all in favour of the Jews before Cyrus B.C. 536, it might be startling enough to one who does not yet believe in prophecy, that, even from Cyrus, the 490 years come within forty-six years of our Lord's Birth; and that, although there were four different edicts, from which the 490 years might begin, these too admit of no vague coincidence. They do but yield four definite dates. There is a distance of 90 years from the 1st of Cyrus to the 20th of Artaxerxes Longimanus, but the dates within those 90 years, from which the prophecy could seem to be fulfilled, are only four. Those dates are, 1) The first year of Cyrus[3], B.C. 536; 2) The third year of Darius Hystaspes, B.C. 518, when he removed the hindrances to the rebuilding of the temple[4], interposed by Pseudo-Smerdis[5];

---

[1] Ezek. iv. 5, 6. [2] ix. 23. יָצָא דָבָר 25. מֹצָא דָבָר מִן. [3] Ezr. i. 1-4. vi. 3-5.

[4] Ezr. vi. 1-12. Zerubbabel and Shealtiel, encouraged by Haggai and Zechariah, resumed the building of the temple in the second year of Darius; (Ezr. iv. 24. v. 1. 2.) they were accused to Darius, (v. 3-end) and thereon they received the decree, which would be in the next year.

[5] The grounds for identifying Artaxerxes (Ezra iv. 7, 11, 23.) with Pseudo-Smerdis are; 1) the enemies of the Jews seem to have sent to each successive king of Persia. They hired counsellors in the days of Cyrus, (iv. 5.) They accused the Jews in the days of Ahasuerus. (iv. 6.) They wrote to Artaxerxes,

3) The commission to Ezra in the 7th year of Artaxerxes Longimanus, B.C. 45$\frac{6}{7}$[6]; 4) That to Nehemiah, in the 20th (iv. 7, &c.) and subsequently to Darius. (v. 6 sqq.) But Darius belng Darius Hystaspes, the two intervening names can be no other than Cambyses and Pseudo-Smerdis. Ezra, who mentions them, says that the temple was finished in the 6th year of Darius, (vi. 15.) and so, before Artaxerxes Longimanus. 2) Pseudo-Smerdis was a religious persecutor, destroying temples and worship. (Behistun Inscr. c. i. par. 14. in Rawl. Herod. ii. 595.) 3) We know that Darius undid acts of the usurper, (Ib.) and this is more likely than that kings of Persia should reverse their own formal acts, (which were held sacrosanct, from the relation in which they were supposed to stand to Ormuzd,) or those of their predecessors. Both names, Ahasuerus (i. q. Xerxes, see Ges. Thes. v. עֲחַשְׁוֵרוֹשׁ p. 75.) and Artaxerxes, were names of honor.

[6] I have adhered to the authoritative Chronology of the reigns of Xerxes and Artaxerxes. Diodorus (xi. 69.) says that Xerxes was murdered by Artabanus, after reigning more than 20 years, when Lysitheus was Archon at Athens. Ol. 78. 4. B.C. 465. "According to the Canon, he died N. E. 283, i. e. *after* Dec. 17. B.C. 466, and *before* Dec. 17. B.C. 465, which coincides with the year of Lysitheus." Clinton. (Fast. Hell. B. C. 465.) Eusebius agrees with this. Manetho also assigns the same length to the reign of Xerxes, 21 years, (quoted by Africanus ap. Syncell. p. 75. D. Clinton, F. H. c. 18. ii. 380. note.) This length of reign corresponds with the dates assigned to his father Darius, and to Artaxerxes, to whom 41 years are given by Manetho, (Ib.) 40 by Diodorus, (Ib. and xi. 69.) which agrees with Thucydides, (iv. 50.) who mentions his death in the Archonship of Stratocles B. C. 42$\frac{3}{4}$. (Clinton, p. 380.) The accession of Artaxerxes, after the 7 months of the assassin Artabanus, would fall in latter parts of 464, B.C.

The difficulties, raised by Krüger and insisted on by Hengstenberg, (Christol. iii. 167-179.) relate to Greek Chronology chiefly, in that Themistocles arrived at the court of Persia when Artaxerxes had recently come to the throne, (Thuc. i. 137.) and addressed his letter to him. (Ib.) But it is said that there are too few events to fill up the time from Platæa B. C. 479, to B. C. 465, and, specifically, that Themistocles, whose flight followed immediately on the death of Pausanias, passed by the Athenian fleet, while besieging Naxos. (Thuc. i. 137.) But, it is alleged, that Pausanias was so precipitate, that the discovery of his treasonable correspondence is not likely to have been delayed until B. C. 466, and that Diodorus places the victories of the Eurymedon, which were later than that of Naxos, B. C. 470. (xi. 60, 1.) But, first, as to Pausanias, although in the first instance, his conceit, at the prospect of Persian greatness, absurdly betrayed him, (Thuc. i. 130.) there is no reason that he should not have learned experience, after he had been twice sent for to Sparta for trial. (Thuc. i. 131. 133.) He must have had prolonged communications with Artabanus, since the suspicions of the bearer of the last letter were aroused by the fact that "no one of the messengers before him had returned," they having, in fact, been put to death at the request of Pausanias. At Sparta, moreover, where he was of course watched, greater precautions were absolutely necessary. He had betrayed himself, when at a distance, in Thrace, at Byzantium and Colonæ of Troy.

year of the same Artaxerxes, B.C. 444.   These would give,
as the close of the 490 years, respectively, the end of 46,
B.C. 29, B.C. 32, A.D. 46, A.D.

(Thuc. i. 130, 1.) Diodorus also (xi. 54, 5.) placed the ostracism of Themistocles, at the earliest, in the Archonship of Praxiergus ; (Ol. 77. 2. B.C. 47½) but
Pausanias did not open his plans to Themistocles until after this time, when Themistocles was in exile at Argos. (Plutarch, Them. c. 23.)   The sojourn also of
Themistocles at Argos was of long duration, since it is said, that " he had his
abode there, but *visited repeatedly*(ἐπιφοιτῶν) the rest of Peloponnesus." (Thuc.
i. 135.)   This agrees with the time ordinarily assigned to his flight, after that
the Lacedæmonians, upon the conviction and death of Pausanias, had demanded
that he should be brought to public trial, viz. 466, two years before the accession
of Artaxerxes B.C. 464.

The date of the siege of Naxos is proximately determined by the expedition
against Thasos which followed after the battle of Eurymedon, which itself
was subsequent to that of Naxos.   For the expedition against Thasos was simultaneous with the attempt to settle 10,000 Athenians and their allies at what
became Amphipolis ; (Thuc. i. 100.) but this attempt was 32 years after the
like destruction of those led by Aristagoras of Miletus. (Ib. iv. 102.)   But his
attempt was in the 3rd year of the Ionian war, B. C. 497. (See Clinton, F. H. A.
497. 465. and T. ii. p. 317. e. 9. Amphipolis.)   The revolt of Thasos then was
in 465, and the siege of Naxos may very probably have been in the preceding
year.   It is by an evident oversight, that Diodorus, having put together the
victories of Cimon, from Eion which was reduced at last by famine (Her. vii.
107.) to the victories at Eurymedon (as he had, just before, the history of Themistocles,) stated that they took place in one year. (xi. 63.)   Probably it was
the date only of the reduction of Scyros. (Grote, v. 410. note.)   The hints of
Thucydides and Herodotus suggest, (as Grote first pointed out,) a large series of
events between B. C. 477, the beginning of Athenian ascendency, and B. C.
465, ample to fill up the period ; viz. the reduction of fortresses held by the Persians ; the gradual change of the Athenian "headship" (hegemony) to "rule ;"
the decline of the Delian synod ; the change made, at the wish of the allies,
when tired of active service, from personal service to contributions in money
and, ultimately, to tribute ; implying also a period of naval and military service on the part of the Athenians, which obtained to them that ascendency.
Eion, Scyros, Carystos, Naxos were the scenes of events, which were but
specimens only of a large whole. (See Grote, Greece, c. 45 p. 390-415.)   Doriscus, when Herodotus wrote, had repeatedly been besieged, and as yet in vain.
(Her. vii. 106. Rawl. iv. 93. note 1.)

Further, Justin (iii. 1.) represents Artabanus, as unapprehensive about Artaxerxes, being "quite a boy" (puer admodum) and, on that ground, feigning that
Xerxes had been murdered by his other son Darius, who was a youth.   It is
said to be improbable, that Artaxerxes should be thus young, if his father had
reigned 21 years.   But Justin contradicts himself.   For, in the same place,
he speaks of Artaxerxes as " a youth," (adolescens) and ascribes to him the rapid counsel and the strength of one matured.   Artaxerxes, he says, on learning
the treason of Artabanus, ordered a review of the army the next day, in which

But further, of these four, two only are principal and leading decrees; that of Cyrus, and that in the *seventh* year of Artaxerxes Longimanus. For that of the 20th year of Artaxerxes is but an enlargement and renewal of his first decree; as the decree of Darius confirmed that of Cyrus. The decrees of Cyrus and Darius relate to the rebuilding of the temple; those of Artaxerxes to the condition of Judah and Jerusalem.

But the decree of Darius was no characteristic decree. It did but support them in doing, what they were already doing without it.

The decree of Artaxerxes was of a different character. The temple was now built. So the decree contains no grant for its building, like those of Cyrus[1] and Darius[2]. Ezra thanks God that "He had put it into the king's heart, to *beautify* (not, to *build*) the house of the Lord in Jerusalem." On the other hand, the special commission of Ezra, was [3] *to enquire concerning Judah and Jerusalem, according to the law of thy God, which is in thy heart, and to set magistrates and judges, which may judge all the people that are beyond the river.* These magistrates had power of life and death, banishment, confiscation, imprisonment, conferred upon them[4]. It looks as if the people were in a state of disorganisation. Ezra had full powers to settle it *according to the law of* his *God,* having absolute authority in ecclesiastical and civil matters. The little colony, which he took with him, of 1683 males (with women and

the skill which each had in arms should be tried; and when Artabanus came armed to it, he proposed to him to change his breastplate with him, (his own, he pretended, being too short,) and then, when he had taken it off, thrust him through with his sword, and had his sons apprehended.

These are the only weighty objections alleged. They have not made any impression on our English writers who have treated of Grecian history. I have considered them, out of respect to Hengstenberg, who attaches much weight to them, and so assumes as the terminus a quo B. C. 455, being, as he thinks, the 20th year of Artaxerxes, but, according to the usual Chronology, his 11th year. His era differs then only by 3 years from that which I have adopted, after Prideaux. (Connection, ii. 14 sqq.) It is also preferred by a Lap. ad loc. and, of older writers, by Aquinas in Dan. Opp. T. xviii. p. 37.

[1] The decree of Cyrus, as relates to the grant, is embodied in that of Darius. vi. 3-5.   [2] vii. 27.   [3] Ib. 14, 25.   [4] Ib. 26.

children, some 8400 souls) was itself a considerable addition to those who had before returned, and involved a rebuilding of Jerusalem. This rebuilding of the city and reorganisation of the polity, begun by Ezra and carried on and perfected by Nehemiah, corresponds with the words in Daniel, *From the going forth of a commandment to restore and to build Jerusalem.*

The term also corresponds. *Unto Messiah the Prince,* shall be *seven weeks and threescore and two weeks,* i. e. the first 483 years of the period, the last 7 being parted off. But 483 years from the month Nisan (March or April, as the year might be,) 458, B.C., in which Ezra had his own mission from Artaxerxes and began his journey[1], were completed at Nisan, 26, A.D. which (according to the ordinary belief that the Nativity was 4 years earlier than our era) would coincide with John's Baptism, soon after the beginning of which, the descent of the Holy Ghost upon our Lord at His Baptism manifested Him to be *the Anointed with the Holy Ghost*[2], *the Christ.*

Further still, the whole period of 70 weeks is divided into three successive periods, 7, 62, 1, and the last week is subdivided into two halves. It is self-evident that, since these parts 7, 62, 1, are equal to the whole, viz. 70, it was intended that they should be. Every writer wishes to be understood; the vision is announced at the beginning, as one which is, on thought, to be understood. [3] *I am come to give thee skill and understanding ; therefore understand the matter and consider the vision.* Yet, on this self-evident fact that the sum of the parts is intended to be the same as the whole, every attempt to explain the prophecy, so that it should end in Antiochus Epiphanes, or in any other than our Lord, (as we shall see,) shivers.

[1] " Upon the first day of the first month, began he to go up from Babylon." (Ezr. vii. 9.) The date " the 7th year of the king " is in v. 8. The Attic year beginning with Hecatombæon, nearly our July, the first year of Artaxerxes, which fell in the Archonship of Lysitheus, coincided with $46\frac{1}{4}$ B.C., the seventh year with $45\frac{2}{4}$, and, since the Jews retained the order of their months, even while they dated the years like their masters, *the first month in the 7th year* would fall in Nisan, i. e. the spring of 458, B.C. [2] Acts x. 38. [3] ix. 22, 23.

On the other hand, the subordinate periods, as well as the whole, fit in with the Christian interpretation. It were not of any account, if we could not interpret these minor details. "De minimis non curat lex." When the whole distance is spanned over, it matters not, whether we can make out some lesser details. Men believe that Mount Athos was severed, because they can trace here and there a portion of the canal. Science assumes, as certain, whatever is presupposed by what it knows already. But, in the prophecy of the 70 weeks, the portions also can be traced. The words are; *From the going forth of a commandment to restore and to build Jerusalem, unto Messiah the Prince,* shall be *seven weeks*[4] *and threescore and two weeks; street and wall*[5] *shall be restored and builded;*

---

[4] The Jews put the main stop of the verse under שִׁבְעָה, meaning to separate the two numbers, 7 and 62. This they must have done dishonestly, לְמַעַן הַמִּינִים (as Jarchi says in rejecting literal expositions which favoured the Christians) "on account of the heretics," i. e. Christians. For the later clause, so divided off, could only mean, "and *during threescore and two weeks* street and wall shall be being restored and builded," i. e. that Jerusalem should be 434 years in rebuilding, which would be senseless. Yet critics, who correct the text ad libitum, have all at once discovered in this case the value of the tradition of the Hebrew accents. Leng. p. 446. Hitz. p. 161.

[5] The construction of the E. V., *street and wall*, is the most natural, both in itself and in the context, since pairs of words are used in this prophecy; "on thy people and on thy holy city;" "to seal vision and prophet;" "to restore and to build;" "the city and the sanctuary;" "sacrifice and oblation." The Verss. also have so understood it. οἰκοδομηθήσεται εἰς πλάτος καὶ εἰς μῆκος, LXX. περίτειχος, Theod. Ald.; τεῖχος, Theod. Vat.; muri, Vulg.; "street," Syr.; σκάμμα, Gr. Ven. They may have had a traditional knowledge, that חָרוּץ, orig. "fosse," may have been used of any "fence." Else a "fosse" was not a "fence" actually used for Jerusalem; for the circuit of Jerusalem then lay along the brows of hills, so that there was no occasion for a fosse, the declivity of the hill being more than any fosse. Nor is there any trace of a fosse around any part of the then Jerusalem. Nor is there any extant instance, in which חָרוּץ or חֲרִיץ is used even of a "fosse." חֲרִיץ in Targ. Job xxxviii. 25. corresponds to תְּעָלָה "watercourse;" and in the Baba kama c. 5. is said to be used of a ditch, broad below, narrow above; (Buxt. Lex. col. 833.) In other instances, in Abulvalid and Kimchi, it is used of a narrow incision. But the word חָרוּץ etymologically signifies, "a thing cut," and may, in the living language, have been used by a metaphor, analogous to בָּצַר, "cut, cut off, inaccessible." The meaning, "watercourse," would itself also have a good sense, "street and watercourse," since the supplies of water so provided were so essential to the well-being of

*and in strait of times.   And after threescore and two weeks
shall Messiah be cut off.*

Obviously, unless there had been a meaning in this division, it would have stood, " shall be *threescore and nine
weeks,*" " not, shall be *seven weeks, and threescore and two
weeks.*"   For every word in this condensed prophecy has
its place and meaning, and the division would be unmeaning, unless something were assigned to this first portion.
The text does assign it.   It says, *the street shall be restored and be builded ; and that, in troublous times.*

The books of Ezra and Nehemiah give the explanation.
Ezra came to Jerusalem, B. C. 458; he laboured in restoring the Jewish polity, within and without, for 13 years
before Nehemiah was sent by Artaxerxes, B.C. 445[1].   Nehemiah, as *governor,* laboured together with Ezra for 12
years, *from the twentieth year* even *unto the two and thirtieth year of Artaxerxes the king, twelve years*[2].   Then
he returned to the king, and after an undefined time, *at
the end of days*[3], he says, *obtained I leave of the king, and
came to Jerusalem.*   The interval probably was not short;
for there had been time for corruptions to creep in, nor
is the king likely to have sent him back soon; else why
should he have returned at all?   The mention of Eliashib's son, Joiada, being high priest then, in place of
his deceased father[4], fixes this second visit probably in
the reign of Darius Nothus, in whose 11th year Eliashib
is said to have died[5].   The expulsion of one of his sons
who had become son-in law to Sanballat, and regulation
of the wards of the priests and Levites, are among the last
acts of reform which Nehemiah mentions in his second vi-

the city and to its defence against an enemy. Still this would involve the use
of an uncommon word in the place and meaning of a common word.

   2. In support of another rendering, *and* the *street shall be built, yea, it is
determined ; and in straitness of times,* is the use of חֲרוּצָה 27. נֶחֱרָצָה 26. and of
חָרוּץ Is. x. 22. explained נֶחֱרָצָה Ib. 23. Probably הֻצַּב Nah. ii. 8. is used with a like
parenthesis; see ib.   But, against it, is the unlikelihood, that words, so naturally conjoined, should be altogether severed.

[1] Neh. ii. 1.   [2] Ib. v. 14.   [3] Ib. xiii. 6.
[4] Neh. xiii. 28. comp. xii. 10, 22.   [5] Chron. Alex. Olymp. 78. p. 162,3.

sit; with them he closes his book. Now from the seventh year of Artaxerxes to the eleventh of Darius Nothus are 45 years. But it was in the period of the high priesthood of Joiada, not precisely in the very first year, that this reform took place. We have any how for the period of the two great restorers of the Jewish polity, Ezra and Nehemiah conjointly, a time somewhat exceeding 45 years; so that we know that the restoration was completed in the latter part of the 7th week of years, and it is probable that it was not closed until the end of it [6]. In regard to *the strait of times*, amid which this restoration was to take place, the books of Ezra and Nehemiah are the commentary. Up to the completion of the walls, there was one succession of vexations on the part of the enemies of the Jews. Their abiding condition they confess in both periods to God; [7] *for our iniquities we have been delivered into the hands of the kings of the lands, to the sword, to captivity, to a spoil, and to confusion of face, as at this day. And now for a little space grace hath been shewed from the Lord, to leave us a remnant to escape—to give us a little reviving in our bondage. For bondsmen are we, and in our bondage our God hath not forsaken us.* In Nehemiah's time, the great public confession of sin closes with the same statement; [8] *Behold we are bondsmen this day, and the land which Thou gavest to our fathers, to eat the fruit thereof and the good thereof, behold, we are bondsmen in it; and it yieldeth much increase unto the kings which Thou hast set over us, because of our sins; and over our bodies they have dominion, and over our cattle at their pleasure, and in great distress are we.*

The next division, 62 weeks, completes the period up to the time of the Messiah. Its two extreme points were marked, its beginning by the close of the 7 weeks or 49 years, its end by the Coming of the long-longed for, the

---

[6] This explanation of the 7 weeks is brought out by Prideaux, Connection, P. 1. B. 5. p. 47-50. and 17 sqq. Even Winer, Real-Lex. v. Nehemiah, admits that he is probably right as to the date of Darius Ochus, the 45 years.

[7] Ezr. ix. 7-9. [8] Neh. ix. 36, 7.

Christ.   It is in harmony with the other prophecies of Daniel, that what is filled up in one place, is bridged over in another.   In the vision of the 4 Empires, the 2nd and 3rd are but slightly touched on; the brief notice is expanded in the viith and xith chapters.   Other prophecies had, as their foreground, the events of world-empires.   The subject of this was the people of God and the Messiah.

The ever-recurring character of prophecy is thus apparent here also, that those two points, which concerned them most, are the most prominent;— the restoration of the polity in the nearer future, and, in the distant future, the crowning acts of God's mercy and judgment, the blessings in Christ and the close of the temporal relation of God to His people.   The intervening period would have occupied a disproportioned place here, and so is omitted.

Not *in*, but *after* those *threescore and two weeks*, it is said, *Messiah shall be cut off; and there shall not be to Him*, i. e. as the context implies, the city and the sanctuary shall be His no more.   Then follows the subdivision of the last week, or seven years, wherein He was to be cut off, since He *was* to be cut off, and yet not in the 69 weeks. *He shall make firm a covenant with many during one week; and in the midst of the week He shall make sacrifice and oblation to cease.*   He speaks not of a temporary suspension of sacrifices, but of the entire abolition of all which had been offered hitherto, *the sacrifice*[1], with the shedding of blood, and *the oblation*[2], the unbloody sacrifice which was its complement.   These the Messiah was *to make to cease three years and a half* after that new covenant began, whether this was at first through the ministry of the Baptist or His own.   It seems to me absolutely certain, that our Lord's ministry lasted for some period above three years.   For S. John mentions by name three Passovers[3]; and S. Matthew's mention of the disciples rubbing the ears of corn[4] relates to a time near upon a Passover, later

---

[1] זֶבַח   [2] מִנְחָה.   [3] ii. 13. vi. 4. and the last.   [4] S. Matt. xii. 1 sqq.

than the first, (for John had been cast into prison[5],) yet earlier than the last but one, for it preceded the feeding of the 5000, which itself preceded that Passover[6]. This bears out the opinion, which is in itself nearly certain, that the intermediate feast, mentioned by S. John, is the Passover[7]. Our Lord's parable of the fig-tree virtually asserts, that a period of some three years of special culture of God's people had preceded. [8]*Behold, these three years I come seeking fruit on this figtree and find none;* and that one year remained, *let it alone this year also.* The cursing of the barren fig-tree and its instant withering[9], just before His Passion and the final pronunciation of its sentence[10], seems to be the symbolical declaration, that that year of respite was over, and its doom was fixed.

The city was devoted, the punishment irreversible; the

[5] Ib. xi. 2.   [6] Ib. xiv. 15. S. John vi. 4-10. Süsskind brought out the argument, (in Bengel's Archiv. i. 186-194.) and observed that, even if the corn were ripe before the Passover, it would not have been ripe some weeks before it, yet the history in S. Matt. xii. must have been, at least, some weeks before that in S. Matt. xiv. which was itself before the Passover.

[7] The feast, S. John v. 1., must have been one of the three great feasts, 1) because of the addition, *and Jesus went up to Jerusalem,* i. e. He went up in consequence of that feast. 2) No other feast is called "*a feast of the Jews,*" i. e. one binding upon all. The dedication-feast and the feast of Purim were not of obligation, and the feast of Purim was kept any where. (Jos. Ant. xi. 6. end.) 3) The first Passover had been spoken of, a few verses before, as *the feast.* (iv. 45. twice.) Had a different feast been intended, it would have been specified. 4) The Passover alone is spoken of in the Gospels as *the feast.* (S. Matt. xxvi. 5. xxvii. 15. S. Mark xv. 6. S. Luke ii. 42. xxiii. 17. S. John above.) The feast of Tabernacles is named, S. John vii. 2. "Since the Jews held the Pascha to be the special and first feast, the Evang. at times defines it further, *the Pascha, the feast of the Jews, was nigh;* at times not, *there was Pascha, feast of the Jews.*" Chron. P. p. 406. S. Irenæus adds *the Pascha* ii. 22, 3. Cod. Sinait. has the art. 5) The events in S. John ii. 23-iv. 54. require more space than from Pascha to the feast of Tabernacles. 6) The words, *there are yet 4 months and then cometh harvest,* (S. John iv. 35.) imply that the next feast was Pascha. The assumption, that *the feast,* S. John v. 1., was the feast of Purim, has nothing in its favour, and is excluded by Süsskind's argument (n. 6.) and by grounds 1, 2, 3, 5. Hengst. notices in addition, (from Reland, Antiq. iv. 9. and Schickard, De Festo Purim, Crit. Sacr. iii. p. 1185.) that the feast of Purim was celebrated in such sort, that our Lord would not have been present at it, and that it was not held on the Sabbath, whereas the festival, S. John v., included the Sabbath.

[8] S. Luke xiii. 7.   [9] S. Matt. xxi. 19.   [10] Ib. xxiii. 34-39.

Messiah's office would be, not with the people as a whole, but with *the many* who would be saved out of it, with whom the new covenant would be confirmed. The remaining 3½ years probably mark the time, during which the Gospel was preached to the Jews, before the preaching to the Samaritans shewed that the special privilege of the Jews were at an end, and that the Gospel embraced the world. We have not the chronological data to fix it.

But the fact of these several periods being prophesied, and the last, above six hundred years before, is the body not the soul of the prophecy; it is not that which bears chief evidence of its divinity.

Human history recurs in cycles. [1] *The thing that hath been, it is that which shall be; and that which is done is that which shall be done; and there is no new thing under the sun.* Empires fall or rise gradually; so the prediction of the fall or rise of an empire within such latitude might have left the fulfilment uncertain. The main subject of Daniel's prediction is single and alone in time, and reaches on through eternity. From eternity to eternity there hath not been nor shall be its like. Men may dispute whether it hath been; they cannot dispute that, for 1800 years, what Daniel predicted has been believed to have been. The conception remains the same, even antecedent to our conviction of its truth. That then, which was foretold to Daniel, in answer to his confession of his own sins and of the sins of his people, of their iniquities and transgressions, and to his prayer for pardon, was a promise of absolute forgiveness of sins. *Seventy seven-times are determined upon thy people and upon thy holy city, to close* [2] *the transgression, and to seal up sins, and to make* [3] *reconci-*

---

[1] Eccl. i. 9. [2] The meaning of לְכַלֵּא is clear from the context, whether it be derived from כָּלָא (i. q. κλείω and κωλύω) "shut, hinder," then, "close;" or i. q. כָּלָה 1) "complete;" 2) "finish," bring to an end. כָּלָא does not indeed occur elsewhere in Piel, but that is no reason why it should not.

[3] כִּפֶּר, when God is the subject, signifies "forgive;" when man, it is the "atoning for," "making the typical propitiation for sin;" covering it by mak-

liation for iniquity. Sin was to be done away, hid out of sight, forgiven. The words, which Daniel had so often repeated in his deep intercessory prayer, *sins, iniquity, transgression,* the thought of which lay so heavy upon him, are now repeated to him in mercy, to assure him the more emphatically through that threefold repetition, that God would put them away as if they had not been. But the mere removal of sin is imperfect. The threefold complement is added; *to bring in everlasting righteousness, and to seal up vision and prophecy, and to anoint a Holy of of holies.* These were to be gifts of God at the close of that 70th week; to be given, as they had never been given before, and the righteousness, so given, to last on to eternity. The very delay is a token of its greatness. God's gifts are with usury. It was no common forgiveness of sins, the publication of which was to be delayed, according to the letter of the prophecy, at least half a thousand years. They were not the past sins of his people, such as had brought upon them the captivity. The words are quite in the abstract, *transgression, sins, iniquity.* The fulfilment would have fallen short of the prophecy, unless, not *their* sins only but, sin in the abstract had been remitted. They were not only to be remitted; they were to be replaced. Hitherto there had been continual sacrifice for sin, a symbolical remission of all sins on the Day of Atonement, wonderful for its completeness as a picture, but incomplete; even because that wonderful picture was, year by year, renewed. Hitherto, there had been many atonements for man's several sins. God here speaks of one act, atoning not for particular sins, but for *sin.* Once, in the future, at the end of the 70 weeks, there should be an atoning for all iniquity, i. e. for all of it, past, present, or to come. *Then,* all sin was to be atoned for, and He Who ended and forgave it, was to *bring in everlasting righteousness. Bring in !* Then, it was to dwell, to make its abode, to have its home, there. *Everlasting !* Then it

ing that offering, for the sake of which it is covered, or put out of God's sight. The context implies, that it would be one act, which should so atone.

was never to be removed, never worn out, never to cease, not to pass with this passing world, but to abide thenceforth, coeternal with God, its Author and Giver.   Righteousness had been promised before, as the gift of the times of the Messiah.   It is what man, being made for God, yearned and yearns for.   [1]*I bring near My righteousness, it shall not be far off; and My salvation shall not tarry; and I will place salvation in Zion for Israel My glory.   [2]My righteousness is near.   Lift up your eyes to the heavens and look upon the earth beneath; for the heavens shall vanish away like smoke, and the earth shall wax old like a garment, and they that dwell therein shall die in like manner; but My salvation shall be for ever, and My righteousness shall not be abolished.   My righteousness shall be for ever, and My salvation from generation to generation.* It was the close of that great prophecy of our Lord's atoning Death; [3]*My righteous servant shall make many righteous.*   Jeremiah had foretold, that God would *raise unto David a Righteous branch,* and that *the name whereby He shall be called* should be, *The Lord our Righteousness.*   Daniel foretells the same; his prophecy joins on with theirs in substance; but he, first, adds the time of its fulfilment.

And in that fulfilment, all prophecy was to be fulfilled. All hitherto had been a longing for that hour.   That hour come, God set His seal upon *vision and prophet.*   Their first office was fulfilled.   To *seal up vision and prophet,* is not, to seal up any one vision or prophet.   The words are purposely placed undefined, in order to mark that they are to be understood without any limitation, not of any one vision or prophet, but of *vision* [4] *and prophet* generally.   As our Lord said, [5]*All the prophets and the law prophesied until John.*   It is all one, whether by the word, *seal,* we understand, *set His seal to,* " accredited," as our Lord speaks, [6]*Him hath God the Father sealed;* or "com-

---

[1] Is. xlvi. 13.   [2] Ib. li. 5, 6, 8. add xlv. 17.   [3] Is. liii. 11. צַדִּיק עַבְדִּי לָרַבִּים יַצְדִּיק,
[4] חָזוֹן is used collectively Is. i. 1. 2 Chr. xxxii. 32.   So both חָזוֹן and חֲזוּת
2 Chr. ix. 21. Kleinert, Aechtheit Ies. p. 11.   [5] S. Matt. xi. 13.
[6] S. John vi. 27.   So of man's corresponding act in believing, Ib. liii. 33. *he*

pleted[7]." Daniel says before, what S. Peter said near 600 years after, when the events came to pass; [8] *those things which God before had shewed by the mouth of all His prophets, that Christ should suffer, He hath so fulfilled.* The remaining clause, *and to anoint an All-holy*, must be spiritual, since all else is spiritual. It cannot be spoken of the natural " holy of holies," which, in contrast to *the holy place*, is always " *the* holy of holies[9];" never "holy of holies." Still less is it the material temple, as a whole, since the temple, as a whole, is never called by the name of a part of it. " Holy of holies," lit. " holiness of holinesses," i. e. All-holiness, is a ritual term, used to express the exceeding holiness, which things acquire by being consecrated to God. It is never used to describe a place, but is always an attribute of the thing, and, in one place, of

that hath received His testimony, has set to his seal, (ἐσφράγισεν) that God is true.   [7] חתם, "sealed," receives its nearer definitions from the object with which a thing is sealed. It is determined by the context. A thing was sealed in a purse, to be retained, Job xiv. 17; a deed, covenant, letter was sealed, to be authenticated, Jer. xxxii. 10, 11, 44. Neh. x. 1, 2. 1 Kings xxi. 8. So in its metaph. use, God is said to *seal the stars*, c. בעד, as it were, "sealed them up," withholding them from shining, Job ix. 7; to *seal the hand of man*, c. ב, hindering him from using it, Job xxxvii. 7; He *sealeth up their* (man's) *instruction*, c. ב, i. e. impresseth it on him, Ib. xxxiii. 16. So here *sin* is " *sealed* up " to be put out of sight, seen no more; *vision and prophecy* are *sealed*, i. e. authenticated. The use of the word, although different in the two clauses, is not ambiguous, being, in each case, ruled by the context. So further Pineda on Job xxxvii. 7.

[8] Acts iii. 18. "What is this which he says, to seal up vision and prophecy? That all prophets announced of Him, that He was to come, and had to suffer. Since then prophecy was fulfilled by His Coming, therefore he said, that vision and prophecy were sealed, because He is the seal of all the prophets, filling up all things which the prophets heretofore announced of Him. For after the Coming of Christ and His Passion, there is no more vision or prophet to announce that Christ should come." Tert. adv. Jud. c. 8. p. 215. Rig.

[9] קדשׁ קדשׁים is used 13 times of " the holy of holies," (Ex. xxvi. 33, 34. Num. iv. 4, 19. 1 Kings vi. 16. vii. 50. viii. 6. 1 Chr. vi. 34. (49. Eng.) 2 Chr. iii. 8, 10. iv. 22. v. 7. Ezek. xli. 4.) and these with one exception (1 Chr. vi. 34.) occurring in the first directions about it, in the law or the building of the temple or Ezekiel's symbolical temple. It is used also in one place of "the holy place," as being relatively the holiest place for that purpose, the consuming of the sacrifice. Num. xviii. 10. " The holy of holies " is even oftener spoken of under another name, דביר (16 times.)

the person, who is spoken of. [1]*It is most holy.* [2]*Aaron was separated, to hallow him all-holy.* The destruction of the temple, as having been previously profaned, is the close of this prophecy[3]. The prophecy promised *an All-holy*, which should be anointed, for *the holy place* which should be destroyed; as our Lord speaks of [4]*the temple of His Body.* At His Birth He was announced as, [5]*the Holy Thing which shall be born of thee.* *The Holy One*[6] became *His* title, Who Alone was without sin. The devils knew him, as *the Holy One of God*[7].

Anointing was the well-known symbol of sanctity through the Spirit of God. *The Lord hath anointed thee,* Samuel said[8] to Saul, *captain over His inheritance;* and then, *the Spirit of the Lord will come upon thee, and thou shalt prophesy and shalt be turned into another man.* When Saul had forfeited the gift, Samuel, at God's command, anointed David, [9]*and the Spirit of the Lord came upon David from that day forward.* The "holy oil" had probably long been lost. Any how, it was among the things which the Jews missed in the 2nd temple. Material anointing had ceased. But anointing had entered into the symbolic language of prophecy in respect to the Christ. [10]*The Spirit of the Lord God is upon Me; because the Lord hath anointed Me, to preach good tidings unto the meek. He hath sent Me to bind up the broken-hearted, to proclaim liberty to the captives, and to those that are bound, a great deliverance*[11], *to proclaim the acceptable year of the Lord:* and, [12]*Thou lovest righteousness and hatest iniquity; therefore God, thy God, hath anointed thee with the oil of gladness above thy fellows.*

This symbolical meaning of the anointing is fixed by the next words of the prophecy; *unto Messiah the Prince.*

---

[1] Ex. xxx. 10, 29, 36. Lev. ii. 3, 10. vi. 10, 18, 22. [17, 25, 29. Eng.] vii. 1, 6. x. 12, 17. xiv. 13. xxiv. 9. xxvii. 28. Ezek. xliii. 12. It is used in apposition to the thing spoken of, Ex. xxix. 37. xl. 10. Ezek. xlv. 3.

[2] 1 Chr. xxiii. 13.   [3] ix. 26, 27.   [4] S. John ii. 19, 21.

[5] S. Luke i. 35. τὸ ἅγιον.   [6] Acts iii. 14. iv. 27, 30. 1 S. John ii. 20. add S. John x. 36. xvii. 19.   [7] S. Mark i. 24. S. Luke iv. 34.   [8] 1 Sam. x. 1. 6.

[9] Ib. xvi. 13.   [10] Is. lxi. 1, 2.   [11] פְּקַח־קוֹחַ, intensive.   [12] Ps. xlv. 7.

The word is repeated. The last of the six blessings was,
to anoint an All-holy; "limshoach kodesh kodashim."
He resumes at once, "unto one Anointed, a Prince." "'ad
Mashiach nagid." No one, wishing to be understood,
would unite so closely words, relating to the same period of time, the end of the 70 weeks, had they not related
to the same object; " to *anoint* an All-holy;" "unto one
Anointed." The words probably fixed the use of the name
Messiah or *the Messiah, Christ* or *the Christ,* as that of
the long-expected Redeemer. In the time of our Lord,
the Name was in the mouth of all, Samaritans as well as
Jews, *the Messiah; Messiah.* *When Messiah cometh*[13], said
the Samaritan woman. *We have found the Messias*[14], was
S. Andrew's announcement to his brother Simon. *Where
Christ should be born*[15], was Herod's enquiry of the Chief
Priests and Scribes. The revelation to Simeon was, *that
he should not see death, until he had seen the Lord's Christ*[16].
The angels so announced His birth to the shepherds,
[17] *Unto you is born in the city of David a Saviour, which
is Christ the Lord.* [18] *All men mused of John, whether he
were the Christ or not.* In answer to the formal deputa-
tion of priests and Levites, [19] *he confessed and denied not,
but confessed, I am not the Christ.* Unbelieving Jews said
to our Lord, [20] *how long holdest Thou us in suspense? If
Thou be the Christ, tell us plainly.* Caiaphas adjured Him
to say[21], whether He were *the Christ, the Son of God.* The
people, impressed by Him, ask [22], *Do the rulers indeed
know that this is the very Christ?* The name was not taught
them by our Lord; they knew it already. It is the Christianity of prophecy, existing, so far, in the minds of the
people, before it was revealed in act. Although, moreover,
the name Messiah occurs absolutely here only in Holy
Scripture —not (as it is every where else [23]) " the Anointed

[13] S. John iv. 25. Μεσσίας as a proper name, without the Article, represented
by the Greek Χριστός.　　　　[14] Ib. i. 41. τὸν Μεσσίαν i. q. τὸν Χριστόν.
　　　　[15] S. Matt. ii. 4.　　[16] S. Luke ii. 26.　　[17] Ib. 11.
　[18] Ib. iii. 15.　　　　[19] S. John i. 20. iii. 28.　　　　[20] Ib. x. 24.
　[21] S. Matt. xxvi. 63. S. Mark xiv. 61. S. Luke xxii. 67.　　[22] S. John vii. 26.
　[23] מְשִׁיחַ יְהוָה occurs 11 times; מְשִׁיחוֹ 10 times; מְשִׁיחָ 6 times; מְשִׁיחַ אֱלֹהֵי יַעֲקֹב

of the Lord," " *Thy* Anointed," " *His* Anointed," " the
Anointed *of the God of Jacob*," or " *the* anointed *priest*,"—
but, as a proper name, *Messiah*, " Anointed," they knew
that He, so spoken of, was the same Whom other Scriptures taught them to look for. They knew, (we learn it
from their own mouths in the Gospel,) where He was to be
born [1], that He was to be of the seed of David [2], that He was
to work miracles [3], that He was to abide for ever [4]; that
He was so to come from God, that *no one* should *know
whence He cometh* [5], that He was to be *the Saviour of the
world* [6]. The contemporary paraphrase of Jonathan used
the name Messiah in explaining 26 passages of the prophets of Him [7]; 17 of them, signal prophecies [8], such as all
Christians have been wont so to interpret, and 9 less obvious [9]. His paraphrase having been, in some measure, tra-
ditionary, the learned Jews before him must have so interpreted Daniel: for from him alone could they have
had the name. Onkelos, a little later, adds two more from
the Pentateuch [10].

Of this Messiah the prophecy goes on to say, *And after
the sixty and two weeks Messiah shall be cut off, and there
shall not be to Him.* What this shall be, which shall be
no more His, is to be supplied from the context, "what
hitherto was His," viz. His people [11], whose *Prince* He

---

[2] Sam. xxiii. 1. In all, 28 times; מָשִׁיחַ הַכֹּהֵן four times, in Leviticus only, Lev.
iv. 3, 5, 16. vi. 22. These are all, except in Daniel. [1] S. Matt. ii. 4-6.
S. John vii. 41, 2. [2] S. John vii. 42. S. Matt. xxii. 42, &c.
[3] S. John vii. 31. [4] Ib. xii. 34. [5] Ib. vii. 27. [6] iv. 42.
[7] They are in Buxtorf, Lex. Chald. col. 1270-2. [8] Is. iv. 2. ix. 6.
xi. 1-6. xvi. 5. xlii. 1. xliii. 10. lii. 13. liii. 10. Jer. xxiii. 5. xxx. 21. xxxiii. 15.
Hos. iii. 5. Mic. iv. 8. v. 2. Zech. iii. 8. vi. 12. besides 2 Sam. xxiii. 3.
[9] Is. x. 27. xv. 2. xvi. 1. xxviii. 5. Jer. xxxiii. 13. Hos. xiv. 8. [7 Eng.] Mic.
v. 1. Zech. iv. 7. x. 4. besides 1 Sam. ii. 10. [10] Gen. xlix. 10. Num. xxiv. 17.
[11] Vulg. "et non erit ejus populus, qui eum negaturus est." Aq. Symm. Syr.
leave it unexplained. (" and there is not to Him," Syr. Aq. οὐκ ὑπάρξει αὐτῷ.
Symm.) Theod. adds κρῖμα οὐκ ἔστιν ἐν αὐτῷ, "matter for judgment is not in
Him." LXX. καὶ οὐκ ἔσται, "and shall not be." אַיִן always includes the substantive verb, "there is not," "there was not," and is the opposite to יֵשׁ and equivalent to יֵשׁ לֹא (Arab. *laisa*, Aram. *laith*) not to לֹא alone. This excludes the Eng.
Vers. *and not for himself*, which must have been לֹא לוֹ. Other renderings, excluded by the meaning of אַיִן, are; 1) *he is not*, (which must have been אֵינֶנּוּ)

heretofore was. The Jews, as a nation, cut themselves off,
when they crucified Him. But, whatever be the precise
explanation of that clause, there is no question as to the
declaration, *Messiah shall be cut off.* The word, *shall be
cut off*, never means anything but excision; death directly inflicted by God, or violent death at the hands of man.
It is never used of mere death, nor to express sudden but
natural death. In the Pentateuch, the word is used of
God's covenant, *he, they, shall be cut off from his, their
people*[12], *from the congregation*[13], *of Israel*[14], which God
explains by His words[15], *I will cut him off from among
his people.* After the Pentateuch, it is more frequently
used absolutely, as in Daniel, *shall be cut off;* and, when
used of national inflictions, it is employed of destruction
of which man was the instrument[16]. Here it obviously
expresses precisely the same which Isaiah had said by an
equivalent word, [17]*He was cut off out of the land of the
living.* Neologist interpreters do not hesitate to admit

2) *he hath nought*, (אין is not "*nought*" but "*is not;*") 3) *he hath none*, (אין is
not" *none.*") But the object to be supplied must be gathered from the context.
Hence it cannot be, 4) " He (Alexander) " shall not have a successor." Bertholdt. 5) "He (Seleucus Philopator) shall not have a son and heir." Rösch,
Ewald. (Seleucus had moreover a son, Demetrius, who succeeded Antiochus Epiphanes.) Nor 6) " *an anointed* (Sel. Ph.) *shall be cut off, and he* shall have *no*
anointed to succeed him ; " in which way " the anointed " is to be both the subject of the original sentence and the person spoken of in relation to that first person. (Maurer.) Such interpretations would soon cease, if people would " interpret Scripture like any other book." (Ess. and Rev. p. 77.) No one, in any
other book, could explain the words, "a king shall be cut off, and to him there
shall not be"—" a king to succeed him." There remains, only, to supply, "and
it (the people) shall have no Messiah more," (Steudel) which, though true, cannot be the meaning here; for the people had nowhere been a subject or object of any previous sentence, and so many substantives had intervened between
this verse and the mention of "thy people and thy holy city," v. 24. One
would even correct אין, owning thereby, that אין לו cannot have its meaning.
[12] Gen. xvii. 14. Ex. xxx. 33, 38. xxxi. 14. Lev. vii. 20, 21, 25, 27. xvii. 4,
9. xviii. 29. xix. 8. xx. 18. xxiii. 29. Num. ix. 13. xv. 30.   [13] Num. xix. 20.
[14] Ex. xii. 19. "from Israel," Ex. xii. 15. Num. xix. 13 ; "from My presence,"
Lev. xxii. 3.   [15] Lev. xvii. 10. xx. 3, 5, 6.
[16] In the Pentateuch three times (Lev. xvii. 14. xx. 17. Num. xv. 31.) else,
Ps. xxxvii. 9, 22, 34. Prov. ii. 22. Is. xxix. 20. Hos. viii. 4. Ob. 10. Mic. v. 8.
[9. Eng.] Nah. ii. 1. [i. 15. Eng.] Zeph. i. 11. Zech. xiii. 8. by the flood, Gen.
ix. 11.   [17] נגזר Is. liii. 8.

this [1], if they can but find out any personage for their theory, who did die a violent death.

The entire cessation of the bloody sacrifices of the law has a twofold aspect, of mercy and of judgment. To those who have believed in Jesus, He *caused the sacrifice and oblation* of the law *to cease,* by re-placing the shadows, which pourtrayed His Atoning Sacrifice, by Himself the Substance, [2] *offering Himself once for all,* [3] *to put away sin by the sacrifice of Himself.* To the Jews who rejected Him, He *caused sacrifice and oblation to cease,* by the destruction of the temple and city, and the dispersion of the people.

On this, the Death of the Messiah, follows the sentence of that utter destruction of the city and temple. The meaning of the prophecy is not, in the least, affected by any variation in rendering or interpreting single words. It is far too broad and explicit.

And the city and the sanctuary the people of a prince who shall come, shall destroy ; and the end thereof shall be with that flood ; and unto the end, war [4]*, and desolatenesses* [5] *decreed.* And after the prophecy of the cessation of sa-

---

[1] So Bleek, Maurer, Lengerke, Ewald, who would have "the Anointed" to be Seleucus IV. Philopator, whose reign was marked by no one event ; Eichhorn, Wieseler, Hitzig, who would make it the aged deposed high-priest Onias III. whose murder had no other public effect than the punishment of the governor who murdered him. (2 Macc. iv. 34-36.) Even Rosenmüller, who would have the Anointed to be Alexander, rendered rightly " exscindetur." Only Bertholdt, with his wonted carelessness, says " Here, as in countless other places, (!) it stands only as a poetic word for מות 'die,' and indicates a rapid and unexpected death." Gesenius followed him in rendering ambiguously "shall perish," contrary to the meaning which he assigns to the word in every other place.   [2] Heb. vii. 27.   [3] Ib. ix. 26, 28.

[4] It can hardly be, *unto the end of the war, desolations are determined,* as in the E. V. For the end of the war was the beginning, not the end, of the desolations. It would also be a tautology. קץ also (Dan. xi. 27.) עת קץ (viii. 17. xi. 35. 40. xii. 4.) מועד קץ (viii. 19.) are terms used by Daniel to designate the close of a period appointed by God. מלחמה has also no article, as בשטף has, referring to " the flood " of war just spoken of, and as it, too, probably would have had, had Daniel meant, *the* war.

[5] שוממות is not an abstract, *desolationes,* but a passive, *loca desolata,* as just before, v. 18. and Is. xlix. 19. lxi. 4. [all.]

crifice ; *and upon the pinnacle of abominations a desolater*[6], *and that, until decreed desolation be outpoured upon the desolated.* The rendering, " upon the pinnacle are the abominations which desolate[6]," comes to the same meaning. In both ways, the temple is the place intended ; in both ways, the cause of the desolation is the same ; in both, the desolation is certain, either described as actually come, or as involved in the purpose of the Divine retribution, in that the abominations which should cause the desolation are there. [7]*Wheresoever the carcase is, thither will the ea-*

---

[6] Gesenius allows (Thes. p. 698.) that the words " ought to be so rendered according to the masorethic points *and* the lawful syntax," but corrects, עַל כְּנַף and translates שִׁקֻּצִים מְשֹׁמֵם, as if it were שֶׁקֶץ מְשֹׁמֵם (citing מַיִם לַחַץ Is. xxx. 20.) and renders, " and on the pinnacle are the abominations of the desolater." He agrees then in the meaning of all the several words, and alters the construction only. He adopts the construction of the LXX. and Theod. καὶ ἐπὶ τὸ ἱερὸν βδέλυγμα τῆς ἐρημώσεως. The analogy of S. Matt. iv. 5. S. Luke iv. 9. τὸ πτερύγιον τοῦ ἱεροῦ, goes far to shew that כָּנָף (orig. " wing ") might have the same meaning as the Greek, i. e. pinnacle. The temple being, in part, the subject of the prophecy, the word " pinnacle " might the more readily mean " *its* pinnacle." Still, if שִׁקֻּצִים מְשֹׁמֵם are united, they must stand in a sort of apposition, " abominations (which are) a desolater," as מַיִם לַחַץ are " waters " (which are, involve,) " affliction." They cannot stand in the relation of the thing caused and its cause, " abominations of (brought by) a desolater." In the phrase מַיִם לַחַץ an abstract noun is added as a sort of adjective, " waters, affliction ;" the phrase שִׁקֻּצִים מְשֹׁמֵם would, according to this analogy, signify as above, " abominations, a desolate-maker ;" i. e. which make desolate. As to the renderings, " wings:" i. e. army, " wing of the temple," כְּנָפַיִם alone means " wings." The substitution of the meaning, " surface of the altar," (Rösch) only illustrates the abuse of so-called Hebrew criticism to rationalist prejudice. כָּנָף might, with equal truth, be said to mean anything else under the sun. Lengerke adopts the construction given above, " and upon the pinnacle of abominations a desolater," but he would have it mean, " a desolater shall come upon a pinnacle, which shall not, when he comes, be a pinnacle of abominations, but which he shall make so," (contrary to all language.) In the words, " upon a pinnacle of abominations a desolater," the " pinnacle of abominations " must, according to all language, express the previous condition. The word, " abomination," must express the moral ground, why, in God's Providence, he came. We should so interpret the like words in any language, " Against the *accursed* race The Avenger came," " upon the *degraded* crew came a destroyer." It would simply not be true, that he " came upon a pinnacle of abominations," if it were not such when he came. The temple was, by God's appointment, " His holy house ; " men " made it a den of thieves." Only desecration from within could make it " a pinnacle of abominations."   [7] S. Matt. xxiv. 28.

gles be gathered together. If, again, the last words be rendered, as in the English margin, "even until decreed desolation shall be poured upon the desola*ter*," (although I think it less probable [1],) it would but carry on the prophecy like those words of our Lord, [2]*Jerusalem shall be trodden down of the Gentiles, until the times of the Gentiles shall be fulfilled.*

Apart from these lesser details of prophecy, the central unmistakeable prophecy lies in the connection of the destruction of the temple and city with their great sin, the cutting off of the Christ. The connection is, not of time, but of cause and effect. Some forty years were allowed, in which individuals might *save*[3] themselves *from* that *untoward generation.* But the doom of the whole was fixed. They had pronounced upon themselves their sentence [4]; *We have no king but Cæsar.* Our Lord, in that tender mourning over Jerusalem, pronounced that its day was past. [5]*If thou hadst known, at least in this thy day, the things which belong unto thy peace, but now they are hid from thine eyes. For the days come upon thee, that thine enemies shall cast a trench about thee, and compass thee round, and keep thee in on every side, and shall lay thee even with the ground and thy children within thee, and they shall not leave in thee one stone upon another, because thou knewest not the time of thy visitation.* Our Lord enlarges what Daniel had said in sum. Both prophecies stand in the same relation. The death of the Messiah entails the destruction of city and temple. *The people of a prince that shall come,* is, by the force of the term, a foreign people with their prince. Before, it was said, *unto Mes-*

---

[1] שֹׁמֵם, as being a different form from מְשֹׁמֵם, is probably used in a different sense. It had been used intransitively in the preceding verse, שֹׁמֵמָה, (v. 26.) as also, (equally in the fem.) v. 18. and in 11 other places (שֹׁמֵם Lam. iii. 11. שֹׁמֵמִין Lam. i. 4. שֹׁמֵמִים Ib. 16. שֹׁמֵמָה 2 Sam. xiii. 20. Is. liv. 1. Lam. i. 13. מְשֹׁמֵם Is. xlix. 8. 19. lxi. 4. (ii.) Ez. xxxvi. 4.) On the other hand, שֹׁמֵם is used twice in Daniel actively, yet not absolutely, (as it stands here,) but as an adj.; and in both places its active meaning is determined by the context, שֹׁמֵם פֶּשַׁע viii. 13. and שֹׁמֵם שִׁקּוּץ xii. 11.   [2] S. Luke xxi. 24.   [3] Acts ii. 40.

[4] S. John xix. 15.   [5] S. Luke xix. 41-44.

siah prince ; now he speaks not of the Messiah at all, but only of *a prince ;* not even *the prince,* as he would have said, had he been speaking of the same. *The Coming.* Daniel habitually used the word *come*[6], of an *invading* power which comes into a land, to conquer it. It is remarkable that, contrary to the facts in the time of Antiochus and conformably to the facts under Titus, the destruction is attributed to *the people of this prince,* not to himself. Antiochus himself was the soul of *his* persecution : Titus wished to save the temple ; his soldiery destroyed it [7]. Then too the destruction was to be final, at least for a long-appointed period. *The end thereof* shall be *with the flood, and unto the end* is *war, desolations decreed. The end thereof* is plainly, " the end of the invaded," not " of the invader." For 1) it stands in the middle of the description of the desolation. The account is progressive. First he says, *the city and sanctuary, the people of a prince who shall come, shall waste :* then he speaks of the violence, the irresistible, all-sweeping flood, with which the desolation shall be ; *the end thereof shall be with that flood.* 2) *That flood* is evidently that overflowing tide of war, just spoken of, the overspreading armies, *the people of the invading Prince.* He had said that that prince should *come ;* now he speaks of his over-flowing power. Daniel never uses the word in any other sense [8]. It is used in Scripture of overflowing for evil, or, twice only, for good [9]. The Psalmist speaks of the *flood of mighty waters* [10], as all languages speak of "a mightier wave," or " sea of troubles." But no where is the word used of the mere sudden death of an individual [11]. *The end thereof* must then be the end of that which has just preceded, the wasting of the city and temple : and this, to the end.

[6] xi. 13, 16, 21, 40, 41.   [7] Jos. B. J. vi. 4, 5-7.

[8] " He so uses it xi. 10, 22, 26, 40. from Is. viii. 8." Hengst. In Nah. i. 8. the allusion is probably to the mode of the destruction. See ib.

[9] Is. x. 22. lxvi. 12.   [10] Ps. xxxii. 6.

[11] The root is used of a large flow of water, Ps. lxxviii. 20. overflowing, 2 Chr. xxxii. 4. washing away, Job xiv. 19. of rains, Job xxxviii. 25. Ezek. xiii. 11, 13.

Look then at this harmonising prophecy as a whole, the completeness of its symmetry, its complicated harmony. Look at the elements which are combined together. There is a whole of time, 490 years, distributed into periods of 49, 434, and 3 ½ years, twice repeated, and these four periods not to be taken any how, but following in this exact order.   Then, in this series of years, as in every other part of prophecy, there is a nearer prophetic foreground of events, whose fulfilment was to guarantee the more distant, the restoration of the city and polity in a period of 49 years from a decree to be issued.   434 years, from the end of those 49, were to reach to the Coming of *Messiah the Prince.*   At a time within the 490 years, but after the first 483, i. e. in the last 7, *Messiah* was to be *cut off;* in the midst of those 7, he was to *make sacrifice to cease,* but to *confirm a covenant,* not with all, but *with the many ; transgression, sin, iniquity* were to be effaced : *everlasting righteousness* was to be *brought in ;* but city and sanctuary were to be destroyed by the overwhelming tide of the armies of a foreign prince; coming down upon the pinnacle of abominations, and the desolation was to endure.

Marvellous blending of mercy and judgment, harmonising with all God's other ways, and with the prophecies that *a remnant* [1] only would accept His mercies : yet inexplicable beforehand, and to be effected only by Divine power.   The destruction and lasting desolation of city, temple, sacrifice, are closing traits of that vision which was to be the consolation of Daniel amid their present desolation, which was coming to an end.   Sin is to be brought to an end and everlasting righteousness brought in ; and yet the desolation is to come, because

xxxviii. 22. of a vessel flooded (l. e. throughly rinsed,) Lev. vi. 28. xv. 12. hands, Ib. 11. blood from the person, Ezek. xvi. 9. a chariot, 1 Kings xxii. 38. metaph. swept away, Ps. lxix. 3, 16. [Heb.] cxxiv. 4. Is. xxviii. 18. Prov. xxvii. 4. sweeping by (rapid rushing) of horse to the battle, Jer. viii. 6. inundating with righteousness, Is. x. 22. of a stream sweeping away, Is. xxx. 28. xliii. 2. Jer. xlvii. 2. Cant. viii. 7. inpouring, Is. lxvi. 12.   [1] See on Joel ii. 32. p. 131.

sin is at its height, and in possession of the holy place itself. The Messiah is to be cut off, and the people no more to be His (as a whole;) and yet He is to confirm the covenant with many; and this covenant must be plainly a new covenant, since the typical atonements for sin were to be abolished.

All this meets in one in the Gospel. He, the so long looked-for, came; He *was* owned as the Messiah; He *did* cause the sacrifices of the law to cease; He *was* cut off; yet He *did* make the covenant with the many; a foreign army *did* desolate city and temple; the temple for these 1800 years has lain desolate; the typical sacrifices have ceased, not through disbelief in their efficacy on the part of those to whom they were once given. The city rose from its ashes, but not for them; long, not for them even to look upon, and, even now, to be strangers in it, not having a house of their own in the Holy City[2].

Now what does the school of Porphyry give us in exchange? The failure in accounting for the periods of time in the prophecy is the least portion of their failure. The heterogeneousness of the events which they bring together, the unmeaningness of the whole, the impossibility of bringing the parts into any one connection, or so as to bear at all on the situation of Daniel or the people, evince yet more, that the unmeaningnesses, which they have brought into the prophecy, cannot be its meaning.

First, as to time. Since the close of the 490 years, if counted even from the edict of Cyrus, falls 118 years after Antiochus, and within 42 years of our Lord's Birth, the 118 years have to be removed. This is, for the most part, effected thus; they assume that the ground of Daniel's

---

[2] This was stated to the Rev. G. Williams, author of "the Holy City," by Signor Pierotti, (Architect under France to the Holy Land and Architect Engineer to Surraya Pasha of Jerusalem) the author of the excellent chart of Jerusalem, who had been for some time employed by the Turkish Government as Chief Surveyor of the public works. I mention this as a fact only, an illustration of its lasting desolation, a superabundance of fulfilment. That desolation of 1800 years would not be less signal, if, at any time, the Jews should anew acquire property in Jerusalem, preparing the way probably for Anti-Christ.

prayer was the nonfulfilment of Jeremiah's prophecy of the restoration of the people and of the city. They say, "[1]the 69th year was now come, and yet there was no appearance that the prophecy would be completed, for city and temple were still desolate. Gabriel is sent to announce to him, that the 70 years of Jeremiah are not to be counted as common years, but as 70 weeks of years." Thus the commencement of the 490 years is to be thrown back to some period of the captivity, and the first 49 years are to be disposed of before the date of the prophecy and the time of Cyrus. Then, because the years would still be too long, the 62 sevens of years are to begin again at the same date. Cyrus is to be the Messiah of v. 25. The Messiah in v. 26. is to be a different person. Those chosen have been, Nebuchadnezzar, or Alexander, both of whom died by a natural death; (Alexander B.C. 323.) or Seleucus Philopator, who was poisoned by his treasurer Heliodorus[2], 175, B.C.; or Onias III. a deposed high priest, who was murdered by one Andronicus, a Syrian governor, at Daphne near Antioch, about 171, B.C., the murderer being put to death by Antiochus Epiphanes[3]. The *prince who* was *to come* is to be Antiochus, whose profanation of the temple was in December or January 16$\frac{4}{7}$, B.C.

The objectors, in this, strangely confuse the actual situation of Daniel in that 69th year of the captivity, and that of their own Pseudo-Daniel 3 centuries and a half afterwards. To Daniel that 69th year was a year of longing expectation. The 70th year brought the fulfilment of the prophecy in Cyrus' decree. In the time of the supposed Pseudo-Daniel, every instructed Jew knew that prophecy to have been fulfilled. The assumed nonfulfilment of the 70 years is in direct contradiction to the admitted testimony of those times. Zechariah alludes to it[4]; Ezra asserts that the proclamation of Cyrus in the first year of his reign was in order to its fulfilment. [5]*In the first year of Cyrus, king of Persia, that the word of*

---

[1] v. Lengerke, p. 407, 8.   [2] see ab. Lect. 3.   [3] 2 Macc. iv. 31-38.

[4] i. 12 sqq.   [5] Ezr. i. 1.

the Lord by the mouth of Jeremiah might be fulfilled, the Lord stirred up the spirit of Cyrus, king of Persia, that he made a proclamation throughout all his kingdom, permitting the Jews to return, and aiding them to rebuild their temple.   But, with this fact, the whole plea for dating back the 490 years is gone.   It was a strange theory, that, on account of the non-fulfilment of a prophecy, at a time before that assigned for its fulfilment, another was commissioned to declare, that the 70 years, which the former prophet had predicted, were not to be 70 years, but 7 times 70 years.   It would have been a mockery, declaring what Jeremiah had said in God's Name to be false. For the words of Jeremiah admitted of no such extension. It was a definite prophecy, which, if not fulfilled, would have failed; which admitted of no eking out, (for 70 years would in no way have meant 490 years,) but which was believed at the time to be fulfilled, and which was fulfilled to the letter.   The theory supposes the prophecy of the 70 weeks to have been written to explain the non-fulfilment of that, which they, to whom this amended prophecy is supposed to have been given, believed and knew to have been fulfilled.

Then too, the words, *from the commandment to restore and to build Jerusalem unto Messiah the prince, is 7 weeks and 62 weeks,* cannot be disjoined.   And this, on account both of the language and substance of the prophecy.

In regard to its substance, the gifts which had just before, in the summary of the prophecy, been promised at the end of the 70 weeks, are those which all other prophets prophesied as gifts through the Messiah.   No critic doubts of this, whether any one believes that those promises were ever fulfilled or no.   No rationalist interpreter questions that those promises were made, and were expected to be fulfilled in that "golden age," the Coming of the Messiah.   No one doubts of this, as to this prophecy. But then, since the times of the Messiah were, according to the admitted meaning of the words of the prophecy, to begin at the close of the 70 weeks, or 490 years, it could not be meant that the Messiah should come, when $\frac{1}{10}$ only of the period had elapsed, at the end of the first 49.

In regard to language; if the words, *and threescore and two weeks,* were joined on to what follows, (as is required by this theory[1],) *and threescore and two weeks, the street shall be built again, and that in troublous times,* then the meaning would be, that the street, i. e. the city, should be in building through that whole period of 434 years[1], which is absurd in itself, and contrary to the theory, in that the first portion of the period, during which it is to be in building, would coincide with that in which it was to lie desolate, in the past Captivity[2]. Further, *a decree to restore and build Jerusalem* is, according to these theories, not to be any decree or commandment of God, but a prophetic promise. This is contrary to the idiom, both in itself and

---

[1] Lengerke acknowledges that Hengstenberg has shewn this. Ewald had laid down as a general rule, " In assigning dates, the accusative is used, if the action belongs to the whole period. But if you would express, that the action falls at a definite moment within a larger period, בְּ must be used, as the Ablative is in Latin." The only apparent exception is, where the larger space is itself very limited, and is used as a sort of adverb; as in German "you might say, diesen Tag, diese Stunde, diese Woche," and we could say colloquially, "this month, this year," for "within this month or this year;" but, "these seventy years," "diese siebenzig Jahre," we or they could not say, except in the sense, " all through these seventy years." הַשָּׁנָה " this year," for, " ' in the course of this year,' (Jer. xxviii. 16.) is so completely an adverb, that you cannot say הַשָּׁנָה הַזֹּאת with the demonstr. Pron., but must say בַּשָּׁנָה הַזֹּאת, as it is in Jer. xxviii. 17. So also בָּאִים Is. xxvii. 6." On the same principle, it would be contrary to the idiom, to construe with Lengerke, as a nominative absolute, *and sixty* and *two weeks—the street shall be built again.* Without the addition of בָּם, " in them," the words would express what was either in doing *throughout* the time, or what was done *at the end* of it, whereas the rebuilding of Jerusalem began, on the rationalist hypotheses, after the first ten, or seven of the 62 weeks; in our belief, during the course of the seven. See Hengst. Christol. iii. 72, 3. Ewald, consistently, rendered, " throughout 62 weeks." (D. Proph. ii. 568.) Maurer theorised that Seleucus *might* have contributed to the improvement of the city; Rösch asserted that the city was then completed. " He [Sel. Phil.] *seems to* have amplified the city which, beyond question, had been long ago restored." Maur. " The completion of the building of the city under Seleucus IV." Rösch, Stud. u. Krit. 1834. p. 288.

[2] " They (Lengerke, &c.) maintain consistently, "that the building of the city Jerusalem was carried on during the captivity, or the time when it lay waste." Wies. p. 103.

in the context also, in that, the identical words having just been used of a direct *command* of God, those same words are now to signify, not a command, but a single prophecy. The words are, "from the going forth of a word," (or "command,") "to restore," &c. It is *word,* not, "*the* word." But "word," simply and indefinitely, is not used to designate *the word of God,* or prophecy, apart from any mention that it *is* "the word of God," any more than our "word" would be. But now, in the immediate context, *the going forth of the word* had been used of the issuing of a command from God to Gabriel, which command he obeyed. In no language would the same idiom be used in different senses in two places so closely adjacent. The prophecy of Jeremiah also, B.C. 606, was a prophecy of the desolation of Jerusalem and of the 70 years of the duration of that desolation. It was, as Daniel speaks of it in this chapter, the *word of the Lord to accomplish 70 years in the desolations of Jerusalem.* A prophecy, in God's Name, of a desolation of the city for a limited period, involves that such desolation should last only for that period; yet it would be unheard-of language to call the prophecy of that temporary desolation *a word* or promise *to restore and rebuild it.* Yet this is the only prophecy of Jeremiah[3], to which Daniel refers. Hosea, Amos, Micah, Isaiah had prophesied the restoration of Judah from captivity; Micah and Isaiah had specifically promised a restoration from Babylon. There is then no more ground to select a prophecy of Jeremiah that God would, after the 70 years, cause them to return to that place, than one of Micah and Isaiah. No one would think of representing those other prophecies as *decrees to restore and build Jerusalem.* Why? Because, when those prophecies were delivered, Jerusalem was not yet besieged, much less destroyed. There is no more reason to select a prophecy of Jeremiah, B.C. 606, than that of Micah, B.C. 758-26; i. e. there is no reason to take either.

But, further, let people (which they will not allow to

---

[3] Jer. xxv. 9-11.

believers) place the beginning of the period where they will, they cannot make either the whole sum, or its several portions, agree with any event in history before Antiochus, if only they adhere to the obvious principle, that the parts are equal to the whole, and so, that $7+62+1$ are the same as the 70 mentioned just before. This was, of course, in any honest way impossible. It was a postulate of " pure intellect," that the prophecy should close in the life-time of the imagined author, accordingly not later than $16\frac{1}{3}$, B.C., the date of the death of Antiochus Epiphanes, which, since, on the hypothesis, the Man of God could not prophesy, he must be supposed to have outlived. But $16\frac{1}{3}+490$ would carry us back to $65\frac{1}{3}$, B.C. in the reign of Manasseh [1], before the birth of Jeremiah, whose prophecy was thus to be explained. Yet the axiom, that there could be no definite prediction, was more self-evident than what to our childhood seemed self-evident, that 2 and 2 make 4. Any how, man willed that the axiom should remain unquestioned, and the science of numbers had to give way before it. Granted, for the time, that Jeremiah's prophecy of the desolation of Jerusalem could, by any human being, be seriously called, " the going forth of a word to restore and to build it ; " still, from 606, B.C. there was an overplus of 48 years on the whole. Or, granted that the actual destruction of Jerusalem by Nebuchadnezzar, when there was no contemporary prophecy of its restoration [2], was that " word to restore and rebuild it," this too, absurd as it was, left 30 years too much. But the difficulty as to the whole period was but the first item. Two other problems had to be worked out in harmony with the solution adopted for this. It was believed by most of the school, with a certainty equal to that claimed for revelation, that *Messiah* the *prince* (v. 26.) was

---

[1] I see that Böhmer consistently adopted this, as the beginning. See below, p. 210.   [2] There is nothing to place the prophecy, Jer. xxx. 18. in that year. Hitzig assumes this as to "its genuine portions," [i. e. what he, Hitzig, allows to be so,] on the ground that, as he thinks, Jer. xxxi. 15. relates to that event.

Cyrus. Another Messias had to be found, who was to be cut off *after the* 62 *weeks*, or 434 years; also some one (since he was not to be the Messiah) who should " make a covenant with the many " for. the last 7 years, in the midst of which 7 years he was to make sacrifice and oblation to cease, and at the end of which he was himself, (so the school agreed,) to come to an end.

These were the impossible problems for unbelief to solve; it had to solve them for itself, which was, so far, easier; for nothing is impossible for unbelief to believe, except what God reveals.

The impossible numbers were to be reduced somehow; men tried their hands all ways.

One [3] only was found to declare the three last verses at least a Rabbinical gloss; one or two only (it is almost strange that no more were found to support the scheme) declared that all the weeks were literal weeks. An essay of an English deist [4], who took this line, was almost unnoticed in England [5]; was translated twice into German, " received with much applause," but, in 7 years, " it was almost forgotten [6]." It was remoulded [7]; but this, we are told, " [8] found least reception of any."

" Not until the light, which rose upon the theological world in the last century, had reached its full lustre," the Germans tell us [9], "could Corrodi and Eichhorn succeed in winning their age to the right understanding of the passage." Only, Corrodi was still so far benighted, that he thought that, take the numbers how men would, they must be real numbers. He saw too that the whole pe-

---

[3] Lowenheim.   [4] A Free Enquiry into Daniel's Vision and Prophecy of 70 weeks. London, 1776. It was translated into German twice, in 1783 by Preiss, and in 1785.   [5] No trace of the book can now be found. It is not in the British Museum, nor in the University Libraries of Oxford or Cambridge. There is no notice of it in any English Bibliographical book, nor can one of our ablest booksellers discover it. It is just alluded to by Wintle on Daniel ix. 24.   [6] Eichhorn, Allgem. Biblioth. iii. 781-790. The English writer " referred " the prophecy to " Cyrus and the fate of the Jews in his time." Ib.

[7] Eckermann, Theol. Beitr. i. 1. p. 133 sqq.   [8] Wieseler, Die 70 Wochen, p. 69.   [9] Bertholdt, Daniel, p. 601.

riod must end with the Messiah. Since then the numbers, like water, did not admit of compression, and could
not be condensed before the time of Epiphanes, and since
there was no Messiah then, he detached the unreducible
49 years from the beginning and added them on to the
end, so that, in lieu of Daniel's divisions, 49, 434, 7, it
was to be 434, 7, 49[1]. The 434 years were to run from
the prophecy of Jeremiah, B.C. 606, to Antiochus Epiphanes' 1st invasion of Judæa, B.C. 170; the 7 years were
to extend to B. C. 16⅓, the death of Antiochus; and the
49 years, which, in Daniel, stand at the beginning, were
to represent a period after the death of Antiochus, when
the Messias is to have been expected to come, but did not.
Corrodi's plan conceded too much of the natural meaning, and was itself too obviously unnatural. It was, so
far, the testimony of an opponent, that the natural interpretation was, that the prophecy should close with the
coming of the Messiah, and that the numbers of years
were to be real bonâ fide years. So Eichhorn tried
another way[2]. He revived a theory, which in Harduin[3]
had been reverential, (for he acknowledged a fuller ful-

---

[1] Corrodi, Krit. Gesch. d. Chil. iii. 253. Wieseler, having first declared his
solution "self-evidently arbitrary and at variance with the text," afterwards
adopted it.   [2] Allg. Bibliothek, d. Bibl. Litt. B. 3. p. 793. Hebr. Proph. iii. 47.

[3] Chronologia Vet. Test. Opera Selecta, p. 592 sqq. defended in his Diss. de
LXX hebdom. Daniel. Ib. p. 880 sqq. Collins (Scheme of Literal Prophecy, p.
175 sqq.) in the main followed Harduin. The discrepancy of the first period, in
this way, he gets over thus; "All which, Chronology proves to have happened.
For, from the 4th year of Jehoiakim, wherein the prophecy of the 70 years' captivity, or of the deliverance from thence at the end of 70 years in the first of
Cyrus, was made to Jeremiah, there are seven weeks or 49 years." i. e. 49 are
the same as 70. The supernumerary years, even from this date, he gets rid of,
by supposing that two persons are prophesied in the words, " unto Messias the
Prince," in v. 25. so that the words should mean, " unto Messias the prince, Cyrus, there shall be seven weeks, and unto another Messias prince there shall be
62 weeks." Cyrus was the first; and "No one can doubt," (he says, p. 182.)
"that the name Messias belongs still better to Judas Maccabæus, since he is called 'the valiant man that delivered Israel,' (1 Macc. ix. 21.) and 'your captain and
fighting the battles of the people.'" (ii. 66.) The difficulty as to the 62 weeks
and the one week he gets over summarily, by counting them together, so that
they should contain the time from the 4th of Jehoiakim to A. S. 148, when the

filment in Christ,) in Marsham[4] was sceptical; and which, having found no soil in England to root in, had been transplanted to Germany, where it met a want, the want to be rid of the prophecy of Daniel. The principle adopted from Marsham was, not to take the 70 weeks or 490 years, as one entire sum, but to divide them into two, so that the first period of 7 weeks or 49 years should somehow run parallel with the first portion of the 63 weeks, and so should not be counted. The selfsame years of time were to serve, as portions both of the 49 and of the 441 years; so that, in fact, the sum total was to be, not 490, but 441; a process like that of the steward, wise in his generation but unjust, who bade his Lord's debtors write "fifty" or "fourscore" instead of a "hundred[5]." Yet, even thus, the numbers 49 and 441 would not fit in to the periods assigned to them. They could not be begun from any common date.

There are 441 years from the 4th year of Jehoiakim, B. C. 606, to B. C. 165, the year when the temple was cleansed after the profanation by Antiochus; but from B. C. 606, to Cyrus, B. C. 536, (if he was to be made the Messiah of v. 25.) there were not 49 years only, but 70. How then was the number 49 to be accounted for at all? Harduin accounted for it in his way, by selecting, for the close of the 49 years, a date of his own, with which the Jews were not directly concerned, B. C. 557, which he assigned as the date of Cyrus' conquest of Media[6]. Marsham, in ignorance of Hebrew, took Daniel's 3 weeks of fasting and prayer, in the third year of Cyrus, to be weeks of years, whereas they are expressly called *weeks of days*[7]; and these 21 invented years were, in some not very intelligible way, to be deducted from the 70 years of the Captivity. The 49 years then were to represent the remaining years of the Captivity, and to be dated from the

sanctuary was cleansed. The death of Antiochus, according to him, lay beyond the 63 weeks. [4] Canon Chron. p. 610 sqq. He closed with the words, meant to hint what he did not care to avow; "An ultra Epiphanem prospexerit Daniel, viderint alii." [5] S. Luke xvi. 6, 7. [6] p. 596. [7] Dan. x. 2. See E. Marg.

expiration of the 21, which were somehow to be its first
21 years; while the 441 years, or, (as Marsham, again in
ignorance of Hebrew [1], made them,) 444½ years, were to
commence from the original date 606, B.C.   The 63½
weeks, = 444½ years, were to last from 4107 of the Julian
Period to 4551 (i. e. from B.C. 607. to B. C. 163;) the 62
weeks were to reach to the beginning of the reign of Epiphanes [2]; the one week was to be the time in which he
had not profaned the temple [3]; the half week, the time
from the capture of the city [3]; the Messias to be cut off,
were to be the high priests generally [4].

Marsham's hypothesis, however, of the 21 years, which
were to explain the 49, was obviously absurd, and in fla-
grant contradiction to the text.   So Eichhorn tried to
mend it in his way.   He began, (as others after him,)
at the end, as being the easiest.   He paraphrased, rather
than translated, but as no one else would; "[5] During a
week of years, religion will shew its power with many [6];"
from A.S. 143, to the re-consecration of the temple at the
beginning of A.S. 148, he counted 6 years, [of course, since
he did not claim to count both extremities inclusively,
from 143 to 148 are 5 years not 6; the actual persecution
up to that time had lasted 3 years only:] "6 years might
very well in poetry count for 7; the suspension of the
daily sacrifice was to be 3½ [really 3] years."   Then he
left the early part of Epiphanes' reign a vacuum, and calculated that 62 weeks or 434 years would go back from
the beginning of the reign of Epiphanes, when Onias was
deposed, B.C. 175, to B. C. 609, 3 years only before Jeremiah's prophecy: but "2 years" he said [7], "cannot come
into account in a reckoning by septennia, since a round

---

[1] Rendering "half of a week," instead of "the half, or midst of *the* week,"
i. e. of the one week just mentioned, as the use of the article requires, חצי השבוע.

[2] p. 615.   [3] p. 617.   [4] p. 616.   [5] Allgem. Biblioth. f. Bibl. Lit. iii. p. 787.

[6] Literally, "the covenant will infuse might into many."   He recognised the
right meaning of the word ברית, God's covenant with man; but 1) if the prophet had meant to change the subject, and make ברית the subject, he would have
placed it before the verb. 2) ברית, often as it occurs as the object of a verb, never
occurs as an agent.   [7] p. 791.

reckoning never troubles itself about a trifle." Then, as to the 7 weeks, he took so far the plain meaning, that the decree to restore Jerusalem must be some actual command to rebuild it, and chose as his starting-point the first year of Cyrus. From 536, B.C. then, he said[8], the years, if counted forward, would come to no year of marked importance to the Jews: *Messiah the prince* must be an oppressor: and Xerxes, although very nearly one, was not. Counted backwards, 49 years would be, he says, only 2 years short of the destruction of Jerusalem by Nebuchadnezzar, [really 3; he himself calls them 52 years.] All then, he says, was plain. It was to be a new interpretation of Jeremiah's prophecy. "Jeremiah, when speaking of the 70 years of misfortune, [Jeremiah spake not of *misfortune* but of *captivity*,] did not mean 70 years in their most special sense, but 70 seven-years. To the end of the captivity, were not 70 years, only 7 weeks or 49 years. But if you take 7 seven-years, and count in addition the 62 seven-years, which elapsed from the time when Jeremiah spoke, to Antiochus Epiphanes, and add the 7 years of his persecution, you have then the exact point of time when the new good-fortune of the Jews was to take its beginning." In other words, because 70 years elapsed from the prophecy of Jeremiah to the end of the Captivity, but only 49 of these after the destruction of Jerusalem, therefore, on the one hand, you were to count 70 weeks of years, viz. 490 years, but, on the other, to deduct from them 49 years. Why? He says, "the word 'after' is used to mark succession of time; since then it is not used here, it is implied that the time is coincident." In this way, by counting at one time backwards, at another forwards, and by dishonest criticism[9], Eichhorn, as

<hr>

[8] p. 792.

[9] According to Eichhorn, the use of אַחֲרֵי was to mark the succession of time, and for this he quoted v. 26, 7. thus, אַחֲרֵי הַשָּׁבֻעִים שִׁשִּׁים וּשְׁנַיִם וְאֵינֶם הַנָּגִיד בְּרִית לָרַבִּים שָׁבֻעַ אֶחָד paraphrasing, "after the 62 weeks of years, is a week of years to be sought, in which religion, &c," but he well knew that he had falsified the text, in which the order depends, not on the אַחֲרֵי, but on the continuity of the narrative; "Messias shall be cut off, and he shall have nought, and city and sanctuary," &c. (וְהִגְבִּיר not וְהִגְבִּיד) "and he shall confirm," &c. So, contrariwise, he knew well that the

far as he could, veiled the fact, that the simple words, " from the going forth of the command to restore and rebuild Jerusalem unto Messiah, (or, as he rendered, an Anointed Prince,) are 7 weeks and 62 weeks, street and wall shall be built," were, according to him, to mean, " from Cyrus' command to restore and build Jerusalem unto the anointed prince Nebuchadnezzar who destroyed it, are 7 weeks, and during threescore and two weeks shall street and wall be rebuilt." Threescore and two weeks from when ? Not from the command to rebuild it which he had selected ; not from the destruction which he had specified ; but from Jeremiah's prophecy, before it was destroyed ; so that the point of time prefixed to the whole, " from the going forth of the command, &c." was, in regard to the first two words [1], " seven years," to mean the decree of Cyrus, and for the next three words [2], " threescore and two weeks," to mean the prophecy of Jeremiah, 70 years before it. Eichhorn owned the unnaturalness of all this, and called it " cabbalistic ; " but the fault was to be with the prophet, not with his own non-natural interpretation. Eichhorn in this way veiled also the fact, that, even from Jeremiah's prophecy, the 62 weeks or 434 years brought him to an unmarked period, the 5th year of Epiphanes [3]; and that so the last week, (really 8 years) had no marked beginning, and that the deposition of Onias III. which, according to him, was to be the cutting-off of the Messias, at the beginning of the reign of Antiochus [4], took place *during*, not, as the text says, *after* the 434 years [5]. Eichhorn, however, was an oracle in those times, and the result was what was wished for ; so it was ruled that all this was an adequate representation of the prophet's meaning. It was received by those [6] who were them-

words חֲצִי הַשָּׁבוּעַ יַשְׁבִּית זֶבַח should be rendered, "*the* half of *the* week," as he had rendered it, p. 786, not "*a* half week," as, contrary to the Hebrew, he rendered, p. 796. But then the words themselves, "half of *the* week," mark that the half-week belongs to the week preceding, not the absence of אֶחָד.   [1] שָׁבֻעִים שִׁבְעָה   [2] שָׁבֻעִים שִׁשִּׁים וּשְׁנַיִם   [3] 606-434 = 172. Antiochus succeeded A. S. 137. (1 Macc. i. 11.) B. C. 176.   [4] 2 Macc. iv. 7-10.   [5] Dan. ix. 26.

[6] " It deserved the applause with which it was received by two of the most

selves received as Theologians. Only, for Nebuchadnezzar, Paulus substituted, as the Messiah, the weak Zedekiah, who imprisoned God's prophet, gave him over to
death, when overborne by his princes[7], did evil in the
sight of God[8], rebelled against God and man, trusting in
man[9], destroyed his country, and died a natural death[10],
as a perjured rebel[11], in the prisons of Babylon. Paulus
tried to cover Eichhorn's arbitrariness by other renderings, as arbitrary. Having reached to Zedekiah from Cyrus, he re-bounded from Zedekiah's captivity, B. C. 588,
to the *murder* of Onias, according to Ussher, B. C. 171. so
far, at least, in conformity with the text. This, however,
being only 417 years, was 17 years before the close of the
434 which he had to fit in. So, by aid of a meaning of
his own, the words were to run, "and during the flowing-by of the times, and after the threescore and two
weeks, shall Messias be cut off, and the people of the
prince which shall come shall destroy the city and sanctuary;" i. e. Onias III. was to be murdered 17 years *before*
the lapse of the 434 years, and Antiochus was to destroy
city and sanctuary *after* them. Only, every one but himself, and probably himself too, knew, that the words must
mean, "in straitness of the times," not, "in the flowing-
by of the times[12];" so the new explanation was only another confession of the difficulty, which it owned by trying
so to solve it and failing.

Yet it was patently unnatural. So then yet another,
who was long the recognised interpreter[13] of Daniel, virtually avowed their incompetency to explain the num-

celebrated and renowned Theologians of our times, (Ammon Bibl. Theol. ii.
207 sqq. ed. 2. Paulus Comm. üb. d. N. T. iii. 415 sqq. ed. 2. note) and other
unknown Scholars in literary journals." Bertholdt, Dan. p. 605, 6.

[7] Jer. xxxviii. 5.   [8] 2 Kgs. xxiv. 19. Jer. xxxvii. 2.   [9] Ezek. xvii. 15.
[10] Jer. lii. 11.   [11] Ezek. xvii. 13, 16, 18-20. 2 Chr. xxxvi. 13.

[12] צוק twice, in kal, is i. q. יצק, "poured," Job xxix. 6. Is. xxvi. 16. once intr.
"was poured out," Job xxviii. 2. The noun מצוק, "column," 1 Sam. ii. 8.
xiv. 5. is connected with הציק i. q. הציג "set up." To "flow by" is quite foreign
from the root.   [13] Bertholdt, Daniel. Rosenmüller abridged Bertholdt's
statements, and (as was his wont) gave them out unacknowledged as his own;
"nostra sententia," i. e. by adoption, in Daniel, p. 322.

bers; only, of course, since the application to Antiochus was infallible, the fault was to rest with the prophet, not with his expositors. It was owned that the 70 years could not so be counted, it was alleged that they were not meant to be counted. They were to be an indefinite prophetical number. The word " weeks " was only to stand, because in sound it resembled " seventy[1]; " a comment or rather "[2] a parody on the 70 years of Jeremiah."

It being assumed, that the 70 years of Jeremiah were not to be taken precisely, so neither, it was assumed, were the 70 weeks of years; and so, neither were the divisions of those years, selected prominently by the prophet, 7, 62, 1; and the number to be compressed was apparently that which had least the character of a round number, 62. Had it but been 60, or 63! These would, at least, have been multiples of other numbers, 10 or 7; but 62 is so solid, angular, unreducible, matter of fact, sort of number, as unlike a " round number " as could be. No process of dividing, subtracting, combining, could make its elements, sacred numbers or " round numbers." There it stood, as if to set at nought the theory of " round numbers," and to require an unevasive matter-of-fact explanation. So then the knot, which could not be solved, was to be cut. The other parts, 7 and 1, were held to be accounted for; and whereas, the more precise these numbers were, the more one should expect the remaining solid number to be so, this was, contrariwise, to be the very reason why it should not. For the first 49 years a very definite period was to be found, that from the destruction of Jerusalem to Cyrus; the last 7 years were to be made seemingly to correspond (which they did not) with the period of the persecution of Antiochus. And then, two periods having been explained, the middle and largest was to be allowed to be false. It was said, that the writer, having once fixed upon the number 70, had to fill it up; and so was obliged to falsify the time from Cyrus to Antiochus Epiphanes,

---

[1] Bertholdt, p. 610, 11.   [2] Ib. p. 612.

making it 62 weeks, or 434 years, instead of 361 years, because otherwise the number 70 could not be made out.

One ground for introducing Epiphanes at all into the prophecy of the 70 weeks was, that he was prophesied of in the 8th and 11th chapters. Bertholdt extended the argument, and, since Alexander was also prophesied of in those chapters, inferred that he must be spoken of here also[3]; and, since there was no other place for him, he was to be *the Messias* to be *cut off.* Since, however, Alexander died a natural death, B.C. 323, and the alleged commencement of Antiochus' persecution was in December, 168, B.C., a century and a half later, therefore the words, "*after* the 62 weeks," were (contrary, of course, to all language,) to mean "[4] *in* their latter half," (in fact when $\frac{2}{3}$ of the period had not expired;) nay, yet more, ("through [5]prolepsis and sullepsis,") it was to be used of events both before and after. According to the new enlightened criticism then, the words were to mean, "And *towards the end* of the threescore and two weeks shall an Anointed [Alexander] be cut off and have no [successor out of his own relations]; and the city and sanctuary shall the army of *a subsequent*[6] prince destroy;" although the death of Alexander was 150 years *before* the expiry of the 62 weeks, and the alleged destruction of the city and temple *after* their close, not to mention the fact, that neither city nor temple were destroyed by or under Antiochus. Such was the new historical and grammatical interpretation, of whose new light Bertholdt boasted[7].

So for 26 years Daniel had rest. The three main plans of getting rid of the superfluous years had been tried. Corrodi had disposed of them beyond the time of Epiphanes; Eichhorn had made them run parallel, and so had thrown them out of the calculation; Bertholdt had declared, that the largest was not to be taken precisely, i. e. no more of it than was convenient. "O ye sons of men, how long will ye love vanity, and seek after leas-

<hr>

[3] Bertholdt, p. 619-23.   [4] "Towards the end," p. 619. 659-61.
     [5] Ib. 616.   [6] משיח.   [7] See above, p. 195.

ing?"   One who should so keep accounts would meet the penalty of dishonesty; one who should so make an astronomical calculation, would be counted a fool.   But anything would do for "scientific theology."   For, God says, "My people love to have it so."   They who *will* to be deceived, are deceived.   No one then had any interest in offering any new solution; for no one doubted that some one of the three solutions would do; and no one heeded, *which.*   So that the reference to our Lord was buried, the rationalists, like the Jews, were hushed, for fear they should awake it.   The less said about it, the better.   Bleek disposed of the whole discussion in two pages[1]; following the same division as Bertholdt, except that he made the 62 weeks end with Seleucus Nicator, (he meant, he said afterwards[2], Philopator;) and he first, (though in courteous terms) assuming the infallibility of their theory, laid the blame of its incompatibility with facts upon the assumed ignorance of the writer.   "The space really meant in the prophecies [of Jeremiah] was defined [in Daniel] to be 70 seven-years, as to which we must needs assume, that the Author, according to *his* calculation of the time elapsed since Jeremiah, *believed, that such was about its length.*"   Else he did not question Bertholdt.

It was otherwise, after Hengstenberg revived from the dust the old belief, that Jesus and His Atoning Death were the end and object of the prophecy, and that we have here a real definite prediction.   Thenceforth, all was commotion to tread out the spark ere the fire should be kindled. Yet the ways already tried had exhausted all practicable methods of making away with the obnoxious years; so the new schemes were only the old ones re-cast, mostly with some fresh monstrousness.

One maintained that the 70 weeks, v. 24, after which those great blessings were to be given, were weeks of days[3]; but the 7, 62, 1, (v. 25-27.) were to be weeks of years; only that the writer did not mean the 7 years to

---

[1] Schleierm. ZS. iii. 291, 2.   [2] Jahrbücher, f. Deutsch.Theol. 1860. v. 87.   [3] Wieseler, Die 70 Wochen, p. 91-4.

be counted at all [4].   He then asks himself the naif question; " [5] If the writer did not mean them to be counted, why did he name them at all ? "   The answer is scarcely credible.   " In part, in order to harmonise with an assumed omission of 7 years of the 70 of Jeremiah's prophecy of the Captivity; in part, lest the 70 weeks of v. 24. should be counted as weeks of years, and so, since there was no room for these seven weeks before Antiochus Epiphanes, any might be tempted to count them afterwards, as Corrodi did."   In other words, the writer, having mentioned 70 weeks, is subsequently to have counted 7, 62, 1, weeks, which make up 70, in order to shew that the *weeks* in both are *not* to be taken in the same sense, as weeks of years.   The framer of this scheme was amazed at the blindness of all critics, Messianic and anti-Messianic.   All, he thought, were biassed, not to see what was so evident [6], yet what he himself afterwards abandoned [7], in order to take up that which he here condemned, as being " [8] self-evidently arbitrary and at variance with the text."   The ground of both his theories, in 'part, was, that he felt how incongruous [9] were the two descriptions ; that of the close of the 70 weeks as described in v. 24, and that of the $7+62+1$ weeks, in v. 27., if the subject in these last was Antiochus Epiphanes.   Then also he saw clearly that the Messiah spoken of must be one and the same [10]. So does error again bear witness to the truth.

Yet another [11] (I take only persons who have been or are held in repute) placed the 7 weeks at the beginning, running parallel with the 62, i.e. not counted at all, and then again at the end, equally not to be counted.   This is a wantonness of contradiction to the text, which can only be explained by the necessity of saying something, when there was nothing to be said.   " The author," he says [12],

---

[4] Ib. p. 101-5.   [5] p. 105.   [6] p. 106.
[7] Gött. gel. Anz. 1846. p. 43 sqq.   [8] p. 71.   [9] p. 93.   [10] p. 103.
[11] Von Lengerke, Daniel, p. 429.   A good deal of his shew of learning was transferred tacitly to his pages from the writer whom he makes it an object to contradict, Hävernick.   [12] p. 429.

"divides the period from the going forth of the word of Jeremiah to the end, seemingly into $7 + 62 + 1$ weeks. It would, however, be an error, if one were to sum up the three numbers, as they follow upon each other. Rather, the number is to be a mystery, and the seeming naturalness, with which it could be summed up, is precisely intended to intensify the mysterious obscurity. The writer divides the period from the terminus a quo (i. e. 588, B. C.) into two, of 62 and 8 weeks. In the first, he marks out a lesser period of 7 weeks to Cyrus, and then again counts from the same terminus a quo [i. e. still 588, B. C.] So then the numbers 7 and 62 run parallel; both start from the same point, but the 7 comes to its close within the 62. This lesser period he names for two reasons; 1) on account of the great importance of Cyrus to the Jews; 2) in this way the sacred number of 3 becomes prominent; and even apart from this, he had no other choice. For since, in order to mark off more precisely the time of Antiochus and so to point him out more distinctly, 1 week (v. 27.) had to stand alone, and the number of 62 weeks was fixed, in that he was compelled, going upwards from the end, to distinguish an *unnamed* period of 8 weeks[1], because the time of Antiochus the Great, since which the Jews again stood under Syrian rule, had

---

[1] Lengerke apparently derived his "8 weeks" from Rösch, (Stud. u. Kritik. 1834. p. 276 sqq.) whom he refutes p. 472, 3. Rösch, by a chronology of his own, placed the destruction of Jerusalem at B. C. 609; whence 49 years reached to 560, B. C. when Cyrus was to have ascended the throne. (Harduin had taken 557, B. C. as the first year of Cyrus in Media. See ab. p. 197.) From the same year 609, 62 weeks, or 434 years, were to come down to the death of Seleucus Philopator, B. C. 175; then 8 more weeks (56 years) would reach down to 120, B. C. [119.] "when John Hyrcanus had raised the condition of the Jews to their best estate." The time of Antiochus Epiphanes was to be marked by the week and the half week taken together. Lengerke answered, 1) that 609 was 22 years before Jerusalem was destroyed; 2) that there is no authority for such a date as to Cyrus; 3) that the death of Philopator was on this theory both to end the 62 weeks, and, (on the hypothesis that he was the Messiah,) to follow after them; 4) that, in the text of Daniel, *the half-week* was plainly a part of *the week*, as expressed by the article חֲצִי הַשָּׁבוּעַ, "in the half," or "the midst of, *the* week;" 6) that there was no occasion for this extension to Hyrcanus. The strange conception of the 8 weeks Lengerke adopted.

to be specially marked, he had no other number but 7 left. The 70 weeks had then a two-fold fulfilment. But the true way of counting is a veiled one. The numbers $7 + 62 + 1$ divide the sacred number 70 outwardly only. The true division is partly a hidden one; since only the period of 62 weeks is named, the other of 8 weeks is passed over in silence."

In plain language, in order to mark out an event, (the transfer of Palestine to Antiochus the Great through the defeat of Ptolemy Epiphanes, B.C. 203,) to which event there is no allusion in this prophecy, which event took place neither at the interval of 62 weeks, (434 years) downwards from the one term assumed, 588, (for this would go down to 154, 10 years after the death of Antiochus Epiphanes) nor at the interval of 8 weeks (56 years) upwards from the other term assumed, the death of Epiphanes, 164, B.C. (for this would reach up to 220, B.C. which is no epoch at all, being 4 years after the accession of Antiochus, and 18 years before the defeat of Ptolemy) —in order, in short, to mark an event to which Lengerke owned that there was no allusion in Daniel, he assumed that the writer mentally divided the 70 weeks into 62 and 8, although neither of the numbers, 62 weeks which are named, or 8 which are not named, could be made to coincide with this unnamed event. And to arrive at this, the writer, dividing 7, 62, 1, is to have placed the 7 where it was not to be counted, and to have interposed the 62 between it and the 1, with which he assumes that it *was* to be counted, and yet not even thus to be counted with the 62 with which it stands connected. And this is given us, as "incontrovertible[2]," as the literal unprejudiced exposition of the sacred text.

[2] Lengerke says (p. 445.) "That the counting [of the 62 weeks] is to Antiochus the Great, becomes *incontrovertibly certain on this ground*, that the Messiah who is to be cut off, *can be* no other than Seleucus Philopator who actually succeeded him, and 'the prince' who follows him is Antiochus Epiphanes, who in xi. 21. also (comp. 20.) is named as the immediate successor of Seleucus Philopator," i. e. from an assumption transparently absurd, that the weak Seleucus Philopator, who attempted to plunder the temple, in order to

So Ewald went back to one of the earlier ways of taking the numbers in their natural order, but making them inaccurate. First[1], he took as his starting point, the 4th year of Jehoiakim, 607, B.C., made Cyrus the Messiah in v. 25., then stretched on to Seleucus Philopator and made him the Messiah of v. 26., and his death, B.C. 176, the end of the 62 weeks or 434 years, and the time of Antiochus, (according to him, *the prince, who should come,*) the 7 years. But the result was that, for 49 years he had 71 ; for 434, 360; for 7, 10; and, the excess in two items not counterbalancing the deficiency of the 3rd, for the whole 490, he had 441. This being unsatisfactory even to Ewald, he took[2] from Hitzig another date, that of the actual destruction of Jerusalem by Nebuchadnezzar, B.C.588, from which there were 49 years to B.C. 539, when, they supposed, that "the Jews may first have heard of Cyrus." The last 7 years were to be from the death of Seleucus Philopator, B.C. 176, or 175, to 168, which was the date of the profanation of the temple by Antiochus. Every date assumed is alike arbitrary. At the destruction of Jerusalem by Nebuchadnezzar, no decree from God or man went forth to restore it. The approach of Cyrus was no marked epoch either at the time or afterwards. Not at the time, upon the unbelieving hypothesis. It had no interest for the Jews *then,* except on the ground of their belief in Isaiah's prophecy, that God would restore them through Cyrus. Conquerors are not wont to give up a portion of their conquest, or to release the slaves of the vanquished, who, by right of conquest, have become their own. They do not trouble themselves about the details of the component parts of the dissolved empire, which they incorporate into their own. It passes, as a whole, into the empire which subdues and absorbs it. Nineveh

pay his Roman tribute, but, in the 12 years of his reign, did nothing to be recorded, was spoken of as a Messiah cut off; it is to follow "incontrovertibly," that the 62 weeks, after which the Messiah was to be cut off, were to end early in the reign of his father, 45 years before his death.

[1] Die Propheten, ii. p. 569, 70.　　　　[2] Jahrbücher d. Bibl. Wiss. vi. p. 194.

had been conquered by the Medo-Persians and Babylonians, but the 10 tribes remained where their conquerors
had placed them.   The change of masters does not alter
the condition of slaves.   Men were the strength of the
country, the riches of their masters.   The Jews were a
peaceful, industrious, faithful population, inured, for the
most part, (as the event shewed,) to their condition.   No
human policy suggested their restoration; past memories
and present interests forbad it.

As they had no ground to expect release beforehand,
except from Divine prophecy, so, when the release came,
the release itself became the memorable date, not the
first anticipation of it.   Even to a contemporary, the first
twilight of dawning hope disappears in the full brightness
of the reality when risen and effulgent.   This is true of all
history.   The birth, not the travail-pangs the first fore-
runners of that birth, is the date of the new existence
which is called into being.   It is according to a law of
our nature, that the date, when the Jews or Babylonians
first heard of the approach of Cyrus, left no trace in history.   Immediately after their deliverance, the first year
of Cyrus, the date of that deliverance, became the marked
era in their history.   It is even absurd to suppose, that a
date, at which no marked event, no change of relations or
of outward circumstances, took place, from which nothing
dated, should, (as this theory requires,) have become a
date nearly 3 centuries and a half afterwards.

The death of Seleucus Philopator, the supposed commencement of the last period, had no interest whatever for
the Jewish people.   At the beginning of his reign, he too[1]
had sought to secure the good-will of the Jews by bearing
the expense of their sacrifices out of his own resources.
After his attempt to plunder the temple, no mention is
made of him in Jewish history.   Secular history speaks
of him, as reigning inactively and weakly on account of

---

[1] " Insomuch that Seleucus too (και Σέλευκον) the king of Asia," &c. i. e. he,
as well as his ancestors; or, "even he who afterward sought to plunder the
temple." 2 Macc. iii. 3.

his father's misfortune [1].   His death absolutely changed nothing, since the first years of Epiphanes were peaceable.

The selection of the date of Antiochus' desecration of the temple for the close of this last period is in direct contradiction to the prophecy to be explained.   For the cessation of the sacrifice was to be in the midst of the week, i. e. after 3½ years, not at the close of the 7 years. Such is the accurate agreement at the beginning and the end of the period, which, Ewald thought, determined the Pseudo-Daniel to place the 62 weeks, or 434 years, in the middle, although the actual years were not 434, but 361, i. e. 73 less.   Yet even thus conscience seems to require that some explanation, whether good coin or bad, should at least be tendered.   So Ewald gave the solution, that seventy of the superfluous years may not have been counted, as being Sabbatical years, and the 3 other superfluous years might be employed to make up the period of Antiochus from 7 into 10.   This is, of course, in the one case, much as if we were to say that there were only 313 days in our solar year because 52 days are Sundays; or as if two inaccurate sums became accurate, because the excess of the one was the same as the deficiency of the other. These solutions are so many idiosyncrasies; every one sees their arbitrariness except their parents.

Rationalists have pleased themselves in exaggerating the variety of ways in which they say that Christians have counted the 70 weeks.   Let them look at home.   I have recounted twelve variations of the anti-Messianic school, and I will add one more as a rare specimen of " scientific exposition."   [2]One following Hitzig, yet owning that the 7 weeks must precede the 62, counts them back from B.C. 605, the date of Jeremiah's prophecy, to B.C. 654, which he assumes to have been the date of Manasseh's conversion.[3]

And so, the weary changes were rung, each refuting

---

[1] App. Syr. 66.   [2] Böhmer, (Deutsch. Zeitschr. f. Christl. *Wissenschaft* u. Christl. Leben. Jan. 1857. p. 39 sqq.) quoted by Auberl. p. 169.
[3] 2 Chr. xxxiii. 16.

his predecessor, the last awaiting his refutation from his successor, or ofttimes taking up that which he had before condemned. Lengerke refuted Rösch, and Wieseler refuted Lengerke, and Hitzig, Wieseler; or they mutually exchanged with each other. Wieseler took up with Corrodi; and Hofmann exchanged his theory for Ewald's; and Ewald gave up what Hofmann took, for Hitzig's[4]; and, at last, since the assumption, that the prophecy is no prophecy but a description of Antiochus, was to be infallible, and yet the periods given by Daniel were hopelessly irreconcileable with that assumption, the fault is to be thrown, not on the infallible theory, but on what, (whether men will it or no,) abides what it was, the word of God. Hitzig, in his arrogant way, says, "[5]If, in this way, the reckoning does not agree, then Daniel has erred, and the only question is to explain the error." "The 7 weeks form the $\pi\rho\hat{\omega}\tau o\nu$ $\psi\epsilon\hat{\upsilon}\delta o\varsigma$ in the calculation." "The Hebrews had no Chronology and no connected history of the Persian period." Those who are more courteous to the aged Prophet say the same more courteously. "[6]The assumption of such an artificial and unnatural calculation is in reality contrary to the text. For it is said, 'throughout 62 weeks shall Jerusalem be rebuilt.' The beginning of this period then cannot be the year of the prophecy; it can only be that of the return under Cyrus. Why should not the author have found and adopted a calculation for the time from Cyrus to Epiphanes, wrong by 70 years?" "Any how, one must assume here a blending of different calculations, if one will not content one's self with a mere erroneousness of the hereditary chronology. But the numbers are too important to allow of a mere accident,

---

[4] This is noticed by Auberlen, Dan. p. 171.

[5] On Dan. p. 169, 70. See *Bleek*, (above and Jahrb. d. Deutsch. Theol. v. 84.) "This space [from Cyrus to Epiph.] is really shorter, is some 9 weeks of years [56 years] less, but this cannot make us doubt an interpretation, supported by grounds so weighty, if we consider that there are in the Canon no chronological data for this period, so that at least a later writer might *easily follow an inaccurate* calculation, especially if *led by a special interest.*" [i. e. ignorance guided by fraud.]   [6] Bunsen, Gott in d. Gesch. i. 527, 29.

and so one has, either, [with Hitzig] to assume that arbitrary double starting-point of the calculation downwards, together with that strange twice-counting, or [with Ewald] to include the 70 years as their number, whereas, according to the literal meaning of the prophecy of Jeremiah, these might seem to be independent of any interpretation by weeks of years."

Such then is the result of this "scientific" criticism. It fixes the interpretation beforehand, at its own will; then it endeavours, in every way it can, to adjust with its theory the clear and definite statements of the text as to the seventy weeks of years, as divided into the periods of 7, 62, 1, and this one into its two halves. It adjusts the numbers, adapts the descriptions of those spoken of, as it wills; no one for the time interferes with it; it has free scope; it adjusts, re-adjusts, turns, re-turns, in every way it wills. It gives its explanations authoritatively; no failure damps its confidence; it has but to please itself; and it cannot. After 80 years of twisting, untwisting, hewing at the knot, the knot is to them as fast and indissoluble as ever. "Except the Lord build the house, their labour is but lost that build it." They form a rope of sand, and wonder that it does not cohere; that, twist it how they will, it is but sand. And so at last they throw up the problem; and, like insolent scholars, accuse not their own ignorance, but their Master's. "It is not we who erred, but Daniel. The problem is insoluble in our way; therefore it cannot be solved at all."

And yet, in this very charge of error on the writer of the book of Daniel, they forgot their own previous charges. This school objects to the book, that the writer had too minute a knowledge of the history of Alexander's successors. "God does not," they say, "so minutely reveal the future." Good. So far then it is conceded that the account is accurate. Again, it says, that the writer was ignorant of the Persian history; that he believed that there were only 4 Persian kings in all, and that the Persian empire lasted but 54 years; that the empire of Alexander was divided immediately after his death[1]. Good, again. It concerns not us, whether God revealed to Daniel more of the future, than he has actually set down. But how this is to help the adaptation of the 70 weeks to the period from Jehoiakim or Cyrus to Antiochus Epiphanes, these theorists have to explain. According to them, the writer knew accurately the period from the battle of Ipsus, B. C. 301, to B. C. 164. This gives 137 years. Add the 54 years, during which these assume the writer to have believed the Persian Empire to have lasted, and the 10 of Alexander's Asiatic wars. This gives us 201 years, which the writer is supposed to have believed to have elapsed from Cyrus to the death of Antiochus Epiphanes. And yet they would have us to accept this as an explanation, why the writer of the book of Daniel should have supposed 63 weeks of years or 441 years to have elapsed from the 4th year of Jehoiakim or, if they would be but decently honest, from Cyrus, when a decree did go forth to *restore and to build Jerusalem*, to Epiphanes. They assume that the writer of the book of Daniel supposed the period from Cyrus to Antiochus Epiphanes, to have been *little more than half of what it was,* viz. 201 years instead of 374[2]; and then, retaining the general term, "inaccuracy of Chronology," they urge this as an argument why the writer may have fixed a period[3], *more than twice the length of the time* which they themselves suppose him to have imagined the actual time to be. Their charge of "inaccuracy of chronology" tells against themselves.

And yet what one, the more bold because the least believing, speaks out, must have been in the consciences of many. "[4]After the death of Jesus, the Son of man, it was inevitable that they, to whom He was the Messiah, should refer to Him the words, [5]*Messiah shall be cut off.*" "[6]One might easily be tempted to interpret *Messiah,* v. 26,

<hr>

[1] Lengerke, p. 514. quoting also Bertholdt. [2] Date of prophecy, B.C. 538—164 = 374. [3] Even if the 7 weeks, = 49 years, are got rid of, there remain 63 weeks = 441 years. [4] Hitzig, Dan. p. 170. [5] ix. 26. [6] Ib. P. 160.

who was to die by a violent death, of Jesus and His Death; and if one thought of this *Messias*, notwithstanding the absence of the Article, as, *the Messias*, (as *Christ* stands in Greek for *the Christ*,) they with whom the Name had weight, naturally understood Messias, v. 25, also to be Jesus Christ." Yet with a strange inconsistency, *any* chronological difficulty was a solid ground not to believe that Jesus was foretold; *no* chronological difficulty was any ground against believing any one else to be spoken of.

The harmony of unbelieving criticism has been contrasted with the disagreements among believers[1]. It were no harm, were these disagreements as great as they allege; for the exposition of particular texts, closely or incidentally as it may at times bear upon the faith, is not, in itself, matter of faith. Not the meaning of texts in detail, but truths, on which they bear, are mostly[2] matters of faith. But the alleged unanimity of this unbelieving criticism has been in pulling down, not in building up. It has been agreed in rejecting Christ. It would, if it could, blot the mention of Him out of the Old Testament. But when the question is, how to replace it, quot homines, tot sententiæ. All agree in bearing witness against Him. But it is still, as of old[3], *their witness agreed not together.* If they waited, until they found those whose witness would agree together, the old faith would not have been parted with till now.

In regard to the 70 weeks, agreement on certain points was a necessity of the case. It was essential to any exposition which should exclude our Lord, that the Messiah of v. 25. should be Cyrus; it was their axiom that the last week should be part of the reign of Epiphanes; they had then next to no choice as to the *Messias* who was to be *cut off.* Without religious indifference they could not have

---

[1] "Among German commentators there is, for the first time in the history of the world, an approach to agreement and certainty." Prof. Jowett, Essays and Rev. p. 340.   [2] I say, " mostly, " because our Lord's words, and so His expositions of the Old Testament also, are of course matters of faith. And so too whatever any inspired writer asserts, apart from translations of words, which, as not affecting the sense, he leaves unaltered.   [3] S. Mark xiv. 56.

lighted upon more than one. The following table will shew their unanimity as to the rest.

	70 WEEKS BEGIN B.C.	FIRST 7 END	MESSIAH V. 25.	68 WEEKS BEGIN	68 WEEKS END	MESSIAH V. 2.	LAST WEEK BEGINS	LAST WEEK ENDS
Harduin	606.	557.[4]	Cyrus, typically.	606.	172.	Onias (type of Christ.)	171.	165.
Marsham	607.	538.	Cyrus.	607.	175.		175.	168.
Collins followed Harduin. Cyrus and, better, Judas Maccabæus.								
Ecker-mann	537.	537.	Zerub-babel.	536.	536. Jewish high priest suspended by Antiochus.		174.	165.
Corrodi	588.	none.	The Christ.	588.	170.	Onias death, 172.	170.	164.[5]
Eich-horn Ammon	536.	588.	Nebu-chadnezzar.	606.	175.	Onias de-posed, 175.	170. hiatus 5 years.	165.
Paulus	536.	586.	Zedekiah.	588.	154.	Jewish high priesthood between Onias and Jonathan. 175-157.	175.	165.[6]
Ber-tholdt Rosen-müller	588.	536.	Cyrus.	536.	170.	Alexander.[7]	170.	164.
Bleek	588. or Je-remiah's time of prophesying generally.	536.	Cyrus.	536.	175.	Seleucus Philopator (at first Nicator.)	175.	164.
Maurer	588.	Cyrus.	Cyrus.	Cyrus.	176.	Sel. Phil.		165.
Hitzig, 1st	588.	539.	Cyrus.	588.	175.	Sel. Phil.	170.	164. hiatus 5 years.
Hitzig, 2nd	606, but the 7 at 588.	536.	Cyrus.	606.	172.	Onias.	172.	165.
Rösch	609.	560.	Cyrus.	609.	175.	Sel. Phil.	175.	164.[8]
Lengerke	588.	538.	Cyrus.	588.	220.	Sel. Phil.	178.	164.
Wieseler, 1st	606.	none.	Onias iii.	606.	172.	Onias.	172.	164, Feb.
Wieseler, 2nd	606.	none.	The Christ.	606.	175.	Onias.	172.	165, Dec.[9] hiatus 3 years.
Ewald, 1st	607.	Cyrus.	Cyrus.	Cyrus.	176.	Sel. Phil.	Philop.	16¾.[10]
Ewald, 2nd	588.	539.	Cyrus.	539.	176.[11]			
Bohmer	654.	605.		605.	171.			
Hilgenfeld as Harduin but dropping the types.								
Herzfeld	587.	538.	Joshua.	538.	170.	priesthood after Jason.	170.	

[4] Really 559; see in Clinton, F. H. ii. 2. Conquest of Media. [5] But 7 weeks =49 years, i. e. undefined time, to be added. [6] "Whether 8 weeks, =56 years, to be added at the end, the Pseudo-Daniel left to the future to explain."

[7] So also Gesenius, v. קציץ and Hupfeld on Ps. ii. T. i. p. 17. [8] 8 more weeks from 175, B.C. to 120, B.C. John Hyrcanus. [9] 7 more weeks, =49 years (a definite for an indefinite time) when the Christ was to come lying beyond 164, B.C. [10] The last 3½ lying beyond. [11] Sabbath years not counted.

But beyond this their utter inability to account for the whole period of four hundred years, in any way plausible enough to command the assent and unity of their own school, they cannot make a theory, to satisfy one another even as to the last week.   Here the harmony was to be so perfect, that we were to be ready, on the ground of such signal coincidence, to surrender at discretion, and accept the rest as an insoluble problem, with that same faith which Christians have, that all difficulties in God's word must needs be soluble, even though they know not the solution.   Rationalists required of us implicit unreasoning faith as to the rest of their theory, on account of the self-evidence of this portion of it.   But is it then so?   Do these seven years so exactly correspond to the persecution of Antiochus?   Here, on the rationalist hypothesis, we are in the writer's own time.   He is to be speaking, not of what he saw, as we know, enlightened by God, but of what he is, by the hypothesis, to have seen with his bodily eyes and heard with his bodily ears.

The facts are not disputed.   There is no question of research or intricate chronology.   In his first years, Antiochus was otherwise engaged.   A portion of the Jews were apostatising, rationalising probably.   They were adopting Greek ways, and Greek unbelief[1].   They sought the king[2], not the king them.   The date of Antiochus' first attack on Jerusalem is given very precisely.   "[3]After that Antiochus had smitten Egypt, he returned again in the hundred forty and third year [of the Seleucidæ, B. C. $1\frac{70}{69}$] and went up against Israel and Jerusalem with a great multitude."

---

[1] 1 Macc. i. 11-15.   [2] "They went unto the king, *who gave them licence* to do after the ordinances of the heathen, whereupon they built a gymnasium at Jerusalem according to the customs of the heathen, and made themselves uncircumcised, and forsook the holy covenant, and joined themselves to the heathen, and were sold to do mischief." Ib, 13-15.   The gymnasium, adorned with emblems of Greek idolatry, and containing schools of Greek philosophy, was meant to Grecise the Jewish youth.   The key to the unbelief was the "becoming uncircumcised," an effacing of the outward mark of the covenant with God, (see Lightfoot on 1 Cor. vii. 18.) resorted to subsequently in time of persecution, now undertaken voluntarily, to assimilate themselves to the heathen.   "Let us make a covenant with the heathen," was their resolve; "to do after the ordinances of the heathen," was the permission of Antiochus. Jos. Ant. xii. 5,   [3] 1 Macc. i. 20.

Then he plundered the temple, (as had been done by other conquerors before him,) to supply his reckless expenditure[4]; but it was a passing storm. It is said expressly[5], "when he had taken all away, he went into his own land." The real lasting persecution began two years later, when he returned in great anger at the discomfiture of his plan by the decisiveness of Popilius, at some time in the early autumn of B.C. 168. It is again said expressly, "[6]*After two full years* the king sent his chief collector of tribute unto the cities of Judah, who came unto Jerusalem with a great multitude." Jerusalem and Judæa had been meantime unmolested from without. The collector of tribute came to the cities of Judah, when "two years were fully expired." Jerusalem lay secure within its strong walls, which held out so many sieges. It is again expressly recorded that "[7]he [Apollonius] spake peaceable words unto them, but it was all deceit; for when they had given him credence, he fell suddenly upon the city and smote it very sore, and set it on fire and pulled down the houses and walls thereof on every side, and built the city of David [Mount Zion] with a great and strong wall, and with mighty towers, and made a strong hold for them and put a garrison of apostates in it." It is clear then from the whole account, that, up to this time, autumn[8] 168, B.C., there had been no permanent

[4] "He committed sacrilege on very many temples." Polyb. xxxi. 4.

[5] 1 Macc. i. 24.　　[6] Ib. 29.　　[7] Ib. 30-34.　　[8] "Both Livy (xlv. 10.) and Polybius (xxix. 11. Legat. 92.) shew that Popilius did not proceed to Egypt till after the battle of Pydna ; and as that battle was on the 23rd of June, his interview with Antiochus must be placed in July or August; and Antiochus would reach Palestine in the Autumn." Clinton, Fasti Hell. iii. 323. The date of the battle of Pydna is fixed by an eclipse. "The eclipse, which preceded the battle of Pydna, fell upon June 21, which would fix the battle to June 22, and the preceding notes of times agree with this date.—Porphyry in Euseb. Chron. 1. 38. p. 177. rightly places the battle within Olymp. 152. 4. i. e. before July, B.C. 168." Id. on B.C. 168. Tables, iii. p. 84. Popilius did not leave Delos, until the news of the the battle of Pydna reached him at Delos ; they sailed by Rhodes, where they spent 5 days. (Liv. xlv. 10.) There had been time for Alexandria to be "reduced to extremities." (Polyb. xxix. 11. Leg. 92.) Polybius too thinks that "Antiochus would not have obeyed, unless the overthrow of Perseus had taken place and been credited." (πιστευθέντος) Ib.

possession of Judæa by Antiochus.   The persecution then commenced; on the 15th of Chisleu[1] (December, 168, or January, 167, B.C.) the temple was desecrated by the idol-altar built upon the altar of God; on the 25th, the first sacrifice was offered upon it.   Three years afterwards, on that same day in that month, the temple was cleansed.

This was, of course, December, 165, or January, 164, B.C.   Judas proceeded to fortify the sanctuary, as before, and Bethsur.   Antiochus was at this time engaged in war with "the Satraps of the upper provinces," probably with Artaxias[2].   The tidings must have been dispatched soon after the defensive preparations of Judas, for no later tidings reached him.   But the subsequent campaign of Judas Maccabæus against the petty nations who harassed Israel had come to a close, while Epiphanes was still in Persia, attempting to plunder the temple in Elymais[3]. On his retreat after its failure, he heard how the Jews had defeated Lysias, undone his desecration of the temple, "[4]fortified the sanctuary and *his* city Bethsur," and he died, while yet in Persia[5], of a wasting disease[6], 149, A.S.[7] 16$\frac{4}{3}$, B.C.   The exact month it is impossible to determine[8].

Popilius then probably proceeded leisurely, in order to give full time for the news, on which the success of his embassy depended, to be fully accredited.

[1] 1 Macc. i. 54.   There is no reason to change the date against all authority, in order to identify it with v. 59.   The *sacrifices* to God were renewed on the day, on which the first idol-sacrifices were offered.   (1 Macc. iv. 52.) This is the point of contrast between i. 59. and iv. 52.   The fact in i. 54. is additional.

[2] See ab. p. 150. 1.   [3] 1 Macc. vi. 1.   [4] Ib. 7.   [5] Ib. 5. so too Polyb. Fragm. xxxi. 11. Porph. in S. Jer. on Dan. xi. 44.   [6] φθίνων. App. Syr. 66. "He laid him down upon his bed, and fell sick for grief, and there he continued many days, for his grief was ever more and more, and he made account that he should die." 1 Macc. vi. 8, 9.   [7] Ib. 16. Jos. Ant. xii. 9. 2.

[8] Demetrius probably escaped from Rome so as to succeed at the very beginning of A. S. 151, i. e. Oct. B.C. 162.   For the death of Lysias and Eupator, and the two expeditions against Judæa took place before the close of the Adar ensuing.   If then Eupator reigned 2 years, (as Josephus Ant. xii. 10. 1. and Eusebius, Can. p. 356. say,) the death of Epiphanes must have fallen at the beginning of 149, A.S. the autumn of 164, B.C.   But Eusebius (in his Table, ii. 260.) and his Chronographer (i. 194.) assign 1 year 6 months to the reign of Eupator. And it may be, that Josephus took his period of 2 years from the more general statements of the first book of Maccabees, that Epiphanes died A. S. 149.

But his death was no relief; rather it was the signal for renewed hostilities. Antiochus being far away, Lysias had remained inactive in the interval, gathering a fresh army at Antioch[9], perhaps awaiting the return of the messenger and further instructions. After the death of Epiphanes, Lysias, in the name of his youthful son [10] Antiochus Eupator, renewed the war; it was carried on by Demetrius, after he had murdered Lysias and Eupator; and the first rest in the war was, when Nicanor, the second general sent against the Jews by Demetrius, had been defeated and slain in Adar, 151, A. S. [11] i. e. early in 161, B.C. It is then remarked for the first time, "Thus the land of Judah had rest for a little while." The first stage of the war then, and apparently that marked in Daniel himself in the prophecy specially relating to the persecution by Antiochus [12], was probably more than two years after the death of Epiphanes. How then do the events

and that Demetrius escaped from Rome, A. S. 151. The uncertainty extends to 6 months.   [9] 1 Macc. iv. 35.   [10] Eusebius (p. 187.) says that he was 12 years old; Appian, that he was 9. (Syr. i. 46, 66.) [11] 1 Macc. vii. 1. 43-50.

[12] The term assigned in Daniel viii. 14. (which belongs to this Old Testament Anti-Christ) is 2300 days, i. e. 6 years, 4 months, 2 days. This is any thing but a "round number." The time between the dates specified in the first book of Maccabees from Chisleu 15, A. S. 145, (the day when the idol-altar was erected) to Adar 13, A. S. 151, is only a month of 29 days short of the whole sum. The lunar year had 354 days; in 6 years, there would be two intercalary months of 30 days. The remainder of Chisleu adds 15 days; the two months before Adar, 59 days; of Adar there were 13 days. The sum then stands thus;

$$354 \times 6 = 2124$$

2 intercalary months	60
2 intervening months	59
parts of Chisleu and Adar	28

$$\overline{}$$

$$2271$$

leaving a deficit of a month of 29 days. But the desecration of the altar was not the beginning of the persecution. (1 Macc. i. 33-53.) A month then may well have elapsed before, in which all public worship of God was suspended. (Ib. 39.) This is the calculation of Hävernick, and, in the main, that of Dereser and even Bertholdt; only that Bertholdt tries to make room at the end for the month unaccounted for.

Another period, however, equally harmonises in point of time, that from the first invasion, in 143, A. S. to the death of Antiochus, *if* the death of Antiochus did not take place until the spring of A. S. 149, i.e. that of 163, B. C. For, since

of the last week or their dates agree with this history?
Those events are, the cutting off of Messiah, the confirming of a covenant with the many during the whole 7 years,
the causing of all sacrifice to cease at the end of the first
3½ years.   Anti-Messianic interpreters place in it, and
must place in it, the utter destruction of city and temple,
and (as they will have it) the destruction of the destroyer.

The prophecy says, that at the end of the 3½ first years,
the 2nd invasion, that of 145, A. S., was "two full years" after the first, the
first also must have been in Autumn, the previous part of our year B. C. 170,
i. e. the close of A. S. 142, having been spent in the Egyptian expedition.   For
this invasion was "after he had smitten Egypt." (1 Macc. i. 20.)   If then we
suppose this first invasion to have been near the middle of the 2nd month of 143,
A. S. i. e. Nov. 15. B.C. 170, this would give the following result, the era of the
Seleucidæ beginning at Tisri 1, i. e. at the month in the lunar year answering
to our October ;

10 months of 143, A. S. and 13 days		308 days
A. S. 144, 5, 6, 7, 8; 354 × 5.		1770
A. S. 149, 5 months of	30 × 3	90
	29 × 2	58
6th month, 14 days of		14
two intercalary months		60

———

2300

There is then good space, *if* the reign of Eupator was only 1½ year ; and the
events were marked in themselves, the first aggression of Antiochus against
the people of God, and the issue of his persecution in his death.   If this were
so, the number was twice remarkably fulfilled.   This way was adopted by à
Lapide, although not entering into its proof.

The Anti-Messianic interpreters, who could not satisfy themselves with the
expedient of halving the days, have taken this plan ; only in order to make Dan.
xii. 11, 12. relate to events in the life of Antiochus, they re-modelled, in different ways, the beginning of the era of the Seleucidæ and history.   The shift of
halving the days is one of of those monsters, which have disgraced "scientific
expositions" of Hebrew.   The simple words עֶרֶב בֹּקֶר אֶלְפַּיִם וּשְׁלֹשׁ מֵאוֹת, "evening-
morning two thousand and three hundred," (according to the analogy of
νυχθήμερον, 2 Cor. xi. 25. and the summary of each day in Gen. i. 5, &c.
"And evening was, and morning was, the first, second, third, &c. day,") were
to mean 1500 mornings on account of the morning sacrifice, and 1500 even-
ings on account of the evening sacrifice, and yet עֶרֶב of course means "evening," and בֹּקֶר "morning."   But could they, per impossibile, mean "morning and
evening sacrifices," the matter would not be mended.   Standing as the words
do before the numeral, the numeral must, according to the principles of all language, apply to the whole.   Conceive any one rendering "noctes diesque
triginta," "15 nights and 15 days."

all sacrifice was to cease; it implies that it was to cease
altogether; the temple, where alone it could be offered,
was to be utterly destroyed; no word is said of its restoration. Ruin broods over its desolate places. Anti-Messianic interpreters have diverted attention from the first
3½ years, at the expiration of which all sacrifice was to
cease, to the last 3½ years, after which they supposed
it to be restored. Of this, there is nothing in the text;
and the desecration of the temple lasted for three years
precisely, not for 3½ years. Again, counting back the 7
years from the only date, which these interpreters can
make out for themselves, the death of Antiochus, (if it was
so) in the spring of 163, B. C., we arrive at the spring of
170, B.C. in the middle of 142, A.S. This was 2 years and
9 months before the desecration of the temple, but it was
itself absolutely no era at all. It was eight months before even that first passing storm, when Antiochus plundered the temple of Jerusalem, as he did so many besides.
It was a happy eventless year for the Jews, when they
were living *every man under his vine, and under his fig-tree,*
with no signs even of that first hurricane; much less of
their long desolation. Onias too, the exiled high-priest,
having been deposed by Epiphanes on his accession [1] towards the close of A. S. 137[2], in the middle of B. C. 175,
had been murdered three years subsequently[3], B. C. 172;
consequently two years before this date. Lastly, the heathenising party of the Jews also applied to Antiochus at
the very beginning of his reign[4]. Even then on the Anti-Messianic theory, that "the confirming the covenant
for one week" was meant of the encouragement given by
Antiochus to the apostates who applied to him, this also
was prior by 4 years to the week or 7 years of which it
was to be a characteristic.

Not a fact then, nor a date coincides. Granting these
interpreters all which they ask for, allowing, which is utterly unnatural, that it should be said of one and the same

---

[1] 2 Macc. iv. 7-10.　　[2] Clinton, F. H. iii. 323.　　[3] 2 Macc. iv. 23. 32-4.
[4] 2 Macc. iv. 7-10. 1 Macc. i. 10-15.

earthly king, that he should destroy the city and sanctuary, confirm a covenant with many for one week, and that, after half of the week, he should make sacrifice and oblation to cease; and this, in the sense that he shewed favour to apostates and deserters, and made war upon the city and people—even supposing all this granted, they can give no account of those very dates in which all these things are supposed to have taken place, and which are to be the key to all the rest. Antiochus did not confirm any covenant for 7 years, nor did he make sacrifice to cease for half of those 7 years, nor was any Messias, or any one alleged to be a Messias, cut off during those 7 years; nor was the temple destroyed; nor were there any 7 years, in the period selected, of one uniform marked character. Rather the 7 years selected were of a most chequered character; first, nearly a year of entire peace; then horrible and cruel treachery and bloodshed; then nearly two years more of peace; then three years of intense persecution; then a respite, at least from the general of Epiphanes for a year and 5 months, and victory over the petty heathen nations who assailed them.

And yet the writer, living, according to their hypothesis, in Judæa, writing, as they say, to encourage their countrymen "[1] in their great struggle against Antiochus," could not be mistaken about what he is to have seen with his own eyes.

The scheme then of connecting the prophecy of the 70 weeks with Antiochus Epiphanes fails, evidently, palpably, as to the very point upon which it is mainly brought to bear, the end and object of it. The impossibility of accounting for the whole period of 490 years or the two periods of 49 and 434 years is not in the least relieved, but is aggravated by the impossibility of explaining the last 7. The writer is supposed to have had no object, except to describe his own times and their issue, so far as it lay before him; there was no call to mention time at all; and, having a tabula rasa, on which, according to

[1] Ess. and Rev. p. 76.

the hypothesis, he had to describe, as future, events before his eyes, he is to have written them with marks, patently at variance with those events which he saw and knew. In order, on the hypothesis, to explain Jeremiah's prediction, in the fulfilment of which all of his time believed and of which they desired no explanation, he is to have written, as relating to his own times, a prophecy, which no one can adapt to them, explaining what was clear by what was inexplicable, irradiating light by darkness.

Yet this failure, as to time, although a mark against these interpretations, is not so great a failure as the objectless character of the whole.

According to these dislocating interpretations, the whole promise of the blessings to come is to lie in that first verse of the prophecy; and yet, since, according to them, to "anoint one all-holy" was to be the mere cleansing of the visible sanctuary, these too were to be quite impersonal. The promise does indeed contain what our spiritual nature most longs for, forgiveness of sins and the gift of righteousness, but, the personal Christ being blotted out, they were to be connected only with that outward purification of the profaned temple. All the rest of the prophecy is to relate, either to their restoration through Cyrus 370 years before, or to that chequered state in which they were, or to events in which they were no way concerned, or actual visitations of God upon them, in which the picture is to close. What to them was the death of Alexander, or Seleucus Philopator, or even of the ejected high-priest Onias III, whom these have substituted for the Christ? Shocked they were doubtless at the murder of the blameless old man; but it in no way affected them, since he was far removed from them at Antioch, and his death was the result of mere private malice, avenged even by Antiochus on the perpetrator. But, according to these men, the central part of the prophecy are the desolations and profanations of Antiochus, a long abiding desolation decreed by God. Whether they in-

terpret "to the end" or "to the end of the war," it was
to an end, which they were not to see, a night of which
their eyes were not to behold the first faint streak of the
dawn.

Contrast together the text and the interpretation. On
the 24th verse, I will refer only to those who are consistent. For of all anomalies, one of the strangest is, to assume that v. 24, with all its fulness of spiritual promise,
had its fulfilment in Jesus, and yet to maintain that the
rest, which is a filling up of that outline, relates to persons with whom the spiritual history of the world is no
way concerned.

They then, who are consistent, paraphrase thus ; ("not
seventy years but) seventy seven-years are determined on
thy people and on thy holy city, until iniquity is perfected,
and the mass of sins is full, and transgression is atoned by the suffering of punishment, and the prosperity of
old times is brought back, and the prophet's (Jeremiah's)
saying is fulfilled, and the all-holy (the temple) is consecrated (by Judas Maccabæus.")

We are told in explanation, "[1] the Jews in the Hasmonæan age, according to the moral-deterministic principles of their nation [2], looked upon the time from the destruction of the Jewish state until that when Judas Maccabæus, after driving out the Syrians, could undertake
the consecration of the temple, as one, in which the people of Israel was to make the measure of its sins full ; and
on the same principles they believed, that henceforth the
anger of God would turn away from the people, and the
long-heaped guilt be looked upon by God as atoned." As
far as this has any truth, the point of departure is arbitrarily selected. A greater than Daniel said [3], *Fill ye up
the measure of your fathers.* Unrepented sin does accumulate, whether upon the individual or the nation, until

---

[1] Bertholdt, Daniel, p. 616, 8.   [2] " Dan. viii. 23." This school continually draws its statements as to " the Hasmonæan age " from Daniel alone,
and is seemingly unconscious that it is " begging the question."
[3] S. Matt. xxiii. 32.

it brings down God's chastisements [4].   Persevering disobedience to God's warnings by the former prophets brought on the first captivity [5]; disobedience, ending in the heathenising under Antiochus Epiphanes, brought on his fierce persecution; disobedience, culminating in the rejection and murder of Christ, ended in their last destruction and dispersion. But on each occasion, they were put on a new trial. The sins, of which Antiochus became the scourge, were not those of their fathers *before* the Captivity, but their own. The ground assigned then for dating from the first destruction of Jerusalem is arbitrary and false. It is either too early or too late. In one way, a nation takes its character from all its previous history, since it became a nation; in this sense the date of the first destruction of Jerusalem is too late. In another, Israel was put on a new trial, after the restoration under Cyrus, and in this way the date from Jeremiah is too early.

The exposition is also self-contradictory, in that it assigns the same date for the filling up the measure of sin, and for its forgiveness. The filling up the measure of sin is the time, not of forgiveness but of punishment. If the punishment is, in its nature or in God's purpose, temporary, the restoration comes at *its* close. In that 69th year of the captivity, in regard to which this prophecy is supposed by all these expositors to have been given, that punishment was coming to an end. Israel had not been, for those 69 years, filling up iniquity, but had been bearing its punishment.

Apart from this acknowledgement, that sin is, not in itself but in the mind of the Hebrews, a cause of affliction, the rest is more heathen than heathenism; it is not on a par with Virgil's description of the golden age to come, as borrowed from the Jewish Sibyl.

To proceed with their exposition, I will take the most

---

[4] See Butler's Analogy, i. 2.

[5] Lev. xxvi. 14-39. (on the gradually accumulating punishment,) 2 Kings xvii. 7-23. Jer. xxv. 3-11. xxix. 18, 19. Ezek. xx.

plausible, leaving out monsters, unless they have been followed by many ;

From the going forth of the commandment to restore and to build Jerusalem, [i. e. from Jeremiah's prophecy of its 70 years' desolation,] *unto Messiah the Prince* [i. e. to Cyrus] *shall be 7 weeks,* [49 years, being a round number for the round number 70,] *and threescore and two weeks,* [i. e. during 434 years, yet not so, really, but during 360 years,] *street and wall shall be built, and in strait of times ;* [contrariwise, the greater part of the time, all that with which the Pseudo-Daniel is to have been most familiar, the time after Alexander, was a prosperous time.] *After the 62 weeks* [i. e. really before their close] *Messiah shall be cut off* [i. e. a high priest shall be deposed, or, having been deposed, shall be assassinated out of private malice ; or a foreign king shall die a natural death, or shall be poisoned,] *and there shall not be to him* [a successor or a legitimate successor, or one of his own kin ; although all had successors, and one might just as well supply anything else whatever, which they had not,] *and the people of a prince that shall come shall destroy city and temple* [i. e. shall fire [1] some houses in the city, yet leaving it, as a whole, unhurt and inhabited as before [2], and displacing not one stone or ornament of the temple, nay nor touching it ; for the idol-altar was built on the brazen altar outside [3];] *and his end shall be in that flood,* [not in that, nor in any other flood of war ; but, rather more than 3 years afterwards, after he had been victorious in his own wars, he wasted away of a disease which Jew [4] and Gentile [5] alike looked upon as a Divine infliction,] *and unto the end is war,* [not to *his* end, nor to any one's end, but *to the end* of the war, i. e. there shall be war, till there is peace,] *and desolations determined* [i. e. upon Jerusalem, which, after three years, and a year or $1\frac{1}{2}$ year before the death of Antiochus, was again reoccupied and fortified by the Jews.]

[1] 1 Macc. i. 31.   [2] Ib. 38, 55.   [3] Ib. 54, 59.   [4] Jos. xii. 9, 1.
[5] Polyb. xxxi. 11. T. iv. 513. Schw.

And he shall confirm the covenant with the many for one week, [the *prince* had not been the subject of any former sentence; the *covenant* is, in Daniel, the covenant with God; *the many* were not apostates; but, apart from all this, Antiochus made no covenant with any; to give licence to forsake God's law is no covenant; there were no seven years in which Antiochus was in any relation with any Jews; he gave that licence at the beginning of his reign; in the period of the war, i. e. during the 7 years, in which it is supposed to have been made, it came to an end of itself;] *in the midst of the week he shall cause the sacrifice and oblation to cease,* [there is no era from which those 3½ years can be dated,] *and on the pinnacle of abominations a desolater,* [the temple was not then a place of abominations, (as the Jews in our Lord's time made it a den of thieves; and afterwards, in their last war, more fearfully desecrated it;) yet it is so called from what it was before the desolation, not as what the desolation made it;] *and until decreed desolation shall be poured on the desolate;* [even if this be rendered, *on the desolater,* the death of Antiochus, although an awful judgment of God, formed no era, made no change, was received as no relief by the Jews. For their war, all this time, had been with his generals, not with himself who was warring far away; and with those same generals the war was renewed, when he was dead.] If any one can believe this to be the meaning of the prophecy, of a truth, unbelief imposes hard laws upon the intellect of man.

Or look again at the prophecy, in the light of those times for which the Anti-Messianic interpreters will have it to be written after the event, and of those for which it was really given.

The supposed object of this prophecy, according to the rationalist interpretation, is to account for the prophecies with regard to the Messiah not having been fulfilled at the time of the return from the Captivity, by promising their fulfilment at the time of Antiochus Epiphanes. Where is there a trace that the Jews ever looked for their fulfilment then, or were disappointed at His not coming? This is no negative argument. We have, in Ezra and Nehemiah, a graphic account of their condition at different dates during 126 years after their return. We see them struggling with their present difficulties, but no more looking for our Lord's first Coming in which they believed, as somewhat immediate or near, than we look for His second Coming, which we daily confess, as proximate. We have also Prophets, whose early date no one questions. Haggai promises that He should come in that temple, which was then in building[1]; Zechariah speaks of His Coming, but of the events under Alexander before it[2]; Malachi, a century, probably, after their return, foretells His coming *suddenly to His temple*[3], and *the messenger* who should come before Him. This was, any how, two centuries and a half before Antiochus. Then, as to the times in which the hypothetical writer of Daniel is to have lived and written, we have authentic, detailed histories of times, before, under, and after, Antiochus Epiphanes; we have books of edification written then, the two books of Wisdom and Baruch. In none of them is there any expectation of any deliverer. The books of Maccabees speak calmly of the great tribulation in Israel after Epiphanes, such as had not been since there had not been a prophet among them[4]; the Jews laid aside the stones of the profaned altar, "[5]in the mountain of the temple in a convenient place, until there should come a prophet to shew what should be done with them." They laid them by carefully as for many days. Twenty years afterwards, B.C. 141[6], the Jews, "[7]the great congregation of the priests and people and rulers of the nation, and elders of the country," made the priesthood hereditary in Simon's family "in perpetuity[8], until a faithful prophet should arise." Israel is still a people of the future. In their prosperity as in their

---

[1] Hagg. ii. 6-9.   [2] Zech. ix. 1-8. See further Lect. v.
[3] Mal. iii. 1. iv. 5.   [4] 1 Macc. ix. 27.·   [5] Ib. iv. 46.
[6] "18 Elul, 172," Sel. 1 Macc. xiv. 27.   [7] Ib. 28.   [8] *εἰς τὸν αἰῶνα* Ib. 41.

adversity, they look on calmly to the future. The time came, and there was a general expectation. All men's minds were stirred; the pious were waiting; men were on the look-out; there was no doubt among them, that He was coming; they were like men in a city, when some great one of the earth is expected; as the time came nearer, they watched each token that it might be He: [9]*Art thou He that should come, or do we look for another?* [10]*If Thou be the Christ, tell us plainly."* The poor Samaritan woman said, "[11]I know that Messias cometh, which is called Christ; *when* He is come, He shall tell us all things." Ambitious bad men availed themselves of the general stir, and said[12], *I am Christ,* [13]*and drew away much people after* them. In all their afflictions, amid all that former pressure and noble struggle for their faith and country, there arose men zealous for the law of their God and for Israel, but no false Messias arose. False Christs could not somehow come, until about the time of the true. They were darkness cast, where *the true Light*[14] was obstructed; fantastic, cold-engendered, fleeting, parhelia around [15] *the Sun of Righteousness,* which owed their existence to His Presence.

Whence then,—contrary to what those perverters of the truth of history as well as of Holy Scripture say,— whence that long-enduring patience after the Captivity, in the troublous times in which the temple was rebuilt, the city and polity restored, amid the partial oppressions of some of Alexander's earlier successors or the concentrated deadly enmity of Antiochus Epiphanes, and Eupator, and Demetrius, amid all the hopes and fears of that nearly 60 years' strife of the Maccabees[16], until about a century before our Lord; whence all this tranquil looking to a distant future, through more than five checquered centuries, when Christ did *not* come, and then, all at once, all that out-bursting of those long pent-up hopes,

<hr>

[9] S. Matt. xi. 3. [10] S. John x. 24. [11] Ib. iv. 25. [12] S. Matt. xxiv. 5.
[13] Acts v. 36, 7. [14] S. John i. 9. [15] Mal. iv. 2. [16] 167, B.C.
Mattathias; 109, B.C. the close of the wars of John Hyrcanus.

all that stirring expectation of Him, as at their doors, as
to come before that generation should be gathered to their
fathers?

The prophecies of Daniel explain both the previous
tranquillity in that long winter which lay upon them, and
that sudden burst and glow of spring-like hope, all nature ready to expand and welcome Him, when the Sun
was indeed to come and put forth His power. Daniel
had pointed out a long time, lasting, at the least, five centuries, during which the Messiah should not come. The
people believed him, and, during all those centuries, looked
not for Him *then* to come. The latest edict in behalf of
Jerusalem having been given B. C. 445, there remained
only 91 years, at certain periods in which the prophecy
of Daniel could be fulfilled[1]. Of these, 42 only[2] had
elapsed, when the then tributary *king, and all Jerusalem
with him, was troubled* at the announcement, that strangers from the East were enquiring for the new-born king
of the Jews, whom they were come to worship. Nearly
30 years more, and one appeared, arresting the thoughts
of all by the austere garb of Elijah, which preached that
he was living not for this world, while his herald-voice
proclaimed in Daniel's words, *the kingdom of heaven is at
hand.* A few months more, and *He* came, who spake not
as man spake, who did miracles which man could not do,
who drew hearts, men knew not how. Expectation was
created; men's souls were prepared; they who were His
listened to the Voice which man had so long waited to
hear. But the awful freedom of the human will was
respected by its Maker. Messiah was cut off, as Daniel
foretold, legal sacrifices end, sin is forgiven, everlasting
righteousness is brought in, the new covenant is confirmed.

Look steadily at the emptiness, irrelevancy, inharmo-
niousness, of those things, which men have fastened,—
not meanings but unmeaningnesses— on the book of Da-

---

[1] See ab. p. 166-9.   [2] 536, B. C.—(490 + 42) = 4, B. C. the probable date
of our Lord's Birth.

niel, and then look how that book lights up with its true meaning, reflecting beforehand Him who had not yet risen ; and you cannot hesitate to choose between the darkness and the light.

LECTURE V.

*The minuteness of a portion of Daniel's prophecies is in
harmony with the whole system of Old Testament Prophecy, in that God, throughout, gave a nearer foreground
of prophecy, whose completion should, to each age, accredit the more distant and as yet unfulfilled prophecies.*

PORPHYRY's objection to the book of Daniel, that it contained such definite prophecies of the reign of Antiochus
Epiphanes, was consistent in him, if he had become altogether a heathen, and meant to deny *all* definite prediction.   To maintain it, he must have denied the truth
of most of the Old Testament, and contradicted the spirit and character of the whole.   For the Old Testament
is full of definite prophecies.   Definite prediction, prediction as definite as those in the Book of Daniel, is an
essential part of its system.   Porphyry's German followers accepted this issue.   They rejected the definite predictions of Daniel, but only in common with all other
definite prediction of the Old and New Testament.   It
is the character of English minds to take things piece-
meal.   They admit an objection in detail, without observing whither it tends, and become inconsistent alike
in their belief and their unbelief.   When it is proposed
to you to disbelieve the book of Daniel, because there is
"[1] not only minute description of Antiochus' reign, but

---

[1] Dr. Williams, Essays and Rev. p. 76. Again, "In the case of Daniel, he
may doubt whether all parts of the book are of the same age," [which now
not even a rationalist questions,] "or what is the startingpoint of the 70 weeks ;

a stoppage of such description at the precise date 169, B. C.," or to deny the genuineness of the later chapters of Isaiah because Cyrus is there predicted by name [2], you are in fact asked to admit a principle, which involves the disbelief of all definite prediction. For the objection is one à priori, as to the character of all God's revelations of the future. The prediction of a person by name can be no proof, that it is a seeming prediction only, written by one contemporary with that person, except on the principle, that God did not, on any ground or under any circumstances, vouchsafe to His creatures such definite knowledge of the future; that the Bible, so far, stands on the level of any human book. The argument against the book of Daniel involves broadly, that there are no true definite predictions in Holy Scripture, beyond the reach of human sagacity; else it could be no objection to the book of Daniel, that, if his, it has definite and minute predictions.

The Germans, from whom the objections were taken, saw this. They laid down broadly; "[3] Most convincing

but two results are clear beyond fair doubt, that the period of weeks ended in the reign of Antiochus Epiphanes," [i. e. what account can be given of the 70 weeks is to be a matter of doubt; only, no doubt is to be admitted that it does not relate to our Lord,] "and that those portions of the book, supposed to be specially predictive, are a history of past events up to that reign." Ib. p. 69.

[2] Prof. Jowett, Ib. p. 243.

[3] Lengerke, p. lxxv. lxxvii. "That the events of a distant future, and the fates of kingdoms, not then existing, yet only as far as Antiochus Epiphanes, are evidently predicted after they had occurred (post eventum) most definitely and accurately, even with data as to time." De Wette, Einl. § 225[6]. So also Bertholdt, Dan. Einl. § 2. Eichhorn, Einl. § 615, 6. Rosenm. Proœm. n. iii. Herzfeld holds other alleged grounds unconvincing; Bleek alone held that this would be unconvincing, *but for* those other alleged grounds. Herzfeld says, (Gesch. Isr. Exc. 2. § 13.) "That the prophecies of this book, so detailed throughout, *must* have been committed to writing *after the events*, [there being, it is assumed, no prophecy,] is, as is well known, one of the very chiefest proofs, that it is to be placed in the times of the Syrian persecutions. This proof is not to be confined to the Hebrew portion, but is to be extended to the Chaldee also. For ch. vii. contains, in prophetic form, an equally detailed late history (see vv. 7, 8, 21, 24, 25.) and even ch. ii. cannot have been written earlier, although it only mentions the intermarriages between the Macedonian [not so, see ab. p. 139.] kingdoms, and not the Syrian persecutions. This [omission]

against the genuineness (of Daniel) is the character of
the prophecy, and specially its definiteness.　1) The prophets speak mostly of the future in indefinite images and
hints.　Where they individualise, it is poetic language,

can be satisfactorily explained, in that the author conceived of the succession
and main relations of those empires, not the persecutions of the Jews, as of interest to Nebuchadnezzar, whose he feigned this dream to be; whereas, in Daniel's own visions, these persecutions must needs be of chief moment.　The
assumption (ii. 44.) that the kingdom of God would dawn in the days of the
Greek kings [Roman empire] *cannot* have arisen before their persecutions.
The intermediate chapters (iii-vi.) are closely connected with ch. ii. and each
other.　*Of other proofs of so late date*, which people will have it they have
found in these chapters, *I hold one only to be perfectly sound.*　The prayer
three times a day (vi. 11.) points to a time when religious ideas out of India [!]
penetrated into the neighbouring countries." [see below Lect. viii.]　Bleek
said contrariwise; "if Daniel is author of the six last chapters, we can only
look on them as containing actual visions, predictions of the future, which were
unfolded to Daniel in visions.　But it has been remarked with justice, that
these are strikingly distinguished from the prophecies of other prophets by the
definiteness and clearness of the predictions.　Most striking is this difference
in the accurate chronological fixing of future events, viii. 14. ix. 25-27. xii.
11, 12.—Not less surprising is the definiteness of the prophecy in regard to
the succession of the single events, especially ch. x-xii, where the several struggles of the Ptolemies and the Seleucidæ are described so accurately, that one
seems to read history rather than prophecy.　This too, it will be confessed, is
out of analogy with the other Hebrew prophets.　At least, most of the prophecies, preserved to us, are of this other sort; they are general threatenings
or consolations and promises, rather than intended to impart knowledge of single events in the future, and what, in them, appears as prediction of such events,
is commonly only the poetical side of the prophecy, in that the prophet indivi-
dualises, like a poet, depicting in single traits the general truth, which he
wishes to express; in which case we can neither shew, nor are we entitled to
look for, an accurate literal fulfilment of the single traits of the prophecy in the
events of subsequent times.　This applies to the prophecies as to the Messiah
also.　Yet it is not to be denied that, among the prophecies of the Hebrew
prophets, there are several, even though few in comparison, which relate to single
incidents of the future, and predict them.　None of these indeed can be compared to the predictions of the book of Daniel; in none of them e. g. do we
find described the single destinies of kingdoms, which, at the time of the announcement, did not exist.　*Yet we ought not, in this respect, to pass any
over-positive judgment, since we are not in a condition to draw defined and
sharp lines, how far and to what degree of definiteness the spirit of pro-
phcey opens the future or not.*　I do not then believe that, if the book of Daniel had all other marks of genuineness, the above-noticed character of the
prophecies contained in it could be alleged as any certain proof of their later
date."　Schleierm. ZS. iii. 233-5.

and the predictions are really not such, or did not come
to pass in the way marked out.   But if the prophets enter upon events, which lie centuries beyond and really
happened, their prophecies are acknowledged to be spurious,—or a right interpretation guards from false assumptions [1];—or, lastly, the prophet stands actually in the
time which he describes so accurately; it is his *present*."—
" 2) [2] The author further departs from the custom of other
prophets in the accurate chronological statements, in
which he enters even upon days."   " 3) [3] In no prophecy
of the Old Testament, except in Daniel, are detailed
events of kingdoms described, which kingdoms did not
exist in the time of the prophet."

These two last statements, although untrue, involve
seemingly, not the denial of all prediction as such, but
only two sorts of prediction, which, if true, are unmistakeable ; that of precise dates, and that relating to Empires unknown to the prophet except by revelation.   If
these statements were true, they would have no force of
proof against the book of Daniel, so long as it is not altogether disproved, that God ever vouchsafed prediction.   For if God has revealed the future in any definite way, beyond the reach of the most piercing human
intelligence, the whole principle is admitted.   Mere variety as to details, in the character of that superhuman
definiteness of prediction, is one of the properties of Old

[1] I regret to see this language adopted by Dr. Stanley, Jewish Church, p. 465.
"The secular events are (with a few possible exceptions) within the horizon of
the Prophet's age," and " They are either confessedly exceptional, or else admit,
(on quite independent grounds) of another interpretation." (Ib. note)   Yet he
himself doubts not of the prophecy of Balaam ; although, how he could think
that " the ships of Cyprus, of Greece and of Europe, were *then* [1450, B.C. half
a millennium before Homer and some 700 years before the foundation of Rome]
just seen in the horizon of human hopes and fears," (Ib. p. 192.) I cannot imagine.   The real question at issue between Christians and those whose language
Dr. Stanley partially adopts, is," whether prophecy is human sagacity or Divine
knowledge?" Dr. Stanley, who believes the prophecy of Balaam to include
" Asshur and Babylon, Assyria, Chaldæa and Persia, no less than the wild hordes
of the desert," (Ib. 193) must believe it to be a prescience given supernaturally
by God.   It is the more to be regretted, that he accepts the language of unbelievers.   [2] Leng. lxxviii.   [3] Ib. lxxix.

Testament prophecy. It is the very summary of Old Testament prophecy, that [1]*God in many portions and in divers manners spake in time past unto the fathers by the prophets.*

The point, which is really at issue and which underlies all this denial of definite prophecies, is, whether prophecy is human or Divine. Disguise it how men will, what is really meant is, that God acted through the natural powers of man[2]. It is the old question of Pelagianism, which, speak how it would about the help of God, always meant, underneath, that succour which God supplied to or through the natural powers of the mind, intellect, reason, moral sense, as distinct from and excluding any operation of Divine grace. So all prediction is at best to be some "inexplicable capacity of anticipating[3]," founded on the knowledge of human nature and of God's Providence; prophecy, which these men limit to the fore-announcing of our Lord's Coming, is to be " [4] a striving

---

[1] Heb. i. 1.

[2] "What the prophet can, with perfect right, announce as the word of his God, is, in its contents, nothing but the application of some general Divine truth to a given moral condition, or a clear contemplation as to the confusions or unevennesses of moral life before him, springing out of the clear light of the spirit. What belongs to it falls within the province of the purer, i. e. the Divine spirit; and if a prophet knows any thing more, and can give answer as to other questions, this is something accidental." Ewald, Die Proph. i. 12.

[3] Schleiermacher distinguishes a "prediction, which is to be exclusively united to a heightened and pious stirring of the soul, and that which can arise out of an intelligent survey of human relations and a correct and deep sympathy," and adds, "that to no prediction, whatever its contents or however great its accuracy, or however wonderfully the images of a stimulated power of anticipation may sometimes be confirmed, can a sacred character be attributed." (D. Christl. Glaube, § 103. p. 134, 5. referred to by Tholuck, Die Propheten, § 9. p. 76.) He sums up, "All predictions, both those which arise out of historical tact, and those which spring from an inexplicable power of anticipating, are" to be "made over to the investigation of the nature of the soul." Ib.

[4] "When belief in the Redeemer already exists, we can dwell with much contentment on the expressions of a longing for redemption, awakened by earlier revelations, in themselves inadequate. And this is the proper import of the prophecies of the Messiah, (an import certainly both strengthening and confirming,) wherever they occur and in however dark anticipation they may be shrouded, that they discover to us a striving of human nature towards Christianity, and, at the same time, as the confession of the best and most ensouled out

of human nature towards Christianity." Both purely human. But, although the correspondence of the Gospel with our spiritual needs is, in fact, one of the strongest bands by which God holds fast our faith, yet our need, as sinners, to be reconciled with God, and to be made at one with Him from Whom we feel, by nature, severed, could not and did not lead human nature to expect *beforehand* that God would meet that need. Much less could heart of man imagine, that He would give His Only-Begotten Son (of Whose Being human nature could, of itself, know nothing,) to die for our sins, or that He would give His regenerating Spirit to those who believe in Jesus. Prophecy of the Supernatural must be itself supernatu-

of the earlier pious communities, express, that they were only to be looked upon as preliminary and passing institutions." Schleierm. § 14. i. 105, 6. Schleiermacher led others into the land which he did not enter, being in antagonism with shallow rationalism, though short of Christian truth. Nitzsch, who retains the distinction of prophecy and prediction, owns both as supernatural, i. e. from God. Only he thinks, that "prediction must be rare, in order not to destroy the whole relation of man to history, the more so, because, in the cases to which it extends, it can only become altogether perfect through the most definite statements of the special marks of the fact." System d. Christl. Lehre, § 35. It is not clear to me, what Nitzsch, and those who have adopted his maxim, mean by it. God does not interfere with His creature's free-agency ; but the most definite prediction does not interfere with this. What bad men do not like, they disbelieve, and accomplish, while disbelieving it. *Of a truth against Thy holy Child Jesus, Whom Thou hast anointed, both Herod and Pontius Pilate with the Gentiles and people of Israel were gathered together, for to do whatsoever Thy hand and Thy counsel determined before to be done.* Acts iv. 27, 28. Even when any one received a prediction as to himself, his way of acting upon that prediction rested with his free-agency. Hazael fulfilled his through murder ; (2 Kgs. viii. 13-15.) Jeroboam sought to establish his through sin ; (1 Kgs. xii. 26-33.) Jehu fulfilled his in the letter, not in the spirit. (2 Kgs. x. 31.) All abused their free-agency ; the prediction did not "destroy the relation of man to history." The whole history of Jeroboam's house, God says, and so of Israel, would have been different, had he been faithful to God. (1 Kgs. xi. 38.) Tholuck points out an oversight in this whole distinction between prediction and prophecy. The greatness of prophecy is proportioned to the greatness of its subject. Prophecies then as to the Christ were greater than any temporal prophecies. But, even as to our Lord Himself, prophecy foretold, at times, the greatest things, at others what formed a subordinate part, yet all were parts of one whole in the Mind of God. "Prophecy," says Tholuck in reference to the distinction of Schleiermacher, "even if not without exception, became the concrete view of the future ; prediction has every where prophecy as its background." Die Propheten, § 9. end p. 78.

ral. His temporal judgments, *when they fall*, find more response in the souls of us sinners. Yet, although God, in His judgments of the world throughout the history of the world [1], acts, of course, in His varied dealings with His creatures, on one law of His All-wise Justice, man cannot tell beforehand, either whom He will punish, or how. Those predicted punishments mostly come upon one nation by another. "God punishes the guilty." True; but which? Man could not know beforehand, on any ground of the Divine justice. The executioner was mostly as guilty as the criminal.

Good and evil are so variedly mingled in nations or individuals, that, even when we know that persevering infringements of the Divine laws entail in the end, by God's appointment, certain punishments, yet we cannot usurp the prerogative of God, and, of our own minds, pronounce His judgments. The forms too of God's judgments are so manifold; the time, when they burst, is so hastened or withheld upon grounds which we know not, that, although we know enough to see the justice of those judgments when they have come, we do *not* know enough to foresee those judgments before they come, still less their time or their ultimate issue [2].

But, in the time of Old Testament prophecy, mankind had yet to learn, both that there was a judgment of the world, and that there was One Judge, the One True God. Theorists, here as elsewhere, abuse ungratefully the knowledge which, as matter of fact, they have gained from revelation, to trick out human nature in its fallen state, and claim that, as their inherent endowment, which God gave them as a mitigation of their ills.

All along the times before Christ came, prophecy was no *mere* prediction, no mere strengthening of faith by the fact of God's revealed foreknowledge. All along, its subjects were those of the Psalmist's song [3], *mercy and judg-*

---

[1] "The world's-history is the world's-judgment," conciser in the original, "Die Weltgeschichte ist das Weltgericht." quoted by Tholuck, Die. Proph. p. 79.   [2] Ewald rests his idea of temporal prophecy simply on the anticipation of Divine justice.   [3] Ps. ci. 1.

ment. All along it withdrew the veil, not only from things invisible as yet by reason of distance, but from that which is to man more invisible still, because he would fain not see it, God's minute, righteous Providence, to Whose serene Omniscience nothing is too small to see, to Whose Omnipresent Justice nothing is too mighty to control or to punish. Even more perplexing yet, than the separate announcement of mercy or judgment, is the blending of both. Man cannot, of himself anticipate mercy after judgment; without direct revelation, it is clean contrary to man's "anticipations." Presumption or despair are alike natural to the heart of man, as conscience is awakened or unawakened. To faith only it is revealed, that *whom the Lord loveth, He chasteneth.* Those detailed minute prophecies had their own especial office, to mark out, that God's Judgments were not mere chance, (as men, now also, often think,) nor again, (what lies nearer to the depths of man's heart, who feels himself in the power of the Invisible) a mere fated thing, but the discriminating sentence of the One Ruler of the world.

So far from those minute temporal prophecies, such as we have in Daniel, being alien from Old Testament prophecy, they are, in fact, a part of God's whole way of acting under the old dispensation.

I would first point out the general indications of such a system of minute prophecy running along the whole course of the Old Testament history, presupposed by what is related in that history, but extending beyond the specific instances which are recorded.

1) Such prophecies are presupposed by the test, through which, at all times, the true prophet was to be distinguished from the false. The fulfilment or non-fulfilment of definite prophecies is the God-given test of the truth or falsehood of the prophet. *⁴And if thou shalt say in thine heart, How shall we know the word which the Lord hath not spoken? When a prophet speaketh in the name of the Lord*

⁴ Deut. xviii. 21, 2. I am glad to see this recognised by Dr. Stanley, Jewish Church, p. 462.

*if the thing follow not nor come to pass, that is the thing
which the Lord hath not spoken ; the prophet hath spoken
it presumptuously ; thou shalt not be afraid of them.*   God
forewarned His people of the struggle which there should
be between the true prophets and the false, and gave them
a test of the true.   But that test in itself implies a near
fulfilment of definite prophecy ; else it would have been
no test at all, by which true prophecy could be tried.
Such definite prophecy is presupposed by all that long
actual struggle between the false prophets and the true[2],
which closed only with the suspension of true prophecy,
and which shall yet be revived before the end of the world.
Sometimes it comes to a more solemn issue, as in that
grand appeal of the one true prophet of God, when standing against the 400 court-prophets of Ahab[3].   The repeated challenge of Isaiah, that the gods of the nations
had not uttered and could not utter predictions such as he
had given in the Name of God[4], and as had been fulfilled,
was a challenge of the same sort to the heathen world,
as Daniel's exposition of the dreams of Nebuchadnezzar
or of the hand-writing on the wall, when the wise men
of Babylon had failed, was in act.   Accurate fulfilment,
of which men were cognizant, is implied by the simple
declaration, with which Amos winds up his series of like-

[1] See Introd. to Micah, p. 289. False prophecy reappeared after the captivity.
Neh. vi. 12, 14.   Zechariah prophesied its cessation under the Gospel, xiii. 4.
Dr. Stanley instances " the prophetess Noadiah and the rest of the prophets,"
(Neh. vi.)" " as indications of the prophetic spirit," "among the Samaritans,"
(Ib. p. 423.) as if there were any real connection between the false prophets
and the true, between those who *prophesied out of their own hearts*, and uttered lies in the name of God, and those *to whom the word of God came*, and
who *spake as they were moved by the Holy Ghost.*   Bitter and sweet are both
tastes, truth and falsehood are both in word, yet most opposite.   It is no less
confusion to blend those, who stood in directest antagonism, the instruments
of God or the instruments of Satan, e. g. p. 429. " The prophets were to be
found in considerable numbers, fifty, or even 400 at a time.   The 50 (2 Kgs.
ii. 16.) were prophets of God ; the 400, false prophets of an idol, 1 Kgs. xxii. 6.

[2] Rev. xvi. 13. xix. 20. xx. 10.   [3] 1 Kgs. xxii. 6.   Probably the 400
Ashtaroth-prophets *which did eat at Jezebel's table.*   Ib. xviii. 19.

[4] xli. 21-23. 26-28. xlii. 9. xliii. 9-12. xliv. 7, 8, 25-28. xlv. 11, 19, 21. xlvi. 9.
xlviii. 3-7, 14-16.

nesses; [5] *Surely the Lord God will do nothing, but He revealeth His secret unto His servants the prophets.*

2) Still further, there are, in the earliest provisions of the law and in the history of Samuel, indications, that God condescended to shew His individual care and superintendence of human things by a more minute personal foretelling, than is recorded.   It was a part of the office of[6] *Eleazar the High Priest to ask counsel for* Joshua, *after the judgment of Urim and Thummim.*   We see, in a few instances in the history of David, how habitually he consulted God thereby, and what minute answers as to the proximate future were given him, when his own human sagacity was utterly at fault[7].   The defence of the high priest, when accused by Doeg of having consulted God for him against Saul, implies that he had so done for him in times past.   He consulted for him, as for one employed by the king, and knew nothing of these changes.   *"Did I now begin*[8] to enquire of God for him?—Thy servant knew nothing of all this, less or more."*   And indeed on that self-same occasion, we know the fact, that David *then* so consulted Ahimelech, only through Doeg's accusation and the High-Priest's admission[9].   Even Saul, in his short-lived better days, had so enquired of the Lord, though with his characteristic fitfulness[10].   Then, for a long time, he disused it.   It would lie in his character, to have disused it from the day when God answered him not[11].   As is the wont of faith without love, he recurred, in the extremity of his fortunes, to all the means whereby God would be consulted, and, when God would not answer, had resort to evil powers.   [12]*When Saul enquired of the*

---

[5] See on Am. iii. 7.   [6] Num. xxvii. 21.

[7] 1 Sam. xxiii. 2, 4, 6, 9-12. xxx. 7, 8. 2 Sam. ii. 1. v. 19, 23. xxi. 1.   Probably it was in reference to Zadok's office, as priest, that David said to him, *Art thou not a Seer?* 2 Sam. xv. 27.   It is noticed that, in the 3 days' pestilence inflicted for the pride in numbering the people, *David could not go before it (the tabernacle of the Lord, being at Gibeon) to enquire of God; for he was afraid, because of the sword of the Angel of the Lord.* 1 Chr. xxi. 30.

[8] הַחִלֹּתִי הַיּוֹם 1 Sam. xxii. 15.   [9] Ib. 9, 10.   [10] Ib. xiv. 18, 19.

[11] Ib. 37.   [12] Ib. xxviii. 6.

R

Lord, the Lord answered him not, neither by dreams, nor by Urim, nor by prophets. [1] *God is departed from me, and answereth me no more, neither by prophets nor by dreams.*

The use of the Urim lasted, probably, until the Captivity; since after the Captivity it is spoken of as something which might perhaps still be restored [2], if God so willed.

3) But this was apparently reserved for persons in eminent station, whose acts concerned the well-being of the whole. The relation of Samuel to the people, at the close of that disorganised period of the Judges, belongs more to private life. It is expressly mentioned, at the beginning of God's revelation to him [3], *The word of God was rare in those days; there was no vision spread abroad.* This scarcity must stand in contrast with fulness, before, or after, or both; for it is said, *in those days.* Samuel's foretellings were frequent, and had that characteristic of Divine truth, that they never failed. His prophetic office was so authenticated. Samuel *grew* [4], it is said after that first revelation, *and the Lord was with him and did let none of his words fall to the ground. And all Israel, from Dan even to Beersheba, knew that Samuel was established a prophet of the Lord. And the Lord appeared again in Shiloh : for the Lord revealed Himself to Samuel in Shiloh by the word of the Lord ;* not in vision only, but by inward inspiration. The name of *Seer* implies a habitual "foreseeing" of things which others saw not. To ask God through him was a common every-day thing. [5] *Beforetime in Israel, when a man went to enquire of God, thus he spake, Come, and let us go to the Seer.* Saul's servant was cognizant of the fact, that [6] *all that he saith cometh surely to pass.* His proposal to consult Samuel about the lost asses causes no surprise, beforehand, in the event, or when related to Saul's uncle [7]. It is ac-

---

[1] Ib. 15.　　　　[2] "And the Tirshatha said, that they should not eat of the most holy things, till there stood up a priest with Urim and with Thummim." Ezr. ii. 63. Neh. vii. 65.　　　[3] 1 Sam. iii. 1.　　　[4] Ib. 19-21.　　　[5] Ib. ix. 9.
[6] Ib. 6.　　　　[7] Ib. 6-10. 20. x. 2. 16.

cepted as the natural solution of the visit to Samuel which had seemed remarkable. Yet this too had its parallel in the Gospel. Saul's heart was prepared for the religious influence of the company of the prophets who, Samuel had predicted, would meet him, by the fulfilment of previous prophecy as to ordinary wayfarers[8]. The hearts of the disciples were prepared for the great mysteries of the Passion[9] and of the Holy Eucharist[10] by the minute prophecy as to the place where they should find the ass and the colt tied, and the answer of the owner, when they should loose them[9]; and by that other of the *man, bearing a pitcher of water,* who should *shew* them *a large upper room furnished and prepared*[10]. Those prophecies of the Old Testament are not more minute, nor do they relate to circumstances more apparently incidental, than these two of our Lord Himself.

4) It would seem, from the breadth of the expression used, on occasion of Samuel, that this habit of enquiring and obtaining answers from God did not begin in his time. *Beforetime in Israel, when a man went to enquire of God thus he spake, &c.—he, that is now called a prophet,* (Nabi) *was before called a Seer* (Roeh.) This seems to go beyond the case of Samuel's contemporaries. As, habitually, in after times, people consulted the "prophet" (Nabi) in their emergencies, so now the "Seer" (Roeh.) The two offices were thenceforth united. In the early times, the title 'prophet' mostly described those who were recipients of Divine revelation or inspiration, but did not themselves predict the future[11]. Abraham was entitled a pro-

---

[8] Ib. x. 2-10.   [9] S. Matt. xxi. 1-3. S. Luke xix. 29-34.

[10] S. Mark xiv. 13-16. S. Luke xxii. 10-13.

[11] The title is given to Abraham ; (Gen. xx. 7. see Ps. cv. 15.) Aaron, as the speaker for Moses; (Ex. vii. 1.) Miriam ; (Ex. xv. 20.) the 70, on whom the Spirit of God came, by implication ; (the title Nebiim, *would that all God's people were* (Nebiim) *prophets,* corresponding to the word, *they prophesied,* i. e. praised God by inspiration of God. Num. xi. 25-9.) The prophet, sent by God, Judg. vi. 8, exercised the pastoral office of the prophet only. He was (like *the man of God,* sent to reprove Eli, 1 Sam. ii. 29.) sent on a specific message of rebuke, but was no bearer of prophecy. In Judg. ii. 20-22, it is not said, who was the organ of the prophecy. It is, in substance, the same as that at the be-

phet, received great prophecies, but did not himself prophesy. Jacob prophesied, but is not called a prophet.
Prophecies of Moses contained the whole future of Israel,
yet he is called a prophet by implication only.

5) The title also, *Gad,* [1]*David's Seer,* [2]*Heman, the king's
seer in the words of God,* [3]*Jeduthun, the king's seer,* implies
apparently some special relation of those prophets to David, as "seeing" for him what he saw not. On one occasion, Gad gave him prophetic advice as to his safety, which
he obeyed [4].

6) To *enquire of the Lord* was as received an idiom before the return from the Captivity, as to "consult" a physician or a lawyer is among us. The language occurs
throughout the Old Testament.   Not to repeat what has
been cited, Rebekkah, before Esau and Jacob were born,
went to [5]*enquire of the Lord,* and received a prophecy as
to the future of the nations to be born of her unborn sons.
Immediately [6]*after the death of Joshua, the children of Israel asked of the Lord, who shall go up for us against the
Canaanites first, to fight against them ? And the Lord
said, Judah shall go up.   Behold, I have delivered the land
into his hand.   Again,* they cried unto God, when oppres-

ginning of ch. ii. 1-4, which was delivered through an angel. *Deborah the prophetess* (Judg. iv. 41.) uttered a signal prophecy, but there is no trace that she
was a seer.   The other cases, in which the word is used, are themselves prophecies ; (Num. xii. 6. Deut. xiii. 1, 3, 5. xviii. 15, 18, 20, 22.) they foretell what
should be, they do not speak of what *was* then.   Deut. xxxiv. 10. only says
what was *not,* not what was.   *There arose not a prophet since in Israel, like
unto Moses.*   The writer of the book of Samuel states, that in his time the
nabi, prophet of God, was the organ of answering those who "enquired of God,"
as, in Samuel's time, "the seer."   He does not say, that this was the only office of
the prophet, nor that there had not been any *prophets* (Nebiim) before Samuel ;
only that those who exercised that one office, had not that name in his time.
Colenso's argument then against the Pentateuch drawn from it (n. 248.) is a
mistake of his own.   Even after this, prophets are mentioned collectively,
whose only office apparently was that, corresponding to the use of the word
in Num. xi. 29, the inspired praise of God.   1 Sam. x. 5. 10-12. xix. 19.   In both
cases, they are designated by ancient words ; the one, "company" (לַהֲקַת)
of prophets," occurring there only, (xix. 19 ;) the other, (חֶבֶל) "band of prophets," occurring probably in that sense in x. 5. 10. only.   [1] 2 Sam. xxiv. 11.
1 Chron. xxi. 9. 2 Chron. xxix. 25.   [2] 1 Chron. xxv. 5.
   [3] 2 Chron. xxxv. 15.   [4] 1 Sam. xxii. 5.   [5] Gen. xxv. 22.   [6] Judg. i. 1, 2.

sed by Philistines and Ammonites, and received an answer[7], rejecting them for awhile, it is not said through whom.   After the defeat at Gibeah, in the time of the Judges, the collected tribes thrice "enquired of" God[8] as to their punishment of Benjamin.   Having previously enquired by lot, as to the king to be given them, when *Saul was taken*, they were told verbally, on enquiry, where he was to be found[9].   It is remarked, as something unwonted, [10] *we enquired not at it* (the ark) *in the days of Saul*, i. e. after his degeneracy.   In David's days, it was a proverb of the acute practical sagacity of Ahitophel, [11] *The counsel of Ahitophel, which he counselled in those days, was as if a man had enquired at the oracle of God.   So was all the counsel of Ahitophel both with David and with Absalom.*   Jehoshaphat asks Ahab[12], *Enquire, I pray thee, at the word of the Lord to-day*, and would not be put off with the 400 Ashtaroth prophets; *Is there not still here a prophet of the Lord, that we may enquire of him?*   When the king of Israel desponded in the war with Moab, Jehoshaphat's instant resource was, as before[13], *Is there not here a prophet of the Lord, that we may enquire of the Lord by him?*   He says at once of Elisha, *The word of the Lord is with him.*   When the neglected book of the law had been found in the temple, Josiah sent to Huldah the prophetess, *to enquire* as to the future of Judah, and was answered that God had heard his prayers and that the evil should not be in his days[14].   The godless Zedekiah still sent to *enquire of the Lord* by Jeremiah[15].   In the Captivity, people, estranged from God, enquired of Him by Ezekiel[16], and were told that it would be to their hurt[17].   In the idolatrous kingdom of Israel too, Jeroboam sent to the prophet Ahijah, to enquire as to the issue of his son's sickness[18].   God also, by Elijah, pronounced that Ahaziah should not recover, be-

---

[7] Ib. x. 10-14.   [8] Ib. xx. 18, 23, (with mention of the ark) 27, 8.
[9] 1 Sam. x. 21.   [10] 1 Chr. xiii. 3.   [11] 2 Sam. xvi. 23.   [12] 1 Kgs. xxii. 5, 7.
[13] 2 Kings iii. 11, 12.   [14] Ib. xxii. 12-20.   [15] Jer. xxi. 2. xxxvii. 17.
[16] Ezek. xiv. 1-3. xx. 3.   [17] Ib. xiv. 4, 5, 7-10.   [18] 1 Kings xiv. 2-14.

cause he had enquired of the god of Ekron, not of God [1]. Even Benhadad sent to Elisha, to enquire whether he should recover of his disease [2]; and a messenger from Edom came to ask Isaiah as to the issue of the night of calamity which threatened them : they were bidden, if they would indeed enquire, to enquire with earnestness, and so to *return, come* [3].

Prophecies, on one principle yet so varied, declaring, all along, what the natural heart of man is still so slow to believe, that all human things are minutely ordered by *His* Will, Who knows alike the number of the stars and of the hairs of our heads which He alike created, the fall of a sparrow or of a kingdom to the ground, are any thing but " [4] exceptional."   Sometimes, through the importance of the occasion and of the answer, they became a part of those prophecies, which declared the nearer temporal future of Israel.

The prophecies, which God has willed to preserve to us as the main system of Old Testament prophecy, had these three chief subjects ; 1) God's purpose of love in the promised Seed, the pure unlooked-for unanticipated effluence of the love of the Creator.   2) Temporal judgments, the images, earnests, heralds, of the Judgment to come. 3) Temporal mercies, in, amid, through, those temporal judgments.

Of these three distinct distances of prophecy, prophecy as to *Him*, Whose Coming was the main object of the choice of the Jewish people, *the Seed* in Whom *all the nations of the earth* should *be blessed* [5], was expanded or defined the most slowly.   Forgiveness, through *the* Sacrifice, was impressed by the rite of sacrifice.   Else, the promise stood, like a beacon-light at the end of a long vista, of which the whole was foreshortened, yet that first long future shewed that it was a great way off.   Time and circumstance as to His earthly Origin, Birth of a Virgin, Birthplace, Character, Offices, Life, Death, Divinity,

<hr>

[1] 2 Kings i. 3, 4-6, 16, 17.   [2] Ib. viii. 8, 14.   [3] Is. xxi. 11, 12.
[4] Stähelin, p. 191.   [5] Gen. xxii. 18.

Atonement, Sufferings, rejection by His own, acceptance by us Gentiles, Glory, everlasting Kingdom, were expanded gradually, and most towards the time, when the gradual setting-in and deepening of God's temporal judgments might shake faith as to His yet distant purpose of love.

Of the two nearer distances of temporal prophecy, the furthest point was, to Abraham, the deliverance of his descendants from Egypt after the 400 years of affliction, and the judgment on the nation whom they should serve and who should afflict them [6]. The nearer events of prophecy to the Patriarchs, as time went on, were, the destruction of Sodom and Gomorrha [7]; the preternatural birth of Isaac [8]; the increase of Ishmael and the character of his descendants [9]; the beginning of the future of Esau and his descendants [10]; the temporal predictions to Jacob [11]; the elevation of Joseph [12], the seven years' plenty and seven years' famine of Egypt [13].

The prediction to Abraham, as to the deliverance from Egypt, was the first of a series of prophecies of judgment on the world, that first separation of the people of God from those who *would* be His enemies, and of God's opposite dealings with each; faint, yet, *as* a separation, expressive shadow of the great separation at the End. [14]*That nation, whom they shall serve, will I judge, and afterward they shall come out with great substance.* It was the first of the prophecies against the Heathen nations, not *as* Heathen, (for *as* Heathen, or simply *as* enemies of the Jews, no nation is threatened,) but as transgressors of God's unwritten law, graven, as it is until obliterated by man's will, on every human heart. And, if the people of God should become *not God's people* [15], the like or severer judgments were foretold to them; nay, judgment was evermore prophesied as to [16]*begin with the house of*

---

[6] Ib. xv. 13, 14.   [7] Ib. xviii. 17-21. xix. 13.

[8] Ib. xv. 4-6. xvii. 1-19. comp. Rom. iv. 3. 16-21.   [9] Ib. xvi. 10-12. xvii. 20. xxi. 18.   [10] Ib. xxv. 23. xxvii. 39, 40. (comp. xxxvi. 6, 7.)   [11] Ib. xxviii. 15. xxxi. 3 sqq. xxxii. 9, 28. (comp. Hos. xii. 4.)   [12] Ib. xxxvii. 6-9.

[13] Ib. xli.   [14] Gen. xv. 14.   [15] Hos. i. 9.   [16] 1 Pet. iv. 17.

God, and to fall on the heathen instruments of its execution, only for exceeding or abusing their commission. Those judgments on Israel were to have several stages; they were to increase, Moses foretold[1], in severity: at last, on impenitence, they were to end in a temporary captivity; and that, on repentance, was to issue in restoration to their own land. Such, at the distance of 850 years, was the furthest horizon of their then future.

But, within this period, there were marked lesser periods, each with its own prophecies of weal or woe. Nor were these any chance unsystematic predictions. Varied, often minute, seldom repeated identically, they were one in their end and purpose, to fix in men's minds, that God held in His hands His creature's destiny, that good and evil came from Him, and were apportioned by *Him* who foretold them ere they came,—good of His own free goodness, evil as drawn upon His creatures by their own evil.

One such period, the prophesied 40 years[2], during which they were to wander in the wilderness, until the former generation should have died there, had already elapsed.

The next period, that of comparative obedience under Joshua, was chiefly one of fulfilment of prophecy. Yet here too prophecy accompanied even miracle, (as at the passage of the Jordan, or the fall of the walls of Jericho,) and the leading events of the conquest, as the capture of Ai, the defeat of the five kings, and the crowning victory by the waters of Merom. Over and above the fulfilment of the larger prophecy, that they should inherit the land promised to their fathers, the blessings of Jacob and Moses, so far as they related to temporal things, began their course of fulfilment. The lot, directed by God, fulfilled the specific promises to Asher, Zebulon, Issachar, and as to the territorial portions of Ephraim and Judah[3].

---

[1] Lev. xxvi.   [2] Num. xiv. 33. xxxii. 13. Deut. ii. 14.

[3] The portions of Judah, Ephraim, and Manasseh, were assigned to them by lot, only before the rest. (Josh. xv. 1. xvi. 1. xvii. 1, 2.) " By lot was their inheritance, as the Lord commanded by the hand of Moses, *for the nine tribes and the half tribe*, Josh. xiv. 2.

The tribes, in the nature of their temporal blessings, had a perpetual memory, not of the goodness only, but of the Providence of God, who brought about for each, what He had promised to each. The vines of Judah[4]; the exceeding fruitfulness of the portion of Ephraim and Manasseh[5]; the olive-groves of Asher[6], its iron and brass from its near Tyrian merchandise[7]; the active commerce of Zebulon[8], and the glass of its sands[9]; the resting enrichment of Is-

---

[4] Gen. xlix. 11. Hebron, below which lay the valley of Eshcol, was given to Caleb on condition of expelling its giant inhabitants. (Josh. xiv. 12, 13.) The Vineyards of Engedi (Cant. i. 14.) also lay in Judah. Its vines and balsams were still famed in the time of Origen (in Cant. Opp. iii. 67.) " Uzziah had vine-dressers in the mountains and in Carmel," [of Judah.] 2 Chr. xxvi. 10. The terraces, on the sides of the now barren mountains of Judah, were noticed by Clarke (Travels, ii. 520.) and by General Straton as "vestiges of ancient luxuriance." (in Keith on Prophecy, p. 109.)

[5] Gen. xlix. 25. Deut. xxxiii. 13, 14. Jer. iii. 19. "All travellers bear testimony to the 'general growing richness' and beauty of the country in going north-wards from Jerusalem, the 'innumerable fountains' and streamlets, the villages more thickly scattered than any where in the south, the continuous cornfields and orchards, the moist vapoury atmosphere." (Martineau, 516. 521. V. d. Velde, i. 386, 8. Stanley, 234, 5.) Grote, in Smith Bibl. Dict. v. Ephraim. Add Von Schubert, iii. 127. Drew, Scripture Lands, p. 95.

[6] Deut. xxxiii. 24. It included Carmel, (on its richness see on Am. i. 2.) the Western end of the valley of Esdraelon, and a rich lowland on the shore from Carmel to Zidon. (Jos. Ant. v. i. 22.)

[7] It is foretold, that the metals should be in abundant use in a manufactured state, not, that they should be found in Asher. The language is different from that in Deut. viii. 9. where Moses speaks of Palestine generally as "a land whose stones are iron, and out of whose hills thou mayest dig brass." Iron was supplied in abundance by the basalt of Hauran, and is found in Lebanon. Volney, i. 233. Russegger, i. 693, 4. Palestine has not, however, been explored geologically, so as to show whether there are worked-out mines.

[8] Gen. xlix. 13. Deut. xxxiii. 19. All have remarked on the difficulty of tracing exactly the boundaries of each tribe, partly because many places are not yet identified, partly because, the distribution being (as Keith observed) that of towns with their districts, the line was probably very irregular, as in some of our English counties. Josephus says, " They of Zabulon received the country, extending to the lake of Gennesareth, and around Carmel and the sea." Ant. v. 1. 22.

[9] Deut. xxxiii. 19. " Two miles from Ptolemais a very little stream runs by, called Beleus, where by the tomb of Memnon is a wondrous place of 100 cubits. It is circular and hollow, and yields the sand for glass ; after it has been emptied, many shiploads having been taken, it is filled up again." Jos. B. J. ii. 10. 2. " A tiny shore, but unexhausted." Tac. Hist. v. 7. " A shore of not above

sachar, through which that commerce passed[1]; the enriching neighbourhood of the sea of Galilee to Naphtali[2];— these were no mere natural gifts of God's Providence. Their several blessings were, in a manner, the heraldic mottoes of each tribe, and spoke of God's foreordaining love. Still more, those portions of the prophecy which pourtrayed the character of the tribes. They are the banner of God hanging over them, when faithful to Him. The lion-might of Judah, of Gad, and of Dan[3], Ephraim's horns of power, the swift energy of Benjamin[4], could be put forth, on each occasion, as strength which God had pledged to them. In that reeling strife which Jacob fore-

half a mile, it has sufficed for yielding glass during so many centuries." Plin. N. H. xxxvi. 26. Ps. Jon. on Deut. xxxiii. 19. has, "they produced mirrors and vessels of glass from the shore."

[1] Gen. xlix. 14, 15. Deut. xxxiii. 18. "Rejoice, Zebulun, in thy going out, and, Issachar, in thy tents." The rule of Hebrew parallelism, whereby each hemistich may be supplied out of the other, hardly applies here, where the main subject of each hemistich is a distinct tribe. For, if it were paraphrased, "Rejoice, Zebulun and Issachar, in thy going out and in thy tents," there would be nothing assigned as characteristic of either, contrary to the character of the other prophecies. The mention of the tents, in contrast to the "going out" of Issachar, corresponds with the image in Gen. xlix. Their joint enrichment is expressed in Deut. xxxiii. 19. The rich "great plain" of Esdraelon fell almost wholly to Issachar.

[2] Naphtali stretched far Northward from the N. W. end of the sea of Galilee to Anti-libanus, with which Mount Naphtali was connected. Josephus says, "The Naphtalites received the parts turned towards the East unto Damascus, and the upper parts of Galilee to Mount Lebanus and the sources of Jordan." (Ant. v. l. 22.) It would thus become the channel of the trade from Damascus southwards. The description, "He giveth goodly words," (Gen. xlix. 21.) has no known explanation in those times. Yet the Eng. Vers. "Naphtali is a hind let loose, he giveth goodly words," (which Dr. Stanley pronounces, "mistranslated," Pal. 363.) is right. The rendering, "is a spreading terebinth; he giveth forth goodly boughs;" Ib. (originally from Bochart, ii. 258. Leipz.) is founded on an altered text, אֵילָה for אַיָּלָה, and אֲבָרֵי, for אֲמִירֵי, from אָמִיר, which occurs only in Is. xvii. 6, 9. has no known plural, and in its own nature would not have one, since it means, not "bough," generally, but, as we say, "a leader." "Leaders" would, of course, be a defect. Onk. Vulg. Syr. Saad. Sam.-Ar. agree so far against the LXX.

[3] The title "lion's whelp," etymologically would signify the cub, not yet separated from its mother, and (Ezek. xix. 2, 3, 5.) is used of the age before it has grown to be the "young lion," כְּפִיר, which catches prey. Yet there is apparently no such emphasis here, since it is used of Judah. (Gen. xlix. 9.)

[4] Gen. xlix. 27.

told of Gad, and which, at the Eastern outskirts of the
land, he had ever to wage, now pressed in, but *at the last
overcoming* [5], he bore, a more than "charmed," a God-
protected "life."   So Dan, trampled upon in the dust by
the horse-hoofs of the enemy, was still, out of the dust, to
cast backward the horse and his rider, deadly as a serpent's bite [6].   And yet, although Dan was then little inferior in numbers to Judah [7], and larger than either Ephraim or Manasseh separately, the brunt of the conflict was to
be borne by Judah and Ephraim.   The blessing to Judah,
[8] *Thou wilt bring him back to his people ; his hands strive
for him ; and help from his enemies Thou wilt be*, was the
abiding hope of the wives and mothers of Judah, when its
armies went forth to the field.

Three tribes had, for the misdeeds of their first fathers.
lost, successively, the primogeniture ; existence alone was
promised them; but Reuben was excluded from eminence;
Simeon and Levi were to be dispersed in Israel.   In the
wilderness, Reuben, 7th in point of numbers, sought to
recover the primogeniture [9]; Simeon appears to have been
prominent in the abominations of Baal Peor [10], and had lost
nearly two thirds of its numbers, since the first numbering
in the wilderness [11]; Levi's fierceness had become a sanctified zeal.   Simeon then disappeared from the blessing of
Moses [12]; Reuben's perilous pride was stayed by the prophecy of the fewness of his numbers [13]; the sentence on

[5] Ib. 19.   [6] Ib. 17.   [7] Dan, in the 2nd year, Ib. 62,700 ; (Num. i. 38, 39.)
Judah, 74,600. (Ib. 26, 7.) Dan, in the 39th year, 64,400 ; (Ib. xxvi. 42, 3.)
Judah 76,500. (Ib. 22.)   [8] Deut. xxxiii. 7.

[9] Such seems to have been the object of the rebellion of Dathan and Abiram,
claiming civil, as Korah and his company of Levites claimed ecclesiastical, dignity, Num. xvi.   [10] Num. xxv. 14.   [11] It had 59, 300,
Num. i. 23. but 22, 200 only, Ib. xxvi. 14.

[12] The remarkableness of its omission gave rise to an incorrect correction in
the Alex. MS. of the LXX. which got over two seeming difficulties at once by
inserting it in the verse relating to Reuben ; "and let Simeon be many in number."   Apollinaris observes that "the accurate copies do not mention Simeon."

[13] " Let Reuben live and not die ; and let his men be few."   The E. V., following Aben-Ezra, has supplied the "not" from the preceding clause ; but this,
although not infrequent, when the negative is in the main clause, is not ad-

Levi, although unreversed, was turned into a blessing and
an occasion of greater nearness to God.   So was there
stamped on the history of the people the great law of the
justice and love of God, that irreversible chastisement
deepens on persevering impenitence, but, on repentance,
became, through the rich exuberance of His mercy, the
channel of His choicest favours.   In the subsequent history, although Simeon and Reuben still lived, Reuben so
dwindled away, that we find his cities completely in the
possession of Moab and Ammon; Simeon had a scanty
settlement taken out of Judah [1], yet, if the tradition be
true, he too gained by the breaking of his fierce might,
and while some of his sons, in search of pastoral wealth,
broke out beyond the borders of the promised land [2], and
probably became an Arab tribe [3], others became the teachers of the little children of Israel [4].   These prophecies had
their continuous fulfilment, and so, when, after nearly $3\frac{1}{2}$
centuries, Judah, from being an eminent, became the
royal tribe, the promise that it should not be dissolved
until Shiloh should *come* [5], gained the more impressive

missible when (as here) it is in a subordinate clause.   The Verss. then rightly
omit the negative, although the Vulg. alone has the rendering, et sit parvus
in numero."   [1] Josh. xix. 9.   [2] 1 Chr. iv. 39-43.

[3] Tebrizi, in his Comm. on the Hammasa, mentions three Jewish Arab tribes
as existing up to the times of Mohammed.

[4] "Another exposition, ' there shall not be to thee poor scribes and teachers
of infants, save from Simeon.' " Rashi ad loc.   The Jerus. Targ. has, " I will
divide the tribe of Simeon, able teachers of the law in the congregation of Jacob."   That of Ps. Jon. " I will divide the possession of the sons of Simeon
into two parts ; one part shall go forth to it out of the midst of the sons of
Judah, and part among the rest of the tribes of Jacob."

[5] שִׁלֹה (as it stands in the Hebrew text) would be an old form, which, becoming a proper name thus early, never entered into the ordinary language.
In this case Ezekiel's paraphrase, which any how attests that he recognised
the prophecy as relating to the Messias, would indicate also that the original
meaning of the name was not familiar to his hearers.   *Remove the diadem and
take off the crown—I will overturn, overturn, overturn it, and it shall be no
more, until He come Whose right it is ; and I will give it.* (xxi. 31, 2. Heb.)
Ezekiel's עַד-בֹּא אֲשֶׁר לֹו הַמִּשְׁפָּט may have been chosen to bring out the personal sense
of the word שׁילה, (if written and pointed שֵׁלֹה for שִׁלֹה, as, in the next verse, מותה,
עילה,) which was not expressed by the form of the word itself.   Ezekiel's paraphrase apparently determined Onkelos to render, "until Messias shall come,

significance, was fixed by Ezekiel, and became the centre
of the temporal hopes of Israel's continuance, when it was
hemmed in to the two tribes whose permanence was promised or hinted at, Judah and Benjamin. So, largest and
least met in these two great prophecies, the obedience of

Whose is the kingdom," (retained in the Targ. Hieros.) and the Greek translators, the Syriac, and Saadias, (τὰ ἀποκείμενα αὐτῷ, LXX. and Theod. in Eus.
Dem. Ev. p. 370. ᾧ ἀποκεῖται, Aq. Symm. " he whose it is," Syr. Saad.) There
is nothing to be said against this, since, (apart from Gen. vi. 3.) ש = שֶׁ certainly occurs in the ancient song of Deborah, (Judg. v. 7.) and, being also Phœnician, is an early, not a late form of the relative. (See Introd. to Jonah, p. 250.)

The reading שלה, however, is attested by the paraphrase of Ps.Jon. "until
the time that the king Messiah shall come, the little one of his sons," (from שַׁי,
i. q. שלל, "embryo," or the Arab. *Saleel*, "the new-born male child taken from
its mother's womb." (So Abulw. & Kim.) The authority of the MSS is also
for it; 38 MSS only having the defective שלה, none the punctuation שִׁלֹה. The
exstant Samaritan text also omits the ', but the Samaritan version retains the
word as a proper name; an Arab.Sam. Comm. on Genesis comments on the ';
one Sam.Arab. version substitutes Solomon, or peacemaker, while another renders, " he who is worthy of it." De Rossi Varr. Lect. iv. App. p. 217, 219.
There are traces of a Kri and Kethiv, שלה Keth. שילה Kri in the Echa Rabbathi,
f. 586. Ven. 1545 (but שלה Keth. in Mart. Pug. Fid. f. 531.) and of a Kri שלו
in Mattan Chehun. in Norzi ap. de R. p. 218. An etymology שי לה, " to him
are gifts," occurs in the Beresh. Ketsara in Mart. f. 251. and in the Talmud
Horaioth in Yalkut Shimeoni, f. 49. 3 and in Jarchi in de Rossi, p. 219. In
this case the form would be according to the analogy of שׁילֹם from שׁלה and גלה
from גלה &c, (see Hengst. Christ. i. 68. ed. 1.) This must any how be the etymology of the name of the place *Shiloh*, " rest," a name given probably after
Israel rested there. The etymology remains the same, if שילה be regarded as
an abridged form for שִׁילוֹן, (Hengst. i. 68. ed. 2.) Nothing turns on the etymology; the only question raised grammatically, is, whether the proper name
Shiloh be the Nom. or the Acc.; *until Shiloh come,* or *until he come to Shiloh.*

The rendering, " until he come to Shiloh," is obviously the reverse of the fact,
since the eminence of Judah was, not *before* he came to Shiloh, but afterwards.
The words, " staff, sceptre," must relate either to the rule *in* Judah or *of* Judah; i. e. of the tribe within itself, or towards the other tribes. Of the tribe
within itself, it would be unmeaning, if limited to the entrance into the promised land; since it was equally true of every other tribe. Of rule towards
others, it would be untrue; since, although the most numerous tribe and first
in dignity, (the birthright, forfeited by the elder sons, Reuben, Simeon, Levi,
having descended to it,) it had absolutely no authority. The sole authority,
which was lodged any where, was that given directly by God to Moses of the tribe
of Levi, and subsequently to Joshua of the tribe of Ephraim. Caleb was faithful as well as Joshua, but Joshua had entire authority given him; Caleb, the
chief prince of Judah, was as subordinate as any other. Rationalist interpreters have no choice but to call the prophecy, one " framed after the event,"

the heathen to Him our Peace, the calling of the Gentiles by those Northern tribes, where Jesus lived and whence Apostles came, and which were, above the rest, the high-way of Palestine.   Then Zebulon indeed rejoiced in its going out, and, with Naphtali, [1]*called the people to the mount,* i. e. the Holy Mount of God.

(e. g. Davidson, i. 198.) i. e. a falsehood. But then they are bound to shew that it agrees with the event. They cannot deny that, on the Jewish and Christian interpretation, it does. Judah did maintain its corporate existence until Jesus came, and then was dissolved. On the Anti-Christian, it had no fulfilment. The facts, that it was the most numerous tribe, that it marched first in the wilderness, that it drew its lot first for its inheritance, involve no authority. In numbers, it was little more than Joseph, (i. e. Ephraim and Manasseh collectively,) ⅓th only larger than Dan. In the wilderness, it marched at the head of two tribes, East of the Ark, as did Reuben on the South, Ephraim on the West, Dan on the North. This was dignity, not authority. The camp of Judah (Num. ii. 9.) had no other character than that of Reuben, (Ib. 10.) Ephraim, (24.) Dan. (31.) In the whole conquest of Canaan under Joshua, it has not even any priority ; although, if it had, a regiment or tribe, ordered to march first, has dignity, not authority. It is *under*, not *in* command. But, in a marked way, throughout that history, (except when, *after the conquest*, Caleb volunteered, and Ephraim asked for a larger lot,) the children of Israel are spoken of as one whole. It is throughout, *Israel, all Israel, the children of Israel.* The several tribes are merged in the whole. Twice in the book of Judges, Judah is related to have gone first to battle, by command of God. (Judg. i. 1, 2. xx. 18.) On the first occasion, he fought only as a tribe, joining in mutual alliance with Simeon, whose lot was taken out of his. (Judg. i. 3.) But both cases shew that it had no such prerogative ; else, there had been no occasion to enquire of God.

Still more unmeaning does the other clause become, "and to him [i. e. Judah] shall be the obedience of the nations," i. e. (as these writers explain it) " Judah will be the leader of the other tribes till Canaan be subdued, and, after obtaining a quiet and sure abode in the country, shall *still maintain its superiority.*" (Davids. i. 200.) But "superiority" is not receiving "obedience," still less, as the word meant doubtless, "loving obedience."   comp. יִקְּהַת אֵם "reverent obedience to a mother," Prov. xxx. 17. and the connected יָקֶה (prop. name) and the Arabic *wakeha*, "obeyed ;" *wakai*, viii. "was reverent to God." עַמִּים also are " the peoples, nations," not " the Jewish people." Obedience also is rendered to an individual, or a whole, not to a part. Obedience, when rendered, was rendered to the kings, not to Judah. Judah was a large part and, after the two first reigns, almost the whole of the people who obeyed. They were the obeyers, not the obeyed.

[1] Deut. xxxiii. 9. The prophecy, like that as to the "goodly words" of Naphtali, has no explanation at those times. The notion, that "a common sanctuary was intended for them in Mount Tabor," was one of Herder's crotchets, which I regret to see in Stanley's Jewish Church, p. 662.

The prophecy, (in the sense, in which all understood it, until, in the last century, it was in the interest of unbelief not to understand it,) fixed, at the new era of the people, the promise to Abraham. The promise, "in thy seed shall all the nations of the earth be blessed," was expanded in both its parts. Judah was pointed out as the line, in which that Seed should come; the blessing was, that he should be "Peace;" that blessing was to reach the Gentiles through obedience to Him. The name Shiloh was enlarged in the later prophecies of "the Prince Peace."

The book of Judges almost opens with the prophecy, that the nations whom they had left should be as [2]*thorns in their sides, and their gods a snare.* Its history contains the fulfilment of this, and is the first stage of the completion of Moses' prophecy. The deliverances on repentance are sometimes without, yet, in the cases of Barak[3] and Gideon[4] and Sampson[5], with prophecy.

The chain of individual personal prophecy was continued on in the predicted judgments on Eli's sons[6], and on his house[7]; on Saul[8]; even on David in the threefold punishment on his great sin[9]; on Solomon[10]; as to each there had been preceding promises[11]. Yet the predictions are not scattered profusely. That upon Eli's house, as it was fulfilled in successive generations, remained, one continued warning to the priesthood. One prophecy of woe overshadowed all the later years of David. The prophecy as to Jericho[12] brooded over its mighty ruins for some six centuries. Else, prophecy comes as the harbinger and forerunner of changes, not in tranquil times. Once only[13], when preaching repentance to Israel, Samuel foretold to them their deliverance from the Philistines. Twice God revealed himself to Solomon in dreams, at his first choice[14], and after the dedication of the temple[15]: then,

[2] Judg. ii. 3.   [3] Ib. iv. 6, 7, 9.   [4] Ib. vi. 12-16. vii. 2-7.   [5] Ib. xiii. 3-5.
[6] 1 Sam. ii. 34.   [7] Ib. 31-3. 36.   [8] Ib. xiii. 14. xv. 26, 28, 29. xxviii. 19.
[9] 2 Sam. xii. 10-14.   [10] 1 Kgs. xi. 9-12.   [11] To Saul, 1 Sam. x. 1-6; to David, Ib. xvi. 1-13. 2 Sam. vii. 11-16. xii. 25; to Solomon, 1 Kgs. iii. 5-14. ix. 2-9.   [12] Josh. vi. 26.   [13] 1 Sam. vii. 3.   [14] 1 Kgs. iii. 5-15.   [15] Ib. ix. 2-20.

having gifted him with wisdom, He once more only [1] revealed Himself outwardly to him [2], to pronounce the sentence, mitigated for David's sake.   On and after the division of the ten tribes, prophecy and miracle were even more bestowed on the schismatic kingdom of Israel than upon Judah, which had the temple-worship and *the teaching priesthood* [3], until the conflict of unbelief had set in in Judah too, and corruption was, although at the distance of two centuries, preparing its destruction.   The temporal kingdom of Israel was inaugurated by the prophecy of Ahijah to Jeroboam [4].   On the morn of the consecration

[1] "The Lord God was angry with Solomon, because his heart was turned from the Lord God of Israel, which *had appeared to him twice.*" Ib. xi. 9.

[2] Ib. 11-13.

[3] 2 Chr. xv. 3.   The prophet Ahaziah described the condition of Israel, in contrast with Judah, *for a long season Israel hath been without the true God, and without a teaching priesthood, and without law.*   Dr Stanley says of this period, "they, [the prophets,] maintained the true religion in the northern tribes, *at times when in Judah it was crushed to the ground,* and when in Israel it had to struggle against severe persecution or sluggish apathy."   J. Ch. 421.   The prophets were God's instruments for maintaining what remained of religion in Israel against the state-corruption, but Dr Stanley's account of Judah, and of the relative condition of Israel, is unhistorical.   The bad reign of Rehoboam lasted but 17 years; Abijah's (with an interval of good, 2 Chr. xiii.) 3; Asa's declension lasted 5 years; (Ib. xvi.) Jehoram, under the influence of Ahab's daughter Athaliah, reigned 8 evil years; Athaliah, 6; Joash after Jehoiada's death, seemingly 1; in all, thus far, 39; whereas the good part of Asa's reign was 36 years; that of Jehoshaphat, 25; of Joash, seemingly 39 years; in all, about a century.   Most of Amaziah's reign was also good, as also of Uzziah's.   The increased corruption of Judah seems to have set in, somewhat before the reign of Jotham. (2 Chr. xxvii. 3.)   Yet Hosea bears witness to the relatively good state of Judah. (xi. 12. iv. 15.)   In Israel, the idolatry, which all its kings encouraged, must (according to St. Paul's statement, Rom. i.) have been an intense source of immorality.   All concurred in "making Israel to sin," besides the yet worse corruptions of the house of Omri. (See Introd. to Hosea, p. 2, 3.)

[4] 1 Kgs. xi. 29-38.   Dr Stanley says, "It was in the disorders at the close of Solomon's reign, that the Prophetic Order assumed an importance in the state, such as it had never acquired before.   Samuel had transferred the crown from Saul to David; Nathan, from Adonijah to Solomon; but Ahijah, in transferring it from Rehoboam to Jeroboam, created not merely a new dynasty but a kingdom." (J. Ch. p. 420.)   Scripture says, that Samuel anointed David at God's command *against his own judgment,* for he would have chosen Eliab; (1 Sam. xvi. 6.) and against his own wishes, since he *mourned for Saul.* (Ib.

of the state-apostacy, its final desecration and the name of its overthrower were foretold 3½ centuries before [5]. The beginning of two of its four first dynasties [6], the close of all the four [7], was foretold. In the reign of Ahab, miracle and prophecy were put forth against the new corruption of Baal. The great famine and its close [8]; Ahab's twofold victory over Benhadad [9]; his death [10], and the specific retribution of the innocent blood of Naboth upon himself [11] and upon Jezebel [12]; the extirpation of Ahab's house [13], and its respite [14], are minutely foretold. Yet again no mere foretelling. It is chastisement; mercy; then, at last, excision. This striving, on God's part, to win Ahab who *sold himself to work wickedness,* is one of those marvellous touches of the long-suffering of Divine love, which meet us in the Old Testament. God even complains, that Ahaziah, the son of Ahab, did not enquire of Him, instead of the god of Ekron, as to the issue of his illness [15]. Even the last of the doomed house received promise of victory from Elisha, when united with Jehoshaphat [16], deliverance from peril through Elisha's supernatural knowledge of the king of Syria's counsels [17], and in the siege of Samaria [18]. Then followed the guardian-promise to the house of Jehu. Contrary to all experience as to the

xv. 35.) David says also that God appointed, that Solomon should succeed him. (1 Chr. xxii. 9, 10. xxviii. 5, 6.) Nathan was very probably the organ of communicating that will of God; but, when Adonijah would have reversed God's appointment which David had confirmed by oath to Bathsheba, (1 Kgs. i. 13.) Nathan simply advised Bathsheba, how to save her own life and Solomon's by informing David. (Ib. ii. 13.) Ahijah the prophet declared himself the organ of God, *Thus saith the Lord, the God of Israel.* 1 Kgs. xi. 13. It is misleading, to speak only of the human agents and *their* acts, and to ignore that they acted at the express command of God. And this the more, since, although Dr Stanley speaks of their "endeavours on both sides to keep up a sentiment of humanity," (p. 421.) he says also, " at times, they increased the bitterness of the division," (p. 457) and "they were not without grievous shortcomings," (p. 450.) as if they had not acted and spoken under inspiration of the Spirit of God.   [5] Ib. xiii. 2.

[6] Jeroboam's and Jehu's.   [7] Jeroboam's by Ahijah, Ib. xiv. 6-16. Baasha's by Jehu son of Hanani, Ib. xvi. 1-4.   [8] Ib. xvii. 1. xviii. 1.   [9] Ib. xx. 13, 14, 28.   [10] Ib. 42. xxii. 17-23. 28.   [11] xxi. 19.   [12] 2 Kgs. ix. 36, 7.   [13] 1 Kgs. xxi. 21-24.   [14] Ib. 29.   [15] 2 Kgs. i. 2-4. 16.   [16] Ib. iii. 17, 18.   [17] Ib. vi. 8-23.   [18] Ib. vii. 1.

former kings of Israel and the history of those who came after, the house of Jehu was to last till the 4th generation [1]. The 3 promised victories of Jehoash [2] were Elisha's last bequest to his people; Jonah, amid the weakness of the kingdom, predicted the great extension of the kingdom of Jeroboam II. [3]; when this had been fulfilled, Amos, at the moment of the separated kingdom's greatest might, reversed the prediction and pronounced the affliction of Israel in the scene of its recent victories [4]. Hosea foretold the breaking of its might in the valley of Jezreel [5]. The Syrians, who had smitten them but by whose aid, after this, they sought to gain Jerusalem for themselves [6], (perhaps as a support against Assyria,) should, Amos foretold, be carried captive to Kir [7], a country loosely connected with Assyria, and, at that time, in rebellion against it [8]. Contemporaneous are the two prophets' predictions of the final extinction of its kingdom [9]; and, in regard to it and its kings, the close of all these particular prophecies, of all this care which they had wasted, follows in those vast comprehensive prophecies, which above 2600 years have not yet exhausted, that they should *abidingly* be *wanderers among the nations* [10], despised among the nations [11], sifted as in a sieve in the four corners in the earth, yet every real grain under the care of God [12].

The recorded prophecies in the early times of the kingdom of Judah were also given on emergencies. But these were the fewer, since God's promise to David secured the calm succession in the kingdom [13], in strange contrast with the broken dynasties of Israel and the anarchy in which they expired. The sacred historians were of the kingdom of Judah; yet they have only preserved four temporal prophecies in its early history; that of Shemaiah to Reho-

---

[1] 2 Kgs. x. 30.   [2] Ib. xiii. 14-19.   [3] Ib. xiv. 25.   [4] See on Am. vi. 14. p. 208, 9.   [5] See on Hos. i. 5. p. 9. x. 14. p. 69, 70.   [6] Is. vii. 2-6.   [7] See on Am. i. 5. p. 160, 1.   [8] Niebuhr, Gesch. Ass. p. 156.   [9] See on Am. ix. 8. p. 222.   [10] See on Hos. ix. 17. p. 61, 2.   [11] See on Hos. viii. 8. p. 52.   [12] See on Am. ix. 9.   [13] 2 Sam. vii. 12-16. 1 Kgs. viii. 25. xi. 13. 32. 36. 2 Chr. vi. 16. Ps. cxxxii. 11, 12.

boam[14], during the invasion of Shishak; that of Hanani
the Seer to Asa[15], on his alliance with Syria; that of Ja-
haziel to Jehoshaphat[16], when Moab, Ammon, and Edom,
conspired to extirpate Judah; and the personal prophecy
of Elisha against Jehoram[17]. Yet a fifth is referred to,
[18] *the vision of Iddo the Seer against Jeroboam the son of
Nebat.* But Judah had its prophets throughout. Nathan the prophet probably even survived Solomon, since
[18] *the acts of Solomon, first and last,* were *written in the
words of Nathan the prophet, and in the prophecy of Ahijah the Shilonite, and in the vision of Iddo the seer against
Jeroboam.* But the prophecies of Ahijah and Iddo being
apparently specific prophecies, it would follow that Nathan lived to write the latter acts of Solomon also. Iddo
survived Rehoboam and Abijah, since he wrote their histories in two distinct works[19]. Azariah the prophet, son
of Oded[20], awakened Asa to a great reformation, which
drew back many of Israel too to the worship of God, a reformation deeper apparently than those of Hezekiah or
Josiah. Jehu, son of Hanani, who had prophesied against
Baasha[21], appears as a prophet in the kingdom of Judah
under Jehoshaphat[22], whose acts, first and last, he wrote,
in his old age[23]. Both Jehu son of Hanani, and Eliezer
son of Dodavah of Mareshah[24], rebuked Jehoshaphat for
his alliance with Ahab, which, by the intermarriage of
his son Jehoram with Athaliah, so fatally corrupted Judah. Few as are the prophecies which are preserved at
this period, the title Seer, given to Iddo, Hanani, and

---

[14] 2 Chr. xii. 7, 8.   [15] Ib. xvi. 7-9.   [16] Ib. xx. 14-17.

[17] Ib. xxi. 12-15.   [18] Ib. ix. 29.   [19] 2 Chr. xii. 15. It is said that he
wrote להתיחש, lit. "to genealogise," paraphrased by the Vulg. "diligenter ex-
posita." In xiii. 22. the title מדרש implies a diligent commentary, and it is
said to contain "the matters of Abijah and his ways and his words." It is
assumed that Ye'do or Ye'di, יעדי or יעדו, (2 Chr. ix. 29.) is the same as Iddo,
עדו. (xii. 15. xiii. 22.)

[20] Ib. xv. 8-15. All suppose Oded, v. 8. to be the same as Azariah the son
of Oded, v. 1.   [21] 1 Kgs. xvi. 1-4, 12.   [22] 2 Chr. xix. 2.

[23] Ib. xx. 34. From the middle of the reign of Baasha to the end of Jehoshaphat's, are about 50 years. There is then no reason to doubt the identity of the prophet.   [24] Ib. xx. 37.

Jehu son of Hanani, implies a habitual gift of prophecy; nor was the title *Nabi*, "prophet," ever given in those times to any individual, who was not the organ of prophecy, as well as the interpreter of the Divine will. Nathan the prophet had conveyed to David the promise, that [1] *his kingdom* should *be established for ever before God*, his *throne should be for ever;* a promise which, in itself, enlarged while it limited the prophecy of Jacob. This prophecy had been expanded in the Psalms of David and Solomon. The great mystery which lay in the original promise of victory over the Evil one through the Suffering of the Seed of the woman, had been unfolded to David in the Passion, Death, continued Life, session at God's right hand, [2] of Him to Whom alone God said, *Thou art My Son, this day have I begotten Thee*, to Whom the kingdoms of the world should be converted. Hence the special religious interest in the continuance of David's line, around which the prophecies of the Messiah in Hosea and Amos[3] among the ten tribes chiefly turned; hence the great prophecy of Joel, the type of so many later prophecies, predicted that wide outpouring of the Spirit of God, beginning in Judah and Jerusalem.

In the network of prophecy, the definite predictions of the earlier prophets became the all-but-present of the later. Hosea and Amos had foretold the captivity of Syria and Israel; Isaiah fixes the spoiling of both within one year[4], the breaking up of Ephraim, as a people, in 65 years[5]. As usual, the men of God do not point out the detail of the fulfilment of their prophecies; yet, by a combination of scattered dates, out of which the number, 65, could not have been put together, even as a marginal gloss, we find that the 65 years were fufilled to the exact year[6].

---

[1] 2 Sam. vii. 12-16.   [2] Ps. ii. xvi. xxii. cx.

[3] Hos. iii. Am. ix. 11, 12.   [4] Is. viii. 4.   [5] Ib. vii. 8.

[6] Two contradictory modes of escaping the definiteness of this prophecy were adopted; 1) that it was a gloss; 2) that, since the captivity of Israel fell probably some 20 years after this date, it had no fulfilment. They are contradictory, because a gloss, as it would have been written after the event, would have been adapted to the event, and 65 years could not have been adapted, in reference to a period, manifestly not much exceeding 20. Isaiah however speaks,

Isaiah and Nahum foretold the deliverance of Jerusalem from Sennacherib, when he counted it an easy prey, and his own death[7]. Both foretell the suddenness, easiness, utterness of the overthrow. *[8]At eventide, behold terror : before morning, he is not. He shall shake his hand against the mount of the daughter of Zion.* God would accept the challenge. *The Lord, the Lord of hosts, shall lop the bough with terror.* Micah[9] and Isaiah[10] foretell the captivity at Babylon, when Assyria, not Babylon, was the object of Judah's dread, and the tributary king of Babylon, under plea of congratulation on Hezekiah's recovery[11], was probably courting his alliance against Assyria. Isaiah foretells the conquest of Babylon by Medes and Persians[12], in the "night of its festivity," and its utter desolation[13]; the recovery of Tyre, after 70 years *as the years*

not of a captivity of Ephraim, but of its entire dissolution, as a separate people; "shall be broken from being a people." This plainly was, when Esarhaddon brought others in their stead, (Ezr. iv. 2, 10.) and since those by whom he replaced them came in part from Babylon, (Ib. & 2 Kings xvii. 24.) it took place doubtless at a time when Esarhaddon had subdued some revolt at Babylon. But, since the reign of Esarhaddon at Babylon was from about, B.C. 680, to B.C. 667, 13 years, (see Rawl. Herod. i. p. 482.) Pekah's invasion of Judah, not before his 17th year, B.C. 742. when the reign of Ahaz began, yet, (on account of the number of events in the remaining 3 years of Pekah's reign,) probably in that year, the close of the 65 years would fall in the third year of Esarhaddon's reign at Babylon, B.C. 677. But Babylon did revolt in Esarhaddon's reign, (Niebuhr, Assyrien, quoted by Tholuck, Proph. p. 190.) and Esarhaddon was there when his generals brought Manasseh captive. (2 Chr. xxxiii. 11.) This event, again, (according to the Seder Olam, p. 67.) took place in the 22nd year of Manasseh; so that we have the fact of an Assyrian expedition to Judæa from the Assyrian king at Babylon in the 65th year from the first of Ahaz. (Ahaz 14 years, + Hezekiah 29, + Manasseh 22, = 65.) Manasseh is mentioned in an inscription of Esarhaddon, as a tributary. (Rawl. Her. i. p. 483.) This was the close of the existence of Ephraim, as a separate people, since the seat of the separated kingdom was given to heathen. But then neither have the words the character of a gloss. The Hebrew expression is too poetic. Even Ewald, being able to persuade himself that 65 was a "round number," being "somewhat less than a human life," and that it meant "before a human life" [just born] "shall have passed away," admits that "the words have a genuine old Hebrew tint," and thinks that they were "derived from an older oracle of some unknown prophet." d. Proph. i. 211. Thol. ib.

[7] Ib. xxxvii. 6, 7, 29, 33-5. x. 24-34. Nah. i. 11-15.   [8] Is. xvii. 14. x. 32, 34. add Nah. i. 12.   [9] iv. 10.   [10] Is. xxxix. 6, 7.   [11] Ib. 1.   [12] See Lect. iii. p. 125, 6.   [13] xiii. 19-22. xiv. 22, 3.

of one *king*[1], (i. e. as in Daniel, one kingdom,) when it was yet flourishing and in security.   In the prophecy of the 70 years, after which Tyre should resume her traffic, Isaiah anticipates the prophecy of the 70 years of the captivity of Judah; the Chaldæans are foretold as the destroyers of Tyre[2]; and the breaking of the Chaldee yoke was to set it free; as, in fact, although under Persian rule, it was still allowed to refuse to Cambyses the aid of its fleet against its colonies and to baffle his plans[3].   Isaiah foretold the destruction of Moab in *three* exact *years, like the years of an hireling*[4], who counts his years to the very day.   Isaiah's prophecy of the capture of Ashdod within 3 years was in act also[5].   He fixes it in the minds and imaginations of his people, and stakes his truth, as a prophet, on the fact that the strong city, memorable afterwards for enduring the longest siege in human memory, 29 years[6], against Psammetichus king of Egypt close by, should fall within 3, before the general of a distant empire.   He fixes, within one precise year, the conquest of an Arabian tribe, which ordinarily so easily eludes assault.   And yet Sennacherib had the title of king of Arabians[7].   To Hezekiah himself Isaiah foretold the prolongation of his life for 15 years[8].

It is said that[9] we should remember that, when Nahum prophesied, "the Babylonian power threw its shadow

---

[1] xxiii. 15.   [2] Ib. 13.   [3] See below p. 288.

[4] xvi. 14. "In v. 13, 14. every syllable sounds like the majestic tone of Isaiah." Ewald d. Proph. i. 236.   Stähelin follows him. Einl. p. 229.   Even Davidson admits the principle, "The silence of history is no good argument against the verification of the prophecy in some unknown Syrian expedition." iii. 13.

[5] Is. xx.   [6] Herod. ii. 157.   [7] Herod. ii. 141.   Even Ewald observes, (Gesch. Isr. iii. 628.) "The fulfilment is self-evident from the prophecy; for such prophecies would not have been preserved in writing, had they not been confirmed by the event." in Tholuck, d. Proph. p. 119.

[8] xxxviii. 5. "The announcement of 15 years being added to the days of Hezekiah are contrary to the nature of prophetic foresight.   *They are too exact and precise to be predicted;* and *must* therefore have been written after the things mentioned were known and past." Davids. iii. 31. i. e. it being settled à priori that there is no such exact prediction, it *must* be assumed that the writer of these chapters put a prophecy into Isaiah's mouth falsely.

[9] Dr Williams, Ess. and Rev. p. 68.

across Asia." The internal notes mark Nahum's prophecy to belong to the time of Hezekiah [10]. Even then, human wisdom could not foresee the issue of the strife[10]. But Nahum also foretells its destruction by means of the river which was its defence [11], and that fire should devour her[12].

Babylon was tributary to Assyria until the end of the Assyrian Empire. Not Babylonian power, but a revolted Babylonian general[13], spoiled Nineveh of the armies which might have resisted in the field the Median invasion.

Equally minute are the characters of the desolation foretold. Of Zion alone, of all the cities to be destroyed, it was predicted, that it should *be ploughed as a field*[14]; strange blending of desolation and inhabiting, and it has been so. Tyre was to be for the spreading of nets [15]; Nineveh[16] and Babylon [17] for the habitation of the wild animals of the desert; Rabbah of Ammon was to be [18] *a stable for camels; and the Ammonites a couching place for flocks;* Egypt, amidst its great and almost indomitable fertility, was to be a desolation [19], and [20] *a base kingdom.*

For forty one years, from the 13th of Josiah to the last of Zedekiah, Jeremiah declared one future for Israel, destruction from the North, captivity in Babylon. After Josiah's death, his life was sought by those of his native place[21], it continued to be plotted against [22]; he was defamed [23], reproached, derided, all day long [24], cursed by the people man by man, as they curse those who grind them with usury[25], accused falsely[26], placed in the stocks[27], put on trial for the truth[28], imprisoned[29], given over to death [30]: yet he had foretold from the first, that God would preserve him to the end, and that he should be treated kindly by *the enemy at the latter end*[31]. He went about among

---

[10] See Introd. to Nahum.   [11] Nah. ii. 6.   [12] Ib. iii. 13, 15.
[13] Abyden. in Eus. Chron. Arm. i. 54. Rawl. on Herod. l. p. 487.
[14] See on Mic. iii. 12.   [15] Ezek. xxvi. 14.   [16] Zeph. ii. 13, 14.   [17] Is. xiii. 19-22.   [18] Ezek. xxv. 5.   [19] See on Joel iii. 19. p. 152-4.   [20] Ezek. xxix. 14, 15.   [21] xi. 19-23.   [22] xviii. 18, 20, 22, 3.   [23] xx. 10.   [24] Ib. 7, 8. add xxiii. 33-40.   [25] xv. 10.   [26] xxxvii. 13-15.   [27] xx. 2, 3.   [28] xxvi. 8-24.   [29] xxxii.   [30] xxxviii. 4, 5. xxxvii. 15-21. xxxviii. 6-20.   [31] xv. 11.

them, persecuted by all, but invulnerable. For God was his invisible defence. *I have made thee this day*, were the words of his inauguration [1], *a defenced city and an iron pillar and brasen walls against the whole land, against the kings of Judah and the princes thereof, and against the people of the land : and they shall fight against thee ; but they shall not prevail against thee ; for I am with thee to deliver thee.* False prophets contradicted him ; the people loved this contradiction, and greedily swallowed every delusion ; the great men of the city were bent on defence; the petty kings around leagued to resist the king of Babylon ; Egypt, at the first and the last, had warlike and able monarchs, Pharaoh Necho and Pharaoh Hophra. One voice alone peremptorily from the the first pronounced the distinct issue. Before Nineveh fell, while Babylon was still dependent, while Judæa, amid the weakness of the last Assyrian king, was in perfect repose, that voice was first heard, which sounded on for those 41 years ; [2]*Out of the north evil shall break forth upon all the inhabitants of the land. For lo, I will call all the families of the kingdoms of the north, saith the Lord, and they shall come and set every one his throne at the entering of the gates of Jerusalem.* That voice never wavered. During 18 years of Nebuchadnezzar's reign, it announced uniformly, that he should be its destroyer [3]. What if, like Alexander or Cyrus, he had died prematurely? What, if in the first 18 years of his reign? Jeremiah knew that he would live, until God's word should be accomplished. And during this interval, nothing moved him. At one time Nebuchadnezzar sent only bands of the Chaldæans against Jerusalem [4]; at another, the approach of Pharaoh's army compelled him to raise the siege [5]. Jeremiah only prophesied its destruction with the more emphatic energy.

---

[1] i. 18, 19. add xv. 20, l. xx. 11.   [2] l. 14, 15. iv. 6. vi. 1. 22, 23. x. 22. xiii. 20. add v. 15. viii. 14-16, 19. xxxvi. 29. "king of Babylon."

[3] Jer. xxiv. (4th of Jehoiakim,) xxvii. 1-11. (beginning of the reign of Jehoiakim,) xxii. 24, 25. (Jeconiah,) xxix. (beginning of Zedekiah's reign,) xxviii. (4th of Zedekiah,) xxxiv. (9th of Zedekiah.)   [4] 2 Kgs. xxiv. 2. xxxii. (10th of Zed.)   [5] Jer. xxxvii. 5.

When it was most straitly besieged, he bought, at God's command, a field in his native village, foretelling that, as he had done, so should others do thereafter [6], *for I will cause their captivity to return, saith the Lord of hosts.* It was nothing less than "[7] despair before the Chaldæans." It was knowledge from God. Isaiah knew from God that Sennacherib would not prevail; Micah, Isaiah, Jeremiah, alike knew of the captivity at Babylon; all alike knew of the deliverance from it. The captivity, contrary to the judgment of the nations around him and of his own people, was to be but the travail-pangs of the restoration which was to follow [8]. The prophets foretold both with equal confidence. The fulfilment of the prophecy of the captivity was to be the earnest of the fulfilment of the prophecy of the restoration. And during the long respite, which men abused to discredit the truth of the prophet, God manifoldly bore witness to His prophet's words. The people looked for the restoration of Jehoahaz, the prince of their own choice [9], from Egypt; Jeremiah foretold his death in his exile [10]; *he shall see this land no more.* And he died in Egypt. Jeremiah foretold that Jehoiachin and his mother [11] should lose their crown; they were carried captive [12]. To Jehoiakim he prophesied disgrace; that after death, his corpse should be [13]*dragged along,* like that of a malefactor, *and cast forth* beyond the gate of Jerusalem. The capture of Jerusalem, ending the 3 months'[14] reign of his son, gave opportunity for this; and the contumely to the rebellious vassal would be in conformity with what Jeremiah had prophesied more ge-

---

[6] Ib. xxxii. 44.   [7] "Contrast Isaiah's confidence against Assyria with Jeremiah's despair before Chaldæa." (Stanley, J. Church, p. 457. in illustration of the "changing of the Prophetical teaching with the events of their time.")

[8] Micah iv. 10. Is. xl. sqq. Jer. xii. 15. xvi. 15. xxiii. 1-8. xxiv. 5-7. xxvii. 22. xxix. 10-14. xxx. xxxi. xxxiii.

[9] 2 Kgs. xxiii. 30. 2 Chr. xxxvi. 1. He is ranked the 4th of the sons of Josiah, being also named Shallum, 1 Chr. iii. 15. Jer. xxii. 11. He was younger than Jehoiakim, much older than Zedekiah. 2 Chr. xxxvi. 2, 5, 11.   [10] xxii. 11, 12.

[11] xiii. 18.   [12] 2 Kgs. xxiv. 12.

[13] מחוץ והשלך מהלאה לשערי ירושלם Jer. xxii. 19. add xxxvi. 30.   [14] 2 Kgs. xxiv. 8.

nerally[1]. He alone of the four last wretched kings of
Judah, rebel though he was, did not die in captivity. The
political circumstances of Nebuchadnezzar, which detain-
ed him elsewhere, so that he sent against Jehoiakim
bands of the Chaldæans[2], with auxiliaries of *Ammonites,
Tyrians, Moabites*, were shaped so, as to leave room for
the fulfilment of the words of Jeremiah.

Then follow the signal prophecies, as to Zedekiah; first,
when the king enquired of God by him, defeat, capture
by Nebuchadnezzar[3]; then, when the last siege set in, Jeremiah promised him, that it should be well with him if
he should surrender; else, he foretold the mockery of his
harem[4]; that he should speak to the king of Babylon
mouth to mouth, see him eye to eye, be led to Babylon[5].
Minuter still was the prophecy of Ezekiel in the captivity, while the scoffers mocked him[6], *the days are prolonged and every vision faileth.* It is as if he saw in a vision the flight of Zedekiah, probably disguised, [7]*by the way
of the gate between the two walls by the king's garden*, fleeing *towards the plain*, at the last, a solitary fugitive, *his
army scattered from him*, pursued and overtaken by the
Chaldees, brought before the king for judgment, his eyes
put out, and himself carried to Babylon. Probably he did
so see it. For when, by the symbolical act of *digging
through the wall* of his house, removing his goods through
it *on his shoulders at twilight* with his *face covered, as they
that go forth into captivity*, he thus explains his act; [8]*the*

---

[1] viii. 1, 2. This seems to me more probable than that it was done by his
own subjects, stained though he was with "innocent blood" and oppression
to supply his luxuries. Jer. xxii. 13-17.　　[2] 2 Kgs. xxiv. 1, 2.

[3] Jer. xxi. 4-7. add xxiv. 8.　　[4] xxxviii. 22.　　[5] xxxii. 4, 5. xxxiv. 3.
　　　　　　[6] Ezek. xii. 22.　　　　[7] 2 Kgs. xxv. 4-7.

[8] Ezek. xii. 12-14. Ewald generalised the prophecy and accepted it. (Proph.
ii. 255. 213.) Stähelin (p. 306) says, "in truth, the blinding of Zedekiah is
not *necessarily* prophesied in xii. 13. but this passage *can* also be understood
only of his imprisonment; and as to xxiv. 1. the possibility of so clear an *anticipation* ought not to be denied." So he half-retracts his explanation, that
" Ezekiel recast his prophecies, and so e. g. xii. 13. xxiv. 1. prophesied what is
so special; *involuntarily* in the later recasting he introduced the fact into the
prophecy;" (p. 305.) in other words, said that he had prophesied what he had

prince that is among you shall bear upon his shoulder in the twilight, and shall go forth ; they shall dig through the wall to carry out thereby : he shall cover his face, that he see not the ground with his eyes : My net also will I spread over him, and he shall be taken in My snare : and I will bring him to Babylon to the land of the Chaldeans; yet shall he not see it, though he shall die there ; and I will scatter toward every wind all that are about him to help him, and all his bands.

And yet to the Jews nothing seemed less likely than all this. Hananiah ventured to predict the restoration of Jeconiah, (Jehoiachin,) and the vessels of God's house within two years[9]. Jeremiah predicted the false prophet's death within that year, and he *died in* that *year in the seventh month*[10]. The judgment predicted on the individual was itself not insulated. Such had been aforetime that on the disobedient prophet[11]; on Gehazi[12]; on the false counsellor Shebna[13]; the false prophet Amaziah[14]. Such were the predictions of Jeremiah himself to the false priest Pashur[15]; to the false prophets Ahab and Zedekiah[16], and Shemaiah[17]; such in the N. T. were those of St. Peter to Sapphira[18], and of St. Paul to Elymas the

not. So then if the prophecy imply mere human knowledge, it is to stand ; if more, it is to be assumed to be recast. And this is to be criticism ! Davidson follows Stähelin's first solution of subsequent revision and introduction of "later knowledge." (iii. 150.) " Ezek. xii. 13. *must* have been written after the event," iii. 147. i. e. because it contains so distinct a prophecy. (In ii. 460. Davidson had apparently given it as an instance of *admissible* definite prophecy.) " In like manner ch. xxiv. *could* only have been written after the destruction of Jerusalem," (iii. 147.) although Ezekiel distinctly says, that he was directed to note that it was delivered on the very day that the king of Babylon set himself against Jerusalem. (xxiv. 2.) On the like definite prophecy, (ch. xxi.) Ewald writes, as if he had been there, " One day it came vividly into the Prophet's mind, (who, although far removed from the scene of action, yet with his spirit ever followed the march with stretched expectation,) as if the army must be arrived before Jerusalem on that very day. His *anticipation* must very nearly or altogether have hit right, since the statement xxiv. 1. agrees quite historically with 2 Kgs. xxv. 1."   [9] Jer. xxviii. 1-4.   [10] Ib. 15-17.

[11] 1 Kgs. xiii. 21, 22.   [12] 2 Kgs. v. 27.   [13] Is. xxii. 15-19.
[14] See Introd. to Amos, p. 153. on Am. vii. 16, 17. p. 214.   [15] xx. 1-6.
[16] xxix. 21-23.   [17] Ib. 24-32.   [18] Acts v. 9.

sorcerer [1].   Contrariwise, the prediction to the Rechabites [2] has remained in force unto this day [3].

The prophecy of the capture of Babylon is so graphic, that it takes its place in history, accrediting the accounts of Herodotus and Xenophon.   Its mighty men " forbear to fight; they remain in their strong holds; they become as women.   Post shall run to meet post, and messenger to meet messenger, to tell the king of Babylon that *his city is taken at the end* [4] thereof, and that the passages are stopped, and the reeds they have burned with fire, and the men of war are affrighted."

The title " vision " justifies us in conceiving, that vivid pictures, such as those of the capture of Babylon in Jeremiah and Isaiah, (and the like in other prophets,) were first spread before the prophets' minds, and then described by them in God-given words.   The traits are characteristic of this siege, not of sieges in general.   The idolatrous festival of Belshazzar; its night of revelry; its sudden interruption; the fruitless cry " to arms;" the drying up of the Euphrates as by fire; the possession of the passages; the vast city taken, ere it was aware; the hurrying of the posts to tell the king;— we see it all vividly with our own eyes, as much as in the historical relations of the capture. Yet neither prophet supplies the whole history.   Both see the besieging armies; Jeremiah, the kings of the Medes and of the North; Isaiah, the Persians also [5]; both, the destruction of Babylon, the breaking in pieces of her gods [6]. Isaiah alone sees the festive night, the sudden surprise amidst their revelry.   [7]*The night of my pleasure He hath turned to terror to me.   They prepare the table; watch the watch; eat, drink; 'arise, ye princes; anoint the shield.'* In another vision he sees the slaughter of the king, his

---

[1] Acts xiii. 11.   [2] Jer. xxxv.

[3] The first notice of the Rechabites was given by Dr. Wolff in his Journal from 1827 to 1838, Lond. 1839. p. 388, 9.   He gave a further account, Travels and Adventures, T. ii. p. 298-300. Lond. 1861. and p. 508. of an edit. in one Vol., also 1861.   R. Schwarz of Jerusalem speaks of them, Das Heilige Land, p. 407-10. [Rev. G. Williams.]   [4] Jer. li. 30-32.   [5] See ab. p. 125, 6.

[6] Is. xxi. 9. Jer. l. 2. li. 44.   [7] xxi. 4, 5.

burial not among the tombs of his fathers [8]. Jeremiah alone sees the mode of the capture, the completeness of the slumber of repose in which they were wrapped. Daniel, Xenophon [9], Herodotus [10], relate the festival-revelry; Herodotus and Xenophon, state that Cyrus knew of it, and entered by the Euphrates. Daniel and Xenophon [11] relate the death of the king; Xenophon relates that the assault was in the night [12], that the watch was surprised drinking [13], the city captured through the death of the king, in that same night [14], as Daniel relates that in the night the king was slain; Herodotus adds, that the river-gates were left open, those same passages which Jeremiah beholds as siezed. The complete security of Babylon is related by both the Greek historians [15]; its deliberated unwarlikeness stands in strange contrast to its subsequent energy in rebelling [16]. Coarser rationalism assumed that both predictions were "framed after the events[17],"i.e. were lies; more refined rationalism assumed that they were delivered during the siege, yet on no other ground than the assumption, that prophets did not predict events which "lay beyond their political horizon[18]." The assumption

[8] xiv. 15, 22.   [9] Xen. Cyrop. vii. 5. 9.   [10] i. 191.   [11] Ib. § 11.
[12] Ib. 9.   [13] Ib. 10.   [14] Ib. 11, 12.   [15] Her. i. 190. Xen. l. c. § 7.
[16] See ab. p. 127. Berosus too mentions the single battle. c. Ap. i. 21.

[17] Eichhorn, Paulus, Rosenm., Koppe, as to Is. xxi. in Ges. on Is. xxi. i. 649. At that date, 1822, "no one," he said, "had pronounced the oracle of Jeremiah (li.) to be spurious." (p. 650.) He maintains that both were written before the event, because they contained nothing which might not be foreseen. "In Jer. li. 32," he says, "the taking of the fords and shallow places of the Euphrates is spoken of: if one would combine this with the account of Xenophon, that the soldiers of Cyrus had to creep along shallow places in the bed of the Euphrates, it would follow that it was written later and was spurious," i. e. if it contained undeniable prophecy.

[18] This is Gesenius' primary argument, on Is. xiii. xiv. xxi. Ies. i. 448. Then follows, 2) the allegation of embittered enmity and love of revenge; assuming again that the Prophet was not pronouncing God's judgments: 3) an argument, in like way, in a circle, from the similarity of the language with other parts of Isaiah, assumed *on the like grounds* to be spurious. 4) Of actual indications of a later style in the three chapters, Gesenius finds 3 only to allege, admitting at the same time that the language is " pure." His instances are, 1) רעה "began to speak." Both cases, xiv. 10. xxi. 9., are implied answers. Besides, this meaning " began to speak," lies nearest to the original meaning of the root,

was repeated by turns as to each case in which the prophets do so predict the future, yet on each occasion, as if in entire unconsciousness, that the critics were repeating dogmatically the very point which they had to prove.

When Jeremiah had been removed to Egypt, the pro-

and occurs in Deuteronomy, Job, Canticles. 2) The "unemphatic use of the pronoun xiii. 3. xiv. 13. 19;" but, in all 3 places, (as is to be expected in a prophecy so energetic,) it is very emphatic. 3) מרגעה xiv. 4. The reading is itself doubtful; any how, it is a word framed by the writer, and a poetic form. Knobel's instances (out of which Davidson selected his, iii. 9.) have not the slightest force of proof. There is not one characteristic expression among them. נלו xiv. 3. occurs in Job, רגז Joel ii. 1, &c.; השקיפה, "look forth," in Cant. ii. 9. Ps. xxxiii. 14. only; שגל Deut. xxviii. 30., twice only besides, Jer. iii. 2. Zech. xiv. 2. 5., in Zech. probably repeated from Isaiah; דמות, "*the likeness of* a great people," xiii. 4. see Ps. lviii. 5. (David's.) "פתח 'loose, set free,' xiv. 17. earlier, 'open.'" Knob. פתח is to "open *a thing*," and פתח to "loose *a person*," Ps. cii. 21. cv. 20.; "loosed" the camels from their load, Gen. xxiv. 32. The difference is not of date, but of idiom. שעיר xiii. 21. recurs in this sense once xxxiv. 14.; פצח רנה an expression of Isaiah, xiv. 7. xliv. 23. xlix. 13. lv. 12. It is the common Hebrew idiom, whereby a noun is added to a neuter verb, in cases where we use a preposition. In Is. lii. 9. the two verbs פצחו רננו are used, as in Ps. xcviii. 4. It is the usual argument in a circle, to assume the spuriousness of Is. xl-lxvi. and then to argue that another prophecy of Isaiah is also spurious, because the prophet used the same expressions in both.

With such proofs as these, it would be easy to prove any work in any language, not to have been written by its author.

The positive evidence for the genuineness of ch. xiii. xiv. has been given well by Hävernick, § 208. Only the heads need be stated here. 1. The title, which ascribes it to Isaiah, is, like other titles in this portion of the book ch. xiii-xxiii., closely united with the prophecy. It is the only indication of the object of the prophecy, until v. 19, where Babylon is first named in the body of the prophecy. The titles in this portion are varied, historical, (xx. 1.) symbolical, (xxi. 1. 11. xxii. 1.) as an author only would vary them, sometimes omitted as xviii. xxii. 15., whereas a later hand would be uniform. 2) It stands connected with the prophecies, before and after. 3) xiv. 24-27., which is *its* close, refers to the prophecy against Asshur which preceded it, and is a summary of God's judgments on the world. The prophecies then against Asshur and Babylon must have formed one whole, as they stand in Isaiah now. Jeremiah, who adopted the language of Isaiah, (ch. l. li.) united them in the same way. 4) Isaiah, in these chapters, uses language of Joel alone, (see Introd. to Joel, p. 96.) his language here is used by later prophets, Habakkuk, Zephaniah, Jeremiah. 5) The language and thoughts recur in undisputed chapters of Isaiah.

The prophecies of Jeremiah (ch. l. li.) bear, even to an English reader, so evidently the impress of his style, that to attempt to convince one who did not see it, would be to try to give sight to the blind. Here, however, another antidogmatic prejudice came in. Jeremiah, in these chapters, as was especially

phecy of the conquest of Pharaoh Hophra in Egypt is as definite as that of Zedekiah [1].

The first prophecy which Ezekiel receives, after the visions which contain his inauguration to his office [2] *in the 5th year of king Jehoiachin's captivity,* is conveyed in the symbolical act which he was bidden to do[3], lying 390 *days on the left side,* according to *the years of* the *iniquity* of Israel, and *forty days on* his *right side* for the *iniquity of the house of Judah.* The days are explained to represent

his wont, embodies language of earlier prophets. But among these, he uses that of the latter chapters of Isaiah. The whole boasted theory then, as to the " Pseudo-Isaiah," was at stake, and, with it, the whole undeifying of prophecy. Gesenius satisfied himself, that Jeremiah did not employ those chapters, and that what he there foretold in ch. l. li., he could have foreseen by human sagacity; so he had no doubts as to the genuineness of ch. l. li. (Ies. Einl. ii. 26.) nor at that time De Wette. (Einl. ed. 1822.) In 1839 De W. still said only, "ch. 52, 50, 51. are from later hands, *at least* the false addition li. 59 sqq.." (p. 277.) Those who, on antidoctrinal grounds, deny the chapters to be Jeremiah's, are forced to concede the likeness of the style. This was shewn by Küper, Jerem. libr. sacr. Int. p. 106-32. They have had recourse to the expedients; 1) that the chapters are "a learned imitation of Jeremiah, in order to make them pass for his;" (Ewald, Proph. li, 491. after Gramberg, Rel. Id. li. 400.) 2) that " they were written by Jeremiah but recast by the Pseudo-Isaiah;" (Movers, de utr. recens. Jer. indole 1837. De Wette, Einl. 1852. § 217. a.) 3) that a prophecy of Jeremiah was really taken by Seraiah to Babylon, (Jer. li. 59.) and, when the fall of the Chaldee power was confidently expected, was published, interpolated out of other prophets and out of Jeremiah himself to gain it the more credit. (Stähelin, Einl. p. 278.) 4) that the chapters were written by some unknown prophet about B.C. 556, (Maurer, ad loc.) 550, (Knobel, Proph. ii. 355.) perhaps Baruch, (Id. 353. Bunsen, Gott in d. Gesch. i. 437.) while a defender of their genuineness maintains conversely that they were imitated by the author of the latter chapters of Isaiah. (Graf. Jeremiah, p. 584.) So do they shew, in attack or defence, where the real pressure is. Yet the words of one of the extremest writers are virtually the confession of all, as to these chapters of Jeremiah; " In truth, this section yields many proofs of its genuineness. Language, (l. 16. li. 1. 3. 7. 14. 45. 55.) imagery, (li. 7. 8. 34. 37.) style, (l. 2. 3. 7. 10.) especially in turns, (as li. 2.) the subscription, (li. 57.) the unannounced dialogues, (li. 51.) indicate Jeremiah unmistakeably. And chronological data confirm this. Assyria is fallen, (l. 18.) &c." (Hitzig, Jeremiah, p. 391.) Of the rest it may suffice to add, that Nebuchadnezzar is spoken of as the reigning king of Babylon, (" and *last, this* Nebuchadnezzar," l. 17.) and that, in contrast with an unnamed king of Babylon, upon whom the punishment should fall. (l. 18.)

¹ Jer. xliv. 30. xlvi. 26.   ² Ezek. i. 2. the next date is in ch. viii. 1. " in the 6th year, in the 6th month, on the 5th of the month."   ³ iv. 4-6.

years; *I have appointed thee each day for a year;* the symbolical act itself follows upon another, representing the siege of Jerusalem [1], its separation from God [2], and is a prophecy against it [2]. It is agreed on all hands [3], that the 390 years begin with the division of the two kingdoms, B. C. 975; the 40 years, with the reformation of Josiah, either that in his twelfth year [4], B.C. 630, or the more complete reformation in his eighteenth year [5], B.C. 624. But 390 years after B.C. 975, end in the year of the last deportation by Nebuzaradan in the 23rd year of Nebuchadnezzar B.C. 585; and 40 years, from B.C. 624, end within a year of the same date.

In relation to his people, the prophecies of Ezekiel coincide with those in the later part of Jeremiah's ministry: he foretells, in exile, the vanity of the resistance of the kings of Judah. In regard to Egypt he has a remarkable definite prophecy, that her land should be *desolate forty years,* that at the end of forty years, the Egyptians should be gathered, but that *they shall be there, a base kingdom. It shall be the basest of kingdoms, neither shall it exalt itself any more above the nations; for I will diminish them, that they shall rule no more over the nations* [6].

It has been a superabundance of fulfilment, that this has been the history of Egypt, a prey successively to the ·Persians, Macedonians, Romans, Arabs, Georgians, Ottoman Turks.

With this amplitude of fulfilment, it is even absurd to raise the question as to the fulfilment of the 40 years. The larger prophecy, which 2500 years have not exhausted, that it *shall be a base kingdom, neither shall it exalt itself any more among the nations,* is *as* definite, *as* unlikely to be fulfilled. It was not, that the internal energy of its people was exhausted. Even of this there was no sign, when Ezekiel prophesied. Pharaoh Hophra had disputed energetically, and to human sight hopefully,

---

[1] Ezek. iv. 1, 2, 8.   [2] Ib. 7.   [3] as by Eichhorn, Rosenmüller, and "others," ap. Maurer.   [4] 2 Chr. xxxiv. 3.   [5] Ib. 8. 2 Kgs. xxii. 3.   [6] Ezek. xxix. 14, 15.

with *the hammer of the whole earth*[7]. They continued their struggles with the Persian power[8]; Alexander replenished their population with his Greeks, and founded Alexandria as the emporium of the world. The first Ptolemies developed its resources, and its commerce by land and sea, with Libya, India, Italy; its new masters gained for themselves, for a time, territories wider than it had in its most prosperous days[9], but Egyptians had no share in the greatness, except to supply taxation; Ptolemy Euergetes, who shewed favor to his native subjects, was the third and last of its great Ptolemies. Thenceforth was decay. When Egypt became Roman, Roman Emperors dreaded its advantageous position for revolt, under the rule of an ambitious governor, and kept it in close dependence on themselves. Yet it never *exalted itself any more.* The means which its governors adopted to recruit it, or to strengthen themselves, turned to its permanent weakness. Its population, native, Greek, Jewish, Arab, was energetic, but divided[10]. But the first step in this division was long after the prophecy of Ezekiel.

The difficulty of fixing the particular period of forty years arises from the fact, that the systematic accounts of Egypt at that time, those in Herodotus, are from Egyptian priests, who are known to have cast a veil over their disgraces. They tell us of Necho's fleets[11], his circumnavigation of Africa[12], his victory over the Syrians at Megiddo and his capture of Cadytis, but nothing of the first victory of Nebuchadnezzar over Egypt in his father's life-time[13], or of the defeat at Carchemish[14], after which apparently Necho[15] *came not again any more out of his land, for the king of Babylon had taken from the river of Egypt unto*

---

[7] Jer. l. 23.   [8] See ab. p. 71. 136.

[9] Ptolemy Philad. held Egypt, with parts of Ethiopia, Arabia, Libya; Cyrene; Phœnicia, Cœle-Syria, Cyprus, and parts of Asia Minor: his son, Ptol. Euerg., had the coast of Asia Minor as far as the Hellespont, and even maritime towns of Thrace.   [10] "Of every hundred mummies derived from the Necropolite receptacles of Memphis, 70 have lost their Coptic peculiarities." Smith, Geogr. Dict. v. Ægyptus, p. 46. from Sharpe, Hist. of Eg. p. 133. ed. 2.

[11] Her. ii. 159.   [12] Ib. iv. 42.   [13] see ab. p. 60.

[14] Jer. xlvi. 2.   [15] 2 Kings xxiv. 7.

the river Euphrates all which pertained to the king of Egypt. On this, and all of the rest of Necho's "sixteen years," Egyptian history is silent; and in the six of his son Psammis it names only an "attack" on Ethiopia just before his death[1]. In the 25 years of Apries, they had nothing to relate, but a march against Sidon, and a naval battle with the king of Tyre[2], (in neither of which did they venture to say that he was victorious,) and the unsuccessful expedition against Cyrene to which they attributed his destruction. The Bible only adds the speedily quelled march to relieve Jerusalem when besieged by the Chaldeans[3]. The boast of pride related by Ezekiel, [4]*My river is my own, and I have made it for myself,* as well as the corresponding boast in Herodotus[5], both imply strength in *defence* only, and that in Ezekiel a strength against attack, derived from the situation of Egypt. The employment of a foreign mercenary army, a sure sign of decay, commenced with Psammetichus I. the great grandfather of Hophra, it is said[6], in civil strife. The ground of the desertion of the native troops stated by Diodorus[7], that the post of honor, the right wing, was assigned to the strangers, implies a very large enrolment of foreign troops and chief dependence upon them. The desertion of the native warrior-caste, which Herodotus states at 240,000[8], is substantiated by monuments[9]. This, (whatever was its real extent,) must have been a great

---

[1] Her. ii. 161.

[2] Ib. Diodorus makes him victorious against the Cypriotes too, and take Sidon, so that the rest of Phœnicia surrendered out of fear. (i. 68.) Herodotus (ii. 182.) says that Cyprus was first *subdued* by Amasis. Herodotus would hardly have omitted to speak of such successful results of the expeditions which he speaks of, had they been true. The Egyptian monuments add nothing of greatness. It does not appear from them that Necho II. was son of Psammetichus, whose daughter, (his half-sister, if he was son of Psammetichus,) he married. (Brugsch, l'Egypte, p. 252.) " His few monumental memorials do not deserve much attention." (Id. p. 254.) The monuments confirm the fact of the one expedition of Psammis. (Ib. p. 255, 6.) "The monumental traces, recalling the name of Apries, are dispersed throughout Egypt." (Id. 257.) No one contains any historical statement.   [3] Jer. xxii. 5-8. 2 Kgs. xxv. 1-4.

[4] xxix. 3, 9.   [5] ii. 169.   [6] Her. ii. 152.   [7] i. 67.   [8] ii. 30.

[9] See Sir G. W. in Rawl. Her. T. ii. p. 44, 5. n. 3. add note 2. p. 43.

source of weakness, breaking the military traditions of Egypt, and throwing them more upon their foreign mercenaries, of whom Hophra is said to have had 30,000[10]. With these indications and occasions of weakness, before the time of Necho, it is not improbable, that Berosus, under the Satrap in those parts who had rebelled[11], meant the king of Egypt; that Egypt was already tributary, (as the successor of Hophra, Amasis, was probably in reality a Babylonian Vice-king,) and that the inaction of Necho, after his two great defeats, was owing to his weakness. There is, then, ample room for the 40 years of desolation before the death of Hophra. The intense hatred of the Egyptians towards Apries, expressed by the title "the hated[12]" on the monuments, and which, according to Herodotus too, was slaked only by his blood, when Amasis unwillingly gave him into their hands, being, as they complained, "[13] the bitterest of enemies to them and to him," implies any thing rather than a prosperous reign or a prosperous condition of Egypt under him. The internal prosperity in the reign of Amasis[14] stands in contrast with the former distress. This represents exactly what Ezekiel foretold, a restoration of internal prosperity, without any restoration of external power. Whether or no Egypt was engaged in the alliance with Crœsus against Cyrus as a tributary to Babylon, and whether or no its troops, in consequence of that alliance, fought against Cyrus[15], it fell, an easy conquest, at the first appearance of Cambyses.

[10] Her. ii. 163. [11] See ab. p. 62. and below Lect. vii. [12] In Rosellini, Monum. Storichi, i. 275. quoted Winer, Reallex. v. Hophra, see Thol. Proph. p. 131.
[13] Her. ii. 169. [14] Ib. 177. and Sir G. W. in Rawl. Her. ii. p. 387. "The traces of monumental memorials are dispersed over the whole country, from Alexandria to Syene. Although of little value for the political history of the times of Amasis, yet they serve notably to prove the assertion of Herodotus as to the developement of architecture and sculpture under Amasis." Brugsch, p. 262.
[15] Herodotus (i. 77. 79.) distinctly says, that Cyrus' rapid march on Sardis anticipated the reinforcements which Crœsus hoped for from Babylon, Egypt, Sparta. Xenophon, on the other hand, circumstantially relates the Egyptian way of fighting there, their valour, and the colonization of the survivors. (Cyr. i. 2. 10. vii. i. 30-45.)

I have dwelt upon this prophecy the rather, because sceptics have made their boast of its assumed failure. Knowing, as we *do* know, the divinity of the Old Testament as a whole, it cannot be essential to our faith, that the truth of details too should be matter of demonstration. We believe as to the parts, because we believe the whole. It is a poor, unintelligent, human faith, ignorant of the real character or grounds of faith, which cannot say, unconcerned, about details, "I do not know." Those immediate prophecies were an evidence to those to whom they were given. Our faith indeed must be independent of minute points of obscure secular history. To us, (as far as temporal prophecy is an auxiliary to faith,) those long continuous prophecies are given. It is a wilfully false issue which scepticism puts it upon, when, ignoring that large tangible prophecy which it cannot deny, that Egypt should, on its restoration, *no more exalt itself above the nations,* and, unable to account for a patent fact of history, which, in Ezekiel's time, there was no human ground to anticipate, it diverts the attention from an unmistakeable prophecy, by alleging that another part of the prophecy was not true prophecy, simply because we, for whom that prophecy was not given as evidence, have not the data fully to substantiate it.

The prophecies as to Egypt led far into the Captivity. Then, there was a term of 70 years, which, counted from that year, when captives were first taken to Babylon, the first of a long series of such removals, viz. the 3rd year of Jehoiakim, were fulfilled to the exact year[1]. It is,

[1] Sixty six years are furnished by the length of the reigns given in the Canon of Ptolemy;

Nabocolassarus	Nebuchadnezzar	43
Ilvarodamus	Evil Merodach	2
Nericassolassarus	Neriglissar	4
Nabonadius	Nabunahit	17
		66

To these should be added probably a year or 18 months preceding that part of the fourth year of Jehoiakim, with which Nebuchadnezzar's accession to his father's throne coincides, (see below, Lect. vii.) and the two years during which Darius the Mede was Viceroy; the permission to return not having been

primâ facie, absurd to suppose that the author of the first chapter of Ezra and Zechariah were mistaken about the number of years in which they were so deeply interested[2].

After the Captivity, not to speak now of the prophecy of the 4 Empires in Zechariah, as bearing on that of Daniel[3], there is a distinct prediction of the conflict of the Jews with the Greeks and of their victories over them. And, before this war, there is a prophecy of a heavy calamity, which falls in succession upon Damascus, Hamath, Tyre, Zidon, and the maritime cities of Philistia, Ashkelon, Gaza, Ekron, Ashdod, in which calamity the temple of God was to be guarded, not by human power, but by His unseen Presence. *[4]I will encamp about Mine house, because of the army, because of him that passeth by, and because of him that returneth.* And this, while God should *smite the power of Tyre in the sea.* The selection of the places and of the whole line of country corresponds very exactly to the march of Alexander after the battle of Issus, when the capture of Damascus, which Darius had

given until the 1st of Cyrus at Babylon B.C. 536. See Prideaux, Connection, A. 538. B. ii. T. i. p. 179. Davison on Prophecy, Lect. 6. Clinton, F. H. T. 2. c. 18. p. 367 sqq. Tholuck adopts what he calls "an approximative number;" (Die Proph. p. 103.) what in our ordinary idiom is called "a round number," not what the rationalists mean by it. A "round number" idiomatically means "a number, in which fractions are disregarded." It must then be the nearest number above or below. We might say, for 2556, "in round numbers, 2600;" or for 68 ¼ years, "in round numbers, 70," and so on. But the very idiom implies that the number shall be the nearest number which is obtained, either by filling up or dropping the fractions above or below it. 70 might be "a round number" for 68 or 72. It could not be for 62 or 78. The principle then would introduce no vagueness into prophecy; although I see no occasion for its introduction; and that the less, since Daniel understood the numbers on consideration, as he says, ix. 2. Davidson's real objection lies, as usual, in the definiteness of the prophecy. "We may go farther with Hitzig, and pronounce 11 b-14 a, suppositious, because the 70 years' captivity in Babylon is *too specific* to be pronounced in the fourth year of Jeholakim." iii. 98. His plea, "Jeremiah would not have uttered what is not strictly correct, because the captivity did not last 70 years," (ii. 462.) stands in sad contrast with the respectful words of Niebuhr, "Since the number 70 is a typical number, this slight difference, [68 for 70 as he supposes,] should fill us with respect, instead of raising doubts as to the truth of the prophecy, or leading us to doubt the Babylonian chronology." Gesch. Assurs u. Babels, p. 90. in Tholuck, Die Proph. p. 112, 13. ² See above, p. 190. ³ See below, Lect. vi. ⁴ Zech. ix. 8.

chosen as the strong depository of his wealth, of Persian women of rank, confidential officers and envoys [1], opened Cœle-Syria; Zidon surrendered; Tyre, specially marked out by Zechariah [2], was taken with great effort after a 7 months' siege [3]; Gaza too resisted for 5 months, was taken, and, it is said, plucked up [4]; but Alexander passed by with his victorious army and returned, and Jerusalem remained uninjured. History gives no other explanation of Zechariah's prophecy than this conquest by Alexander; that conquest agrees minutely with the prophecy. No other event in history does. But, apart from this, the victory of the Jews over Greeks was, of all events of history, then the most improbable. There was not the most distant likelihood of collision between them; they had no point of contact. The name of Greece was known to the Jews, only as that of one of the many countries which traded with Tyre; a distant nation, to whom Tyre and Zidon had, in their slave-trade, sold Jewish youths, *that* they *might remove them far from their border;* but the guilt and the punishment belonged to Tyre and Zidon, not to them. Joel had, for this sin, prophesied the punishment of Tyre, not of Greece. Eichhorn, whose form of unbelief exempted him from any necessity to explain prophecy of any other than its true object, avowed that this prophecy of Zechariah *did* relate to the march of Alexander and the victories of Jews over Greeks at the later critical period of their history. He said plainly, "[5]The conquests of Alexander are described so clearly, that they

---

[1] Grote, Greece, xii. 173, 4.   [2] ix. 3, 4.   [3] Diod. Sic. xvii. 40-45. Arr. ii. 16-24. Curt. iv. 2.   [4] $\kappa\alpha\tau\epsilon\sigma\pi\alpha\sigma\mu\acute{\epsilon}\nu\eta$ Strabo, xvi. 2. 30.

[5] Einl. T. iv. § 605. He persuaded himself, as his way was, that it was a description of past events, and so invented a prophet, not earlier than Alexander. He supposed the name of the Greeks, in the subsequent prophecy, to stand for that " of the most powerful enemies of the Jews." But Alexander had been their friend. On any human aspect of prophecy, it were absurd to suppose that, in the time of Alexander, Jews should anticipate conquering the conquerors of the world. The prophecy of Zech. xiii. 7-14, 21. he explained of Judas Maccabæus (p. 450.) and so put it in the time of the Maccabees. Corrodi, (according to Köster in Zech. p. 25,) followed him, (Bibelcanon, i. 107.) and found Antiochus Epiphanes in c. 14. (I do not find the passage.)

cannot be mistaken."   " In what is said of Tyre, who can mistake Alexander's wonderful conquest ? "   "All the chief places, which Alexander, after the battle of Issus, either took possession of or conquered, are named one by one, the land of Hadrach, Damascus and Hamath, Tyre and Zidon, Ashkelon, Gaza, Ekron and Ashdod."   Unbelieving interpretation vacillated according to the requirements of the theory of each.   If any would own that the prophecy related to the march of Alexander and to real victories of Jews over Greeks, they placed it in those times[6].   If any felt constrained to place it earlier, they would not see, what to others, who believed prophecy as little, was so plain, and took up with any thing[7] which

---

[6] Rosenm. said generally, "Jahn refers the prophecy to the wars, which the Jews, after Alexander, waged with the Greeks who held Syria.   Other interpreters who, in like way, think that the victories, gained by the Maccabee leaders over Antiochus Epiphanes, are meant here, infer that this was written after the Maccabee times." on Zech. ix. 13.

[7] *Paulus* said, that the prophecy expressed what *might* be the hopes of the Jews after Hyrcanus had subdued Edom, and so placed it at that time, about 129, B.C. (üb. d. N. T. iii. 131-5.)   *Rosenmüller* said, "the *uncertain hopes* of the future, expressed here by the prophet, are not to be referred to *certain events*."   *Bertholdt* ruled that, if it related to Alexander's victories, " it *must* have been written by a prophet who flourished after Zechariah at the end of the Persian period."   (Einl. T. iv. § 430. p. 1714.)   But he thought it was written in the time of Ahaz, before the Syro-Samaritan war ; (2 Kgs. xvi. 5, 6.) and so "that it was probable that the Assyrians gave the unknown prophet *some occasion* for his strong threatenings against Hamath, Tyre and Zidon ; but that it could not be proved, for want of historical data."   In plain words, the object of the prophecy could not be Alexander, in whom it was exactly fulfilled, because then there would be prophecy.   But no other account could be given of it, therefore we must imagine one.   *Gramberg* would have it, that the Prophet, in the first prophecy as to Damascus, &c, used the language of the former prophets without any special meaning, and in that of the victory over the Greeks meant only, " that so mighty and warlike a people *could* only be conquered by Jehovah with His Israelites." (Rel. Id. i. 529, 30.)   *De Wette* (ed. iv. when he acknowledged its genuineness) would have the prophecy to be a concealed denunciation against Persia, "against which Zech. did not wish to prophesy openly." (p. 311.) "ix. 13. [against Greece] x. 6 sqq. are archaisms, resting at the same time on the hoped-for restoration of the people;" (Ib.) or, later, "a prophetic antiquarian style whereby the Prophet cast a veil of mystery over his prophecies." (p. 337. ed. 7.)   *Knobel*, supposing it to date before 740, B.C., says, " It was *expected*, that the Egyptians, to try their strength against Egypt, would march through Syria, Phœnicia, and Philistia, as they

would fit in with any part of the prophecy or (if need were) with nothing.   Greece was, until Alexander, a colonising, not a conquering nation; the Hebrews had no human knowledge of the site of Greece.   There was not a little cloud, like a man's hand, when Zechariah thus absolutely foretold the conflict and its issue.   Yet here we have a definite prophecy, given later than Daniel, fitting in with his temporal prophecy, expanding a part of it, reaching beyond the time of Antiochus, and foreannouncing the help of God in two definite ways of protection; 1) *without war*, against the army of Alexander ; 2) *in*

did once later, (Is. xx.) and that the kingdom of Israel too, (Zech. x. 9-12.) and in a lesser degree that of Judah, (ix. 8, 9.) would be affected by it.   That plan of the Assyrians was probably not carried out then ; for the history of that time does not mention it." (Proph. ii. 169, 70.) *Hitzig* would have the first prophecy to be a mere imitation of the beginning of Amos, and that against the Greeks to be a prophecy, that the Jewish slaves, scattered among the Greeks, should rebel against them and conquer them.   He admits, " peculiar is the expectation, that his people should fight against the Greeks;" (174.)—contrary to the whole character of prophecy, which bade the Jews in captivity to be still, seeking the good of those under whom they lived ; and absurd in itself, as if some scattered slaves could be called Judah and Ephraim ! *Ewald* (D. Proph. ii. 314, 5.) would make it an encouragement to the Jews to make war on the Greeks for detaining their banished," [those sold as slaves.] *Herzfeld* (Gesch. Isr. Exc. 2. § 3. i. 283.) would make the first prophecy relate to the expedition of Shalmaneser, and, substituting פרץ for פך, would make the latter relate to a civil war, to be encouraged by God.   *Stähelin*, for the first part, followed De Wette ; but called ix. 13. a prophecy against Greece ; (p. 327.) how, he does not explain. *Bleek*, in his strange compromising way, in which he admitted right principles but excepted to their application, owned that there are such definite distant prophecies in Holy Scripture, but, on à priori grounds, preferred to suppose that the words related to something unknown, rather than own that they related to that in which he confessed that they were fulfilled.   "Certainly one may find in these glorious battles of the Jews, in a certain sense, a fulfilment of what is here foretold by the Prophet.   But if we are not to deny to this utterance all moral character, and to consider it purely as the production of a mantic predictiveness—a gift which I do not deny to be possible and actual, but which, in the Bible prophets, appears, if at all, yet very seldom, then, I believe, we may consider ourselves justified in assuming, that the prophet here named the Greeks individually, instead of the enemies of the Covenant-people generally, not because he saw in spirit before him the later battles of the Jews with the Seleucidæ, but because he had, in the historical relations of the past or present, a special occasion to give them prominence in this respect."   Theol. Stud. u. Krit. 1852. H. 2. p. 266, 7.

the war of the Maccabees; and those, two of the most critical periods in their history after the captivity. Yet, being expansions of part of the prophecy of Daniel, the period to which they belong became clearer in the event by aid of the more comprehensive prophecies. They were two points in the larger prediction of the 3rd empire.

The partial minuteness of Daniel's prophecies belongs to the transition-state of the period for which those prophecies were given. They are in one sense a link between the Old and New Testament. God was preparing His people to depend more on His invisible presence. In the captivity itself, the three great bodies of His people dispersed among the heathen, those in Assyria, in Egypt, and in Babylon, had still each their own great prophet, Ezekiel among the *captives by the river of Chebar*, Jeremiah in Egypt, Daniel in Babylon. After the captivity, there were but three prophets more. Of these, the prophecies of Haggai, preserved to us, fall in the space of four months in the 2nd year of Darius Hystaspes [1], 16 years after their return; Zechariah began two months [2] later than Haggai, and has no known date beyond the 4th year of Darius [3]. The prophecy of Malachi is probably contemporaneous with the second visit of Nehemiah, about 400, B.C. Then prophecy ceased in act. It was exceptional, while it lasted. For those five centuries, in the first instance, the book of Daniel was written. God no longer willed to interfere visibly. Israel, a petty nation, hated, envied, on account of its magnificent claims, that its God was the God of the whole world, was placed in the high-way of the world, to be trampled upon by each in turn. Forerunner of the Christian Church, and itself shortly, the whole true Israel, to pass into it, it lay for the time, resting on the unseen Providence of God, and awaiting, with keener expectation, the Deliverer of itself and of the world. It was no longer to have single Prophets raised up, to explain to it or to point out God's dealings with it, to preach submission, or to promise mitigation of suffering or de-

---

[1] Hag. i. 1. ii. 1-10. 20.   [2] Zech. i. 1.   [3] vii. 1.

liverance upon its repentance. But God *left Himself not without witness.* Details of prophecy, such as aforetime had been given by different prophets, in succession, were spread out before them at once, culminating in that great trial of faith, the last before our Lord's first Coming, when Antiochus Epiphanes used all artifice and force to extirpate the worship of the One God. Daniel foreshewed to them his power, his artifices, his partial success in abolishing the public worship of God, his sudden destruction without human hand. They should need no human might; they had but to endure, and the victory was God's.

These more detailed prophecies of Daniel, then, so far from being exceptional in God's dealings with His people, were in conformity with all His ways, as recorded for us, before the captivity; so far from being retrogressive, in introducing a more limited character of, so to speak, civil prophecy, his prophecy was adapted to a state of progress, a condition more like our own, in which, instead of the living, revealing, prophet, they were cast upon the written book. But in that book God taught them that, however the world might rage, it was in His hands. He who beforehand told the course which ambitious, selfish, crafty, oppressive, sensual, monarchs would take, and how it would fare with them, shewed that He Himself ruled and overruled the affairs of men which He foreknew. The book of Daniel said in fact, at each stage of its fulfilment, what God said in words by Isaiah, *Behold, the former things are come to pass, and new things do I declare unto you ; before they spring forth, I tell you of them* [1].

The same relations of a large future and a minute foreground of prophecy, which should be an assurance to men, until those large prophecies had time for their fulfilment, recurs in the Gospel. What is now to us a primary evidence, the conversion of the nations, was to the Apostles matter of faith. To us it is a marvellous evidence, which our own eyes see, that, as it was foretold, "the Holy

[1] Is. xlii. 9.

Church throughout the world," millions upon millions, yea, a hundred millions thrice-told, worship Him Who, when it was foretold, was worshipped only by a small handful of men in a space not so large as one of our English counties; that they worship Him, as it was foretold, Who came, was rejected, was crucified by them as a malefactor, and so atoned for them who crucified Him, and for the whole world. The shame of the Cross is the triumph of prophecy. Jesus suffered, as was written of Him; He reigns and is worshipped, as was also written of Him. He endured, what mere man could not endure; He reigns, as man could not reign. He has won the world to the Cross, as He foretold, and as man could not win it. The Church of all times and climes is large enough to be its own witness. It was foretold of, and, after eighteen centuries, endowed with the perpetuity of its Author and Founder, it IS. But while it was struggling into being, and man yet hoped to trample out its life, there was all that nearer minuter foreground around the Person of our Lord. His acts and history were the fulfilment of minute prophecy. Even those things which man could have fulfilled, had he willed, as that entrance into Jerusalem [2], belonged to a character which none, save He Whose it was, could sustain, greatness in lowliness [3]. Such too were, the preaching of the Gospel to the meek [4]; the binding up the broken-hearted; the liberty to the captives; the glorious light to the despised land of Galilee [5]. Such and much more was all that sorrowful history of His Passion, *the 30 pieces of silver* [6], *the shame, the spitting* [7], *the smiting on the cheek*, the gall and the vinegar [8], the piercing [9], and that, *of the hands and the feet* [10], the violent Death [11] by His people for whom He died. These would have been the end of all human pretensions. They were the beginning of His Divine kingdom, Who said by His

[2] Zech. ix. 9.　　　[3] The Jews themselves saw that lowliness was the characteristic of the prophecy. See ab. p. 84.　　　[4] Is. lxi. 1. S. Luke iv. 18.
[5] Is. ix. 1.　　　[6] Zech. xi. 13.　　　[7] Is. l. 6.
[8] Ps. lxix. 21. S. John xix. 29.　　　[9] Zech. xii. 10. S. John xix. 34, 37.
[10] Ps. xxii. 16.　　　[11] Is. liii. 8. Dan. ix. 26.

prophet, *They shall look on Me Whom they have pierced;* of Whom it was said[1], *Him Whom man despiseth, Him Whom the nation abhorreth, a servant of rulers, kings shall see and arise, princes also shall worship.* Human wisdom could not conceive, human power could not accomplish, that such a death should be the regeneration of the world. Salvation through the Crucified was the stamp of foolishness which the Gospel bore in the eyes of the followers of Socrates.

That same characteristic of prophecy, the larger distance and the nearer earnest, occurs too in our Lord's prophecies. We know His prophecies, that He shall come to be our Judge. He told it often and most distinctly. But, this being unseen, His judgment on the devoted city was the first earnest of that Judgment to come, with which accordingly He in His prophecy closely connected it, as closely and upon the same principle, as Daniel, under inspiration of the Holy Ghost, connected the Resurrection with Anti-Christ, and Anti-Christ with his Jewish type, Antiochus Epiphanes. Our Lord also used the same minuteness of prophecy, in that He directed His disciples to flee from Jerusalem after it had been encompassed by armies, a command which only became possible through the un-Roman retreat of Cestius Gallus. It is noticed also that, out of 17 sieges which Jerusalem sustained, once only, in consequence of its rocky site, was it encircled with a wall; and that once was foretold by Jesus[2]. Minuter yet were His predictions of the details of the contumelies heaped upon Him, the mode of His death, the threefold denial of S. Peter, the treason of Judas.

In this long array of prophecy, which I have exhibited to you, it has been impossible to vindicate each against the cavils brought against it. This was not our problem. It was alleged, in prejudice against the book of Daniel, that its prophecies, if really such, were out of harmony with the other prophecies of the Old Testament, that other prophecy was not so minute or definite. I under-

<hr>

[1] Is. xlix. 7.　　　　[2] Tholuck, Proph. p. 194.

took to point out to you, that the truth was the exact contrary to this; that the prophecies in Daniel, so far from being out of harmony with those in the rest of the Old Testament, were altogether in conformity with them. Impugners of the book of Daniel alleged an unlikeness on the surface; I undertook to point out to you the real harmony. If any one deny all Divine prophecy, a single lecture cannot suffice to assure him. But the argument, if honest, assumed the truth of prophecy generally. People, who so argue, act the believers in prophecy. For the alleged difference between the prophecies of Daniel and other prophecy could have no weight in disproving that they are Divine prophecy, unless it could be shewn, that they were so different in character from Divine prophecy, that it would be a contradiction to think that both came from the same Author.

But opponents have, for the most part, granted the agreement of other prophecy with the event. The assumption, that definite prophecies are "prophecies after the event," would, if true, make the Bible the most dishonest book which ever was written, with one all-pervading dishonesty, coextensive with its actual Divinity. But it concedes the fact of the agreement. It cuts the knot, which it cannot untie.

Of the vast range of definite prophecy, it is even strange that men should venture to attack any, when on their own shewing they can attack so little. Thus, the most laborious impugner of Daniel, in denying *all* definite prophecy, attacked definitely but very few, and even in these he mostly falsified prophecies, in order to accuse them of failure. When Isaiah prophesied the invasion of Judah by Assyria which *was* fulfilled, Lengerke substituted "destruction" which Isaiah did not prophesy; when Isaiah prophesied the spoiling of Samaria and Damascus within the year, he substituted, "the *destruction* of both within the year." When Isaiah foretold the fruitless invasion of Sennacherib and his sudden overthrow, Lengerke ignored the fulfilment of this prediction, which he tacitly admitted, in order to allege, that Isaiah in error predicted details of a siege which he did not predict.   Hosea foretold that Israelites should return to Egypt, and eat unclean things in Assyria [1].   Lengerke said, "According to Hosea [2], the ten tribes were to be carried back to Egypt, which was never fulfilled."   But clearly, since Hosea prophesied in the same verse, that Israel should *eat unclean things in Assyria*, he could not mean that the "ten tribes" should return to Egypt.   He could have meant it only of individuals of them.   Hosea, moreover, said distinctly, "he shall *not* return into the land of Egypt, *and the Assyrian shall be his king* [3];" marking the former statement to be partial or metaphorical.   To Assyria also was to be carried the calf of Bethel [4], the centre of their idolatry and of their national existence.   Humanly too, it is a poor and petty criticism, which fixes itself on this subordinate expression, limited, as it is, by the context, and ignores those vast prophecies, which describe the condition of Israel for 2600 years, as a nation, that they should be despised wanderers among the nations.

A miscellaneous group has been exhibited to you, in proof of an alleged fault among us, that "[5]the failure of a prophecy is never admitted, in spite of Scripture and of history."   Yet of the prophecies alleged to have failed, that of Amos, that the house of Jeroboam should fall by the sword, came true in the next generation; not the prophet's saying, but the false priest Amaziah's perversion of it, failed.   The sentence, pronounced by Jeremiah on Jehoiakim, points to a dragging of his corpse in contumely, which history does not contradict, but, in itself, leaves as probable [6].

In regard to the capture of Tyre by Nebuchadnezzar, stress has been laid on the silence of the Tyrian historian Menander, and the statement in Ezekiel, that Nebuchadnezzar and his army should find in Egypt the reward for

[1] ix. 3.   [2] He quotes p. lxxvi, vii." ix. 3. xi. 5." after Gesenius (Ies. ii. 827.) xi. 5. should probably be viii. 13. since in xi. 5, Hosea says the contrary.   [3] xi. 5.   [4] x. 6.   [5] Prof. Jowett, Essays and Rev. p. 343.   [6] See ab. p. 265, 6.

his services against Tyre, which he had not found from Tyre. Both imply the capture of Tyre. Menander, who makes a boast of its resistance to Salmanassar[7], would doubtless have related the issue of the siege of Nebuchadnezzar, had it been honourable for Tyre[8]. He himself lets out the facts, that the reign of the king, who resisted Nebuchadnezzar, ended with the close of the war[9]; that after the next, probably tributary, king, Baal, (to whom he attributes no relation to the deceased king, as he does to others,) judges were appointed[10]; that the line of kings was broken ; that, just before the close of the Babylonian monarchy, they had to send to Babylon for two brothers of their royal family in succession[11]. All this points to the ordinary treatment of conquered provinces, that, first, a native tributary king was appointed, then, if need were, severer measures were taken. Ezekiel speaks of Nebuchadnezzar as an instrument of God against Tyre. [12]*I have given him the land of Egypt for the labour which he served against her, because they wrought for Me.* The service, which he executed for God against Tyre, was the accomplishment of God's purpose to bring down its pride. Ezekiel says that he did that service[13]. Further, he only says that Nebuchadnezzar and his army had no adequate return for a 13 years' laborious siege. S. Jerome, who had access to histories now lost, relates as a fact, that when Tyre was all but taken, "they put all their valuables, gold, silver, vestments, and other goods, on board their vessels, and transported them to the islands, so that, when he took the city, Nebuchadnezzar found nothing worthy of his toil." The expedient is so obvious[14], that even a scepti-

---

[7] in Jos. Ant. ix. 14. 2.   [8] Hengstenberg's argument, de rebb. Tyr.

[9] c. Ap. i. 21. He is giving the chronology, and says, "In the time of Ittobaal Nebuchadnezzar besieged Tyre 13 years." But whether or no Ittobaal began his reign before, he could not have reigned after the siege ; for Menander is counting the years from Ittobaal to Cyrus, and if the 13 years of Ittobaal had not been any how his last 13 years, they would have furnished no date.

[10] κατεστάθησαν. This does not express that it was their own act.

[11] See ab. p. 119.   [12] Ezek. xxix. 18.   [13] Häv. on Ezek. p. 428.

[14] Diodorus relates that, in the siege of Alexander, the Tyrians purposed to remove, and in part removed, to Carthage their wives, children, and aged.

cal critic finds in it nothing to question[1]. Isaiah foretold that it should be so. [2]*Pass ye over to Tarshish; howl, ye inhabitants of the isle.* The state of Tyre also was changed by that capture. Although its fleet was still so powerful, that their refusal to take part in the expedition against Carthage frustrated the plan of Cambyses[3], it had submitted of its own free-will to the Persians, and ranked after Sidon[4]. The assertion of Josephus[5], that it was recorded in the Tyrian archives, that Nebuchadnezzar subdued the whole of Phœnicia, would, in itself, far out-weigh the silence of Menander. Rationalism retreated then in presence of the facts, and admitted a capitulation of Tyre[6], with which even Petavius[7] had been satisfied; but, therewith, it resigned its sole argument, the silence of Menander, who says no more of a capitulation than of a surrender. It has no support of its assertion but its own will.

Baffled in the attempt to find direct failure of prophecy, rationalism assumed that prophecy always related to the immediate future, and so, when the prophet, beholding that future in a long perspective, spoke of·the future of a city or nation without reference to time, it assumed that

Diod. xvii. 41. Curt. iv. 1-5. Häv. p. 429. Herodotus (i. 164.) relates the same of the Phocæans, and attributes to Harpagus, the general of Cyrus, the knowledge of their intentions.

[1] Ewald on Ezek. d. Proph. ii. 324. "Although we do not know the historical source, out of which he [St. Jerome] drew, yet it agrees perfectly with the brief words which Ezekiel held to suffice. True, that the prophet does not say in so many words that Neb. entered island-Tyre; but the converse, that the Tyrians at last vanquished him, lies still less in the words; and, whether, or no, he entered upon the empty houses, is, in regard to the sequel, which is the only question in Ezekiel, indifferent. All which Ezekiel has to say here is, that Egypt will, through the ordering of Jahve [God,] be the more certainly abandoned to be plundered by the Chaldæans, the less he found his hard toil, employed at Tyre for higher ends, rewarded." [2] Is. xxiii. 6.

[3] Herod. iii. 19. [4] Ezr. iii. 7. Herod. vii. 98. viii. 67. "In the first seat sat the king of Sidon; after him the king of Tyre." Häv. p. 433,4.

[5] "Nay, even in the archives of the Phœnicians are written things, agreeing with what is said by Berosus about the king of Babylon, that he subdued Syria too and the whole of Phœnicia." c. Ap. i. 20.

[6] Movers, d. Phœn. ii. 1. p. 428. 448 sqq. who however admits the complete subjugation of Phœnicia, including Tyre. "We *allow* that the Syrians capitulated." Davidson, ii. 467. [7] De Doctr. Temp. ix. c. 69.

the prophecy failed, if it was not fulfilled at once. But it was a simple falsifying of the prophet's words, when men said, e. g. "[8] the complete destruction of Babylon *by the Medo-Persians* is prophesied by Isaiah." "[9]Ezekiel predicts its [Tyre's] utter destruction *by Nebuchadnezzar,* so that it should be like the top of a rock, and never rebuilt."

It is strange that they who insist so much, that prophecy is not definite, who assert, even untruly, that dates are no matter of prophecy, will yet have it that these prophecies were not fulfilled, nay, that the prophets were deceived, because the whole of each prophecy was not fulfilled at once. No one denies that Babylon has long been in the condition which Isaiah [10] and Jeremiah [11] foretold; and that Idumæa is in that predicted by Obadiah [12], Isaiah [13], Jeremiah [14], Ezekiel[15]; and that Tyre and Rabbah of Ammon are what Ezekiel foretold they should become [16]. All these prophets say, what punishments should come upon those nations; no prophet says, as to the completed desolations, *when* they should be. They described apparently, in God-given words, the vision which God spread before their souls. We know that, as to our Lord's first Coming, they, for the most part, knew not the time. Only they knew, St. Peter tells us also, that it was not to be in their own; and this, by revelation of God. They knew by revelation the things themselves; *the Spirit of Christ in them testified beforehand the sufferings of Christ, and the glory which should follow*[17]. Very different from the fanatical expectations of later times, which have ever been outrunning prophecy, *it was revealed to* them, St. Peter continues [18], *that not unto themselves, but unto us, they did minister the things which are now reported unto you.* Further, as to what was not revealed to them, they were left, St. Peter says, to their own pious search into the meaning

[8] Lengerke, Dan. lxxvi.   [9] Davidson, ii. 468.
[10] Is. xiii. 19-22. xiv. 23.   [11] Jer. l. 12, 13, 39, 40. li. 26, 37-43.
[12] Obad. 9, 18. see my Comm. p. 242, 3.   [13] Is. xxxiv. 11-15.
[14] Jer. xlix. 17, 18.   [15] Ezek. xxxv. 7, 9.   [16] Ib. xxvi. 14.
[17] 1 S. Pet. i. 11.   [18] Ib. 12.

of what was revealed through them [1]. *Of which salvation the prophets enquired and searched diligently, who prophesied of the grace* that should *come unto you.* Vision is independent of time. When then the prophets say nothing of time, we have no right to assume, that they fixed any definite time for that future, which God spread out before them as *what* should be, irrespective of the time *when* it should be. At times the succession is marked in the prophecy itself; as, when Obadiah, after foretelling the destruction of Edom by Nebuchadnezzar, foretells a second chastisement through the Jews, which came upon them through John Hyrcanus, accordingly four centuries after Nebuchadnezzar. The assumption, that the omission of any mark of duration implies a disbelief that there would be any long interval, would be contrary to the authority of our Lord Himself, Who spake of the destruction of the world in connection with that of Jerusalem, without any note of time. Yet even apart from our knowledge of His Divinity and Infallibility, we know that elsewhere His words presuppose a long interval. The question is too, not how much the Prophets knew, but what God the Holy Ghost, Who spake by them, meant by the words which He gave them.

It belongs to the character of prophecy, to [2] *declare the end from the beginning.* It belongs to God's mercy, that His judgments break in gradually, at intervals, leaving space for repentance. "[3]Therefore chastenest Thou them by little and little that offend, and warnest them by putting them in remembrance wherein they have offended, that leaving their wickedness they may believe in Thee, O Lord." "Executing Thy judgments upon them by little and little, Thou gavest them place of repentance." What God's word declared has come.

The attempts then to disjoin the prophecies of Daniel, as something unlike in kind from those of the rest of the Old Testament, fails in both ways of stating it. Rather, we have that characteristic of unity, which is stamped

[1] 1 S. Pet. i. 10. [2] Is. xlvi. 10. [3] Wisdom xii. 2. 10.

upon all God's works of nature and of grace, likeness amid variety. Daniel, as being for that dreary time, when the living prophets ceased, a microcosm of prophecy, has in one all the character of prophecy. Largest and least, the remote future and the near, the conflict of the evil and the good, and its final issue, man's free-agency and God's overruling Providence, Judgment and Mercy, the Death of the Redeemer and His everlasting Kingdom, His Presence, as Man yet more than man, at the Right Hand of God, the passing away of the old Covenant and its sacrifices and the bringing in of the New, forgiveness of sins and the gift of rightcousness, are all concentred in him. The form in part varies, the centre is the same. The minute is not severed from the vast, nor the near from the remote, nor predictions as to time from the eternal issues of this fleeting world, nor the glories of Christ from His humiliation and Death : but in Daniel, as in all the prophets, and in God's other prophets as in him, we see God, working through man's free-agency, knowing, in His ever-present Eternity, the events of His creatures' varying and conflicting wills, beholding things which are not as those which are, present with His creatures in all the intricacies of this eddying life, Himself, in all, the ever-present God, the pitying Father, the all-just Judge. Prophecy, like God's physical creation, bears witness to the Oneness of its Author, by that marvellous oneness which underlies its beautiful variety, reappearing without repetition ; varying without deviation of principle ; one without identity : manifold, yet never departing from its one type.

LECTURE VI.

-----

*On the proof of the genuineness of the Book of Daniel,
furnished by the date of the closing of the Canon of the
Old Testament, and by the direct reference to it in the
Canonical Scriptures, and in other books before or of the
Maccabee period.*

THE account of the close of the Canon of the Old Testament, as given by those to whom the books themselves
were entrusted, is very definite, and proceeds on a definite principle. Josephus, in a controversial work, in
answer to an impugner of Judaism, states, in the name
of his countrymen, when it was closed, and why no later
writings were admitted into it. It was closed, he says,
in the reign of Artaxerxes, son of Xerxes, and that, because the succession of prophets closed then. "With
us," he says [1], in contrast to the contradictions of Greek
history [2], "there are, not myriads of books inharmonious
and conflicting, but two and twenty books only, containing the records of the whole time, and rightly believed
to be Divine. Of these, five are those of Moses, which
comprise as well the matters of law as the account of
the generations of man, to the time of his death. This
period is little short of 3000 years. But from the death
of Moses to the reign of Artaxerxes, the king of Persia

-----

[1] c. Ap. i. 8. Eus. H. E. iii. 10.   [2] Ib. 3. "I should be a busy body,
if I would teach those who know better than I, how Hellanicus differed about
genealogies from Acusilaus, or how Acusilaus corrects Hesiod, or how Ephorus
points out that Hellanicus in most things lied, and Timæus as to Ephorus, and
subsequent writers as to Timæus ; and as to Herodotus, all, &c."

after Xerxes, the prophets after Moses wrote what was done in their times, in 13 books. The 4 remaining books contain hymns to God, and suggestions to men as to their lives. From Artaxerxes down to our own times, events have been recorded, but they have not been accounted worthy of the same credit as those before them, because the exact succession of Prophets existed no longer. And it is evident in deed, how we stand affected to our own writings. For, so long a period having now elapsed, no one has dared either to add or to take away from them, or to change any thing; it being a thing implanted in all the Jews from their first birth, that they should account them as oracles of God, and abide by them, and, if need were, gladly die for them."

The unchangeable adherence of the Jews to the Old Testament, that wonderful faith, which has for 1800 years since, in the main, characterised their nation, even while forced, if they would remain Jews, to explain away the prophecies which they believed and attested, is stated at the same time by one of the mystical school. Philo, of a character the most opposite to that of Josephus, says, "[3] They change not even a word of the things written by him, [Moses,] but would rather endure 10,000 deaths than be persuaded to what is contrary to his laws and customs."

Josephus somewhat varied the distribution of the books, within the three divisions in which the Jews class-ed the books of Holy Scripture. For the question at issue with Apion was the historical faithfulness of the Old Testament. "[4] Since I see many attending to the blasphemies uttered by some out of hostility, and disbe-lieving what I have written about our antiquities, and making it a token of the modernness of our race, that the celebrated Grecian historians have not accounted it worthy of mention, I thought it needful to write briefly of all these things, &c." On this ground Josephus classes in one all which we call the historical books with Job and

<hr>

[3] In Euseb. Præp. Ev. viii. 6. p. 357.   [4] c. Ap. i. init.

the Prophets. His 13 books are, 1) Joshua; 2) Judges and Ruth; 3) Samuel i. ii; 4) Kings i. ii; 5) Job; 6) Isaiah; 7) Jeremiah and Lamentations; 8) Ezekiel; 9) The Twelve (minor prophets;) 10) Daniel; 11) Ezra i. ii; (i. e. Ezra, Nehemiah;) 12) Chronicles i. ii; 13) Esther. His four books of hymns and ethics are owned to be, 1) Psalms; 2) Proverbs; 3) Ecclesiastes; 4) Canticles. No one now disputes that such were the 22 books intended by Josephus, so numbered by a sort of memoria technica, in conformity to the 22 Hebrew letters[1]. No one now ever questions that he meant to include all the books of the Hebrew Scriptures, and those only. It has only been alleged, in transparent contradiction to his own words, that it is "a private account" of his own. He speaks of it as "an implanted belief of all the Jews, for which they would gladly die."

The date at which the Jews, in the time of Josephus, believed the Canon of their Scriptures to have been closed, was about four centuries before the birth of our Lord. Josephus probably fixed on the reign of Artaxerxes, as being the period of Nehemiah's great work of restoration[2], although the actual closing of the Canon probably took place during the second visit to his country, the probable date of the prophet Malachi, under the son and successor of Artaxerxes, Darius Nothus. The period which lay between was a long one; the time of Antiochus Epiphanes lay some 250 years nearer. Yet it was a period of the most active human intelligence. It reached back into no ages, really or hypothetically "dark." Socrates was a contemporary of Malachi; the source of the two philosophies, which have influenced the world, was of the same date as the last of the Hebrew Prophets. Better might we suppose the Greeks ignorant as to the dates of *their* philosophers, than imagine the Jews, to whom the word of God was dearer than life, ignorant as to the date

---

[1] S. Jerome in Prolog. galeato. Opp. ix. 454. "The books of the Old law are in like way 22; Moses, 5; the Prophets, 8; the Hagiographa, 9."

[2] Neh. i. 1. xiii. 6.

of *their* prophets. The term, moreover, was measured by something besides years. Josephus speaks of it as a period of mental activity in Judæa. "From that time down to our own, events were recorded; but they have not been accounted worthy of the same credit as those before them." This describes a portion of the deutero-canonical books of the Old Testament; books held in estimation among the Jews as well as by Christians, but not received by the Jews into their Canon, because Israel had no more prophets, who had authority to receive them.

The Canon of the New Testament closed with the Revelation of St. John, and his death was, it is supposed, about A. D. 101.   Now, conceive the parallel case, that a Christian writer, early in our 6th Century, e. g. Procopius, had stated in an Apology, that the history of Christ and His Apostles had been written in five books, and that there were 22 other books written by Apostles between the Resurrection of Christ and the reign of Trajan; that, after the reign of Trajan, down to his own times, other books had been written; yet that these were not esteemed worthy of the like credit, since there had been no Apostle later than the reign of Trajan; and that so, since the time of Trajan, no one had taken from or added to the number of the sacred books;—what would be thought of a writer, who should assert that the Epistle to the Hebrews was not written until 25 years after the Council of Nice, and so, about A. D. 350?   Apart from all other evidence, it would be thought inconceivable, that Procopius could assert, that the Christian Canon had been unalterable since the death of the last Apostle, if a book had been added to the Canon two centuries and a half after his decease.

One of the earliest of the books, written during that period of reflection and expectation, after the close of the Canon,—the Wisdom of the son of Sirach, furnishes a probable date as to itself. The preface, written by the grandson of the author, who translated it into Greek, defines that date more closely. The author, after devoting six chapters to the praise of great men, whom God had raised up in Israel during the period of the sacred books, winds up with the praise of the earliest progenitors or renewers of the human race, Shem and Seth, and closes at the beginning, with Adam.   Then follows abruptly the praise of Simon, the high priest, the son of Onias, whom he describes as one, still fresh in men's memory, mentioning even his personal stature rising above that of the other priests, like a young cedar among the palm-trees [1], and his personal beauty.   Now, although there were two high-priests, Simon son of Onias, and Simon II. son of Onias II., it is in itself the most probable, that the writer is describing the first Simon, both on the ground of his own greater eminence, and because the writer calls him simply, " Simon the high Priest, the son of Onias." The first is the Simon who, Josephus says [2], " was surnamed ' the Just,' on account both of his piety to God and his benevolence towards his countrymen."   He is the Simon singled out in an early tract of the Mishnah [3], as one of the last remnants of the great Synagogue.

The grandson relates that he himself " [4] came into Egypt, Euergetes being king."   The date of the well-known Ptolemy Euergetes agrees with the date of Simon the Just.   For, Simon having been contemporary with Ptolemy son of Lagus, the grandson of his contemporary, the son of Sirach, might well come into Egypt in the reign of Ptolemy Euergetes, the grandson of Ptolemy I., himself also a great patron of letters.   The title of honour naturally belongs to the eminent person who bore it.   A writer, wishing to designate his own date, would not use an ambiguous title.   The name Euergetes would recall to the Alexandrian, Jew or Heathen, the real "benefactor " to his country, not that later king, who, however he usurped both name and kingdom, was, from his bloated person, called Physcon, " big-bellied," from his deeds, Kakergetes, " malefactor ; " retaining, says the

---

[1] Ecclus. l. 12.   [2] Ant. xii. 2, 5.   [3] Pirke Aboth, c. 2.   [4] Prologue.

historian [5], "through his daily excess," neither the form nor the feelings of a man. A pious Jew would not have named Euergetes, one who, for incest, aggravated, cold-blooded murder of his own offspring, promiscuous massacre, hideous, inconceivable, diabolical, revenge, was a disgrace to human nature. Nor would Euergetes have been a correct title. Those, who called him at all by the name, entitled him " Euergetes the second," or " Euergetes Physcon," to distinguish him from the Ptolemy to whom the title belonged [6].

Simon the Just having been high-priest at the time of Ptolemy Lagi, the son of Sirach probably lived and wrote early in the 3rd century B. C.; his grandson went into Egypt somewhere in the reign of Ptolemy Euergetes 247-221, aged 38, and translated the book after some little interval.

The grandson's account is most distinct. He says, that his grandfather studied the Old Testament as a whole, and proceeded to write further, drawing his thoughts from it. " Whereas many and great things have been *delivered to us by the law and the prophets and by the rest who followed their steps,*—whereof not only the readers must needs become skilful themselves, but also they that desire to learn be able to profit them which are without both by speaking and writing, my grandfather Jesus, when he had given himself to the study *of the law and the prophets and the other books of our fathers,* and had gotten therein good judgment, was drawn on himself also to write something pertaining to learning and wisdom, to the intent that those who are desirous to learn and are addicted to these things, might profit much more in living according to the law." The book, (according to

---

[5] quotidiana luxuria ita marcenti, ut —sensu hominis nimia sagina careret. Just. 34, 2. sagina ventris non homini sed belluæ similis. Id. 38, 8.

[6] " His (Ptol. Epiphanes') two sons succeeded him, the eldest surnamed Philometor, the younger, Euergetes the second." Porphyry. (in Eus. Chron. Arm. i. 238.) " Ptolemy, the 2nd Euergetes." (Id. p. 241.) " Philometor his brother succeeded, the second Euergetes, whom they call Physcon." (Strabo, 17, 1, 11.) " Euergetes Physcon," (Ib. 12.) Justin gives him no surname.

the grandson's impression or knowledge,) was intended chiefly as a sort of epitome of practical teaching drawn and recast from Holy Scripture, to win those without to live according to the law. Three times, in this short preface, the grandson speaks of the Old Testament, as one completed whole; 1) in his own person, as the body of teaching which had been *delivered to Israel;* 2) as the source whence his grandfather derived his knowledge, 3) in reference to his own work of translation. "The same things uttered in Hebrew, and translated into another tongue, have not the same force in them; and not only these things [his grandfather's book which he had translated] but *the law and the prophets and the rest of the books,* have no small difference when they are spoken in their own language." He could not more explicitly have contrasted this book, on which he had been engaged, with those of the three classes before it. They, then fore-existing; this, derived from them; they, of primary authority; this, applying them; they, such as might be expected to retain, to a greater degree, their native force in a translation; this, as what might (obviously, from its less Divine power) lose more in translation.

The grandson is a good witness as to the religious habits of his thoughtful and pious grandfather. He could not fail to know them. The son of Sirach then had before him, as the authoritative source of instruction, the Scriptures of the Old Testament, in that same threefold division in which they existed in our Lord's time. The last class, although more miscellaneous, was as complete and as authoritative as the others. He does not say, "others who followed him," but "*the* others;" not, "other books of our fathers," but, "*the* other books[2]," "[3]*the* rest of the books." They were a complete whole, as authoritative as the rest; for the son of Sirach drew from all without distinction, as authorities to and above himself.

---

[1] διὰ τοῦ νόμου καὶ τῶν προφητῶν καὶ τῶν ἄλλων τῶν κατ' αὐτοὺς ἠκολουθηκότων. Præf.   [2] τήν τε τοῦ νόμου καὶ τῶν προφητῶν καὶ τῶν ἄλλων πατρίων βιβλίων ἀνάγνωσιν.   [3] αὐτὸς ὁ νόμος καὶ αἱ προφητεῖαι καὶ τὰ λοιπὰ τῶν βιβλίων.

According to the date of the Wisdom of Sirach, as given by his grandson, the question of external evidence as to the book of Daniel is decided. For the question lies only between the real date at which the book of Daniel was closed, B. C. 534, and the date of the death of Antiochus Epiphanes, B.C. 164. The prophecies in the book exclude any other. All must be true or all imposture. The prophecies as to Antiochus Epiphanes himself are too minute to be human, if written before the event at all. No human sagacity could have foreseen them. If we take "Simon the son of Onias" in the book itself to be the great "Simon the Just," and the "Euergetes" in the grandson's prologue to be *the* well-known Ptolemy Euergetes, then the grandson must have come into Egypt between B. C. 247-221 [2]. Supposing him to have come thither, as he says, at 38, at the close of the reign of Ptolemy Epiphanes, his father must have been born at the least some 60 years before, and the date of his grandfather must have fallen, any how, 280, B.C.; the Canon must have been then closed; and the book of Daniel had its place there. But taking him who is spoken of as Simon, *the* great Simon, him who would be known by readers as " Simon son of Onias," not to be the high-priest who was celebrated by Jewish writers subsequently, but a later Simon, comparatively unknown; taking also him who is called Euergetes to be one whom all Egypt justly execrated as Kakergetes; assuming also that people dated, (as there is no proof that any one but himself ever dated,) from the time of his first accession, before he was driven out for his repeated and wanton aggression on his forbearing brother; that " the 38th year in the time of Euergetes " meant what it does not naturally mean [3], " the 38th year

---

[2] Ptolemy Euergetes came to the throne, B. C. 247, died B.C. 22¼. Clinton, F. H. iii. 386.

[3] No one would doubt, in any ordinary Greek, that the sentence, ἐν γὰρ τῷ ὀγδόῳ καὶ τριακοστῷ ἔτει, ἐπὶ τοῦ Ἐυεργέτου βασιλέως παραγενηθεὶς εἰς Ἀίγυπτον καὶ συγχρονίσας, meant, "for having, in the 38th year, in the time of king Euergetes, arrived in Egypt and continued some time with them." The context relates to his own work of translation, its difficulties, and the way in which

of Euergetes," just 2 years before Egypt rose up, unable to endure the monster any longer, and expelled him from them ; supposing this to be the date of the grandson's coming to Egypt, still the opponents of Daniel would gain nothing. The 38th year of Ptolemy Physcon, counted even thus, would fall 13¾ B.C [1]. The grandfather's book was a well-known book : it was then in repute ; his grandfather himself must have been somewhile dead, and yet, during those long years of thought and study, which must have prepared for such a book as the Wisdom of Sirach, the complete Canon of the Old Testament was (his grandson says,) the subject of that study. Let the date of the son of Sirach, when he so studied the Holy Scripture and laboured, as he says, for all time to come, have been as low as 180, B.C.[2], the case of the opponents of the book of Daniel is still as hopeless as ever, since the book of Daniel must have been earlier than this ; and, being earlier, must have been prophetic.

he qualified himself for it. " I found," he says, " a copy of no small learning, and held it most necessary to apply some labour and study to translate this book." The date, "the 38th year," is, in the natural construction of the Greek, distinct from the date by the reign of Epiphanes. In Greek, no more than in English, would "in the 38th year in the time of Epiphanes " mean "in the 38th year of Epiphanes." It would rather signify a concurrent date, as, in the Maccabees, the phrase, "in the first year in the time of Simon the high priest," means, "in the first year of their freedom." (1 Macc. xiii. 42. add xiv. 27.) It is then most natural to understand " the 38th year " of his own life, and the beginning of his Hellenistic studies of which he is speaking. The language of this preface does not contain a single Hebrew idiom. And it is, moreover, no Hebrew idiom, that the single translator of Haggai and Zechariah has rendered, בִּשְׁנַת שְׁתַּיִם לְדָרְיָוֶשׁ, ἐν τῷ δευτέρῳ ἔτει ἐπὶ Δαρείου. It is no natural translation, not the way in which a Hebrew would think in Greek, and so, not an Hellenistic idiom, but a mere rendering of one man. It is no authority then for rendering the words of the preface, which we have in their original Greek, otherwise than they would be rendered in any other Greek.

[1] Ptolemy Physcon dated back to the 12th year of his brother Philometor, when the Alexandrians made him king, his brother being for the time a puppet in the hands of Epiphanes. But his brother having succeeded his father, 181, B. C., his 12th year and Physcon's 1st was 1¼⅞ B.C.; his 38th, 13¾ B. C. See Porphyry in Clinton, F. H. ii. 390, 1. and table of kings of Egypt, ii. 408.

[2] Even Fritzsche supposes the work to have been completed 40 or 60 years before B. C. 132, and so between B. C. 192-172. Weish. Jesus Sirach's. Einl. p. xvi.

The existence of the Wisdom of Sirach, out of the Hebrew Canon, in itself implies that the Canon was closed, when it was written. His grandson avers that it was written in Hebrew; weighty Jewish authorities[3] attest its existence in Hebrew for a long period. "[4] Its high reputation appears from the way in which it is mentioned and its contents are applied. Very weighty authorities, chiefly of Palestine[5], appeal to Sirach, and sometimes in a way, used only of passages of Scripture. Even in the beginning of the 4th century, the book is counted among the Kethubim[6]." "[7] Sirach's proverbs passed into moral writings, were recommended by the wise, and spread abroad in public addresses. Including the anonymous citations, some 40 sentences, mostly in an abridged form, are given us in these writings, some of which are missing both in the Greek and Syriac text. All but three are in Hebrew, and, if the quotations are literal, they yield not unimportant contributions to the Hebrew of that time."

No ground can be alleged, why a Hebrew work written in Palestine, of such character as the Wisdom of Sirach, so praised, so approved, so full of wisdom, should not have

---

[3] Zunz (a Jewish Sceptic) quotes the *Tosefta*, (Yadaim, c. 3. "the book Ben Sira and all the books written since,") the *Jerusalem Talmud*, (j. Berachoth c. 7. j. Chagiga 2. 1. j. Nasir 5. 3. R. Akiba cites the books of Ben Sira j. Sanhedr. 10. 1.) *Babylonian Talmud*, (Chagiga 13. a. Yebamoth 63. b. [also R. Nissim relations f. 16. a.] Kethuboth 110. b. Baba Bathra 98 b. 146 a. Sanhedrin 100. b. Nidda 16. b.) *S. Jerome*, [as representing his Jewish instructors,] *Bereshith Rabba*, (c. 8. f. 10. a. f. 12. a. 73. f. 82. c. 91. f. 101 c. *Vaiikra Rabba*, (c. 33. f. 203. b.) *Midrash Coheleth*, (f. 102. c. 116. a.) *Tanchuma*, (f. 13. a. 15. d. 69. a.) "and some later writers besides." "Rapoport has already proved that R. *Nissim* quotes out of Sirach, in his life, p. 8." Gottesdienstl. Vorträge d. Juden, p. 101.   [4] Id. p. 101, 2.

[5] "As *Rab*, (Erubin 65. a. [comp. Sanh. 44. b.] 54. a. Beza 32. b.) *Jochanan*, (Nidda f. 16. b.) *Elasar*, (j. Taanith 3, 6. j. Chagiga 2, 1. Bereshith Rabba f. 10. a. Tanchuma f. 15. d.) *Rabba bar Mare*, (Yebamoth 63. b. Baba Kama 92. b.)

[6] "שאמר, says Rab, (Erubin 65. a.) וכתיב R. Chanina (1, 1.) and the Babylonian Talmud; (Berachoth f. 48. a.) Rabba Bar Mare uses the same expression with the addition בכתובים, and sets it over against the Law and the Prophets, (Baba Kama 1. 1.) Eliahu Rabba has הכתוב אומר of the same passage, in Yalkut, Gen. f. 23. d, but in the editions, c. 12. f. 61. b., there stands for it, 'The wise say.'" Ib. p. 102. a.   [7] Zunz, p. 102-4.

been received into the Canon, but either that inspired authority was then lacking to receive it, or that its author had not the same tokens of Divine authority as the writers of the Old Testament; or both.

The writer himself speaks with authority; he sums up his book, as a source of practical wisdom; "[1] Jesus, the son of Sirach of Jerusalem, hath written in this book the instruction of understanding and knowledge; who out of his heart poured forth wisdom. Blessed is he that shall be exercised in these things; and he that layeth them up in his heart shall become wise. For if he do them, he shall be strong to do all things; for the light of the Lord shall lead him, Who giveth wisdom to the godly." Yet at the same time, he speaks of himself, as coming *after* the writers of Holy Scripture, a mere gleaner after them. "[2] I awaked up last of all, as *one that gathereth after the grape-gatherers;* by the blessing of the Lord I profited, and filled my winepress like a gatherer of grapes. Consider, that I laboured not for myself only, but for all them that seek learning. Hear me, O ye great men of the people, and hearken with your ears, ye rulers of the congregation."

The son of Sirach himself, in praising great men of Holy Scripture, mentions generally, rulers, wise counsellors, "rich men furnished with ability," and, with all ranks and conditions of life, two classes of writers, those who "[3] announced in prophecies," and those who "[4] narrated verses in writing," [setting them forth at length.] By these last he manifestly intends the Psalmists, (as of David especially he says, that "[5] he praised the Lord most High with words of glory; with his whole heart he sang songs;") and hagiographical writers, (as of Solomon he says, "[6] The countries marvelled at thee for thy songs and proverbs and parables and interpretations,") and even

---

[1] l. 27-29.   [2] xxxiii. 16-18. In xxiv. 33. it is Wisdom, not the author, who says, " I will yet pour out doctrine as prophecy."

[3] ἀπηγγελκότες ἐν προφητείαις, xliv. 3.   [4] διηγούμενοι ἔπη ἐν γραφῇ, Ib. 5.

[5] xlvii. 8.   [6] Ib. 17.

especially such lengthened works, forming one whole, as Job, or the Canticles[7], or Ecclesiastes. So then[8] we have in the author himself, those two divisions of Holy Scripture, the "prophecies" and "the writings," as, in praising Moses, he adds "the law." "God gave him commandments, even the law of life and knowledge." Besides this, that long panegyric in itself bears witness to the greater part of our existing Canon, and to nothing besides that Canon.

This same division of the Old Testament into the same three classes occurs in a document, attributed to Nehemiah in a letter which stands at the beginning of the 2nd book of Maccabees.   The book itself closes with the death of Nicanor[9], B. C. 161, and the subsequent peaceful possession of Jerusalem by the Jews; "from that time forth the Hebrews had the city in their power." The work of Jason of Cyrene, which the author epitomised, did not extend beyond the reign of Antiochus Eupator[10], who died in the autumn B.C. 162[11]. To one, probably the former[12] of the two letters, there is added a date, 188[13], i. e. 125, B.C. There is no indication of any later date. This letter quotes from some writings, called "commentaries of Nehemiah[14]," that Nehemiah, "founding a library, gathered together the matters as to the kings and the prophets and the things of David, and the epistles of the kings concurring the holy gifts." The "library" was doubtless connected with the temple, in the treasury or Archives of which we know other documents to have been deposited[15]. What document the writers of the Epistle had before them, we have no clue.

Nor do the words contain anything as to the formation or closing of the Canon, or any act whatever in regard

---

[7] Fritzsche, ad loc. owns this.   [8] This argument is from Häv. Einl. i. p. 32. [9] xv. 37.   [10] ii. 20-3.   [11] Clinton, Fast. Hell. iii. 325.   [12] In 2 Macc. xi. 21, 33, and 38, the date is at the end of the letter.   [13] i. 10. It would then be divided, "in the month Chasleu, in the hundred fourscore and eighth year." Judas, whose name is prefixed to the 2nd letter, fell in battle, B. C. 161.   [14] ἐν τοῖς ὑπομνηματισμοῖς τοῖς κατὰ τὸν Νεεμίαν, lit. "the commentaries *according to* Nehemiah," ii. 13.   [15] 1 Macc. xiv. 49.

to it.   But the passage proves thus much, that a writing was in existence a century before our Lord, under the name of Nehemiah, presupposing the existence of the Canon in the time of Nehemiah, in that he gathered together into a library the books of which it was composed. Doubtless they were authentic copies which he was believed so to have collected, in like way as "the Epistles of kings concerning gifts" were, doubtless, the original letters of the kings of Persia, copies of which are preserved in the book of Ezra, to which originals, when need arose, appeal might be made.   The law had been already spoken of [1].   "The matters of the kings" doubtless comprised what are now called "the former prophets;" "the things of the Prophets," "the later Prophets;" "the things of David," the hagiographa; the third miscellaneous section being designated from the Psalms, the first book in it, precisely as our Lord speaks of [2] *all things, written in the law of Moses, and the prophets, and the Psalms, concerning* Himself, in language familiar to those to whom he spake. The writers of the Epistle speak of the act of Nehemiah in gathering together those former books into the library, as a place of safe keeping, in just the same way as they speak of the act of Judas in "gathering together all those things which were lost by reason of the war we had, and they remain with us."   "In like manner [3]," they say.   As then the writers, when they spoke of this act of Judas in "gathering together" those later documents, could not mean to speak of any gathering for the first time into a collection, (for they speak of them as having previously "fallen asunder [4]" and being "lost,") so neither could their meaning be, that Nehemiah, with whose act they compare that of Judas, for the first time collected those former books into the Canon.

Let people place this letter at what date they will, be-

---

[1] ii. 2. 3.   [2] S. Luke xxiv. 44.   [3] ὡσαύτως, ii. 14.

[4] διαπεπτωκότα διὰ τὸν πόλεμον.   Herzfeld would translate this, "what happened in the war," i. e. that he gathered its events in a history, (i. p. 444, 5.) which is, of course, impossible.

fore our Lord, (and no one would now place it later,) it were absurd to suppose that a writing, attributed to Nehemiah, and speaking of the Canon as existing in his time, could have obtained belief, had the Canon been closed subsequently to the times of the Maccabees. But the validity and accuracy of the tradition has even been insisted upon by opponents of the book of Daniel. For, mistaking it for an account of a formation of the Canon, they thought that it could be used, as an argument, that the Hagiographa, in the time of Nehemiah, was as yet unfixed. And so they committed themselves to admit the correctness of a tradition which is evidence against them [5].

These traditions or indications of the close of the Canon of the Old Testament coincide with the data which

[5] "The second place is 2 Macc. ii. 13. where a notice has been preserved out of lost memoirs of Nehemiah. The correctness of this account we have certainly no ground to doubt. The only question is, what writing we are to suppose to be intended." Bleek, Schl. ZS. iii. 201. "Nehemiah directed his attention to the commenced collection of a holy national library, as is expressly related in 2 Macc. ii. 13. Probably he succeeded in gaining several books, not yet found; and the passage quoted contains in fact very clear indications, that through him *some* [τὰ περὶ τῶν προφητῶν could not, of course, mean, *some*] prophetic books, as also the books of Samuel, here called 'the books of David,' (τὰ τοῦ Δαυΐδ,) because they treat chiefly of David; and 'the books of Kings' (τὰ περὶ τῶν βασιλέων) were added to the national library." Berth. Einl. § 28. p. 75, 6. Movers would have the whole to relate to a commenced formation of the Hagiographa. "The matters as to the kings," were to be the Chronicles; "David," "the first book of the Psalms;" "the Epistles," Ezra. Loci quid. Can. T. &c. p. 15. Stähelin leaves it open to mean, "either the books of the prophets according to their two divisions, or at least the books of Samuel and Kings, perhaps the Chronicles also, the documents contained in Ezr. vi. 2 sqq. vii. 11. and the Psalms." Einl. § 3. p. 9. Herzfeld is at pains to prove the genuineness of the two Epistles, (which he counts as one, Gesch. Isr. Exc. 18. i. 443 sqq.) but will have it, that ἐπισυνήγαγε, in ii. 14. means "compiled;" but in ii. 13. with which the statement stands parallel, means "collected." He too maintains that the threefold division of the Old Testament was intended by the writer of that letter; the first division being what are now the earlier prophets (i. e. the historical books written by prophets, Joshua, Judges, Samuel, Kings;) the 2nd, what the Jews count the later prophets, "Isaiah, although only to ch. 39; Jeremiah, with the Lamentations; Ezekiel and the 12 lesser prophets; only it may be that Jonah was added later; lastly, a collection of Psalms viz. Ps. 2-41., all attributed to David, and Ps. 42-50. from the sons of Korah and Asaph." Gesch. Isr. ii. 50. and Excurs. 22. p. 92 sqq.

X

we have of its gradual formation before and in the captivity. I cannot, of course, here condense the evidence for the genuineness and Divinity of the several books of the Old Testament. I can only point out traces of the gradual formation of the Canon, what books must have been received into it before the Captivity, and so, how little remained to be done after the return from it. The harmony of the account throughout involves an antecedent probability, that the Canon was closed, as Josephus states it to have been, while there were yet persons living, who had a recognised Divine authority to receive books into it.

The wildest criticism does not now doubt that the whole Pentateuch was before the Captivity. The objections which have lately been raised against it are but *like the chaff of the summer-threshing-floors*. They are but the arguments of persons, who wish to be deceived and so are deceived.   But although, had their charges been true, the Old Testament would have been as Satanic as it is Divine, they concede all which is needed for this argument. I will then here state, i) The indications, in the Old Testament itself, that a Canon was formed and enlarged ; ii) what books were manifestly of recognised authority before the Captivity.

i) The close of the Pentateuch contains a solemn account, with what earnest protest Moses, when ready to depart, delivered the law to *the priests, the Levites, and all the elders of the people*, to be read publicly at the Feast of Tabernacles in the 7th year, the year of release [1], when hearts would be gladliest. Besides this public gift and public use, Moses gave a copy of it to be laid up by the side of the ark. [2]*Moses commanded the Levites who bare the ark of the covenant of the Lord, saying, Take this book of the law, and place it at the side of the ark of the covenant of the Lord your God, and it shall be a witness against you.* It was deposited there, not as a mere place of safety, but close by the place of the typical atone-

____

[1] Deut. xxxi. 10, 11.   [2] Ib. 26, 7.

ment for sin, *the Ark of the covenant,* as the protest against their national breach of that covenant by idolatry. There was yet further the provision, that the king, when he should come to the throne, should [3] *write for himself the copy of this law in a book, from that which is before the priests, the Levites, and it shall be with him, and he shall read therein all the days of his life.* This book, it is plain from the Pentateuch itself, was not a section only of it, since the word, *the book,* is used in the larger sense in the Pentateuch itself. In regard to Amalek, Moses is commanded; "[4] write this for a memorial *in the book* and rehearse it in the ears of Joshua." Moses "[5]took *the book* of the covenant, and read in the audience of the people." The curse is threatened to Israel, "[6]if thou wilt not observe to do all the words of *this law* that are written in *this book.*" To this book Joshua added. Without entering into the details, how much he added, the fact of his so adding is stated clearly at the close of his book [7], "Joshua wrote these words in *the book of the law of the Lord.*" The very form, in which Joshua and the other historical books (except the Chronicles) begin, *And it was,* shews that the writers intended to join them on to previous books [8]. A Hebrew writer would not use the form, any more than we should, unless he intended by it to join on his book to a previous whole. In the book of Chronicles, which is a whole by itself, Ezra does not use it; nor does Daniel.

Samuel again, when he had "[9]told the people the law of the kingdom, *wrote it in the book* and laid it up before the Lord;" on the same ground on which Moses had so laid up the law, as a memorial against its infraction.

So also as to the books of the prophets. Isaiah bids his people[10], *Search ye out of the book of the Lord and read;*

[3] Ib. xvii. 18.   [4] Ex. xvii. 14.   [5] Ex. xxiv. 7.

[6] Deut. xxviii. 58. add 61. "every plague not written in the book of this law," xxix. 21, "according to all the curses of the covenant that are written in this book of the law;" 27, "to bring upon it [the land] all the curses written in this book."   [7] Josh. xxiv. 26.   [8] See on Jonah i. 1. p. 265.

[9] 1 Sam. x. 25.   [10] Is. xxxiv. 16. " דִּרְשׁוּ מֵעַל סֵפֶר.

x 2

using the corresponding word to that which our Lord used, [1]*Search the Scriptures.* Isaiah appeals here, as elsewhere[2], to the evident fulfilment of prophecy. But he speaks of it as a whole, as one book of the Lord, of which his own should form a part, in which they who should search should find, in which God's word and the coming events which he foretold were accurately paired, one with the other. *No one of these* [predicted things] *shall fail, none shall want her mate.* Even an opponent has owned this, in his heathenish language[3].

The use of the law by the prophets, and of the earlier prophets by those who succeeded them, implies the same thing. It has been pointed out, how prophets of Israel, Hosea and Amos, appeal to or presuppose the law of Moses, as well known in the schismatic kingdom of Israel[4], and so, how certain it is, that the law, as contained in the Pentateuch, was an existing authority, which Jeroboam could not shake off, but had to adapt his corruption of religion, as well as he could, to it. It has been pointed out too, how the citations of each earlier prophet by those who came after, presuppose that those former books were of recognised authority. Amos, when he opens and almost closes his prophecy with words of Joel[5], or applies more extensively those of Hosea[6], intends manifestly to carry on a message, already recognised as Divine. So also Obadiah, when he uses words of the prophecies of Balaam, Joel, Amos, and a Psalm[7]. Micah alludes emphatically to those parting words of his great predecesssor in the book of Kings[8], to expressions of the Psalms and Proverbs[9], to Joshua, to David's elegy over Saul and Jonathan, as well as to the Pentateuch; Habakkuk, Zepha-

---

[1] S. John v. 39. ἐρευνᾶτε τὰς γραφάς.   [2] xlii. 9. (coll. xli. 21-23.) xliii. 9-12. xliv. 7, 8. xlv. 19, 21. xlvi. 8-11. xlviii. 3-8. 14-16.

[3] " The poet seems to think of the insertion of his Oracle in a collection of Oracles and sacred writings, from which posterity could judge hereafter as to the correctness of his prophecy." Gesen. on Is. xxxiv. 16. i. p. 921.

[4] Hengstenberg, Auth. d. Pent. i. 48-125.

[5] See on Joel, p. 94, 5. on Amos, p. 154.   [6] See on Amos, p. 153.

[7] See on Obadiah, p. 230, 1.   [8] See on Micah, p. 289. Hengstenb. Christol. i. 475.   [9] See at length in Caspari Micha: and on Micah, p. 294, &c.

niah, Ezekiel, employ words or thoughts of his.   Jonah, by adopting the form *And*, joins on his prophetic history to the sacred histories before him, and blends his mission to the heathen with the history of the people of God.

Nahum, in the opening of his prophecy against Nineveh, manifestly refers to Jonah's appeal to God in regard to it.   For Nahum had to exhibit the stricter side of God's dealings as to that same city.   God had said in Jonah, how He forgave on repentance; Nahum opens his book by saying in that self-same form of words, that He was indeed long-suffering, but would not finally spare the guilty.   Nahum and Zephaniah use language of Isaiah[10]; Zephaniah uses that of Habakkuk, as also of Joel, Amos, Micah; Habakkuk's hymn shews one well-acquainted with the Psalms.   Whom does not Jeremiah employ?

The appeal in his day to the great prophecy of the destruction of Jerusalem in Micah[11], in its own words, shews that the book must have been in public use.

Even before the captivity God by Ezekiel speaks of the prophets before him as one whole[12].   *Thus saith the Lord God; Art thou* [Gog] *he of whom I have spoken in old time by My servants the prophets of Israel, which prophesied in those days many years, that I would bring thee against them?*

When then Daniel, studying Jeremiah's prophecy of the 70 years of the Captivity, says, *I understood by the books*[13], i. e. the biblia, scriptures, *the number of the years, which the word of God was to Jeremiah the prophet, to fulfil as to the desolations of Jerusalem, seventy years,* this exactly expresses what we see from the writings of the prophets before the captivity to have been the fact, that the books of the prophets were collected together.

The captivity set God's seal on the true prophets of God over against the false prophets, and gained a reverence for them among those also of the people who had derided and persecuted or slain them before.   *The for-*

---

[10] On this and the following I hope to write in the Introduction to those Prophets.   [11] See on Micah, p. 290.   [12] Ezek. xxxviii. 17.   [13] ix. 2.

mer prophets[1] is a standing expression for the prophets before the Captivity.

The historical books were, at all times, an essential part of the teaching of Israel. They were a mirror in which God exhibited to them in act, in their own history, what in the law He had taught them in word, the fruits of obedience and disobedience to Himself. Much as the several series of histories vary in their character, this line runs through them and holds them in one, as, outwardly too, they are joined on together. Their difference of character marks their independence; the unity of design marks one guiding principle.

On ground of language the book of Joshua must have been very early; for its language has so much in common with the Pentateuch, although the Pentateuch has marks of greater antiquity, having archaisms, which the book of Joshua has not, and not having language which the book of Joshua has[2]. On historical grounds[3] the books of

---

[1] " Be ye not as your fathers, unto whom the former prophets have cried, saying, Thus saith the Lord of hosts, Turn ye now from your evil ways—Your fathers, where are they? and the prophets do they live for ever? But My words and My statutes which I commanded my servants the prophets, did they not take hold of your fathers?" Zech. i. 4-6. " Should ye not hear the words which the Lord hath cried by the former prophets, when Jerusalem was inhabited and in prosperity?" vii. 7. "lest they should hear the law, and the words which the Lord of Hosts hath sent by His Spirit by the former prophets." vii. 12.

[2] " The book of Joshua 1) has not the Archaisms which pervade all the five books of Moses equally, and, 2) notwithstanding great agreement of language with the Pentateuch, resulting from the common subject, yet it had distinct expressions and forms, varying from and unknown to the Pentateuch." Keil, Einl. § 42. p. 166. Of archaic forms of the Pentateuch, unknown to Joshua, Keil counts about 18 ; words and idioms, about 47; (Einl. § 15. 2. p. 40-2.) of new idioms or forms he also counts 18. (Einl. § 42. 4. § 16. 1. p. 46.)

[3] Keil (Einl. § 44. p. 172.) has these arguments ; 1) The Jebusites were not then driven out of Jerusalem (xv. 63.) which David did in the 8th year of his reign. (2 Sam. v. 5-9.) 2) "The place which God should choose ;" He had not yet chosen, (Josh. ix. 27,) as it was chosen under David. (2 Sam. xxiv. 18 sqq. 1 Chr. xxi. 18 sqq. xxii. 1.) 3) The Gibeonites were still "hewers of wood and drawers of water for the congregation and the altar ; " (Ib.) whereas Saul slew them as enemies of Israel and Judah (2 Sam. xxi. 2.) and (it follows) dispersed whom he did not slay. 4) "Great Zidon," (xi. 8. xix. 28.) not Tyre, was still the chief city of Phœnicia. 5) "The Sidonians " were still a people to be ex-

Joshua and Judges must have been written before the time of David, the Judges probably by Samuel [4].

The two books of Samuel were completed probably soon after the death of David [5]. They are far separated from the books of the Kings by the language, as well as by the style of the narrative. You must all have felt the difference between the full, almost biographical, character of the books of Samuel, and the brief extracts in the Kings from the fuller histories of the kings of Israel and Judah. The books of Samuel too contain no quotation of any written book, except the book of Jashar, and that in common with the book of Joshua [5]. The books of Kings, with a few very characteristic exceptions [6], close the reigns of

pelled; (xiii. 4-6.) whereas in David's time they were friendly, (2 Sam. v. 11. 1 Kgs. v. 15. 1 Chr. xiv. 1.) and brothers. (See on Am. i. 9.) Later times than Solomon's are excluded by the fact, that the Canaanites were dwelling at Gezer, (xvi. 10.) whereas Pharaoh drove them out and gave the city, as a dowry for his daughter. (1 Kgs. ix. 16.) Keil added (Comm. Einl. p. xxxv.) 6) Psalm 1. (which I also doubt not to have been a Psalm of David,) embodies God's command to Joshua in His own words; וְהָגִיתָ בּו יוֹמָם וָלַיְלָה Jos. i. 8. בְּתוֹרָתוֹ יֶהְגֶּה יוֹמָם וָלָיְלָה Ps. i. 2. König adds, 7) that it was probably written, before the shortlived conquest of Gaza, Ashkelon, Ekron. Judg. i. 18. comp. Josh. xiii. 3. Since the writer speaks in the first person, ("until *we* were passed over," v. 1. " the Lord sware that he would not shew them the land, which the Lord sware unto their fathers that he would give *us*, v. 6.) it is most probable that the book was written by Joshua; which was the Jewish tradition. Baba bathra, f. 14. 2.

[4] The book of Judges also, which is so manifestly one whole, was written before David had driven the Jebusites from Jerusalem. (i. 21.) It speaks of a forty-years subjection to the Philistines from the days of Samson, and so must have been written, after the victory under Samuel had interrupted that subjection. (1 Sam. vii. 3-13.) The repeated contrast of the state in those days with a more ordered state under a king, (xvii. 6. xviii. 1. xix. 1. xxi. 25.) makes it probable that it was written after the time of Saul. "Until the day of the captivity of the land," xviii. 30. evidently marks the same period as, "all the time that the house of God was in Shiloh." ib. 31. But this ended in that battle in which the ark of God was brought from Shiloh, and taken. 1 Sam. iv. 3-11. It went back, not to Shiloh, but to Kirjath Jearim. (1 Sam. vii. 2.) There is no reason to question the Jewish tradition, that the book was written by Samuel. Baba Bathra, f. 14. 2. 15. 1. [5] 2 Sam. i. 18. Josh. x. 13. Both are poetry.

[6] The exceptions are, Jehoram king of Israel and Ahaziah king of Judah, slain by Jehu; Athaliah, the usurping Queen, who was slain; Hoshea, the last king of Israel; Jehoahaz, removed after a 3 months' reign; (2 Kgs. xxiii. 31-34.) Jehoiachin, removed in like way; (Ib. xxiv. 8, 12.) and Zedekiah, the last king of Judah.

the kings, both of Israel and Judah, with the reference to the larger chronicles of the respective kingdoms. And this is the more remarkable, since the books of Samuel must be founded on the words of Samuel, Nathan and Gad[1], in which the acts of David were written. In language also the books of Samuel are wholly free from Chaldaisms, and from later language generally. The statement, [2]*Ziklag belongeth to the kings of Judah to this day, may* refer to a time when there were kings of *Israel* also. It is not indeed necessary, since it seems to be stated that it was a crown-property, and, whereas it originally fell to Judah[3], then was given to Simeon[4], now it came back to Judah in its kings. There are no other marks of time, and the absence of allusion to any later event fixes the books of Samuel probably, at latest, in the early part of the divided kingdoms[5].

The book of Ruth contains no marks of its date. It is most likely to have been written, when the memory was most fresh. The only custom which is related, that of giving the shoe in witness of a covenant[6], belongs to a very simple time, and may well have fallen into desuetude soon after David's time. The language has this remarkable characteristic, that the forms, which look like Chaldaisms, occur in conversation, and so represent the language of peasant life; the narrative Hebrew being good. The history itself took place a century before David. The right of kindred in redeeming the land[7] is a Levitical law[8]; the custom, that such redemption

---

[1] 1 Chr. xxix. 29.   [2] 1 Sam. xxvii. 6.   [3] Josh. xv. 31.   [4] Ib. xix. 5.

[5] The explanation 1 Sam. ix. 9., as to the office of the *Roeh* having passed to the *Nabi*, requires no later date than the full establishment of the *Nebiim*, "prophets," by Samuel. The dress of the king's daughters (2 Sam. xiii. 18.) might very possibly be changed in the days of Solomon. We could speak of the "long dresses" of 20 years ago. The cases, in which customs or things are said to have lasted *unto this day*, do not require any long period. They are, 1 Sam. v. 5. Dagon's priests not treading on his threshold; vi. 18. the great stone in the field of Joshua, the Bethshemite; xxx. 25. David's rule about the equal division of spoils; 2 Sam. iv. 3. the sojourning of the Beerothites at Gittaim; vi. 8. the name, *Perez-Uzzah*; xviii. 18. the name, *Absalom's place.*

[6] iv. 7.   [7] iv. 3, 4.   [8] Lev. xxv. 25.

in the case of a childless widow involved marriage with her[9], is something beyond, not against, the Levitical law; for the deceased had no brothers left.

The books of Kings close with the life of Jehoiachin, whom Evilmerodach, in his first year, took out of prison in the 37th year of his captivity[10]. He was then in his 55th year[11]. It seems probable that he died within the 2 years of the reign of Evilmerodach, since it is said that the king, i. e. Evilmerodach, gave him a daily allowance all the days of his life. The kings of Judah had become a shortlived race[12]. In this case, the last event in the book falls about B.C. 559, the restoration of Jehoiachin being, as an act of kindness, a mitigation of their captivity, 22 years before its close. Since the book does not allude to that close, there is no doubt that it was completed before. The manner and language of the books fall in with the Talmudic tradition, that the books of Kings were written by Jeremiah[13]. The Hebrew of the books of Kings is indeed purer than that of Jeremiah, hardly any instance of what are alleged as Aramaisms occurring in the narrative[14]. But this, probably, results from the careful embo-

---

[9] Ruth iv. 5.　　[10] 2 Kgs. xxv. 27.　　[11] He was 18 at his accession. (2 Kings xxiv. 8.) "Eight," in 2 Chron. xxxvi. 9., must be an error of a copyist. For he was old enough to do deeds of oppression, if not of blood. (Ezek. xix. 6, 7.) The long imprisonment too implies more of wilful rebellion against the king of Babylon, than an 8-year-old child is capable of.

[12] Manasseh alone reached 67. (2 Kings xxi. 1.) Jotham died at 41; (Ib. xv. 33.) Ahaz at 36; (Ib. xvi. 2.) Hezekiah's life was prolonged, but only to 54; (Ib. xviii. 2.) Jehoiakim died at 36. (Ib. xxiii. 36.) (Amon and Josiah do not come into account here, having been slain, Amon at 24, Ib. xxi. 19. Josiah at 39. Ib. xxii. 1.) Of the uncles of Jehoiachin, Jehoahaz was dead in Egypt, (Ib. xxiii. 34.) and Zedekiah, who was 3 years older than himself, (Ib. xxiv. 18.) was doubtless already dead, since he is not mentioned.

[13] Baba bathra f. 15. 1.

[14] לכּי, 2 Kings iv. 2. בנינכי, נשיכי, Ib. 7. את, 1 Kgs. xiv. 2. 2 Kgs. iv. 16. 23. viii. 1. are, of course, in conversation: but so also is את for את with the affixes אתהם 2 Kgs. vi. 16. אתכם Ib. iii. 11. 12. viii. 8. and thence perhaps, (though an angel is speaking,) Ib. i. 15. So is והשקותים Ib. v. 18. and (if this were modern) סאלטן 2 Kgs. vi. 11. (but on ט see on Jonah p. 250.) There remain only קָבָל 2 Kgs. xiv. 10. and the two words ending in ן, 1 Kgs. xi. 33. 2 Kgs. xi. 13. (the one a proper name, the other, the name of an office; רִצִין, עדִין,) לכתיב (2 Kgs. viii. 21.) is probably an error of MSS.

dying of the original documents, so regularly referred to, which accounts for some variations in the language also. The carefulness of that embodying is shewn in the retention of the words "unto this day [1]," as to things which, at the time of the completion of the whole, had ceased to be; and in the dates, in that the age of the kings of Israel at their accession is not mentioned, nor that of the kings of Judah before Jehoshaphat, whereas it is not omitted as to any king of Judah after Jehoshaphat. Still there is a certain agreement of style between Jeremiah and the books of Kings, and even verbal agreement has been noticed where the writer of the books of Kings writes most reflectively [2]. The insertion of the history of the captivities of Judah at the end of Jeremiah [3] is unaccountable, except on the ground that it was Jeremiah's; and yet the corresponding statement in the book of Kings [4] is not a mere abridgement of it, and so is, probably, from the prophet [5].

This, however, was but the completion of what, in substance, existed long before. The basis of the present books was, from the time of Samuel, furnished by contemporary prophets. The history of David was written by three, Samuel, Nathan, Gad [6]; that of Solomon by Nathan, Ahijah, Ye'di [7]; Rehoboam's by Shemaiah and Iddo [8]; his son Abijah's by Iddo [9]; Jehoshaphat's by Jehu son of Hanani [10]; Uzziah's and Hezekiah's by Isaiah [11];

---

[1] Of the position of the staves of the ark in the temple, 1 Kgs. viii. 8; Solomon's levying a tribute of bondservice of the Amorites &c., Ib. ix. 21; the rebellion of Israel against the house of David, xii. 19; of Edom from under the hand of Judah, 2 Kgs. viii. 22; the disgrace of the house of Baal, 2 Kgs. x. 27. The name of Joktheel (2 Kgs. xiv. 7.) and the dwelling of the Syrians at Elath (xvi. 6.) which are mentioned with the same formula, are not necessarily so limited; but still the formula is probably retained out of the old document.

[2] "comp. 2 Kgs. xvii. 14, and Jer. vii. 26; xvii. 15, and Jer. ii. 5; xvii. 20, and Jer. vii. 15." Häv. Einl. ii. 1. p. 171. Häv. also dwells on the correspondence of Jer. xxxix. with 2 Kgs. xxv.; and the way in which both allude to God's promise to the house of David, His choice of Jerusalem, and the special employment of the language of the Pentateuch in both, p. 171, 2.

[3] ch. lii.   [4] 2 Kgs. xxiv. 18-20. xxv.   [5] Häv. p. 172-4.

[6] 1 Chr. xxix. 29.   [7] 2 Chr. ix. 29.   [8] Ib. xii. 15.   [9] Ib. xiii. 22.

[10] Ib. xx. 34.   [11] Ib. xxvi. 22. xxxii. 32.

Manasseh's by Chosai [12].   These, it is clear, were incorporated in the book of the Chronicles of the kings of Israel and Judah, so often referred to in the books of Kings.

The books of Kings having been completed in their present form before the close of the Captivity, then, on this ground alone, it is clear that the previous books must have been written from the pre-existing prophetic materials before that time.

So as to the third division.   The Psalms, being intended for devotional use in the Temple, must have been early collected.   They were needed for that vast elaborate system of instrumental and vocal music which David instituted, setting apart 4000 Levites [13] *to praise the Lord with the instruments which I made,* said David, *to praise therewith.*   The office of those set over them, was to [14]*prophesy with harps, to give thanks and to praise the Lord.*   The two first collections or books of the Psalms, 1-41, 42-72, contain only 7 anonymous Psalms.   The first is entirely ascribed to David, except four anonymous Psalms [15], three of which are certainly, the fourth probably, his [16]; the 2nd

---

[12] Ib. xxxiii. 19. חֹזֶה "Seer of the Lord."   The name is according to the analogy of many other Proper names; there is then no reason to assume a rare and doubtful plural ending, with Kim.   The Vulg. and Ch. keep it as an appellative.

[13] 1 Chr. xxiii. 5.   [14] Ib. xxv. 1, 2, 4.   [15] Ps. i. ii. x. xxxiii.

[16] Ps. ii. is quoted by the collected Apostles (Acts iv. 25.) as David's, not as a name for the Psalter generally, but specifically, "Who by the mouth of Thy servant David hast said."   It corresponds also with Ps. cx. which our Lord Himself quotes as David's in a conviction of the Jews, which turns upon the Psalm's being David's.   But Ps. i. is distinctly written as a pair with Ps. ii, as well as an introduction to the whole Psalter.   The *Blessed,* with which it begins, corresponds with the *Blessed* with which Ps. ii. closes; the end of Ps. i. *the way of the ungodly shall perish,* וְדֶרֶךְ רְשָׁעִים תֹּאבֵד, bears on, *and ye perish* as to *the way,* וְתֹאבְדוּ דֶרֶךְ, the close of Ps. ii.   They correspond too in subject.   Each exhibits the 2 classes into which the world is divided, those who accept and those who reject God, in their way and in their end.   Ps. i. describes them in relation to the Law of God, the one studying and delighting in it, the other, in practice and in words, scorning and scoffing at it. (i. 1.) Ps. ii. exhibits them in relation to Christ, the one in concerted rebellion against Him, the other trusting in Him; the one, His inheritance to the ends of the earth and *blessed;* the other, perishing.   One cannot doubt the unity of the author in the unity of thought.

Ps. x. is so closely connected with Ps. ix. which is ascribed to David, that the only question has been, whether it is altogether one Psalm with it. It is connected with it in outward form, in that both together form a partially alphabetic Psalm. In Ps. ix. the alternate verses, 2, 4, 6, 10, 12, 14, 16, 18, begin, in the order of the alphabet, with eight of the first eleven letters of the alphabet, א, ב, ג, ו, ז, ח, ט, י, to which the ninth is to be added, if ק, v. 20., is used to replace כ; in which case two only, ד, ה, would be omitted. Ps. x. has verses beginning with 5 out of the remaining eleven. Both Psalms also have verses where the alphabetic arrangement is broken. The xth, omitting 6 letters, between the ל with which it begins and the four last letters (ק, ר, ש, ת, v. 12, 14, 15, 17,) with which it closes, has 3 tetrastichs, (i. e. 2 verses divided in the middle,) 3, 4 ; 6, 7; 10, 11; and 3 tristichs (verses divided into 3) 5. 8. 9. corresponding to the number of the omitted letters, מ, נ, ס, ע, פ, צ, and so in a degree marking the omission. The omission in Ps. ix. is also marked by four verses, successively beginning with ו, of which one only belongs to the alphabetic order. Their subject is the same, the overthrow of the ungodly, who forget (Ps. ix. 19.) and despise God, and oppress the humble and *afflicted*, (עָנִי ix. 10. x. 18 ; else only Ps. lxxiv. 21.) who trust in Him. There is a connection too in their language, as especially in the remarkable phrase, לְעִתּוֹת בַּצָּרָה, which occurs only in these two Psalms, and which in Ps. x. manifestly refers to Ps. ix. In Ps. ix. 10. he says, "The Lord will be a refuge *at needful times in the trouble*." Ps. x. 1. asks, " Why hidest thou Thyself *at needful times in the trouble*?" Both end in the same way, the prayer against the prevailing of *weak man* (אֱנוֹש) against God, (ix. 20. x. 18.) and with the judgment of the heathen, יִשָּׁפְטוּ גוֹיִם ix. 20. אָבְדוּ גוֹיִם x. 16. לְשַׁפֹּט יָתוֹם וָדָךְ 18. Both have the appeal, קוּמָה יהוה ix. 20. x. 12. Both Psalms are complete in themselves, and yet are, in structure, essentially different. Ps. ix. is a Psalm of thanksgiving for God's judgments, as past, and has only two brief prayers, v. 13, 19, 20. Ps. x. describes the wicked in the period of his prosperity, when he thinks that all things are given into his hands, and briefly concludes with the judgment. In Ps. ix. the Psalmist thanks chiefly in his own name, "I will praise thee, &c." (ix. 1, 2, 3, 4, 13, 14.) In Ps. x. the prayer expressed or implied, and the thanksgiving, are for a class, " the poor," &c. in the 3rd person. (x. 2, 8, 9, 10, 12, 14, 17, 18.) In like way, Ps. ix. 13, 19. declares that God *does* not " forget (שכח) the poor ; " Ps. x. 12. prays that He *will* not, in contrast with the boast of the ungodly that He " has forgotten," x. 11. Ps. ix. speaks of it as an attribute of God, that He "maketh inquisition for blood," דֹּרֵשׁ דָּמִים ; the turning-point of Ps. x. is the boast of the ungodly, that God does not enquire בַּל יִדְרֹשׁ x. 4. לֹא תִדְרֹשׁ x. 13.

Ps. xxxiii. begins where Ps. xxxii. ended. Ps. xxxii. closes with the exhortation, " rejoice in the Lord, ye righteous, and jubilate, all ye upright in heart ; " Ps. xxxiii. takes up the key in words too used in Ps. xxxii, "Jubilate, ye righteous, in the Lord," and then follows the wonderful jubilee of praise for the marvels of His creation and of His Providence, how full the earth is of His tender mercy ; and the whole Psalm has only one brief prayer at the end, making, as it were, all this universal love their own. The Psalm appears then to have been written, as a sequel to Ps. xxxii. Its beginning connects it with a Psalm of David's ; there is a presumption that it is David's, from its being placed in this first book of Psalms ; there is nothing *against* its being his. Even Hüpfeld (Ps. T. iv. p. 458.) thinks it probable that the לְדָוִד was once there, and fell out subsequently.

contains, in addition to his[1], only a kindred Psalm of Asaph *the seer*[2] and Psalms of the choir which he instituted, "the sons of Korah[3]," one of Solomon's[4], and three anonymous[5]. To this second book is subjoined the remarkable subscription, "The Psalms of David, the son of Jesse, are ended;" and thereon follow two books, the 3rd and 4th, each of 17 Psalms, of which the 3rd, i. e. Ps. 73-89, contains one Psalm ascribed to David; the fourth, i. e. Ps. 90-106, two only. The subscription of the Psalms of the 2nd book seems to have a bearing on the two following books, separating off those books which had most of David's Psalms, in contrast with those which had fewest. The third book is, moreover, with the exception of the one Psalm of David[6], composed of Psalms attributed to the sons of Korah[7], and Asaph[8], which it completes, one Psalm being apparently left uncertain, with a double traditional title, those, who affixed those titles, being unable to decide between them and honestly admitting their inability[9]. The 88th Psalm, which is ascribed in the second title to David's seer, Heman[10], stands by itself also, as the Psalm expressive of the deepest woe in the whole Psalter, the only Psalm which ends in unmitigated woe. The 89th also, alone ascribed to its author, Ethan[11], is again characteristic, in its lengthened, unwavering, confession to God of His faithfulness, and the unperplexed simple pleading of the apparent contrast of the actual

---

[1] li-lxv. lxviii-lxx.   [2] Ps. l.

[3] Ps. xlii. (to which Ps. xliii. is manifestly a sequel) xliv-xlix.   [4] Ps. lxxii.

[5] Ps. lxvi. lxvii. lxxi. Hüpfeld says, "Perhaps the title, לְדָוִד has only dropped out. It is extant in lxvi. lxvii. in some MSS." Ps. T. iv. p. 459.

[6] Ps. lxxxvi.   [7] Ps. lxxxiv. lxxxv. lxxxvii.   [8] Ps. lxxiii-lxxxiii.

[9] In itself the mention of Heman the Ezrahite might, (however insulated the case,) fix the individual among the sons of Korah who composed the Psalm. But the completeness of each title, שִׁיר מִזְמוֹר לִבְנֵי קֹרַח and מַשְׂכִּיל לְהֵימָן הָאֶזְרָחִי, makes me think it probable that they are two titles.

[10] 1 Chr. xxv. 5, 6. add Ib. vi. 33. Eng. 18. Heb.

[11] I think (with A. C. H. in Smith, Bibl. Dict. i. 939) that Ethan is probably the same person as Jeduthun. ("comp. 1 Chr. xv. 17, 19. with xvi. 41, 42. xxv. 1, 3, 6. 2 Chr. xxxv. 15.") The name, "Jeduthun," "great praise," may have been formed by David.

state of things with that promise. The 4th book, on the contrary, is made up wholly of anonymous Psalms, except that of Moses which stands at the head, and the two of David[1]. And then again, in the last large book, i. e. Ps. 107-150, we have what seem to be gleanings of 15 of David's Psalms[2], whencesoever they were gathered, among that larger mass of anonymous Psalms, no other human author being named, except Solomon [3].

The large proportion of Psalms left anonymous is a proof of the conscientiousness of the collector in not adding doubtful names. Nay, we know that some Psalms were David's, which do not bear his name, since Ezra, probably, relates that, when David brought the ark to Jerusalem, he[4] *on that day first gave into the hands of Asaph* and his *brethren, to thank the Lord,* a Psalm, whose two component parts in the Psalter[5] bear no name. On this ground too then, it is apparent that these Psalms were inserted in the third book of the Psalter, before the time of Ezra, and, if so, before the Captivity. For had Ezra inserted them, he would have entitled them Psalms of David, as he does in effect in the Chronicles. The Psalm ends also with a prayer and doxology, with which Psalm cvi. is now closed[6]; a Psalm which stands in the Psalter as a pair with Ps. cv., rehearsing exclusively the mercies of God to Israel; while Ps. cvi. sets forth the ingratitude of Israel for those mercies. The prayer and the doxology form no integral part of Ps. cvi., the doxology closing the Psalm, like our Gloria Patri, and, with it, that book of the Psalms.

But the character also of the Psalms in the several books gives evidence of the gradual formation of the Psalter. In the first of the three books there is no one Psalm, of any later date than David. The second, in the main, ends with Solomon; only that, among the Psalms of the sons of Korah, two are inserted, which seem to corres-

---

[1] Ps. ci. ciii.   [2] Ps. cviii—cx. cxxii. cxxiv. cxxxi. cxxxiii. cxxxviii—cxlv.   [3] Ps. cxlvii.   [4] 1 Chr. xvi. 7.

[5] Ps. cv. 1-15. xcvi. 1-13.   [6] Ps. cvi. 47, 48.

pond best to the time of Jehoshaphat or Hezekiah[7]. In the 3rd book, there is one Psalm relating to Jehoshaphat's time[8], one to Sennacherib's overthrow[9]; and two of Asaph[10], referring to the destruction of Jerusalem, and the Captivity. But since this collection completed the Psalms of Asaph, it may be, that later Psalms of one of the choir of Asaph may have been inserted in the collection. In the great festival of Hezekiah, at the restoration of the worship which Ahaz had suspended[11], he[12] *and the princes commanded the Levites to sing praise unto the Lord in the words of David and of Asaph the Seer.* It may be that he collected a book of Psalms, as his *men*[13], we know, collected Proverbs.

Yet the fourth book also, which opens with a Psalm of Moses[14], contains only one Psalm[15] belonging to the Captivity. In the 5th and last book there are, for the first time, thanksgivings for the restoration from the great captivity[16]. The reference to idolatry also, as foreign and heathen, probably belongs to times when their own national idolatry had ceased[17]. Some of the gradual Psalms suit well to the habitual low estate of the returned exiles[18], beset by the enemies who hindered the rebuilding of the temple; one Psalm at least seems to belong to its dedication[19]. The cxixth Psalm, every verse of which, save one, has one of the ten words, denoting the law[20], and every verse of which, after the introduction, is directed to God, suits no one so well as the pious restorer of the law, Ezra. The five Halleluia Psalms, with which the book closes in one varied thanksgiving, all mourning done away and

---

[7] Ps. xlvi. xlviii, as describing a great gathering and raging of enemies and their instantaneous dispersion; xlvi. 6. xlviii. 45.　　　　[8] Ps. lxxxiii.

　　[9] Ps. lxxvi.　　　[10] Ps. lxxiv. lxxix.　　　[11] 2 Chr. xxviii. 24.

　　　　　[12] 2 Chr. xxix. 30.　　　[13] Prov. xxv. 1.

[14] Ps. xc.　　[15] Ps. cii.　　[16] Ps. cvii. cxxvi. perhaps Ps. cxxix. and cxxxvi.

[17] Ps. cxv. cxxxv.　　　[18] Ps. cxx. (alluding probably to the calumnies mentioned in Ezra,) cxxiii. cxxv. cxxvi. cxxix. cxxx.　　　[19] Ps. cxviii.

[20] "In every verse," is the observation of the Masora on v. 122, "except the 122nd, occurs one of the 10 words, (pointing to the x fundamental commandments of the Law of Sinai, אִמְרָה, דָּבָר, עֵדוֹת, הֶרֶךְ, מִשְׁפָּט, פִּקֻּד, מִצְוָה, תּוֹרָה, חֹק, אֹמֶר, (another reading, צֶדֶק.") Delitzsch, Psalmen, ii. 187. note.

even prayer for the time absorbed in praise[1], suits no time so well as the completed restoration under Nehemiah, when the Lord *built up Jerusalem* and *strengthened the bars of her gates.*

These facts, that the Psalms were gradually collected; that their earlier portions were the oldest; that the latest belong to the times shortly after the Captivity; and that there are no Maccabee Psalms; have impressed critics, whose interest it was to maintain their later date, in order to establish the late closing of the Canon.

I will give the summary of one of this school; "[2]All the later Psalms, which admit of or require an historical explanation, can be perfectly explained out of the history of Israel down to Nehemiah, and can only be explained out of it. A reference to later relations does not hold good, even as matter of interpretation." The Psalms most plausibly, as he thinks, alleged[3], "are all Psalms of penitence or complaint to God; in all, the congregation, in its strait, calls on its God for help. Throughout, those who so pray speak of themselves, as the congregation, the whole of it. There is not the faintest hint of a division of the people into two portions, contending against each other with extremest embitterment, which division is acknowledged to have lasted during the whole of the Maccabee wars. No one hint is there of the foreign enemy of the Maccabee combatants, Greek heathenism, and the Syrians[4]. The main points at issue then, the being or not-being of the true religion, abolition of the worship of God, prohibition of the keeping of the sabbaths and festivals, annihilation of the book of the law and of the other holy books, eating of unclean food, sacrificing to heathen gods, acceptance of the Greek religion, martyrdom of so many of the godly, are no where even alluded to, (for even the words Ps. xliv. 23. lxxiv. 9. are far too

---

[1] Hengst. Delitzsch. See Ewald, Poet. Büch. i. 188 sqq.

[2] Dillmann, üb. d. Bildung d. Sammlung d. heil. Schr. d. A. T. in Dorner, Jahrb. d. Deutsch. Theol. iii. 460-462.

[3] Ps. xliv. lx. lxxiv. lxxix. lxxx. lxxxiii.

[4] Dillmann adds, "which the book of Daniel describes clearly enough."

weak for this.)   The expressions, *Thine enemies, O God; the enemy blasphemeth the name of God; arise, O God, plead Thine own cause;* and the like, are far from establishing that those wars were properly religious wars; else many other passages of the Psalms and of the rest of the Old Testament must be referred to the Syrian religious war.   Then too we read nothing of appeals to victories already won by them over these adversaries, which could not fail in hymns of Maccabee warriors: on the contrary, Ps. xliv. 2-9. refers back to God's deliverances in old times, as the ground of the fresh entreaty.   Contrariwise, most of these Psalms [5] contain clear references to the Captivity, lament over the still-continuing abandonment to the Heathen, or pray for fuller restoration out of banishment;—prayers and laments, removed far enough from the Maccabee times.   Others allude to the mockery and malicious joy of the neighbouring people [6] at the ill-treatment of Israel through the peoples and kingdoms, just as it happened at the time of the destruction of Jerusalem by the Chaldæans [7].   Almost all exhibit the condition bewailed, as one which had long lasted; they entreat, that God would not be angry for ever, would now at the last help, would no longer behold with indifference the long-enduring misery [8].   What meaning could such expressions have in the period, to which the modern expositors would force these Psalms down?"

The LXX translation of the Psalms is in itself a clear evidence, that the Psalter, together with its titles, existed long before it, for it misunderstands many of the titles [9]; yet, of course, the translators of the Psalms would be among the best of their day, since the use of the Psalms

[5] Ps. xliv. 12 sqq. 15. lx. 3. lxxix. 11. lxxx.   [6] Ps. xliv. 14. lxxix. 4 sqq. 12.

[7] Ezek. xxv. Jer. xlix. 7. Obadiah. Is. xxxiv. lxiii. Ps. cxxxvii.

[8] See the expressions Ps. xliv. 24. lxxiv. 1, 3, 10, 19. lxxix. 5. lxxx. 5.

[9] Ewald uses this argument, Poet. Büch. i. 206., "The translator of the LXX. followed, in the Psalter, a MS., which only in less important things departs from the Masorethic text, yet, in the inscriptions, this latest part of the whole, [as Ewald thinks,] misunderstands much, or alters it on his own authority; whence it follows that a considerable space must have elapsed between its date and that of the completion of the present book."

entered into the congregational as well as the personal religious life of the Hebrew, as of ours. The translation, however, of the LXX. was made long before the Greek of the first book of the Maccabees, since Ps. 79. is quoted in that book by memory from the Greek translation[1], and so must have been already familiar to the Alexandrian Jews. Probably, the translation was completed before the Maccabee times.

If completed before the Maccabee times, it is an evidence, of course, that the whole Psalter was then completed; if not, it would still be remarkable, that, ascribing four Psalms, in the Greek five, to Haggai and Zechariah[2], they knew of no later author; whereas, had any Psalm in the Canon been written in Maccabee times, it must have been written by a contemporary.

The book of Proverbs also bears evidence of gradual collection. The statement prefixed to the third portion of it, that "[3] the men of Hezekiah transcribed them," is of course evidence, that the two former portions, which are identical in language, were formed into one whole before that time. "The men of Hezekiah transferred" them from one written document to another, i. e. from a written collection, previously existing, to that in the Canon. The words, "*These also*[4] are proverbs of Solomon," imply plainly that, in the belief of the persons so trans-

[1] 1 Macc. vii. 17. Σάρκας ὁσίων σου καὶ αἵματα αὐτῶν ἐξέχεαν κύκλῳ Ἱερουσαλὴμ καὶ οὐκ ἦν αὐτοῖς ὁ θάπτων. Ps. lxxviii. 2, 3. LXX. τὰς σάρκας τῶν ὁσίων σου τοῖς θηρίοις τῆς γῆς. Ἐξέχεαν τὸ αἷμα αὐτῶν ὡς ὕδωρ κύκλῳ Ἱερουσαλήμ, καὶ οὐκ ἦν ὁ θάπτων.

[2] Ps. cxlv-viii. [cxlvi-viii. Heb. Eng.] They add also the name of Haggai and Zechariah to that of David before Ps. cxlvii., ψαλμὸς τῷ Δαυὶδ Ἀγγαίου καὶ Ζαχαρίου, in the same form as they do that of Jeremiah to Ps. cxxxvi. [cxxxvii. Heb. Eng.] τῷ Δαυὶδ Ἱερεμίου.

[3] Prov. xxv. 1. הֶעְתִּיקוּ, "removed," then "transferred" from one place to another. It means then, not simply "copied out," but "copied into," i. e. into the book already existing. μετῆραν Aq., transtulerunt LXX., μετήνεγκαν Gr. Ven., ἐξεγράψαντο LXX. Gesenius himself quotes from Buxtorf, p. 686. that the Talm. העתיק is either "transcribed," or "translated," (Buxtorf gives מעתיקים "translators.") It is then an arbitrary quid pro quo, when to the right explanation, "transcripsit ex uno libro in alium," Gesenius adds a wholly different meaning, "inde i. q. congessit."   [4] גַּם אֵלֶּה

ferring, both collections, both that into which the proverbs were so transferred, and the proverbs themselves
which were transferred, were Solomon's. There remain
then only the two last chapters, inscribed severally, "the
words of Agur" and "the words of king Lemuel," (obviously a symbolical name [5],) which can have been admitted
into the book later than Hezekiah. Both are entitled by
names, claiming for them Divine inspiration [6], although
we have no data as to the authors.

It is mostly admitted now by the revolutionary school,
that the book of Job is any how earlier than the Proverbs,
in which Solomon uses some, although but little, of its
language and idioms [7]. The adoption of its language by

---

[5] למואל xxxi. 1. למואל Ib. 4. "unto God," i. e. devoted to God, after the analogy of לאל, Num. iii. 24. The idea, that Lemuel is said to be "king of Mas-
sah," is, in Germany, probably now confined to Hitzig. The imaginary kingdom was founded on the mention of Massa among the sons of Ishmael, Gen.
xxv. 14. 1 Chr. i. 30. The stress, laid upon the name *Ithiel,* "God is," "God
is," would incline one to think that it too might be symbolical, in contradiction to some school of unbelief, against which the beginning of the chapter
v. 2-5. is directed. With this the other name, *Ucal,* "I am enabled," (אכל,
other copies אכל for אכל) would, though not obviously, agree. But even then,
if אגור too could (like קהלת Eccl. i. 1.) be a symbolical name for Solomon, ("collector," as St. Jerome's teacher and Judah ben Karish explained it,) it would
still be a degree of symbolism beyond what one would expect, that *the son
of Yakeh,* which looks like a real genealogy, should be symbolic too.

[6] מקרא xxxi. 31.   מראה and נאם xxx. 1.

[7] Some few of the instances given by Keil (Häv. Einl. iii. p. 354.) seem to
me satisfactory. Job xv. 7. לפני גבעות חוללת Prov. viii. 25. ל..נ.חוללתי. Job xxi. 17.
פעם נר רשעים ידעך Prov. xiii. 9. ונר רשעים ידעך xxiv. 20. נר רשעים ידעך. In Job xxviii. 18.
Prov. viii. 16. the only resemblance is the setting the value of wisdom above פנינים;
and this the Kethib in Prov. writes פנים. In Job v. 17. מוסר שדי אל תמאס, Prov.
iii. 11. מוסר יהוה בני אל תמאס, the resemblance is in very simple words. Of single
words, in common to them only, תחבלות "guidances," (of God, Job xxxvii. 12.)
(written תחבלות) Prov. i. 5. xi. 14. xx. 18. xxiv. 6. in a good sense, xii. 5. in a
bad sense: איד, "destruction," Job xxx. 24. xxxi. 29. Prov. xxiv. 22. (Arab.:) תושיה
"solid wisdom," Job v. 12. vi. 13. xi. 6. xii. 16. xxvi. 3. xxx. 22. Prov. ii. 7.
iii. 21. viii. 14. xviii. 1. (else in Mic. vi. 9. Is. xxviii. 29. only :) אבדון "Abaddon,"
Kri. (אבדה Keth.) "place of destruction," Job xxvi. 6. xxviii. 22. xxxi. 12. Prov.
xv. 11. xxvii. 20, also Ps. xxxviii. 12, and still more the thought, Job xxvi. 6,
Prov. xv. 11, are characteristic. Less so, are ידכאו בשער "are crushed in the gate,"
Job v. 4. ואל תדכא עני בשער "crush not the poor in the gate," Prov. xxii. 22. Of
the rest, the use of the form עלם, once in Proverbs, vii. 18. twice in Job,
whereas the Proverbs have also עליו once, and עלין twice, seems to me not cha-

David [1], Solomon, Amos [2], Isaiah [3], Jeremiah [4], attests
that it was received as a sacred book.   Each case is slight
in itself; together, they shew that the book was quoted
from early times.

The antiquity of the Canticles is conceded by those who,
without ground, question that it is Solomon's.   No one
had any interest to question the age of the Lamentations
of Jeremiah.   Only one or two [5] raised an unheeded doubt,

racteristic ; nor פֹּתֶה "foolish" "one easily misled," Job v. 2. but probably, "en-
ticing," i. q. Piel, Prov. xx. 19 ; nor אָכַף, Job xxxiii. 7.(LXX Kim.i. q.כָּף as אָוְילֵץ
for וְיֹעֵץ, oth. " weight," from כָּפַף, " bowed,") comp. אָכַף, with עַל, "impelled,"
Prov. xvi. 26 ; nor שָׁתָה " drink," i. e. " iniquity like water," Job xv. 16. " scorning like water," Ib. xxxiv. 7.; in which two places the idea is of eagerness,
whereas "drinking damage," Prov. xxvi. 6, is against one's will.   Of those
quoted by others, Prov. i. 7. יְרָאַת יי רֵאשִׁית חָעַת, Job xxviii. 28. יִרְאַת אֲדֹנָי הִיא חָכְמָה,
there is, in the *words*, not more than unavoidable resemblance.   So again in
Job xxii. 29. and Prov. xvi. 18. xviii. 12. xxix. 23.   In Job xiii. 5, the wisdom of
silence is real, in Prov. xvii. 28, only apparent ; the thought that the perfection
of God is higher than heaven, deeper than hell, עֲמֻקָּה מִשְּׁאוֹל, Job xi. 8, has no
bearing on Prov. ix. 18, " her guests are in the depths of hell ; " בְּעִמְקֵי שְׁאוֹל.   Of
like words for " calamity " Job vi. 2. xxx. 13. has הַיָּה Keth. Prov. xix. 13, הַוֹּת.

[1] Ps. xxxix. 14. has different reminiscences of Job's language ; הָשַׁע מִמֶּנִּי, Job
vii. 19. שִׁית סָמַי וְאַבְלִיגָה פֶּן אֵלֵךְ בְּטֶרֶם ; עַתָּה לֹא חָשָׁה סָמַי, Job x. 20, 1. אֵלֵךְ.   Ps. lxix. 33. רָאוּ עֲנָוִים יִשְׂמָחוּ resembles in thought, partly in word, Job
xxii. 19. יִרְאוּ צַדִּיקִים וְיִשְׂמָחוּ.   Ps. ciii. 16. וְלֹא יַכִּירֶנּוּ עוֹד מְקוֹמוֹ is identical with Job
vii. 10.   Ps. lviii. 9. נֵפֶל אֵשֶׁת בַּל חָזוּ שָׁמֶשׁ reminds of Job iii. 16. כְּנֵפֶל ;
נֵפֶל־תְּעֻלְלִים לֹא רָאוּ שָׁמֶשׁ ; and Ps. ciii. 15. has the special comparison of man's brief life with the צִיץ, in
common with Job xiv. 2. Ps. כְּצִיץ יָצָא וַיִּמַּל. Job. כְּצִיץ הַשָּׂדֶה כֵּן יָצִיץ.

[2] Am. iv. 13, דֹרֵךְ עַל בָּמֳתֵי אָרֶץ, looks like a reminiscence of Job ix. 8, דֹרֵךְ עַל
בָּמֳתֵי יָם which is the bolder expression, and Amos has in the same verse the word,
עֵיפָה, which else occurs only in the form עֵיפָתָה, Job x. 22.   In v. 8. עֹשֵׂה כִימָה וּכְסִיל,
Amos combines the same constellations as Job xxxviii. 31, and in the words
of Job ix. 9, only omitting עַיִשׁ, עֹשֶׂה עָשׁ כְּסִיל וְכִימָה. Keil in Häv. iii. 353.

[3] Is. הָרוֹ עָמָל וְהוֹלִיד אָוֶן Is. xiv. 11. is verbatim from Job xiv. 11. וְנָהָר יֶחֱרַב וְיָבֵשׁ
xxxviii. 4. seems to be from Job xv. 35. הָרֹה עָמָל וְיָלֹד אָוֶן, Keil Ib.

[4] The likeness in Jeremiah seems to me to lie chiefly in the woe on the day
of his birth, Jer. xx. 14-18. from Job iii.   Of other places quoted, in Jer. xx.
7, 8. Job xii. 4. the specific likeness is only in the Job. שְׂחֹק אָנֹכִי Jer. חָיִיתִי לִשְׂחֹק.
Jer. xlix. 19. and Job ix. 19. have מִי יוֹעִידֶנִּי ; Lam. ii. 16, and Job xvi. 9, 10,
xxvii. 23, have no characteristic expression in common ; Lam. iii. 14, and Job
xxx. 9, both say that the speaker is נְגִינָתָם ; Lam. iii. 7, 9, and Job xix. 7, 8,
have only the word גָּדֵר in common, גָּדַר בַּעֲדִי, גָּדַר דְּרָכַי בְּגָזִית Lam. אֶחְיֵי גָדֵר Job, and
the unheard cry; Lam. iii. 15. and Job ix. 18. have an idiom almost identical,
יַשְׂבִּיעֵנִי בַמְּרֹרִים Job, הִשְׂבִּיעַנִי בַמְּרוֹרִים Lam.

[5] Augusti, (Einl.) Conz, (in Bengel's Archiv. B. iv.) Kalkar (Lam. p. 57 sqq.)
and Thenius, (Comm. p. 120.) chiefly on the ground that it is improbable, that

to vindicate the sovereign power of criticism to call every
thing sacred into question.

The basis then of the third division of the Canon was
beyond question laid before the Captivity, Job, the Proverbs, except, at most, the last two chapters, the larger
portion of the Psalms; the Canticles; and probably the
Lamentations.   Ruth occupied originally its place as the
sequel of the Judges, and was removed here, only on account of its festival use, together with the four other Me-
gilloth.   Ecclesiastes alone is questioned.

Ecclesiastes would probably never have been questioned, but that, on the one hand, it contained so clearly the
doctrine of a future judgment and retribution according
to our works; on the other hand, people gained a plea
for the result which they wished, by ignoring the simple
fact, that language must be adapted to its subject.   Most
of the words, selected to prove its late date, are simply
abstract words, formed naturally from ordinary Hebrew
roots [6].   No one word has been found to characterise an
age later than Solomon's.

"a poet should write five times on the same subject."   Stähelin accounted
"the question as of no great moment, since they any how belonged to the time
of Jeremiah, and confessedly had his language."   Einl. p. 285.

[6] Several of Gesenius' list of words, which were to prove the late date of Ecclesiastes, were such abstract words, ending in ן, ן, ת, Gesch. d. Hebr. Sprache,
p. 36, a work written, if any ever was, in support of preconceived opinions,
only, in his case, anti-doctrinal.

The invalidity of such proof was, at last, observed by Herzfeld, who, in 1838,
swept away most of the rubbish which had hitherto been relied upon. (Kohe-
leth, p. 12-22.) He, however, had the same anti-doctrinal prejudice, that the Bible was indebted to Magianism for the belief in the life to come.   (Gesch. Isr.
ii. 305.) And so, on that ground, it was to be written after the captivity. (Ib.
ii. 66.) He admits that, " the Chaldaisms in it would not require that it should
be brought lower than the time of the Chaldee invasions; only (he adds) the
stage at which the doctrine of immortality appears in it, and its 11 or 15 modern Hebrew expressions speak for its having been composed, at least a century after the Captivity." (Ib. 67.) Five only of the words accumulated by his
predecessors, as marks of modern Hebrew, passed muster with him.   1) The in-
terjection אי, " woe," iv. 10. x. 16. an onomapoeticum, which must have been
very old in the language, since the word אנפה (of some shrill-voiced bird, in Lev.
and Deut.) is formed from it.   Both it and אוי lived on in Talmudic.   2) Granting
that ש, for אשר, is Phœnician and old, the conjunction של viii. 17. is to be mo-

The Canon then was almost completed before the return from the captivity.   Of the books of the former pro-

dern.   But שׁל too is Phœnician.   See Ges. Thes. p. 1346. and my Introd. to Jonah, p. 250.   3) בְּכֵן is to be modern, "because it only occurs besides in Esth. iv. 16;" and 4) אֵלּוּ, vi. 6, "because it only occurs besides in Esth. vii. 4, and the coalition of two conjunctions points to a late time.   Ew. Kr. Gr. 632 n. 7." It is utterly unlikely that אֵלּוּ should be a compound of אִם and לֹא; 1. because they are incompatible conjunctions; 2. because אֵלּוּ (for אִם) is a simple conjunction in Ch. Syr. Sam.   And very probably אֵלּוּ in Hebrew is the same conjunction, only pointed wrong.   Both אִלּוּ and בְּכֵן are rare conjunctions; but there is no principle on which בְּכֵן should be thought to be late, being formed in the same way as לָכֵן, עַל-כֵּן, אַחֲרֵי-כֵן.   It has a meaning, which there was not often occasion to express in the simple construction of Hebrew, "it being thus."   In Esther both words occur in conversation.   5) "מַדָּע, occurring x. 20. and else only in Daniel and Chronicles, instead of the old דַעַת or מַחֲשָׁבָה."   But מַדָּע, Eccl. x. 20, is not "knowledge," but "the place of knowledge," "conscience."   It is the word by which (as Gesenius remarks) the Peshito renders συνείδησις, 2 Cor. v. 11. Neither דַעַת, "knowledge," nor מַחֲשָׁבָה, "device, purpose," would have expressed the idea.   6) "יוֹתֵר, as a particle of comparison, whereas, earlier, the comparison had been expressed by the syntax only."   It is clear from the cases in which יֹתֵר occurs, that it is no mere particle of comparison.   "Wisdom is good with (i. e. as) an inheritance; and better (וְיֹתֵר) to them that see the sun." (vii. 11.)   "And more than these," יֹתֵר מֵהֵמָּה, Eccl. xii. 12. יֹתֵר עָלֶיהָ "over and above that."

The expressions which Herzfeld himself adds are of no more account; 1) עָמַד לְ "stand for," (ii. 19.) is a genuine Hebrew use of לְ.   2) יָרֵא מִלִּפְנֵי, (instead of מֵאֵת,) iii. 14. viii. 12, 13. recurs, he says, in 1 Sam. xviii. 12; which is an odd argument for its lateness.   Probably Solomon used the word, thinking of the presence of God.   3) מְדִינָה, city, lit. "place of jurisdiction," and hence used alike of cities and provinces; of which Solomon, ruling to the Euphrates, doubtless had many. (See further Note B at the end.)   4) He allows that the root כשׁר is not modern, since, in Ps. lxviii. 7, there is כּוֹשָׁרוֹת and in Prov. xxxi. 19, כִּישׁוֹר, and so, since abstracts are so much used in Eccl., כִּשְׁרוֹן (Eccl. ii. 21. iv. 4. v. 10.) need not be modern; but מַכְשִׁיר (equally abstract,) "making to prosper," x. 10. is to be modern, because it is part of the verb. (Herzf. Koh. p. 18.)   5) and lastly, the use of the personal pronoun with the personal verb, אָמַרְתִּי אֲנִי.   Of course, if it is emphatic, it is no mark at all of modernness.   Solomon is giving his own personal experience, in a matter in which no other had experience so large, of the vanity of every thing human, out of God.   If any one will examine the cases in which אֲנִי is added, and those in which it is not, in Ecclesiastes, he will see that it has been added, not pleonastically, but on a definite principle.   The occurrences of eleven *such* words could not be the real ground of making Ecclesiastes one of the latest books in the Canon.

In regard to the so-called Chaldee, or foreign, words; 1) פִּשְׁגָּם "ditch," x. 10. 2) עֲבָדִים "doings," ix. 1. both ἅπ. λεγ. and 3) כְּבָר "formerly," 7 times in Eccl. and peculiar to it, occur in Syriac also, כְּבַר in Nasor. too;   4) פִּתְגָם viii. 11. is a foreign word, older than Pehlevi, naturalised in Syriac equally.   5) בְּבֶל, Eccl. xii.

phets, or historical books, the Kings at most had yet to be formally added to it. Of the later prophets, there re-

3. is a Semitic word common to every dialect, Arab. Æth. Melit. Syr. Ch. Zab. see Ges. 6) עת καιρός (Eccl. iii. 1.) is also common to Arab. Æth. Melit. as well as Chald.; the ז also remains in Sam., although in the present Syr. and Zab. it is זמן; מועד also would not (as Ges. says it would) represent it, for מועד is "appointed time," עת, Eccl. iii. 1, is "fitting time." There remain then only the punctuations of מצא vii. 26. מצה viii. 12. ix. 18.; and the interchange of the ה for the א, in מלאת (viii. 1.) מצא (x. 4.) מצא (x. 5.;) and this, "although, in unquestioned Hebrew books, verbs ל״א and ל״ה borrow each others' forms, yet, on the ground of the more frequent borrowing." Yet of the five words, in מצא the א is not "borrowed" but original, as is attested by the Phœn. and Arab. (see Ges.) It occurs also twice in the Proverbs, xiv. 30. xv. 4. The punctuation of מצה and מצא, Herzfeld himself rightly calls "Syriac." (p. 120.) Syria was part of Solomon's dominions; what marvel then in a few Syriac words? Herzfeld himself would not make these Aramaic words (there is not one purely Chaldee among them) any test of such extreme lateness of the book, as would bear upon the history of the Canon.

As to history, it is said that "Solomon, whose father had chosen Jerusalem for a residence, could not say, i. 16. ii. 7. *above every one who was before me in Jerusalem.*" Solomon does not even say, "every *king*," but Jerusalem was an ancient city, and was a royal city at the time of the Exodus, probably in that of Abraham. (Gen. xiv. 18.) It strengthens his statement, that in those centuries, patriarchal, heathen, and lately Hebrew, none had made such trial as himself, and he too had failed. "Nor could he recommend (viii. 5, 6.) to wait circumspectly the opportunity for rebellion against a tyrant." Solomon does not recommend it, but submission. (viii. 1-5.) "Judgment," (משפט,) 5. 6. is not man's but God's. "Nor could he give a description of princely gluttons." (x. 16, 17.) He gives no such description; why should not God move *him*, as much as Isaiah, to speak of the woe of princely petulance and intemperance, and the blessedness of their nobility and temperance? Well had it been for Rehoboam, had he followed the warning against petulance. "Nor was the people in his time so unhappy as is presupposed in iv. 1. v. 7." Solomon is speaking of individual cases, and doubtless in such large rule, ill held together, there were cases of oppression. The next argument Herzfeld answers himself. "The complaints against unjust judges, iii. 17, violence, iv. 1. v. 7. [8 Eng.,] unworthy filling of posts of honor, x. 5-7, have often been urged against a royal authorship; contrariwise, it might be said, that all this does not appear unsuited to a regent, who has taken the point of view of a popular teacher; yet, taken together with the other arguments against Solomon's authorship, it has some weight." He wrote the book, not as a royal teacher, but as a royal penitent, and in him it would be unnatural not to refer to the past misgovernment. Lastly, comes the real ground; "Further, the assumption of the return of the soul to God hereafter, which is questioned iii. 21, yet popular enough to be spoken of in writing for the people, and which is even victorious, xii. 7, cannot be ascribed to Solomon, since after him no trace of it re-appears until after the captivity." (!) On this subject see Lect. viii.

mained, perhaps, the formal reception of Ezekiel; the three last prophets only had not yet been sent [1].   Of the hagiographa, there remained the collection of some later Psalms; some, in the last book of the Psalms, were not yet written; Daniel perhaps was then formally added; the historical books of Ezra, Nehemiah, Esther, the Chronicles, alone were as yet unwritten.

In no one of these books is there any thing, which requires a date, later than that which Josephus probably meant to fix, the date of Malachi and of the second visit of Nehemiah.

The book of Esther marks itself to have been written by a contemporary.   With this agrees the very accurate yet simple description of Persian customs, entering naturally into minute details [2]; its exact yet incidental agreement with the chronology of the reign of Ahasuerus, (in Greek, Xerxes [3];) the touching traits of her relation to her uncle Mordecai.   The difficulties alleged are but illustrations of its accuracy.   Ending, as it does, with the ele-

---

[1] On Jonah see the Introduction to Jonah, p. 247 sqq ; on Obadiah, the Introduction, p. 227 sqq.   Those who rend off from Isaiah such chapters as they see good, still admit them to have been written and *received* before the return from the captivity.

[2] Heeren, looking upon it, (as the way then was in Germany,) as a fictitious narrative, yet allowed that it was "a faithful picture of the manners of the Persian Court." (i. 1. p. 132.) "The interior of the Harem is pictured to us most exactly in the history of Esther." (Ib. 466.)   Baumgarten, de fide libri Esther, pointed out in detail the agreement with Persian customs ; then Hävernick, Einl. § 192, "on the historical character of the book Esther," p. 338-357 ; so that even Stähelin accepts the history, § 51.

[3] Achashverosh (Esth. i. 1, &c) is formed from the Persian Kh.sh.w.e.r.sh.e. (see Grotefend in Ges. p. 75,) only by the addition of vowels, which should make it pronounceable in Hebrew.   "That Ahasuerus is Xerxes remains the most probable opinion, and will be the more confirmed, when we compare with it the old Persian form." Lassen, D. Altpers. Keilschr. p. 33 sqq.   Rödiger (App. p. 68.) gives it KH.SHa.Y.A.R.SH.A. from Lassen, p. 165. with which Sir H. Rawlinson agrees. (in Rawl. Her. iv. p. 264.)   The feast given in the 3rd year (Esth. i. 3.) agrees with the special assembly of the noblest Persians," (Her. vii. 8.) which followed on the subdual of Egypt, which was in his second ; (Ib. vii. 7.) but Esther did not become Queen till the close of his 7th year ; (Esth. ii. 16.) when the king returned to Susa, after the battle of Platæa. (Her. ix. 107, 8.)

vation of Mordecai [4], and appealing for further accounts to the Chronicles of Media and Persia [5], it was very probably written by Mordecai himself; and it would be an unmarked coincidence, that the historical books of the times in or after the captivity, the historical parts of Daniel, Ezra, Nehemiah, Esther, were written by those concerned in them. The book of Esther does not imply that it was written by Mordecai, but it does that it was written very shortly after the events [6].

The books of Chronicles are marked to have been written prior to the book of Ezra by their close. Ezra, by repeating, at the beginning of his book, the two verses with which he had closed the books of Chronicles, identifies the two works. He breaks off the Chronicles in the middle of the decree of Cyrus, yet so as to give a perfect sense; and begins the book which bears his name, with those two verses, finishing the decree of Cyrus, so far as relates to his then object, the permission to return. A similarity of style and object has been observed between the books; so that believing and unbelieving critics [7] have been agreed, that they were written by the same hand. The only question, of late, has been, whether Ezra is the author of both, or whether both have been compiled by a later hand [8].

---

[4] Esth. x. 3.   [5] Ib. 2.

[6] Ib. ix. 30-32. "And he (Mordecai) sent the letters unto all the Jews in the 127 Provinces of the kingdom of Ahasuerus, *words of peace and truth*, to confirm these days of Purim in their times, as Mordecai the Jew and Esther the Queen confirmed them, and as they had confirmed them for themselves and for their seed, the matters of the fastings and of their cry, and the word of Esther confirmed these matters of Purim; *and it was written in the book*." The expression, "and it was written in the book," implies that it was a consequence, which followed upon what preceded, as we should say, "so it was written, &c; and *the book* can, I think, be no other than this our book of Esther.

[7] Zunz, (Gottesd. Vortr. p. 21-24) Ewald, (Gesch. Isr. i. 252-3.) and still more Stähelin, (Einl. § 45.) are at pains to shew the identity of the authors of the books of Ezra and the Chronicles. Herzfeld (Gesch. Isr. Excurs 2. p. 302.) says, "1 agree perfectly with the result of Zunz, even although not with all his proofs."

[8] "It is indeed commonly accepted, that at least Ezra vii. 27—ix. comes from Ezra himself; but the too close relationship of this section with the pre-

The only plea, alleged for assigning a later date to the books of Chronicles, has been obtained by making the genealogy, at the close of the 3rd chapter of the first book [1], consecutive, which any one can see, even from a translation, that it is not. In this way, six generations were obtained after Zerubbabel, and the date was carried down to the end of the Persian Empire in the time of Alexander. Yet there is a manifest break at the 2nd generation after Zerubbabel; "[2] And the sons of Hananiah, Pelatiah and Iesaiah." There his genealogy closes. What follows, "the sons of Rephaiah, the sons of Arnan, the sons of Obadiah, the sons of Shechaniah," obviously stands in no relation to what went before, since no parent of any of those named, Rephaiah, Arnan, Obadiah, or Shechaniah, had been mentioned. The phrase, "the sons of Shechaniah," and the like, throughout this genealogy, introduces the next link of the genealogy downwards. These families stand in no connection with that of Zerubbabel. The want of relation to the preceding, and of any grammatical connection with it, gives to the section the appearance of an ancient gloss [3]. Yet even

ceding [part of Ezra] to my mind speaks against it, unless indeed one were to accept, that all, and so the Chronicles too, comes from Ezra, which, on account of the genealogy, 1 Chron. iii. 18 sqq. is not possible." Stähelin, p. 161. Even Zunz, (p. 28.) Herzfeld, (p. 316.) Ewald, (i. 258.) grant that Ezr. vii. 27,—ix. fin. is Ezra's, (except that Herzfeld deducts viii. 35, 6). Zunz adds iv. 1-6. x. 18-44. Herzfeld says, "whether x. 18—44. was in Ezra's document, or was appended from some other source, can naturally not be made out." (p. 306.) They all agree that the rest is by the writer of the Chronicles.

          [1] 1 Chr. iii. 21-24.   [2] v. 21.

  [3] This was the opinion not only of the older critical school, Vitringa, Heidegger, Carpzov, but even of Le Clerc, I. D. Michaelis, (Bibl. Or. T. xx. p. 28.) and Eichhorn. (Einl. iii. 596. ed. 4. quoted by Keil, Apol. Vers. p. 45.) Herzfeld too says, "A further descent [than Pelatiah and Ieshaia] is evidently not given there; the 'sons' of Rephaia, of Arnan, Obadiah, and Shechaniah, are doubtless families descended from David, whose descent the writer of the Chronicles either could not or would not specify, and which he therefore only recounts, parallel with one another." (Gesch. Isr. Excurs 8. p.378,9.) De Wette too who, (ed. 2.) in 1822, said positively, "the genealogy of Serubabel is (1 Chr. iii. 19-24.) carried down to the time of Alexander," (§ 189.) modified the statement. "In the (it must be confessed) confused passage, 1 Chr. iii. 19-24. the genealogy of the house of David is carried down to the 2nd generation after

if it be part of the book, the six generations, required to bring down the date of the books of Chronicles, are only obtained by introducing into the text what is not there, viz. that Shechaniah, whose sons are mentioned, was himself the son of Hananiah [4]. Ezra speaks of the "sons of Shechaniah [5]," as a well-known family, at the time of the return from the captivity, without mentioning any genealogy of their's. Probably they were too well known

Serubabel, and doubtless yet further ;" he acknowledges, "the passage is commonly looked upon as a later addition," ed. 7. 1852. Ewald (Gesch. Isr. i. 229. ed. 2.) says, that the "order is difficult to be recognised," but gives it, without explanation, as positively as if there were no difficulty ; "the somewhat-difficult-to-be-recognised consecutive order is, 1 Zerubabel, 2 Chananiah, 3 Shechaniah, &c," overleaping the difficulty. Bleek says, equally without attempting any explanation, "The passage is not *quite* clear ; the text too is not certain, since the LXX differs from the Hebrew text. Yet probably the last is *in the main* the original. There too, according to the most probable interpretation, it is contained that, after Serubabel, 6 generations of his descendants are cited." (Einl. p. 395.) Stähelin only appeals to 1 Chr. ii. 42. "The sons of Caleb the brother of Jerahmeel were, Mesha, his first-born, which was the father of Ziph, and the sons of Mareshah the father of Hebron." But this passage is itself obscure ; for Mareshah is not before mentioned among the sons of "Caleb, brother of Jerahmeel," ii. 18-24, where his sons by three, if not four, wives are mentioned and even a posthumous child, v. 24. In an early forefather like Caleb, the grandfather of Caleb the spy, it is natural to class a whole family of descendants in one. A Scotchman might say of a distant forefather, that he was "the father of the Campbells, or the Stewarts," &c. but it would not be said, in any near interval, when families had not had time to ramify. Moreover in 1 Chr. ii. 43, the words stand connected, "The sons of Caleb the brother of Jerahmeel were Mesha his first born—and the sons of Mareshah." The very way of speaking implies a tradition, that "the sons of Mareshah" were known traditionally to be descended from this Caleb, but that the links were lost. In iii. 21. "the sons of Rephaiah, &c." are not connected. They stand quite distinct. On the same ground then, that we believe "the sons of Mareshah" to have been descendants of that Caleb, viz. that they stand connected with one who is stated to have been his descendant, we believe that the sons of Rephaiah, &c. were not descendants of Hananiah, because it is not expressed that they are, in the way in which the author of the Chronicles, in the like case, expressed it.

[4] If 21-24 is part of the text, it must be pointed ; "And the sons of Hananiah, Pelatiah and Iesaiah. The sons of Rephaiah, the sons of Arnan, the sons of Obadiah, the sons of Shechaniah. And the sons of Shechaniah, Shemaiah, &c." In this way, although the statement is rather abrupt, they would stand as Davidic families, of which the writer, in any case, gives the succession of the last only. [5] viii. 3.

to need it.   He mentions Hattush apparently as one "[1] of the sons of Shechaniah."   If, (as seems probable,) he is the same person as Hattush in the Chronicles, he would be at least a grandson of Shechaniah [2], but could not be the grandson's grandson of Zerubbabel, who returned 79 years before.   If he be the same Hattush, then the generations in the Chronicles go down to the great nephew of one who returned with Ezra [3]; which, as nothing is said of the age of Hattush at his return, involves no later date than Ezra may have seen.   This then, which is admitted to be the only ground for attributing to the Chronicles a date, later than Ezra [4], coincides with the account given by Ezra.

There being no ground, then, why the books of Chronicles should be later than Ezra, and the two books being confessedly by the same hand, the only remaining

---

[1] In the text it is divided, "Of the sons of Phinehas, Gershom; of the sons of Ithamar, Daniel: of the sons of David, Hattush. Of the sons of Shechaniah, of the sons of Pharosh, Zechariah."   But in Ezr. ii. 2. "the sons of Pharosh" are mentioned as a separate family, without being subordinated to "the sons of Shechaniah;" and here too "the sons of Shechaniah" are mentioned apart after an interval.   It seems then the simplest way, to join it thus; "of the sons of David, Hattush, of the sons of Shechaniah: of the sons of Pharosh, Zechariah."   [2] Hattush was one of the sons of Shemaiah, who was of the sons of Shechaniah, 1 Chr. iii. 21, 22.

[3] The genealogy is continued, not in the line of Hattush but in that of his brother Neariah, of whose eldest son Elioenal, 7 sons are mentioned, 22-24.

[4] "On the age of the Chronicles the genealogy, 1 Chr. iii. 18. can alone give any result."   Stähelin, § 43. p. 356.   Bleek only adds 1) The place which it occupies in the Canon, (according to which, he must allow that Daniel was written before Ezra, which would be to give up the whole object of this bringing down of the Canon;) and 2) the coin Darics, 1 Chr. xxix. 7.   Darics are mentioned by Ezra (viii. 27.) in the reign of Artaxerxes, grandson of Darius Hystaspes.   If then they were named from this Darius, they would furnish no argument as to the date of the Chronicles; not to dwell on the Greek tradition that they were named from some earlier Darius, (see ab. p. 124.) or the conjecture that they may have been named directly from *dara*, "king."   Scott and Lidd. v. δαρεικός.   This argument has been retorted, that, after the times of Alexander, Greek, not Persian, money would become the coin of Palestine, as being a Greek appanage.   Davidson would have it, that "Shemaiah son of Shechaniah," Neh. iii. 29. is the same as the Shemaiah in the Chronicles; Herzfeld answers the objection, that, being *the keeper of the East gate*, (Ib.) he was (he supposed) a Levite. Ib.

question is, whether there be any ground to think, that
the book of Ezra is later than the time of Ezra. The
use of the first person in a portion of it has made all but
the extremest scepticism allow that a portion is from his
hand [5]. The likeness of all the Hebrew parts of it has
also been admitted. But Ezra's thanksgiving at the beginning of this admitted portion, that [6] *God hath put it
into the the king's heart to beautify the house of the Lord
which is in Jerusalem, and hath extended mercy unto me
before the king,* is connected with the decree before it [7];
and the insertion of that decree involves such a preface
as that prefixed to it [8]; and that preface, beginning, "[9]And
after these things, in the reign of Artaxerxes king of Persia," involves a previous history, and that, of events prior
to the reign of Artaxerxes, which is just what the previous chapters contain. But those chapters are evidently,
as they stand, one whole ; i. e. the whole is one history of
the rebuilding the temple, from the first permission of
Cyrus to rebuild it until its dedication and the celebra-
tion of the first passover afterwards. It is one progressive history. First, there is the permission of Cyrus to
return [10], and the preparation of the Jews [11]; then his restoration of the vessels of the temple [12], their amount [13],
and the number of those who returned [14]; the setting up
the brazen altar, and restoration of sacrifice [15]; the collection of materials for the temple [16]; the laying the foundation of the temple, with that natural and touching mixture
of the joy of the young and the weeping of the old who remembered its former glories [17]; the cause of the opposition
to its rebuilding [18], and the means employed to hinder it
under Cyrus [19], Ahasuerus [20], [i. e. Cambyses,] Artaxerxes, [i.e. Pseudo-Smerdis [21];] the renewed efforts to rebuild

f See p. 329, 30. note 8. [6] vii. 27. [7] vii. 11-26. Even Herzfeld admits
this to be genuine. [8] Ib. 1-10. [9] Ib. 1. [10] i. 1-4. [11] i. 5, 6.
[12] i. 7, 8. [13] i. 9-11. [14] ii. [15] iii. 1-6. [16] Ib. 7. [17] Ib. 8-13.
[18] iv. 1-4. [19] iv. 5. [20] iv. 6. [21] iv. 7-23. see ab. p. 166, 7.
Keil illustrates this adoption of a 2nd more briliant name by the like act of Ochus,
who on his accession took the name of Darius (Nothus ;) of Arsaces, who took
that of Artaxerxes (Mnemon ;) of another Ochus, who took that of Artaxerxes

it under the new dynasty of Darius[1]; the fresh attempt to hinder it and the baffling of the attempt[2]; the favor of Darius[3]; the completion of the temple[4], its dedication[5], and the first passover held in it[6].

It has been thought most probable that the Chaldee portion, which embodies the letters addressed to the kings of Persia and their rescripts previous to the return of Ezra, were written by a contemporary and inserted by Ezra as a whole. This thread of history does not, in all, exceed 20 verses, the rest of these chapters being taken up with the original documents. It seems to me, too, probable, that this was a distinct whole, part of a larger account[7] which Ezra embodied in his book, beginning his extract with a few verses just preceding the first document, and closing, a few verses after the last. For the first person is used in this section, not as to any important event, in which it might be thought that Ezra associated himself with them, but in a simple statement that those who were concerned in the building gave their names to the governor and his companions who demanded them. It was a strictly personal act. [8] *Then accordingly we said to them,*

(Diod. xv. 39;) and of the last Persian king, Codomannus, who took that of Darius ; (Justin, x. 3.) as also of Cyrus himself, whose name, before his accession, was Agradates. (Strabo, xv. 3. 6. p. 729. Cas.) Pott says, "The name Artaxerxes was, we may safely say, a mere title, and when Bessus, 'taking the royal apparel, commanded that he should be called Artaxerxes,' (Curt. vi. 6.) he therewith declared himself the 'great king of kings,' which lies in the word." Etym. Forsch. i. p. lxiii sqq. in Häv. Einl. ii. p. 294.

[1] iv. 24-v. 2. [2] v. 3-17. [3] vi. 1-13. [4] Ib. 14, 15. [5] Ib. 16-18. [6] Ib. 19-23. [7] By itself, the beginning of the Chaldee, ("Rehum the Chancellor, &c." iv. 8.) might have been a sort of docket on the letter. Even then one should not have expected it to stand, "wrote a letter." But there follows further (iv. 9.) "*Then* Rehum, &c," which implies that it is a sequel of a preceding history : it might have joined on to iv. 6, but not, I think, with iv. 7.

[8] v. 4. Gesen. (Thes. p. 652.) notices that כְּנֵמָא in vi. 13. manifestly refers to the past, [" according to that which Darius the king sent, *accordingly*, כְּנֵמָא, they did perfectly,"] and joins this instance with it. Our translators, following the usual meaning of כְּנֵמָא, "so to speak," (for כְּנֵמָר, כְּדֵין,) "after this manner," put that as a question into the mouth of the Jews, which was in fact a question *to* them, v. 10. "Then said we unto them *after this manner*, What are the names, &c ?" instead of, "Then said we unto them, what the names

what were the names of the men who build this building.
But since this was 63 years before Ezra's return[9], and
since Ezra was engaged in the work of restoration with
Nehemiah whose visit was 13 years later[10], it is not likely,
though possible, that dying, as he did, an old man[11], he
should have been present at that early time. The contrary too is implied, in that he mentions himself for the
first time in the 7th year of Artarxerxes.

Ezra, however, it has been observed, had the Chaldee
document before him, as appears from his adopting into
his Hebrew three remarkable Persian words[12], which are
found exactly in this form, only in his Hebrew.

It has been attempted to make out the Hebrew of Ezra to have been later than Ezra, partly by falsifying the
history in the Chaldee, and then asserting truly that Ezra must have known such history to be false; partly on
the old childish grounds, that Ezra writes in the third
person as well as the first, and praises himself, and also
that he calls the King of Persia, King of Assyria.

1) They assume that Artachshasht, mentioned before

were, &c." Herzfeld admits that it may be taken as in the text, only saying
" that v. 4. would thus contain an oblique construction which would be very
unusual even in later Hebrew." Gesch. Isr. Excurs 2. p. 304. He observes
also, that it is not the answer to the preceding question. Ib. But it stands in
connection with what follows, that God gave them courage to persevere until
the answer came from Darius. They gave their names, and made themselves
responsible for their act. The answer to the former question is given in the
letter to Darius, v. 11-16. Unless this verse contains the statement that the
Jews did answer the question, which the governors state that they did put,
(v. 10.) there would be no such statement at all. According to the present text,
then, the verse does contain an additional fact, but bears witness that the
Chaldee statement was written by a contemporary. Herzfeld, by altering the
text שׁבוּ into יתיבו, would get rid of the evidence, but introduce tautology. It
is contrary of course to all criticism to have recourse to conjectural emenda-
tion, when the text gives a good sense.

[9] 2nd year of Darius, B.C. 520; 7th of Artarxerxes, B.C. 457.

[10] 20th of Artaxerxes, Neh. ii. 1.   [11] Jos. Ant. xi. 5. 5. A very late Jewish
tradition supposed him to have lived to 120. (Benj. Tud. Itin. p. 85.)

[12] אִגְּרָה, " Epistle," Ezr. iv. 7. vii. 11. Heb. iv. 18. 23. v. 5. Ch. (In Neh. and
Esth. אִגֶּרֶת,) פַּרְשֶׁגֶן, " transcript " (of letter,) iv. 11. 23. v. 6. Ch. vii. 11. Heb. but
פַּתְשֶׁגֶן Esth. iii. 14. iv. 8. (See Röd. App. to Ges. p. 108.) גִּזְבָּר, " treasurer," i. 8.
גִּזַבְרַיָּא vii. 21. but גְּדָבְרַיָּא Dan. iii. 2, 3.

Darius under whom the temple was finished, was Longimanus, that the building hindered by him was that of the
walls not of the temple, and that the account, which related to times after Darius, was placed by the writer, before him [1].

Yet in Ezra, the names of the sovereigns of Persia
stand in chronological order, three before Darius [2]; and,
both in Chaldee and Hebrew, an Artaxerxes after Darius [3]. Since then the hindrance of the building by the
Magian impostor is in keeping with what we know of
him from the monuments, whereas it was contrary to the
first principles of Persian belief for its kings to repeal
their own decrees [4]; since moreover there is no reason
whatever to think that Artaxerxes, in the first six years
of his reign, passed any decree against the Jews, whom
he favored ever afterwards; it is mere gratuitous falsifying of the history to say that the king, called Artaxerxes
but placed before Darius, is meant by the author to be
the same whom he placed after him. The enemies of the
Jews do not indeed speak of the rebuilding of the temple, which was what they wished to hinder, but only of
the wall. But the restoration of the temple involved ultimately the restoration of the city. Angry and rival
accusers do not confine themselves to facts, when appealing to a distant authority.

2) The praise of Ezra amounts to this, that he gives to
himself his title in his own book. For it has been observed [5], that, since the title, *scribe of the law of the God of
heaven*, is twice [6] given to him in the decree of Artaxer-

---

[1] Herzfeld, Gesch. Isr. Excurs 2. § 17. p. 303. The באדין, "then," iv. 24,
marks that the history belongs, (according to the writer,) to the times before
Darius. Davidson translates him, ii. 128.

[2] iv. 5-7. 23, 4.   [3] vi. 14. 15. vii. 1. 7.

[4] See ab. p. 166, 7. Herzfeld too observes (p. 306.) that throughout ch. iv.
the orthography is ארתחששתא (or אר) with ש, iv. 7. bis. 8. 11. 23. but throughout ch. vii. (of Artaxerxes Longimanus) with ס, ארתחשסתא vii. 12. 21. as it is also
in Neh. ii. 1. xiii. 6. The difference, though slight, is remarkable for its uniformity, except that, in the addition to the original, Ezr. vi. 14. ארתחששתא, the
form with ש is used of Artax. Longimanus.

[5] Häv. Einl. ii. 1. p. 281.   [6] vii. 12. 21.

xes, such was his official title. It is added only, that he was a *ready*, fluent, expositor of it. He mentions of himself, what others have observed of him in the books of Chronicles, that the law of his God was the great study of his life, and that he made progress in it. Perhaps he meant, as one of the Psalmists, whose expression he used, said before him, that he was a "ready writer [7]" of what he was taught by God, ascribing to himself only that he was, what he was, the instrument of God. Now, if there be any truth in the tradition, that Ezra, in various ways, did so much for the preservation of the Canon, it may have been of especial moment for those generations, until our Lord should set His seal upon the whole [8], that his fitness for the office should be authenticated in the Canon itself. It is not self-exaltation to speak the simple truth. It is not so accounted in St. John [9]. I suppose that, in this day, some of the critics of Ezra would not think it much to let it be known that they were good Hebraists [10], or understood the prophets by human skill, or knew of them (whether they did or no) more than others did before them. All which we hear about "enlightened criticism," and the like, if it were true, would mean, in Scripture language, that they are "ready scribes" in the law of God.

3) Cyrus, under whom the Jews first returned, had made Babylon the royal residence for seven months in the

---

[7] Ps. xlv. 2. *My tongue is the pen of* סוֹפֵר מָהִיר.

[8] S. Luke xxiv. 44.   [9] See ab. p. 22, 23.

[10] Zunz thinks that he understands the title ספר better than the writer of the book of Ezra. "The panegyrics of Ezra [vii.] 6, 10, 11. can not only not belong to this man, but not even to his time, since (v. 11.) they give an explanation of the expression ספר, which is over and above incorrect." (p. 23.) Apart from inspiration, most of us will think that the writer of the book of Ezra knew best. Hävernick observes that the title, which is given to Ezra by Nehemiah also, (viii. 1, 2, 9, 13. xii. 26.) is also, [in Nehemiah's second visit,] given to another, Zadok. Neh. xiii. 13. Davidson paraphrases Zunz, "The way in which Ezra is spoken of in vv. 6, 10, 11. shews that he himself could not have so written. He is termed 'a ready scribe in the law of Moses;' it is said that 'he had prepared his heart to seek the law of the Lord and to do it,' and an explanation of ספר is given in v. 11. which is unsuitable to Ezra himself." p. 129.

year [1]; it had been the centre of the captivity ; out of its temples were the sacred vessels given back to them by the command of Cyrus [2]; it was, probably in the time of Ezra, still one province with Assyria [3]; the kings of Persia liked to connect themselves with Perseus [4], and held him to have been an Assyrian [5]. It is then nothing strange that the Jews, in appealing to the edict of Cyrus whereby he restored them, should have called him king of Babylon [6]; or that Nehemiah should so have called Artaxerxes[7]; or that Ezra, speaking of the king of Persia, apart from his name [8], should have said that God [9] *had turned the heart of the king of Assyria unto them.* But for this petty controversial spirit, which grasps at any straw, people would have seen how these various titles bear upon, and bear out, one another. The *Persian* rulers of Assyria undid towards the Jews what its former rulers had done. In the 2nd letter prefixed to the 2nd book of Maccabees, it is even said, " [10] our fathers were led unto Persia," and critics [11] have found nothing strange in the expression [12].

---

[1] Xen. Cyrop. viii. 7.   [2] Ezr. i. 7. v. 14.

[3] Herod. iii. 92. In vii. 63. the " Chaldæans " are recounted as serving " *among the* Assyrians," i. e. as subordinate to them. Babylonia and Assyria are counted separately in the lists of Darius. (in Rawl. Herod. ii. p. 485.) Herodotus (i. 192.) uses " the Babylonian country," and " the Assyrian country," as identical, says, " thus the Assyrian country is in wealth, $\frac{1}{3}$ of the rest of Asia," and speaks of this as far the wealthiest of the Persian Satrapies. Hävernick (Einl. ii. p. 289.) refers further to Lassen, D. Altpers. Keilinschr. v. Persepolis, p. 67 sqq. 72. in proof of its eminence.   [4] Her. vi. 54. vii. 61. 150. Häv.

[5] Her. vi. 54.   [6] Ezr. v. 13.   [7] Neh. xiii. 6.   [8] Ezra uses " King of Persia " after the name ; " Cyrus King of P." i. 1, 2, 8. iii. 7. iv. 3, 5. "Darius K. of P." iv. 5, 24. "Artaxerxes K. of P." iv. 7. vi. 14. vii. 1.   [9] vi. 22.

[10] 2 Macc. i. 19.   [11] Grimm, ad loc. Exeg. Handb. z. d. Apocr. iv. p. 43.

[12] Zunz (p. 24.) adds the argument, " Ezra goes into the chamber of Johanan, son of Eliashib, (x. 6.) although this high-priest lived long after Nehemiah." (Neh. xii. 22, 23.) Ezra does not say that either was high priest at that time. But Joiada the son of Eliakim was high-priest in Nehemiah's 2nd visit, (Neh. xiii. 28.) and Johanan, who succeeded him, may well have been old enough for Ezra to resort to. Davidson fills up Zunz wrongly, " of the high priest Eliashib who lived after Nehemiah." ii. 130. The natural construction of Neh. xiii. 28, one " of the sons of Joiada, son of Eliashib, the high priest," is that Joiada was high-priest then. Any how Eliashib did not "live

In the book of Nehemiah, Nehemiah himself relates, in the first person, in one consecutive vivid narrative, the history of the rebuilding of the walls of Jerusalem, from the time that God first put the desire into his mind at the court of Persia until it was completed and he had made over the charge of the city[13], and ends with his gathering the people together[14]. The next portion describes what they did, when so gathered[15]. The acts being religious, not civil, the prominent part belonged to Ezra. Nehemiah joins himself in, with the rest of the congregation, saying no longer, "I," but "we[16]." The 11th chapter gave no occasion for the first person, being an account of measures taken by the people themselves for the re-peopling of Jerusalem. In the 12th and 13th Nehemiah had again occasion to speak of himself. The act, with which the history closes, falls soon after B.C. 414. The whole then of the book which admits of it (ch. i-vii. x. 28-39. xii. 27-47. xiii.) is written in the 1st person. Where Nehemiah acted alone, (ch. i-vii.) he necessarily speaks of himself, " I ;" where the first part belonged to another, he classes himself with others, "we." (ch. i-vii.) Wherever then the first person could be used, it is used; and the parts in which it is not used stand closely connected with these; as, the sealing of the covenant[17], ("we *make* a sure covenant," in the present,) with the confession of sin and humiliation before it[18], and this with the previous festival in which, [19]*day by day, from the first day unto the last day,* Ezra *read* to them *in the book of the law of God.* So then all marks itself as contemporary, except the arrangement of the re-peopling of Jerusalem, and the enumeration of some towns and villages in which the rest dwelt[20], and a list of priests and Levites[21]. And yet these too are really

after Nehemiah," since (as Dr. Dav. too states) Nehemiah expelled his grandson;—" a grandson of Eliashib the high priest had become son-in law to Sanballat the Horonite, and was expelled by Nehemiah." (Dav. ii. 137.) According to the natural meaning of the text, Nehemiah survived Eliashib.

[13] Neh. i-vii. 4.   [14] Ib. vii. 5.   [15] viii-x.   [16] ix. 38. (x. 1. Heb.) x. 29-39. [30-40. Heb.]   [17] כֹּרְתִים־וְכֹתְבִים x. 1. Heb. (ix. 38. Eng.) [18] "And because of all this." Ib.   [19] viii. 18.   [20] xi. 25-36.   [21] xii. 1-26.

connected.   For the re-peopling of Jerusalem was a measure which Nehemiah says he had at heart[1]; and the enumeration of the priests and Levites seems to be mentioned in connection with the dedication of the wall[2]. This is more evidence than can be alleged as to most books, out of Holy Scripture.

The objections raised to the genuineness of a small portion of the book amount to this, 1) that expressions of Nehemiah's personal feelings do not occur, where Nehemiah had no occasion to speak of himself; 2) that he speaks of Almighty God under different titles, *The Lord, God of heaven, my God,* (his own favorite, loving and beautiful, title,) *our God, their God, their Lord,* or simply, *God,* according to the varying circumstances, under which he spoke.   "My God," "our God," in that it expresses the relation of the creature to the Creator, is as distinct a title of Almighty God, as His Name Jehovah, or Lord, or God.   A Christian has no title of deeper love than *my God.*   This way of counting the names of God, *Adonai,* YHVH, *Elohim, El,* without any reference to the shades of feeling expressed by them, or any modification of those names by the mention of our relation to God, is a mere disease of the criticism to which it belongs.   But the statement is, over and above, inaccurate, and a seeming contrast only.   As imported to us, it would be more exact, if reversed[3].   It is not, of course, enough to count on the fingers, that the one or other name occurs most often in this or that part of Nehemiah, unless it could be shewn that they had been so used under exactly the same circumstances.   But, in fact, the main usage of the book

[1] vii. 4, 5.   [2] xii. 27 sqq.

[3] De Wette said, from Kleinert p. 132 ; "The names *Jehovah, Adonai,* and *Elohim,* are used promiscuously viii. 1, 6, 8, 9 sqq. 14, 16,&c, whereas, except i. 5, 11. iv. 8, *Elohim* is prevalent in Nehemiah, (especially 'God of Heaven' i. 4. ii. 4. 20.)" Einl. § 197 a p. 263.   (Davidson adopts the words as his own, omitting the title "the God of Heaven," ii. 141.)   The names being "used promiscuously" is of course no real contrast with the one name being prominent. The title Adonai is not used in the chapters, in which it is stated that it is used, and is used where it is implied that it is not.   "Lord," with the personal pronoun, ("their, our Lord,") is used in both.

is one [4]. The result of a careful examination is, 1) that
the proper Name of God (YHVH) is nowhere, through-

[4] The following are all the ways in which the name of God is used in Nehemiah ;

1) The title, *my God*, occurs in the phrases, *the good hand of my God upon
me*, ii. 8. *I told them of the hand of my God, which was good upon me*, Ib.
18. (in reference to 8 ;) *my God put in my heart*, ii. 12. vii. 5 ; *the house of
my God*, xiii. 14. Remember to *me, my God*, v. 19. xiii. 14, 22, 31. *Remember to Tobiah*, &c. *O my God*, vi. 14. *Remember to them, O my God*.
xiii. 29.

2) He prays, *O our God*, in what concerns others too, iv. 4. [iii. 36. Heb.]
as the Levites too pray, "*our God*, the great and terrible God," ix. 32. Or
he relates, "we made our prayer unto *our God*," iv. 9. [3. Heb.]; or speaks to
others, "*our God* shall fight for us," iv. 20. [14. Heb.]; "ought ye not to walk
in the fear of *our God?*" v. 9. "did not *our God* bring all this evil upon us?"
xiii. 18. "shall we hearken unto you—to transgress against *our God?*" Ib. 27.
Also, in the history of what they pledged themselves in common to do, he speaks
in common, "*we* made ordinances upon *us*, to charge *ourselves* for the service
of the house of *our God*, for all the work of the house of *our God; we* cast
lots—to bring it into the house of *our God*," "that minister in the house of
our God;" "to the chambers of the house of *our God*," "unto the house of
our God;" "we will not forsake *the house of our God;*" x. 32-4. 36. bis. 37.
38, 39. [33-34. 37, 38, 39, 40. Heb.] In all which there occurs once only, "the
altar of the Lord, (YHVH) our God," x. 34. [35. Heb.]; (*the altar of the
Lord*, [YHVH] being, with the exception of Ps. xliii. 4, the uniform idiom,
see Ges. Thes. 579.) and once, "the house of the Lord," (YHVH) x. 35. (36. H.)
which again is the common idiom. The expression, *the house of our God*,
recurs xiii. 4. "*Our God*" he had just said, "turned the curse of Balaam
into a blessing," xiii. 2. Contrariwise, *the house of God* occurs in the message of Shemaiah to Nehemiah, vi. 10, and in the contrasted chapters alike,
viii. 16. xi. 11, 16, 22. xii. 40.

3) *His God*, is used, with emphasis, of Solomon, "beloved of his God;"
xiii. 26. and,

4) *Their God*, xii. 45. "they kept the ward of *their God*."

5) *Their Lord* (אֲדֹנֵיהֶם) occurs iii. 5, "their nobles put not their necks to the
work of *their Lord;*" as does, *our Lord*, viii. 10, "this day is holy unto *our
Lord*," (לַאֲדֹנֵינוּ.) x. 30, [29. Eng.] "the commandments of the Lord, *our
Lord*."

6) *The God of heaven*, is used in the two first chapters only, where the context relates to the power of God, in relation to those who were not Jews. i. 4,
"I prayed before *the God of heaven;*" Ib. 5, "and said, I beseech Thee, O
Lord, (YHVH) *God of heaven, the great and terrible God*. ii. 4, "I prayed
to *the God of heaven;*" ii. 20, "*The God of heaven* He will prosper us."
(against Sanballat and the others.)

7) In a title taken from the Pentateuch, "the great and terrible God," he
uses the word אֵל, i. 5. as do the Levites, ix. 32.

8) Besides this he prays simply, O Lord, (יהוה) i. 11.

out Nehemiah, the subject of any sentence; 2) that God is
addressed by that Name throughout Nehemiah; 3) that

9) *The Lord*, אָדוֹן, is used once only, iv. 8. Heb. [14. Eng.]

There are different phrases in which the name of God, or the Lord, are in
Hebrew predominantly united; and these uses of the word God, or Lord,
should be considered in reference to the idioms.

YHVH being the Name by which God revealed Himself, "the commandments of the Lord," x. 30. [29. Eng.] is the received Hebrew phrase; (see
Ges. Thes. p. 579.) here it is added, "our Lord." Corresponding to this is
the expression, "the *law* which the Lord *commanded* Israel," (viii. 1.) "the
law which the Lord *commanded* by the hand of Moses," viii. 14. "The law
of the Lord *their* God," occurs ix. 3, but, simply the *law of God* (אֱלֹהִים) in
viii. 8, 18. x. 29, 30. (28. 29. Eng.) The "law of the Lord" occurs in Exod.
xiii. 9. "the law of God," Josh. xxiv. 26. "*Praise* (הַלֵּל) the Lord" (v. 13.)
is again the common Hebrew idiom. So is, "*worship* (הִשְׁתַּחֲוָה) the Lord,"
(viii. 6. In ix. 3. is added, "their God,") and, although less exclusively, "*blessed* (בֵּרַךְ) the Lord;" (it is added, "*the great God*," viii. 6.) and "they
cried unto the Lord," (זָעַק אֶל) with, or without, the addition "their God."
ix. 4. (see Ges. Thes. p. 426.)

The man of God, xii. 24, 36. is the only idiom used.

"Moses, *the servant of God*," x. 29. [30. Heb.] occurs besides only in
1 Chron. vi. 34. [49. Eng.] 2 Chr. xxiv. 9. Dan. ix. 11; but Moses, *the servant
of* the Lord, also occurs twice in the Chronicles, (2 Chr. i. 3. xxiv. 6.) as well
as in the earlier books, Deut. xxxiv. 5. Joshua 13 times, 2 Kgs. xviii. 12. The
title is used of Joshua in Judg. ii. 8. and of David in the titles of Ps. xviii. and
xxxvi.

The title "congregation of the Lord" was never largely used. It occurs
twice only out of the Pentateuch, Mic. ii. 5. 1 Chr. xxviii. 8. and, in the Pentateuch, chiefly in one set of laws, *who* were not to be received in "the congregation of the Lord." Deut. xxiii. 2, 3. [bis] 4. [bis] 9. [1, 2, 3, 8. Eng.] Else
only Num. xvi. 3. xx. 4. *The congregation of God* occurs only Neh. xiii. 1.

To "make to *swear by God*," Neh. xiii. 25. also occurs only 2 Chr. xxxvi.
13. where it is used of a heathen, Nebuchadnezzar, who did not know His
Name. On the same ground Abimelech says to Abraham, and the Egyptian
slave to David, *Swear to me by God*, Gen. xxi. 23. 1 Sam. xxx. 15. Isaiah,
prophesying of the Gospel, also has, *shall swear by the God of truth*, בֵּאלֹהֵי אָמֵן.
The phrase *shall swear by* the Lord, occurs, in all, 11 times; Josh. ii. 12. ix. 18.
19. Judg. xxi. 7. 1 Sam. xxiv. 22. [21. Eng.] xxviii. 10. 2 Sam. xix. 8. (7. Eng.)
1 Kgs. i. 17. ii. 8, 23. and Hif. ib. 42. Abraham unites both to his servant,
I will make thee swear by the Lord, *the God of heaven, and the God of earth.*
Gen. xxiv. 3.

"Thanksgiving unto *God*," הוֹדוֹת לֵאלֹהִים xii. 46, occurs here only. הוֹדוֹת לַי׳
occurs 1 Chr. xvi. 41. 2 Chr. v. 13. vii. 3, 6. Ezr. iii. 11. but in 2 Chr. v. 13.
vii. 3. Ezr. iii. 11. with the full addition, "for He is good, for His mercy endureth for ever;" in 1 Chr. xvi. 41. 2 Chr. vii. 6. with the last clause only.
Absolutely לְהוֹדוֹת לַי׳ stands only 1 Chr. xvi. 7, but there too premised to a Psalm
which opens הוֹדוּ לַי׳ Ib. 8.

throughout Nehemiah God is addressed and spoken of as, "our God;" 4) That in each part of his book, that in which Nehemiah speaks in the first person, and that in which he does not, God is spoken of as the "Lord of" His creatures, "their Lord," "our Lord;" 5) That titles, such as, *house of God, law of God,* occur throughout; 6) That the expressions, *the congregation of God, servant of God, fear of God, thanksgiving unto God,* cannot be made use of, to identify the parts of Nehemiah in which they occur with the books of Chronicles, since the other expressions, *the servant of the Lord, the fear of the Lord,* occur in the book of Chronicles; and those, *the congregation of God, thanksgiving unto God,* do not occur there, but the expressions, "thanksgiving unto the Lord," "congregation of the Lord," only. 6) That the fuller and more solemn language is used upon the more solemn occasions[1]. In part too it occurs in spoken words[2]. It has been said truly, "[3]The variation is a guarantee to the accuracy of the relation, that the Levites (ch. 9.) pray differently from Nehemiah." It would probably be the office of Ezra, the priest, not that of Nehemiah, the civil governor, to prepare that prayer.

The historical ground alleged is, that the name of Jaddua who, according to Josephus[4], was high priest in the time of Alexander, occurs in the book of Nehemiah. We ought, of course, to be slow to assume any gloss in Holy Scripture, unless the context absolutely requires it. But there is, I think, evidence that the name of Jaddua did not stand in Nehemiah. Ch. xii. opens with two lists of priests and Levites, those which went up with Zerubbabel and Jeshua, and those in the days of Joiakim the son of

---

The fear (יִרְאַת) *of God* (Neh. v. 15.) recurs in the remarkable prophecy, 2 Sam. xxiii. 3. In the Psalms (3 times) Proverbs (16 times) Isaiah (xi. 2, 3. xxxiii. 6.) and 2 Chr. xix. 9, (charge of Jehoshaphat,) *the fear of the Lord* is used. Neither occurs in narrative. (פַּחַד אֱלֹהִים occurs Ps. xxxvi. 2. of "fear towards God," פַּחַד being used of "terror inspired by God," 1 Sam. xi. 7. 2 Chr. xiv. 13. [14. Eng.] xvii. 10. Is. ii. 10, 19, 21. and פַּחַד אֱלֹהִים only in 2 Chr. xx. 29. in the same sense.) [1] viii. 5, 9, 10. ix. 3, 4, 5. [2] viii. 9, 10. ix. 5. [3] Keil, Einl. p. 523. [4] Ant. xi. 8.

Jeshua. They are the priests and Levites, then, in two generations. The Levites are, in both cases, distributed into two classes, 1) those *over the thanksgiving*, 2) those who kept ward. These enumerations follow in an exact order; first, the priests who went up with Jeshua [1], then the Levites [2]; then again, the priests in the days of Joiakim [3], the sons of those mentioned before, (except that no son of Hattush is named;) and, after them, the chief of the Levites according to the former division [4]; lastly, the summary, [5] *These were in the days of Joiakim the son of Jeshua,—in the days of Nehemiah the governor, and of Ezra the priest, the scribe.*

But in the midst of these connected accounts which give two generations of high-priests, priests, and Levites, that of Jeshua and the next, there occur two lists of high-priests, which go down to the 6th generation from Jeshua [6], of the two last links of which no notice whatever is taken in this context. Elsewhere also, in the history of Nehemiah, the last mentioned in the line of the high-priesthood is an unnamed son of the high-priest Joiada, the son of Eliashib, who was himself the son of Joiakim [7], the last mentioned in this context; so that the history stops short of Jaddua.

In the first of the two lists, even if it stands in part, it seems probable that some generations have any how been added. If it stood, " And Jeshua begat Joiakim," the words would introduce the following statement of the *priests in the days of Joiakim.* But, as there is no sort of addition more easily made, than that of some links of a genealogy, it is probable that at all events the latest links were added, which go beyond the history of Nehemiah.

The two verses, containing the 2nd list of names, are evidently altogether out of place. For they come be-

---

[1] xii. 1-7.   [2] Ib. 8, 9.   [3] Ib. 12-21.   [4] Ib. 24, 25.   [5] Ib. 26.

[6] xii. 10, 11, "And Jeshua begat Joiakim, and Joiakim begat Eliashib, and Eliashib begat Joiada, and Joiada begat Jonathan, and Jonathan begat Jaddua." xii. 22, " The Levites in the days of Eliashib, Joiada, and Johanan, and Jaddua."   [7] xiii. 28.

tween the statement as to the Priests and the Levites, which before were closely joined[7]. Further, the name of Jaddua makes the two terms, which the verses assign, inconsistent. The first states, "[8]The Levites in the days of Eliashib, Joiada, and Johanan, and Jaddua, were written, chief fathers; and the priests in," or during[9], "the reign of Darius the Persian." According to which, Jaddua is apparently the last high-priest. But the statement immediately following makes the list to end in the high-priesthood before Jaddua. "[10]The sons of Levi, the chief of the fathers, were written in the book of the chronicles, even until the days of Johanan, the son of Eliashib."

They would only be consistent between themselves, and with the history of Nehemiah, if the name of Jaddua were omitted.

But these verses have so evidently the character of a marginal note[11], which has by some inadvertence been brought into the text, that it needs not to discuss details in them. They are evidently supplemental to the account in Nehemiah. *That* gives the priests and Levites in the times of Jeshua and Joiakim; *this* supplement makes a statement as to three or four generations, *subsequent* to that account, omitting those mentioned by Nehemiah. As a supplemental statement, written on the margin, they were transcribed into a wrong place. It is characteristic, that a school, which rejects with scorn the statement of Josephus, that a high-priest Jaddua shewed the pro-

---

[8] xii. 22. Johanan, in this list, occupies the same place as Jonathan in the former, xii. 11. It may be, that the one was the son of Joiada, whom Nehemiah expelled. [9] על מלכות. [10] Ib. 23.

[11] Even Herzfeld says p. 314, "v. 22, 23. are any how of later origin; for they interrupt yet more strongly [than 10, 11.] the context, which requires that, as in v. 8, 'the heads of the Levites' in Joiakim's days should follow upon 'the heads of the priests.' I do not account them interpolated, but rather as erroneously come from the margin into the text. I assign also each verse to a separate author, &c." In p. 307. he speaks of them as "acknowledged by all to be interpolated." But they suit the theory of Zunz too well to part with, (p. 26, 27.) and from him have been accepted by those who impugn the rest, De Wette, Ewald, (G. Isr. i. 230.) Stähelin, Davidson, ii. 147, 8.

phecy of Daniel to Alexander, accepts the unhistorical
confusion in the same context, whereby Josephus made
"Sanballat the Horonite," the contemporary and adver-
sary of Nehemiah, in the 20th year of Artaxerxes, B.C.
445, to be a contemporary of Alexander, 113 years afterwards [1].

No other, even plausible, ground has been alleged, for
separating what is plainly one coherent whole.   The rest
which has been said are mostly mere insolent assumptions against Holy Scripture, grounded on unbelief [2].

It has long ago been observed, that offences which

[1] Nehemiah says that a son of Joiada the high-priest, the son of Eliashib,
married a daughter of Sanballat the Horonite, and that he himself expelled
him from Jerusalem. (xiii. 28.) Josephus omits all mention of Sanballat at the
time of Nehemiah, whom he places under Xerxes, and makes Sanballat "a satrap sent by the last king Darius to Samaria," who married his daughter, Ni-
caso, to Manasseh, the brother of Jaddua, and son of John, the son of Judas,
the son of Eliashib, (Ant. xi. 7.) who are the Johanan, son of Joiada, son of
Eliashib, in Neh. ii. 22.

[2] 1) It was mere carelessness, when De Wette said, "The words סְגָנִים, (sagans, rulers,) חֹרִים (nobles,) characteristic of Nehemiah, ii. 16. iv. 8, 13. v. 7, 17.
vi. 17. vii. 5. xii. 40. xiii. 11. do not occur in ch. viii. ix. x., and instead, רָאשֵׁי אָבוֹת
occurs viii. 13." (followed by Dav. ii. 141.) "Sagans" is not so characteristic of
Nehemiah, since it occurs of Jewish civil prefects in Ezra; (ix. 2.) still less חֹרִים
"nobles," since it occurs in Eccl. x. 17. 1 Kgs. xxi. 8, 11. Is. xxxiv. 12. Jer.
xxvii. 20. xxxix. 6.   But in all the places of Nehemiah except one, being civil titles, they are used in civil matters.   In that one, xii. 40. Nehemiah says,
how, on the day of the dedication of the city-wall, there were two processions
round the wall, in which laity, priests, singers, were each divided into
halves, and in consequence of that division half of the sagans were with him,
half of the princes of Judah, (he used the words as equivalent s. xii. 31, 32,
40.) headed the other company.   It was a religious ceremonial on the completion of the great civil work which God had prospered.   On the other occasion, which was purely religious, a public exposition of Holy Scripture by Ezra,
he classifies those present only as, "people, levites, priests;" much as we
might speak of clergy and people, without speaking of noblemen or State-Offi-
cers.   But, to express that those who were present were "the heads of families," he used the well-known Pentateuch expression "heads of the fathers,"
which he himself used in a chapter, admitted to be his, vii. 70, 71.   "Heads
of the fathers to all the people" expressed what the terms "sagans and nobility" would not express, unless "all the heads of families" in London meant
its aristocracy.

2) The title *Tirshatha* is a title which the Persian prefects of Judæa had.
It is used absolutely of Zerubbabel, (Ezr. ii. 63. Neh. vii. 65.) added by Nehemiah, in his signature to a document, (x. 2.) [1. Eng.] and on one public oc-

Malachi upbraids are so precisely the same as those
which Nehemiah corrected on his return as governor,

casion, when he was joined with Ezra, (viii. 9.) and under which, without his
name, he records a gift of his to the treasury for the expenses apparently of re-
peopling Jerusalem. (vii. 70.)   It is used 5 times in all; in three cases, of Nehemiah.   *Pechah* is of much more extensive use.   It is used, after the captivity, of the Governor of Judæa, by Haggai of Zerubbabel, and by Malachi in
the time of Nehemiah.   Nehemiah speaks of *the bread of the Pechah* (i. e. the
allowance made to him) v. 14, 18; of "all the time in which he was *their Pechah*" (פחם) v. 14; "the [Persian] Pechahs beyond the river," ii. 7, 9; of "the
throne of the Pechah on this side the river," at Jerusalem, iii. 7.   In the list
of priests and Levites in ch. xii. alone, he is called "Nehemiah the Pechah,"
xii. 26.   Why this case, which does not occur in the narrative, is to rule the
other cases, or, since both names are given to Zerubbabel, both should not be
given to Nehemiah, I know not.

3) No histories can well be more evidently distinct, than Ezra iii. and x. are
from Neh. viii.   Yet Zunz speaks of "a relation, partly dressing out what had
been already related, partly repeating, as belonging to Ezra and Nehemiah, what
had already been related of Zerubabel." (p. 24. translated by Dav. ii. 142, 3.)
"It is conformable to the character of the Chronicle-writer, that he forgets to
make the people take notice of the day of atonement, which occurs five days only
before the feast of Tabernacles, directly contradicts (v. 17.) his own account of
the former festival, (Ezr. iii. 4.) and even (v. 15.) quotes passages from the Pentateuch which are not there." (p. 25. also nearly translated, Dav. ii. 143.)   Nehemiah quotes no *passage* at all.   He says that they found written in the law,
that they should dwell in booths in the feast of the 7th month, and that they
should proclaim that boughs should be brought *to make booths, as was written.*   But it is contained in the law that the three great feasts were to be *proclaimed.* (Lev. xxiii. 4.)   The sort of trees also, of which the booths were to
be made, are mentioned, *fruit*-bearing *boughs of goodly trees, branches of
palm-trees,* and *boughs of thick trees, and willows of the brook.* (Ib. 40.)   It
was directed also that they should *dwell in booths.* (Ib. 42, 3.)   It is hardly
credible that language so insolent should be used, either because, in Nehemiah's
time, it was understood that the proclaiming of the festival involved the proclamation to make preparations for it, or that they specified as trees, the olive and
oleaster and myrtle, as explanations or applications of the directions in the
Law.   Most enlightened and large-hearted criticism!   The words, "since the
days of Joshua the son of Nun unto that day had not the children of Israel done
so," are, Zunz himself owns, like those sayings in the Chronicles, (2) xxxv. 18.
"there was no passover, like to that, kept in Israel from the days of Samuel
the prophet," &c. or of Hezekiah's passover, "since the time of Solomon—
there was not the like in Jerusalem." (Ib. xxx. 26.)   And so in the book of
Kings also. (2 Kgs. xxiii. 22.)   But then what Nehemiah speaks of is the
greatness of the festival, which, of course, does not in the least contradict the
fact, that there had been a festival kept in the depressed condition of the first
band of returned exiles, amid the "fear upon them because of the people of
those countries." Ezr. iii. 3, 4.   The prospect of a Commentary on Ezra and

that the two probably co-operated in their reformation; Malachi, as the prophet; Nehemiah, as the civil Governor. Yet two classes of the offences stand in no evident connection. They were against God and man. Out of avarice, they offered imperfect and worthless sacrifices, and withheld the tithes; they had put away their wives, to marry heathen women. To these is added, that priests were not correctors of the evil, but corruptors [1].

So then, from the examination of the later books themselves, we come back to the statement of Josephus, that the canon closed with the last prophet, the last historical book ending with the reform of those same varied abuses, which the last prophet denounced in the name of God; and the canon was closed about the beginning of the fourth century before our Lord, above two centuries before Antiochus Epiphanes.

With this agrees the tradition in the Talmud, that "[2] the men of the great Synagogue wrote Ezekiel, the twelve, [minor prophets] Daniel, and the book of Esther; Ezra wrote his book and the genealogy of the Chronicles down to *lo*. Rab says, Ezra did not go up from Babylon until he wrote his genealogy, and so he went up. And who finished it? Nehemiah."

It is clear, both from the context of the whole, and from the details, that by "wrote," they did not mean "composed," but "inscribed." For in no other sense could they be said to write the twelve minor prophets, of whom it is there said, "[3] our fathers made a large volume of them, that they might not be lost for their littleness." As they inscribed in the Canon [4] the twelve, so they inscribed in it Ezekiel, Daniel, and the book of Esther, which could not have been inscribed in it before, being written in the Captivity.

What historical grounds then are there to allege, why

Nehemiah, by an able writer, in the series already begun, relieves me from further details.   [1] Neh. xiii. 4, 5, 7, 28. Mal. ii. 1-9.   [2] Baba bathra, f. 15. 1.
[3] Ib. f. 14. 2. [4] So Kimchi says, "they wrote it [the Psalter] in the canon of the Kethubim, כתבוה בכלל הכתובים, not in that of the prophets." Præf. in Ps.

Daniel had not his place in the Canon then, when every other book now in the Canon had?

Grounds alleged have been these; 1) that, had he written in the Captivity, he must have been quoted, or alluded to, by subsequent writers, especially by the son of Sirach. 2) The Jews disparaged him by placing his book, not among the prophets, but in the Hagiographa.

Now, since the place where people have missed him in Ecclesiasticus is among the prophets, in that the author *does* mention Isaiah, Ezekiel, Jeremiah, and perhaps, (though this is doubtful) the twelve, and does *not* mention Daniel, plainly his not mentioning him *there* implies no more than that the Jews in his time had the same arrangement as they have now. If they had any good ground for the arrangement, this plainly is no disparagement at all, any more than it is as to David. The arrangement of the Canon among the Jews, although different from that of the Christian Church, proceeded on definite and legitimate principles. 1) The law, as the original fountain-head of revelation, stands at the head; 2) then all those books, believed to have been written by men exercising the prophetic office, whether those called the first prophets (the historical books from Joshua to the Kings,) or what *we* call the prophets, *they* the later prophets; 3) then, a more miscellaneous class, " Scriptures," sacred writings, Hagiographa, written by persons who, whether endowed with the gift of prophecy or no, had not the pastoral office of the prophet. This last class consisted even chiefly of persons in high secular office. There were kings, as David who, in that wider sense, was eminently a Prophet; Solomon, who wrote at least one glorious Psalm[5], prophetic of Christ; Ezra, who had charge to lead his people back from their captivity, *the priest, the scribe*[6], yet who speaks of Haggai and Zechariah, as having an office of " prophets[7] " distinct from his own;— Ezra, the author of the Chronicles as well as of the book which bears his name; Nehemiah; probably

<hr>

[5] Ps. lxxii.   [6] Ezr. vii. 6, 11, 12. Neh. viii. 4, 9, 13. xii. 26, 36.   [7] Ezr. v. 1.

Mordecai also, the author of the book of Esther. The distribution is allowable; since plainly it is as permissible to class books according to the offices borne by their authors, as according to the subjects of the books themselves. But according to this distribution, the book of Daniel could occupy no other place than it does. Daniel had no immediate office of a practical teacher of his people. He was the statesman, the protector probably, not the direct teacher of his people. The historical portion of his book contains some great dispensations of God, set down in the order in which they took place, but with no account of the date of its composition. The prophetic portions of his book, in which he himself was the organ of prophecy, belong to the last years of a life beyond the common age of man. His first vision was probably not vouchsafed, until he had reached the fourscore years, after which man's ordinary lot is suffering and sorrow. Even at this period, those visions were but insulated events in his life, gifts vouchsafed to him in the midst of a secular life. Daniel, in the four visions which, in the last years of his life, were vouchsafed to him, was the recipient and transmitter of great revelations. Still his office was different from that of those whom God sent, *daily rising up early and sending them*[1], to speak in His Name the words which He gave them. *Their's* was an abiding spirit of prophecy resting upon them; to *him*, as far as we are told, insulated revelations only were disclosed.

It does not affect us, whether the later Jews were right or wrong in distinguishing between those who wrote "[2] through the spirit of prophecy," and those who wrote "through the Holy Ghost." The distinction might be true, if they meant to express, by "the spirit of prophecy," the habitual gift of the Holy Ghost to those called to the office of prophet; and by "the Holy Ghost," the occasional or specific gifts of the Holy Ghost to write what

---

[1] Jer. vii. 13, 25. xi. 7. xxv. 3, 4. xxvi. 5. xxix. 19. xxxii. 33. xxxv. 14, 15. xliv. 4. 2 Chr. xxxvi. 15.   [2] Maimon. More Neboch. ii. 45. p. 317 sqq. Kim. l. c. Praef. ad Psalm.

He willed to be written by them. The distinction belongs to the inspired persons, not to the substance of the things conveyed by them. For in both cases alike the language implies, that these men of God [3] *spake, moved by the Holy Ghost,* and that what they taught was infallible. The distinction appears to be altogether a late one; and probably was erroneous in the character which the modern Jews ascribed to "the spirit of prophecy," in that they imagined those under its influence to be deprived of the ministry of the outward senses. Still they did not mean by the distinction to disparage the greatness of Daniel's prophecies.

Josephus says, that he was "[4] one of the greatest prophets." And whereas the Talmud mentions a saying, that "Haggai, Zechariah, Malachi, had this above him, that they were prophets, and he was not a prophet[5]," yet they themselves explain this to mean "[6] that he was not sent to Israel for the office of prophecy;" i. e. as said above, that he had not the prophetic office. It was part of that same saying, that, in another respect, "[7] he was greater than they, in that he saw the vision which they saw not." And the Talmud says, "[8] if all the wise of the nations were in one scale of the balance, and Daniel in the other, he would outweigh them all." "And Abarbanel says, that "[9] he stood in the secret of God and heard His words," and assents to the Rabbins who, in the Seder Olam, count him among the prophets, and "this they said, not in the way of metaphor, or of mission, but in the way of precision and truth."

In the one sense, then, as the organs of prophecy, David and Daniel were prophets and very great prophets.

[3] 2 Pet. i. 21.　　　　[4] Ant. x. 11. 7.

[5] ‏נביא לא היה‎ Sanhedr. c. xi. Megill. c. l. quoted by Carpz. Intr. iii. 235, 6. and Voisin on Mart. Pug. Fid. P. ii. c. iii. § iii. p. 295.　　[6] The tradition is a childish one, that those three prophets were Daniel's companions who saw not the vision. Dan. x. 7. But it may be a vehicle of real meaning. Any how the tradition, that he was superior to the three in some way, is of the same value as the other, in regard to the Jewish belief, which is the only point at issue.

[7] En Israel in Megilla f. 144. c. 3 ap. Carpz. ib. 236.　　[8] Yoma quoted in Carpz. ib.　　[9] Abarb. in Dan. p. 17, 3.

If the term "prophet" be taken in the meaning of "exercising the prophetic office," then, to deny that they were, in this sense, "prophets," is only to own that God called David to be the shepherd of His people, and, in His Providence, raised the captive Daniel to high secular office in a heathen court. What no one imagines to be a disparagement to the Patriarch David, whose memory was so reverenced, cannot have been meant as a discredit to Daniel.

Nor, clearly, is it any argument against the existence of the book of Daniel, in the time of the son of Sirach, that, that writer did not speak of its author in a place which he did not occupy in the Canon. The panegyric is no catalogue. Its leading principle seems to be to praise men, eminent for their place along the line of history from the creation, the Patriarchs, Adam, Seth, Enoch, before the flood; Noah, Shem, Abraham, Isaac, Jacob, Joseph, before the Exodus; Moses, Aaron, Phinehas, in the wilderness; Joshua, Caleb, and the Judges generally, in the first period in the promised land; Samuel; then Nathan, David, Solomon, Hezekiah, Josiah; and, on occasion of Hezekiah, the prophecies of Isaiah; then, Jeremiah, as prophesying the captivity; Ezekiel; and, in the present text, the Twelve[1]; after the captivity, Zorobbabel, Joshua son

---

[1] All important MSS. and Versions have the words, "And of the 12 prophets let the memorial be blessed, and their bones flourish again out of their place;" yet, as they stand, what follows can hardly be construed, παρεκάλεσε δὲ τὸν Ἰακὼβ καὶ ἐλυτρώσατο αὐτοὺς ἐν πίστει ἐλπίδος, "but he [sing.] comforted Jacob, and redeemed [sing.] them in faith of hope." For the MSS. authorities are just as decided in retaining the singular, as in the insertion of the half-verse on the minor Prophets. So then there is the double anomaly, that the Imperatives are inserted in the midst of the narrative form, and the number is changed. It has been proposed to remedy this, by placing the clauses as to the Twelve prophets after the words, παρεκάλεσε—ἐλπίδος; so that the clause, "he comforted Jacob," &c. should be a continuation of what he said of Ezekiel. Only, there is no more authority for transposing the words, than for omitting them. The words, "let their bones flourish again out of their place," had already occurred, xlvi. 12. The only way, in which the words can be construed, is to understand them to be spoken of God. Yet this too is not according to the analogy of the other verses, in which that is attributed to the prophets, which God did by them. (xlviii. 2, 6, 23. xlix. 7, 9.) The construction and course of thought would certainly be easier, if the clause as to the Twelve were omitted. The writer had alluded to Malachi's closing prophecy, xlviii. 10.

of Josedech, who rebuilt the temple; Nehemiah, who restored the walls. Daniel had not so marked an office for his people, as Ezra, who yet is equally omitted. It is not as a man, that we miss him in the enumeration, but that he does not occupy the place among the prophets, where we are accustomed to see him.

The argument " from silence " is precarious at all times. Here it is the more nugatory, because it stands in conflict not only with the history of the canon generally, but with facts as to the book of Daniel itself.

We have language of his prayer used in Nehemiah; reference to his visions in Zechariah; and, at the times in which the writer must have lived, had he not been the prophet, viz. the Maccabee times, we have quotations not of the book only, but of its Greek translation, in the 3rd (the Jewish) Sibylline book. It is quoted in the 1st book of Maccabees, and at some time, at the least not later, in the book of Baruch; and, men allow too *now*, in the book of Enoch. I stated in a former lecture, how Ezekiel speaks of Daniel in two respects, his wisdom and his righteousness, just as he appears in his book.

i. The correspondence between the prayer of Daniel and that in Nehemiah has been acknowledged and even exaggerated by the opponents of the book of Daniel. First they urged, that if the book had been written by Daniel, it would have been referred to in the later books[2]. When the reference was observed, they quietly assumed as self-evident, that the prayer in Daniel was copied from that of Nehemiah[3]. They alleged in proof of the lateness

[2] In regard to Zechariah, the argument is continued even in the posthumous " Introduction " by Bleek; " Had the book been composed by Daniel, and so, extant from the time of Cyrus and known among the Jews, one should expect to find use made of it in the Prophets after the captivity, Haggai, Malachi, and especially Zechariah i-viii.—But there is nothing of the sort. Jeremiah's prophecies of the Messiah have exercised an influence over Zechariah's conception of the idea of the Messiah; but the visions of Daniel, none." Einl. 1860. p. 589. Davidson, iii. 171, translates Bleek.

[3] " The passage ch. ix. contains verbal imitations of Nehemiah." Leng. p. lx. " Through the expression הספרים ix. 2. [see ab. p. 309.] we are directed to the time after Nehemiah, and also by the employment of the book of Nehemiah,

of the book of Daniel, what had itself first to be proved, and which is not true.

Nothing can be less like one another, than the two long prayers of Daniel and of the Levites in Nehemiah in the main. They are alike only, in so far as both are confessions of sin. But the prayer in Nehemiah[1], like some of the historical Psalms, turns wholly upon facts. It is a confession of God's mercies from the call of Abraham, of their own disobedience from the wilderness onwards, and of the justice of their punishment, ending with a profession of amendment. It proceeds in one steady unbroken course of narrative, from first to last. It contains scarcely a petition. Just towards the end, there is that one, [2]*let not all the trouble seem little to Thee, which hath come upon us.* But they expected no marked interposition *then ;* they confessed their sins, owned God's long-suffering and their unrighteousness, renewed the covenant, and left the future to God. It is the prayer of one, whose memory is well and exactly stored with the precise words in which Moses had written. Throughout that part of the prayer, which relates to the history in the Pentateuch, idioms and sentences of the Pentateuch are worked in[3];

v. 4; comp. i. 5. ix. 32; v. 15, Neh. ix. 10; v. 8, Neh. ix. 34." Id. p. 411. In p. lxi. he speaks of "the *great* use of the book of Neh. in ch. ix." De W. adopted the argument, ed. 7. " Daniel employs not only Ezekiel, who, in the case of the genuineness of the book, stood near him, but also (ch. ix.) Neh. ix." Einl. p. 347 ; then Stähelin, p. 349. and Dav. iii. 194.

[1] ix. 6-36.   [2] Ib. 32.

[3] Neh. ix. 8. לָסֵת לְזַרְעֶךָ—לָסֵת אֶת אֶרֶץ הַבְּרִית עָשׂוּ וְכָרוֹת Gen. xv. 18. אֶת אַבְרָם יְיָ כָּרַת בְּרִית לֵאמֹר לְזַרְעֲךָ נָתַתִּי אֶת הָאָרֶץ. The names of the nations follow in each. Neh. ix. 9. וַתֵּרֶא אֶת עֳנִי אֲבֹתֵינוּ בְּמִצְרָיִם Ex. iii. 7. רָאִיתִי אֶת עֳנִי עַמִּי אֲשֶׁר בְּמִצְרָיִם. Neh. ix. 10. וָאֶתֵּן אֹתֹת וּמֹפְתִים בְּפַרְעֹה וּבְכָל עֲבָדָיו Deut. vi. 22. וַיִּתֵּן יְיָ אֹתֹת וּמֹפְתִים—בְּפַרְעֹה וּבְכָל בֵּיתוֹ Neh. ix. 11. תְּהֹמֹת אֶת יָדְךָ עַל הַיָּם וּבְקָעֵהוּ וְיָבֹאוּ—בְתוֹךְ Ex. xiv. 16. וְהַיָּם בָּקַעְתָּ לִפְנֵיהֶם וַיַּעַבְרוּ בְתוֹךְ הַיָּם בַּיַּבָּשָׁה Neh. Ib. Is. xliii. 16. בְּמָיִם עַזִּים בִּמְצוּלֹת כְּמוֹ אָבֶן. Neh. Ib. Ex. xv. 4. הַיָּם בַּיַּבָּשָׁה add 22. יוֹמָם בְּעַמּוּד עָנָן Ex. xiii. 21. וּבְעַמּוּד עָנָן הִנְחִיתָם יוֹמָם וּבְעַמּוּד אֵשׁ לַיְלָה לְהָאִיר לָהֶם Neh. ix. 12. וְלָהֶם שָׂמְתָּ. Ps. cv. 40. וְלָהֶם מְשָׁמַיִם לַנְתָם הֹרַדְתָּ וְלַיְלָה בְּעַמּוּד אֵשׁ לְהָאִיר לָהֶם Neh. ix. 15. בֹּאוּ וּרְשׁוּ אֶת Deut. i. 8. וַתֹּאמֶר לָהֶם לָבוֹא לָרֶשֶׁת אֶת הָאָרֶץ אֲשֶׁר נָשָׂאתָ אֶת יָדְךָ לָתֵת לָהֶם Neh. Ib. וַהֲבֵאתִי אֶתְכֶם אֶל הָאָרֶץ אֲשֶׁר נָשָׂאתִי אֶת יָדִי לָתֵת Ex. vi. 8. הָאָרֶץ אֲשֶׁר נִשְׁבַּע יְיָ לַאֲבֹתֵיכֶם-לָתֵת לָהֶם בִּקֵּשׁ אֶת Neh. ix. 16. 2 Kgs. xvii. 14. Jer. vii. 26. לְאַבְרָהָם לְיִצְחָק וּלְיַעֲקֹב וְנָתַתִּי אֹתָהּ לָכֶם חַנּוּן וְרַחוּם אֶרֶךְ אַפַּיִם וְרַב חָסֶד from Ex. xxxiv. 6 transposing עָרְפָּם (from Pent.) Neh. ix. 17. רַחוּם וְחַנּוּן. Neh. ix. 18. עָשׂוּ לָהֶם עֵגֶל מַסֵּכָה וַיֹּאמְרוּ זֶה אֱלֹהֶיךָ אֲשֶׁר הֶעֶלְךָ מִמִּצְרָיִם, with the remarkable change into the singular, from Ex. xxxii. 8. עָשׂוּ לָהֶם עֵגֶל מַסֵּכָה–

even the precise words are retained, in which Moses reminds them that their *clothes waxed not old, and* their
feet swelled not, although the last word occurs in those
two places alone. This was done of set purpose; for the
writer used, where he willed, language of his own. In
the same way in which he used the language of the
Pentateuch and of other earlier Scripture, the writer of
that long confession used also language of Daniel's
prayer.

Daniel's prayer, on the contrary, is rhetorical, so to
say, not historical. Its subject is, what must be a creature's confession of sin, God's righteousness, man's unrighteousness. But it is one eloquent, fervid, tide of
prayer. The prayer rises and falls alternately, in a prolonged chequered cadence, as it sets forth or owns successively God's faithfulness, their unfaithfulness; God's
righteousness, their confusion through their unrighteousness; God's property of mercy, their sins calling down
His foreannounced justice; then one brief reference to
the deliverance from Egypt, and an impassioned gush of
prayer rolling on and on, until the last, *Lord, tarry not,
Lord, hearken and do,* overcometh God, and his prayer
is answered. Apart from evidence, no one could doubt
which had used the language of the other.

It is not much which the two prayers have in common,
except what is common to all prayer in distress, the confession of sins past and present which bring down God's

רֹחַם Ps. cxliii. 10. וְרֹחַ תְּשׁוּבָה Neh. ix. 20. וַיֹּאמְרוּ אֵלֶּה אֱלֹהֶיךָ יִשְׂרָאֵל אֲשֶׁר הֶעֱלוּךָ מֵאֶרֶץ מִצְרַיִם
אֱלֹהֶיךָ Deut. ii. 7. וְאַרְבָּעִים שָׁנָה כִּלְכַּלְתָּם בַּמִּדְבָּר לֹא חָסֵר Neh. ix. 21. מוֹבָה זֶה אַרְבָּעִים שָׁנָה יי
שִׂמְלָתְךָ לֹא בָלְתָה Deut. viii. 4. שַׂלְמֹתֵיהֶם לֹא בָלוּ וְרַגְלֵיהֶם לֹא בָצֵקוּ Neh. Ib. עִמָּךְ לֹא חָסֵרְתָּ דָּבָר
אַרְבֶּה אֶת זַרְעֲךָ Gen. xxii. 17. וּבְנֵיהֶם הִרְבִּיתָ כְּכוֹכְבֵי הַשָּׁמַיִם Neh. ix. 23. מֵעָלֶיךָ וְרַגְלְךָ לֹא בָצֵקָה
וְהוּא יַכְנִיעֵם לְפָנֶיךָ Deut. ix. 3. וַתַּכְנַע לִפְנֵיהֶם אֵת יֹשְׁבֵי הָאָרֶץ Neh. ix. 24. כְּכוֹכְבֵי הַשָּׁמַיִם Neh.
ix. 25. בָּתִּים מְלֵאִים כָּל טוּב בֹּרוֹת חֲצוּבִים כְּרָמִים וְזֵיתִים-וַיֹּאכְלוּ וַיִּשְׂבְּעוּ Deut. vi. 11. וּבָתִּים מְלֵאִים
תִּתֵּן לָהֶם מוֹשִׁיעִים וְיוֹשִׁיעוּם Neh. ix. 27. כָּל טוּב אֲשֶׁר לֹא מִלֵּאן וּבֹרוֹת חֲצוּבִים כְּרָמִים וְזֵיתִים-וְאָכְלָה וְשָׂבֵעַ
וּבְמִשְׁפָּטֶיךָ חָטְאוּ בָם אֲשֶׁר יַעֲשֶׂה אָדָם Neh. ix. 29. וַיָּקֶם יי מוֹשִׁיעַ לִבְנֵי יִשְׂרָאֵל וַיּוֹשִׁיעֵם Jud. iii. 9.
וְאֵת מִשְׁפָּטַי אֲשֶׁר יַעֲשֶׂה אוֹתָם הָאָדָם וָחַי בָּהֶם Neh. Ib. Zech. vii. 11. Lev. xviii. 5. וָחָיָה בָּהֶם
וְלֹא עָשִׂיתִי אוֹתָם כָּלָה בַּמִּדְבָּר Ezek. xx. 17. לֹא עֲשִׂיתָם כָּלָה Neh. ix. 31. וַיִּתְּנוּ כָתֵף סֹרָרֶת
Neh. ix. 32. Num. xx. 14. אֵת כָּל הַתְּלָאָה אֲשֶׁר מְצָאַתְנוּ add Ex. xviii. 8. Neh. ix. 35, 6.
מַּחַת אֲשֶׁר לֹא עָבַדְתָּ אֶת יי.—Deut. xxviii. 47, 8. וְהֵם-וּבְמַשְׂמַנֵּי הָרָב-לֹא עֲבָדוּךָ-הִנֵּה אֲנַחְנוּ הַיּוֹם עֲבָדִים
וּבְטוֹב לֵבָב סָרֹב כֹּל וְתָעַבְדָ אֶת אֹיְבֶיךָ

chastisement upon the sinner, or the sinful nation, and thereon, what was peculiar to Israel, the pleading of the promise that God would, on their repentance, restore them. The prayer in Nehemiah had almost come to its close, before there is any point of contact with that of Daniel. The first words of Daniel's prayer, however, which are themselves a re-moulding of a doctrinal statement in the Pentateuch, so reappear in the two prayers in Nehemiah[1], as to shew that those of his day were familiar with that great deep prayer of Daniel.

[1] Dan. ix. 4. Neh. ix. 32. i. 4. The basis of the passages is Deut. vii. 9. "know that יְהוָה אֱלֹהֶיךָ הוּא הָאֱלֹהִים הָאֵל הַנֶּאֱמָן שֹׁמֵר הַבְּרִית וְהַחֶסֶד לְאֹהֲבָיו וּלְשֹׁמְרֵי מִצְוֹתָו." The last clause is slightly modified from the decalogue, Ex. xx. 6, וְעֹשֶׂה חֶסֶד לַאֲלָפִים לְאֹהֲבַי וּלְשֹׁמְרֵי מִצְוֹתָי (Deut. v. 10.) This, as being a fundamental statement of God's relation to His people, was variously applied. Solomon, in memory of his father and of God's promises to him, addressed it in thankfulness, "*Lord God of Israel, there is no God like Thee—Who keepest covenant and mercy with Thy servants, that walk before Thee with a perfect heart.*" שֹׁמֵר הַבְּרִית וְהַחֶסֶד לַעֲבָדֶיךָ הַהֹלְכִים לְפָנֶיךָ בְּכָל לִבָּם 1 Kgs. viii. 23. 2 Chr. vi. 14. Those times of faithfulness were gone. Daniel took the words of Deuteronomy, but instead of "the faithful," he spake to God, as "the great, the aweful," אָנָּא אֲדֹנָי הָאֵל הַגָּדוֹל וְהַנּוֹרָא שֹׁמֵר הַבְּרִית וְהַחֶסֶד לְאֹהֲבָיו וּלְשֹׁמְרֵי מִצְוֹתָיו ix. 4. The attribute of God is twice pleaded to Him in Nehemiah; but, both times, so as to shew that he took it from Daniel, not from Deuteronomy, for in each case he takes words, which are in Daniel, and are not in Deuteronomy. In both he uses the characteristic words, *the great, the aweful God;*" in i. 5. he begins with the word of entreaty, which Daniel had revived from the Pentateuch, אָנָּא. (Gen. l. 17. Ex. xxxii. 31. Dan. ix. 4. Neh. i. 5. else only in Ps. cxviii. 25. the Psalm doubtless of dedication of the second temple, and so, posterior to Daniel. The word is written אָנָּה 2 Kgs. xx. 3. Is. xxxviii. 3. Jon. i. 14. iv. 2. Ps. cxvi. 4, 16.) In both prayers in Nehemiah, something is added. In i. 5, he uses his own title, "God of heaven;" ix. 32, he adds the title, *the mighty* (הַגִּבּוֹר) and stops at "keeping covenant and mercy." While both prayers of Nehemiah could be founded on that of Daniel, that of Daniel could not be taken from either of Nehemiah; not from Neh. ix. 32, because it is incomplete; not from that in Neh. i. 5, because, although it is natural that Nehemiah should have added the title which he uses elsewhere, "God of heaven," there would have been no reason why Daniel, had he used his words, should have omitted them.

Of two other expressions, which Daniel and Nehemiah have in common, the one, ix. 15, *and Thou madest for Thee a Name as at this day*, וַתַּעַשׂ לְךָ שֵׁם כַּיּוֹם הַזֶּה was, in Daniel, certainly a reminiscence of Jeremiah, (xxxii. 20.) since the context is so. The words, with which Daniel introduces it, "And now, O Lord our God, Who broughtest Thy people forth from the land of Egypt," are nearly identical with those which follow it in Jeremiah. (xxxii. 21.) Dan. וְעַתָּה אֲדֹנָי אֱלֹהֵינוּ אֲשֶׁר הוֹצֵאתָ אֶת עַמְּךָ מֵאֶרֶץ מִצְרַיִם בְּיָד חֲזָקָה וַתַּעַשׂ לְךָ אֶת עַמְּךָ אֶת יִשְׂרָאֵל

ii. Nehemiah could naturally allude only to *language* of Daniel; his history had no natural bearing on the history or prophecies of Daniel.   Two in the brief series of Zechariah's visions presuppose Daniel's prophecies of the four world-empires.   They were given to those, who were already in possession of the full disclosures to Daniel, and cannot be understood without them.   They are visions, describing in different pictures the gradual restoration of God's people until the Coming of Christ.   Babylon had fallen; Israel had been partially, yet only very partially, restored.   Zechariah's prayer, like that of Daniel, had been, "[2] Lord, how long?"   In answer to the prayer, there are exhibited to him the four horns, as the obstacle to its complete restoration, and those who should fray them away[3]. The four horns were together symbols of all world-empire,

כְּאֶרֶץ מִצְרַיִם בְּאֹתָה וּכְמִשְׁפָּטִים וְיִד חֲזָקָה Jer.   Only, Daniel used the יָצָא for the יְצִיאָה of Jeremiah.   That same form occurs in Nehemiah, and since the context in Nehemiah is a reminiscence of the Pentateuch not of Jeremiah, and the whole passage has several such reminiscences, there is a probability that these words too were taken from Daniel in whom they occur exactly, not from Jeremiah.

The third place in Daniel is a reminiscence of Jeremiah.   The accumulation, "our kings, our princes, our fathers," or the like, appears repeatedly in Jeremiah.   Daniel owns, "we have not hearkened unto Thy servants the prophets, which spake in Thy Name to our kings, our princes, and our fathers, and to all the people of the land." ix. 6.   This is especially the complaint in Jeremiah. (see ab. p. 341.)   Then he confesses that "righteousness is God's, confusion of face," theirs; and enumerates again those on whom that shame had fallen, "to us, our kings, our princes, and our fathers," and "to the men of Judah and the inhabitants of Jerusalem."   This is also a favorite enumeration in Jeremiah, (xi. 2. xviii. 11. xxxv. 13. and the like, xvii. 20. xxv. 2. xxxv. 17.)   Both enumerations occur in Jer. xxxii. 32.   אֲשֶׁר עָשׂוּ לְהַכְעִסֵנִי הֵמָּה מַלְכֵיהֶם שָׂרֵיהֶם כֹּהֲנֵיהֶם וּנְבִיאֵיהֶם וְאִישׁ יְהוּדָה וְיֹשְׁבֵי יְרוּשָׁלָ͏ִם   Again in these same verses, the phrase, "the near and the far," הַקְּרֹבִים וְהָרְחוֹקִים, Dan. ix. 7. is also Jeremiah's, xxv. 26. (originally in Deut. xiii. 8.) and that, "in all lands whither Thou hast driven them," כָּל־הָאֲרָצוֹת אֲשֶׁר הִדַּחְתָּם שָׁם Dan. ix. 7. Jer. xxiii. 3, 8. xxxii. 37.

The passage in Nehemiah, ix. 32, is also probably a reminiscence of Jeremiah, since two classes are enumerated, "our priests and our prophets," which do not occur in Daniel, but do occur in Jeremiah, ii. 26, where the context is the same as in Nehemiah and, in part, in Daniel; "so is the house of Israel ashamed, they, their kings, their princes, and their priests, and their prophets." כֵּן הֹבִישׁוּ בֵּית יִשְׂרָאֵל הֵמָּה מַלְכֵיהֶם שָׂרֵיהֶם כֹּהֲנֵיהֶם וּנְבִיאֵיהֶם.   In this case then the likeness probably arises from both Daniel and the writer of the prayer in Nehemiah having their minds stored with the prophecies of Jeremiah.

[2] i. 12.   [3] i. 18-21.

yet were in themselves hardly significant, either as to their number or their power, apart from the symbol of the animal which, in Daniel's visions, wielded them. The same four-fold division of power recurs in the vision of the four chariots[1] which issue from between the two mountains of brass, with horses red, black, white, grizzled, strong, (for so only can the word[2] be rendered.) Those who have not explained this vision by aid of Daniel's four world-empires have been puzzled, 1) why the title *strong* should have been given to one set only of these symbols of power; 2) why, in the explanation of the Angel, the first symbol, the chariot with the *red* horses, disappears. Four symbols of earthly power are exhibited to the prophet; three only are explained. Obviously, since the symbols represent the same as in Daniel, there was nothing to be said about the first monarchy; for it was gone. Of the black horses, the symbol of the second, it is said[3], *they have made My anger to rest on the North country*, i. e. on Babylon, of which the former prophets had ever spoken, as *the North*. The third, it is said[4], *go forth after them;* for the Greek empire occupied the same portion of the earth as the Persian. The fourth, the Roman, is designated by the grizzled and strong horses, corresponding to those characteristics of strength and mingled character, so prominent in the fourth empire in Daniel. These also are represented in two relations, 1) in their specific bearing on the Jewish people, they [4]*go forth into the south coun-*

---

[1] vi. 1–3.

[2] אֲמֻצִּים. The root, which is so common in Hebrew, has no other meaning than that of "strength," as Aquila and Vulg. render, καρτεροί, fortes. The guess, that it was a colour, seems to have arisen from its being joined with other colours; hence LXX ψαροί, "dapple-gray," Jon. קִטְמוֹנִין from "ashes." Both then took it to be equivalent to בְּרֻדִּים, with which it is joined. The further guess, that אָמֹץ might be i. q. חָמֵץ, Is. xliii. 1, (Boch. Hieroz. i. p. 111.) was founded on the idea, that the "*red* horses" *must* be meant in vi. 7. But, over and above the presumption that אָמֹץ must be taken in the uniform sense of the root, it is inconceivable, that an epithet, used to describe the horses of the 4th chariot in vi. 3. should be used to describe those of the first chariot in vi. 7. Gesenius (Thes. p. 118.) and even Maurer, Hitzig, gave up the conjectural meaning; Ewald would retain it.   [3] vi. 8.   [4] vi. 6.

try, 2) in their wide-spread solid empire, by permission
of God, '*they walk to and fro in the earth.*   Upon this
their establishment there follows, as in Daniel, the prophecy of the Coming of Christ, '*the Man Whose name is
the Branch.*

This, which was in the main the old interpretation of
Jews[7] and Christians, is free from those difficulties, from
which those who forsook it have not been able to extricate
themselves; but it presupposes the existence of the book
of Daniel.   Daniel's visions could not have been expanded out of this vision of Zechariah.   Zechariah's vision
would not be suggestive of them.   It is not a mere fragment or sketch, which could be expanded.   It itself requires the explanation, which Daniel's visions, in themselves so full and so one, on the very points upon which
this is obscure, supply.

iii. The book of Baruch consists apparently of two
portions, the former[8] probably translated from the Hebrew[9], the latter bearing no marks of a translation.   The
former which is, with an historical introduction, a prayer
for the Jews in Jerusalem to offer for their brethren, is
chiefly in the language of the ancient Hebrew Scriptures,
using largely the language of the law, of Jeremiah, of Daniel.   The great prayer of Daniel is made the basis of the
early portion of the prayer in Baruch, and that, with
one exception, in the order in which the passages lie in
Daniel.   The agreement then can be no chance coincidence, as if two persons under the same circumstances

[5] vi. 7.   [6] vi. 12.

[7] See e. g. Kimchi on Zech. Dr. Mc. Caul's translation, p. 55.   [8] i—iii. 8.

[9] There is no historical statement, that there ever was a Hebrew original.
In St. Jerome's time there was none.   "Among the Hebrews, it is neither
read, nor possessed." (Præf. in expos. Jer.)   Yet the direction, that it was to
be used "in the house of the Lord," (i. 14.) implies a Hebrew or Chaldee original of the prayer; as does also some of the Greek, (I think, with Fritzsche,
Exeg. Hdb. z. d. Apokr. i. 171, 2. and others,) μαναὰ (for מִנְחָה,) i. 10. οὐ—
ἐπ' αὐτῷ, ii. 26. ὡς ἡ ἡμέρα αὕτη, (כַּיּוֹם הַזֶּה,) i. 15. ἀποστολή, ii. 25. βόμβησις,
(for הָמוֹן) ii. 29. ἡμέραι καιροῦ, for יְמֵי מוֹעֵד, i. 14. ἐργάζεσθαι with Dat. "serve,"
(for עָבַד) ii. 22. προσεύξασθε εἰς, i. 11. (מָצָאתִי לָהֶם Ezr. viii. 10.) ἐννοεῖν εἰς,
(בִּין אֶל) i. 16.

"[1]had used formulæ, then in general use." The agreement is not in formulæ, but in whole verses, and that in the same order[2]. Nor can there be any doubt, that Daniel is the original, which is filled up and expanded in Baruch[3]. The prayer of Daniel is one whole, whose inspired thoughts, like those in the Psalms, have formed the devotions of 2300 years, ever gushing forth in renewed fulness. It is the prayer of one, whose mind had been moulded by the writings of the great prophet of the decline of Israel; and the tones of Moses and Jeremiah sound anew in this fresh deep burst of trustful love. But the human instrument, which the Spirit of God struck, was not Jeremiah or Moses, but Daniel's soul. The prayer in Baruch, on the contrary, is a mosaic, formed of jewels from Daniel, Nehemiah, and Jeremiah, blended together, yet not forming one distinct whole.

The book of Baruch bears witness to Daniel on the historical side also. For, in that the author mistook apparently the relation of Nebuchadnezzar and Belshazzar, speaking of them as contemporaries[4], he probably wrote at a time when the memory of the Chaldee monarchs had faded, and the book of Daniel was the only source of information. The mistake, as it seems to be, might arise naturally from Daniel's omission of the

[1] Jahn's solution, Einl. iv. p. 864.

[2] Dan. ix. 7, Bar. i. 15 ; Dan. ix. 8, Bar. i. 16; Dan. ix. 10, Bar. i. 21 ; Dan. ix. 11, Bar. i. 20; Dan. ix. 12, Bar. ii. 1, 2; Dan. ix. 13, Bar. ii. 8; Dan. ix. 14, Bar. ii. 9, 10. (10 expanded ;) Dan. ix. 15, Bar. ii. 11 ; Dan. ix. 19, end of Bar. ii. 15 ; Dan. ix. 18, end of Bar. ii. 16, 17; Dan. ix. 18 end, Bar. ii. 19.

[3] The unbelieving school are bound by their disbelief to disbelieve this, unless they find some date for the book of Baruch, later than Antiochus Epiphanes. So Dillmann, (in Dorner, Jahrb. iii. p. 480) who thinks the book of Baruch "a later off-shoot of the older prophetic literature, not to be so slightly estimated," speaks of "its employment in the book of Daniel." Herzfeld hinted the same, Gesch. Isr. Exc. 2. p. 318, 19. Davidson, assuming B. C. 300 to be the date of Baruch, lays down, " the author of Daniel made use of the Hebrew Baruch in ix. 4-19 which is taken from Bar. i. 15-ii. 17." iii. p. 428. Fritzsche, on the other hand, who puts the book late on inadequate grounds, can afford to see that the book of Daniel was used in it, and makes it the chief ground for the late date of Baruch. Einl. p. 173. So also De Wette, Einl. § 323. p. 427. Bertholdt, Einl. § 427. p. 1750. [4] i. 11, 12. See Lect. vii.

wretched kings between Nebuchadnezzar and Belshazzar, who were of no interest to mankind. But then it implies, not only the existence of the book of Daniel, as historical authority, but that there were then no sources, from which people's Pseudo-Daniel could have compiled his history.

But although there seem, to me, insuperable difficulties against supposing the book of Baruch to have been written at the date assigned in the book itself, the fifth year of the Captivity [5], there is no ground to place it at any late date. For, although the latter portion of the book quotes a Psalm [6], probably of the age of Nehemiah, that mostly original and beautiful section was probably written not so long after the close of the Canon. It is written amid hopes of a speedy restoration [7]; but in a calm atmosphere

[5] "The fifth year" (i. 2.) is doubtless the same date as that in Ezekiel i. 2, "the fifth year of Jehoiachin's captivity." For "the house of the Lord" is spoken of, as still standing, so that "the feasts and solemn days" could be kept, and prayer said, there. (Ib. 14.) Nor is there any difficulty in the statement, that Jerusalem was "burnt with fire," (i. 2.) since it may have been burnt, and the temple have escaped; nor in the account of "the silver vessels" having been "made by Zedekiah," (Ib. 8.) which is indeed in itself likely, although it does not appear, how they could have been carried off in the five first years of Zedekiah's reign; at least, there is no account of his rebellion until his 9th year. It may however have been. It is not right to argue from silence. The expression, "that thou art *waxen old* in a strange land," (iii. 10.) probably means "decay," not length of time, ἐπαλαιώθης having probably the meaning of בָּלָה given to it. But in the prayer, ii. 26, "the house of the Lord" is "desolate," and the captivity is spoken of, as complete, ("we are but a few left among the heathen, where Thou hast scattered us," ii. 13,) and Jeremiah's prophecy of the desolation of Jerusalem and the whole land, as fulfilled, ii. 21-23. add ii. 29-31. In the fifth year of Jehoiachin's captivity, B. C. 594, also, Belshazzar, who was associated in his father's throne about B.C. 541, was probably not born; nor would he then have been connected with Nebuchadnezzar, as *the* king, under whose shadow Israel should live, and serve many days; for there were yet 32 years of Nebuchadnezzar's reign remaining, and probably 20 years of the intervening kings, including 14 years of Belshazzar's father, Labynetus; nor was Belshazzar in the direct line to the throne. But even supposing Balthasar to have been a name of one of the intervening kings or of an elder brother of Evil-merodach who never reigned, (it can hardly be a name for Evil-merodach himself, since they are named from different patrongods,) still there remains the difficulty that Daniel's prayer was not uttered until B. C. 538, and could not have been taken from Baruch's.

[6] Ps. cxlvii. 4. Baruch iii. 34.   [7] iv. 22, 24, 25.

of trust, in the consciousness of no troubles beyond those which were the results of the Captivity, and with no anticipation of the distresses of the Maccabee period. It was then doubtless written before Antiochus Epiphanes.

iv. The LXX translation of *the Pentateuch* at least will not be placed by any later than Ptolemy Philadelphus. But it has been with good reason remarked that the LXX version, in rendering, "[1] when the Most High divided the nations, when He dispersed the sons of Adam, He established the bounds of the nations according to the number of *the angels of God*," instead of "the number of the children of Israel," introduced into the Pentateuch the doctrine, that Angels are guardians over the several nations, a doctrine which is no where found out of Holy Scripture, and which, within Holy Scripture, is only found in Daniel. Of course, some answer must be made, and it is answered that the LXX *may* have drawn it from the general belief of the Jews. This only throws the question further back; for, however the Jews may have expanded any doctrine, the source of their belief is Holy Scripture, rightly or, in later times, wrongly understood, and in this case, we have the fountain of the belief before us, the book of Daniel. It is found no where else [2].

v. The next evidence in point of time is quite apart from the religious writings of the Jews, a work of an Alexandrian Jew, the writer of the Jewish Sibylline book.

Since the investigations of Bleek[3], Friedlieb[4], Alexander[5], it is certain that the work, which now is found as the 3rd Book of the Sibylline Oracles, is entirely distinct from the others, that it has (with the exception of very few manifest interpolations) no traces of Christianity, and that it was written by a Jew about 170 B.C.[6]

---

[1] Deut. xxxii. 8.   [2] See Lect. viii.   [3] Schleierm. ZS. Heft i. p. 120 sqq.
[4] Orac. Sib. 1852. Einl. § 10-17. p. xxii-xxxix.   [5] Orac. Sibyll. Exc. 5. c. l. T. ii. p. 314 sqq. 1856.   [6] Bleek too saw that the date must be between 170-168 B.C. (Heft ii. p. 222, 3.) The first and successful expedition of Antiochus against Ptolemy Philometor, was 171, B.C. the 2nd, after which he first attacked Jerusalem, 170, B.C.; that from which the final persecution began was 168, B.C. Ptolemy Philometor was a minor at the time of the first expedition. See above p. 152, and Clinton, Fasti Hell. ii. 320, 1.

Friedlieb sums up his analysis of the book thus, "[7] If you remove from the third book the later foreign accessions, viz. its present beginning, 1-45, and the last ten lines, as the latest addition to it; also v. 47-96, which were written about 40-31, B.C., and if you restore to it the Preface which originally belonged to it, such as it has for the most part been preserved in Theophilus, you have, as an independent whole, the Sibyl, composed by a Jew about 160, B. C., in regard to which it may be unhesitatingly assumed that it is the old præ-Christian Erythræan Sibyl, known to Alexander Polyhistor, Varro, Josephus, &c, which Theophilus and Athenagoras used, to which Lactantius assigned a very especial preeminence, estimating the number of its verses at about 1000[8]. From this it appears, that little is wanting to our Sibyl; for, after deducting what is extraneous and adding the genuine fragments, it contains 905 verses, so that in all only 95 verses are missing, of which some belonged to the Preface, the rest to the book itself.

" This Erythræan was the old Hebrew Sibyl, as it is expressly called by Clement, Pausanias, &c. It deserved this name the more, since it was composed by a Jew, and the Old Testament was the chief source of its Oracles.

"All portions which, according to the accounts of the old authorities, stood in the Erythræan or Hebrew Sibyl, occur in our's; a proof that our inference is well-founded. We can go a step further. Virgil has in his fourth Eclogue the prophecy of the golden age, and ascribes it to the Cumæan Sibyl. This prophecy, which is founded on Isaiah xi, also stands in our Sibyl, v. 784-794, so that we may attribute to this Sibyl the name of Cumæan, though in this indeed there is a confusion, which however could easily arise, since, according to Varro, the Cumæan had also the names Amalthæa, Demophile, and Herophile."

The writer three times fixes his date by annexing the prophecies of the conversion of the heathen to the date

---

[7] p. xxxviii, ix.   [8] Lact. Inst. Div. i. 6.

of the 7th king, who should rule over Egypt, of Grecian race [1]. In the early years of that king or of his reign [2], it mentions the 1st expedition of Antiochus Epiphanes against Egypt, his overthrow of the kingdom, his return to Asia with great wealth [3]; but the writer knows nothing later of Antiochus, nothing of Maccabæan wars, nor of any attempts of Antiochus against his people or the temple. Contrariwise he foretells, in language taken from ancient prophecy, from Joel and Zechariah, the fruitless seige, not by one but by many kings, against Jerusalem and the temple, their utter overthrow by the direct interposition of God; and the entire peace of the sons of God, in cities and in the country, God placing around them, as it were, a wall of fire. On this was to follow the conversion of the heathen [5].

The date then of the writer cannot be later than about B.C. 170, and before the commencement of the persecution by Antiochus.

Yet at this date he quotes the prophecy of the ten horns and the horn which should spring up at their side [6];

Ἐκ δέκα δὴ κεράτων παρὰ δὴ φυτὸν ἄλλο φυτεύσει

—καὶ τότε δὴ παραφυόμενον κέρας ἄρξει.

On the other hand, it is even remarkable that, in regard to the Messiah, employing, as he does, prophecies of Isaiah and Zechariah, he scarcely alludes to those of Daniel. It may be, that in the words, "[7] Then from sun-

---

[1] iii. 192, 3. 318. 608-10. ed. Friedl.   [2] Βασιλεὺς νέος, 608.   [3] 611-15.
[4] iii. 663-709.   [5] Ib. 710-731.   [6] Sib. iii. 397. 400.
[7] Ib. 652-5. Καὶ τότ' ἀπ' ἠελίοιο θεὸς πέμψει βασιλῆα

Ὅς πᾶσαν γαῖαν παύσει πολέμοιο κακοῖο,

Οὓς μὲν ἄρα κτείνας, οἷς δ' ὅρκια πιστὰ τελέσσας.   Lengerke, after Voss, understands ἀπ' ἠελίοιο to mean, that the Messiah was to come from the sun, i. e. from heaven. (p. 337, comp. p. 334.)   This would have been expressed by ἀπ' οὐρανόθεν. ἀπ' ἠελίοιο, "from the sun-rising," is the converse of Homer's, πρὸς 'Ηῶ τ' 'Ηέλιόν τε, "towards the morning and the sun," i. e. the East. The author of the 2nd Sibylline book, (a Christian heretic) unites the language. of Daniel with that of the N. T., but does not use this expression:
"But there shall come in a cloud to the Immortal, Immortal Himself,
Christ in glory, with the excellent angels,
And He shall sit on the right on a lofty throne, judging
The life and ways of men, holy and unholy." ii. 242-5.

rising God shall send a king, who shall stay all the earth from evil war, slaying some, to others fulfilling faithful oaths," he may allude to those words in ch. ix, *He shall confirm the covenant with many in one week.* But his omission, for the most part, of the prophecies of Daniel as to the Messiah, is a striking answer to those who say that the prophecies of Daniel were forged for those times. The Sibylline writer was a fanatic; a modern school would class Daniel with him; and yet, on this subject of the common hopes of the Jews, the Coming of the Messiah, he found nothing in Daniel to use for *his* hopes.

The first of the modern assailants of the book of Daniel, pointed out the correspondence of the ten horns and the other collateral horn with the prophecy of Daniel, and also the early date of the Sibyl, and had no other solution than that both "[8]the Daniel of Palestine and the Egyptian author of the Sibylline book drew from an earlier and common source," and that, "yet earlier, it was not uncommon to represent Alexander and the kingdoms formed after his death under the image of an animal with ten horns," whereas, in the time of Antiochus, there had not been ten kings, and there never were ten kingdoms. "Who could believe it?" said a later opponent [9],

[8] Bleek l. c.

[9] Hilgenfeld, D. Judische Apocalyptik, p. 69. note. Hilgenfeld's expedient was to bring the Sibylline book down to 137, B.C. This was to be effected by interpreting of Antiochus Epiphanes, what must relate to Alexander, and then explaining the sequel, of times after Epiphanes. The words are, " But Macedon shall bring forth heavy woe for Asia, And greatest grief of Europe shall shoot forth From bastards of the race of the Cronidæ and the race of slaves. She [Macedon] shall o'ercome Babylon too, the strong city ; And, of the whole earth which the sun surveys Entitled lady, she shall perish by an evil fate, Having no law for the late, much-bewailed descendants. Once too shall there come unexpectedly to the happy soil of Asia, A man clad with purple robe on his shoulders, Fierce, unjust, fiery, lightning-born ; But all Asia shall bear the yoke, and the bedewed earth shall drink much slaughter. But thus too shall Ades take charge of every one in utter destruction. Whose race he willeth utterly to destroy, From their race shall his race utterly perish, Giving forth one sucker ; which too the destroyer shall cut off From ten horns ; but shall plant another plant close by. He shall cut off the warrior father of the purple race, And himself by sons, to whom war becomes an auspicious, likeminded [friend], Shall perish, and then shall the horn, planted hard by, rule." (iii. 381-400.) There

who thought that he had escaped the difficulty in another way.   " Credulity of the incredulous ! "

is no question, but the fierce conqueror of all Asia and Babylon is Alexander; the term "bastard" "is probably an allusion to Zech. ix. 6, and to his claim to descent from Jupiter, (Sib. v. 6, 7.) as it is explained distinctly Sib. ix. [xi] 195-8. The "one sucker" is perhaps Alexander's son, who was murdered. But, in secular history, it is in vain to look for minute meaning in such a writer as the author of the 3rd Sibylline. He has one great contrast, Asia and Europe, of which Asia, in the empire of the Messiah, was to requite to Europe the ills it had received. The description does not suit Epiphanes. He came, not as a conqueror, but redeemed from being a hostage at Rome by his brother, whose throne he occupied peacefully, and, in the absence of his nephew Demetrius at Rome, lawfully; he sought to extirpate no race, neither the Ptolemies nor that of Demetrius. But with the groundwork the whole theory is gone. The wars with the Parthians, in which Demetrius II. lost his liberty, and his brother Antiochus Sidetes his life, were to be the explanation of " war becoming to the sons their favourer and friend."(Zündel, Daniel, p. 143.) Zündel (although he inadvertently accepted the explanation of Hilgenfeld) has pointed out the following additional evidence that the 3rd Sibylline was not later than B.C. 160. 1) The passage about the tower of Babel is cited as the Sibyl's by Alexander Polyhistor. (Eus. Chron. Arm. i. 38.)   But he had it from Eupolemus. (Eus. Præp. Evang. iv. 17.)   But " the work of Eupolemus cannot be later than 160." (Kuhlmey, Diss. Inaug.)   But connected with this, is a prophecy of empires, not world-empires like Daniel's, but successive powers, so as to be an imitation of his prophecy. " He raised up the kingdom of Egypt, then that of the Persians, Medes, Egyptians, and Babylon of Assyria; then of the Macedonians, again of Egypt, then of Rome." iii. 159-161.   2) That kingdom was also in its beginning. " But thereon will be the rule of another kingdom, Hoary and many-headed, [the senate] and from the western sea, Which shall rule much land, and shake many, And cause fear to all kings afterward, And amass much gold and silver from many cities....In those days, there shall be great affliction among men, and shall confuse all, And cut all to pieces and fill all with ill, By disgraceful avarice, ill-gained wealth, In many countries, and Macedonia most. Until the 7th reign, which a king of Egypt shall reign who shall be of the race of the Greeks." (iii. 175-193.)   This suits the state of Macedonia, before its subdual; not after it had become a Roman Province, 168, B.C. 3) Tribute from Asia was but recent. "Know, then, evil race of Egypt, that thou art near destruction, And then will the past year have been best for the Alexandrians, When Rome received the tribute-bearers of Asia." (348-50.) But then the writer threatens requital to Rome. The tribute from Asia began with the enormous sum, put upon Antiochus the Great, after the battle of Magnesia, 190, B.C.; but the threat could not have been after the battle of Pydna, 168, B.C.   The utmost ambition even of Mithridates was to recover Asia. The most decisive proof of the age of the 3rd Sibylline book seems to me that given in the text p. 364. the rest harmonise with it. Philometor too, though probably about 10 at his accession, B.C. 181, could hardly have been accounted βασιλεὺς νέος, 21 years afterwards, B.C. 160.

vi. The extreme accuracy of the first Book of Maccabees
is acknowledged on all hands.   It is *the* history of the Jews
in that complicated period, wherein they were brought
into varied relations with contending powers.   The writer gives us an outline of the persecution of Epiphanes,
as connected with his expeditions against Egypt[1], and
then, in order of years, the struggles of the Maccabees,
from the first bold act of Mattathias to the death of the
last of his sons, Simon.   In this period of 34 years, he
gives 20 dates[2], names of various persons who claimed
the throne of Syria, sometimes outlines of their end.
His facts are in accordance with other history, wherever
they come in contact ; he inserts written documents [3], and

---

[1] 1 Macc. i. 16, 20, 29, 54. with three important dates, that of his accession,
A. S. 137 ; an expedition to Egypt, on the return from which he spoiled Jeru-
salem, A.S. 143 ; the beginning of his persecution of the Jews, A.S. 145 ;
Caslen 15.

[2] ii. 70, A.S. 146, death of Mattathias ; iii. 37, A.S. 147, Antiochus' expedition to the East ; iv. 28, expedition of Lysias, "the next year ;" iv. 52, A.S.
148, cleansing of the temple by Judas ; vi. 16, A.S. 149. death of Epiphanes ;
vi. 20, A.S. 150, Judas' ill success against Lysias, and relief by rivalry of Philip, returning from Persia ; vii. 1. A.S. 151, Demetrius' escape from Rome,
murder of Lysias and Eupator by army ; Ib. 43, Adar 13, defeat and death of
Nicanor ; ix. 3, A.S. 152, expedition of Bacchides, in which Judas was slain ;
Ib. 57. rest for two years after the death of Alcimus ; x. 1, A.S. 160, war between Alexander (Balas,) "son of Ant. Epiph.," and Demetrius ; in the 7th
month Alexander makes Jonathan high-priest ; x. 57, 8, A.S. 162, Ptolemy
marries his daughter Cleopatra to Alexander ; Ib. 67, A.S. 165, "Demetrius
son of Demetrius" [i. e. Nicator II.] comes from Crete ; xi. 19, A.S, 167, Demetrius is established on the throne by death of Ptolemy on 3rd day after he
had received the head of Balas ; xiii. 41, 42, A.S. 170, yoke of the heathen taken away by grant from Demetrius, 1st year of Simon ; Ib. 51, A.S. 171, Simon
recovers at last "the tower in Jerusalem ;" xiv. 1-3, A.S. 172, Demetrius taken prisoner by Arsaces ; Ib. 27, 35, A.S. 172, 3rd year of Simon, Simon chosen governor and high-priest by the people ; xv. 10, A.S. 174, Antiochus (Sidetes) "returns from the isles of the sea," (" Rhodes," App. Syr. 68.) to "the
land of his fathers ;" xvi. 14-16, A.S. 177, Simon and two of his sons assassinated treacherously.

[3] In the answer from the Roman senate, viii. 23-32, the Latin gleams
through in three places. (see Grimm ad loc.) The author gives a transcript
(ἀντίγραφα) Ib. 22, as also of the letter to the Lacedæmonians, (xii. 5.) and
their answer, (Ib. 19.) and of a second letter, (xiv. 20.) and of the decree in
favour of Simon. (xiv. 27.) Also he inserts a brief letter of Alexander Balas, (x.
18-20 ;) a letter of his rival Demetrius, (whose beginning is characteristic, ad-

there is nothing to contravene their genuineness; his dates and names even remarkably stand the test of coins [4]. Sharing singularly Judas Maccabæus' simple trustful estimate of the Roman character [5], relating the reports which reached Judæa just as they reached it [6], the writer is the more remarkable for the knowledge of customs and facts, which come within the scope of his relation [7].

dressed " to the people of the Jews," and ignoring Jonathan, who had just received the high-priesthood at the hand of Alexander, Ib. 20, 21.) Ib. 25-45; a letter of Demetrius in favour of the Jews, (xi. 32-36.) of which a copy was to be sent to Jonathan, (Ib. 37.) and another of Demetrius to Simon, xiii. 35-40; a letter of Antiochus Sidetes to Simon, xv. 1-9.

[4] e. g. in the remarkable title, x. 1, "Alexander, the son of Antiochus, Epiphanes," in which the writer attributes the title Epiphanes to Alexander Balas, whereas every one imagined that it must belong to Antiochus Epiphanes, whose son Balas claimed to be. But a coin of Balas (in Eckhel, Doctr. num. I. III. 228,) bears the title Epiphanes, agreeing with the text. Grimm ad loc.

[5] viii. 1-20. See ab. p. 160, 1. In speaking of "the terms of studied equality" in the treaty granted by the Romans, I did not observe the claim of superiority, unoffensively conveyed in the twice-repeated, "as it hath seemed good to Rome," noticed by Grimm ad loc. p. 129.

[6] e. g. as to the capture of Antiochus III. alive by the Romans, viii. 7; the cession of India and Media as well as Lydia, by Antiochus and the grant of them to Eumenes. Ib. 8. The writer expressly says, "Judas had *heard*," Ib. 1. "it was *told* him also." Ib. 2. He tells accurately an inaccurate report which altogether determined Judas. Grimm remarks on the mention of the Gauls, (Ib. 2.) that Livy says, "the victory over Antiochus was more glorious to the *Romans;* that over the Gauls gladder to the *allies*." xxxvii. 37. The prominence given to Spain, (viii. 3.) and the policy and perseveringness of the Romans, (Ib. 4.) are striking, as is the allusion to the Ætolian threat, to carry the war into Italy, (Ib. 9); the amazement so natural in one, hitherto in contact only with Eastern ambition, that no one sought to be Sovereign, (Ib. 14); and that hitherto they had been free from internal discord. Ib. 16.

[7] These are naturally most observable in the series of persons, kings and others, who come in contact with the Jews. The incidental traits are in keeping; e. g. the silence observed by Ptol. Philom., when Jonathan's enemies tried to irritate him against Jonathan, (xi. 5); the way in which Demetrius got rid of Lysias and Eupator, without ordering them to be murdered, (vii. 2-4); Epiphanes' extravagance in gifts and consequent needs, (iii. 30); that Lysias was of the blood royal, (Ib. 32); the mention of "*the* great pit" at Bezeth, (vii. 19); Nicanor's hatred, (vii. 26.) connected probably with his previous defeat, (iii. 38); minute statement of taxation, very oppressive yet not unexampled, (see Grimm) mentioned not in complaint, but in treaty promising its abolition, (x. 29, 30); complex manœuvring, beyond what appears on the surface, (Ib, 80, 1); the service rendered by the Jewish troops sent by Jonathan

He also tells simply the retreats, defeats, flight, diminution, increase, of the Maccabee armies[5]; how their chiefs,

to Demetrius, (xi. 44-51) ; hindrance of relief of besieged in the tower at Jerusalem by deep fall of snow, (xiii. 22 ; deep snow is mentioned else, once only in Holy Scripture ; 2 Sam. xxiii. 20.) the decree of the Romans on receiving the shield from Simon, (xv. 20.) that all "pestilent fellows" should be given' up to Simon, who had fled to other kings and countries, (Ib. 21.) Grimm quotes the remark of Josephus (B. J. i. 24. 2.) on a similar grant to Herod ; "To no other king did Cæsar give such honor, that he should recover one who had fled from him even from a city not appertaining to him." Probably the grant was made the more readily to Jews, the offences being religious, which Romans did not care about, not civil. The names of kings and countries, to which these letters were sent from Rome, are remarkable, in that no one, without accurate information, would have selected all the names of kings, (e. g. Arsaces ;) and that the names of countries are put down without reference to relative situation ; yet even Sampsames, which was an enigma in old times, (the Vulg. has Lampsacus,) is now recognised to be Samsum, a town, "held in considerable respect," in the gulf of S. (Ker Porter, Trav. ii. 690.) between Sinope and Trebizond, mentioned by Abulfeda, (I. D. Mich. ad loc.) The Epistle to the king of Syria was addressed to Demetrius, (xv. 22.) who was king when it was despatched, but, when it arrived, was a prisoner in Parthia.

Of customs, may be named ; slave-merchants attending a conquering army, (iii. 41); intoxicating drink given to, and even set before, elephants to stimulate them, (vi. 34) ; their "Indian," (Ib. 37) ; the "clasp of gold," as a token of royal favour, (x. 89. xi. 58); that there were different classes of "the friends of the king," (x. 65) ; the office of στρατηγός in Syrian rule, (Ib.); "leave to drink in gold," xi. 58.

[5] Judas, in the second battle at Bethoron, had "a small company,"(iii. 16) ; then 3000, but ill-armed, (iv. 6); after the victory over Gorgias, he had 10,000, (iv. 29) ; after the retreat of Lysias, he and his brother had 11,000, besides a reserve, (v. 17-21.) which must have been considerable, since its commander, fighting against orders, lost in one battle 2000 men. (Ib. 60.) Against Lysias with his larger army he is unsuccessful ; probably by a bold charge, he destroys 600 men, (vi. 42) ; his brother sacrifices himself in vain, (Ib. 43-6) ; his army retreats. (Ib. 47.) After the intrigues of Alcimus, he had only 3000 men, (vii. 40.) with which he defeated Nicanor, probably through his own personal prowess, since Nicanor's death determined the battle. (Ib. 43, 4.) He has again only 3000 against Bacchides, of whom all but 800 fled in the battle in which he fell. (ix. 5-6, 18.) After this Jonathan had but a company, whom his opponents thought to take in one night, (ix. 58.) who were besieged in a city "in the wilderness" (of Tekoa.) Ib. 62. He does not appear at the head of an army, until Demetrius, (over against Alexander Balas, x. 4, 5,) gave him authority to gather an host, and released the hostages. (Ib. 6-8.) After Alexander had made him Meridarch, (Ib. 65.) he could select 10,000 men from Jerusalem, besides those under Simon. (x. 74.) In a battle with an army of Demetrius, on a surprise, almost all his men flee, but return. (xi. 72, 3.) "Horsemen" appear in the Jewish armies for the first time under Simon, yet then too were

in their openhearted character, fell into snares [1] ; and how they were relieved by events in their assailants' history, rather than by their own power [2]. He writes in a simple unimpassioned way, leaving the history to make its own impression.

We have then good ground to think, that the few simple words of the dying Mattathias, the parent of the Maccabee heroes, are likely to have been faithfully preserved. They are a few energetic short discriminating sentences, such as such a man would speak, when transmitting to his sons the cause of the faith, around which he had rallied them. The direction, as to the part to be taken by his sons, is not what men have looked for, but is verified by thoughtful attention to the history [3]. Two

very inferior in numbers, (xvi. 4, 7.) He then "chooses out of the country 20,000 men of war." (Ib. 4.)

[1] xii. 46-48. xvi. 11-16. In the same simplicity, the Asidæans trusted Alcimus and Bacchides, because "he, a priest of the seed of Aaron, is come with this army and he will do us no wrong," (vii. 14.) and those in Jerusalem admitted Lysias and Eupator into mount Zion, whereon they destroyed its walls, vi. 61, 2.

[2] The peace with Antiochus Eupator was granted to them in their extremities, on advice of Lysias, on the ground of the return of Philip, the rival of Lysias, vi. 54-63. Bacchides left them in peace for 2 years, the king of Syria having all the strong places in the country, ix. 50-7. Demetrius, in dread of his rival Alexander Balas, authorised Jonathan to raise an army, (x. 6.) whereon Jonathan re-fortified Jerusalem, (Ib. 10, 11.) Grant of high-priesthood from Alexander, (Ib. 18-20) ; immunities offered to the Jews by Demetrius on the condition of their supplying him with 30,000 men, (Ib. 22-45) ; rejected, because Demetrius was not believed, whereas Alexander was, (Ib. 46, 7.) Favor shewn to Jonathan by Alexander when successful. (Ib. 59-66.) Further favor, when he had defeated Apollonius, general of Demetrius II. (Ib. 88, 9.) After Alexander's death (xi. 17.) good terms given by Demetrius, (Ib. 23-37.) but troops asked for and sent. (Ib. 42-44.) After his breach of promise, (Ib. 53.) Jonathan accepts favours from Antiochus son of Balas and Tryphon, (Ib. 57-60.) renews the alliance with Rome, (xii. 3.) On Tryphon's treacherous murder of Jonathan, (Ib. 42-48. xiii. 23.) and of Antiochus, (xiii. 31.) Simon sought and obtained recognition by Demetrius, (Ib. 34-40.) renewed treaties with Rome, (xiv. 16-19.) with present. (Ib. 24.) Terms renewed by Antiochus Sidetes, when trying to regain his father's kingdom, (xv. 1-9.) broken, when successful. (Ib. 27.) Letters from Rome to different kings and countries in favor of the Jews, in acknowledgment of their present. (Ib. 15-24.) The book closes with the murder of Simon by his son-in-law shortly afterwards.

[3] Mattathias designates Simon as "a man of counsel," and bids them "give

points have been observed in that speech, as bearing on
the book of Daniel.   1) His mention of Daniel's companions and of Daniel in the same simple way, in which he
had named other Scripture-examples before them, Abraham, Joseph, Phinehas, Joshua, Caleb, David, Elias [4];
and that, in the order in which their deliverances are related in the book, Daniel's companions being named before himself.   Their histories too are touched on in a single word, as recorded in Daniel.   "[5] Ananias, Asarias,
and Misael, *by believing* were saved out of the flame.
[6] Daniel, *for his innocency,* was delivered from the mouth
of lions."   2) His acknowledgement that a time of destruction was come [7], such as Daniel had foretold; and
his absolute certainty as to the issue, such as the knowledge of the prophecies of Daniel would justify.

"The words of dying men are not written down,"
they say.   True! but the glowing words of faith of such
a father as Mattathias are written in the table of the
heart, and live there in the breasts of sons, and, if need
were, of sons' sons.

ear to him, he shall be a father to you," whereas Judas he describes as " mighty
and strong from his youth ; let him be your captain." (1 Macc. ii. 65, 6.) Grimm
criticises this, as a mere mistake of the relater, since Simon too had the sole
command, *after* the deaths of Judas and Jonathan, and Judas might have
" shewn counsel, *had* he lived."   But the characteristic of Judas, which fitted
him to be captain *then* with their handful of men, was the personal lion-heart-
ed strength and courage, by which he made those sudden assaults which threw
superior numbers into confusion, (1 Macc. iii. 11, 23. iv. 3, 4. v. 28, 33. ix. 14,
15.) in one of which assaults, surrounded by superior numbers, he fell. (ix. 16,
18.)   Simon was associated in a subordinated command by Judas, (1 Macc. v.
17-23.) and afterwards was joined with Jonathan, (Ib. ix. 33.) yet still as subordinate, (Ib. 65. xi. 59, 64. xii. 33, 38.) the authority remaining with Jonathan. (Ib. x—xii.)   Not until all his brethren were dead, did he have the
chief command.   [4] ii. 52-60.

  [5] Ib. 59. comp. Dan. iii. 17, 18, 28.   [6] Ib. 60. comp. Dan. vi. 22.

  [7] On the one side, the strong word ἰστηρίχθη is used ii. 49. (νῦν ἰστηρίχθη
ὑπερηφανία καὶ ἰλεγμὸς καὶ καιρὸς καταστροφῆς καὶ ὀργὴ θυμοῦ ;) on the other,
Mattathias bids them confidently, not to fear " the words of a sinful man."
(ἀνδρὸς ἁμαρτωλοῦ.) Ib. 62.   This is independent of the question whether, in
the καιρὸς καταστροφῆς, there be any reference to the καιρὸς συντελείας in Dan.
viii. 19. xi. 35.   The word " sinner " is not applied to the heathen as such, (as
Grimm says, on i. 34,) but to some special antagonism to God and His laws.

But the date of the book itself, embodying this mention of the two miraculous deliverances in Daniel, as well as that of the "[1] abomination of desolation," in those same Greek words, by which the LXX had translated those of Daniel, was, probably, early in the life of John Hyrcanus. For the first book of Maccabees breaks off with the account of the assassination of Simon, and the carrying of the tidings to his son John.   The rest of the history of John was contained "[2] in the chronicles of his priesthood, from the time he was made high priest after his father." The writer's ground for breaking off was, he says, that what remained had been written already.   But the fact of the history of Hyrcanus having been written would not have shewn this, had Hyrcanus been dead and had there been a period beyond him.   This history of their former war had also a special history, before the war of freedom was over.   The expression also, "[2] the rest of the acts, &c. they are written in the chronicles of," naturally signifies that they were written in chronicles kept contemporaneously year by year.   He refers, as do the older writers whose language he adopts[3], to chronicles officially kept, not to any book publicly circulated[4].   The writer only names the time when they began, to signify that they left no gap from the time when he left off.   Nor do the facts, which he says were contained in those chronicles, necessarily go down far in the life of Hyrcanus.   "[2] The rebuilding of the walls of Jerusalem" was naturally his first act on throwing off the Syrian yoke, when he heard

---

[1] $\beta\delta\epsilon\lambda\nu\gamma\mu\alpha$ $\dot{\epsilon}\rho\eta\mu\dot{\omega}\sigma\epsilon\omega s$, i. 54, from Dan. ix. 27. xi. 31.   [2] I Macc. end.
[3] 1 Kgs. [3 Kgs. LXX.] xiv. 19, 29, &c.   [4] Grimm rests his argument solely on the supposed circulation.   He says, "Our writer refers to these annals, as to a book *in extensive circulation*, accessible to his readers.   But it cannot be well supposed, that it came *into public use* before it was completed at the death of John Hyrcanus." p. xxiv. But it is one thing that writings should be "accessible;" quite another, that they should be "in circulation."   As it is quite certain that those other chronicles of the Kings of Judah and Israel were *not* in circulation, so, doubtless, this phrase, adopted from the old books, meant what it meant before, that they were state-documents, accessible but *not* in circulation.   Those documents, if kept annually, were *accessible*, in any year of the reign of Hyrcanus, down to that period.

of the death of Antiochus Sidetes[5], B.C. 127[6]. The wars were ended soon after, and a long peace was secured by the Syrian civil wars[7]. The main wars were over then, B.C. 125, and all which the writer of the 1st book of Maccabees speaks of, as contained in the chronicles of Hyrcanus, falls in that period. Probably then it was written about B.C. 125. Soon after, Samaria was destroyed, and the last ashes of war extinguished, B.C. 109. Any how a very accurate and simple writer, who lived before the death of Hyrcanus, B.C. 105, writing of a period at most 60, probably only some 40, years before, having access also to written documents[8], relates that Mattathias, the father of those whose history he relates, on his deathbed encouraged his sons with histories taken from the book of Daniel together with other canonical Scriptures. And this, three years before the time, when, on the rationalist hypothesis, the book is to have been written. He himself quotes the book of Daniel, as bearing on those times.

But, beyond the direct citations, the whole history of the Maccabees, as recorded in that book, is inconsistent with men's invention of a Pseudo-Daniel in the time of the Maccabees; while the absence of any expectation or

---

[5] The wars, in which he subdued Samaria and incorporated Edom, followed immediately after the death of Antiochus, and were probably not long protracted; for "most of the cities were void of fighting-men." Medaba alone resisted for six months. The temple of Samaria was destroyed, some "200 years after" it had been built by permission of Alexander, B.C. 332. (Jos. Ant. xiii. 9. 1.) Soon after, was the Roman edict which confirmed Hyrcanus. (Ib. § 2.) After a long interval of peace, Samaria was destroyed, one of the generals of Antiochus Cyzicenus perished, the other sold to Hyrcanus what remained in the hands of Syria. (Ib. xiii. 10. 1-3.)

[6] See Clinton, F. Hell. T. iii. p. 335.　　[7] First, between Antiochus Grypus and Alexander Zebina; then, between Antiochus Grypus and Cyzicenus. Josephus says; "After the death of Antiochus (Sidetes,) Hyrcanus revolted from the Macedonians, and neither as subject, nor as friend, did he yield them anything. But his affairs were advancing greatly, and were at their height, in the times of Alexander Zebina and especially of those two brothers. For their war with each other gave Hyrcanus leisure, &c."

[8] The identity of the formula used at the death of Judas (ix. 22.) with that as to Hyrcanus (xvi. 23.) and those in the books of Kings, leaves me no doubt that the writer meant, that the other acts of Judas and his wars, &c. were "not written" in the document from which he took the rest.

looking for the Messiah *then*, falls in, as I said[1], with the natural exposition of the prophecy of the 70 weeks.   The Pseudo-Daniel, men say, wrote to "[2]encourage his countrymen in their great struggle against Antiochus."   Then, we should have the phænomenon of a contemporary, writing to inspire his countrymen with the belief that their struggles would be ended by the coming of the Great Deliverer, and a minute, natural, accurate, history of 34 years of those struggles, written in all the simplicity of trust in God, that He, Who had delivered their forefathers, would, in His ordinary Providence, give them the victory, but without the slightest thought of any unusual intervention[3].   There is not one hope of a future temporal deliverance, but a calm waiting in religious matters for the time, when a "[4]Prophet should arise."   "We miss," says a writer[5], candid on the whole but unbelieving, "we miss something essential in those speeches of the book. For although no tradition had been preserved to us, we must have pre-supposed, as necessarily involved in the religious mind[6] [of the people,] that the hopes of the Messiah should scarcely ever have kindled up clearer and more glowing than in that extreme trouble under Antiochus Epiphanes, and that those hopes would have been the mightiest impulse to animate to the most dauntless, boldest, struggle, and the most joyous endurance."   Yet the history is too vivid, too graphic, not to be true to the life. It is consistent with itself.   The actors in it look to God's ordinary Providence, that He will give to the few the victory over the many, on the whole; they are not dejected by defeat; they look around and avail themselves ably of human help; they act as religious men, with the belief that God willed to preserve His people, looking for no extraordinary interposition, but with what we should call good practical wisdom.   They expect a prophet, but

---

[1] Lect. iv. p. 228-30.   [2] Dr. Williams, Ess. and Rev. p. 76.
[3] iii. 18-22. 43, 4. 52, 3, 59, 60. iv. 10, 11. 24, 5. 30-3. v. 32, 3. vii. 37, 8. 41, 2. ix. 46.   [4] See ab. p. 228.   [5] Grimm, Kurzgef. Hdb. z. d. Apokr. T. iii. p. xix.   [6] lit." a religious-psychological necessity."

hereafter. The book of Daniel, according to the authorship and object imputed by these men, would be at variance with all this; and all this, with the imputed purpose of the book of Daniel. The Pseudo-Daniel is to have
written a series of prophecies, bearing upon the times of
Antiochus; he is to have ascribed them to an ancient prophet, and to have stated that they were to be kept concealed until his own time: those prophecies are to have
been produced at the time of the Maccabees, in order to
awaken the expectation of a supernatural deliverer, who
should give them the victory, and establish a temporal
"kingdom of the saints," i. e. of the Jews. The prophecies, framed, as is alleged, for this end, are to have been
received largely and at once, and are to have been placed
unhesitatingly at once among their sacred scriptures;
they are to have been referred to thenceforth as prophetic truth, and yet there is not one trace of their having
the slightest influence on the minds of the people, in in-
spiring those hopes, which they are to have been forged
to create. The history of the Maccabees, as the authentic history of those times, contradicts the unbelieving
theories as to Daniel.

The first book of Maccabees was, I think, probably
written in Hebrew[7]. Had the Greek been the original,

---

[7] S. Jerome doubtless means to say that he had seen the original Hebrew of
the first book of Maccabees. "Maccabæorum primum librum hebraicum reperi;
secundus græcus est, quod ex ipsa quoque phrasi probari potest." (Prol. gal.)
For the fact, that the language itself of the 2nd book shewed that it was Greek,
would have had no bearing on the former statement, unless he had meant that
the first was originally Hebrew. Origen's statement that they had a Hebrew
title implies the same. "External to these [the canonical books] are the Maccabees which are entitled Sarbēth Sarbane el." (in Eus. H. E. vi. 25.) For
they would not have been known to the Greek-speaking Church by a Hebrew
title, unless such had been the original title. Hebraisms, of course, in themselves prove nothing; for one, who thinks in his own language and writes in
another, is, in fact, translating, although mentally. One e. g. who had the
word לפני in his mind, might just as well use ἐναντίον for it, instead of ἐνώπιον,
as one who had it before his eyes; and so on. But mistakes in translating
shew that the writer and translator were different. The "two and thirty
strong men" upon each elephant seem likely to be for "two or three;" (שלש
שנים for שנים שלש. (vi. 37.) The difficult words, "At Saramel," (xiv. 28.)

the quotation of the LXX[1] would have been by the original writer, about 125-109; and in that case, the book of Maccabees would have involved an earlier date of the book of Daniel, on the ground of the following argument also. If the original was Hebrew, it is only the Greek translator of the Maccabees, who has adopted the translation of the LXX for the term in Daniel.

vii. It is admitted that a considerable interval elapsed between the writing of the book of Daniel and its translation; and that, on the ground both of the additions to Daniel, contained in the LXX and admitted to be contemporary with it; (viz. the prayer and song of the three children, the history of Susanna, and that of the destruction of Bel and the Dragon,) and also of the character of the translation itself. 1) The history of Susanna was confessedly written in Greek[2]. In regard to the other additions there are no data. But, since they were not in the Hebrew, and since the history of Bel and the Dragon is evidently founded *in part* on the history of Daniel in the Hebrew Canon, some interval must have elapsed between the writing of the book of Daniel, and the gathering of these additions to it.

But 2) the LXX translation of the book itself is, even in important places, so remarkable a modification of it, that a long interval must have elapsed between the time when it was written and when it was so translated. The Greek itself is, in many parts, purer and more elegant than that of any other of the LXX translations.

seem to be most easily explained by a mistake of וֹ for בֹ, רֹאשׁ עַם אֵל, so that it should run, " Simon the high priest and prince of the people of God," (Wernsdorf's conjecture.) " Elam " is called a " city," (vi. 1.) perhaps as a faulty translation of מְדִינָה, " city " or " country ;" but perhaps also in that the name of the country is given to the capital, as Arabic writers call Memphis or Cairo, " Misr," originally Egypt." (Grimm, p. 91.) Still most of the cases alleged, although possible, are not decisive. Thus the words, " be ye instead of me and my brother," (xvi. 3.) probably allude to the last brother with whom he was so long associated, (Jonathan ;) so that there is no reason to think that it is a mistake of אַחַי for אָחִי. Yet there are other minute expressions, which seemed to me, on the whole, indicative of a translation. [1] See ab. p. 372. n. 1.

[2] No other explanation can be given of the verbal allusions, 54, 5. 58, 9.

The translator avoided Hebraisms, which Theodotion subsequently restored, and, in some places, substituted a classical Greek word. But in the same mind of recommending it and his people to the readers, he manifoldly glossed the text. In the historical portion, he inserted statements, more or less full, which he thought would make the narrative easier, or would explain it, or would increase its effect, or meet some lesser difficulties. On the other hand, he omitted or changed statements, which he thought would be unacceptable to his reader, and modified some doctrines. He made both Nebuchadnezzar and Darius more religious and more thoroughly converted, than Daniel states them to have been. He explained, who, he believed, Darius was. The miraculous accounts place us in quite a different atmosphere from that in which we live in Daniel. The translator made large additions, condensed, transposed, repeated, as he thought would be acceptable. In some cases, his thoughts must have turned on the times in which he lived ; as, when he made the insanity of Nebuchadnezzar the punishment for his sacrilege against the house of God, and placed the dream, which predicted it a year before, in his 18th year, the year of the capture of Jerusalem, and of the destruction of the temple [3].

The translation of the later historical prophecy, (ch. xi.) is remarkable in another way. The prediction is to have been, (Porphyry and his school say,) history in the form of prophecy, because it is so exact. Of all this historical prophecy, the translator understood well one part, just that which a Jew, living at the time at Alexandria, would know, or what happened in Egypt itself. He paraphrases rightly the words, "[4]there shall come ships of chittim," by, "And the Romans shall come and shall expel him, and shall rebuke him strongly," in allusion to the peremptory way in which Popilius cut short the subterfuges of Epiphanes. But in the whole previous pro-

---

[3] All this will be seen most vividly by an actual comparison of the LXX with the text, for which see Note E.   [4] Dan. xi. 30.

phecy, from the successors of Cyrus to Antiochus Epiphanes, at every stage, in every step of every stage, he shews himself to be ignorant of the history. He trusts himself with it as little as he can. A literal translation would, of course, have guided him aright, wherever there was no uncertainty of construction; but, on whatever ground, down to the time of Antiochus Epiphanes, he almost always distorts the facts, because he would not trust himself with a literal translation. Porphyry and his school have maintained that it would have been an easy thing, in the time of Epiphanes, to write the prophecies of Daniel, on the ground that *they* could understand them by aid of the histories at their command[1]. The case was very different, when those histories were not written[2]. Tradition, or ordinary learning, did not suffice. The remarkable failure of a Jew at the time of Epiphanes, even with the prophecy of Daniel before him, well-read as he was in Greek, (as the character of his Greek, here and there, shews,) is an argument, which must strike any mind, which wills not to be blind. It is even strange that the translator of Daniel could have failed so uniformly. The exception as to Popilius, in which he even added, (as his way was,) what was not in Daniel, marks his own date. There was nothing to fix this one fact in the memory of a later generation, more than so many which he distorted for want of any traditional or historical knowledge of the past. In this case, he added real facts to those foretold by Daniel, as, in other cases, he perverted the facts which lay before his eyes in the prophet. Yet all this was not

[1] " To understand the latter part of Daniel, manifold Greek history is necessary; viz. Callinicus Sutorius [3rd cent. A.D.] Diodorus, Hieronymus, [3rd cent. B.C.] Polybius, Posidonius, Claudius, (about 100, B.C. Smith, Biogr. Dict. v. Quadrigarius) Theon, and Andronicus Alipius, (about 112-51, B.C. Smith) whom Porphyry too says that he followed; Josephus also and those whom Josephus puts down, and especially our Livy, and Pomponius Trogus and Justin, who relate the whole history of the last vision, and after Alexander down to Cæsar Augustus describe the wars of Syria and Egypt, i. e. of Seleucus, Antiochus, and the Ptolemies." S. Jerome, Præf. to Daniel.

[2] Polybius did not apparently begin his history until after 145, B.C. See Smith, Dict. iii. 144.

for want of knowledge of the original language, which he understood well, except perhaps, in places, some antiquated words of the prophet's date.

In the prophecy of the 70 weeks, the translator again repeatedly falsifies the time, in order to make it fit in with that of Epiphanes. For the dates of the original, he twice substitutes seven, and seventy, and sixty two, making 139. This, according to the era of the Seleucidæ which the Jews used, comprised the second year of the reign of Epiphanes, soon after whose accession Onias was deposed, to which act this writer probably alluded in his unfaithful paraphrase, "chrism shall be removed." Apparently, he meant the first date of "seventy weeks" to be literal weeks, since he renders, as if Daniel himself were to see them; in his next numbers he supplied "years," capriciously effacing the word "weeks;" and then, at the end, under the "week," "weeks," means again literal "weeks of days." Thus he makes the later part of the prophecy a prophecy of the chequered but successful resistance to Antiochus, ending not in the destruction of the city and of the sanctuary, but in a second rebuilding of the city[3]. And this he does, altering

[3] This will be seen best by a translation of the whole. (In order to represent the original more exactly, I have not supplied the article where it is omitted.) " Seventy weeks are determined upon thy people and upon the city of Sion ; that the sin be accomplished and the iniquities become rare, and to wipe away the iniquities and the vision be thoroughly understood, and everlasting righteousness be given, and the visions and a prophet be consummated, and to gladden a holy of holies. And thou shalt be gladdened, and shalt find commands that answer be made, and shalt build Jerusalem, a city to the Lord. And after seven and seventy and sixty two, chrism shall be removed and shall not be ; and a kingdom of gentiles shall corrupt the city and the holy place with the anointed ; and the consummation thereof shall come with anger, and unto time of consummation it shall be warred upon by war. And the covenant shall have might towards many, and it shall return and shall be built again in length and breadth, and at consummation of times ; and after seventy and seven times and in sixty two years, unto time of consummation of war, and the desolation shall be taken away, through the prevailing of the covenant for many weeks, and at the end of the week the sacrifice and the drink-offering shall be taken away, and on the temple shall be an abomination of the desolations unto end, and end shall be given upon the desolation."

No theory of different readings will explain these variations. The translator seems to have taken like words suggested by the text, ad libitum, yet with-

and transposing the words of the text as suited his purpose, repeating of the later time what belonged to the earlier, so that it has even been thought that we had a confusion of different translations [1]. He did, in effect, make his translation, what a modern school has accused the writer of making the book, a direct but fraudulent encouragement in the Maccabee struggle. But he effected it by falsifying the text of the Prophet; whence the Church rejected his translation [2] alone out of the LXX. People out any possibility of uniting them in a Hebrew construction. The first deviation no change could account for. He gives apparently a double translation of וְחָתוֹם חָזוֹן, reading the 2nd time, וְלַהֲתֵם "and to bring to an end a vision;" "gladden," he obtains by substituting לְשַׂמֵחַ for לִמְשֹׁחַ. It is mere guess-work, how he came to add "thou shalt be gladdened," (one conjecture is as good as another; it may be a mere repetition.) Then, in מִן־מֹצָא דָבָר לְהָשִׁיב וְלִבְנוֹת, there are materials for his words, "find," "command," "answer," "build," but not so that any Hebrew could put them together: for עַד he has עִיר, "city," and for "Messias prince" he substitutes "Lord." Then he springs to v. 26, substitutes for the הַשָּׁבֻעִים the שָׁבֻעִים שִׁבְעָה of v. 25. and renders, as if it were שָׁבֻעִים. Then having got through, as best he could, to the first words of v. 27. "and he shall confirm a covenant with many," he goes back to the end of v. 25. which he had omitted, substituting however "consummation of times," for "strait of times." Then he repeats again the date at the beginning of v. 26. but passes over to the end of it, which had before suggested the words, "and unto time of consummation it shall be warred upon by war," and translates, "and unto time of consummation of war;" and out of שֹׁמֵמוֹת נֶחֱרֶצֶת, "decreed desolations," he gains his, "desolations shall be taken away;" (much as if we were to say that "decision" meant "cutting off," "ending:") then he inserts again the prevailing of the covenant, but, this time, "for many" (he adds) "weeks," supplying "weeks" from the שָׁבֻעַ following: חֵצִי "half" seems, by its sound, to have suggested קֵץ, "end," and then he gets tolerably to the end of the prophecy.

[1] Zündel, (p. 177-182.) who makes it an argument for the higher date of the original, in that there had been time for successive translations. To me it seems too continuous a whole, to be the result of chance combinations of different translations.

[2] "Except the LXX translators, who passed over all this, I know not why, the three other interpreted, 'colleague.' Whence, by *the judgment of the doctors of the Church*, their edition *was repudiated* in this volume, and Theodotion's is commonly read, which agrees both with the Hebrew and with the other translators." S. Jerome on Dan. iv. 5. In his Preface to his version, he expresses doubt how the LXX translation of Daniel came to be bad, but asserts, in the same way, that it was deliberately rejected for its defects. "The Churches do not read Daniel according to the LXX translators, using the version of Theodotion. And why this happened, I know not. Whether,

do not gloss the book of a contemporary.   It is not until a book has long had authority, and has had its place in the minds or souls of men, that men write glosses upon it.   They do so, because their text has authority.   Further, this proceeding of the LXX translator attests that the book, actually in existence and acknowledged, was not the encouragement which human policy wanted, to stimulate the people in their resistance.   The book of Daniel, as written, was an encouragement to persevere under trial; as falsified, it became a stimulus to religious, which ended in becoming a political, resistance.   It is remarkable that, in the prophecy of the 70 weeks, it effaces the doctrine of the Messiah, teaching people, as far as its influence went, to look for nothing beyond the present.

The opponents of the book of Daniel admit that a long interval must have elapsed between the writing and the translation[3].   But the translation bears marks of being of the time of Epiphanes.   There is then no room for such an interval, unless the book of Daniel was written, when, place it where men will, if they place it before Epiphanes, it contained prophecy of events utterly undiscernible by man.

viii. I will only add briefly that there is one more evidence to Daniel in these times, the book of Enoch.   A writer or writers of a portion of it had studied the book

because the language is Chaldee and in some peculiarities differs from our idiom, the LXX were unwilling to retain in the translation the same lineaments of language, or whether the book was published under their name by another, (I know not whom,) not adequately acquainted with Chaldee, or whether there was any other cause, I know not; this one thing I can affirm, that it differs much from the truth, and was, by a sound judgment, repudiated." Præf. in vers. Dan.   S. Justin and Tertullian used the LXX.   "Origen asserts in the 9th volume of his 'miscellanies,' (stromateis,) that from this place (iv. 5. Ch. 8. Eng.) in the prophet Daniel he comments not according to the LXX, who vary much from the Hebrew truth, but according to the edition of Theodotion." (S. Jer. on Dan. iv. 5.)

[3] Lengerke said, p. xxvi, " For its composition a space of from 50-60 years was fully sufficient."   De Wette at one time "maintained that the LXX translation of Daniel must, from its character, have been made a considerable time after the publication of Daniel."   Einl. p. 358. quoted by Häv. Einl. ii. p. 458.   In De Wette's last edition, this statement was removed.

of Daniel, so that both his language and thoughts re-appear in it, combined with those of other prophetic writings. It does not, like the Sibylline book, simply quote one or two remarkable predictions. Its writers were diligent students of the prophetic Scriptures, and had combined their teaching into a whole, partly right partly wrong, in the way of uninspired reflection. But the use of the prophet Daniel is the more remarkable, because it is the result of reflection upon his writings as part of a whole, and that whole, Holy Scripture. I will name only two chief subjects, the doctrine of the Messiah and of Angels.

1) The inculcation of a day of retribution is the chief object and moral of the book of Enoch. The chief doctrine then, as to the Messiah, selected in it from Daniel, is that of "the Son of Man, sitting" in His glory. With this title of " the Son of Man" is combined that of " the Chosen," from Isaiah; and "the Chosen" is even the most frequent name, although the two names alternate. The then future worship of all nations is spoken of, in language of the Psalms, and the gifts of His Humanity in that of Isaiah, and the then present revelation of Him by the prophets; still the central thought, which introduces the mention of Him, is judgment to come, as in Daniel[1].

[1] xlv. 3-5. "On that day will the Chosen sit on the throne of glory, and will make choice among their deeds and abodes innumerable, and their spirit will be strong within them when they see My Chosen, and those who have prayed to My holy and glorious Name. And on that Day will I let My Chosen dwell among them, and will transform the heaven and make it everlasting blessing and light. And I will transform the earth and make it a blessing, and will make my chosen dwell in it, &c." So the sequel of the passage already quoted as to the Son of Man (p. 84.) is, " because the Lord of hosts has *chosen* Him, and His lot before the Lord of spirits has excelled all through righteousness for ever. And this Son of Man, Whom thou hast seen, will arouse the kings and the mighty from their beds and the violent from their thrones, and will loose the bands of the violent, and break in pieces the teeth (Ps. lii. 8, &c.) of sinners. And He will drive kings from their thrones and their kingdoms, because they magnify Him not, nor praise Him, nor thankfully acknowledge Him by Whom their kingdom was given them. And He will repel the face of the violent, and shame shall fill them; darkness will be their habitation, and worms their bed; (Is. xiv. 11.) and they will have no hope to rise from their beds, because they magnify not the Name of the Lord of spirits, &c." xlvi. 3-6. "And in those days I saw the Ancient of days, as He sat upon the throne of

Reflection had taught the Jews of his day to believe iu

His glory, and *the books of the living were opened* before Him ; and His whole host, which is above in heaven and around Him, stood before Him." (xlvii. 3.) " And on that day I saw a well of righteousness inexhaustible ; round it were many wells of wisdom, and all thirsty drank out of them, and became full of wisdom, and had their dwellings with the Righteous and Holy and Chosen One. And at that hour was that Son of Man named before the Lord of spirits, and His Name before the Ancient of days.   He will be a staff to the righteous and to the holy, that they may stay themselves thereon and not fall ; and He will be the light of the people, [Is. xlix. 4.] and the hope of those who are troubled in heart.   All who dwell on the earth will fall down and worship before Him, (Ps. xxii. 27-29. lxxii. 9-11.) and will exalt and praise and celebrate the Name of the Lord of spirits.   And therefore was He chosen and hidden before Him, ere the world was created, and to eternity will He be before Him."   [" In that he says," observes D. "that *He* (not His Name) was hidden before God, before the creation of the world, and that to eternity He would be before God, it is clear even from the analogy of the second part of this declaration, that the hidden Being cannot be understood to be merely ideal, but must be understood as real." comp. also lxii. 7.   " For before was the Son of Man hidden, and the Highest has reserved Him for His Might, and has revealed Him, the Chosen."] " And the wisdom of the Lord of spirits has revealed (i. e. by prophecy) Him, the Holy and Righteous ; for He maintains the lot of the righteous, because they have hated this world of unrighteousness and all its works and ways : for in His days the kings of the earth, and the violent who possess the fortresses, are of downcast look, for the work of their hands ; for in the days of their fear and need they will not deliver their souls.   And I will give them into the hands of My chosen, as straw in fire and as lead in water ; so will they burn in presence of the righteous and sink in presence of the holy, and no more trace of them will be to be found.   And in the day of their distress there will be rest on the earth ; for they will fall before Him, and will not rise again ; and there will be no one to take them in his hands and lift them up ; for they have denied the Lord of spirits and His Anointed.   Praised be the Name of the Lord of spirits. For wisdom is poured out like water, and glory ceaseth not from eternity to eternity.   For He is mighty in all mysteries of righteousness ; and unrighteousness will pass away like a shadow, and have no stay ; for the Chosen hath stood up before the Lord of spirits, and His glory is from eternity to eternity, and His might from generation to generation.   In Him dwelleth the spirit of wisdom, and the spirit of Him Who giveth insight, and the spirit of teaching and of power, (Is. xi,) and the spirit of those who have fallen asleep in righteousness. And He will judge the secret things, (Eccl. xii. 14.) and no one will be able to bring an idle word before Him ; for He was chosen before the Lord of spirits according to His good pleasure." ch. xlviii. xlix.   " And in those days the earth will give back its deposit, and the kingdom of death will give back its deposit which it has received, and hell will give back what it owes.   And He will choose the righteous and holy among them, for the day is come that they should be delivered.   And the Chosen will sit on His throne in those days, and all mysteries of wisdom will stream from the thoughts of His mouth ; for the Lord

Him Who was to come, as the Son of God[1], eternally

of spirits has given it Him and glorified Him : and in those days the mountains will leap like rams, and the hills skip like lambs (Ps. cxiv. 4.) which are satisfied with milk ; and they will all be like angels in heaven. Their countenance will beam for joy, because in those days the Chosen has stood up, and the earth will rejoice, and the righteous will dwell in it and the chosen will go and walk in it." (ch. li.) "And he [the angel] said to me, All these things, which thou hast seen, serve the rule of His Anointed, that He may be powerful and mighty on the earth.—And those hills which thou hast seen of iron and of copper, and of silver and gold, all will melt before the Chosen, as wax before the fire, and as water which flows down (Mic. l. 4.) over those mountains, and will be weak before His feet. And in that day men will not be able to deliver themselves by gold or silver, nor to deliver themselves, nor flee away. All these things will disappear and be annihilated from the face of the earth, when the Chosen shall appear before the Lord of spirits." (lii. 4. 6. 7. 9.) " And after this, the Righteous and Chosen shall manifest the house of His congregation, which shall not be henceforth hindered, in the Name of the Lord of spirits." (liii. 6.) " The chosen will dwell with the Chosen One." (lxi. 4. add lxxi. 17.) "The Lord of spirits sat on the throne of His glory, and the spirit of righteousness was poured out upon Him, [the Chosen, See D. p. 196, 7.] and the speech of His mouth slew all sinners [from Is. xi. 4.] and unrighteous, and before His Presence they perish. (Ps. lxviii. 2.) And pain will seize them, when they see that Son of the woman sitting on the throne of His glory." [lxii. 2. 5.] " And the Lord of spirits will dwell above them, and with that Son of man will they dwell together and eat and lie down and rise up from eternity to eternity." (lxii. 14.) " And He sat down on the throne of His glory, and the sum of judgment was given over to Him, the Son of man, and He will remove and destroy sinners from the face of the earth, and those who have seduced the world—And thenceforth shall there be nothing transitory ; for He, the Son of the Man, hath appeared, and sitteth on the throne of His glory, and all evil shall disappear and pass away before Him ; but the word of that Son of the Man will avail before the Lord of spirits." (lxix. 27. 29.) "And after this, his [Enoch's] name [i. e. his person] was lifted up to that Son of man, to the Lord of spirits." (lxx. i.)

[1] "And in those days, saith the Lord, shall they call all the sons of the earth together, and bear witness to the wisdom thereof [of the books of Enoch ;] shew them to them, for ye are their guides and rewards over the whole earth. For I and My Son will unite ourselves with them for ever, and ever, in the ways of righteousness during their life." c. cv. Yet the Chosen is named as one who should praise the Lord of spirits. "And the whole army of heaven, and all holy ones above, and the army of God, the Cherubim and Seraphim and Ophannim, and all angels of power, and all angels of dominion, and the Chosen, and the other powers which are upon the firmament over the water, will call and will begin with one voice and praise and glorify and extol and magnify in the spirit of faith [or faithfulness,] and in the spirit of wisdom and patience, and in the spirit of compassion, and in the spirit of right and of peace, and in the spirit of goodness, and will all say with one voice, Praise to Him and praised be the Name of the Lord of spirits for ever and ever." lxi. 10, 11. This is, of course, not

præexisting with God[2], but also as the Son of Man Who shall come to be our Judge. His office for us on earth was, with this writer, subordinate. Having little thought of any but the deadliest sin, and thinking but poorly of repentance[3], he looked to the Rewarder, not to the Redeemer. Still, on this side, the book implies a long study of Daniel, in connection with other Scripture and as equally authoritative with it, utterly inconceivable, had the book of Daniel been written 164, B.C.

2) The doctrine of Angels varies in the book itself. Yet it implies, even in its errors, a meditative use of Holy Scripture. It has not much, which bears directly on Daniel, only the names of Michael and Gabriel, the office of Michael towards the Jewish people, and the title, "Watchers," applied to the holy Angels. The common truths as to the holy Angels are, in part, largely expanded, and that by aid of other Scripture; in part they are modified, and that untruly. The book of Enoch has some names of chief angels, which occur rarely even in later Jewish writings, or which do not even occur in them[4].

Christian language; for Jesus receives the worship of all the creation, and although the Manhood of Jesus is a worshipper of the Trinity, yet Jesus, being God and Man, could not be so spoken of; much less, together with creatures.

[2] See ch. xlviii. lxii. 7. lxx. 1. in p. 384. note.   [3] " In the day of trouble, evil will accumulate on sinners, and the righteous will prevail in the Name of the Lord of spirits: and He will let the rest see it, that they may repent and cease the works of their hands. They will have *no honour* before the Lord of spirits; but in His Name they will be delivered, and the Lord of spirits will have compassion upon them: for His compassion is great," 1. 2, 7.

[4] In ch. xl. there are " 4 forms on the four sides of the Lord of Hosts, different from " " the thousands of thousands and thousands of thousands," (taken from Dan. vii. 10. "there being in Æth. no one term for 10,000," Dillm. p. 20.) " which stood by." " The first voice praised the Lord of spirits from eternity to eternity. The second I heard praising the Elect, and the elect who are weighed before the Lord of spirits. The third praying for the dwellers on the earth, and beseeching in the Name of the Lord of spirits. The fourth I heard, keeping off Satans and not allowing them to come before the Lord of spirits to accuse the dwellers on the earth." The angel, who comes with Enoch, tells him their names. These are, " 1) the holy Michael, the pitying and long-suffering; 2) Rufael, set over all diseases and wounds of the sons of men; 3) the holy Gabriel, set over all powers; 4) Fanuel, set over the repentance and hopes of those who inherit eternal life. These are the 4 angels of God most High."

It supposes that there are angels, presiding over each of the ordinary changes in the physical world[1], thunder and lightning, hoar-frost, hail, snow, mist, dew, rain ; and of

(mentioned again liv. 6. lxxi. 8. 9. 13. in the same connection with the "thousands of thousands.") In ch. ix. "departed souls" "cry to the holy ones of heaven" to obtain vengeance against the giants (before the flood;) and four Angels, "Michael, Gabriel, Surian, and Urian," ("Suriel, Uriel," Dillm. p. 97.) present their cry. "The name Suriel occurs in this place only and in Berachoth, f. 51. 1." [the only place mentioned by Buxtorf, p. 1453.] Dillm. Ib. In the Greek, they are the four names received in the Church, Michael, Uriel, Raphael, and Gabriel; but probably the translation is more exact than the extract of G. Syncellus, who probably corrected it. In ch. x. for Urian is Arsyalalyur [compounded of חמשאל, "Sun of God," אליאור, "my God is light." D.] and for Surian is Rufael. In ch. xx. there are *six* "holy angels who watch ; "*Uriel*, the angel of thunder and earthquake ; *Rufael*, the angel of the spirits of men ; *Raguel*, (רעואל, "friend of God."] who exercises vengeance on the world and on the lights ; *Michael*, set over the best part of men, the people ; *Sarachael*, [סרכאל "president of God"] set over the spirits of the sons of men, whom the spirits seduce to sin ; *Gabriel*, set over the serpents and over Paradise and over the Cherubim." An angel *Zutel* or *Zutuel* or *Zuteel* (זוטאל D. p. 135.) is once mentioned, xxxii. 2. The *Ophannim* ("wheels") from Ezek. i. and x. are mentioned with the Cherubim and Seraphim, (as in Rosh Hashana, f. 24, 2. Buxt. p. 187.) and angels of power (ἐξουσίαι Col. i. 16. add Eph. i. 21.) and of dominions (κυριότητες ib.) lxi. 10. The Seraphim, Cherubim, Ophannim are mentioned as round the house of God. "These are they who sleep not and who guard the throne of His glory." lxxi. 7.

The Archangel, who is supposed to accompany him, is called "the angel of peace;" (lvi. 2. lx. 24.) whence probably the ἄγγελος εἰρήνης in S. Chrysostom's liturgy, of the guardian angel.

Perhaps it is in contrast with "the sons of men," that there occur the phrases, "the children of the holy angels," (lxix. 4, 5.) "the sons of the angels," (lxxi. 1.) "the children of the angels of heaven." (cvi. 5.) Yet there occurs the strange and unexplained statement, "in those days [i. e. "when the congregation of the just shall appear," ch. xxxviii.] the elect and holy children shall come down from the high heavens: and their seed shall unite itself with the children of men." (xxxix. 1.)

The "avenging angels" are, in one case certainly, (lxvi. 1. those employed in the flood,) good angels. Yet lvi. 1-3. they seem to be evil angels. In lxii. 11. lxiii. 1. nothing is expressed ; nor in liii. 3.

[1] lx. 14-21. The term applied to each is "spirit," "the spirit of the sea ;" but it is also said, "the spirit of the hoarfrost is its angel, and the spirit of the hail is a good angel ;" 17. "And he [the spirit of the mist] is its angel," 19. "When the spirit of the rain moves forth out of its containing vessel, the angels come and open the vessel, and lead him forth," &c ; and then follows the mention of "those angels," who are described, (in imitation of Zechariah,) as sent to measure in the North country, but here to measure the righteous, ch. lxi.

the sea also; "angels over the powers of the waters[2]."
In the Noah-portion of the book, there is an angel who
stands in the fountain which, the writer says, "[3] produces
lead and tin." It expands the title, "hosts of heaven,"
to mean, that angels "watch over the stars, that they
should appear in their season," and names "leaders of
the four seasons," "heads over thousands," with "other
subordinate guides[4]." The 15 names mentioned do not
occur elsewhere. It speaks of "[5] the leaders of the heads
of the thousands, set over the whole creation and over
the stars." Of fallen angels, it is very full on that one
point, for which it gained for a time extensive yet not
complete reception in the Church, viz. the idea that the
sons of God, who were the parents of the giants before
the flood, were, not "the sons of Seth," but angels. Their
number it asserts to have been 200[6], gives the names of
their 20 or 21 leaders, and states, what arts some of them
are to have taught to men[7]. The giants born of them are
said to have been 3000 ells high[8]. On the other hand,
it mentions but little of Satan or of continued evil-
agency[9].

It is a remarkable change from the book of Daniel,
that the title "watcher," which, in the prophet apparently

[2] ch. lxvi.　　　[3] lxv. 8.　　　[4] lxxxii. 11-20.

[5] lxxv. 1. Enoch is said to have "seen the paths of the angels," xviii. 5.
Of these it is said, (lxxx. 6.) "many heads of the stars set over will go astray,"
(or "fail." D. who conjectures that he may mean the planets. p. 344.)

[6] ch. vi-xi. lxix. Extracts in G. Syncell. Chron. p. 20-23. ed. Dind. The 20
bear a relation to the two hundred; they are supposed to be "leaders of tens."
In lxix, the chief, Semyaza, (שמחזאי Buxt. p. 2444. from Ps. Jon.) is counted
apart. Dillmann corrects the corrupted names. p. 93, 4.

[7] In ch. viii, seven such are named: in Sync., 9: in ch. lxix. 4-12, attributed
to Noah, 5 others are mentioned, inconsistent with those lists.　　　[8] vii. 2.
omitted by Sync. D. states, "one MS has, 300," evidently a correction.

[9] "Satans" are mentioned as accusers of mankind; (from Job i. and Zech.
iii.) xl. 7; (see p. 385. note 4;) "all mysteries of the angels and all violence
of the Satans," lxv. 6; "the avenging angels prepared all instruments [of
punishment, liv. 3-5.] for Satan," liii. 3. "The hosts of Azazel" were to be
"laid in the depths of all damnation," (D. p. 171.) "because they were subject to Satan and seduced those who dwell on the earth," (liv. 5, 6. but this
too only relates to that one supposed set of acts before the flood.)

is given to the angels to designate their sleepless being [1], is, in Enoch, almost exclusively used of those whom this later writer reputed to have fallen before the flood [2].

In some of this account of angels we are in an entirely different atmosphere from the book of Daniel. It is not an expansion of the book of Daniel; but the result of a meditation on various passages of Holy Scripture, to which the book of Daniel gave no impulse, since it contained no example of it. Fables, not from Daniel, are mixed up with truths which are from Daniel.

There is, besides, detached use of the language of Daniel, as of other Scripture, in the book of Enoch.

The book of Enoch is professedly made up of several

[1] Dan. iv. 10, 14, 20. [13, 17, 23. Eng.] See below Lect. viii.

[2] i. 5. "the watchers shall tremble;" x. 7. "that all the children of men may not perish through the mystery of all that which the watchers have uttered and have taught their sons;" Ib. 9. "go forth, and destroy the children of the watchers from among men;" Ib. 15. "destroy the wanton souls and the children of the watchers, because they have mishandled men;" xiii. 10. "I began to speak those words of righteousness and rebuke those watchers of heaven;" xiv. 1. "what follows written here is the word of righteousness and of correction of the eternal watchers;" Ib. 3. "He has created me and given to me to rebuke the watchers, the sons of heaven;" xv. 2. "go and say to the watchers of heaven, who have sent thee to intercede for them." xvi. 1. 2. "So will they putrefy, until the day when the great Judgment shall be fulfilled upon the great world, upon the watchers and the ungodly; and now, to the watchers who have sent thee to intercede for them, to them who aforetime were in heaven, &c." xci. 15. "In the 10th week in the 7th portion will be the judgment for eternity, that is held upon the watchers."

On the other hand, the adjuncts, "who watch," "who sleep not," are used to denote the unceasing praise and obedience in heaven, xxxix. 12, 13. "Thee they praise who sleep not; they stand before Thy Majesty, and praise, bless, and exalt Thee, saying, holy, holy, holy, is the Lord of spirits; He fills the earth with spirits. And then my eyes saw those who sleep not, as they stand before Him and praise, &c." lxi. 12. "Him shall all they praise, who sleep not above in heaven." lxxi. 6, 7. "Around it were the Cherubim and Ophannim; these are they who sleep not and who watch the throne of His glory." xiv. 23. "The holy ones, who were near Him, departed not day or night, and went not away from Him." See also xx. 1. in note 4. p. 386.

The title "watchers" is only once given to good angels, xii. 2, 3, and then in antithesis to those who had fallen, "All his [Enoch's] life was with the holy ones and the watchers, and I, Enoch, was praising the great Lord and King of the world, when the watchers called me, me Enoch the scribe, and said to me, 'Enoch, thou scribe of righteousness, go, carry tidings to the watchers of heaven who have left the high heaven, &c."

books[3]. Its parts are very unequal. Its moral exhortations are earnest; then again there are those miserable false and childish physics, unrelieved in some places by any moral tone[4], to which however one of the writers attaches primary importance with a foolish vanity[5]. The introduction is so loosely connected with the other parts, that it may easily have been joined on afterwards, and the passage in it, which resembles that quoted by S. Jude

---

[3] The parts, of which the book of Enoch consists, are; 1) the brief introduction, ch. i-v, declaring that God would come to judgment, and how all nature obeyed Him, great and small, except man. In this, which is loosely connected with the book, occurs a passage very like to, but not absolutely identical with, that quoted by St. Jude. Then, unconnected with this, is the story founded on Gen. vi. 2, and Enoch's embassy from the fallen angels to God, ch. vi-xvi. Then follows a story, now detached, but connected by its beginning with something which once preceded it; "*And they* took me to a place." It is Enoch's travels in the unseen world, in which he mixes up some childish and impossible physics, ch. xvii-xxxvi. Then follows what is called (ch. xxxvii.) a second vision, distributed in 3 "figured discourses," in which he describes what he saw in heaven, the abode of the blessed, ch. xxxviii-xiv.the Messiah, with the prophecy of His Coming, ch. xlv-lvii. The third, ch. lviii-lxix, is in utter confusion; a short prophecy of the lot of the righteous, ch. lviii; a statement that the writer saw the mysteries of thunder and lightning, ch. lix; another as to fabulous creatures, Leviathan, Behemoth, and angels of the elements, ch. lx. (in the mouth of Noah, lx. 8.;) the world to come and judgment by the Chosen, ch. lxi-liv; a revelation of Enoch to Noah as to the flood and the punishment of fallen angels, with digressions about the formation of metals and hot springs, ch. lxv-lxviii. It winds up with a declaration of the might of the oath by the Name of God, whereby the world was created, lxix. 16-19, and preserved, 21-23, and praises God, 24, 5, whence it passes to the revelation of the Name of the Son of Man and of Judgment, 26-29. Then follows the assumption of Enoch, and his sight of heaven, ch. lxx. lxxi. Then " the book of the courses of the light of heaven," fabulous physics, ch. lxxii-lxxviii; a revelation addressed to his son Methuselah, ch. lxxix; a prophecy of preternatural changes of nature for men's wickedness, ch. lxxx; Enoch's return to earth and his charge to Methuselah to hand down this knowledge, chiefly as to the physics, ch. lxxxi, ii. Then two visions, early in the life of Enoch, related by him to his son Methuselah, (the second being a sketch from Adam to his own time,) ch. lxxxiii-xc. an address to Methuselah and his brothers, ch. xci. with a disjointed fragment, Ib. 12-17. The "doctrine of wisdom, written by Enoch the scribe," an exhortation, mingled with prophecy, founded on judgment to come, ch. xcii-cv. Marvels at the birth of Noah, ch. cvi, vii. " Another writing which Enoch wrote for his son Methuselah and for those who shall come after him, and hold the law in his last days;" a brief exhortation, ch. cvii.   [4] ch. lxxii-lxxviii.

[5] xxxvii. lix. lxxxii. 3, 4. xciii. 10, 11, &c.

from the book of Enoch, may very probably have been fitted in by a later writer[1].   But the main substance of the book is doubtless old.   The latest event spoken of in it relates to the time of the Maccabees[2].   It has been interpreted to relate to John Hyrcanus, professedly in order to leave room for the later date of the book of Da-

---

[1] The short preface contains the statement, that Enoch had observed that all trees were deciduous, except 14, which is a Greek statement, Geopon. xi. 1. See in Dillm. p. 91.

[2] The only indication of time in the whole book lies in the vision, in which, under an allegory, its writer gives chief points of sacred history from Adam to the Maccabees.   It indicates the restoration of the temple, then adds, in language taken from Malachi, " they began again to put a table before the tower [temple,] but all the bread thereon was defiled and impure."   So the eyes of all these sheep were blinded as to everything, and their "shepherds too, and they were given over to their shepherds to destroy, very many ; and the Lord of the sheep abode still, until all the sheep were scattered on the field, and *mingled with them*, and they delivered them not from the hands of the beasts," (lxxxix. 73-5.) until a new generation arose, which tried to rouse the elders, but fruitlessly.   That generation acquired horns, and their destroyers cast them down, until a great horn shot forth, which they assembled themselves to cast down, but could not.   Ravenous birds preyed on them, until there remained only their skeletons, and these too sank to the ground and few sheep were left, (xc. 2-4.)   Thus far, there are the grinding oppressions by foreign governors, and their own heathenising, as described 1 Macc. i. 11-13.   Then follow three stages of recovery; 1) a new but defenceless generation, "lambs," whose eyes were opened, who cried to their deaf and blinded parents, the sheep ; the ravens flew at them and carried off one of the lambs. (Ib. 6-8.) 2) a time when the lambs gained horns, and the ravens cast down their horns. (Ib. 9. The interval is marked by the formula, taken from Daniel, "And I beheld until" (see ab. p. 78.) 3) a time when a great horn shot up, of one of the sheep, the young ran to him, the ravens and ravenous birds tried to destroy the horn ; and availed not, (Ib. 9-13) ; until, at last, they had exceeded the measure of destruction allowed, (Zech. i. 15) ; the Lord of the sheep came and smote the earth with the rod of his anger ; the earth opened and swallowed up the gathered foes, (14-18.) a sword was given to the sheep to destroy, and all the beasts and birds of the air fled before them. (19.)   On this follows the Day of Judgment. (20.)   A throne is set up in "the pleasant land," (Dan.) and the sealed books were opened. (Dan. vii. 10.)   Now as this is confessedly not prophecy, but imitation of prophecy, it must have been written before the Maccabee struggles were closed.   For it represents the struggles of the enemy to destroy the one great horn ; and these struggles were to be ended supernaturally.   But since there was no supernatural end, then this part of the book must any how have been written before the end, i. e. before the end of the wars of John Hyrcanus.   But the whole description also suits better to the time before Hyrcanus.   The first stage was unresisted persecution, when men's eyes were

niel with which the writers were so deeply imbued[3].
It suits more naturally to Judas Maccabæus, or Simon.

opened, but before they began to resist. This suits the first Maccabee sufferings. (1 Macc i-62-4. ii. 1-41. 2 Macc. v. 27-vii. 42.) The one lamb who was
taken, may have been Eleazar, (2 Macc. vi.18-31.) or possibly Onias III. The
second was the beginning of the Maccabee wars, when they were only a handful of men. The third suits with the time of Judas, or Jonathan, or Simon,
under whom "the yoke of the heathen was taken away from Israel." (1 Macc.
xiii. 41.) In one respect, it suits Judas Maccabæus best, because he was the
first "great horn" who was raised up; but it suits either of the three better
than Hyrcanus; for, after the first siege of Jerusalem in which he surrendered,
he fought, not against, but under Antiochus, (Jos. Ant. xiii. 8. 4.) and when
Antiochus was dead, he had no resistance from Syria to meet, until a slight
ineffectual effort at the end, not to subdue him, but to relieve Samaria. (Ib.
10. 2.)

The mention of the Parthians and Medes, as the nations whose kings should
in the last days be stirred up by angels against Jerusalem, is of no account in
fixing the date, as if the writer would not know of the Parthians until after
Hyrcanus had fought in the army of Antiochus against them. The statement
is a mere imitation of Zechariah. (ch. xiv.) Parthians and Medes stand only as
representatives of Eastern nations, "in those days shall the angels gather themselves, and direct their heads towards the East, towards the Parthians and
Medes, to stir up a spirit of uprising among the kings, &c." (lvi. 5.) The two
names stand, as in 1 Macc. xiv. 2. Arsaces is called "the king of Persia and
Media;" Philip "returned from P. and M."Ib. vi. 56. The Jews knew of Arsaces, king of Parthia, in the time of Simon. 1 Macc. xiv. 2, 3. xv. 22.

I do not take account of the numbers of the rulers indicated in this section;
for I do not think that they are any definite persons. Only it is clear that foreign rulers are meant.

A writer, whom Dillmann accounts later than the chief writer of the book,
places himself and his revelation at the end of the 7th week of the world. But
the 6th week ended with the Captivity. (xciii. 8.) Of the 7th week he says;
"In the 7th week will a rebellious generation arise, and many will be its deeds,
and all its words will be rebellion. And at the end thereof will the chosen and
righteous be rewarded from the everlasting plant of righteousness, in that sevenfold instruction [his own] will be given them as to His whole creation." (Ib.
9, 10.) But the 7th week was not yet closed, for the 8th was to begin with
the times of the Messiah and with a power given to them over their enemies.
(xci. 12.) And this was to follow a miraculous destruction of the enemy. (xc.
19. comp. 18.) Since then the 7th age was not completed, the calculation of
Dillmann, that each week was to contain six generations, would, (if true) argue for the earlier composition of the book. For, according to him, the 14
generations would reach to John Hyrcanus. (p. 390, 1.) Since then they were
not completed, the book would, in this way too, fall before that time.

[3] "Of all our canonical books in the Old Testament, the author (as is admitted
and universally owned) took for his pattern chiefly the book of Daniel. He

But, at latest, the period of John Hyrcanus, B.C. 130-109, leaves no room for such a developement of doctrine after B.C. 163. Yet there is absolutely no choice, it has never been pretended that there is any choice, except between true prophecy in the time from Nebuchadnezzar to Cyrus, and false prophecy in, or rather after, the death of Antiochus.

I cannot, as some religious and eminent defenders of the book of Daniel have done, add to these human evi-

rested on that book, or developed from it, many of his chief doctrines, (those of the Messiah, the kingdom of Heaven, the resurrection, the judgment by the Messiah, the times of the 70 shepherds;) and he imitated it in many details of his descriptions and in expressions, (e. g. entitling the Israelites 'stars of heaven,' xlvi. 7. xliii. 3, 4 ; the conception of the shining of the righteous in the kingdom of the Messiah, civ. 2, or the descriptions of the throne of the Majesty of God, and what encircles it, &c.;) and not merely the second part of the book, but the 4th also, and in single reminiscences the 5th also, betray this dependence on the book of Daniel. And this too of such sort, that it presupposes, not merely that the writer was acquainted with that book, but that he completely lived in its fundamental thoughts and firmly believed in them. This one circumstance would suffice to refute those, who would have it, that one portion of the book, (most of it except ch. xxxvii-lxxii,) was written at the beginning of the Maccabee wars, and suppose that the last important person in Jewish history, whom the writer had lived to see, (ch. xc. 9 sqq.) was Judas Maccabæus, not John Hyrcanus. Contrariwise, this circumstance compels us to assume, that a long time had elapsed since the writing of the book of Daniel, in which it had not only come into circulation and was much read, but had already attained a high, almost canonical, estimation in the congregation. Such an estimation it could, however, have attained in the half century before the writing ofthe book of Enoch." Dillmann, Das B. Henoch, Einl. p. xlv. His other grounds for placing the book in the time of Hyrcanus, are, that 1) a book so full, with such comprehensive objects and presupposing such learned studies, was not suited to such stormy times as those of the Maccabee wars, but "suits a time of rest after the struggle, in which people sought to maintain, settle, and defend, theoretically and scientifically, what had been practically fought for and won." p. xlvi. Certainly the Maccabee wars were not times for any writing, the book of Daniel as little as any other, unless by inspiration. But 1) it is not made out that the book of Enoch was written in Palestine. 2) In Palestine itself things were quiet, after the death of Antiochus Sidetes, B.C. 126. (Clinton, F. H. iii. 335.) 3) The book of Enoch is childish, except where borrowed from Holy Scripture. To assume then the later date, on account of this period of reflection on Holy Scripture, is the usual " begging the question," the lateness of the book of Daniel. Of the two other grounds, on 2) the mention of the Parthians, and 3) the weeks of the world, see note 1. p. 391. It is plain that the assumed date of the book of Daniel is the real ground, upon which the date of the book of Enoch is fixed.

dences the testimony of our Lord, or use Divine authority as a makeweight to human proof.   There, we are altogether on different grounds, in a different atmosphere. What I have proposed to myself in this course of lectures is to meet a boastful criticism upon its own grounds, and to shew its failure, where it claims to be most triumphant.   The authority of our Lord stands alone.   It is all in all, or, we should have nothing.   It is the word of Him Who, being God, spake with a Divine knowledge, Perfect, Infallible.   If His knowledge could have failed in any one thing, if He could (God forbid!) have set His seal on one thing which is not true, Divine authority would be gone.   Hesitate how men will for the while, it was truly said by one of the most powerful intellects of this day [1], " there is but one choice, Infallibility or infidelity."

[1] Dr Newman.   People rely, for this infallible teaching, personally on our Lord, or on the divinity of Holy Scripture, by virtue of His promise (S. John xvi. 13. xiv. 26) ; or on the witness of the universal and undivided Church (which sanctioned the Creeds, and the doctrines of Grace, and of the Sacraments) by virtue of our Lord's promise, (S. Matt. xxviii. 20. xvi. 18. "the gates of hell shall not prevail against it ;") or on the manifold promises that God will bestow on us the gift of faith in what He has revealed ; so that we have not human, but Divine, faith.   In all these ways, people have an authority out of themselves and their own opinions.   But we must have, subjectively, a supernatural faith, by gift of God the Holy Ghost, in that which has been supernaturally revealed, or we should have no faith at all.

LECTURE VII.

On the " historical inaccuracies " falsely imputed to the book of Daniel, and the "improbabilities" alleged.

THE charges of " historical inaccuracies " have been lavished with a reckless hand.   They are gathered into one in the following statement of Lengerke [1], who exhibits in them the current charges of the German rationalists [2]. They have been recently transferred among us by a dissenting writer [3].

"5) The lateness of its date is clear also through *the historical inaccuracies.*   Errors in chronology and antiqui-

---

[1] Daniel Einl. § 13. p. lxiii.

[2] De Wette, in his Einl. § 255. a. Ed. 7. (as became his practice) epitomised Lengerke.   "That Daniel is not the author of this book, is clear, 1) out of the fabulous contents of the historical portion, which is full of improbabilities, (ii. 3 sqq. 46 sqq. iii. 1, 5 sqq. 20, 22, 28 sqq. iv. 31 sqq. v. 11 sqq. 18 sqq. 29. vi. 8 sqq. 26 sqq.) of monstrous miracles, (ii. 28. iii. 23 sqq. v. 5. vi. 23, 25.) and even of historical incorrectnesses, (such as no other prophetical book of the O. T. contains ;)" "incorrect representations of the wise men of Babylon, Daniel's inconceivable admission among them ; (ii. 2. iv. 7. v. 7, 11.) Darius the Mede instead of Cyaxares II ; (vi. 1. [v. 31. Eng.] ix. 1. xi. 1.) mention of the (Persian) institution of satraps under Nebuchadnezzar, (iii. 3.) and Darius the Mede, vi. 2. [1. Eng.] Ahasuerus, father of Darius the Mede, (Cyaxares II.) instead of Astyages ; (ix. 1.) Belshazzar, son of Nebuchadnezzar, last king of Babylon : (v. 11, 13, 18, 22, 30. contrary to Berosus in Jos. c. Ap. i. 20.) conception of the lion's den as a pit, (vi. 17.)" "Its relations moreover are formed so much upon the same type. (comp. ii. 2-11. with iv. 4-8. v. 8 ; iii. 4-12. 24-30. with vi. 8-18. 21-24.)   This love of miracles and the religious fanaticism, as nourished by persecution, which it breathes, evince, that it is akin to the 2nd book of Maccabees, and a fruit of the times of Antiochus Epiphanes, and this uniformity betrays the fiction."

[3] Davidson, Introd. T. iii. p. 174, 5. 180-92.

ties, and embellishment of the history, remove the author
far from the prophetic period.   For, only in regard to the
Maccabee times, does he give accurate and detailed accounts.   As historical inaccuracies must be accounted;
1) the date of the first deportation ch. i. 1; 2) the historical
contradiction between ch. i. 21. and ii. 1; 3) the false idea of
the lion's den, ch. vi. and 4) of the Magi. (ch. ii.)   It excites
at least the gravest suspicion, that Daniel (ch. viii.) in the
reign of the Mede Cyaxares II. [Belshazzar,] 5) sees himself in vision at Susa, as a residence of the Persian kings;
for although Susa was already built in the reign of Darius, it did not become a royal residence until the time of
Cyrus. 6) He speaks of satraps and government by satraps,
which cannot be imagined under the Babylonians, nor under Medes and Persians at the time of the capture of Babylon.   7) He calls Nebuchadnezzar erroneously the father
of the last king, gives that king a false name, makes him of
royal blood, and follows a false legend as to the capture of
Babylon and the fate of the last king.   8) He brings on
the stage a Cyaxares II., Darius the Mede, who never lived.   9) He makes the supremacy of the Medes still subsist
at the time of the capture of Babylon; and 10) is in ignorance as to the order of succession of Persian kings."

Of this list of errors, attributed to the writer of the book
of Daniel, but, in truth, the inventions of the neologist
school, I have already shown the baselessness of the imputation as to the account of the Medes and Persians [4].
1) It is quite clear that Daniel does *not* speak of the Median preeminence as still lasting at the time of the capture of Babylon [5].   He twice expresses the contrary, that
" Darius the Mede received the kingdom " i. e. from another, and " was made king " i. e. by another [6].   2) It is
probable [7] that there was a Cyaxares II ; but the identification of Cyaxares II. with Darius the Mede is only a probable historical conjecture, with which Daniel is in no
way concerned.

---

[4] Obj. 9.   [5] See Lect. iii. p. 122 sqq.   [6] Ib. p. 122, 3.
[7] Obj. 8. See Ib. p. 124, 5.

It is directly false, on the surface of the book, to say [1], that Daniel gives an accurate account of the times of the Maccabees alone. The accuracy of the prophecy of the victories of Alexander, of his sudden untimely end at his full strength, of the fourfold division of his empire, and of some chief events in the two houses of the Ptolemies and the Seleucidæ for 7 or 8 generations previous to the time of Antiochus Epiphanes and the Maccabees, have been used by the Porphyry-school as arguments against their being prophecy. "They are too accurate and minute," these men say, "to be prophecies." Then they cannot be inaccurate also; nor has there been an attempt to point out an inaccuracy.

The hypocritical argument is plainly nihil ad rem. It is to be an argument against the genuineness of Daniel that he was ignorant of the Persian succession [2]. What? In the minds of these writers, who disbelieve in prophecy, it is to be an argument that Daniel did not write the book, because he did not know events yet future in the time of Daniel! So then each is alike to be an argument against the genuineness of Daniel, that, on the hypothesis, he did, and did not know the future! Be it that he did not know more of the Persian succession than he sets down in his book, that God only revealed to him certain marked points of history and not the rest. We cannot tell. Perhaps it is the most probable. But this ignorance, if it were such, would have its obvious ground, if he knew what he knew, by revelation from God. In that case, he did not know it, because God did not reveal this unimportant series of kings, which even human historians have revolted from dwelling on. The alleged ignorance is perfectly consistent with the real character of Daniel, as a prophet. For God revealed to His prophets so much of the future, as He willed His people to be forewarned of. It is utterly inconsistent with the character of the assumed Pseudo-Daniel. For it is absurd to suppose a person to know by human knowledge the number of kings from Cy-

---

rus to Xerxes, and then again the chief events from Alexander onwards, and to have been absolutely ignorant of the whole intermediate history, or that there was any history intervening.

I will take the other charges in order.

i. The date[3] in ch. i. accurately agrees with Berosus, and is not contradicted by any authority; the date in ch. ii. agrees exactly with that in ch. i. Daniel says, ch. i., that Nebuchadnezzar besieged Jerusalem in the third year of Jehoiakim; that God gave Jehoiakim into his hands and a portion of the vessels of the house of the Lord; and that certain of the seed-royal and of the nobles were carried to Babylon. He does not say, whether Jerusalem was taken or no. The mention that, not Jerusalem but, Jehoiakim fell into the hands of Nebuchadnezzar, rather implies that it was not. Daniel states the expedition and its results. Nebuchadnezzar besieged Jerusalem, and took Jehoiakim. Jehoiakim became tributary to Nebuchadnezzar, as we read in the book of Kings, [4]*and became his servant three years.* Perhaps the profane king, (such as we know Jehoiakim to have been[5],) redeemed himself with treasures out of the temple, a portion of the vessels, and hostages. The book of Chronicles relates the two leading facts of the capture of Jehoiakim and the carrying away of some of the vessels of the Lord, equally without relating any capture of Jerusalem. [6]*Against him came up Nebuchadnezzar, king of Babylon, and bound him in fetters, to carry him to Babylon. Nebuchadnezzar also carried of the vessels of the Lord to Babylon, and put them in his temple in Babylon.* It is the more probable, that the writer of the book of Chronicles is speaking of the same event as Daniel, in that both speak of a portion[7] only of the vessels of the house of the Lord being taken; but Daniel alone supplies the date.

The first year of Nebuchadnezzar falling, according to Jeremiah[8], in some part of the 4th of Jehoiakim, this ex-

---

[3] Obj. 1 and 2. [4] 2 Kgs. xxiv. 1. [5] Jer. xxxvi. 23-25. [6] 2 Chr. xxxvi. 6, 7. [7] מִקְצָת כְּלֵי בֵית הָאֱלֹהִים Dan. i. 2. מִכְּלֵי בֵית יהוה 2 Chr. xxxvi. 7. [8] Jer. xxv. 1.

pedition, in the course of which he besieged Jerusalem, was before his accession to the throne. This coincides with the account in Berosus[1] of Nebuchadnezzar's successful expedition, when sent by his father Nabopolassar, from which he brought to Babylon *Jewish* captives, as well as Syrian, Phœnician, and Egyptian; and "[2] from the spoils" of which war " he ornamented splendidly the temple of Bel," who was specially his god. In Daniel, whose king Nebuchadnezzar had been from boyhood, it is nothing surprising, that he should speak of Nebuchadnezzar in no other way, than, "king Nebuchadnezzar," even when speaking of the time before his accession. Daniel does not ordinarily mention kings by their name only, Nebuchadnezzar, Belshazzar, Cyrus, but adds the royal title also[3]. We should naturally say, " Queen Victoria was carefully educated by her mother," or " the Emperor Napoleon passed some years of his life in England," although the education of our Queen was concluded before her early accession to the throne, and the Emperor's residence here, was before his accession and while he was in exile.

Daniel then having been carried captive in the third year of Jehoiakim, there is no discrepancy, but perfect agreement, between the dates in the first and second chapters. Daniel was to be educated for three years[4] *in the learning and tongue of the Chaldæans; at the end of the days* he was examined before the king; and in the course of the 2nd year of the reign of Nebuchadnezzar, he was counted among the wise men, and was to

---

[1] See Lect. ii. p. 60. [2] Jos. c. Ap. i. 19.

[3] Nebuchadnezzar king of *Babylon*, (in contrast with Jerusalem,) i. 1. the king Neb., ii. 46. iii. 1,2,3,5,7, 24. v. 11. Belshazzar the king, v. 1,9. Belshazzar king of Babylon, vii. 1. viii. 1. Darius the king, vi. 6, 9, 25. Cyrus king of Persia, x. 1. In other places, in which the name stands alone, some attribute of the royal title has been mentioned, or the title itself had occurred in the context, as Dan. i. 18. "in the reign of Neb.," ii. 1. iii. 9, 13, 14, 16, 19. "Belshazzar commanded," v. 2. (the title " king " had occurred in v. 1.) " Darius the Median received the kingdom," v. 31. " It pleased Darius," vi. 1. " In the first year of Darius, which was made king," ix. 1. [4] i. 1, 18.

share their lot. For this period of three years there is ample space.

Jehoiakim himself, probably, came to the throne in the middle of B.C. 609. For since the expedition of Pharaoh Necho against Asshur was probably in the spring, when campaigns commonly began, Josiah, who was slain when Necho reached Megiddo, probably died in that spring. Let us suppose it the end of April, for clearness. Then the three months' reign of Jehoahaz would have been broken off at the end of July, B.C. 609. The 3rd year of Jehoiakim, whom Pharaoh placed on the throne in his stead, would begin at the end of July, B.C. 607. In that year Nebuchadnezzar, according to Daniel, came against him. If Jehoiakim submitted in November of that year, the three years of Daniel would close, late in 604 or early in 603. If, again, Nebuchadnezzar returned to Babylon from that extensive expedition against Phœnicia, Cœle-Syria, Egypt, and succeeded his father near the end of the 4th year of Jehoiakim, B.C. 605, then the second year of Nebuchadnezzar would not be completed till B.C. 603, and the close of Daniel's three years would fall in the latter part of that his second year.

But it is probable that the submission of Jerusalem did take place in November, B.C. 607. For although Jeremiah only mentions that the fast was proclaimed *in the ninth month*[5], yet, as this must have been a civil fast, the analogy of the four fasts in four several months[6], after the final capture of Jerusalem, makes it probable that this day was fixed in connection with some recent event which men mourned. And that the more, because November would otherwise hardly have been selected for a fast, which, at that season, must have been the more trying for those who had to come up to Jerusalem. There is no recent event at that time, except the siege of Jerusalem.

At that time, the access to Jerusalem was open on all sides. For the words were to be *read in the ears of all*

---

[5] Jer. xxxvi. 9.   [6] Zech. viii. 19.

Judah, that are coming out of their cities, that are coming from the cities of Judah to Jerusalem[1].

In the following year Jehoiakim rebelled. `In his days, it is related[2], Nebuchadnezzar king of Babylon came up, and Jehoiakim became his servant three years; then he turned and rebelled against him.* Jehoiakim must have been already plotting that rebellion at the time of the fast, a year before he avowed it. And this explains his extreme anger at the predictions of Jeremiah, that he burnt the roll and directed that Jeremiah and Baruch should be seized[3]. For Jeremiah had foretold the fruitlessness and destructiveness of that policy, upon which the reckless king was bent. At that time, the sixth year of Jehoiakim, Nebuchadnezzar was probably engaged elsewhere; for he did not himself come up against him, as he had before and did afterwards. For it is said[4]; *The Lord sent against him bands of the Chaldees, and bands of the Syrians, and bands of the Moabites, and bands of the children of Ammon.* The mention of *bands* of these several nations points to irregular incursions, made to harass him, not to any formal effort directed by any chief general.

With this agrees the mention, made by the Rechabites, of *the [5]army of the Chaldæans, and the army of the Syrians,* which constrained them, so far, contrary to their father's injunctions, to *dwell at Jerusalem.*

The expedition, led first by generals of Nebuchadnezzar, and then by himself in person *in* his *7th year*[6], when he *carried captive three thousand Jews and three and twenty,* was doubtless in the first instance directed against Jehoiakim. The 7th year of Nebuchadnezzar coincided with the latter part of the reign of Jehoiakim, and the three months of the reign of his son Jehoiakin. But

---

[1] הבאים Jer. xxxvi. 6. and again ver. 9.

[2] 2 Kgs. xxiv. 1. He had probably been placed on the throne by Necho, as being in the interests of Egypt, as, contrariwise, he had been passed over after the death of his father, and his younger brother had been made king by the people, probably to continue the policy of Josiah.   [3] Jer. xxxvi. 23-26.

[4] 2 Kgs. xxiv. 2.   [5] Jer. xxxv. 11.   [6] Ib. lii. 28.

those three months were not enough to furnish the occasion of the expedition to begin and to complete it. Jehoiakim very possibly slept with his fathers, before the siege began, and people may have thought for those three months, that he had escaped the disgrace foretold by the Prophet. The dragging of his corpse was probably meant as a warning to bad successors, not to rebel.

The first siege of Jerusalem falling in the third year of Jehoiakim, must have preceded the defeat of Pharaoh Necho at Carchemish, which took place in the 4th year. But, as we know not one fact beyond these dates, except the relative position of the places; not one circumstance as to the campaign, except its success; since too the conquering party does not even name Necho, unless the Assyrians contemptuously regarded his authority as delegated, and himself as the rebellious Satrap, we have nothing, upon which to build a theory of the campaign. Sennacherib aforetime, and Nebuchadnezzar afterwards in the time of Zedekiah, were engaged in the subdual of Judæa before they attacked Egypt, and were withdrawn from the siege by reports of an expedition from Egypt. Necho took Carchemish three years before, after defeating Josiah. Why Nebuchadnezzar should have placed his army between Carchemish and Egypt, preferring first to recover the king of Jerusalem to his dependence on himself, of course we cannot know. The fact is implied by Berosus as well as by Daniel. But the measure has no such improbability, as to throw a doubt on any statement even of ordinary history. Independent dates, such as these in Daniel, which are perfectly consistent with each other and with history, yet which could not have been suggested by other history, bear the characteristic mark of an original authority, viz. that it states what it knows, regardless whether it agree primâ facie with other history or no.

It is even strange how a difficulty could be raised about an account so simple and consistent. It *was* raised by remodelling history, contradicting Berosus' account of the campaign before Nebuchadnezzar came to the throne, asserting, that when Jeremiah said, the fourth year of Jehoiakim was the first of Nebuchadnezzar, he did not really mean his first year, but the "first, in which the Jews heard of him[1];" contradicting the account in the book of Kings, that on Jehoiakim's rebellion, after being tributary for three years, God sent bands of Chaldees, Syrians, Moabites, Ammonites, against him, and so placing Nebuchadnezzar's first invasion in the 6th year of Jehoiakim, and, (contrary to the explicit statement in Jeremiah,) denying that, which was probably directed against Jehoiakim in his last year, although it fell upon his son.

And yet for all this contradiction of Scripture, there is not even a plea, except a mistaken arrangement of the events in Josephus[2], and a preconceived opinion that Nebuchadnezzar invaded Judæa once only, and an impatience at the inability to gather scattered notices into systematic history.

ii. Rationalists must now retract the assertion that "[3] the last king of Babylon has a false name in Daniel;" since it is now an admitted fact, that the name of Belshazzar occurs on Babylonian Cylinders, as that of the eldest son of Nabunahit, (the Nabonidus of Berosus, the Labynetus of Herodotus,) the last king of Babylon, and being associated with his father in the empire, and slain at Babylon. The history was read at one and the same time in Lower Chaldæa by Oppert[4], and by Sir H. Rawlinson[5] in England. The three monograms, by which the name is expressed, are each well known, as being of

---

[1] Lengerke, p. 3. from Griesenger, Neue Ansicht, &c. p. 39.

[2] Ant. x. 6.   [3] Obj. 7.

[4] "In Abu Shahrein in Lower Chaldæa, cylinders of Nabonid have been discovered, wherein mention is made of his eldest son and co-regent Belsarussur. He was slain in Babylon, and is the Belshazzar of Scripture." Oppert, letter to Prof. Olshausen, Jan. 16. 1854, in Zeitschr. d. Deutsch. morg. Ges. viii. 598.

[5] "Mr. J. Taylor—has lately discovered a number of clay cylinders at Um-Qeer, the modern Arab capital of Sook-ess-shoohd on the Euphrates. Two of these cylinders have already reached me.—The most important fact which they disclose is that of the name Belsharezer, and that he was admitted by his father to a share in the government." Sir H. Rawl. in Athenæum, March 1854. p. 341.

frequent occurrence[6]. The fact, that Belshazzar was slain, is illustrated "[7] by the inscription of Bisutun, in that the impostor, who caused the Babylonians to revolt against Darius Hystaspes, and who personated the heir to the throne, did not take the name of the eldest son[8] of Nabonidus, Belsharezer, but of the second son Nabukudurusur." Berosus, then, gives the history of the open campaign of the father Nabonetus, who, having been defeated, shut himself up in Borsippa, and was there taken after the capture of Babylon. Daniel relates the prediction of the fall of the Babylonian Empire in the capital, given to the son Belshazzar in the midst of his idolatrous insolence, and its fulfilment. The two àccounts, which unbelievers have insolently contrasted, and which believers have been unable to harmonise, appear as distinct portions of the same history, the downfall of Babylon. But men might well ask themselves, which is the most likely to have known the name of Bel-

[6] "The name is expressed by three monograms, the first signifying the god *Bel;* the second, *shar, a king;* and the third being the same sign which terminates the name of Nabopolassar, Nebuchadnezzar, Nergalshareser, &c." Ib. note. Nergalshareser is, by a like contraction, called Neriglissoor by Berosus in Jos. c. Ap. i. 21; Neriglisar, by Megasthenes, Alex. Polyh. in Eus. Chron.; Niglisar by Jos. Ant. x. 11. 2. Belshazzar is not much abbreviated from Bel-shar-usur, and is abbreviated according to that common principle of languages, by giving it a more Aramaic form. The א is retained, although not pronounced; the *r* alone is lost, and that is replaced by the double *z*. We have בלשאצר for בלשרצר. Perhaps Daniel wróte it, as it was pronounced. We, English, strangely change the pronunciation of our proper names. I remember, Saxby being Sauceby; Birmingham being Brummegem; Cirencester is pronounced Ciceter; Leicester, Lester; Worcester, Worster; Malvern, Mawvern; Magdalene *College* was, in Oxford, Maudlen; in London, the Magdalen *Penitentiary* was pronounced as it is spelt. [7] Sir H. Rawl. in Athenæum l. c. Prof. Rawl. Herod. Ess. 8. i. 525. note 8, from Behistun Inscr. i. par. 17. iii. par. 13. re-edited, Ib. T. ii. p. 595, 6. 608.

[8] The fact, that Belshazzar was the eldest son, is stated in an inscription, thus decyphered by Dr. Hincks; (Journal for Sacr. Lit. T. xiv. p. 412.) "Save thou me; as to posterity, distant days to an extending extend thou; also as to Belshazzar the son, the beginning of the issue of my heart, on the worship of thy great godhead his heart make to abide." Prof. Rawlinson informs me, that no name is mentioned in the inscriptions, together with that of the reigning monarch, unless he were co-regent. Dr. Hincks speaks of Belshazzar, as being, according to the inscriptions, "heir apparent." Ib. p. 409.

shazzar, which remained unknown to Babylonian, Persian, or Greek historians, the prophet who lived in Babylon, or a Jew who is to have lived in Palestine nearly four centuries afterwards?

iii. In what way this Belsharusur was descended from Nebuchadnezzar, since his father was not of the royal family, may yet be discovered, or may, without detriment, remain unknown. Intermarriage with the family of a conquered monarch, or with a displaced line, is so obvious a way of strengthening the newly acquired throne[1], that it is à priori probable, that Nabunahit would so fortify his claim. The fact, that two impostors took the title of "Nabocodrossor son of Nabonid," completely establishes the fact, that Nabonidus wished to associate his family and dynasty with that of the great conqueror and the benefactor of Babylon.   No one would hesitate to accept such an explanation in secular history.   It is unphilosophical to set historical statements at variance, when they admit of a ready solution.

iv. But, it is said, the Queen-mother and Daniel speak of Nebuchadnezzar to Belshazzar, as his father, and to Belshazzar, as being his son, whereas the relation was, anyhow, that of grandfather and grandson, so that, although, by God's Providence, men have unexpected external evidence that the name is right, still the relation is to be wrong. These men teach the old prophet, that he ought to have said, "Nebuchadnezzar, thy grandfather," "and thou, his grandson."   Most accurate advice! Daniel would doubtless have followed it, had he been speaking English. But what if, in Chaldee, it was impossible, without coining a new word?   Neither in He-

---

[1] Prof. Rawlinson (Bampton L. p. 443, 4.) gives as instances, "so Amasis married a daughter of Psammetik III. (Wilkinson in Rawl. Herod. ii. 387.) and Atossa was taken to wife both by the Pseudo-Smerdis and by Darius Hystaspes. (Her. iii. 68, and 88.) On the same grounds Herod the Great married Marianne. (Jos. B. J. i. 12. 3.)" Even Mr. F. Newman acknowledges the principle in regard to the committing of Zedekiah's daughters to Gedaliah : (Jer. xli. 10.) quoted ib. The same principle was probably involved in Absalom's incest, (2 Sam. xvi. 22, 23.) and Adonijah's request, 1 Kgs. ii. 23.

brew, nor in Chaldee, is there any word for "grandfather,"
"grandson [2]." "Forefathers" are called "fathers" or
"fathers' fathers." But a single grandfather, or forefather, is never called "father's father," but always "fa-
ther" only. This is so, alike in early and late Hebrew,
and the Chaldee follows the idiom. Jacob says, [3] *The
God of my father, the God of Abraham, and the fear of
Isaac.* God says to Aaron, [4] *the tribe of Levi, the tribe of
thy father.* The confession, to be made at the offering
of the first fruits, began; [5] *A Syrian, ready to perish, was
my father;* and in the same sense, probably, Moses says,
[6] *the God of my father.* David said to Mephibosheth [7], *I
will surely shew thee kindness, for Jonathan thy father's
sake, and will restore to thee all the land of Saul thy father.*
And Asa is related to have [8] *removed Maachah his mother
from being queen,* though it is said in the same chapter,
that she was the mother of Abijam his father [9]. Maacha
herself, who is called *daughter of Absalom* [9], was really
his granddaughter, he having left one only daughter, Ta-
mar [10], and her own father being Uriel [11]. Again, it is
said, [12] *Asa did right in the eyes of the Lord, as did David
his father,* and in like way of Hezekiah [13]. Contrariwise,
it is said that [14] *Ahaz did not right, like David his father;*
that [15] *Amaziah did right—yet not like David his father; he
did according to all things as Joash his father did.* Here,
in one verse, the actual father and the remote grandfather
are alike called *his father;* as, before, the father and grandfather of Mephibosheth [7] were called, in the same verse,
his father. [16] *Josiah,* it is said, *walked in the ways of David his father; he began to seek the God of David his father.* In Isaiah there occur, [17] *Jacob thy father;* [18] *thy first
father,* i. e. Adam; and to Hezekiah he said, [19] *Thus saith*

---

[2] Even in Rabbinic, Buxtorf only mentions the terms, זְקֵנִי, זְקֵנְתִּי "my old man,
my old woman," for "my grandfather," "my grandmother." col. 684.

[3] Gen. xxxi. 42. [4] Num. xviii. 2. [5] Deut. xxvi. 5. [6] Ex. xviii. 4.
[7] 2 Sam. ix. 7. [8] 1 Kgs. xv. 13. [9] Ib. 2. [10] 2 Sam. xiv. 27.
[11] 2 Chr. xiii. 2. [12] 1 Kgs. xv. 11. [13] 2 Kgs. xviii. 3. 2 Chr.
xxix. 2. [14] 2 Kgs. xvi. 2. 2 Chr. xxviii. 1. [15] 2 Kgs. xiv. 3.
[16] 2 Chr. xxxiv. 2, 3. [17] Is. lviii. 14. [18] Ib. xliii. 27. [19] Ib. xxxviii. 5.

the Lord, the God of David thy father. So, on the other hand, there is no one Hebrew or Chaldee word to express "grandson." In laws, if the relation has to be expressed, the idiom is [1] *thy son's daughter,* [2] or *thy daughter's daughter;* or it is said, [3] *thou shalt tell it to thy son's son;* [4] *rule thou over us, thou and thy son, and thy son's son.* The relation can be expressed in this way in the abstract, but there is no way in Hebrew or Chaldee to mark, that one person was the grandson of another, except in the way of genealogy, " Jehu the son of Jehoshaphat, the son of Nimshi." And so, the name *son* stands for the "grandson," and a person is at times called the son of the more remarkable grandfather, the link of the father's name being omitted. Thus Jacob asked for [5]*Laban the son of Nahor,* omitting the immediate father, Bethuel[6]; Jehu is called *the son of Nimshi*[7], omitting his own father, Jehoshaphat[8]. The prophet Zechariah is called the son of Iddo[9], his own father being Berachiah[10]. Hence the Rechabites said, as a matter of course, [11]*Jonadab the son of Rechab our father commanded us ; we have obeyed in all things the voice of Jonadab the son of Rechab our father;* although Jonadab lived some 180 years before[12]. And reciprocally God says, [13]*the words of Jonadab the son of Rechab, that he commanded his sons, are performed;* and, *Because ye have obeyed the commandment of Jonadab your father, and kept all his precepts.*

In the Assyrian inscriptions, Sargon speaks of the "[14]kings my fathers," although himself probably connected with the former line of kings, only through intermarriage ; and Isaiah speaks of " [15] Merodach Baladan, *son* of Baladan," the immediate father of Merodach Baladan having been " Yagina[16]."

The requisition then, that Daniel or the Queen-mother

---

[1] Lev. xviii. 10. [2] Ib. and 17. [3] Ex. x. 2.
[4] Jud. viii. 22. [5] Gen. xxix. 5. [6] Ib. xxviii. 5. [7] 1 Kgs. xix. 16.
2 Kgs. ix. 20. [8] 2 Kgs. ix. 2. 14. [9] Ezr. v. 1. vi. 14. [10] Zech. i. 1.
[11] Jer. xxxv. 6, 8. [12] in Jehu's time B.C. 884. (2 Kgs. x. 15.) Jeremiah's prophecy was about B.C. 707. [13] Ib. 14. 16. [14] Athenæum l. c. Rawl. Herod. T. i. p 472. [15] xxxix. 1. [16] Rawl. B. Lect. p. 443. note 4.

should have expressed to Belshazzar the exact relation in which he stood to Nebuchadnezzar, is a thing simply impracticable according to the genius of the language. But further, it would have been false to nature. The object of the Queen-mother was to influence Belshazzar; that of Daniel, to impress him by the contrast of his conduct and his grandfather's. The words "son's son" are used, (where they are used,) to express distance. The idiom expresses the continuing-on of the line. It is, as I said, never used of an individual. Daniel used the only idiom, existing in the language, to express the relation; and at the same time, instead of mentioning an inglorious father, he set before Belshazzar the history of his renowned father, the father of his greatness, the neglected example of God's judgment on the proud, and of His mercy on humbled pride.

v. In regard to Susa[17], rationalism, credulous, as usual, *against* the Bible, snatched at first at a statement of Pliny, "[18] Susiana, in which Susa, the ancient regal city of the Persians, was built by Darius the son of Hystaspes." It also mistranslated Daniel, as though he said, that he was actually in Susa[19], whereas he says, that in his vision he was there, (as Ezekiel speaks of his being in his vision at Jerusalem[20].) Then it tried to establish, that Elam was not conquered by Nebuchadnezzar[21], so that Daniel was to have stated that he was in a place, not then built and not in the Babylonian empire. All these allegations were plainly contrary to the facts.

Xenophon calls the city, Susa, in the time of Cyrus, saying that he "[22] passed the three spring months in Susa." Cambyses sent Prexaspes to Susa to put his brother to death[23]; then, on hearing of the revolt of Pseudo-Smerdis, he set off himself to march to Susa[24] against him, but died; the two Magi reigned there[25]. Darius Hystaspes

---

[17] Obj. 5.

[18] N. H. vi. 27. 31.　[19] Bertholdt defended this at length, (p. 510, 4.) followed by Bachiene (Heil. Geogr. p. 615.) and others; which every one now sees to be wrong.　[20] Ezek. viii-xi.　[21] See ab. Lect. iii. p. 117, 8.　[22] Cyrop. viii. 6. ult.　[23] Herod. iii. 30.　[24] Ib. 64.　[25] Ib. 65.

came thither from Persia Proper, of which his father was Satrap[1]. Herodotus too calls it "[2]the Susa of Memnon," a name which carries its date back to the fabulous times of Greece. Strabo says, that the Persian kings chose it as their residence, in part, "[3]on account of the dignity of the city;" and so, as long præ-existing. Greek traditions placed "[4]Memnon son of Tithonus and his Susianians" in the time of the Trojan war. Pliny does not contradict all this, if we understand that he used the word "built," in regard to Susa, in the way in which it is so often said of one who rebuilds, beautifies, enlarges or fortifies. In that sense he must clearly have used it of Ecbatana, when he says, "[5]King Seleucus built Ecbatana, the capital of Media." So Nebuchadnezzar said, [6]*Is not this great Babylon that I have built for the house of the kingdom?* and, in this sense, Solomon doubtless is said to have "[7]built Tadmor," and Rehoboam to have "[8]built" Bethlehem, Tekoah, and other towns, which existed long before.

Rationalism then had to retreat from all those former charges, step by step. What remains resolves itself into a mere denial of prophecy. Daniel saw Susa, as a representative of Persian empire. Probably it was already the seat of that empire. For it is in itself unlikely, that Cyrus should have abandoned his Persians, and made the Median capital his only seat of empire. The one authority, who states that he made Susa the Persian residence, does not hint that he made it so *after* the conquest of Babylon. Contrariwise one of the grounds, which Strabo assigns for the choice[9], its "bordering upon Babylon," suits the times before its capture better than those subsequent. Before the capture, Susa was a good point, whence to invade Babylon; a three months' residence

---

[1] "Darius, son of Hystaspes, arrived at Susa, having come from the Persians. For of these his father was governor," (ὕπαρχος, i. q. Satrap.) Ib. 70.

[2] vii. 151. In v. 54. he calls it "the Memnonian city;" v. 53, "the Memnonian palace."   [3] xv. 3. 2. p. 728.   [4] Diod. ii. 22.

[5] N. H. vi. 14. 17.   [6] Dan. iv. 30. Eng. 27. Ch.   [7] 1 Kgs. ix. 18.

[8] 2 Chr. xi. 6.   [9] l. c.

there was of no special value in regard to Babylon, when Babylon was already their's. The account of the march of Cyrus against Babylon, given by Herodotus, also falls in with the probability, that Susa was already his capital. Herodotus first [10] mentions the water of the Choaspes, which the Persian kings took with them on their expeditions; then, the crossing of the Gyndes [11]; but from Susa on the Choaspes to the Gyndes was the first part of the royal road [12], which connected Susa with the extremity of the Persian empire on the west.

In the 3rd year of Belshazzar, probably shortly before the close of the Babylonian empire, God foreshowed to Daniel the rise, the growth, the fall of the 2nd world-empire, which was about to destroy the first. This could not be more graphically shewn than by the symbolic animal, close by the capital of Persia whence its conqueror issued. Ecbatana would have symbolised chiefly the inferior, the Median, portion of the conquering empire. The name of Susa symbolises the superior element, the Persian. The slight touch is another indication, that Daniel knew the relation of the two races, of which these writers would fain make him out to be ignorant.

vi. The mention of Satraps is to yield a twofold argument against the book of Daniel; 1) that they are mentioned at all as Babylonian officers; 2) that there were so many as 120 under Darius the Mede. True! Berosus, the Babylonian historian, who is an infallible authority, if he can be made to seem to contradict Holy Scripture, mentions them too. He speaks, as we saw [13], of the Satrap who rebelled against Nabopolassar. But this too is to be an anachronism [14]; for there are to have been no Satraps in Egypt before the time of Cambyses, and those, of course, Persian. True again; " [15] The government of the Asiatic

---

[10] i. 188. [11] i. 189. [12] v. 52.

[13] See above Lect. ii. p. 60. [14] Lengerke on Dan. iii. 3. p. 117.

[15] " We know from other places, that the government [of the Medes,] as in other Asiatic empires, was a government by Satraps; in that the foreign populations were under Median Satraps." Heeren, Ideen, i. 1. 143. "The government

states, Assyrians, Babylonians, Medians, and Persians, was a government by Generals, Princes[1], who at the same time were Stadtholders, Governors general." Subdued, but warlike nations, uncemented into one with the conquering empire, and at a distance from its capital, must be held in allegiance by the strong hand and will of some delegated authority, to whom the distant government is confided. The Governors in our colonies or conquests, the Cape, Calcutta, Madras, Bombay, New Zealand, would, when government was less organised, have been Satraps. Governor, or Governor-General, is the title equivalent to Satrap. But further, the Assyrian boast in Isaiah, [1]*Are not my princes altogether kings?* exactly expresses the character of the Satrap, an officer who lived in almost royal state, almost independent of his distant suzerain, so that he provided the contingent of tribute, or, if need were, of soldiers, and was often in a condition, and tempted, to assert his complete independence. In the great wars or invasions of the king, the Satrap brought his contingent of troops, and became one of the *great king's*[2] attendant *princes.* The title of Nebuchadnezzar himself, *king of kings*[3], expresses the same relation. The title involves this, that he was *king of* those who governed as *kings*, under him. Merodach-baladan, entitled king of Babylon by Isaiah[4], was probably one of the vice-kings or Satraps of the king of Assyria. For Babylon was, before and after this time, dependent on Nineveh. Sennacherib made Belib his viceroy there[5]; his son Esarhaddon transplanted Babylonians to Samaria[6], and carried Manasseh captive to Babylon[7]. As-

by Satraps, which had in Xenophon's time attained its full organisation, was common to the Persian Empire with all great despotic empires." Id. p. 489. " It belongs to the peculiar constitution of the Assyrian, Chaldean, and Persian Empires, that the provinces were governed by Satraps or Vice-kings, who were often relations, brothers, sons, or step-sons, of the king, at times extremely powerful, rivalled the royal court in pomp, but often withdrew themselves from its supremacy, and made themselves independent."   [1] Is. x. 8.
    [2] 2 Kgs. xviii. 19. Is. xxxvi. 4.   [3] Ezek. xxvi. 7. Dan. ii. 37. as of Artaxerxes, Ezr. vii. 12.   [4] Is. xxxix. 1.   [5] as Elibus, (Polyhistor) or Belib. (Can. Ptol.) see Rawl. Herod. i. 504.   [6] Ezra iv. 2.   [7] 2 Chr. xxxiii. 11.

syrian viceroys appear as Babylonian kings in the Canon of Ptolemy[5]. The name, Satrap, being of Sanskrit origin, may have come in at any time. The relation, expressed by the name, neither began nor ended with the Persians, being inseparable from the loose organisation of the vast Eastern Empires. Berosus speaks of a Satrap under Nabopolassar; Diodorus uses the term of the governor set by Ninus over Media[8], and speaks of the " Satrapy of Babylonia," as having been promised to Belesys[9]. The name continued on under the Grecian Alexander[10], and after his death. There is not then a shadow of ground, because Xenophon says that Cyrus, "[11] when he was in Babylon, thought good at once to send Satraps to the conquered nations," to assume that he was the *first* who sent Satraps to conquered provinces, or that he was instituting a new office. Xenophon says, "[12] having selected those of his friends whom he thought the fittest, he sent Satraps to Arabia, Cappadocia, the Greater Phrygia, Lycia and Ionia, Caria, Phrygia on the Hellespont, and Æolis. But over Cilicia and Cyprus and the Paphlagonians he sent not *Persian* Satraps, because they seemed to join willingly the campaign against Babylon :" and again, "[13] The Cilicians and Cyprians joined his army very readily. Wherefore he never sent any *Persian* Satrap over either Cilicians or Cyprians, but their native kings sufficed him." This is precisely the same policy which we find in Alexander and his immediate successors, who left certain kingdoms under their native kings, making them, as did Cyrus also, tributaries. The king was in these cases the Satrap, as elsewhere the Satraps became little kings. Herodotus himself says generally, that the Persians adopted the polity of the Medes[14]. Xenophon is obviously relating no new institution, but how Cyrus chose fitting *Persians* for the office, which itself was an integral part of all Asiatic rule. The point insisted on in

[8] Diod. ii. 2.　[9] Ib. 24.　[10] See ab. p. 154-6.　[11] viii. 6. 1.　[12] Ib. 4.
[13] vi. 4. 1.　[14] 1. 134. see Bähr ad loc. following Heeren, l. l. p. 142.

each case is, that they were *Persian* [1] Satraps. The statement presupposes that the office existed before. It was manifestly also a mere partial, unsystematic, arrangement or account, since, of the six Persian Satraps, five were placed in Asia Minor [2]; and, in all his other territories, one only, and that, in Arabia. Cyrus appears rather to have modified the existing system of Satraps, by "[3]placing the governors of the citadels and the captains of guards at the different posts in the country," as checks upon them. Herodotus also mentions a Persian Satrap of Sardis under Cyrus [4], and of Egypt under Cambyses [5]. In regard to the number, it is evident that either Darius diminished the existing number, or that *his* Satraps mean something different from the office under Cyrus. For in Asia Minor alone the Satraps under Cyrus were twice as many as those mentioned in that division by Darius [6]. The number of *twenty*, under which Herodotus sums them up, is itself uncertain. In the Behistun inscription, Darius mentions incidentally a "[7] Satrap of Arachosia" not included in the list of Herodotus, whereas the province is mentioned in "[8] the three authentic lists of the Persian provinces, which are contained in the Inscriptions of Darius."

The several lists of the provinces in those three inscriptions are moreover imperfect, not exactly agreeing with one another, yet each exceeding in number that given by Herodotus [9]. They shew, that variations took place even

[1] mentioned both in viii. 6. 4. and vi. 4. 1. [2] viii. 6. 4. [3] Ib. 1. [4] iii. 120.

[5] iv. 166. [6] In addition to the five Persian Satraps there were, under Cyrus, the three native Satraps of Cilicia, and Paphlagonia, and the neighbouring Cyprus. Xenophon, in his own time, names the Persian "rulers" of two more divisions of Asia Minor, through which he passed, the Bithynians, and the Phasians (to the East of Pontus,) with the Hesperians. Anab. vii. 8. pen. Polyænus (vii. 21. 7.) mentions, in regard to the times of Artaxerxes Memnon, a Satrap of Catonia, (one of the ten divisions of Cappadocia. Strabo xii. 1. 4. p. 534.) Under Darius, Herodotus mentions four Satrapies only in Asia Minor.

[7] Beh. Inscr. col. 3. par. 9. §.2.

[8] The lists are given in Rawl. Her. T. ii. p. 485, n. 6. on Her. iii. 94.

[9] The list at Behistun (given by Rawl. ib. and in the inscription itself, p. 591,) mentions 23 provinces including Persia, (which it alone counts,) and the "Islands of the sea;" (col. 1. par. 6. in Rawl. Her. ii. 591.) but not containing

in the reign of Darius himself. Several, which occur as
one Satrapy in the system given by Herodotus, are given
in the lists as distinct provinces [10].   In all, those lists furnish the names of 33 provinces, instead of the 20 Satrapies, or, (including [11] the Arabians, Ethiopians, Colchians,
who brought presents instead of tribute, and the Persians, who were exempt from tribute,) the 24 divisions of
Herodotus.   Yet they omit the fifth Satrapy, " all Phœnicia, Palestine-Syria, and Cyprus."   Then also, since, in
the third year of the reign of Xerxes, his dominions were
divided into 127 provinces, it is in itself likely that the
division into 20, which Herodotus himself speaks of as
something peculiar [12], did not exclude a division into more
numerous provinces.   A trace of such subdivision occurs
probably in the " [13] nome *in* Dascyleium."   One of those
larger Satrapies can hardly have been included under the
title.   Æolis continued to be a separate Satrapy in the
time of Artaxerxes.   It was held under Pharnabazus, and
given by him to whom he willed [14].   Yet its Satrap, Mania, was in a condition to hold her own and to make war
with towns in the Troad [15], and to incorporate them in her
satrapy.   She also joined Pharnabazus [16] in his invasions
of the Mysians and Pisidians, gave him tribute and presents, and received him in a more distinguished way, than

Sagartia, which that at Persepolis has, nor India, which is in the lists at Persepolis and Nakhsh-i-Rustam.   The list at Persepolis (Ib.) alone has not " the isles
of the sea."   That of Nakhsh-i-Rustam (Ib.) has not Mecia nor Sagartia, but
has eight, which the others have not.   The four Satrapies of Asia Minor (Her.
iii. 90.) appear probably in the Nakhsh-i-R. list alone, as Cappadocia, Saparda,
and Ionia repeated twice; the two others have three only.

[10] Babylonia and Assyria are one Satrapy, but are two provinces in the lists;
(as they were also in Xenophon's time, Anab. vii. 8. pen.;) the Sagartians, Sa-
rangians, Mycians, part only of the fourteenth Satrapy, are three provinces;
the Parthians, Chorasmians, Sogdians, Arians, the sixteenth Satrapy, are four
provinces in the lists; the Sattagydians and Gandarians, part of the seventh
Satrapy, are two provinces.   [11] Herod. iii. 97.

[12] Her. iii. 89.   " It was only now, that the empire was divided only into
20 Satrapies, and that it was defined, how much each was to pay."   Flügel,
in Hall. Enc. Art. Perser. Gesch. p. 374.

[13] Her. iii. 120. In 126, Orœtes is called " the lieutenant-governor of Dasc."
in vi. 33, "*in* Dasc."   Thucydides also speaks of "the Satrapy of Dascyleium."
i. 129.   [14] Xen. Hell. 3, 1. 8.   [15] Larissa, Hamaxitus and Colonæ.   [16] Ib. 10.

the *other* lieutenant-governors.   Pharnabazus, then, had many subordinate governors, who had, equally with himself, the title of Satrap [1].   Palestine itself, after the captivity and immediately after Daniel's time, is spoken of as "[2] a province."   In the same book of Ezra it is related, that[3] *the commissions of the king were given to the satraps of the king and to the governors on this side the river, and they furthered the people*, whereas, according to the later arrangement of Darius, there was in that district one Satrapy only.   In the book of Esther also, the Satraps are spoken of with reference to the one hundred and twenty seven provinces [4], (Medinoth.)

The result then is, that the government by Satraps was, according to heathen historians too, Babylonian also, and was, under whatever name, an essential part of those large Eastern empires; that Cyrus sent *Persian* Satraps, continuing, but modifying, the old office; sending Satraps, on whom he could rely, and limiting the power of the Satraps; and that the division by Darius Hystaspes, mentioned by Herodotus, which, as appears from the monuments of Darius himself, needs correction, did not interfere with the previous distribution into smaller provinces, of which we have notice before and after him.   Plato asserts [5], on the other hand, that Darius made another distribution into seven only, the Governors of which must have borne the common title of Satraps.   The title, signifying, (it is thought [6],) "lord or protector of a kingdom or province," might relate equally to a larger or lesser province, although history, as is natural, has occasion mostly to speak of the greater Satraps.   A Governor-general of

---

[1] The word " Satrap " is used in regard to Mania, n. 8-10; she is compared with " *the other* ὕπαρχοι."   The word then must be used, as it is in Herodotus, (see Bähr on Her. iii. 70. note, v. 25. note.) as the Greek equivalent for Satrap.

[2] Ezra ii. 1. Neh. vii. 6. xi. 3.   [3] Ezra viii. 36.

[4] viii. 9. In iii. 12, the number of the provinces is not mentioned, but the letters were written to the king's Satraps in each province, (Medinah) of which it is said, i. 1. viii. 9, and ix. 30. that there were 127.

[5] " He divided [the empire] into seven parts." de Legg. iii. p. 144. Bip.

[6] See in Rödiger's App. to Gesen. Thes. p. 68.

India would be likely to be mentioned in history; not so probably a governor of the Cape or of Bombay.

vii. Unbelief counted, it did not weigh, arguments, when it would make an argument out of the description of the den of lions[7]. The den is to have been a cistern, (much like that, I suppose, in which the white bears used to be kept in the Zoological gardens,) and the stone is to have been laid over the whole opening, excluding light and air, so that no animal could live in it. Such is the description which Lengerke would insolently foist upon the book of Daniel[8].

It is, of course, foreign from Daniel, who represents[9] the king as speaking, and himself, as hearing and answering, ere the stone was removed. This is, of course, as essential a part of the description as the rest. The den was, for safety, below ground. Such a den must needs have some approach from above, in order to admit of its being cleaned by the keepers, and the bones of the animals, on which the animals were fed, being removed. There is nothing in the meaning of the word to determine further the shape of the den[10]. But the way, by which

[7] Obj. 3.

[8] p. 272. 283. Davidson adopts the insolence of Lengerke, "How did the animals live in a *cistern-like* den? Did an angel give them air to breathe, whose vitalising property could not be exhausted? It is difficult to see how life could have been long supported in the place. Lions would soon have died in it." iii. 175. Leng. had said, p. 272. "Hengstenberg (p. 134.) and Hävernick (p. 223.) decline considering the preservation of Daniel in the lion's den, as a natural event, but forget that the lions too could not have held out in a hole, void of air, covered with a stone. Over these no angel watched, as over Daniel (v. 21.) and yet it were necessary to assume a 2nd miracle, to make their preservation, and so the miracle of the deliverance of Daniel, possible."

[9] vi. 19-21.

[10] גּוּב. "In Syriac, *goobo* is used of 'a prison,' Barh. Chron. p. 178. l. 10. of 'caves' Ib. p. 317. l. 15, &c." Häv. Neue Unters. p. 65. *Jauba*, in Arab. is used of a cleft between two mountains, a ravine; the opening between clouds; space between houses or lands; a pit or ditch, a small inn." Freyt. Lex. Arab. l. 321. In Syriac, it seems to be a hollow. The Rev. Payne Smith has kindly furnished me with these instances from the collectanea of Bernstein and Quatremère with his own; "the hollow receptacle of a bolt," Gest. Al. 88. 7; "vessel," Ecclus. xxi. 14. Judith vii. 20; "cistern," Ib. viii. 31. Jer. ii. 13; from which flocks drank, Rel. Jur. 123. 9; "well," (at Bethlehem) 2 Sam. xxiii. 15, 16; it is used of "pits" in which people hid themselves and

the keepers descended, might obviously form a way of escape for one whom the lions spared, when first cast to them. The Jews, the keepers of the Emperor's lions in Fez, contrived, at times, to rescue their compatriots whom the Emperor had had cast in[1]. The word rendered, *mouth*, is evidently the entrance. Of a well the whole was, and often still is, covered in the East by a stone, to reserve it for the time of use[2], to keep it free from uncleanly things, or from being stopped by sand. The object of the princes, in laying a stone on the mouth of the den and sealing it with the seal of the king and of his lords, was simply to prevent the removal of Daniel. To this end, it was only necessary to close the entrance, where the stairs or ladder, by which the keepers went down into the den, abutted at the top. Such an entrance from above is described, in regard to a lions' den in Fez, where state-prisoners and Jews were often thrown. "[1] The lions' den was a large quadrangular hole in the ground, divided by a partition into two chambers. This wall has a door, which can be opened and shut from above. The keepers

dwelt, 1 Sam. xiii. 6 ; the large "pit" of Beth-Eked, 2 Kgs. x .14 ; "pit of mud," deep enough for a prison, Barh. Chr. p. 118; "a dungeon," Jer. xxxvii. 16; "a prison," Wisd. x. 13. S. Ephr. ii. 416. Bar. Hebr. Chr. p. 178. 303. 338, (*beit goobo* prison-house, Acta Mart. ii. 239.;) "den" of lions, Dan. vi. 7, 12. Hist. Drac. 31. S. Ephr. in Ass. B. O. i. 78; a *hollow* in a wood, (perhaps i. q. χάσμα, LXX) 2 Sam. xviii. 17. S. Ephr. ii. 48 ; "deep pit," for, "the pit of hell," Ecclus. xxi. 10 ; it is explained by שׁוּחַ, "large cisterns," Ass. B. O. iii. 1. p. 499. It is also used (as my son has noted) for מַסְגֵּר, "prison," Ps. cxlii. 7; בּוֹר, "prison," Gen. xli. 14; and in the phrases, "go down to the pit," Ps. xxviii. 1. lxxxviii. 4 ; "in the lowest pit," Ps. lxxxviii. 6 ; a pit, into which an ass or ox might fall and be killed, Ex. xxi. 33. In Jer. xli. 7, 9. it is used of the large pit, originally dug by Asa "for fear of Baasha," whether to bury things in, or, as Bochart thought, (T. ii. p. 65. Leipz.) as a subterranean hiding place, or as a large reservoir. In any case it must have been a large one. Ishmael cast 70 men into it. From the same meaning of "hollow," is perhaps derived that of "bridge." In Hebrew too גֶּשֶׁר is an "arched building," Ezek. xvi. 24, 31, 39. The arch was known in Babylon in Nebuchadnezzar's time ; for the "hanging gardens" of Babylon were supported by arches, and were over the river, Strabo xvi. 1. 5. p. 738. Cas. In Samaritan also, it stands for "well," Gen. xxvi. 25 ; "cistern," Lev. xi. 36; "dungeon," Gen. xli. 14. Ex. xii. 29. Cast. Lex. col. 505. [1] Höst, Nachr. v. Fez u. Marokko, p. 77. 290.

[2] Gen. xxix. 2, 3. As to the present practice see Robins. Pal. i. 490. and note 1. 2.

of the lions, (mostly Jews,) throw food into the one division, and so entice the lions thither, then they shut the
door from above and clean the other division. The whole
is under the open sky, and is only encircled with a wall,
over which* people can look down in. The Emperor
sometimes has men cast in."

Of course, we cannot tell whether such was the structure of the den into which Daniel was thrown. Daniel
wrote for believers, not for antiquarians. Enough, that
a den of such sort would answer the description in Daniel,
and that, the entrance being closed by the stone laid on
it, the purpose of the princes could be effected without
the absurdity imputed. But to invent absurdities betrays
the malus animus of the critic; the prophet remains un-
harmed, as he was in the lions' den.

vi. The imputations of " ignorance about the Magi[3]" are
to be made up of an alleged discrepancy of the statements
of Daniel from those of Porphyry and S. Jerome. These,
it is said, divide the Magi into three classes, whereas Daniel, it is affirmed, enumerates five. As though, even if
their accounts were at variance, such a change as to the
number of classes into which an institute was divided, could
not take place in nearly eight centuries! But there is
no discrepancy. The four[4] classes, enumerated by Daniel,
magicians, astrologers, soothsayers, Chaldæans, are a division of *kind,* according to the character of their employment. The distinction in Porphyry is one, not of *kind,* but
of *degree.* They are three *orders,* like the different ranks
of the initiated, or of the Free-masons to this day. The
three orders of Magi, mentioned by Porphyry[5], (from
whom S. Jerome gives an extract[6],) were degrees in the

---

[3] Obj. 4.   [4] Lengerke (p. 48.) overlooked, that the title מכשׁפים occurs
once only in the *Hebrew,* (Dan. ii. 2.) not in the Chaldee; and that in the Chaldee enumerations there stands גזרין, (ii. 10. 27. iv. 4. v. 7. 11.) which is not in
the Hebrew of Daniel. They are then doubtless equivalents. Compare especially ii. 48. *he made him chief of the sagans of all the wise of Babylon* with
ii. 2. on the one hand in which four classes are mentioned, including the Heb.
מכשׁפים, and on the other, v. 11. in which there are also *four,* but the Chald.
גזרין stands for the Heb. מכשׁפים.   [5] De Abstin. iv. 16.

[6] " Eubulus, who unfolded the history of Mithra in many volumes, relates

highest, the priestly order. Porphyry distinctly calls them ministers of the Deity. "[1]Among the Persians, those who are wise as to the Deity, and are its ministers, are called Magi. For Magos means this in their native language. This race is accounted so great and venerable among the Persians, that even Darius son of Hystaspes inscribed on his monument, in addition to the rest, that he was a teacher of the things of the Magi. These were divided into three classes, as Symbulus [Eubulus[2]] says, who wrote the history of Mithra in many books. The first and most learned class neither eat any living thing, nor slay it, but abide in the ancient abstinence from animal food[3]. The second class use animal food, but do not kill any tame animal; nor do the third touch all things, like ordinary people. For the transmigration of souls is a doctrine of all the first."

This last statement of Eubulus, which he assigned as the ground of the whole abstinence from animal food, is a manifest error, since the metempsychosis was no part of the Magian system; and the whole is directly contradicted by Herodotus[4].

There may, of course, still have been three classes of priests, although all besides is erroneous. So the evidence for the threefold division was to be eked out by an alleged threefold division of the ancient Egyptian and of the Parsee priesthood. This, if true, would manifestly be nothing to the purpose, unless it were shewn that the Magi were all priests, or that the modern ritual-priesthood of the Parsee and the priesthood of the Egyptians

---

that among the Persians there are three kinds of Magi, of whom the first, who are the most learned and eloquent, take no other food than meal and vegetables." S. Jer. adv. Jovin. ii. 14. [1] l. c. [2] S. Jer. l. c. [3] Leng. adds, of his own apparently, that " they abstained from wine and marriage." (p. 46.) The classes of Parsee priests are hereditary, and so involve marriage.

[4] "The Magi are much severed both from other men and from the priests of Egypt. For these hold it matter of conscience not to kill any living thing, except what they sacrifice. But the Magi kill with their own hands all, save dog and man, and indeed shew great earnestness in it, killing alike ants and serpents, and the other reptiles and fowls." i. 140.

were identical with that of the Magi. In Christian times however, in which alone we have any account of the division of the Egyptian priesthood [5], the number was *not* three. It consisted of four [6] or five more learned classes, besides others, to whom the general name of "priest" is also given. S. Clement of Alexandria recounts five [7], as entering into the Egyptian processions of his day. All these were entrusted with books of Hermes, and four were engaged in secular learning also.

The distribution of the Parsee priesthood into the Desturs, Mobeds, Herbads, is also a division of degrees; its antiquity is altogether uncertain. The names are not old, but modern Persian. They do not occur in the Zendavesta. Any how, this is not a division of the Magi generally, and it relates to ritual only. Those who distinguish the Destur and the Mobed most, say, "[8]that the office of the Mobed is to utter the prayers, to enact the ceremonies, and to this end he must know the whole Zendavesta by heart, but without necessarily understanding

---

[5] Herodotus (ii. 36. 58.) whom Leng. quotes, has nothing on the subject. In ii. 37. he says contrariwise, "Each god has, not one priest, but many, of whom one is chief priest; if any die, his son is appointed in his stead." In Exod. vii. 11. it is not clear that three classes are mentioned. It is literally, "And Pharaoh too called the wise men and enchanters; and they too, the writers of the sacred writing, did so with their enchantments." It is not clear, then, whether Moses speaks of two classes, or of three; any how, he does not say, that there were only three.

[6] "The true philosophising exists in the prophetæ and hierostolistæ, and hierogrammateis, and the horologi. But the other multitude of the priests, and shrine-bearers, and temple-sweepers, and ministers of the gods, exercise cleanness in like way, but not with so much accuracy or continence." Porph. de abstin. iv. 8. p. 321.

[7] Strom. vi. 4. p. 757, 8. Pott. Porphyry n. 9, p. 324. mentions the hymn-singer, as "employed in the worship of Sarapis by fire and water, making a libation with the water and strewing the fire, when, standing on the threshold, he, in the native language of the Egyptians, awakens the god."

[8] Haug, die Gâthâs Abth. 2. p. xiii. from the Destur at Poonah. Spiegel, (Avesta ii. p. xv. c. 1.) whom Haug criticises, quotes the Persian translation of the Ardâ-virâf-nâme, "the Desturs of the law, they are the Mobeds," and refers to Hyde Rel. Vett. Perss. p. 367. ed. 1. The name Mobed, for the chief priest of the Magi, occurs often in accounts of Syriac martyrdom. Lorsbach, Museum, p. 132. and Syriac collectanea of Quatremère.

it. The Destur has the superintendence of all the cerc-monies and of the whole fire-worship, without being re-quired to perform it, this being done at his direction by the Mobeds. He is to understand and to be able to ex-pound the Zendavesta, and in all matters of belief he alone is appealed to." The Herbads are acknowledged to be the lowest class of fire-priests.

This too is a division wholly different in principle from that of Daniel. On the other hand the well-known ac-count of Strabo corresponds so far with this of Daniel, that he speaks of *several* kinds of Magi. "[1] Of the astro-nomical Chaldæans there are many kinds[2]. For some are called Orchians, and others Borsippians, and *many others*, as, according to sects, speaking different things concerning the same dogmas."

Three of the classes in Daniel are also marked classes.

The *Chaldæans* were known to Greek writers also, as the priests[3] among the Magi. These are the spokesmen of all the wise men, in that first trial by Nebuchadnezzar[4]. The title is not used (as some have said) as a name for all the Magi, but historically only on this one occasion. Elsewhere, and even by "the Chaldæans" themselves, they are mentioned as one class only among others[5]. The generic title, used in Daniel, is not Chaldæans, but, *all the wise men of Babylon*[6]. This, as to Nebuchadnezzar's time[7], included four classes; in the single case, mentioned in Belshazzar's reign[8], three only are named.

---

[1] xvi. 1. 6.   [2] γένη.

[3] "The Chaldæans, being priests of this god," [Bel.] Her. i. 181. "On the greater altar, the Chaldæans burn 1000 talents of frankincense every year, when they celebrate the festival of this god." ib. 183. "The priests, whom the Baby-lonians call Chaldæans." Diod. Sic. ii. 24. "The Chaldæans, being of the oldest Babylonians, in the distribution of the polity have the like rank with the priests of Egypt. For they are appointed to the service, and study wisdom during the whole period of their lives, having their greatest glory from astrology." Ib. 29. "Chaldæans, a kind (γένος) of Magians." Hesych. (Häv. Dan. p. 48, 9.)

[4] ii. 4, 5, 10.   [5] with the מְכַשְּׁפִים, אַשָּׁפִים, חַרְטֻמִּים, Dan. ii. 2; with two classes only, by the Chaldæans themselves, ii. 10. viz. כל חרטם ואשף וכשׂדי ; with the same two classes and the גזרין iv. 4. and v. 11. referring to Nebuchadnezzar's time; and, of Belshazzar's, without the כשׂדים, v. 7.   [6] ii. 12, 13, 14, 18, 24, (bis) 48. iv. 3. Ch. [6. Eng.] v. 7, 11.   [7] ii. 48. comp. ii. 2. and v. 11.   [8] v. 7.

A 2nd class, *ashshafim,* as has been already mentioned, occurs only in Daniel and in West Aramaic[9].

A 3rd, *chartummim,* (which probably signifies, etymologically, *writers of sacred writing,*) occurs besides only of Egyptian magicians[10]. But the connection of Babylonian and Egyptian idolatry makes it, in itself, probable, that it was one and the same institution in both ; and we are directly told that Democritus, (who died B.C. 357,) wrote "[11] on the sacred writings in Babylon."

The 4th class is, at least, characterised in this way, that a different name is given to it in the Chaldee and Hebrew ; which at least shews, (contrary to what has been stated so carelessly,) that discrimination was used in the naming of the several classes.

But it is said, that it was improbable that Daniel should, with his strict principles, have been willing to be taught among the Magi ; or that they should have received him among them, being an hereditary caste; or that he should have been set over them, or should have accepted such a charge[12].

In regard to his willingness to be taught, Moses too, we know, [13]*was learned in all the wisdom of the Egyptians.* As Moses acquired their secular knowledge without their debasing superstitions, so Daniel. As Moses was educated by the priests, who were sole possessors of Egyptian learning, so Daniel by the Magi, the possessors of the Babylonian. In both nations the learning was ordi-

[9] See Lect. i. p. 40.

[10] Gen. xli. 24. Ex. vii. 11. In Exodus, it stands connected with the חכמים and מכשפים, whether including them, or no. The rendering of the LXX, ἱερογραμματεῖς, (acquainted as they were with Egyptian customs,) makes it morally certain that the word is compounded of חרט "style" and חרט "sacred."

[11] περὶ τῶν ἐν Βαβυλῶνι ἱερῶν γραμμάτων. Diog. Laert. vit. Democr. The Hierogrammateus, according to S. Clement Al., "had to know, what are called Hieroglyphics, and about cosmography, and geography, the order of the sun and of the moon and of the five planets ; the ground-plan of Egypt, and the diagram of the Nile ; the register of the ornaments of the temples, and of the spots consecrated to them ; about the measures, and the things of use in the temples." Strom. vi. 4. p. 268. Sylb.

[12] Lengerke, Dan. p. 50, 1. Bleek (Einl. p. 598,) only excepts to his undertaking the charge, followed by Dav. iii. 183.   [13] Acts vii. 22.

narily transmitted from father to son : of the Persian
Magi it is expressly said, "[1]The Persian Magi never educated non-Persians, *unless the king enjoin it.*"   In such a
monarchy as the Babylonian or Persian, the king's will
was, of course, law.   As the Egyptian priesthood had a
large province of secular knowledge, so all tradition tells
us of the varied learning of the Chaldæans, and their astronomy.   Heathen knowledge was, of course, *made subject to vanity*; and astronomy was subjected to astrology.
Still astrology, however intense the interest in it might be
to those who believed in it, was only a subordinate study.   "In Babylonia," Strabo says [2], "an abode was set
apart for the native philosophers, called Chaldees, who
are chiefly engaged about astronomy; but some claim to
cast nativities, which others do not admit."   Their astronomical observations, were received in Greece as of
acknowledged accuracy, and, from their extent, made a
change in Greek astronomy [3].   Greeks[4] too have thought
that the birthplace of philosophy was "among the Magi of
Persia, the Chaldees of Babylonia or Assyria."   We have
also received unexpected notices of a very large literature
on "[5]political and social legislation, philosophy, medicine,
botany, natural history, and the history of man."   There

[1] Philostr. de vit. Soph. Protag. Opp. p. 498. Mor.   [2] l. c.

[3] Simplicius notices Aristotle's acknowledgment of his uncertainty about
the motions of the planets, and subjoins; "We ought then, persuaded by
Aristotle, to follow the later writers, because they best adhere to the phænomena, whereas the earlier neither perfectly adhere to them, nor knew so
many, because the observations, sent by Callisthenes from Babylon, had not
yet arrived in Greece, which Aristotle had besought him to send ; which observations Porphyry relates to be for 1903 years, being preserved down to the
times of Alexander of Macedon." (on Aristot. de cœlo L. ii. f. 123. ed. 1526.
quoted by Prideaux, Conn. A. 570.) Epigenes (in Plin. N. H. vii. 57.) adds
the fact, that the observations were recorded on bricks, the well-known material of inscriptions. The uneven numbers in Porphyry are an internal
evidence of truth, against the vague exaggerations of the 720,000 years of
Epigenes, 490,000 of Berosus and Critodemus, (in Plin. l. c.) 473,000 of Diodorus Sic. (ii. 31.) 470,000 of Cicero, (de Div. i. 19.) 270,000 of Hipparchus,
(in Procl. in Timæum p. 31.) which Diodorus and Cicero too held to be incredible.   [4] Diog. Laert. Procem. init. He mentions also the Gymnoso-
phists among the Indians, and the Druids among the Celts and Galatians.

[5] See on Obadiah, p. 243 from Chwolson, &c.

was then a large field for Daniel to study or to regulate, without entering upon their superstitions or misbelief.

His office, also, as described by himself, seems to point to a general supervision of the whole, rather than to direct connection with details. He is not called Rab-Mag, chief of the Magi; but is simply said to have been *head of the sagans (or governors) over all the wise men of Babylon;* perhaps a sort of minister of public instruction.

But even in that which was most connected with superstition, the astrological predictions of the wise men, there may have been very large scope for correcting abuses and superstitions. The wise men of Babylon certainly had the reputation of a very great political sagacity. The character of human prediction is "to see events while beginning [6], and to anticipate." To discern their purport and tendencies from the first, is the province of human long-sightedness. To see events in their superhuman causality in the mind of God, is His gift to the prophet. The Chaldee politicians had, apparently, extraordinary natural gifts of human sagacity, which, from youth onwards, were diligently cultivated [7]. "They say," says Diodorus [8], "that predictions have been made to other kings not a few, and especially to Alexander the conqueror of Darius, and to Antigonus, and Seleucus Nicator, who reigned after him; and in all the aforesaid they seem to have guessed well. They predict, also, to indivi-

---

[6] "Take accurate account, if you will, of those things for which an orator is responsible; I decline it not. What are these? To see, &c (as in text) and foretell them to others." Demosth. de corona, p. 308. Dind. quoted by Strachey On the Prophets of the O. T. p. 2. 29. (Tracts for priests and people.)

[7] Diodorus (ii. 39.) contrasts the early, traditional, hereditary, persevering training of the Chaldees in philosophy and astrology, with the Greek want of training, late cultivation of philosophy, distracted pursuit of it, and the search after novelty and speculations, not for truth's sake, but to attract disciples and gain a livelihood.

[8] ii. 31. The two cases mentioned by Herodotus of the Magi are intrinsically improbable, and inaccurate as related. As to the dream of Astyages, there was nothing to alarm him, that his descendant should flood all Asia ; (i. 167.) nor, if true, is it likely that he should have married his daughter into the royal family of Persia. In both cases too the Magi are related to have fallen into complete error. (i. 120. vii. 19.)

duals what is about to happen, so successfully, that those who have made trial marvel at what happens, and deem that it is beyond what belongs to man."

If this was so, the fraud lay in their claiming Divine authority for that which was human. And this, their fraud, was the occasion of two of their defeats. In the belief, which they encouraged, that the interpretation was Divine, it was nothing unreasonable in Nebuchadnezzar, to ask of them to recall to him the half-forgotten dream[1]. God did reveal both to Daniel. The unknown character on the wall became the like test in the time of Belshazzar.

II. The incorrectnesses then of Daniel being correct, they are to be eked out by "[2] a number of improbable and suspicious statements." Of these we may sever off at once, what is called "[3] the rigorism of the Jews," i. e. the obedience of Daniel and his companions to the law of God; "[4] the detestable self-will and fanaticism of the Jewish Officers of state," i. e. the plain-spoken refusal of Daniel's companions to be guilty of idolatry; "[5] the fanaticism of Daniel," i. e. his refusal to cease to pray to God, because a king commanded; and contrariwise[6] the non-mention of Daniel, when he was not attacked; and "[7] the senseless requisition of Nebuchadnezzar, that the wise men should tell him his dream;" which tacitly assumes the falsehood of the history, since it would only be "senseless," if it was not calculated to be a test between truth and falsehood.

[1] Nothing is more common than an indistinct memory of a dream, of such sort, that a person can be sure what the dream was *not*, although he cannot recall what it *was*. Even Stähelin quotes from the Mémoires de l' Acad. d. Inscr. T. 48. p. 647, [extracts from Masudi, Sirat alresool, by De Sacy,] a like account of Rebia ben Nasr king of Yemen, who made the selfsame requisition on the same ground. "Prince," the diviners said, "tell us the vision and we will give you the interpretation." "No! for then I could not be certain of the truth of your interpretation. He alone can know the meaning, who can know the vision before I relate it." De Sacy's transl. The story has no historical evidence; since Almasudi died near the end of our 10th cent.; but it illustrates the principle. [2] Lengerke, xiii. 6. p. lxiv, v. [3] Improb. 1. See ab. Lect. i. p. 17, 18. [4] Improb. 6. [5] Improb. 17. See p. 446. [6] Improb. 4. see ab. Lect. i. p. 14. and below, p. 460. [7] Improb. 2. See in text.

There remain, [8] the want of proportion in his golden image; [9] the religious persecution of Nebuchadnezzar; [10] Nebuchadnezzar's seven years' insanity; [11] that he prays before he [wholly] recovers his reason; [12] that he gives an account of his insanity in an edict to his subjects; and that [13] yet, in that edict, he does not show his belief in the God of the Jews, as the only God; that [14] Daniel did not come with the rest of the Magi, and was unknown to Belshazzar; that [15] Belshazzar was courteous towards Daniel, and [16] Daniel inconsistent in declining, and then accepting, the king's gift; [17] that the sacred vessels were so coarsely profaned; [18] that Daniel was proclaimed the third ruler of the kingdom in the night of the capture of Babylon; [19] the frantic law of Darius; [20] traces that a Jew wrote the edict of Darius; and (which is the same as the 16th) [21] the incredible intolerance of the king.

It seems as incredible to these writers, that human nature should be sinful and arrogant, as that man, through the grace of God, should obey God. Strange that any one, ever so little acquainted with the drunkenness of human power and pride, should venture to represent Belshazzar's insolence, or the law into which the vanity or policy of Darius was entrapped, as any thing incredible for human nature to venture upon. When such things are swept together, we are at least sure, that no refuse has been left behind. I will take the miscellaneous list in the order of their interest.

i. It is now conceded that the madness of Nebuchadnezzar [10] agrees with the description of a rare sort of disease, called Lycanthropy, from one form of it, of which our earliest notice is in a Greek medical writer of the 4th century after our Lord, in which the sufferer retains his consciousness in other respects, but imagines himself to be changed into some animal, and acts, up to a certain

---

[8] Improb. 3.   [9] Improb. 5.   [10] Improb. 7.   [11] Improb. 9.
[12] Improb. 8.   [13] Improb. 10.   [14] Improb. 11.   [15] Improb. 12.
[16] Improb. 13.   [17] Improb. 14.   [18] Improb. 15.   [19] Improb. 16.
[20] Improb. 18.   [21] Improb. 19.

point, in conformity with that persuasion. Those who imagined themselves changed into wolves howled like wolves, and, (there is reason to believe, falsely,) accused themselves of bloodshed [1]. Others imitated the cries of dogs; it is said that others thought themselves nightingales, lions, cats, or cocks, and these crowed like a cock. It was no dissimilar form of disease, that others imagined that their bodies were, wholly or in part, changed into some brittle substance, whence they avoided contact, lest they should be broken. Others had other similar delusions, varying incidentally from each other.

The monotony of the descriptions of the disease seems to imply that it was very rare. Marcellus (4th Cent.[2]) mentions two sorts. "They who are siezed by the kynanthropic or lycanthropic disease, in the month of February go forth by night, imitating in all things wolves or dogs, and until day especially live near tombs." Aetius [3], (end of the 5th Cent.[4]) quotes the exact statement; giving his account also of the symptoms, and of remedies. Paulus of Ægina [latter half of 7th Cent.] omits only the kynanthropy[5]. Further, Galen, I believe, only mentions one case, of one who acted like a cock. "[6]Another, hearing cocks crow, as they, before they crow, flap their

[1] Single instances of the disease are given in Calmeil, La Folie considérée sous le point de vue pathologique, philosophique, historique, et judiciaire. Paris. 1845. T. i. p. 276, 336. 416. (who also gives an account of an epidemic attack of it in the Jura, Ib. 310.) and in Dr Arnold's Observations on the nature, kinds, causes, and prevention of Insanity, (published 1782,) p. 122-5. To both these works Dr Browne kindly directed me. The references to other medical writers, quoted below, were supplied to me by Arnold's work. Welcker's work, Die Lycanthropie ein Aberglaube u. eine Krankheit, (Kl. Schriften, iii. 157 sqq.) contains no facts, only a theory that such was the origin of the fable about Lycaon.   [2] Biogr. Univ. xxvi. 597.

[3] L. vi. c. ii. p. 104. v. reprinted also in Galen. Opp. T. x. p. 502, 3. ed. Chart.

[4] These dates are taken from Dr. Greenhill's articles in Smith's Biogr. Dict.

[5] iii. 16. He also says generally, "some think themselves some brute animals, and imitate their noises. Some think themselves earthenware vessels, and fear that they shall be broken." iii. 14.

[6] de loc. affect. iii. 10. Opp. vii. 442. The context is of actual mental delusion. "Fear besets all the melancholic; but not always the same sort of unnatural phantasy. For one thought he was earthenware, and so gave way to those whom he met, lest he should be broken." &c. as in text.

wings, so he, flapping against his sides with his arms, imitated the noise of the animals." Trallian again (in the 6th century[7]) mentioned the same form of disease only; "[8]Others think they are a cock, and imitate its crowing." The notices moreover in the middle ages are rare. Mostly, one only occurs in an author, writing on the subject of melancholic alienation[9]; and the repetition of the same stories in modern writers shews how little, in addition, modern experience furnishes. The disease is one from which there have been recoveries. Mercurialis says; "[10]The disease is horrible, yet not destructive to life, even if it last for months; nay, I have *read* that it have been thoroughly cured after years." The exact form of the disease, which would be Boanthropy, I have not found any notice of[11]; perhaps, because the howling of

---

[7] Dr. Greenhill l. c. (v. Alexander) i. 126.   [8] De Art. Med. i. 17. p. 165.

[9] The authorities, quoted by Dr. Arnold, mostly mentioned single cases. Van Swieten (Comm. in Boerhaave, iii. p. 521. says that Forest (L. x. obs. 25. p. 441.) had "seen one countryman, seized with this species of mania, who in spring wandered about a cemetery, and had all the signs mentioned by the ancient physicians," (which last remark implies that it was *then* unknown.) William of Brabant mentioned one case, one at Padua, A.D. 1541, who said that he was a wolf, with the hair turned inside. (quoted by Wier, De Præstig. Dæmon. iv. 23. p. 335.) Zacut, a Portuguese writer, also mentions a single case. (Praxis Med. Obs. 51. p. 12.) Riverius writes more generally, " Others think that they are dogs, cats, wolves, cuckoos, nightingales, cocks, and imitate the noises of these or other animals. Others think that they are dead, and that they must neither eat nor drink." (Praxis Med. i. 14. p. 34.) But, as this last was doubtless the celebrated case, in which the sufferer was led to think that other dead ate, and so was recovered, probably the other rarer sorts, if authentic, were but single cases. Besides these, Actuarius, (end of the 13th cent.) mentions the case, but not as knowing it; " Of the same sort would that disease be, called lycanthropy, as if men had put on a wolf's nature." (De Math. Med. i. p. 48.)

[10] Med. Pract. i. 13. He gives much the same account as Paul. Æg.; "by day they lie hid in the house. At night-fall, forthwith they go forth, and coursing hither and thither, they howl, avoid any who meet them, seek the tombs, are hollow-eyed, and of foul and black complexion."

[11] Arnold (on Insanity, i. 223.) suggests that such may have been meant by the story of the Prœtides in Virg. Ecl. vi. 48. Virgil describes a partial insanity of this sort, lowing, looking for their horns, fearing to be yoked, while he states it to have been in one respect partial. But this form of insanity is not mentioned by any other writer who mentions the insanity of the Prœtides, Apol-

wolves, or dogs, or the crowing of cocks, are most heard by night, and are more piercing sounds, and so make most impression on a diseased brain. The remarkable expressions, [1] *his heart was made like the beast's,* [2] *let a beast's heart be given him,* fit most naturally with this form of disease. This would be its most literal, and exhaustive, explanation. The rest of the description would be in conformity with this, that Nebuchadnezzar, when affected with this disease, ate grass as an ox, and allowed his hair and nails to grow, unshorn and unpared [3], as if he was the animal.

The growth of the nails described is exactly that which modern physiologists have stated to be their growth, when so neglected. *His nails,* Daniel says, *were like bird's claws.* "The nails," says Kölliker [4], "*so long as they are cut,* grow unremittingly; when this is omitted, their growth is confined. In this case, as may be observed in the sick when long bedridden, and in the people of Eastern Asia, the nails become 1½ or 2 inches long, (among the Chinese, according to Hamilton, 2 inches,) and *curve* round the fingers and ends of the toes." The principles, which regulate the excessive growth of hair, are, Dr. Rolleston tells me, less ascertained [5]. Both be-

lodorus, (ii. 2. 2.) or Pherecydes, (in Schol. on Hom. Od. xv. 225.) or Herodotus, (speaking of the Argive women generally, ix. 33.) or Ælian, (Var. Hist. iii. 42.) or Diod. Sic. (iv. 68.) or Pausanias, (viii. 18.) or Pliny, (xxv. 21.) or the Scholiast on Pindar, (Pyth. iii. 96.) or even by Ovid. (Met. xv. 325.) Perizonius, (on Ælian l. c.) says that it is equally unknown to Callimachus, Vitruvius, (viii. 3.) to the author of the Epigram which he quotes, and to Stephanus Byz.   [1] Dan. v. 21.   [2] Dan. iv. 16, Eng. 13, Ch.
[3] iv. 33, Eng. 30, Ch.   [4] Gewebelehre d. Menschen, 1859. § 54. p. 126. furnished me by Dr Rolleston.

[5] "Whereon an excessive growth of the hair which occurs, and its diseased falling-off, together with a frequent reproduction in great masses, depends, cannot be stated with precision. Probably the increased or diminished exsudation from the vessels of the papillæ and bulb of the hair, are the chief causes; more distant causes are probably the condition of the skin and of the whole frame." Kölliker, Ib. p. 150. furnished me by Dr. Rolleston. Dr. R., in answer to my enquiries about the condition of those boys and girls who have run wild, tells me, "Linnæus (Amœnitates Academ. T .vi. p. 65.) says that all the histories of them were to the effect, *quod omnes fuerint hirsuti;* and Ludwig (Grundriss d. Naturgeschichte) speaks of some of these cases, which he gives a

ing, I believe, called excremental, the excessive growth of both would probably be simultaneous. But both may have been the result of that personal neglect, which is so strangely humiliating, a part of a most distressing form of mental disease, and which I have seen as the result of disappointed pride.

The expression, however, *let a beast's heart be given unto him,* may only signify the privation of the characteristic of man, reason, as the king wrote of himself, '*my reason returned unto me.* And there is a distinct form of insanity, in which the eating of grass is one of the characteristic features. "In many classes of the insane," the eminent Commissioner of the Board of Lunacy for Scotland, Dr. Browne, informs me [7], "the eating garbage, excrement, even grass, is a symptom both of general debasement and of perverted appetites. I was accustomed to distinguish a class of my patients as *fæcophagi* or eaters of ordure; and there are met with in asylums *sarcophagi*, individuals who have desired to eat, or who conceive that they have eaten, or who have attempted to eat, human flesh; and *phytophagi*, who devour grass, leaves, twigs, &c. I have had such cases; as well as stone-swallowers, hair-eaters, &c."

"If Nebuchadnezzar's punishment then be regarded as 'alienation,' involving the greatest conceivable amount of degradation, the 'eating grass as oxen,' the expulsion from the society of his fellow-men, and the exposure to the elements, may be viewed as most graphic features of his disease, and of the cruel treatment, to which, in those and in much more recent days, such an affliction subjected the sufferer."

Whichever was the form of Nebuchadnezzar's disease, not even the extreme form of insanity interferes with the resumé of in 1796, as being 'long-haired;' (p. 147.) but in summing up he says, ' Their *skin* was not more hairy, nor of a different complexion, nor thicker than usual.' I have failed to find any statement as to a correlation between the hair and mental alienation, but I hear that such a correlation does exist; The hair becoming bristly, &c. was looked upon as symptomatic."

  6 iv. 33, Ch. 36, Eng.   7 in one of the letters, which he kindly wrote to me, in answer to my enquiries.

inner consciousness, or, consequently, with the power to pray[1]. Altomar gives an instance of lycanthropy[2], which he had himself witnessed, in which neither consciousness nor memory were at all impaired. The person, who had thought himself a wolf, asked him afterwards, whether he was not afraid of him.

An eyewitness has related to me, how, when visiting an asylum, one accompanied him, who made such acute observations on the several forms of insanity of the other patients severally, that the visitor expressed his surprise, how he came to be confined there. "O, I am a cock," was the instant answer, and he began crowing, and flapping his arms; just as the disease is described by Galen.

The Père Surin, who, in exorcising others, fell for many years into a strange malady, in which he believed himself to be possessed[3], gives a most vivid account how, outwardly he was wholly powerless, spoke what was put into his mouth, rolled on the ground, and was, meanwhile, within, in the most perfect peace and communion with God. His description of himself is a most wonderful specimen of acute mental analysis[4], while outwardly he was a maniac. The inner consciousness remains un-

[1] Improb. 9.　[2] De Medend. Morbis. c. 9. in Schenk, Obss. Med. L. i. p. 229.

[3] I believe that no authorised opinion was ever given as to the exact nature of the P. Surin's disease.

[4] "For three months and a half I have never been without having a devil near me, and that actively. Things are come to that pass, that God has permitted, I think, for my sins, what has perhaps never been seen in the Church, that, in the exercise of my ministry, that devil passes from the body of the person possessed, and, coming into mine, assaults and prostrates me, agitates and crosses me visibly, possessing me for several hours like an energumen. I could not express to you what takes place in me during this time, and how that spirit unites itself with mine, without taking from me either the knowledge or the liberty of my soul, acting nevertheless as a second self, and as if I had two souls, one of which is dispossessed of its body and of the use of its organs, and holds itself apart, looking on at the other which introduced itself into its body, as it acts. The two spirits fight on the same field, the body; and the soul is, as it were, divided. In one part of itself, it is subject to diabolical impressions; in the other, it has the emotions proper to it, or those which God gives it.

"At the same time I feel great peace under the good pleasure of God, without knowing how there comes to me an extreme rage and aversion to Him, which produces a sort of impetuous motions to separate myself from Him,

changed, while, up to a certain point, the sufferer thinks,
speaks, acts, as if he were another.   Dr. Browne, who has

which amaze those who witness them ; and, at the same time, a great joy and
sweetness, which shews itself by lamentations and cries like those of demons.
I feel the state of damnation and apprehend it, and feel myself pierced, as it
were, with the points of despair in that stranger soul which seems to me my
own ; while the other soul, which feels itself in perfect confidence, mocks at such
sentiments and, in all freedom, curses him who causes them—nay, I feel that
the same cries, which escape my mouth, come equally from these two souls,
and I have difficulty to discern whether it is the joyousness which produces
them, or the extreme fury which fills me.   The extreme tremblings which
seized me, when the holy Sacrament was brought near to me, proceed, it appears
to me, equally from a horror at its presence which is unsupportable to me, and
a cordial and sweet reverence, without my being able to ascribe it to the one
rather than the other, and without having it in my power to restrain them.   If,
by a motion of one of these two souls, I wish to make a sign of the cross on
my mouth, the other turns aside my hand with the greatest rapidity, and seizes
my finger in my teeth to bite it out of rage.   I never find orison more easy or
more tranquil than amid these agitations.   While my body rolls on the ground,
and the ministers of the Church address me as a devil, and load me with maledictions, I could not tell you the joy which I feel, having become devil, not
by rebellion against God, but by the calamity which represents to me vividly
the condition to which sin has reduced me ; and appropriating to myself, as
being such, all the maledictions bestowed upon me, my soul has reason to sink
in the abyss of its nothingness.

. " When the possessed see me in this state, it is a pleasure to see how they
triumph, and how the devils make a mock of me, saying, ' Physician, heal thyself, go now this moment mount the pulpit ; how glorious it will be to see him
preach, after having rolled on the ground !' what ground of benediction to see
one's self the sport of the devils, and that the justice of God takes account of
my sins in this world.   Such is my condition at this moment almost daily.
There are great disputes about it, whether this be possession or no, whether
ministers of the Gospel can fall into conditions so unsuited to their state.
Some say that it is a chastisement of God upon me, in punishment of some
illusion ; others say something else ; and for me, I am content as I am, and
would not change my lot with another, being firmly convinced that there is
nothing better than to be reduced to great extremities.   My own extremity
is such, that I have few operations free ; if I wish to speak, my utterance is stopped ; at mass, I am stopped quite short.   At table, I cannot carry the food to
my mouth ; at confession, all at once I forget my sins, and I feel the devil entering me, as into his own house.

" As soon as I awake, he is there at orison.   He takes away all thought from
me, when he pleases ; when the heart begins to expand in God, he fills it
with rage ; he casts me asleep when I wish to watch, and publicly by the mouth
of the possessed [the Prioress] he boasts that he is my master, which I have
nothing to gainsay : having the reproach of my conscience, and on my head
the sentence pronounced against sinners, I ought to undergo it, and revere

done more, I am told, than any other of our day for mental disease, tells me, as the result of the experience of
above 30 years; "My opinion is that of all mental powers
or conditions, the idea of personal identity is but rarely
enfeebled, and that it never is extinguished. The Ego
and non-Ego may be confused. The Ego, however, continues to preserve the personality. All the Angels, Devils,
Dukes, Lords, Kings, 'gods many,' that I have had under
my care, remained what they were, before they became
Angels, Dukes, &c, in a sense and even nominally. I have
seen a man, declaring himself the Saviour, or St. Paul,
sign himself *James Thomson*, and attend worship as regularly, as if the notion of Divinity had never entered into his head."

"I think it probable,—because consistent with experience in similar forms of mental affection,—that Nebuchadnezzar retained a perfect consciousness, that he *was*
Nebuchadnezzar, during the whole course of his degradation, and while he ate 'grass as oxen,' and that he may
have prayed fervently that the cup might pass from him."

"A very large proportion of the insane pray, and to the
living God, and in the words supplied at their mother's
knee or by Mother Church, and this whatever may be
the form or extent of the alienation under which they laboured, and whatever the transformation, in the light of
their own delusions, they may have undergone. There
is no doubt that the sincerity, and the devotional feeling,
is as strong in these worshippers as in the sane. I do
not say that all madmen pray, or can pray; but, as you
suppose, monomaniacs, and melancholics, chronic mani-
acs, and ements, (in vast numbers) the hallucinated, &c.

the order of Divine Providence, to which every creature ought to submit."
Letter to the Père d' Attichi, May 3. 1635. quoted by Calmeil, La Folie, ii. 59-64,
from Hist. des Diables de Loudun, p. 217 sqq. This condition lasted first for
two, then for 20 years, with few intervals, 1638-58. in which he composed a
much-valued work on the spiritual life, Catéchisme Spirituel, 2 voll. In 1658 he
was wholly restored; but was not allowed to go back to the place, where his
sufferings first came upon him. A brief notice of him, from the Biographie
Universelle, is prefixed to the translation of his " Foundations of the Spiritual
Life,"(London, 1847.)with such illustrations from his letters, as I then could find.

Those of the Edinburgh school of Philosophy and educated medical men would not, I conceive, take any exception to the view which I have given, because the very conception of partial Insanity involves the possibility of the sentiment of devotion and the recognition of a Supreme Being remaining intact, while other powers are diseased."

There is scarcely any stronger internal evidence of truth, than circumstances, on the surface unlikely, which, on careful examination, appear to be in harmony with the rest of the history. And this the more, when the scientific knowledge of that truth belongs to a later age. Thus, in secular history, Herodotus' account of the circumnavigation of Africa is now undoubted, because of the fact of the position of the sun [1], which one would not have known who had not crossed the line. So, in this account of Nebuchadnezzar, if the disease was some form of Lycanthropy, we should have an account of a rare disease, mentioned by no author before the Christian era, with physical facts, not obvious, but in harmony with it; but in any case, and still more remarkably, we have the psychological fact, that one, perhaps with *a beast's heart*, imagining himself an ox, any how in a very degraded form of insanity, could still pray as a man. Although it be not certain, yet it is highly probable, that the [2]*band of iron and brass*, which, in the dream, was to be around *the stump of the tree*, the symbol of Nebuchadnezzar, relates to that mode of restraint, which, in Palestine, in the times of the Gospel [3], and down to a late period, was thought necessary to secure the poor sufferer from self-injury, or from injuring others. Any how, this dwelling with the wild animals, and feeding like them, look like the state of one, whose return to reason was wholly despaired of. And yet, before he recovers, he prayed. This is related in Daniel with the simplicity of truth; ignorant scepticism pronounces it impossible; true physics and psychology attest the reality of the description.

ii. So from physics, men turn to historical evidence.

---

[1] Her. iv. 42.　　　[2] Dan. iv. 15. Eng. 12. Ch.　　　[3] S. Mark v. 3, 4.

"No one else relates it[1]." What, if they did not? Where are the full annals of Nebuchadnezzar's reign, that men should pronounce any event related in Holy Scripture, untrue, unless it were related in his secular history? It is an hypocritical issue to put it on. They who do so, do not believe themselves. They do not limit their belief of Nebuchadnezzar's history to the few surviving fragments of Berosus. What are those facts? Just that sketch of his campaign before he was king, his captives, his succession to his father, and his honoring Bel, his god; his adding a second city to Babylon, and its strong walls; his palace; his hanging gardens; his falling sick; and the length of his reign[2]. Until the decyphering of the monuments[3], our knowledge of most of his great and useful works came from Abydenus[3]; who also has the tradition, that he knew of the future desolation of his Empire by the Medes and Persians[4]. Even for his conquests, Josephus was obliged to supplement his account from Megasthenes, Diocles, and Philostratus. Berosus does not relate the battle of Carchemish; Egyptian annals do not record it. These men eagerly believe it on the authority of Jeremiah, set it down as a certain fact, because they think they can employ it against Daniel. But why believe one fact of Holy Scripture, not another? The only principle of belief or unbelief of this historical criticism seems to be, whether a fact can seemingly be pressed or no into the support of its preconceived opinions.

Enough, that there is neither external nor internal evidence against the history of Nebuchadnezzar's insanity. Almost all ancient or modern history is a mosaic, made up of the fragments of single authorities. If we were to strike out of it what is related by one author only, we should

---

[1] Lengerke gave up the old objections to the disease, and rested his objections on this. "Granted that the condition, into which N. sinks, is explicable, yet in no writer is there any allusion to an event, which must have occasioned such changes in the kingdom, that no one, who ever so briefly related the reign of that king, could have failed to touch on it." p. 145. Davidson re-writes the statement of Leng. iii. 185.   [2] in Jos. c. Ap. i. 19. See ab. p. 60.

[3] See ab. p. 119, 20.   [4] See ab. p. 126.

often have but a threadbare history, a few hard outlines, unrelieved and unshaded by all those minuter touches, which supply the proportions and symmetry and beauty and instructiveness of history. These critics would turn aside from the dry bones of secular history, which alone their system would leave. But that can be no canon for the writing of Daniel, which would not hold as to secular history; which the wildest criticism has not consistently applied to sacred history. Even unbelief writes it's history of "the Hebrew Monarchy," disbelieving of it only what is Divine.

The singular tradition, preserved by Abydenus[5], contains an account of a supernatural state, which befel Nebuchadnezzar on the roof of his palace, in which he is said to have prophesied the conquest of Babylon by the Medo-Persians, and which, being in his mouth, looks like a strange reminiscence of his illness. The statement can hardly be put together out of Daniel himself. For it is not likely, that Abydenus should have combined into one whole materials scattered in the book, standing in no relation to one another, and in part very subordinate, whereas the history, with which they are connected in Daniel, is so characteristic. As they stand in Daniel and Abydenus, they are too unlike, to have been directly borrowed. And yet, as we read Abydenus, they sound like reminiscences of the facts in Daniel blended together, as unauthentic tradition is wont to connect things heterogeneously[6]. Eusebius was struck with the resemblance.

[5] "I found in the writing of Abydenus about the Assyrians, what follows about Nebuchadnezzar. Megasthenes says &c" [see ab. p. 117.] Then, after the prediction of the conquest of Babylon by a Medo-Persian, which tradition put into the mouth of Nebuchadnezzar, (given above p. 126.) it made him continue; "Would, before my people were given [to him,] some Charybdis or sea would receive him, and utterly extinguish him ; or, turned aside otherwhither, he were borne through the desert, where are neither cities nor step of man, but beasts do feed and birds roam, wandering alone among rocks and ravines, and that I, before these things had come into my mind, had met with a happier end. Having foretold this, forthwith he disappeared." Præp. Ev. ix. 41.

[6] Even Lengerke (p. 151.) "agrees with Jahn (Arch. ii. 1. p. 214.) in thinking the tradition of Abydenus a late patchwork, put together partly out of the prophecies, c. 2 and 4, partly out of the relation of the insanity c. 4. and lastly

"[1] In the history of Daniel, it is related of Nebuchadnezzar, how and in what manner he became insane; but if the Greek, or Chaldee historians, conceal the disease, and state that it came from God, and call that madness, which seized him, some god or dæmon, we need not marvel. For it is their custom to ascribe such things to God, and to call gods, daimones." A sickness of his, which apparently was remarkable, because it is recorded, is mentioned by Berosus [2]. An interval, in which he did none of his great works in Babylonia, is mentioned in his inscriptions [3]; and that, the more remarkable, because his works were so stupendous and so extensive. The further doubt which has been raised, how his empire could be preserved to him during those seven years of insanity, finds its solution in the incidental notice of Berosus. One chief Magus kept the government for him on his father's death, until he could return [4]. Much more would they for one, to whom the whole empire owed its great-

out of the explanation of the unknown writing by Daniel c. 5." He accordingly rejects "the assumption of Bertholdt (p. 305 sq.) Bleek (p. 269.) Kirmss (p. 57. 62.)" who (in the way of that school) assumed that the tradition in Abydenus was the basis of the history in Daniel. It is not unlikely, that tradition should have put into the king's mouth a curse taken from his own calamities; but it is, in itself, absurd to suppose, that such a curse, which does not contain any direct allusion to those calamities, should have suggested the history. Again, the incidental mention of the roof of the palace is unmeaning there; in Daniel, Nebuchadnezzar was surveying from it *great Babylon which* he *had built for* himself. Then also, it is the concentration of these reminiscences in one place, which marks the borrower. And what would the Palestine Pseudo-Daniel have had to do with Chaldee traditions?

[1] Chron. Arm. i. 61.

[2] "falling into a state of sickness," ἐμπεσὼν εἰς ἀρρωστίαν. in Jos. c. Ap. i. 20. Berosus connects the illness with Nebuchadnezzar's decease. The accounts then are different, although, probably, his insanity *was* in the later part of his life, since it stands connected with his greatness and completion of his works at Babylon. It is also the last event of his life mentioned by Daniel. In the only other case, in which Berosus mentions the sickness of a sovereign, it stands connected with history, the sickness of Nabopolassar having given occasion to Nebuchadnezzar's first military glory. (Hengst. Beitr. i. 106.) Bertholdt's statement that Berosus, by this expression, marked that a sovereign died a natural death, is directly false, since in our brief fragments he does not use it of Neriglissar or Nabonedus. Hengst. Ib. p. 105, 6.   [3] See Rawlinson Bampton Lect. v. p. 166. and note 29. p. 440.   [4] See ab. p. 60.

ness, nay, its being.　Nor was his son, Evilmerodach, one, whose character would furnish any temptation [5] to antedate his reign by ingratitude to his great father.

iii. Nor is it in any way contrary to human nature, but rather it is in accordance with it[6], that Nebuchadnezzar, while acknowledging the supreme power of the God of Daniel[7], retained his Polytheism [8]. The belief in a supreme God in no way interfered with the acknowledgment of inferior gods. Polytheism is in direct conflict with Monotheism, not with the owning of one Supreme God. The Persian kings owned Ahuramazda to be the supreme God, yet worshipped *gods many*. Cyrus, in his edict, owned the supremacy of the God of Israel[9], Artaxerxes spoke of Him, as *the God of heaven* [10], yet doubtless without abandoning their hereditary Polytheism. Constantine issued an edict, directing the auguries [11], and had on his coins, " Soli invicto [12]," after he had acknowledged the God of Christians to be the One True God, and had professed that he "[13]awaited the judgment of Christ," "the Saviour."

A believer must wish that the great king had known God more thoroughly. The history in Daniel bears the more the character of truth, in that it must have been against the wish of a pious Jew, that the conversion was imperfect [14]. The character of Nebuchadnezzar is one of those, which have so much of nobility, that one longs for them to have been more perfect. He is exhibited, as men are, with their mixture of good and bad. As each of the three proofs of the wisdom or power of the God of Israel

---

[5] See ab. p. 120.　[6] Improb. 10.　[7] *the high God.* iii. 32. Ch. [iv. 2. Eng.]

[8] *Daniel, whose name is Belteshazzar according to the name of my god,* iv. 5. Ch. [8. Eng.] *in whom is the spirit of the holy gods,* ib. and 6. 15. [9. 18. Eng.]　　　　[9] Ezr. i. 3.　　　　[10] Ib. vii. 21, 23.

[11] A.D. 321. Si quid de Palatio. cod. Theod. L. xvi. Tit. x. T. 6. p. 283.

[12] Banduri Num. Impp. Rom. ii. 254. 266. 283-8. 300. There are also coins with the inscription Jovi Conservatori, Ib. 253. 262. 273-5. and Marti Conservatori, Ib. 253, 263, 4, 276, and Herculi Conservatori, Ib. 262.

[13] Epist. ad Episc. Cath. Concil. A.D. 314. i. 1455. ed. Col.

[14] Hengst. points out how " Jewish and Christian interpreters have striven to make the conversion as complete as possible." p. 116.

comes to him, there is the quick, honest, self-forgetful, acknowledgment of the truth. Two periods of power and magnificence have been passed unnoticed, in which the strong convictions faded before his own dazzling greatness. Years of conquest must have passed between that first acknowledgment of Daniel's God, after the explanation of his dream by Daniel, and the hour of pride in which he commanded the image to be worshipped; and then again another, in which he in a manner re-created the cities of his country, and in which he forgot that he, into whose hands God had given the known world, held only a delegated power. In Daniel, (as is always the way of truth,) the two sides of his character stand out unrelieved. Nebuchadnezzar uses in his edict the language of Daniel, as to God, (for what other could he use, having learnt what he did learn of God from him?) and he uses his own heathen language. His relapses are related, not his temptations. He owns the truth, for the time, with his whole soul; what marvel, that, amid such greatness, he did not uniformly persevere, when the marvel would have been, (a crowning marvel of Divine grace and of heathen faithfulness to that grace,) if he had uniformly persevered?

iv. The proclamation, which announced his past malady [1], would only have been strange, had there been nothing remarkable in his restoration. The supposed objection must be, either that it was too humble, or that it might have shaken the confidence of his subjects. But human nature feels, even heathen nature felt still, that it is an exceeding glory to be the special object of the care of God. The god of unbelief must be a more dumb idol than the Pagan gods, that unbelievers feel it not. Nebuchadnezzar, after the event, felt that it was so, even when shewn in the correction of his pride. He who feels it not, shews that he not only knows not God, but that he cannot even imagine the relation of the creature to the Creator, nor see, even dimly, something of the greatness and goodness of the infinitely Great and Good God. The

[1] Improb. 8.

fact, that Nebuchadnezzar felt that it was his own truest honor, that God had so chastened and yet had so restored him, is a great truth as to the soul, which does not lie on the surface; as these men confess, in that they do not see it.

v. Why Nebuchadnezzar so solemnly inaugurated his golden image[2], and whom or what he intended by it, we can have no certain knowledge[3]. It manifestly had a political end, since the officers of all the provinces of the empire were assembled to inaugurate it[4]. The ground, why adoration was claimed for it, was the king's will, that they should [5] *worship the golden image which Nebuchadnezzar the king had set up.* The charge against the three Jewish governors was ingratitude, and, as was so often alleged against Christians, contumacy. Whether the image was formed in reminiscence of that emblem of human might, which Nebuchadnezzar had seen in his

[2] Impr. 5.

[3] Since Bleek, it has been repeated by one after another, that the history was a pure fiction, intended as an example of steadfastness to the Jews, under the persecution of Antiochus. The golden image was to denote a statue which Antiochus is to have set up in the Temple; the refusal of the three youths to worship was to be an encouragement to the contemporaries of the Pseudo-Daniel. Bleek says; "We cannot help thinking of Antiochus Epiphanes, who, after he had caused Jerusalem to be taken by surprise and plundered, desecrated the temple, had it dedicated to Jupiter Olympius, and heathen sacrifices offered on the altar of burnt-offerings, after the βδέλυγμα ἐρημώσεως, 'the abomination of desolation,' doubtless the *statue of Jupiter*, had, on Chisleu 15, 167 B.C. been erected there." (p. 259-60. Einl. p. 602, 3.) This statement, that Ant. Epiph. had any statue of Jupiter set up in the Temple, was itself a pure fiction; as even Lengerke (p. 104, 5.) was constrained to own that Hengstenberg had shewn. (Beitr. i. 86.) No one of the three accounts of the desecration of the temple (1 Macc. i. 44-64. 2 Macc. vi. 1-11. Jos. Ant. xii. 5. 4. B. J. i. 1. 1, 2.) mentions anything of it. On the contrary, the history both of the desecration and purification shews, that what was done was the building of an idol-altar upon the Altar of God. "They *built*," (ῴκοδόμησαν,) it is said, (1 Macc. i. 54.) "an abomination of desolation upon the *altar*." A statue could not be said to be "built." The account goes on, "and in the cities of Judah round about they *built* (ῴκοδόμησαν) altars;" (ib.) and, in relating that desecration of the temple, "and on the 25th day of the month, sacrificing upon the idol-altar (βωμὸν) which was upon the Altar," (θυσιαστηρίου.) ib. 59. In the account of the purification it is said, "they bare out the defiled *stones* into an unclean place." [Ib. iv. 43.] Hengst.   [4] Dan. iii. 2, 3.   [5] Ib. 5-7. 12. 14. 18.

dream, and of which the head was declared to represent himself, or whether it was himself whom he intended to be worshipped in it, it was plainly some test of allegiance, required of all peoples, nations, and languages, in his whole empire.   In Persian times, we should have no doubt that it was the monarch himself, who made himself his people's idol.   A form of idolatry, which the Ethiopians [1] and Egyptians [2] are said to have shewn to their kings; which ran through Persian history; which Alexander adopted; which successors of his, among the Seleucidæ and Ptolemies, stamped on their coins [3], or upon monuments [4]; which reappeared among the Arsacidæ when they extended their empire [5]; which Caligula could not be

[1] The Ethiopians "said, that the accounting the kings to be gods is an Ethiopian institution," (carried with them by the Egyptians.) Diod. iii. 3. "Whomsoever the god, carried about in a festive procession, takes, the people forthwith choose as king, and forthwith worship and honor as a god." Ib. 5.

[2] "The Egyptians seem to worship and honor their kings, as if they were really gods." Diod. i. 90.   "Darius was intimate with the priests in Egypt, and partook of their theology, whence he was so honored, that while living, he alone of (Persian) kings was addressed as a god, while living." Ib. 85.

[3] Antiochus Theus received the title, in flattery, from "the Milesians, for removing a despot." App. Syr. c. 65.   It appears on the coins of Ant. Epiphanes, (Frölich p. 47. 51. 53. in Clint. F. H. iii. 325.) Demetrius Soter, (Vaillant p. 129. in Clint. iii. 326.) Antiochus, son of Balas, (Dr. Smith in his Biogr. Dict. T. i. p. 198.) Demetrius Nicator, (Frölich, p. 71. 87, Vaillant. p. 176, in Clinton p. 336.) Demetrius Eucærus, (Eckhel iii. 245. in Cl. p. 342.) Antiochus son of Ant. Grypus. (Vaillant Hist. Ptol. p. 100. Fröl. p. 113. in Cl. p. 342.) The title "goddess" appears on a coin of Cleopatra, the mother of Ant. Grypus and Cyzic. (Fröl. p. 91. in Cl. p. 339.)   Balas took the title of "Theopator" on his coins. (Vaillant p. 138. 140, Frölich, p. 67, in Clinton p. 328.)   Of the Ptolemies, the title "god" occurs on a coin of Philometor, (Vaillant p. 103. in Cl. iii. 393.) and "goddess" on two of Antony's Cleopatra, (θεὰ νεωτέρα, Vaill. p. 189, 190. in Cl. iii. 406.) Of the Ptolemies before Philometor, a coin of Philopator alone had *any* title beyond that of king.

[4] In the inscription at Adule, "transcribed by Cosmas in the beginning of the reign of Justin," (he reigned A.D. 518-527,) Ptolemy Euergetes gives the title "Saviour gods," to his grandparents, Ptolemy Lagi and Berenice, and that of "gods" to his parents, Ptolemy Philadelphus and Arsinoe, claiming "descent on the father's side from Heracles son of Zeus, and on the mother's from Dionysus son of Zeus." in Montf. Coll. Nov. ii. 141, and thence in Clinton F. H. iii. 387. note o.

[5] Arsaces vii. took the title Theopator, (coin in Smith Biogr. Dict. i. 355.) Arsaces xii. had that of "god." Phlegon in Phot. Cod. 97. p. 84. Bek. ib.

sated with; which was the object of ambition to emperors and empresses of heathen Rome, must have a deep root in human nature. It is an offshoot of the primeval temptation, *ye shall be as God.* We know not enough of Babylonian idolatry to say what Nebuchadnezzar intended. It would have been altogether in keeping, that he, who, like the Lycaonians [6], was ready to shew Divine honors to that which was superhuman, *the spirit of the holy gods* which he believed to be in Daniel, should, in the intoxication of irresistible power, have claimed them for himself. The Babylonians, in the time of Alexander, of their own accord, greeted the conqueror's entrance with "[7] the burning of frankincense and all kinds of odours on silver altars arranged on either side."

vi. The colossal form of the image was, doubtless on purpose, not after the proportions of the human frame [8]. Majestic height was manifestly the idea of a statue 60 cubits high. The apparent height was much increased by the diminished breadth, in that its height, as compared to its breadth, was as 10 to 1, instead of 6 to 1. Not proportion, but ideal effect, is the object of, at least, the sculptures of Nineveh. There is no need that it should have been "like the Amyclæan Apollo, the bust of man on a column, with human [hands and] feet [9]." The sun-images bore no human proportion [10]. Who could

[6] Acts x. 25.   [7] Curt. v. 1. 20. Hav. on D. ii. 46.   [8] Improb. 3.

[9] Munter Relig. d. Bab. p. 59. Hgst. p. 95. This obviously would not interfere with the figure's being an image (צלם); since the human countenance, which specially gave it the character of an image, would remain the same. Pausanias describes the Amyclæan Apollo; "It is not the work of Bathycles, but ancient and made without art. For, except its face and the extremities of the feet and hands, the rest is like a brass column. It has a helmet on its head, and in its hands spear and bow." Lac. iii. 19. 2. K. O. Müller speaks thus of the class of statues to which it belongs; "Nothing is more common than to find unworked stones, stone-pillars, stakes of wood, set up as images for worship.—If, to the honor of the god, the sign was formed more costly and ornamented, it is called an ἄγαλμα.—In order to bring the sign in nearer relation to the god, single significant parts were added, heads, arms which contain the attributes.—In this way was formed the brazen pillar of the Amyclæan Apollo, with helmeted head and armed hands, &c"

[10] עצבים. See Ges. Thes. p. 491. and Max. Tyr. viii. p. 87. ib.

have looked for proportion in the Colossus of Rhodes[1]? "Large colossi and *very long* men-sphinxes[2]" entered into the (probably kindred) idolatry of Egypt. Adversaries also admit, that images are called golden, which are only overlaid with golden plates[3]; but therewith they own that objections have been wantonly multiplied.

vii. "[4]The edict of Darius, that no one should for 30 days ask any petition of God or man, save of himself," is said to have been "insane." Religiously, of course, it was extreme insanity. But that which was in truth insane, to pray of man as if he were God, to neglect God for man, is simple matter of fact. The Persians looked upon their king as the representative of Ormuzd, as indwelt by him, and, as such, gave him Divine honors. Persians,

---

[1] The colossus of Rhodes was 10 ells higher. Plin. H. N. xxxiv. 18. Pliny mentions (ibid.) "a colossal figure 110 feet long, made in his own time by Zenodorus for Nero, which, after his crimes were condemned, was dedicated to the sun." "How little proportion was there in many of the little so-called Etruscan figures!" Munter l. c.   [2] Herod. ii. 175.

[3] "*Some* objections may be removed with little trouble. The statue must have a pedestal, which must be high, in order that the statue might be visible to the far-encircling multitude, and so one may assume, with Thube, that its height was included in the 60 cubits. The statue too with its pedestal may have been of wood within, [S. Chrys. Hom. iv. in S. Matt.] and only overlaid with gold. ($\pi\epsilon\rho\iota\chi\rho\upsilon\sigma\alpha$ $\kappa\alpha\iota$ $\pi\epsilon\rho\iota\alpha\rho\gamma\upsilon\rho\alpha$, Ep. Jerem. 8.) For the inside of idols ($\dot{\eta}$ $\kappa\alpha\rho\delta\iota\alpha$ $\alpha\upsilon\tau\tilde{\omega}\nu$ Ib. 20.) was generally of wood or clay (Bel 7.) and was then covered with gold by the goldsmith. (Is. xl. 19. xli. 7. xliv. 13. Jer. x. 3-5.) And this explanation is supported by the Hebrew idiom, that they were wont to call that 'gold,' or 'copper,' which was only covered with plates of gold or copper. (Ex. xxx. 1-3. xxxix. 38. xl. 5. 26. xxvii. 1, 2.)" Bertholdt Dan. p. 256, 7. J. D. Michaelis, (as his way was,) had the amount of gold calculated, supposing it to have been solid gold. And thenceforth this figured among "objections." Yet in truth Babylonians, as well as Hebrews, called that golden, (as it was,) which was, not gilt, but overlaid with gold. "According to Herodotus, the great gold statue of Bel, the golden table before it, the golden steps, and the golden seat, *together* amounted only to 800 talents of gold, which would not in the least suffice, if these things had all been of massive gold. According to Diodorus, 1000 talents of gold only were employed on a statue 40 feet high, which would be a nothing for a massive image of that height, and of breadth proportionate. Diodorus too (ii. 9.) expressly describes the statue as beaten with the hammer, and so, not massive." Hengst. p. 98. "Such is indeed the idiom of all languages, as in the aurea sella, Cic. Phil. ii. 34: Nep. Eumen. 7." Häv. ad loc. The term "massive gold" implies other use of gold, *not* massive.   [4] Improb. 16.

Persian monuments, contemporary Greek writers, attest this. "With us," said Artabanus[5] to Themistocles, "of many and good laws this is the best, to honor the king, and worship him as the image of god who preserveth all things," i. e. Ormuzd. Curtius says, "[6] the Persians worship their kings among the gods;" Isocrates, "[7] worshipping indeed a mortal man, and addressing him as a Divine being, but dishonoring the gods more than men." Arrian relates[8] that, from the time of Cambyses to that of Alexander, the Magi had had the hereditary charge of the tomb of Cyrus at Pasargadæ, and "received daily from the king a sheep, wheatflour, and wine, and monthly a horse to sacrifice to Cyrus. In Persian inscriptions they are called "[9] offspring of the gods," and "gods." Representations at the royal graves at Persepolis, in whatever way they are to be explained, indicate some very close relation and identification of the king with Ormuzd[10]. The Persians, as they borrowed other things from the Medes, so probably this. Deioces is represented by Herodotus as retiring and keeping himself out of sight[11]. In this ac-

[5] Plutarch Themistocl. c. 27. from Charon of Lampsacus (B.C. 504.) The mention of the custom is not incidental, for the presentation of Themistocles to the king turned on his compliance with it.

[6] viii. 18. in Brisson de reg. Pers. p. 8. sqq. who adds iii. 31. v. 9. 29. viii. 17. and quotes also Herod. vii. 136. Val. Max. iv. 7. vii. 3. Justin vi. 2. Lamprid. in Alex.; Trebell. Pollio in Zenobia; and, of the Parthians, Jos. xx. 3. Xenophon (Ages. i. 34. quoted ib.) is speaking of the Persians generally.

[7] Paneg. v. fin. p. 140, 1. ib.   [8] vi. 29.

[9] "In the Greek inscriptions, corresponding to the cuneiform, at Naksh-i-Rustam, in De Sacy Mémoires sur div. antiq. de la Perse, Pl. 1. p. 27. 31. the Persian kings are called ἔκγονοι θεῶν, ἐκ γένους θεῶν and θεοί." De Sacy translates an inscription, Mem. de l' Instit. hist. anc. T. ii. p. 183,4. 188, "The figure is that of the worshipper of Ormuzd, of the excellent Sapor, king of the kings of Iran and Aniran, heavenly germ of the race of the gods, son of the worshipper of Ormuzd, the excellent Hormuz, king of the kings of Iran and Aniran, heavenly germ of the race of the gods, grandson of the excellent Narses, king of kings." "Grotefend has found on cuneiform inscriptions the title, 'race of the ruler of the world.' comp. Munter l. c. p. 29." Hengst.

[10] See Hengst. p. 129, 30.   [11] Her. i. 199. Brisson notices this, quoting also from Aristotle (de mundo,) "Himself, as is said, was fixed at Susa or Ecbatana, invisible to all;" and Justin, (i. 9.) "Among the Persians, the person of the king, under semblance of greater majesty, is hidden;" and Xen.

count of Darius itself, the unalterableness of the law of
the Medes and Persians is a part of the supposed relation
of the king to Ormuzd. Man, claiming to act through
a Divine presence, could not afford to appear mistaken
or changeable[1]. There was a ready plea for the decree.
It was pressed upon the king by the assembled governors
of the provinces, whom the king had himself created.
They were governors in a conquered realm. The object
of the decree probably was to obtain from the Babylonians and other provinces that special recognition of the
king, as the representative of the Supreme God, invested
with his delegated power, which the Persians already recognised. The decree was for 30 days[2]; for those who,
for such a space, had so recognised that divinity of the
king, would have admitted the principle of submission to
him, as a Divine authority. It came to the king, pressed
by the whole weight of his Councillors : once passed, it
could not be retracted without forfeiting the claim which
it was to establish. Hence the fruitless effort of the king
to evade the decree, and the bold tone of the Councillors
at the last. They represented a characteristic principle
of Medo-Persian Monarchy, while they abused it.

viii. But, it is altogether an assumption, that "intolerance" was unknown to Babylonians[3] or Persians[4]. We
are told from the inscriptions, that the Assyrian wars were
"[5]religious wars;" we also know that the Babylonians had

Ages. ix. 1. 2.   "A reverence was thrown over him, in that he was rarely seen,
and difficult of approach."   [1] This was observed by Heeren i. 259.

[2] " How will any justify the circumstance, that a command, which was to secure the supremacy of the Magian religion, was given only for 30 days ? " Leng.
p. 272. "Why for 30 days only ? " Dav. iii. 192.   [3] Improb. 5.   [4] Improb. 19.

[5] Prof. Rawlinson has pointed this out, Herod. Essay vii. T. i. p. 495.   It
does not depend upon the translation of particular words, whose meaning may
not be as yet established, as " heretics," (in Fox Talbot repeatedly, but also in
Sir H. Rawl. Journal As. Soc. xviii. 1. p. 164. 198.) It is expressed in too
various ways, to depend upon particular words. The following instances are
from the single inscription of Tiglath-Pileser i, translated simultaneously by
Sir H. Rawl. and F. Talbot, and, in part, by Hincks and Oppert. (Ib. 164-219.)
Tiglathp. speaks of subduing "the enemies of Ashur ;" (R. p. 168. R. T. 206, 7.
R. T. H. 202, 3. 214, 5.) "kings hostile to Ashur ; " (R. T. p. 168.) a king, who

taken captive the Assyrian gods[6]; as Cambyses and the Persians afterwards took many of those of Egypt, the recovery of which gained for the 3rd Ptolemy the title of Euergetes[7]. The sacred bull was slain both by Cambyses and Ochus; and the ready submission to Alexander has been attributed to their resentment of the oppression of their religion by their Persian masters[8]. The Zoroastrian system took its rise in intense hatred of the Vedic worshippers[9]; it was established amidst civil wars[10]; and subsequently wars arose on occasion of it.   "Slay these

---

" was not submissive to Ashur my Lord," (R. 192) " did not acknowledge A. my L." (R. 184.) " paid no worship to A. my L." (T. 193.) " worship not A. my L." (T. 184.) " were disobedient to A. my L." (H. 199.) " foreigners hostile to A." (R. H. 214, 5.) " heretics, my enemies and the enemies of A." (T. p. 214.) " who knew not the true religion," (T. p. 188.) "the kings of infidelity who are tributaries without faith [?] ;" (O. p. 189.) " who had not paid tribute and offerings to A. my L." (R. p. 178.) " withheld the tribute and offerings due to A. my L." (R. T. H. O. p. 170, 1.) "the cities of Subarta attached to the worship of A. my L." (R. 178.) "which belong to A. my L." (T. ib.) "undertook (to do homage) before A. my L." (H. ib.) " the subjects of A. my L." (O. p. 185.) Tigl's. own conquests are "in the service of my Lord A." (R. T. p. 192, 3. 198.) " in the martial service of the great gods who rule in the Euphrates land;" (T. 188.) he " rules in the service of the great gods." (R. ib.) Ashur bids him war, (R. T. H. p. 180, 1. R. O. p. 188, 9. R. H. p. 194, 5.) "for the enlargement of the frontiers of his [A's] territory." (R. p. 178.) He goes against those who do not acknowledge A. "in the might and power of A. my L." (R. p. 184.) "in the most high name of A. my L." (T. ib.) "in the execution of the will of A. my L." (O. ib.) He "attached" the conquered " to the worship of A. my L." (R. p? 184.) "with 60 kings victoriously I fought, and the laws and religion of my empire I imposed upon them," (T. p. 168.) " with attachment to the worship of A. my L. I entrusted them, i. e. I caused them to worship A." (R. p. 186.) " their territory I annexed to the special possessions of A. my L." (T. ib.) " with prostrations before god Asur my L. I received their contributions." (O. p. 187.)   " I imposed upon them religious service. "(R. p. 176. 194.) " I left him in life, to learn the worship of the great gods from my city of A." (R. p. 192.)   He took captive their gods, (R. T. H. p. 174, 5. 196, 7. R. T. p. 184, 5. bis.) "25 of their gods," (R. T. O. 186,7.) dedicated them to his own, (R. T. O. 186, 7.) to his guardian god, (R. T. p. 176.) "his guide." H. p. 177. His enemies "took their gods and fled." (R. H. p. 174, 5.)

[6] In the Bavian inscription, Sennacherib records his having "brought back from Babylon the images of the gods, which had been taken from Assyria 418 years before, and had set them in their places." Layard, Babylon p. 212, 3. from Dr. Hincks.   [7] S. Jer. on Dan. xi. 7, 8. Inscription at Adule l. c.

[8] Smith Geogr. Dict. i. 45.   [9] See further Lect. viii.   [10] Gâthâ Ahunav. 5 [Yaçna 32] n. 7. p. 15. 31. Haug. G. Uçtav. 9. (Y. 44.) n. 15. p. 11. 25.

liars with the sword [1]," is a maxim of Zarathustra as well as of Mohammed.   But heathenism, as is now recognised, was tolerant only of those who did not deny itself.

ix. Daniel, however, did not thrust himself on danger. He went into his house; there, he was in the upper chamber, in the uppermost story, where the Orientals retired, that they might be unobserved[2], the usual place of prayer. Unostentatious, yet not even in appearance denying his faith for the sake of the king's command, he did just as he did before.   He was probably out of ordinary sight; for his accusers had to *press tumultuously*[3] in upon him, and *found him*," it is said.   Rationalists have declared this fanatical[4]: then, in their mind, it must be fanatical, to be willing to die rather than deny God.

x. The decree of Darius appears to me a decree of protection for the Jews.   It is not a command to worship the God of Daniel, but to stand in awe of Him.   To me, it seems equivalent to the decree of Nebuchadnezzar, not to speak against Him; only, the punishment, which Nebuchadnezzar annexed to the breach of his decree, is omitted.   The Satraps had combined to extinguish the worship of God.   Darius decrees that, throughout his dominions, men should stand in awe of Him, i. e. that they should not make attempts against His worship, as these had done.   It is not usual for monarchs to write their own decrees; and this decree had no relation to the personal circumstances of the sovereign, as that of Nebuchadnezzar upon his recovery necessarily had.   There seems to me no reason why Daniel himself should not have been commissioned to write it, as first Minister of the Empire, or should not have suggested its language[5].

[1] Gâthâ Ahun. 4. [Y. 31.] n. 18, p. 30.   Under the Sassanidæ it is spoken of as a religious duty to force back any converted from Parsism.   "If any depart from the path of the Yazatas, [gods,] he [the king] has him seized, and brought back to the right way." Minokhired in Spiegel tradit. Schr. d. Pars. p. 135.

[2] David retired to the upper chamber to weep over the death of Absalom. (2 Sam. xviii. 33.) Elijah prayed there for the boy's life. (1 Kgs. xvii. 19.)

[3] vi. 12. ‏וירגשׁו‎.   [4] Lengerke says, "Daniel purposely seeks danger [which is directly untrue] and his conduct must be estimated from the same aspect as that of his three companions, c. 3." p. 279.   [5] Improb. 18.

The objection is again put dishonestly. One who urges that the edict "bears traces of having been written by a Jew," as a separate objection, concedes for the time the fact of the edict itself. But if the edict was written at all, by whom should it have been written, but by Daniel? Granted, that a certain proclamation was made by a sovereign, no one could urge it as an argument against its genuineness, that it bore tokens of the style of the Prime Minister. The objection is added, only to swell the number, and to make it seem as if the supposed forger had betrayed himself.

xi. In the history of Belshazzar, the objections are simply childish. The insolence of Belshazzar, in desecrating the sacred vessels in a festival in honor of his gods, is nothing strange [6]. Excited by wine [7], he would triumph over God, as the Philistines did, when they placed the ark in the temple of Dagon. It is far less strange than the recklessness, with which, in the wantonness of party spirit, the sacred vessels of the altar have been used to adorn the side-boards of wealthy courtiers [8], or, in a time of political animosity against the Church, fonts have been turned into horse-troughs [9]. Nor is it strange [10], that the insolent and sensual boy-king troubled not himself to know of Daniel; but "following," as St. Jerome says [11], "the old and inworn error of his race, called *the astrologers and Chaldæans and soothsayers*, not the prophet of God;" or that Daniel, so neglected, did not appear, uncalled, with the wise men, when he would not be listened to if he

[6] Improb. 14.   [7] בִּטְעֵם חַמְרָא. lit. "in the taste of the wine." The LXX. renders "elevated by wine." Vulg. "jam temulentus." S. Ephr. paraphrases, "exhilarated by the taste of the wine." Even Leng. says, "Ammonius rightly, 'The exceeding wantonness of Belshazzar and his wine-bibbing drew him to this great blasphemy.'" in Mai Scriptt. Vett. T. 1.

[8] "Many private men's parlours were hung with Altar-cloths, their tables and beds covered with copes instead of carpets and coverlids; and many made carousing cups of the sacred chalices, as once Belshazzar celebrated his drunken feast in the sanctified vessels of the temple." Heylyn Hist. of the reformation p. 134. (Hist. of Edward vi.)

[9] This is an authenticated fact after the war of independence of the United States with England, the Episcopalians having been loyalists.   [10] Improb. 11. Dav. iii. 186, 7, extracts out of Leng. 238-40.   [11] on Dan. iv. 7.

spoke contrary to them, but reserved himself until some
opening should dispose the king to listen to him ; or that
Belshazzar, when the Queen Mother had circumstantially
reminded him of the supernatural wisdom which had been
found in Daniel, in the days of Nebuchadnezzar, should
have remembered so much of him, that his father had
brought him from Judæa[1]. Daniel's Hebrew name, which
Nebuchadnezzar (the Queen-Mother had reminded Belshazzar) had changed after the wont of conquerors, suggested his Jewish origin. All the rest Belshazzar professed to have been told[2]. The accurate distinction has
the more the air of truth. Every one knows, how one
little circumstance will awaken a whole train of forgotten
histories of the past. Nor again, bound, as kings ever
held themselves to be, to fulfil, at least, the letter of their
public promises, is it at all strange[3], that, in that night
which Belshazzar knew not to be his last, he fulfilled his
promise to him who should read the mysterious writing.
When objectors charge inconsistency on a history, they,
for the time, presuppose its reality. Their argument
must be, " granted the rest of the circumstances, *this* is
inconsistent with them." Let them place themselves then
in the circumstances of that night. Let them imagine it
(what, as unbelievers, they must,) mesmerism, or whatever else they dare[4], but let them imagine the ungodly
revelry and triumph over God, broken at once by a sight
seemingly supernatural, the man's hand writing characters which no one could decypher ; we may suppose them
the old Hebrew character, which would naturally be unknown to the wise men of Babylon. Let them picture

---

[1] v. 13. Lengerke says, " The author contradicts himself, for, according to the
discourse v. 11, Daniel is utterly unknown to the king ; [not so ; what the Queen-
Mother reminds him of is the extraordinary wisdom found in him ;] but then,
v. 13, he forthwith remembers him, and knows his origin." (p. 238.)

[2] v. 14. 16.   [3] Improb. 12.

[4] Bertholdt, who admitted all the facts of the festival on the night of the capture of Babylon, the profanation of the sacred vessels, and a writing upon the
wall, supposed that the writing might have been contrived by some well-mean-
ing friend of Belshazzar to awaken him, or by some intriguer with Cyrus to
insult the king. Dan. p. 352, 3.

to themselves the confusion of the revellers, impressed, at the height of their idolatrous pride, with a sense of the supernatural which it baffled all the wisdom of the wise to explain; the increasing terror at the failure [5]; that sudden reverse, which changes presumptuous triumph into prostrate fear; the calm, reassuring words of the Queen-mother [6], speaking with dignity and authority [7] of the respect of the great departed king for Daniel, as endowed with a mysterious presence of the gods whom they believed; and then let them view, amid that scene of broken revelry, the silver-haired prophet, of above fourscore years, alone standing fearless, when all feared, the one surviving witness of the departed greatness of their empire, almost as a denizen of another world, since all of his generation had long been numbered with the dead, indifferent as to greatness, regardless of the king's dis-

[5] v. 9.

[6] The "Queen" v. 10. was obviously the Queen-mother, because the *wives*, as well as the concubines, of Belshazzar were, according to the Babylonian custom, already present at the feast. The title שֵׁגַל, (the title of the "wives" in v. 2. 3. 23.) as distinct from the concubines, is used of the wife of the king of Persia in Neh. ii. 6, and of the ideal queen, Ps. xlv. 10. "שֵׁגַל is always the Queen." Rosh hashshana f. 4. 1. quoted Buxtorf Lex. Chald. col. 2327. In like way גְּבִירָה, the title for an Egyptian Queen, (1 Kgs. xi. 19.) is used of the dignity of Queen-mother, 1 Kgs. xv. 13. 2 Chr. xv. 16. Jer. xiii. 18. xxix. 2. (coll. xxii. 26. 2 Kgs. xxiv. 12.) It seems to me also most probable, that " the children of the king, and the children of the queen," (2 Kgs. x. 13.) were different persons, viz. the children of Jehoram and those of the Queen-mother, Jezebel. This was also the statement of Josephus. " Josephus " [Ant. x. 11. 2] "writes that this was the grandmother of Belshazzar; Origen, that it was his mother; whence also she was acquainted with things past, which the king knew not. Let Porphyry then shake off his sleep, who dreams that she was the wife of Belshazzar, and mocks at her knowing more than her husband." S. Jer. on Dan. v. 11. S. Ephrem and Theodoret also speak of her as the king's mother; and even the rationalist school now admits it, Leng. Hitz. Ros. Winer,. Real-Wort. i. 151. (against Bertholdt p. 355. 366.)

[7] The mother of the heir-apparent in Eastern monarchies had, in any case, considerable influence. Heeren p. 500. Herodotus has a remarkable tradition of the great wisdom of the mother of the last king of Babylon, whom he calls Nitocris, (i. 188. The wife of Nebuchadnezzar was Amuhea, Abyd. in Eus. Chr. Arm. i. 54,) attributing to her the same great brick-embankments on the Euphrates, which, Berosus says, were built *in the time of* the last king, (ἐπὶ τούτου in Jos. c. Ap. i. 20. and so Eus. Chron. Arm. i. 72,) and the bricks of which actually bear his name. Athenæum N. 1377. Rawl. Herod. i. p. 521.

pleasure, speaking words of forceful truth, explaining unhesitatingly, in the name of his God, the hitherto inexplicable words, and announcing a doom, founded on the just retribution of God, to which the heart of man in its secret depth responds,—granted, for the time, the supernatural, all the rest is in most perfect harmony with it. Nor is it, in the least, inconsistent[1], that Daniel should have declined the king's honors, when offered to him as a bribe, and that, when his strict, because truthful, message had been listened to, he should have accepted the short-lived honor in the departing kingdom, which might the rather prepare the conqueror to listen to his words in the name of his God.

I said, "granted, for the time, the supernatural;" for the question which has been raised does not relate to the abstract fact, that God reveals Himself and attests His revelation by prophecy or by miracle. The truth of miracles in the abstract, as I said at the outset, does not, on the one side or the other, belong to criticism. Criticism, in regard to a particular book, would, at most, have to do with the harmony or the evidence for the facts recorded in that book, not to the whole question of the intercourse which the Creator vouchsafes to His creature, man. It is consistently, so far, that some have objected to "the objectless prodigality of miracles, which, as miracles, are improbable, and rest on incorrect statements." The "prodigality" of miracles of power, as distinct from the miracle of superhuman knowledge, consists in this, that in seventy years, *three*[2] miracles are recorded ; the deliverance of Daniel's three friends in the furnace, of Daniel

---

[1] Improb. 13.   At last, the objection is to be, that, granted all the rest, the events are to be too many to be crowded into one night. Leng. p. 241. Dav. iii. 187.   Yet the festival began by day and was prolonged into the night.   The events which took place after dark, are only 1) the handwriting, 2) the sending for the Magi and their failure, 3) the Queen-mother's appearance and the sending for Daniel, 4) the short conversation mentioned in Daniel, and 5) the consequent fulfilment of the king's promise, which, as the Court and the attendants were already assembled, could take place at once.

[2] Davidson adopts Leng's., "objectless lavishing of miracles." p. lxii.   "The miracles recorded in the book are *lavishly accumulated,* without any apparent

himself in the lion's den, (which itself, although super-natural, could scarcely be called in the ordinary sense a suspension of a law of nature,) and the miraculous hand-writing in the midst of the idolatrous feast. "Objectless" they can only seem to those, to whom all revelation of God seems to be objectless. I would that they who make the objection could say, what miracle they believed, as having an adequate object. Unless they believe that some miracles are not "objectless," it is mere hypocri-sy to object to any particular miracles, as "objectless." For they allege, as a special ground against certain mi-racles, what they hold to be a ground against all miracles; and act the believer in miracles in the abstract, in order to enforce the disbelief in specific miracles. It was a grand theatre. On the one side, was the world-mo-narchy, irresistible, conquering, as the heathen thought, the God of the vanquished. On the other, a handful of the worshippers of the One only God, captives, scattered, with no visible centre or unity, without organisation or power to resist, save their indomitable faith, inwardly upheld by God, outwardly strengthened by the very ca-lamities which almost ended their national existence; for they were the fulfilment of His word in Whom they believ-ed. Thrice, during the seventy years, human power put itself forth against the faith; twice in edicts which would, if obeyed, have extinguished the true faith on earth; once, in direct insult to God. Faith, as we know, "quench-ed the violence of fire [3]," "stopped the mouths of lions." In all three cases, the assault was signally rolled back; the faith was triumphant in the face of all the representa-tives of the power and intelligence of the empire; in all, the truth of the One God was proclaimed by those who had assailed it. Unbelief, while it remains such, must deny all true miracles and all superhuman prophecy. But, if honest, it dare not designate as "objectless," miracles which decided the cause of truth on such battlefields.

object, and differ from those elsewhere related. Their *prodigal expenditure* is unworthy of the Deity." iii. 174.   [3] Heb. xi. 33, 34.

In like way, as to the "improbable[1]" character of the miracles. Let men grant that any miracles are "probable," or that they have taken place, and then, from that standing-ground, point out wherein these are "improbable." Let one profess his belief that our Blessed Lord walked on the water, multiplied the loaves and fishes, healed by a word one *born* blind, raised one who had been for four days dead, rose Himself from the dead, passed through the sealed tomb and the closed doors, and then let him point out what intrinsic improbability there is, that God, in regard to the three youths who confessed His Name in that great theatre, suspended the power of fire to burn, or that He withheld for a night the wild fierceness of some creatures of His hands, that they should not destroy the prophet who would not, for fear of man, disown Him.

It is alleged that the miracles could not have been wrought to strengthen the faith of God's people, for, 1) "it would be a contradiction to the Divine dispensation, since, at the beginning of the captivity, God had departed from His people and had given it up to its enemies;" nor 2) could they have been to "prepare the restoration of Israel through the recognition of the Omnipotence of the Lord and the authority of Daniel;" nor 3) that the heathen might be brought to recognise the one true God [2].

---

[1] "Hitzig," says Lengerke p. 109, "appositely remarks, (Heidelb. Jahrb. 1832 p. 26,) 'The main improbability, the wondrous deliverance itself, Hengstenberg has passed over in entire silence.' Naturally ; for here he must quit the field, and retire to the province of a faith, ever ready to believe. In truth, a miracle, which changes the nature of its element, is a great one. It is the greatest in the Old Testament, but not therefore the most credible." This is *not* hypocrisy, if either of these writers believed any miracle of the Old Testament. This question of the greater or less of miracles, if spoken of God, is gross anthropomorphism : in regard to its effects on man, such a miracle is, of course, no more amazing than the parting of the Red Sea, or of the Jordan, the ascent of Elijah, or any of the other miracles which could not, like the falling of the walls of Jericho, or the destruction of Sennacherib's army, be, possibly, the operation of natural causes, minutely directed by the Providence of God, Whose wisdom predicted what He willed, in the order of His Providence, at that exact time to fulfil.

[2] Leng.' lxii, lxiii. following Bertholdt against Hengst. Beitr. i. 35-40. The section is, under a different arrangement, closely followed by Davids. iii. 174, 5.

The statements, as usual, "beg the question" of the falsehood of the history, but, this time, of more history than Daniel's. 1) There is no intimation, any where, that God did cast off His people. On the contrary, in the prediction of that captivity in the law, He said, "[3] *yet for all this, when they be in the land of their enemies, I will not cast them away—but I will remember for them the covenant of their ancestors, whom I brought forth out of the land of Egypt in the sight of the heathen, that I might be their God.* And more specifically He had promised, in regard to the captivity at Babylon, that He would visit them there [4], *there* [5] He would redeem them. There too, meanwhile, He had promised them *peace,* [6] *in the peace of the city whither I have caused you to be carried captive.* The captivity was, from the first, part of God's declared purpose towards them. It was the crowning act of God's discipline spoken of in the law, in which He promised that, if they should repent, He would *remember* His *covenant* with their fathers, and *would remember the land* [7]. God raised up Ezekiel, as the prophet of the captivity of the ten tribes; He allowed Jeremiah to be carried down by the refugees in Egypt. It was in harmony with this, that He raised up Daniel in Babylon.

2) Nor was Daniel's position any slight mitigation of the captivity, or any slight protection of his people. Let any one imagine a Christian, as devoted to God as Daniel, and with that same love for his people which his great prayer indicates, First Minister at the Ottoman Court. The change which he would readily imagine in the condition of Christians, now *made like the dust by threshing* [8], may enable him to picture to himself the benefits which Daniel's office yielded to his people. Each miracle resulted in a decree in favor of the Jews. The miraculous and the ordinary history are in harmony, which is what men mean to deny by their word "objectless."

---

[3] Lev. xxvi. 44, 5.   [4] Is. xlviii. 20. Jer. xxix. 10.   [5] Mic. iv. 10.
[6] Jer. xxix. 7.   [7] Lev. xxvi. 40-42.   [8] The expression of a very intelligent Syrian to myself, from 2 Kgs. xiii. 7.

But further, it is most probable that the release of the Jews was one consequence of these miracles. The miracles stand connected in a chain. The superhuman knowledge, shewn to Nebuchadnezzar, was the ground why Daniel was called in on that last night of Belshazzar; his reading of the hand-writing, and the office which he occupied in consequence, were his first commendation to Darius. The restoration of his people was doubtless the fruit of his influence with Darius and Cyrus. It will have surprised most of us, that, according to the chronology in Daniel, the restoration of the Jews was not the immediate result of the conquest of Babylon. Looking upon it, as we did, as the promised result of that capture, and upon Cyrus as its foretold agent, we expected it to have taken place at once. And doubtless, had it been any human result, any political favour to a people who were oppressed by those whom he conquered, Cyrus would have given it at once, or not at all. Now men have the double problem to solve, why he restored them, and why he did not restore them at first. There was no motive of human policy, why he should restore them [1].

[1] Gesenius (on Is. xli. 2.) says, "*Perhaps* Cyrus favored the view of the Jews, [of the similarity of their faith with his own religion, Magism,] because it must have been of moment to him, when about to conquer the lands, in which the Jews lived scattered, to win the confidence and attachment of the people, which cherished the liveliest national hatred to their oppressors." But, 1) with the fall of Babylon, the whole empire, in which the Jews were scattered, except Egypt, was already in his hands. 2) The Jews, (as appears from the fewness of those who returned at first,) were, as a people, well contented with their condition. The religious portion only of them returned. 3) The state of the Jews was not like what people are probably thinking of, and what are now called "the oppressed nationalities." A nation, conquered, imperfectly amalgamated with the empire, longing for independence, is, of course, a formidable source of internal weakness to that empire; a source of strength, if won, to an invader. But the Jews in the Babylonian empire were not a "nationality." They were but scattered captives without organization, without leaders, without military training. There is no ground to think that they could be of any use to the conqueror, as neither is there any hint in history that they were. We know the measures of the campaign against Babylon; a pitched battle, in which Labynetus fled and shut himself in Borsippa, as Belshazzar did in Babylon; the provisioning of Babylon on the one hand, the stratagem whereby Cyrus took it unresisting. Magism was also as much, perhaps more, op-

In the ordinary course of human events, he would not even have known of their existence. There is no indication, that he did know of it before the conquest. The prophecy of Isaiah must have been shewn him; for his decree in favour of the Jews evinces belief in it. But a prophecy, in the language of a scattered population unknown to him, would have had no convincing power[2]. The living authoritative speaker gains admission for the unknown written word. As the history stands in Daniel, Cyrus had reason to trust Daniel; he had no reason to trust any ordinary Jew, who should shew him the, to him unknown, oracle. The accounts in Daniel and Ezra correspond with the facts, that the Jews were released, but not at first. Their restoration, was no part, apparently, of the original plan of Cyrus; because he, who could have done it with a word, did it not. It was no deep plan of human policy; because, two years after he had granted the permission, he restrained his favour ungraciously, persuaded by his councillors. His decree runs; [3]*The Lord God of heaven hath given me all the kingdoms of the earth; and hath charged me to build Him an house at Jerusalem.* The facts of sacred history accord with this; Daniel was accredited to Darius by the events at the close of the kingdom of Babylon; he was accredited personally to Darius by his known *innocency*[4] and by his supernatural deliverance; Darius issued a decree, commanding that people should reverence the God of Daniel. Daniel himself [5]*prospered in the reign of Darius and of Cyrus.* One, then, in high favor at the Court, himself accredited by miracle, accredited the unknown prophecy, and Cyrus acted upon it.

3) Nor, although the miracles did result in great benefits to the Jews, is there any reason to think that such was their sole end. In Babylon God shewed in act, what prophecy all along declared, that He was not a God of

posed to truth, than Babylonian idolatry. The Sassanidæ, who revived it, were deadly persecutors both of Jews and Christians.

[2] Hengstenberg's argument p. 39. from Kleinert Echtheit d. Iesaia p. 134 sqq.   [3] Ezr. i. 2.   [4] Dan. vi. 22.   [5] Ib. 28.

the Jews only.   Nor were they wasted.   It is said, " Nebuchadnezzar had ever to be converted anew.   Especially, in c. 5, Belshazzar and his court, except the Queen-Mother, were wholly unacquainted with Daniel and *his* miracles, which he had as yet wrought[1] ! " Alas !   If man's waste or forgetfulness of God's goodness were to be a proof that God had never shewn it, then we must disbelieve that God has ever shewn any mercies of His Providence or His Grace to our own bad selves ; which yet we, each of us, know that He has.   But, although Nebuchadnezzar's two first convictions of the greatness of the God of the Jews faded in time, we know of no relapse after the last. God triumphed at last, and won Nebuchadnezzar, as He does so many relapsing Christians.   There is no reason to think that the aged Darius ever went back from *his* conviction.   The revelation to Belshazzar was the open temporal judgment on one who had despised God's known dealings. [2] *Thou, his son, O Belshazzar, hast not humbled thine heart, though thou knewest all this, but hast lifted up thyself against the Lord of heaven.*   Belshazzar had forgotten Daniel ; he had *not* forgotten God's ways with Nebuchadnezzar ; but, like too many so-called Christians, he despised known truth.   We know, that God's judgment was fulfilled.   We do not know that it was wasted even on him.   Yet they are not the great of this world, who are mostly converted to God.   Many of those thousands of souls, who were assembled in that plain of Dura, may have been won to the belief of the One true God ; many, at Belshazzar's revelry, may have been awed towards God, before they slept their death-sleep ; many hearts may have been reached through Nebuchadnezzar's affecting

---

[1] Leng. p. lxiii. Davidson follows the inconceivably careless statement, "Belshazzar and his nobles appear to have been unacquainted with Daniel and *his miracles,* as the 5th chapter shews.   Nebuchadnezzar had always to be convinced anew.   The *array* of marvels *wrought through the instrumentality of Daniel* made little impression on the monarchs and their people." p. 174, 5. Again p. 171, "The cases of Ezra and Daniel are different.   The former was a priest and a scribe : the latter a prophet *and worker of miracles.*"

[2] Dan. v. 22, 23.

account of his humiliation, or awed into forbearance towards His people by the edicts of Nebuchadnezzar and Darius. "Many hearts may have been reached," did I say? They who, like the German critics, come to know of the history of Daniel, simply as matter of criticism or of unbelief, may look on that great history, as a matter which could at most affect the then generation, and think that the doings of God failed, because Belshazzar had turned a deaf ear to God's warnings to Nebuchadnezzar. We, most of whose minds must have been arrested in our childhood or boyhood by the impressive fascinating histories, we, to whom, as to the whole Church from the first and the Jewish Church before us, they have been, all our lives long, instructive, know that the works and words of God do "not pass away." Miracles of God did not cease their office of instruction and impressiveness, with the generation before whom they were wrought. Yet, even on that limited field, it is not true, according to the history itself, that God's dealings with Nebuchadnezzar had no effect even on Belshazzar and his Court. Daniel remained in honor among the conquering Medo-Persians, as among the conquered Babylonians. If men cast aside God's word as a fable, it is alas! their loss; but at least, let them not falsify it, in order to prove it to have been useless.

As regards the alleged "exaggeration" of the miracles, objectors must, in their consciences, know, that the only miracle, as to which this is alleged, could not have been lessened, if it was to be a miracle at all. It was more impressive to the great multitude, that Nebuchadnezzar's passion, which made him command that the furnace should be *heated seven times more than it had been thought good to heat it*, turned upon those whom he employed as his instruments. Little things affect us; and the fact, that *the smell of fire had not passed upon* the three confessors of God, set before people's eyes the completeness of the miracle. But when a miracle admits of no degrees, it is mere idleness to speak of "exaggeration."

The result of examining these untrue allegations against
the book of Daniel is not simply negative, that nothing
can be alleged against it, which does not relate to all revelation, as such.   Daniel wrote of certain events, which
he was inspired to record, in detail[1].   He relates them,
(which is a stamp of truth,) without any explanation, in
all simplicity.   He alludes, in his narrative, to kings unknown to Grecian historians, and to the relations of empires; he mentions whole classes of officers, and the
names of their offices, partly Semitic, partly of Aryan
origin, and gradations of their rank; wise men and their
classes; even musical instruments, of different nations,
and names of articles of dress, which Hebrews did not
use; he assigns dates freely; he describes what was probably a marvellous and very rare disease of the great monarch, and the fact of his praying amid extreme mental
alienation, a fact, which seems in the highest degree improbable, but is accordant with known facts; he alludes
to customs, personages ; he gives a scene from the interior of Babylon on the night of its capture, where, contrary to ordinary Eastern custom, he mentions the presence of the ladies of the harem [2], and distinct from these,

---

[1] Hengstenberg has a section, "knowledge of the whole state of things at
the time of Daniel;" Beitr. i. 333-52, from which several of these instances have
been taken.

[2] "Relaxation of manners shewed itself among the Babylonians, especially
as to the other sex.   There was not that retirement, which else prevails in the
harems of the East.   Hence the prophet, when he threatened the city with its
fall, symbolises it as a luxurious and delicate female, who, from her soft couch,
is cast into captivity. (Is. xiii.) [? xlvii. 1-5.]   Even in drinking-bouts their
women appeared ;—Curt. v. 1."   [The passage of Curtius is too revolting to
quote.]   Heeren i. 2. p. 201 sqq.   The presence of a concubine at a drinking-
bout of the last king of Babylon is stated by Xenophon. (Cyrop. v. 2. 28.)
The dancing, united by Herodotus (i. 191.) with the "revelling" of that last
night at Babylon, implies the presence of their women.   Among the Persians,
the drunken command of Ahasuerus, and the queen's refusal, (Esth. i. 10-12.)
imply the contrary custom.   "She, keeping to the Persian laws, which forbid
women to be seen by strangers, did not go the king." Jos. Ant. xi. 6. 1.   The
statement of the Persian Embassadors to king Amyntas, that it was the Persian custom, that the wives and concubines should be present at their feasts,
(Herod. v. 18.) if historical, was a shameless lie, to attain their end.   Plutarch
denies the presence of the wives at Persian feasts, affirms it of concubines. (Sym-

and not present with them at the feast, the Queen-mother, speaking in a tone of authority; he tells even of the plain stucco on the walls of the banquet-room, such as, notwithstanding the prevailing taste for ornament, is still found in the corresponding palaces of Nineveh[3]; he alludes, in one word, even to the custom of Eastern kings, (such as we find it among Persians and Parthians,) to lie at table by themselves, *over against*[4] their guests, probably for safety's sake; he gives events of that night, which fill it up, adversaries have said, even to overflowing, but for which time is left, since the fact is supplied, that the capture was not until towards morning[5]; he describes capital punishments under the Babylonian[6] and Persian kings, varying, in one respect, in conformity with their religion; the furnace he describes, as one only could have described it, who had seen such[7]. In his natural, truthful, and, so, fearless description, he again and again tells us what for us, who have only an antiquarian knowledge of these

pos. i. 1.) So neither among the Parthians were the women present at feasts, (Justin xli. 3. Macrobius adapts the statement of Plutarch to the Parthians. vii. 1.) nor among the ante-Mohammedan Arabs. Häv. on Dan. p. 180. So strange did the presence of the women seem to the LXX translator, that he omitted the mention of them. Hengst. p. 338.

[3] "There were chambers in the palace of Sennacherib, as well as in those of Nimroud and Khorsabad, whose walls were simply coated with plaster, like the walls of Belshazzar's palace at Babylon." Layard Nin. and Bab. p. 651.

[4] "And *over against the thousand* (לָקֳבֵל אַלְפָא) drank he wine." S. Ephr. paraphrases, "Alone he lay over-against all reclined." A Greek Scholiast has, "It was their custom, that each should have his own table." (in Mai.) Athenæus says, on the authority of Heraclides of Cuma, "When the Persian king makes a drinking-feast, (πότον [משתה] ποιῆται,) and he often makes one, those who drink with him are about twelve. And when they have supped, the king, by himself, and the guests, one of the eunuchs calls those who drink with him. And when they come in, they do not drink the same wine as he, and they, sitting on the ground, he lying on a couch with gold legs." Parask. ii. in Athen. iv. 26. "Among the Parthians, in their feasts, the king had the couch, whereon he lay alone, higher than the rest, and his table too apart, placed before himself alone, as a demigod, full of barbaric meats." Posidonius (about 100 B.C.) de Parth. L. v. in Athen. iv. 38.   [5] Xen. Cyrop. vii. 5. 27.

[6] Fire is mentioned, as a capital punishment, under Nebuchadnezzar, Jer. xxix. 22. "whom N. roasted in the fire;" and probably Ezek. xxiii. 25. "thy residue shall be devoured by the fire;" which was, of course, disused by the Persians.   [7] Even Bertholdt owns this. p. 69.

things, it requires thought to harmonise; he explains nothing, as writers do at a period somewhat later than the events which they describe, or when they write for a wider or different circle.   His accounts are minute, graphic; he accumulates the names of the classes, which he mentions, whether of officers, wise men, or musical instruments.   Those, who have been on the watch for his halting, have thought again and again, that they have found some flaw, which should loosen the whole fabric.   Look closer, and you see that the parts fit closely together; that, the more closely you press the expressions, the more exactly they correspond.

And this exactness occurs, even where the antagonistic critics have thought there was only a hap-hazard enumeration.   For example, at Nebuchadnezzar's inauguration, eight classes of officers of state are enumerated.   Nebuchadnezzar gathered them; Shadrach, Meshach, and Abednego, were comprised among them.   Why was not Daniel?   There is no allusion to any excepted class.   Why should there?   Daniel is describing what *was*, the gathering of these officers, not, what was *not*.   Yet, at the end of that eventful day, we find the king conferring with another class near himself, his *councillors*[1], who had not been commanded to worship the image, and of whom Daniel was, from his position, one.   So in other cases.   When you see a picture, representing the life of a people, and see, not a feature, a garb, a gesture, a building, a plant, other than you know to belong to the character of the people and scene which it represents, you doubt not that it is drawn from the life.   No one could imagine a picture of Teniers to have been drawn by one who had not a personal knowledge of what he depicts.   One little flaw detects, that a poetical description is taken from careful research, not from sight.   " Rhododendrons," it has been said[2] of a note on a description of the lake of Gennesareth

---

[1] Dan. iii. 27.

[2] Stanley Palestine p. 371 on Keble's Christian Year, 3rd Sunday in Advent. Again "'Tabor's lonely *peak*' is an inaccurate expression, and 'the mountains

which we all love, "is a mistake for oleanders."   When
then there are *no* "rhododendrons," for "oleanders," when
all these varied touches, so boldly and so freely given, each
and all, come true, what else can one judge, than that
Daniel drew from the life?   The apparent improbability
is, when verified, the surest witness to truth.   The building which, how ever many sides it may present to wind,
storm, flood, cannot be shaken, is founded on the firm
Rock.

terraced high with *mossy* stone ' is an image belonging to the moist atmosphere of the West, not to the bare landscape of the East." Stanley Ib. 372.

LECTURES VIII. AND IX.

The points of doctrine and practice mentioned in the book of Daniel, which are alleged to indicate a date later than that of the prophet, are identical or in harmony with the other Scriptures of the Old and New Testaments; nor was any doctrine or practice, mentioned in the book of Daniel, borrowed from Parsism.

" Later ideas and practices " figure as an argument in all the attacks upon Daniel. Lengerke stated this most diffusively. "[1] The dogmatic ideas are wholly at variance with those which prevailed in the Captivity and immediately after it, but agree accurately with the Maccabee period; and consequently find numerous parallels in the Apocryphal books. [2] The doctrine of the Messiah appears already much more developed than in Ezekiel; the Messiah appears as a superhuman being; traces of the divine nature occur no where besides in the prophets,

[1] Einl. z. Dan. § 13. n. 7. p. lxv. Davidson nearly translates, (iii. p. 177, 8.) " The doctrinal and ethical ideas of the book often differ from the notions entertained at the time of the exile and immediately after, while they agree with the Maccabæan age, as is seen by parallels in the Apocryphal books."

[2] paraphrased by Davidson, ib. " Thus the Christology is much more developed, than it is in the prophets of the Captivity, like Ezekiel. Here the Messiah appears a superhuman being. (vii. 13.)—This doctrine is not found in any other passage of the Old Testament. The original of vii. 13. is evidently Ezek. i. 26-28; but there Jehovah himself is represented as having some resemblance to a human form, whereas Messiah is the subject in Daniel. Though the later Jews transferred qualities and attributes from Jehovah to Messiah, the early ones, [i. e. the earlier inspired writers,] kept both apart, because they did not believe Messiah to be other than human."

but first in the Sibylline books in the time of the Maccabees. That passage [of Daniel] is imitated from Ezekiel; only, in Ezekiel, the human form signifies Jehovah,
here, in Daniel, the Messias; as, altogether, the latest
Jews transferred many attributes from Jehovah to the
Messiah. Further, it is unmistakeable, that the definite
succession of Judgment, Resurrection, the Appearing of
the Messiah, is first most sharply marked in our book,
and the doctrine of the last things appears more developed
than in the earlier books."

" [3] The doctrine of Angels in the book also carries us
into the latest time. The Angels appear already quite
in the form in which they were introduced from the later
Parsism into Judaism. Here first is found the distinction of higher and lower Angels, and the doctrine of guardian angels [4]."   " [5] Peculiar to the book of Daniel are also
the names of Gabriel and Michael, and, like the analogous
Raphael in Tobit, borrowed from a later doctrine of Angels
formed under Persian influence."

" [6] The Asceticism also of the book approaches hard to
Pharisaism. The exaggerated ideas of the later Jews as
to the power of prayer [7], which subsequently were yet
more developed, appear to shew themselves already.

[3] " The Angelology of the book points to a late origin. Thus the names of
Gabriel and Michael first appear in it. Higher and lower angels are distinguished, for Gabriel is commanded by another. (viii. 16.) One of the guardian angels contends with another for 21 days, and helps another. Here we
see the influence of Parsism on Judaism." Dav. p. 178, 9.   [4] x. 13.

[5] from De Wette Allg. Enc. Art. Daniel p. 90.   [6] Leng. ib. n. 8.

[7] vi. 11. ii. 18. ix. 3. x. 2. Davidson thinks this an argument, and gives the
same instances, " Exaggerated and excessive notions of the value of prayer (!)
betray a later Judaism; not later, however, than what may have been developed in Judaism, under the influence of Parsism, a generation or two after
the return from Babylon." [Herzfeld said this of the "Angelology." "The Angelology in iv. 10. 14. is no sign of any considerable lateness of date. If it took
its rise out of the earlier belief of Israel through Persian influence, it need only
be a generation or two later than that influence." Gesch. Isr. Exc. 2. § 13.
p. 295.] " Thus Daniel prays and makes supplication with windows open towards Jerusalem, though (!) he knew that a royal decree was signed, con-
demning any one that did so to be cast into the den of lions. (vi. 11.) He
mourned and fasted three full weeks. (x. 2, 3.) A secret was revealed to him
in answer to prayer, ii. 18." p. 179, 80.

Then too, revelations are imparted to him, in consequence
of frequent prayer. To this head belongs the abstinence
from profane food [1]; the three-weeks fasting; the prayer
three times a day; the searching and grubbing in the
Scripture [2], and the interpretation of a prophetical portion [3]."

Now, apart, for the time, from the facts, and the arrogance and open profaneness of some of this, or the censure on the New Testament and our Blessed Lord which
some of it involves, the argument, as a whole, assumes
the falsehood of revelation. The fact asserted is this;
"None of these doctrines or practices are contained either in the earlier books of Holy Scripture, or in Ezekiel who lived in the Captivity, or in Haggai, Zachariah,
or Malachi after it."   Yet, as Daniel confessedly lived towards the close of that former revelation, there would be
nothing strange, that doctrines, especially as to the Messiah, should be revealed at its close, which had not been
revealed before. Nor, considering the short compass of
the prophets after the Captivity, would it be anything
strange that any doctrine or practice should be contained
in Daniel, which does not occur in the three. God foretold by Haggai, that He would give peace [4] while the 2nd
temple still stood, which does not occur in the others;
Malachi alone foretells the coming of Elias [5]. God revealed Himself *in divers ways* [6] to the Prophets," "[7] dividing to each severally as He would." Granted, that
God did reveal Himself to the Jews, then the mention of
any truth in Daniel alone could be no ground for assuming that it was not revealed to an earlier contemporary of

[1] i. 12. " He also abstained from the king's meat as profane, and lived on
pulse. (i. 12.)" Dav. p. 180.   [2] x. 2.

[3] De Wette summed up thus; " The later expansion of the doctrine of Angels (iv. 14. [17 Eng.] ix. 21. x. 13. 21.) and of the Christ, (vii. 13. sqq.
xii. 1-3.) of doctrine, (xii. 2 sq.) morals, (iv. 24. [27 Eng.] comp. Tob. iv. 11.
xii. 9.) and asceticism, (i. 8-16. comp. Esth. LXX after iv. 17. 2 Macc. v. 27.)
According to Hävernick this only refers to abstinence from meat or drink offered to idols. [See ab. Lect. i. p. 17, 18.] vii. 11. [8 Eng.] comp. Acts ii. 15.
iii. 1. x. 9. 12. [30.]" Einl. § 255. c. ed. 7.

[4] Hagg. ii. 6-9.   [5] Mal. iv. 5.   [6] Heb. i. 1.   [7] 1 Cor. xii. 11.

Haggai and Zechariah. It could be no à priori ground against the genuineness of the book of Daniel. The ground is not historical, but anti-dogmatic. These writers again tacitly assume in the negative the whole matter at issue, whether God revealed Himself to His creatures. They assume that all man's religious knowledge is the result of the workings of his own mind and is developed in certain orders or cycles; and so, that no portion of it could exist before that stage of the developement of the human mind to which they assume that it belongs; and so, again, that the belief in any doctrine or practice, expressed in any writing, is an evidence of the age to which that writing belongs. Some such series of assumptions is necessarily involved in the argument, that the book of Daniel must belong to the time of the Maccabees, if it be true, that such or such beliefs or practices are found in the book of Daniel, and are not found in the three prophets after the Captivity or in those before them.

Another assumption is also involved, that the belief was *not* derived in the Maccabee times from the book of Daniel.

To take these subjects in order:

i. The first statement is untrue, both in what it affirms and what it denies. It affirms that traces of the Divine Nature of the Messiah are *not* found elsewhere in the Prophets, and *are* first found in the Sibylline books. In the Jewish Sibylline book,—the only Sibylline in existence before our Lord,—there is *no* trace of a Divine Nature of the Messiah [9]. The language in the book of Enoch is, obviously and confessedly on all hands, taken from Daniel [10]. There *is*, as we know, in the Prophets, evidence of the belief in the Divinity of Him Who was to save us, before the time of Daniel. This, again, is a statement, affecting not the book of Daniel only, but the Gospel.

a. Our Lord Himself cited the 110th Psalm of Himself, the Christ, awakening up the thoughts of His adversaries, that He, Whom they gainsaid, was in truth an object

---

[8] See ab. Lect. vi. p. 362, 3.   [9] See the passage, alleged by Lengerke, ib. p. 364.   [10] See ib. p. 382 sqq.

of awe to them, and that they were His enemies, to their own great peril. [1]*While the Pharisees were gathered together, Jesus asked them, saying, What think ye of Christ? Whose son is He? They say unto Him, The Son of David. He saith unto them, How then doth David in spirit call Him Lord, saying, The Lord said unto my Lord, Sit Thou on My Right Hand, until I make Thine enemies Thy footstool? If David then call Him Lord, how is He his Son?* The adversaries of Jesus, at that day, had no answer to give. They could not deny that the Messiah was to be of the seed of David; or that David himself spoke *in spirit,* i.e. by inspiration; or that he spake the words of that Psalm; or that he was speaking of the Christ and of His reign, in despite of and over His enemies. They could not deny any of this; nor could they concede the inference which our Lord drew, that, according to their own prophets, the Christ was to be more than man, without taking away the ground of their own opposition to Him, for which, soon after, they condemned Him to death. They had no answer, because there is none, save to confess that David in spirit foretold, that He, the Christ, Who was to be born of him according to the flesh, was, in another mode of being, his Lord. Jesus appealed to their own convictions. The greatness of the Psalm doubtless forced it on them, and, in the face of the Truth, they dared not directly lie. Twice in the brief Psalm, the prophetic asseveration of God is alleged, as pronounced to the Object of the Psalm. *The word*[2] *of the Lord to my Lord, Sit Thou on My Right Hand, until I make Thine enemies Thy footstool.* The appeal of St. Paul is irresistible[3]; *To which of the angels said He at any time, Sit on My Right Hand, until I make Thine enemies Thy footstool? Are they not all ministering spirits &c.* To sit on the right hand of an earthly king involved an association in the dignity of the Sovereign. Human nature, if it have any true belief in God, if it know anything as to God or itself, could not tell the lie to itself, that this *could* be said to an earthly king. Unbelief, unless shameless,

[1] S. Matt. xxii. 41-5.   [2] נאם   [3] Heb. i. 13, 14.

could not say, that David sat on the Right Hand of God, because David had brought in the Ark into the city, where he dwelt. As if any one sat on the Right Hand of God, because his house was by a Church! Nothing in David's life corresponds to the saying. David was a warrior-king; his enemies were subdued through human means and a human arm sustained by God. He himself fought, till his strength failed him [4]; and he fled before Absalom. Rationalism will scarcely say, that this is a fulfilment of that calm reign, which God affirmed, *Sit Thou on My Right Hand, until I make Thine enemies Thy footstool* [5]. And he, who was so to sit, was also to be a Priest, not after any priesthood which existed in David's time. *Thou art a priest for ever after the order of Melchisedek.* A priest for ever! David was no priest. He was soon to pass away, and to be gathered to his fathers. The Psalm must have been written, after Zion had been taken [6]. It were mockery, on any hypothesis, as addressed to David. The whole Psalm is personal. God binds Himself by an unchangeable oath. *Thou art a priest for ever.* To sum up, the king sits in calm majesty at the Right Hand of God, where no human king was ever imagined to sit. While He is enthroned there, God sends forth the rod of His power. He rules, not by subduing only, but amidst His unsubdued enemies; yet He is to reign until all His enemies be beneath His Feet. His people offer themselves willingly in the day of His power, yet clad not in earthly armour, but in the beauties of holiness. He Himself is a priest, and that for ever, yet by a priesthood, superseding the Levitical priesthood, unchangeable, in His own Person. *Thou art a priest for ever.* All corresponds to the truth in Christ. His Human Nature has ever been believed to

---

[4] 2 Sam. xxi. 15-17.

[5] Ewald, I see, does say this. He interprets the whole Psalm of David, (Psalm. p. 23-5.) and " to sit on the Right Hand of God," is, that God would go with him, as it were, on "a chariot of victory" to fight against his enemies.

[6] Even Ewald admits, that " the language of the short Psalm does not contradict its being of the time of David," and supposes it to have been " addressed to David, as he went forth to war against powerful enemies." ib. Dav. ii. 285, follows Ewald.

be in that special nearness to God, expressed by His *Right Hand ;* St. Stephen saw Him there ; Apostles averred it ; the whole Church ever confessed it.   He is there, our Priest as well as our King, King with an unchangeable Priesthood.   His people fight, not with weapons of this world, but in the armour of holiness.   Godliness in them wins fresh subjects to Him.   His kingdom is still upheld amid the hostility of the world.   *He rules in the midst of His enemies.*   The time, when all shall be subdued to Him, is, in the nature of things, yet to come.   Such a waiting lies in the words of the prophecy and is a part of it ; *sit Thou on My Right Hand till—.*   The long expectation, which is the mockery of human hopes, is the fulfilment of the Divine promise.   He rules, He gathers His willing peoples in each generation, until time shall melt away in eternity.   Each century, during which the consummation of all things is delayed, is full of new victories over all the powers of darkness, the resistance of the world, the weakness of the flesh.   Each century is a prolonged victory over the destroyer of all human things, time. What says rationalism ?   "[1]The word 'until' is not to be pressed, but is to be understood ideally of an unending, unclosed, uninclusive term."   But where was it for David ? And what are the objections to the interpretation given by Christ ?   1) "[2] The sitting on the Right Hand of the Fa-

---

[1] Hupfeld Ps. T. iv. p. 183.   Ewald (Ps. p. 25.) refers to Bathsheba's language at David's death-bed, " Let my lord king David live for ever," (1 Kgs. i. 31.) and the Psalms prophetic of Christ xxi. 5. [4 Eng.] xlv. 3. 7. [2. 6. Eng.] and Psalm xli. 13.   Bathsheba did not, like the Persian, greet the king, "Mayest thou reign for ever." (Ælian V. II. i. 32.)   I cannot think that, with the knowledge of the life to come which David had, the words "live for ever" were an unmeaning heartless formula, a mockery to a dying man.

[2] Hupfeld p. 175.   "It is certain that a prophecy of the Messiah in the Christian sense, i. e. with the attributes ascribed to him in the New Testament on the ground of this Psalm, is, in the way in which it is here expressed, utterly inconceivable in a poet of the Old Testament, being irreconcileable with all historical and psychological conceptions and principles of interpretation, acknowledged elsewhere.   *For"* &c (as in the text.)   The remaining grounds are, 3) "that the Object of the Psalm is addressed as present;" as if the Prophet could not in vision, like Balaam, *see Him but not now, behold Him, but not nigh;* and 4) "that God would destroy his enemies;" which is but what our Lord Himself says, *Those Mine enemies who would not that I should reign over them,*

ther in the New Testament is a heavenly, ever united with the Resurrection and Ascension of Jesus, of which, earlier, *no anticipation could come into the heart of man.* 2) The high-priestly, or atoning office of Christ, (as it is taught in the Epistle to the Hebrews in contrast with the Mosaic Priesthood and including the abolition of the Mosaic law,) equally goes too far beyond the position of the Old Testament, and, especially is too foreign to the idea of the Messiah of the Old Testament, that *such a thought could* have come into the mind of an Old Testament poet or prophet." In other words, because the thought could not come in any human way, and, *it is assumed,* was not revealed by God, it could not have come at all.

It was to our Lord as to His Human, not His Divine, Nature, that it was said, *Sit Thou on My Right Hand.* For, as God, He is ever one with the Father. But it was said to Him, *because* He was God. David's Son, *as* Man, would not have been David's Lord. The later prophets, even if any of them were greater prophets, were not the lords of those who went before them. *Among those born of women, there is not,* our Lord said [3], *a greater prophet than John the Baptist.* Nay, he was [4] *more than a prophet.* Yet he was the lord of no one. The angels themselves were the fellowservants of the Apostles and prophets, *and of those who have the testimony of Jesus* [5]. Jesus was David's Lord, because He was God; He was his Son, because He was God Incarnate. To sit on God's Right Hand, was a property of His Human Nature; but it belonged to that Nature, because, in that Nature, He was Lord and God. And so David gave to the Christ a title, which, as Man, did not belong to Him, and he prophesied of Him what did not belong to man. His words, like those of Daniel, ascribe to the Messiah a nearness to

bring them hither and slay them before Me. (S. Luke xix. 27.) Davidson adopts these last arguments, adding, " Not to speak of the psychological impossibility before-mentioned, that a writer should, without the least intimation, *identify himself* with a person who was to live long after." (l. c.) This is mere carelessness. The Psalmist speaks of the subject of the Psalm, as " my Lord."

[3] S. Luke vii. 28. S. Matt. xi. 11.   [4] S. Matt. xi. 9.
[5] Rev. xix. 10. xxii. 9.

Godwhichhas never been said ofany created being. They
foretell that fact, which our Lord predicted of Himself[1],
which has ever been believed by all who ever believed in
Jesus, which ever formed a part of the earliest Creeds,
that Jesus is, as no other is or can be, in that special nearness of glory, which is called the Right Hand of God.   If
men believe the fact, they will find it difficult not to believe
that the Psalmist's words relate to the fact which they
describe.   The Psalmist and Daniel foretold the super-
angelic glory of the Messiah in the same way.

b. A direct statement of the Divinity of the Messiah, in
the Psalms, has the authority of St. Paul, who alleges it
in contrast with even superhuman beings.   [2]*But unto the
Son He saith, Thy Throne, O God, is for ever and ever.*
The attempts to eliminate the meaning betray their origin,
and condemn one another.   No one, but for a preconceived opinion, could interpret the word, *Elohim,* otherwise
than as *God,* and as the title of the being addressed.
No one, acting up to the boasted principle, that " Scripture" is to be "[3] interpreted like any other book," could
hesitate so to render it.   No one, who could evade the
meaning which he wished not to see, has hesitated about
either.   Grotesque as have been the renderings or explanations offered, no one, who thought he could so
construct the sentence, that the word, *Elohim,* need
not designate the being addressed, doubted that *Elohim*
signified "God;" and no one who thought that he could
make out for the word, *Elohim,* any other meaning
than that of " God," doubted that it designated the being
addressed.   A right instinct prevented each class from
doing more violence to grammar or to idiom, than he
needed, in order to escape the truth which he disliked.
If people thought that they might paraphrase, "thy
throne, O judge, or prince[4]," or "image of God[5]," or
"[6]who art as a God to Pharaoh," they hesitated not for

---

[1] S. Matt. xxvi. 64. S. Mark xiv. 62. S. Luke xxii. 69.   [2] Heb. i. 8.
[3] Prof. Jowett Essays and Rev. p. 377.   [4] Rashi.
[5] Obad. Siporno.   [6] Isaac Jabetz, Torath Chesed (as said to Moses.)

a moment to render with us, "Thy throne is for ever and ever."   If men think that they may assume such an idiom as, "thy throne of God," meaning "thy divine throne," or "thy throne is God," meaning "thy throne is the throne of God," they doubt not that *Elohim* means purely and simply "God."   "There are interpreters," says Gesenius[7], "who say that *Elohim* is used, in the singular, of one king, and is the same as *Ben-Elohim*, 'Son of God,' appealing to those almost Divine honours which the Easterns pay to their kings, and the Divine attributes with which they adorn them, as 'Antiochus Deus Epiphanes.'   But the primary place which they allege, Ps. xlv. 7, does not at all prove this. They render, *Thy throne, O God*, (i. e. O divine king,) *shall stand for ever;* but it can scarce be doubted that *Elohim*, the wonted name of God in the Psalms of the sons of Korah, is the same as in countless other places."

Modern criticism, here or elsewhere, has been busy in blinding itself to what it wished not to see.   No one, in the least conversant with Hebrew, and who had any idea of the idiom of language, could doubt how the four simple words are to be rendered.   We could not doubt in Latin, how we must understand the words, "Solium tuum Deus in æternum."   The Hebrew words are as simple as any in any language.   If people could but persuade themselves that the words were a parenthetic address to God, no one would hesitate to own their meaning to be, "Thy throne, O God, is for ever and ever."   They express naturally the eternal dominion of God.   This is their obvious, their only natural grammatical meaning.   In no other Psalm would any one have doubted it.   One may appeal to men's own consiences, that they could not.   When then they strive so hard, in non-natural ways, to force other meanings on the words [8], it is clear that their

---

[7] Thes. p. 99. He used the same arguments on Is. ix. 5. p. 564, 5. note. But on Isaiah, he adopted the one evasion, "thy God's-throne is for ever and ever;" in the Thesaurus, the other, "thy throne shall be ["is" ib. 699.] a throne of God (i. e. fortified and prospered by God.")

[8] These renderings have been, 1) "Thy throne *is* God for ever and ever."

ground for this lies in their own conceptions, what the

Even Hupfeld saw that this was "too bold."   "God is our refuge," nay, "our
dwelling-place," for *in Him we live and move and have our being*.   He is between us and our foes ; so He spoke of Himself, as the "shield" of His own.
He doth that for them, in spirit and in body, which these outward things do
for the body.   But the throne is a symbol of dignity higher than its own, that
of the monarch.   It would be unbefitting to speak of the Creator as the "throne"
of the creature, because it would imply, not that the creature had a glory derived from the Creator, but that the Creator was subordinate to His creature.
So Saadias dropped the rendering, and supplied, "God *shall establish* thy
throne for ever and ever ;" which, however, just requires the additional word,
" shall establish," יָכֵן.   Not in Hebrew, any more than in any other language,
can, " Thy throne God for ever and ever," stand for, " God shall establish thy
throne for ever and ever."

2) " Thy throne, God," is to mean, " Thy throne of, or from, God."   This
is not so expressed in Hebrew.   The throne of Israel was God's throne, because it was a theocracy, its kings were His vicegerents.   Once it is said, *God
chose Solomon to sit upon the throne of the kingdom of the Lord over Israel*,
1 Chr. xxviii. 5 ; and then, *Solomon sat upon the throne of the Lord, as king
over Israel*.   But this cannot make the words, " Thy throne, God," mean
" Thy throne from God."

3) They say, כִּסְאֲךָ אֱלֹהִים is for כִּסֵּא אֱלֹהֶיךָ, the pronoun, *thy*, being, (as, it is
alleged, in some few other instances,) interposed between the nominative and
genitive.   But כִּסֵּא אֱלֹהֶיךָ, itself, must mean, " the throne of thy God ;" it could
not mean, " Thy throne from," " or of God."   No one could seriously maintain that it did.   And this might have shewn people, that that other rare idiom
does not apply to this case.   The few cases are strictly cases of apposition. עֻזִּי
(Ps. lxxi. 7.) or מָעוּזִּי חָיִל (2 Sam. xxii. 33, for הַמְאַזְּרֵנִי חָיִל Ps. xviii. 33.) are not
for עֹז כְּמָחֲסֶה or for מָעוֹז חֵילִי which would rather mean, " the refuge of my
strength," or would, at least, be ambiguous ; but are to be taken simply, "my
refuge, strength," i. e. "and that a strong one."   אֹיְבַי שֶׁקֶר (Ps. xxxv. 19.) is
illustrated by שֹׂנְאַי חִנָּם, with which it is united ; as חִנָּם is an adverb, so שֶׁקֶר.   They
are added absolutely, "my haters gratis," "mine enemies falsely."   So עֶזְרָתֵנוּ הָבֶל,
lit. "our help (which is) vanity." Lam. iv. 17, In like way, סְדִינֵי בַד (Lev. xvi. 13.)
is, "his garment, linen ; " i.e. "consisting of linen ; " דַּרְכֵּךְ זִמָּה (Ezek. xvi. 27.)
"thy way, lewdness," i. e. mere lewdness.   In all the cases, except Lev. xvi. 13,
the words added express a quality ; viz. strength, might, lewdness, falseness, gra-
tuitousness.   Lev. xvi. 13, "his garment, linen," is but the well-known case of
an explanation standing in apposition, as is seen in cases where the chief word
has the article.   סְדִינֵי בַד, "his garment, linen," is the same construction, so far,
as הַכְּתֹנֶת שֵׁשׁ, "the coat, fine linen," Ex. xxviii. 39. הַכְּרוּבִים זָהָב "the cherubs, gold."
1 Chr. xxviii. 18.   But God could stand in no such relation to the "throne"
of man.   Ewald himself gives an explanation of the idiom, similar in principle,
(ausf. Lehrb. § 291. 3. b.) "Poets can easily append the suffix to the first substantive, to which it belongs, and then subordinate the second independently,
as עֻזִּי מָעוֹז, 'my refuge in strength,' i. e. my strong refuge ; אֹיְבַי שָׁוְא, "my lying
enemies,' Ps. lxxi. 7. [מַרְכְּבֹתֶיךָ יְשׁוּעָה, " Thy chariots, which are salvation,"]

words theologically can *not* mean, not in any persuasion
Hab. iii. 8. Ezek. xvi. 27. xviii. 7. [taking חֻבְּלָתו חֹב (both ἅπ. λεγ.) as if it
were "his pledge for a debt," others, as E. V. "debtor."] 2 Sam. xxii. 33."

4) They render, "Thy throne is (a throne of) God," which is, of course, simply impossible. Ewald (Kr. Gramm. § 343 note) said, "Very seldom is the
status constructus wanting in the predicate, when it is the noun immediately
preceding, as כִּסְאֲךָ אֱלֹהִים 'thy throne is God's (throne') for א כִּסֵּא; more easily
with a noun designating the matter, Jer. xxiv. 2." But Jer. xxiv. 2. requires
nothing to be supplied. We have, in English, many such idioms; "The one
basket, very good figs, like the figs first ripe; and the other basket, very bad
figs, which could not be eaten for badness." The cases which others allege are
obviously irrelevant, being cases in which the article has been put anomalously,
yet on a different principle, before the nominative, as הָאָרוֹן הַבְּרִית, " the ark of
the covenant;" הָאֵל בֵּית אֵל, "the God of Bethel." For in these cases, there
is only *one* nominative and *one* genitive; there is nothing really to be supplied.
The saying of Hebrew grammarians, that הָאָרוֹן הַבְּרִית was for הָאָרוֹן אֲרוֹן הַבְּרִית, "the
ark, the ark of the covenant," is, in itself, obviously a mere shift to explain the
anomalous placing of the article; for there is no such emphasis, as this repetition would imply; and, if this anomaly were to be thus accounted for, it would
have no bearing on the passage in the Psalm; since, in those cases, the words
are in apposition; in the Psalm they would be made to stand as subject and
predicate. In his ausf. Lehrg. § 296. b. ed. 7, Ewald quotes, as exactly corresponding, only Cant. i. 15., rendering, (as the E. V.,) "*thy eyes* are *doves'*
eyes." But from Cant. iv. 1, "thy eyes are doves behind thy veil," or "locks,"
and, still more, from v. 12, "His eyes are doves at the rivers of waters, bath-
ing in milk, sitting in fulness," or, "at the fulness" (i. e. of the streams,) it
is clear that the object of comparison, in i. 15, also, is the dove itself, not its
eyes. For in iv. 1. v. 12. there follows on the comparison the mention of the
situation of the dove. Ewald too rendered iv. 1, "thine eyes doves around
thy locks;" v. 1, "His eyes are doves over the water-brooks." Delitsch (ad loc.)
says, "Hitzig, on Pr. vii. 27, rightly questions the correctness of the elliptical
explanation in places such as Deut. viii. 15. 1 Kgs. iv. 13. Ezr. x. 13." Certainly in such idioms as, "who led thee through the great and terrible wilderness, fiery serpents and scorpions and drought," (Deut.) "threescore great
cities, walls and brasen bars," (1 Kgs. iv.) "the people *is* many, and the weather *is* showers," (Ezr.) no one scarcely could think of filling it up "wilderness
of serpents," "cities of walls," or "the weather is weather of showers." Such
renderings ignore the idioms of language. Yet Hitzig now justifies his rendering, "thy throne is a God's throne," by such idioms. (ad loc.) According
to these interpreters, in the 2nd half-verse, where there would be no ambiguity, "a sceptre of righteousness is the sceptre of thy kingdom," שֵׁבֶט מִישֹׁר שֵׁבֶט
מַלְכוּתֶךָ, the nominative is inserted in both clauses; and in the first half-verse,
where (as the Versions shew) the obvious rendering is, "Thy throne, O God,"
the nominative, which would prevent the ambiguity, is omitted. A writer, who
writes fully, not מִישֹׁר only, but שֵׁבֶט מִישֹׁר שֵׁבֶט מַלְכוּתֶךָ would, à fortiori, have written, כִּסְאֲךָ כְּסֵא אֱלֹהִים, *if he had meant it*, since there was the greater need of precision, because its obvious meaning involves an important dogmatic statement.

5) Gesenius (on Is. ix. 5.) adopted yet another construction. "The word

what they grammatically *do* mean. The words are addressed to God [1]; the context shews that He Who is so כִּסֵּא has two genitives, *in different relations*, after it, just as Lev. xxvi. 42, בְּרִיתִי יַעֲקֹב ' my Jacob's covenant,' i. e. my covenant with Jacob." In Lev. xxvi. 42, two constructions are united. In Hebrew, בְּרִית is joined in the genitive very commonly with the name of the person who makes the covenant, (as in the often-repeated," בְּרִית, "·the covenant of the Lord,") and more rarely with that of those, with whom the covenant is made, as Deut. iv. 31. בְּרִית אֲבֹתֶיךָ " the covenant with thy fathers ; " Mal. ii. 10. " with our fathers ; " Ps. lxxxix. 30, עֲבָדְךָ .3 " the cov. with thy servant;" Mal. ii. 8 ; בְּרִית הַלֵּוִי, " the covenant with Levi ; " Is. xlii. 6. xlix. 8. בְּרִית עָם, " a covenant with the people." In the emphatic saying, Lev. xxvi. 42, *I will remember My covenant with Jacob, and also My covenant with Isaac, and also My covenant with Abraham I will remember*, the two constructions are united, which has no difficulty, because, as Gesenius said, " they stand in different relations," well known in the idiom of the language. So in Jeremiah xxxiii. 20, בְּרִיתִי is united with יוֹם and לַיְלָה " *My covenant* with *the day and My covenant* with *the night*, parallel with, *My covenant with David My servant.* (בְּרִיתִי אֶת דָּוִד. v. 21.) The construction ברית את חד in itself suggests, that the construction, ברית היום, is idiomatic and elliptical. In v. 25, the adverb, יוֹמָם, is substituted for הַיּוֹם. The elliptical idiom was doubtless the rather used, on account of the great frequency of the fuller idiom, " made a covenant with " &c. The covenant, of course, implies the two parties between whom it is made. The two persons in (lit.) " the covenant of Me, Jacob," " the covenant of Me, Isaac," " the covenant of Me, Abraham," stand not only in relation with the word, " covenant," but with each other. וְכָרַתִּי אֶת בְּרִיתִי יַעֲקוֹב וְאַף אֶת בְּרִיתִי יִצְחָק וְאַף אֶת בְּרִיתִי אַבְרָהָם אֶזְכֹּר have no ambiguity. It is but the union of known relations. " My covenant," " the covenant of the Lord," is, every where, the covenant which God made ; " the covenant of your fathers," " of your servant," is " the covenant which He made with the fathers, &c ; " and the phrase, " My covenant with Jacob," does but blend them, in the same sense in which they were used apart. There is also no other possible meaning. The words " Thy throne," "the throne of God," equally have definite meanings, but exclusive of each other. They express, each of them, to whom the throne belonged. They are both the genitive of the subject. "The throne of God " never occurs in the sense of " the throne which God gave." We have, " Thy throne (O Lord) is from generation to generation," Lam. v. 19 ; " the Lord's throne is in heaven," Ps. xi. 4 ; " God sitteth on His holy throne," Ps. xlvii. 8 ; " justice and judgment are the habitation of Thy throne," Ps. lxxxix. 14; " the heaven is My throne," Is. lxvi. 1 ; " the throne of the Lord," Jer. iii. 17; " the place of My throne," Ez. xliii. 7. And we have no other meaning. To render, then, "thy throne of God," in the meaning "thy throne entrusted to thee by God," (Ges. on Is. ix. 5.) is to join the words in a sense which they never have, rejecting that which the like phrase actually has. (Lam. v. 19.) Gesenius abandoned this (Thes. p. 98, 699.) for No 3 ; yet rendered (Ib. p. 1036.) " *solium tuum a Deo constitutum* stabit *in æternum*."

[1] " The Versions take *Elohim* as the Vocative ; but neither can this be an address to Jahve, (YHVH) as the Targum takes it ; *nor can the king be so directly taken as God.*" Hitzig. As for Hitzig's supplementary argument, (from Ewald,) it contains its own answer ; " moreover עֹלָם וָעֶד (without לְ, comp. Lam.

addressed as God, is a King among men, but One Whose kingdom is not of this world; His end truth, and meek righteousness; Himself, beauteous above the sons of men; His lips overflowing with Divine grace; and these things in Him, the Source of Divine Unction.   Men would not believe that our Lord was God, or that God foretold this of Him [2]; they dare not deny, that the simplest meaning of the words in themselves is, " Thy Throne, O God, is for ever and ever."

c. A 3rd place, which the whole body of the Apostles quoted [2], while addressing God, which St. Paul alleged to the Jews [3] at Antioch in Pisidia, quoted in the Epistle to the Hebrews [4], and alluded to in the Epistle to the Romans [5], speaks of the Messiah, as, in a special way, " the Son of God."   The second Psalm is a prophecy against the vain attempts of heathen nations to throw off the sovereignty of God and of His Anointed.   It exhibits, as Isaiah and Daniel do, the vain tumults of men, and, over-against them, the calm supremacy of God.   Rebellion against the Lord and against His Anointed, i. e. His Messiah or Christ, is one and the same act.   [6] *The kings of the earth set themselves in array, and the rulers take counsel together, against the Lord and against His Anointed.*   Obedience to God and reverence to the Son are also one and the same.   [7]*Serve the Lord with fear and rejoice with trembling.   Kiss the Son, lest He be angry.*   Trust in Him is the source of manifold blessedness.   *Blessed are all they that put their trust in Him.*   His wrath is destruction. It is one and the same as the wrath of God, as instantaneous in its effects and as fatal.   *Lest He be angry and ye perish from the way, when His wrath is kindled but a*

v. 19.) is uniformly only an incidental determination of the predicate, xlviii. 15. x. 16. lii. 10. not the predicate itself." It is mere straw-splitting, to admit that כִּסְאֲךָ לְדֹר וָדֹר (Lam. v. 19.) signifies, " Thy throne is for ever and ever, and to deny that כִּסְאֲךָ עוֹלָם וָעֶד means the same. The construction, which is the point questioned by Hitzig, is precisely the same.   Ewald had doubtless forgotten Lam. v. 19, when he made the assertion.   עוֹלָם וָעֶד is as near an expression for eternity, as human language admits; it expresses clearly the same as לְדֹר וָדֹר.   [2] Acts iv. 25, 6.   [3] Ib. xiii. 33.   [4] Heb. i. 5.   [5] Rom. i. 4.   [6] Ps. ii. 2.   [7] Ib. 11, 12.

little. His inheritance embraced all nations. [1]*Ask of Me and I will give Thee the heathen for Thine inheritance.* It is given by God, as our Lord says, [2]*All power is given unto Me in heaven and in earth;* but it is coextensive with the earth; *the uttermost parts of the earth for Thy possession;* as our Lord, after mention of that power given to Him, said to His Apostles, and, in them, to His Church unto the end, [3]*Go ye and disciple all nations.* Of Him alone it is said, *Thou art My Son, this day have I begotten Thee.* Others have been and are adopted sons, He alone is a Son by nature; of Him Alone is the word used, which expresses the special relation of nature. Of others whom God *made* His sons, He said; [4]*he shall be My son, and I his Father.* To Him Alone, Who is the Son by Nature, He saith, *This day I have begotten Thee.* The kiss also (as it continues among us to this day,) to a superior was the well-known act of fealty, or of worship [5]. But, beyond the word itself, was the association with God. The

[1] Ps. ii. 8.   [2] S. Matt. xxviii. 18.   [3] Ib. 19.   [4] 1 Chron. xxii. 9.

[5] See on Hos. xiii. 2. p. 82. נשק occurs 34 times in the Bible. Three of these cases are in the idiom, נשקי קשׁת, "drawers of the bow," and are, in fact, from a different root. In all the other 31 cases, it has the one meaning, "kiss." In all cases but one, the object is expressed; in 7 places besides this Psalm, it is in the accusative; 21 times it stands with ל; in Gen. xli. 40. with על; in Ezekiel, iii. 13. of things inanimate, with אל. The one exception, where the object is omitted, is in Ps. lxxxv. 11, צדק ושׁלום נשׁקו, "righteousness and peace have kissed;" obviously, each other. בר occurs once besides, in the undoubted sense, "son." Pr. xxxi. 2. It is not an Aramaic word only, as is commonly stated. It is also a Phœnician word, and so it belongs to the earliest stock of the language. It occurs in Plautus, (Ges. Script. ling. Phœnic. p. 379,) and in proper names; *Vermina,* βερμινᾶς = בר אשׁן; Liv. App. (Ib. p. 415,) *Bar-melech,* בר מלך, "son of the king" i. e. Baal; Inscr. Melit. 2, 4. (Ib. p. 348.) βαρμόκαρος, Polyb. 7, 9. = בר מעקר, "son of Hercules." (Ib. p. 403, coll. p. 353.) Gesenius also explains by it the names, Πάραλος (Diod. xvi. 9,) i. e. בר בעל "son of Baal;" (Ib. p. 412.) *Bogudes* (App. Dio C.) i. e. בר נוד "son of a troop;" (Ib. 404.) and *Bomilcar* (Liv. Pol. App.) בר מלקר "son of Milcar," i. e. Hercules. (ib.) Aramaic are poetic forms. But the form was also probably chosen here, to avoid the repetition of the same sound, בן פן, without any corresponding emphasis. The word נשק then, taken in its uniform meaning, and in a received construction, fits in with the mention of the object, "kiss the Son." The grammatical meaning suits the context. God said, "I have set My king upon My holy hill of Zion." He declared of that king; "Thou art My Son." The world was in rebellion against Him. God exhorts them to shew reverence to the Son, lest He be angry and they perish.

close of the Psalm corresponds with the beginning. It
is an exhortation to those who were in rebellion, to return to obedience to God and to His Son. "⁶The words,

On the ground of this uniform meaning of נשק, its meaning was retained even
by those who did not understand, or who wished to evade, the meaning of בר.
Hence Aquila translated strictly, καταφιλήσατε, "kiss;" Symmachus, in the
derived meaning, "worship," προσκυνήσατε; as St. Jerome too, "adorate."
But then it was inconsistent, not to take בר, as the object of the verb, in either
of its known senses, "Son," or, (from the root ברר,) "pure." For it is unidiomatic, to take as an adverb a word, which is only used as a noun, and that, when
following an active verb, which requires a noun to complete its meaning. Aq.
ἐκλεκτῶς, Symm. καθαρῶς, S. Jer. purè. Yet even thus Aquila, at least, must
have thought that "the king" was the object, since the word "kiss," which
he adopts, could not be applied to God, save through the Incarnation. In regard to the rendering of the late Chaldee Targum, and of the LXX, "lay hold
of instruction," נשק never signifies to "lay hold of," only to "stretch the bow ;"
and בר (if the vowel be changed) is only once used with the affix, ברי, "my purity," and that, when the idiom, בר ידים, had just preceded, and the equivalent
נקים followed. Even thus, "purity" is not "instruction." Hupfeld, rejecting
the real meaning, "son," as inapplicable, (he thought,) so felt that no other
would hold, that he devised a correction of the text, בם for בר, although well
knowing that this was a construction unknown to Hebrew.

⁶ Aben Ezra. The reference to the Christ is acknowledged by the older Jews
of all Schools. It is mentioned as a tradition in the Talmud, tract *Succa*, dist.
Hachalil; "Our Rabbins handed down, ' Messiah ben David, (who is to be revealed, may he be revealed in our days !) God, blessed for ever, said to him, 'ask
something of Me and I will give it Thee,' as is said, *I will declare the decree,
The Lord said unto Me, Thou art My Son &c. Ask of Me &c.*' And when he
shall hear, that Messiah son of Joseph is slain, he shall say, ' Lord of the world,
I ask of Thee nothing but life ;' God shall say to him, ' thou askest life of Me ;
before thou saidst this, David thy father prophesied of thee, *He asked life of
Thee; &c'*" Ps. xxi. 5. (Mart. Pug. Fid. f. 330.) The unworthiness of this representation belongs to the Talmudists; but they are witnesses to the traditional meaning. In the mystical school, the Midrash Tillim says, " kings shall
rise up against him, [Messias ben David,] as it is said, *the kings of the earth* &c.
Ps. ii. 2. Mart. f. 332. (See also ib. f. 604.) and again, " when his hour shall
come, God shall say, ' I must create him by a new creation,' and so He saith,
This day have I begotten thee." on Ps. ii. 2. Mart. f. 285; and on ii. 7, (f. 3, 4.)
Ps. cx. 1. Ps. ii. 7. and Dan. vii. 13. *lo with the clouds of heaven*, are quoted
together of the Messiah. (Schöttg. Hor. Hebr. ii. p. 121.) And on Ps. 21, "R. Je-
hanan says, '*Ask*,' was said to three, Solomon, (1 Kings iii. 5,) Ahaz, (Is. vii. 11.)
and king Messiah, *Ask of me* &c Ps. ii. 8." (Mart. f. 516.) And in the Bereshith
Rabba, " R. Huna in the name of R. Idi, [and R. Joshua B. Levi,] saith, " This
(Jer. xxxi. 21.) is king Messiah, of whom it is said, ' Thou art My Son.'" (in
Mart. f. 284.) In the Pirke R. Elieser c. 28, Mesharshia [4th cent.] is quoted,
interpreting v. 2. of the last " gathering of all nations to fight against Messiah
b. David." (Schöttgen ad loc. p. 227.) So also the Avoda sara f. 3. 2, (ib. p. 228,)
Tanchuma f. 55. 2, (Ib. p. 74,) Pesikta Sotarta, f. 58. 1, (Ib. p. 96,) the Zohar,

serve the Lord, refer to the words, *take counsel against the Lord ;* the words, *kiss the Son*, to the words, *and against His Anointed.*"

The omission of the article gives even an added emphasis to the word *Son* [1], in that the name thereby gains the character of a proper name, belonging to Him, and to no other as it does to Him [2].

(ib. p. 227,) Midrash Esther f. 107. 4, (Ib. p. 68, 9.) interpret the beginning of the Psalm of Gog and Magog.   The Mechilta, quoting the words, *against the Lord and against His Anointed*, has the simile of " a robber, standing behind the royal palace, insulting it, and saying, ' If I find the king's son, I will seize and slay him and crucify him, that he may die a hard death,' but the Holy Spirit shall mock them ; *He that sitteth in the heavens shall mock them.*" (in Yalkut Shimeoni, ii. f. 90. 1. Sch. p. 227.)   The Midrash Tillim has the likeness of " a king who was wroth with his subjects ; but they went to his son and besought him to appease the king.   When they were reconciled, they sang a hymn to the king ; but he said, ' Why sing ye a hymn to me, go rather and present it to my son.   For but for him, I should have destroyed the whole city.'" (f. 4. 2. Sch. p. 229.)   It recognised the interpretation, even while misapplying it to the Jewish people.

[1] So מֶלֶךְ, "king," Ps. xxi. 1, and חֹק, "decree," in this Psalm, v. 7.   Delitzsch remarks, how the omission of the Article is emphatic in Arabic also, quoting Fleischer on Zamakshari, Not. 2 p. 1 sq. and De Sacy Anthol. Gramm. p. 75. Hupfeld (p. 33.) says, that the word, בַּר, "son," would be " unmeaning without יהוה or the article."   Yet he had himself, a few lines before, remarked the similar use of מֶלֶךְ, Ps. xxi. 1. And this, in face of the acknowledged fact, that the article is habitually omitted in poetry, where it would stand in prose, as is said in all grammars. (e. g. Gesen. Lehrg. p. 652. Ewald ausf. Lehrb. § 277 p. 679. ed. 7.) מַלְכֵי אֶרֶץ again occurs in this same Psalm, v. 2.

[2] Dr Williams said, " If he would follow our version in rendering the 2nd Psalm, *kiss the Son*, he knows that Hebrew idiom convinced even Jerome, the true meaning was, *worship purely*," (Ess. and Rev. p. 68.) quoting him, " cavillatur-quod posuerim—*Adorate purè*-ne violentus viderer interpres et Jud. [aicæ calumniæ] locum darem." Hieron. c. Ruffin. [i.] § 19.   This is not an accurate account of S. Jerome's statement.   Ruffinus blamed him for inconsistency, that, " having, in his brief commentary, said, ' adore the Son,' in his translation he put ' adore purely.'"   S. Jerome defends himself, that "' Bar ' had different meanings ; ' Son,' as in Barjona, Bartholomæus, Barthimæus, Bariesus, and Barabbas ; also ' wheat ' and ' a sheaf of corn ' [i. e. '*corn* even standing,' Ps. lxv. 14.] and 'elect' [from Cant. vi. 9.] and ' pure.'"   "What then have I offended," he says, " that I have rendered diversely an ambiguous word, and that while in the little commentary, where there was freedom of discussion, I had said,' *adore the Son*,' in the body of the work, [his translation,] lest I should *seem* to do violence to the text and give occasion to Jewish calumny, I said ' *adore purely*,' or '*in a chosen way*,' as Aquila and Symmachus also translated ?"   It seems to me that S. Jerome preferred the rendering, "the Son," since he adopted it where he could explain it, but gave way to prejudice in

d. The King, who is the subject of the 72nd Psalm, has attributes, which could not belong to any human being, immortality, omniscience, omnipotence. He is the source of an immortality of blessing, by acts strictly personal, so long as this world shall endure[3]. Wherever the needy should cry in the whole world, there and then would He save. This is the special prerogative of God. Omniscience alone hears the cry of every human heart which it framed: Omnipotence alone can deliver every one every where. Human benefactors can do this here and there[4]; God alone every where. [5]*When he cried unto Him, He heard.* [6]*Thou shalt cry, and He shall say, Behold Me!* is the prerogative of an Almighty Helper. [7]*Call upon Me in the day of trouble; I will deliver thee and thou shalt glorify Me,* is God's invitation to all who will seek Him sincerely, and an anticipation of that loving invitation of our Lord, [8]*Come unto Me, all ye that labour and are heavy laden, and I will give you rest.* Yet this is assigned as the ground, [9] why *all kings shall fall down before Him; all nations shall serve Him. For He shall deliver* &c. This is, in truth, the attractive power which has drawn men unto Jesus, before they yet knew what it is to love Him, that He is an Almighty Deliverer.

Yet the government of this King is wholly spiritual. *Peace* is to be the yield of the world, but in *righteousness*[10]; salvation[11], righteous judgment[12], tender compassion[13], de-

rendering "adore purely." But, although S. Jerome had very valuable traditional knowledge of Hebrew, which he acquired with so much cost and pains from his Jewish instructors, no one thinks now that he had an idiomatic knowledge of Hebrew. It was not his line. Yet in rendering פ͏ֿ "adore," he paraphrased rightly on the right grounds.

[3] Ps. lxxii. 5, 7. v. 5. is clearly addressed to the subject of the Psalm. In v. 17, it is said, "His Name shall endure for ever," and in Ps. lxxxix. 29. 36. "his seed shall endure for ever," Ib. 4, "thy seed will I establish for ever;" Ib. 37, "it shall be established for ever;" here only, it is said of the Person.

[4] Job xxix. 12.   [5] Ps. xxii. 24. add Ps. xviii. 7. xxxiv. 4, 5, 6. 15-17. iv. 3. iii. 4. lv. 16. xcix. 6. cxvi. 4-16. cxviii. 5. cxx. 1. cxlv. 18, 19. Jon. ii. 2.

[6] Is. lviii. 9.   [7] Ps. l. 15. add xci. 15. Jer. xxxiii. 3. Is. lviii. 9.

[8] S. Matt. xi. 28.   [9] v. 11, 12.   [10] v. 3. Each hemistich fills up the other, "mountains and hills shall yield peace to the people in righteousness."

[11] v. 4, 13.   [12] v. 2, 4.   [13] v. 13. עַל דַּל

liverance [1], redemption [2], are His acts; the afflicted ones [3] of God, of the people [4], the sons of the needy [4], and generally, the needy [5], afflicted [6], or those in low estate [7], he who hath no helper [8], are the objects of that love; and that, by His coming down from above, as rain upon the herb, when ready to dry up. *Precious in His eyes* should be *the blood* [9] of such as these [10]; as it is said of Almighty God, [11] *Precious in the eyes of the Lord is the death of His saints.* All are strictly personal acts. The King Himself is to do all these things. His empire is to be coextensive with the world, coenduring with time. The confines of the promised land are by turns removed; His dominion is to be *from sea to sea,* from the Mediterranean, their Western boundary, to the encircling sea beyond Asia's utmost verge; and, *from* their Eastern boundary, *the river,* the Euphrates, *unto the ends of the earth* [12]. Some nations are mentioned as specimens; the wild sons of the wilderness [13], countries known to Solomon by commerce only, in the then distant Spain, or the empires on the shores of the Mediterranean [14], the depths of Arabia or the far-removed and wealthy Nubia [15]. But these are instances only of the voluntary submission. The prophecy passes on to universal empire. *All kings, all nations* are to *fall down before Him* and *serve Him.* They are to offer their best, *presents* and *gifts;* yet the most costly offering is to be the oblation of the poor. The kings of Sheba are to be there, but the gold of Sheba is specified as the offering of the poor. *Precious shall their blood be in His eyes. And live he, he will give of the gold of Sheba.* His enemies are voluntarily to submit themselves.

[1] v. 12.   [2] v. 14.   [3] v. 2.   [4] v. 4.

[5] v. 12, 13. [ii]   [6] v. 12.   [7] v. 13.   [8] v. 12.

[9] v. 6. "upon the mown grass," as in Am. vii. 2. E. V. rightly. Striking image of a world, in all appearance, hopelessly dead, but with a hidden capacity for receiving life! V. 7. The like image occurs in the prophecy of Christ, 2 Sam. xxiii. 4.   [10] v. 14.   [11] Ps. cxvi. 15.

[12] אַפְסֵי אֶרֶץ occurs 14 times, and always in this sense, as also קַצְוֹת הָאָרֶץ (4 times) and קְצֵה הָאָרֶץ (20 times.) The plural in itself involves it, as in the Homeric πείρατα γαίης, and we say "the land's *end,*" but "the ends of the earth."

[13] צִיִּים. v. 8.   [14] אִיִּים v. 9.   [15] סְבָא

The abundance of peace in His days is to be *as long as the moon endureth.* He is to be the object of reverent fear, *so long as sun and moon endure.* And yet, by a wondrous coincidence with the fact, it is hinted that He Himself should be out of sight. For it is said, *His Name shall be for ever; His Name shall propagate* [16], gaining, generation after generation, a fresh accession of offspring, *as long as the sun and moon endure;* and yet, again, He is to be the personal source of blessing; men *shall be blessed in Him* [17]. The prophecy of Solomon expands the pro-

[16] The E. V. has, (according to its rule,) followed the kri, יִנּוֹן, " shall be propagated." It is a mere substitution for the bold image of the text. Yet it must be an old correction, since it supplies one of the names of the Messiah. " Pirke R. Elieser c. 3. and Bereshith rabba s. 1. f. 3. 3. ' Six things' (*seven* are counted in Pesachim f. 54. 1. Nedarim f. 39. 2. Midrash Tehillim f. 35, 4. [see in Mart. Pug. fid. f. 335.] and Midrash Mishle f. 53, 3.) ' were before the foundation of the world, and among them the name of the Messiah, *Before the sun, Yinnon is his name.*' Ibid. c. 36, among those six, whose name was known before their birth, the ' name of the Messiah,' is mentioned, with an appeal to this place. [See in Mart. f. 334.] Echa Rabbathi f. 59. 3. and Sanhedrin f. 98, 2, ' They who are of the school of Jannai said, that ' the name of the Messiah is Yinnon,' from this place. Midrash Mishle c. xix. 21. f. 57. 1, ' The name of the Messiah is Yinnon,' also quoting it." Schöttgen de Messia ad loc. In the Bereshith R. l. c. and Midr. Till. l. c. it is explained actively, yet the pass. form seems to have crept in, " Why is his name called יִנּוֹן? Because he shall give birth to (יְנִין) those who sleep in the dust of the earth ? "

[17] There is no pretext for the gloss of Le Clerc, (following Rashi,) that the words, " shall be blessed in Him," are to be limited by the idiom, Gen. xlviii. 20. *By thee Israel shall bless;* which, by force of the conjugation, must have a different sense, and which is explained by the addition, *saying, God make thee as Ephraim and Manasseh.* בָּרַךְ, orig. " bent the knee," " prayed," is used of man's act as to man, in no other sense than, " prayed for a blessing," (as even benediction in God's name is still a prayer.) " Israel shall bless by thee," has then no other meaning than that which is expanded in the sequel, " use thy name in praying a blessing from God." Even apart from the meaning of the word, man cannot "*make* blessed" through man ; self-evidently he cannot bless through forefathers, long since departed. Yet the very fact that the word is explained by the addition, "*saying, God make thee &c.*" shews that it is no ordinary idiom, as indeed it occurs in that one place only of Scripture. From God to His creature, man, to " bless " is to " make blessed." In itself, the Hithpahel or Nifal might be either reflective or passive, " he blessed himself," or, " he was blessed " by God. וְהִתְבָּרֵךְ is reflective Deut. xxix. 18. " shall bless himself in his heart," i. e. "pronounce himself blessed," as explained in the context. In Is. lxv. 16. and Jer. iv. 2, (where it is united with בְּ) it signifies " shall bless himself in," i. e. " seek blessing in." In both cases, the object

mise to Abraham; as it is itself afterwards expanded in those of Micah, Isaiah, and Zechariah [1].

In Isaiah there occurs that wonderful prophecy of One, Who should be born a Child, yet of Whose personal rule there should be no end, Whose reign should not pass away, like that of mortal kings, who succeed others, to be succeeded by others, but which should endure *from thenceforth even for ever* [2]. The line of David had lasted, from father to son, nearly 3 centuries, when Isaiah so prophesied. God had promised to David, [3] *Thine house and thy kingdom shall be established for ever before thee.* Three centuries had verified the promise. Isaiah opens another mode of its fulfilment. It was no longer to be from

is God; "He that blesseth himself in the earth shall bless himself in the God of truth;" (Is.) "the nations shall bless themselves in Him, and in Him shall they glory." (Jer.) In both, it stands connected with an *act* of man, "shall swear by the God of truth;" (Is.) "thou shalt swear, 'The Lord liveth,' in truth, in judgment, and in righteousness, and the nations shall bless themselves in Him." (Jer.) Even then, if יִתְבָּרְכוּ בוֹ were to be rendered in the Psalm reflectively, "shall bless themselves in Him," it would still mean, (according to the idiom in Isaiah and Jeremiah,) "shall seek their blessedness from Him." In the first passage in Genesis xii. 2, God had already said to Abraham, "Thou shalt be a blessing," i. e. in its most natural sense, "a source of blessing," as in Ps. xxi. 7. The Nifal occurs only in these prophecies, Gen. xii. 3. xviii. 18. xxviii. 14. It is not known that it is any where used reflectively. The Hithpael is used twice Gen. xxii. 18. xxvi. 4. After the typical sacrifice of Isaac, the term of the blessing is changed to Abraham, "in thy seed shall all nations be blessed," instead of "in thee." (Gen. xxii. 18. xxvi. 4.) To Jacob, (Gen. xxviii. 14.) both are united, "in thee and in thy seed." The emphasis, laid on the words in the five-times-repeated blessing, also precludes an interpretation, at once so empty and so exaggerated as, that this full promise should mean, that all nations of the world should use this as a formula of blessing, "God bless thee as He blessed Abraham, Jacob, and their descendants." Ammon, and Bertholdt, (de ortu theol. Hebr. p. 102.) got rid of the prophecy by saying that, "all nations of the earth" meant the Canaanitish nations; and that the blessing on them, was that the remnant, which was not destroyed, was associated with the Jews! They admitted thus, that St. Peter (Acts iii. 25, 6.) and St. Paul (Gal. iii. 8. 16.) were right in arguing from the plain meaning of the words, "In thy seed shall all the kindreds of the earth be blessed."

[1] The peace, characteristic of the ruler in this Psalm, reappears in the title, "Prince of peace," in Is. ix. 6.; in the peace foretold Is. xi.; in Micah v. 5. "this Man shall be our peace;" in Zech. ix. 10., quoting this prophecy.

[2] Is. ix. 6. Heb. 7 Eng.   [3] 2 Sam. vii. 16.

father to son, but was to abide in one individual, who
should be born of his seed. Of Him he gives that wondrous prophecy of lowliness and Divinity, united in the
Incarnation. [4]*Unto us a Child is born, unto us a Son is
given, and the government shall be upon His Shoulder, and
His Name shall be called, Wonderful Counsellor, Mighty
God, Eternal Father, Prince of Peace. El*, the name of
God, is no where used absolutely of any but God. The
word is once used relatively, in its first appellative sense,
[5]*the mighty of the nations*, in regard to Nebuchadnezzar.
It occurs absolutely in Hebrew 225 times[6]; and in every
place is used of God. It has been observed,[7]how, in Hebrew too, it is specially used in union with some attribute
of God; " God most High," " God Almighty," " a jealous
God," " the Living God," " God compassionate and gracious," "God, the great and terrible," and the like, as, here,
" Mighty God." This way of rendering the words in
pairs agrees also with the immediate context, in which
the title of the Saviour, Who was to be given, is, in the
three other cases[8], expressed in pairs of words. Decisive, however, is the occurrence of the same phrase in
the next chapter. There, no one could render otherwise than, [9]*A remnant shall return, a remnant shall return, to the Mighty God*. No one can doubt that such is
the natural meaning of the words *El Gibbor*. Any one
acquainted with Hebrew, if asked irrelatively of any context, " what is the meaning of the words *El Gibbor?*"
would answer at once, *Mighty God;* just as one, acquainted with Latin, would answer, that " Deus Omnipotens "
means, " God Almighty." There is no more real doubt
about the one than about the other. Had any Hebrew
writer wished to express might only, he could have been

[4] Is. ix. 5. Heb. 6 Eng.

[5] Ezek. xxxi. 11. It occurs once also in the plural, Ib. xxxii. 21. אֵלֵי גִבּוֹרִים,
where 23 MSS have אֵילֵי.   [6] See Fürst. Conc. p. 48, 9.

[7] Gesen. Thes. p. 48. אֵל עֶלְיוֹן, Gen. xiv. 18, 19, 20, 22. Ps. lxxviii. 35. אֵל שַׁדַּי
Gen. xvii. 1. &c. אֵל קַנָּא, Ex. xx. 5. אֵל רַחוּם וְחַנּוּן Ex. xxxiv. 6. אֵל גָּדוֹל וְנוֹרָא Deut.
vii. 21. אֵל חַי Jos. iii. 10. אֵל גָּדוֹל Ps. xcv. 3. אֵל מִסְתַּתֵּר Is. xlv. 15. אֵל צַדִּיק Ib. 21.
as here אֵל גִּבּוֹר. And so וְהָאֵל הַקָּדוֹשׁ Is. v. 16. הָאֵל הַנֶּאֱמָן Deut. vii. 9. &c.

[8] פֶּלֶא יוֹעֵץ, אֲבִי עַד, שַׂר שָׁלוֹם.   [9] x. 21.

at no loss to do so, without taking words, belonging to God alone. It would then have been simply misleading, to have used those words at all, unless the prophet had used them in their simple meaning. And this, not in a matter of slight moment, but in one touching the centre of the faith. The Jewish people was a witness to the Unity of God the Creator. The doctrine of the Trinity enlarges the doctrine of the Unity, by revealing fully that, of which indications only were given in the Old Testament, the mode of the existence of the One God. The doctrine of the Trinity being true, it is in accordance with all God's other ways of teaching the Jews, that He should have gradually prepared men's minds for the full revelation of the doctrine. No one, who believes the doctrine, doubts that these passages are to be understood in their plain grammatical sense. No one, who had not a repugnance to the doctrine contained in them, would hesitate for a moment about it. Those who, because they disbelieve that doctrine, resort to violent expedients of explaining away the obvious sense of the words, have to suppose, that prophets of God taught in words which, in their only natural sense, contradicted, according to them, the central doctrine as to the Being of God.

The passage does not stand alone in Isaiah. It is nearly connected with that announcement of the Virgin-Birth of Him, of Whom it is said, [1] *she shall call His Name Emmanuel, God with us.*

In the prophecy of the rule of Him Who should spring from the house of David when laid even with the ground, the sucker from its hewn stump [2], Isaiah describes Him

---

[1] vii. 14.

[2] גֵּזַע (xi. 1.) is the "*hewn* stump," according to etymology, usage, and tradition. גדע and גזע, differing only by the omission of the sibilant in ז, survived in Hebrew; גדע only in the verb and in two or three proper names in Numbers and the Judges, (גִּדְעֹם, גִּדְעוֹן, גִּדְעֹנִי,) גזע only in the noun. Both occur, as verbs, in Arabic, גדע, "amputated," גזע, specifically of the "hewing off wood from a tree." (Cast.) In Job xiv. 8, גֶּזַע is the "hewn stump" which may yet revive and shoot forth. "There is hope to the tree, *if it be cut down*, and it shall yet put forth, and its sucker shall not fail. Though its root wax old

as exercising Divine power.   On His will hangs the life
and breath of His creatures.   By His word they were
created; at His word the ungodly perish.   [3]*He shall smite*

in the earth, and its stump (גִּזְעוֹ) die in the ground, through the scent of water it shall shoot, and bring forth boughs like a plant;" (נֶטַע, a tree freshly
planted.)   In Is. xl. 24, the term, גֶּזַע, must necessarily be a part of the tree.
For the mighty, (as so often in Scripture,) is compared, in the different like-
nesses, to the tree itself.   "They are not planted, (like a young tree,) yea,
they are not sown, (like a seedling,) yea, their stump shall not shoot forth root
in the earth."   They themselves would be the stem, and this had just been
mentioned.   The נִטָּעוּ "are planted," corresponds to the נֶטַע, "like a plant," in
Job: the גֶּזַע, "their stump," to the גִּזְעוֹ, "its stump."   It is a frequent contrast in Scripture, that the mighty shall neither prosper, (like the fresh plant,)
nor recover their fall, (like the sucker from the stump.)   In the context,
the גֶּזַע Is. xi. 1. corresponds with the גְּדוּעִים, which had just preceded, Is. x. 33.
They are the two forms of the root, by which, in Hebrew, the action "hewing"
and the "thing hewn," "the stump," are expressed.   It is a continuation of
the metaphor, and the common contrast in Scripture, that the mighty shall be
brought low, the lowly exalted.   "Lo, the Lord, the LORD of hosts, loppeth
the bough with terror, and the high of stature are *hewn down*, (גְּדוּעִים) and the
lofty shall fall—and He shall cut down the thickets of the forest with the iron,
and Lebanon shall fall by a Mighty one; and a rod shall shoot forth from the
stump of Jesse, and a Branch shall shoot forth out of his root."   The image
of a chance shoot from the stem, while yet standing, is also unseemly.   Such
can but come to nothing, at best weakening and disfiguring the tree.   From
the hewn stump, which has vitality, a strong tree will shoot forth.   As such
a sucker, the Messiah is spoken of, both here (xi. 10.) and in Is. liii. 2.   The
mention of Jesse, "the stump *of Jesse*," belongs to the lowest estate of his line.
The book of Ruth mentions its more prosperous condition in the time of Boaz.
Eliab, Jesse's son, speaks of "those *few* sheep in the wilderness," (1 Sam.
xvii. 28.) which yet were his father's whole flock, (Ib. xvi. 19. xvii. 15,) and
David speaks of himself as "a poor man and lightly esteemed." (Ib. xviii. 23.)
Amos had already foretold the coming of the Messiah, when the tabernacle of
David should be fallen; (see on Amos ix. 11. p. 223, 4.) and Micah indicated
the same, when he foretold His birth at Jesse's little village Bethlehem.   (See
on Micah v. 2.)   Aq. Symm. Theod. render κορμὸς, and Kimchi says, "The tree
which is cut down, and its root is left in the earth, is called גֶּזַע."   Is. xi. 1. is
quoted in connection with the preceding x. 34. in the Talmud Jerus. Berachoth f. 5. 1. (in Mart. Pug. fid. f. 279. Lightfoot Hor. Hebr. on S. Matt. ii. 1.
Schöttg. de Mess. p. 529.) in the Sanhedrin f. 93. 2. (in Schöttg. ad loc.) in the
Midrash Tillim on Ps. 72, 1. (Mart. f. 603.) the Bereshith Rabba on Gen.
xxxviii. 18. xlix. 8. (in Schöttg.) Tanchuma in Yalkut Shim. i. p. 247. (Ib.)
as also in Rashi and Abarb.   Subsequent verses of c. xi. are quoted of the Messiah in the Zohar also, and Sanhedrin; xi. 4, is quoted in the Midrash Tillim
on Ps. ii. 2, Midrash Ruth rabba, Pesikta rabb. f. 63, 1, (Sch. ad loc.) Tanchuma, (Sch. p. 77.) Zohar chadash. (Ib. 137.)   [3] Is. xi. 4.

*the earth with the rod of His mouth, and with the breath
of His lips shall He slay the wicked.*   St. Paul describes
in words, slightly varied from them, the destruction of
Anti-Christ.   [1]*Then shall that Wicked be revealed, whom
the Lord shall consume with the spirit of His mouth and
shall destroy with the brightness of His Coming.*

Micah, the contemporary of Isaiah, prophesied the birth
of the Ruler at Bethlehem, as Isaiah had foretold His birth
in low estate.   He too contrasts the *going forth* in time *to
be the Ruler of Israel* with the *going forth from of old,
from the days of eternity*[2]; teaching not a præexistence
only, but an existence before all time, in eternity[3].

Two out of the three prophets after the Captivity contain the same doctrine.   It is God Almighty Who says,
*I will pour upon the house of David and upon the inhabi-
tants of Jerusalem the spirit of grace and supplication*, and
Who adds, in words following at once, *they shall look upon
Me Whom they have pierced.*   But to pour out the Spirit,
issuing in and producing *grace and supplication*, is plainly a Divine act, God alone having the sovereign power
over the heart, alone the power to give the Spirit and
to work in the heart *grace and supplication.*   When Zechariah prophesied, the Jews were familiar with that
great prophecy in Joel[4], in which God speaks of the future
outpouring of the Spirit, *I will pour out My Spirit upon
all flesh,* as the signal act of Divine power and grace.
Here He foretells that same outpouring of the Spirit, and
that, as a fruit of it, they should gaze earnestly on Himself Whom they pierced.   Then, Zechariah prophesied
that He, Whom they first pierced and then penitently gazed
on, was God.   Unbelief, of course, must have its ways of
escape.   It has altered the text; it has ascribed to the
Hebrew word, *dakaru,* a sense which it nowhere has; it
has adopted unnatural constructions.   Here again, each
party concedes all the truth which it can afford.   They,
whose way of escape has been to alter the text, have admitted the genuine meaning of the Hebrew word; they

<hr>

[1] 2 Thess. ii. 8.   [2] v. 1. Heb. 2. Eng.   [3] See further on Mic. v. 2.
[4] See on Joel ii. 28. p. 127-9.

who have evaded the truth by means of a non-natural rendering of one Hebrew word, admitted, as a matter of course, the genuine meaning of the other, or the correctness of the text. A full consent of all the Versions and the oldest MSS attests the correctness of the text; an uniform use of the Hebrew words throughout Holy Scripture attests, that their meaning, here, is that in which St. John quotes them, declaring the actual piercing of the Christ[5].

As Zechariah then, in this place, spoke of Him Who was wounded, as God, so, in another, alleged by our Lord of Himself, God speaks of the Shepherd Who was slain, as equal with Himself. *[6]Awake, O sword, against My Shepherd, and against the Man that is My Fellow, saith the Lord of Hosts.* The word rendered, *My Fellow,* (it has been observed[7],) was revived by Zechariah from the language of the Pentateuch. It was used 11 times in Leviticus, and then was disused. There is no doubt, then, that the word, being revived out of Leviticus, is to be understood as in Leviticus. But in Leviticus it is used strictly of a fellow-man, one who is as himself. The places are, *[8]If a soul sin, and commit a trespass against the Lord and lie unto his neighbour in a deposit &c. or have oppressed his neighbour. [9]With the wife of thy neighbour thou shalt not lie carnally. [10]Ye shall not steal, nor deal falsely, nor lie* (lit.) *a man against his neighbour. [11]Ye shall do no unrighteousness in judgment: thou shalt not respect the person of the poor, nor honour the person of the mighty; but in righteousness thou shalt judge thy neighbour. [12]Thou shalt not hate thy brother in thine heart; thou shalt in any wise rebuke thy neighbour, and not suffer sin upon him. [13]If a man cause a blemish in his neighbour, as he hath done, so shall it be done to him. [14]If ye shall sell ought to thy neighbour or buy from the hand of thy neighbour, oppress not* (lit.) *a man his brother; According to the number of*

---

[5] To avoid needless repetition, I reserve the details of proof for my Commentary on Zechariah, if God wills.   [6] Zech. xiii. 7.   [7] Hengst. Christ. iii. 529, 30. ed. 2.   [8] Lev. v. 21. Heb. vi. 2. Eng.   [9] Ib. xviii. 20.   [10] Ib. xix. 11.   [n] Ib. 15.   [12] Ib. 17. where עליו refers to נפש, as being masc. in meaning, though fem. in form.   [13] Ib. xxiv. 19.   [14] Ib. xxv. 14, 15.

the years after the jubilee, thou shalt buy of thy neighbour.
[1] *Ye shall not oppress* (lit.) *a man his neighbour.*

In all the cases, the ground of the injunction is, that the duty commanded, or the offence prohibited or punished, relates to a fellow man. They are applications of the great law, *Thou shalt love thy neighbour as thy self.* " What, as a man, thou wouldest not have done to thee, do thou not." It is the law of our common humanity. The name designates, not one joined by friendship or covenant, or by any voluntary act, but one, united indissolubly by common bands of nature, which a man may violate, but cannot annihilate; which, when they are violated, turn to his condemnation, and God is offended, the common Father of His creatures. "[2] When then this title is employed of the relation of an individual to God, it is clear that that individual can be no mere man, but must be one, united with God by an unity of Being. The *Fellow* of the Lord is no other than He Who said in the Gospel, [3] *I and My Father are one,* and Who is designated as, [4] *the Only Begotten Son, Who lay in the Bosom of the Father.* The word, it seems, was especially chosen, as being used, in the Pentateuch, only in the laws against injuring a fellow man. The prophet thereby gives prominence to the seeming contradiction between the command of the Lord, *Awake, O sword, against My Shepherd,* and those of His own law, whereby no one is to injure his fellow. He thus points out the greatness of that end, for the sake of which the Lord regards not that relation, whose image among men He commanded to be kept holy. To speak after the manner of men, He draws attention to the greatness of the sacrifice, whereby [5] *He spared not His own Son, but freely gave Him up for us all.* The word *Man* forms a sort of contrast with *My Fellow.* He, Whom the sword is to reach, must unite the Human Nature with the Divine."

On yet a third place in Zechariah [6] I will only say

[1] Lev. xxv. 17.   [2] Hengst. Christ. iii. 530.   [3] S. John x. 30.
[4] Ib. i. 18.   [5] Rom. viii. 32.
[6] Zech. xi. More fully, I hope, in my Comm.   See Hengst. Christol. iii. 410

here, that it is Almighty God Who says, *I will feed the flock*, Who with authority deposes the three shepherds who abused their office; it is He Who said, *give Me My price*, and, when the thirty pieces were given, spoke of it as the price at which He Himself was valued. *The Lord said unto me, Cast it unto the potter, the goodly price that I was priced at.*

Malachi, lastly, gives to the Christ the Name, *the Lord*, which belongs to God only. The ungodly Jews longed for an interference of God in their behalf. *Where*, they said, *is the God of judgment?* *Behold*[7], is the well-known answer, *I will send My messenger, and he shall prepare the way before Me, and the Lord, Whom ye seek, shall suddenly come to His temple, even the Messenger of the covenant, Whom ye delight in;* where the coming of God to His own temple and that of the Messenger of the covenant, [8]*the Mediator of the new covenant*, is one and the same. Our Lord Himself marks the identity, when He says of St. John Baptist; [9]*This is he of whom it is written, Behold I send My messenger before Thy face, which shall prepare Thy way before Thee.*

Daniel does, certainly, foretell of the Christ, that He should be Man and yet more than man. *One like a son of man.* He speaks of Him, not as before His Birth, nor in His days on earth, but, as He is now, since His Ascension, at the Right Hand of God. He speaks of Him, not as "to come," but as already come[10], His life on earth past; (for on earth only could He have become *a Son of man;*) His days of humility ended; not coming from Heaven, but ascended to Heaven, and receiving all power in heaven and earth, which, He said on earth, was given to Him on His Resurrection. We see, in act, what was said in words in David's Psalm, which Jesus quoted as written of Himself, [11]*The Lord said unto my Lord, Sit Thou on My Right Hand until I make Thine enemies Thy foot-*

---

sqq. Dr Mc Caul Obss. appended to his translation of Kimchi on Zech. p. 132.
sqq. [7] Mal. iii. 1. "The Lord whom ye seek." "This is king Messiah, and He is also the Angel of the covenant." Kimchi. [8] Heb. ix. 15
 [9] S. Matt. xi. 10. S. Luke vii. 27. [10] vii. 13. [11] Ps. cx. See ab. p. 465-70.

 Daniel and the rest prophesied alike the same truth.

stool. We see that everlasting dominion given to Him, which has now been acknowledged for above 1800 years; we behold Him, receiving the beginnings of that homage, which has been rendered to Him ever since, and shall be rendered to Him for ever, that [1] *all peoples, nations, and languages should serve Him.* But this prophecy of Daniel, although clear in itself, and understood both by the Jewish [2] and the Christian Church, is not, in the least, clearer than those other prophecies. It is arbitrary to select the one passage of Daniel, as clearly containing the doctrine of the superhuman Being of the Messiah; then, on the à priori ground that Prophets and Psalmists *could* not have meant it, to reject that meaning in other places, where it is not a whit less clearly stated; and, finally, to raise an argument upon the assumed omission of the doctrine in the other Prophets and Psalmists and its mention by Daniel[3], that the book of Daniel must be considerably later than they, because he believed what, in the literal meaning of their words, they believed also. The grammatical meaning of the words is as plain in the other Prophets and in the Psalms as in Daniel. The argument also tacitly assumes, not only the absence of any true revelation under the Old Testament, but the mere humanity of our Lord. For, our Lord being God, then, according to their own witness, the author of the book of Daniel

[1] vii. 14.

[2] There is a remarkable agreement of different Jewish Schools, that the Son of Man, Dan. vii. 13. is the Messiah, much as they shrink from the prophecy of the 70 weeks. "This is king Messiah." Zohar (Parasha Toledoth col. 338. Sultzb. in Eisenm. Entd. Jud. ii. 756.) Rashi. "This is Messiah our righteousness," Saadia, (comparing with it Ps. cx. 1.) "who shall come into the Presence of God," Ibn Yech. adds. Eisenm. quotes even Aben Ezra, as saying הוא המשיח, though in the present copies he explains it of the Jewish people. Martini Pug. Fid. P. ii. i. 13. f. 352, quotes from him; "R. Yeshuah said that this, (Who was) 'like the Son of Man,' is the Messiah, and the saying is right." (עמן הדבר) Add the Tseror Hammor (Mart. p. 214.) the Midrash Tillim, on Ps. ii. 2. comparing Ps. cx. (Mart. f. 423.) "R. Berachiah in the name of R. Samuel," in Midrash Tillim on Ps. xxi. 7. (Mart. f. 504. 517.) See also Bereshith R. on Gen. xxviii. 10. (ab. p. 84.) Tanchuma (ib.) Sanhedrin, Chelek (ib.) Beresh. R. on Gen. xlix. 11. (Mart. f. 656.) Bammidbar R. sect. 13. f. 200, 1. (in Schöttg. de Mess. § iv. p. 63.) [3] "Here he is presented in a higher aspect than in any of the prophets; a heavenly being or messenger." Dav. iii. 177.

truly prophesied (to say the least) His superhuman Nature. They also assume, either the non-credibility of the Gospels, or (God forgive it) error in our Lord Himself, since He quoted that description of His Divinity and Power over all, as fulfilled in Himself. The wound is aimed at Daniel, through the Redeemer's Side.

ii. The statement as to "[4] the definite succession of judgment, resurrection, appearing of the Messiah," is ambiguous. If it were meant, that the second Coming of Christ was to follow upon the judgment upon Anti-Christ, and that then would be the general resurrection, this would be the same as St. Paul also taught[5], and would be true. But then it could be no argument against the genuineness of the book of Daniel, except on the assumption of the falsehood of both. Lengerke, like the Jews, confounded the second Coming with the first, himself disbelieving both. "[6] We must naturally think, in conformity with the parallel places[7], that, at this time, the reign of the Messiah was to burst in. But the author conceives, as connected with this, the Judgment as well as the Resurrection, as in Isaiah[8]." Now, first, if these events do stand so connected in Isaiah, and no critic dreams of placing the chapter of Isaiah later than the close of the Captivity, how is their being so connected in Daniel, to be a proof that the book is later than the times of Daniel? But, secondly, the statement is not true. The great "last things" are predicted in Daniel, independently of time. In c. xii. after the prediction of the last troubles of Anti-Christ, the Resurrection is foretold; but the Judgment and the Second Coming of our Lord are not spoken of there. In c. vii. the presence of our Lord in heaven, as the Son of Man, is predicted, but not His actual Coming to judge, although the judgment on Anti-Christ is thrice spoken of[9]. The fact, if true, would be irrelevant, except on the assumption of the falsehood of the statements in St. Paul; since what, being true, could be known

Leng. p. lxix.   [5] 2 Thess. ii. 2-8.   [6] p. 564. the place referred to in proof of the assertion, p. lxix.   [7] "vii. 14. comp. 11. and ix. 24."   [8] "xxvi. 19. comp. 1-4. 9."   [9] vii. 11. 22. 26.

to St. Paul by revelation only, might equally have been made known to Daniel.

iii. But, apart from the order of these events, we are told that "[1] in Daniel's time they did not yet think of the Resurrection;" and, in order to account for the reception of the doctrine of the Resurrection from the Parsees, it is assumed that "[2] it was first received by the Jews who remained behind in the Captivity and who lived in an atmosphere altogether filled with this doctrine, and at last passed from the Eastern Jews to the Jews, as Jewish." The truth is nearly the reverse, that the doctrine of the Resurrection, i. e. of the body, as distinct from a continued existence of the soul after the death of the body, was not known to the Zoroastrians until after the Christian era, and was borrowed by them, together with much besides, from the Christians.

Man's creation for immortality was, according to Holy Scripture, contained in the history of his creation. Adam knew it. His creation *in the image of God, after His likeness* [3], in itself involved his immortality. All created good is some reflex of its archetype in the Infinity of its Maker's mind. Man alone, of all created things in this our world, was formed in the image and likeness of *Himself*. He *bore* in himself *that*, for which, when it had been defaced by the fall, he has been reborn in Christ, [4] *the image of the heavenly*. But in that he was created in the image of God, he must needs have in himself created gifts, corresponding to the all-perfect attributes of God. Man had then, as endowments wherewith he was created, reason, intelligence, imagination, beauty of soul, justice, goodness, righteousness, love, immortality, as a sort of

---

[1] Berth. Einl. iv. p. 1540.

[2] Herzf. Gesch. Isr. ii. 309.   Earlier rationalism asserted that the Jews borrowed the doctrine of the resurrection from Parsism during the captivity, so e. g. Ges. on Is. xxvi. 19. p. 805.   Davidson follows these; on Ezekiel, iii. 150.   How the Jews in Northern Assyria in the time of Ezekiel should have come in contact with Parsism, or the Jews in Babylonia until the very end of the captivity, these writers do not explain.   The argument against Daniel, of course, falls through, since, if the Jews knew the doctrine in the captivity, its mention in Daniel can be no argument, that he did not write during the captivity.

[3] Gen. i. 26, 27.   [4] 1 Cor. xv. 49.

created reflection of the infinite Wisdom, Beauty, Goodness, Justice, Righteousness, Eternity of Eternal Love,
which is God.   Every thing else may in the end be lost;
every gift of grace, even the capacity of grace, may in
the end be obliterated; every thing good, wherewith he
was endowed, may be forfeited for ever, in the endless
separation from God in hell.   Immortality alone must
remain; and man is conscious of his immortality, because immortality is of the essence of his being.   Thence
doubtless is that almost inextinguishable belief of his
own immortality, however perverted the forms of that
belief may have often become.

And when he fell, and the *image of God* was defaced
in him and His *likeness* was obscured, the sentence pronounced upon him at once implied, that death was not
his original portion, and that God willed to restore him to
life.   In that sentence, [5]*until thou return unto the
ground, for out of it wast thou taken; for dust thou art,
and unto dust shalt thou return*, it lay, that even his body
was not originally formed to be dissolved.   For the death
of the body would not have been pronounced as the sentence on his sin, had it been God's purpose for him if
he had not sinned.   The truth of the Apostle's words, [6]*by
one man sin entered into the world and death by sin; and
so death passed upon all men, for that all have sinned*, lay
in the sentence of God upon Adam.   And so, again, that
first Gospel, the promise of the *Seed of the woman* [7] who
should *bruise* the serpent's *head*, in itself implied man's
immortality.   For the victory over the serpent would not
have been complete, unless man had been restored to what
he was before.   It would have been nothing to *him*, had
he not been immortal.   What of Adam was earthy re-

[5] Gen. iii. 19.

[6] Rom. v. 12. St. Paul is speaking only of the death of *man*, as the fruit of
sin, as is plain from the addition, "and so death passed upon all men &c."
The objection then of some geologists, that death was antecedent to the existence of man, is plainly, in any case, irrelevant.   Not but that, since angels
fell before the creation of man, death may have first existed, and that, even on
this our earth, in consequence of sin.   Only it is not contained in the Apostle's
statement, which relates to man only.   [7] Gen. iii. 15.

turned to the earth, and no redemption was wrought, no victory was won. Then, since God's word is true, its accomplishment lay beyond, and Adam, for whom it was to be wrought, still lived, though unseen.

This belief was expressed by the Patriarchs, as St. Paul developes their meaning [1], when they said that they were *strangers and pilgrims on the earth.* The saying was applied in the law, that each generation had but a life-hold property in the promised land. [2] *The land is Mine; for ye* are *strangers and sojourners with Me.* The much-containing phrase, "sojourners with God," itself lived on. David took up the word [3]. It still expresses our Christian hopes; we use his words in parting for a while from those whom we love. For they, who are *sojourners with* God here, undoubtedly abide with Him for ever. The term in itself expresses, that they who used it *looked for a better country*, their everlasting home with *Him*, with Whom they now were sojourners. So David, in the same Psalm, confessing man's frail condition at his best estate here, owned forthwith, where his own longing expectation lay. [4] *And now, what look I for, O Lord? my longing expectation is to Thee.*

The doctrine of life after death lay, for thoughtful minds, in the continued relation of God to the Patriarchs, expressed in the title, [5] *I am the God of thy father, the God of Abraham, the God of Isaac, and the God of Jacob*, by which God revealed Himself anew to Israel in Egypt. For our Lord would not have blamed the Sadducees so severely, [6] *ye therefore do greatly err*, unless, through their own fault, they had remained ignorant of what they might have known. *God*, our Saviour adds, in explanation of its meaning, *is not the God of the dead, but of the living.* He said not, *I have been*, but "I am the God of Abraham [7]" &c. God, (it lay in the words,) took no transient

---

[1] Heb. xi. 13. from Gen. xxiii. 4. xlvii. 9.

Lev. xxv. 23.   [3] 1 Chron. xxix. 15. Ps. xxxix. 12.   [4] Ps. xxxix. 7.

Ex. iii. 6. 15. 16. iv. 5.   [6] S. Mark xii. 27.

[7] St. Mark follows the original in omitting the *am*, but the present relation is expressed by the force of the terms, "I the God of Abraham." The sim-

care of those who were His; He, the Unchangeable, could not be named from His relation to something so fleeting as man's visible existence here; He, the All-Good, did not enter into a relation to His creature, only, of His own accord, Himself unforsaken, to end it; He, the self-communicating, the Fountain of life, did not leave without some portion of His life, those with whom He deigned to stand in so close communion; they, who lived to Him, lived in Him and by Him, and they who lived by Him, could not wholly die: so then Abraham, the real Abraham, could not be simply that form of earth which was to return to the earth, although that also was a part of Abraham, and therefore in the fact of the life of Abraham was involved not only a continuance of life after death, but a resurrection from the dead. God would not be called the God of the fishes of the sea or of the fowls of the air, or of any of His irrational creation, although they were all the work of His hands and He preserves them all, nor the God of the wicked, although He was yet merciful to them, since one day they would cease to have any portion of Him and had now withdrawn themselves from Him; but only of His saints and of the Holy hosts of heaven. His interest in those whom He loves continued still after they were gathered to their fathers, and was continued on to their children; yet He took not an interest in that which was not. All this, and far more, lay in those deep, simple, words, "I am the God of Abraham, the God of Isaac, the God of Jacob."

The belief in reunion after death lies also in the varied expressions of the association of the soul by death with those who had gone before. It was said first, in the form of a promise, [8]*thou shalt go to thy fathers in peace.* Of Abraham, Ishmael, Isaac, Jacob, it is said, he [9]*was gathered unto his people,* words which do not intend a reunion of the bodies in a common burial-place; for Abraham was not buried with his fathers, nor was Ishmael[10];

ple copula is not, and cannot be expressed in Hebrew; but the past or future would have been expressed.   [8] Gen. xv. 15.

[9] Ib. xxv. 8, 17. xxxv. 29. xlix. 33.   [10] Ib. xlix. 31.

and Jacob speaks of it as something distinct from his burial, [1]*I am gathered unto my people ; bury me with my fathers.* It means also more than a common lot of death. It speaks of the " I," and of a congregation, into which each "I" should be received, the assembly of those, who had been parted with out of sight for a time, but with whom, through death, he should be joined. David's comfort of himself, as to his child, [2]*I shall go to him,* implies the same belief of personal reunion. The later language, he [3]*slept with his fathers,* contained the same truth.

The impression made by the history of Enoch, that *God took him* [4], is marked by the repetition of the word as to the ascension of Elijah [5]. The same word expressed the faith of the Psalmists, the sons of Korah and Asaph, and the faith, so expressed, entered thenceforth into the public worship. From the time of David, Israel drank in that faith in their devotions. " [6]The rule of prayer was the rule of faith." They confessed it, as we do, in their prayers to God, and what we confess with our lips God works into our heart, by the gifts of faith and of certain knowledge.

The subject of the 49th Psalm is the different lot of the brutish who live for this world, as if it were their everlasting dwelling-place, and that of those whose portion is God. As to both, the Psalmist sees beyond the grave; the worldling living, in his thoughts, by a sort of posthumous immortality [7], but in vain. [8]*No brother can indeed redeem a man, or make agreement unto God for him.* They are [9]*laid* together in the stall of *the grave*, with *death* for *their shepherd.* But what man could not do for himself,

---

[1] Gen. xlix. 29.   So also as to Abraham xxv. 9. and Issac xxxv. 29.

[2] 2 Sam. xii. 23.   [3] 1 Kgs. ii. 10. &c.   [4] Gen. v. 24. אֹתוֹ לָקַח.

[5] 2 Kgs. ii. 3. 5. לָקַח, add 9. 10.

[6] " ut legem credendi lex statuat supplicandi."   S. Celestine Ep. ad Episc. Gall. § viii. Conc. iii. 475. ed. Col.   [7] Ps. xlix. 11.

[8] Ib. 7, 8. אָח לֹא פָדֹה יִפְדֶּה אִישׁ. The אָח is placed emphatically at the beginning. The idiom is wholly different from the common, אִישׁ אָחִיו, " a man, his brother," i. e. one another. The construction here brings out the relation of the אָח, "a brother," i. e. " one, who is merely a brother, cannot pay that *great* ransom," (the force of the emphatic פָדֹה יִפְדֶּה) " for a man, and give to *God* his redemption." When then it follows, " God shall *redeem* my soul," (the same word יִפְדֶּה) it follows, that it is altogether a different kind of redemption.   [9] Ib. 14.

God would. *God will redeem my soul from the hand of the grave; for He will receive me*[10]. The grave had a claim upon him; God would "redeem" him. He seems to hint at mysteries which he does not speak. *We* know how God willed to *redeem from the power of the grave;* but the result he expresses; *"for* He will receive me," i. e. to Himself. So far the two classes are separated; the worldlings will be with Death for their shepherd, the godly will be with God. But the Psalmist seems also to speak of a meeting of the righteous and the wicked after this first severance, a Morning yet to come after the night of death, the great Resurrection-morning, *"the* Morning" which has no evening; when there shall be the great public reversal of men's judgments; *the righteous shall have dominion over them.* Then, they, not the wicked, should have the preeminence.

Yet more marked is the 73rd Psalm, because the prosperity of the ungodly had taken more hold of the Psalmist[11], and because it was in *the Sanctuary of God*[12] that he found his answer. The end of the ungodly is evil, sudden destruction[13]; and that end, like that of Korah, Dathan, and Abiram, coming upon an evil life, is the earnest of an evil hereafter. If this life were all, it were all one, how it ended. The Psalmist saw, beyond, the contempt to which they should awaken. [14]*As a dream when one awaketh, O Lord, in the Awakening*[15] *thou shalt despise their image,* their vain unsubstantial being, since it was void of God; a vain show, "full of sound and fury, signifying nothing." What God despises must be full of contempt; and so Asaph forestalls Daniel's words, [16]*some shall rise to shame and everlasting contempt.* On the other

---

[10] Again עָמִי׳ Ib. 16. (Heb. 15 Eng.) [11] Ps. lxxiii. 2-4.

[12] Ib. 17. [13] Ib. 18, 19. [14] Ib. 20.

[15] בְּעִיר for בְּהָעִיר, on the same principle as the ordinary future is formed יָקִיל for יַקְסִיל, and in common nouns, בְּאֵין for בְּהָאֵין. In the Inf. Hif. the contraction is more frequent with לְ, on account of its more frequent use and closer union with the verb, but it occurs with בּ also, בַּעֲשׂוֹ, Neh. x. 39, in Nif. בְּהִוָּסֵל Pr. xxiv. 17. See Ges. Lehrg. § 94. 3. p. 320. Ewald ausf. Lehrb. § 244 b. p. 535. ed. 6. [16] Dan. xii. 2.

hand, he sums up the past, present, future of the godly. *I am continually with thee; Thou hast holden me by my right hand, Thou shalt guide me by Thy counsel, and, after, receive me[1] into glory.* The *after*, when God's guidance is past, can be no other than the great *hereafter:* the word, *receive me,* is the appropriated term for our, "take unto Himself." But the ground of this assurance lies deeper than the assurance itself. And so it sheds its light over much of Holy Scripture besides. Its ground is that same ground which our Lord pointed out in the title, "God of Abraham." God was the Psalmist's own God, and so He could not fail him. All which God had been to him, all which He was, He must be for ever. For He is unchangeable. It is an inner revelation, such as Heathenism could not know, because it could not know of union with God, that God could make Himself belong to the soul, as He had made the soul His own. *Whom have I in heaven?* None had he, save God. But then God, in all that wide heaven, was his. *And with Thee,* together with Thee, and so, having Thee, *I have no delight on earth.* In God he had all, and so he desired nought besides. But then He who was so his, must be his for ever. *My flesh and my heart faileth,* i. e. though flesh and heart be consumed, nay, he speaks of them as consumed already, *God is the strength of my heart and my portion for ever. For ever!* Not then for this little span of life only. Union with God is a pledge of immortality. But then every child of Israel, who had learnt the truth of that Psalm, [2]*O God, Thou art my God,* had in him the assurance of a deathless unbroken unitedness with God.

The like contrast of the future of those who choose this world, and that of those who choose God, for their portion, occurs in a Psalm of David, with the same reference to *the Awakening,* but in the calm self-possession of one who [3]*knows in Whom he has believed,* a Christian before Christ came. He grants that the worldly had their whole heart's desire. They were *men of* (lit. *from) the world*[4];

[1] Again נבקח v. 24.　　[2] Ps. lxiii. 1.　　[3] 2 Tim. i. 12.
[4] υἱοὶ τοῦ αἰῶνος τούτου. S. Luke xvi. 8. ἐκ τοῦ κόσμου τούτου. S. John viii. 23.

they belonged to it, and it to them; *their portion was in this life;* God's choicest temporal treasures, His *hidden store*[5], were theirs; He *filled their belly with* them; they *were sated with children,* and had a sort of posthumous existence in them, and a survival of their wealth, continued, at their will, to their descendants.   In contrast to these, whose portion was in this life and in God's earthly gifts, David says, where his was.   *As for me, I shall behold Thy face in righteousness; I shall be satisfied, in the Awakening, with Thy likeness.*   Satisfying is opposed to satisfying[6]; end to end, all to all.   The portion of the worldly had been pursued to the utmost verge of this life, yea, and to all of this world, which they could in their imagination grasp, after their unwilling departure from it.   And then there stands, in opposition to it, the short summary of David's whole portion; *I shall behold Thy face; I shall be satisfied with Thy likeness.*   David had, before, spoken of that beatific Vision, in contrast with the destruction of the wicked.   *The upright shall behold His Face*[7].   Here, alone, it is repeated, *I shall behold Thy Face.*   This is exactly what God had said to Moses, that man could not see in the flesh and live[8].   God revealed Himself to Moses more nearly than to others[9].   Yet God did not, for him, suspend the law of our mortality, that we cannot, in the flesh, behold God and live.   David, in both places, says that it shall be hereafter, in the consummation of the righteous, as opposed to the consummation of the ungodly.   Here, he says further, *in the Awakening.*   It is the special term, used of the awakening from death, ei-

---

[5] Ps. xvii. 14. צְפוּנְךָ, as צָפוּן Job xx. 26; מַצְפֻּן Deut. xxxiii. 19; and צָפַן, (God) "stored up for," Ps. xxxi. 20, (19 Eng.) Prov. ii. 7; צָפַן with לְ "stored by for," in God's Providence, Ib. xiii. 22; of evil, Job xxi. 19.

[6] יִשְׂבְּעוּ בָנִים v. 14. אֶשְׂבְּעָה—תְּמוּנָתֶךָ v. 15.

[7] Ps. xi. 7.   The two places illustrate one another.   On the other side, "the face of the Lord" is said to be "upon," i. e. turned in displeasure "upon evil-doers," (Ps. xxxiv. 16.) yet, not "the countenance" but "the eyes" are said to "behold."   The renderings then, "His countenance doth behold the upright," or "the thing which is right," are unidiomatic.   [8] Ex. xxxiii. 20. 23.

[9] Num. xii. 8.

ther for a time [1] or for ever [2].   And in that sight will be satisfying fulness.   It is the beatific Vision.   *I shall be satisfied, in the Awakening, with Thy Likeness*, or *Form* [3]. The worldly had their fulness in *children* ; he should have his, in *the Form of God*.

The whole context, each expression, and the harmony with other Scripture, require it to be interpreted of the world to come.   And then not of future life only, but of resurrection [4], and, since of the resurrection, then of the body.

Continued life and resurrection are incompatibles in the same subject.   The soul lives on, sleeps not, continues its unbroken existence; resurrection, awakening, belong to that which was dead, asleep, the dust which had returned to dust.

The 16th Psalm speaks yet more distinctly of the body, since it is a prophecy of the resurrection of the undecayed Body of Jesus.   It expresses a certain future, which, every child of Adam knew, could not be directly fulfilled in himself.   He, of whom he speaks, was to see the grave, but He was not to abide in it ;

   " Therefore My heart was glad, and My glory rejoiced,
    My flesh also shall rest securely ;"

and the ground of this unanxious rest of the body is ;

   "*For* Thou wilt not leave My soul to Hell ;
    Neither wilt Thou suffer Thy Holy One to see corruption."

The force of the words is strengthened by their bearing on each other.   To " leave the soul to Hell," is, in Hebrew as with us, to abandon it to its power [5].   The ground, why the flesh, as distinct from the soul, should " rest securely," is this, "*for* it shall not be left to hell."   It should rest securely ; for it was to be there but for a little while.

---

[1] 2 Kings iv. 31. Jer. li. 39, 57.   [2] Job xiv. 12. Is. xxvi. 19. Dan. xii. 12.

[3] הְמוּנָה corresponds to εἶδος, S. John v. 37. or μορφή, Phil. ii. 6.

[4] This is owned by R. Nehemiah in the Bereshith Rabba on Gen. iii. 23, (Mart. Pug. fid. f. 457) and by R. Rachmon in Rashi, and Rashi himself, (quoted ib. f. 682.) The quotation from Rachmon rests on Martini's MSS.

[5] as in Job xxxix. 14 ; with אֶל, Ib. 11 ; Nif. with לְ, Is. xviii. 6 ; or, in the other sense of our "leave to," i. e. "bequeath to," Ps. xlix. 11 ; or "leave for," Lev. xix. 10. xxiii. 22. Mal. ii. 19. [iv. 1. Eng.]   In each case it is an "abandonment to."

And thereon follows eternal life, to which death is the en-
trance-hall;

> Thou shalt make me know the path of life;
> In Thy Presence is satisfying fulness of joy,
> At Thy Right Hand are pleasures for evermore.

Even apart from the distinct words, " Thou shalt not
suffer Thy Holy One [6] to see corruption [7]," the whole con-

[6] De Rossi counts 158 MSS. of Kennicott and 183 collated by himself, in all 271
MSS., which read חסידך " Thy holy One; " and 40 editions, some of the 15th,
most of the 16th cent. All the old versions render so. He quoted also Talmud Bab., Midras Tehillim, Yalkut Simeoni, and, of later Jews, " Kimchi, Ara-
ma, Aben Sohev, Aben Yachia, Joseph Chivân, Alshech and others in their
published Comm. and R. Immanuel in his MS. Comm." The MSS., both Kenn.
and De Rossi affirm to be the best, although De Rossi states, that there are
" even ancient Spanish MSS., one of Toledo A. 1277 and one A. 1413 Hillel,
and a Neap. Psalter A. 1490 which have חסידך," (Scholl. Critt. p. 99.) Even
when the plur. חֲסִידֶיךָ was brought into the printed editions, it was with the
punctuation of the singular and the note, יתיר, " Yod is superfluous ; " so that
it should be read חסידך, " Thy holy one." In the MS. of the Arab. version of
Saadia (Poc. 281 see my A. E. to Nicoll's Cat. p. 559, 60.) the old Hebrew
text has הסידך, the י being squeezed in, in a different and later ink. Saadias
renders inconsistently, " holy ones," (plur.) but *"see"* (sing.) לא תסלם באריך
אן ידי בדא אלהלאך   In Hunt 416, (see ib.) where this and other missing Psalms
have been supplied in a different hand, the sing. occurs, ליך " thy friend." The
whole context is of the sing. The plural is owing to Jewish anti-Christian
controversy. " Very few MSS.," De Rossi says, "have the points of the plural."

[7] שחת (διαφθορά LXX. Acts) is most naturally rendered corruption in Job
xvii. 14. (where it stands parallel with רמה, " the worm,") and in Ps. lv. 24,
לבאר שחת, " to the pit of corruption " or " destruction." Also in Ps. xlix. 10.
ciii. 4. Jon. ii. 7. it is probably "destruction." Hengstenberg's attempt to maintain that S. Paul too may have taken שחת in the meaning " pit," will not stand
comparison with the text. (Acts xiii. 35-7.) No one could have argued so
briefly ; " He saith, Thou shalt not suffer Thy Holy One to *see the pit*—For David—fell on sleep and was laid unto his fathers, and *saw the pit*. But He Whom
God raised again *saw not the pit*," whereas, if *the pit* meant the grave, Jesus,
as well as David, did *see the pit*, and the Burial of Jesus as well as His Resurrection, is part of our faith, " He was crucified, dead, and buried." Hengst.
tries to save himself from contradicting the Apostles by supposing that they
used the original word in the sense, " pit," and that St. Luke substituted the
LXX word " corruption," although wrong. This would any how have involved an unfaithful rendering of St. Paul's own words. (v. 34. 36. 37.) But
Hengst. says ; *"In the sense*, in which David did, Christ saw not the grave, saw
it not in the sense of the Psalmist." Had this been St. Paul's meaning, the
supposed meaning of " see " must have been drawn out ; whereas, not in any
given sense, but altogether, St. Paul denies *that* of Jesus, which he affirms of
David. This is one of the unhappy compromises in the later theories of one,
who has done so much good service to the truth, which has drawn down on him

nection would be destroyed, if the verse were understood of a mere temporary deliverance from death. Everlasting life does not follow upon the mere delay of death, but the freedom from death and corruption, in which the Psalmist rejoices, is an entrance to the fulness of joy in the everlasting vision of God.

What was fulfilled in Christ redounds to us, for, for our sake, it was fulfilled in Him. The Psalm relates to the Psalmist and to us, reflected back from Christ. What was accomplished perfectly in Him the Head, overflows to us the members; His resurrection was the source and the pledge of ours. So we believe, that God will not abandon our souls to hell. But David knew and impressed the more the belief in the resurrection, in that he set *Him* before his people, over Whom death had no power, and joyed in His joy, which He has made ours.

Besides these passages in the Psalms, which directly express in words the belief in the life to come or the resurrection, there is also much language which implies it. Look at the doings or gifts of God which, the early Psalms say, will be "for ever." [1] *Your heart shall live for ever;* [2] *Thou settest me before Thy face for ever;* [3] *Thou gavest him length of days, for ever and ever.* [4] *Thou hast set him a blessing for ever.* Or reciprocally; [5] *I trust in the tender mercy of God for ever and ever; I will praise Thee for ever;* [6] *I will give thanks unto Thee for ever;* or again, [7] *the fear of the Lord endureth for ever.* An immortality of praise implies an immortality of being; the endless abiding of the reverence of God involves, that they too who so revere Him shall abide alway. Again, [8] *In Thee is the fountain of life; and in Thy light*

the praise of Dr. Williams, "even the conservatism of Hengst. is free and rational, compared to" &c. Essays p. 67. The belief of the later Jews, on the ground of this Psalm, that David's body did not decay, (see e. g. R. Isaac in Midr. Tehillim ap. Mart. P. F. f. 681.) is a strong proof of their interpretation. Perhaps St. Peter alluded to it, and corrected it, " Let me *freely speak unto you* of the Patriarch David, that he is both dead and buried," &c. Acts ii. 29.

[1] Ps. xxii. 26.　[2] Ib. xli. 12.　[3] Ib. xxi. 4.　[4] Ib. 6.　[5] Ib. lii. 8. 9.　[6] Ib. xxx. 12.　[7] Ib. xix. 9.　Add Ib. lxi. 5. עולמים the "ages all along" of the Veni Creator.　[8] Ib. xxxvi. 9.

shall we see light. What can it mean, but that, when we shall be plunged into that Ocean of Light which God is, all darkness shall cease; then, admitted to Himself, the Fountain of life, we shall see in Him, what on earth we never saw, the true eternal Light? What is this, but the vision of God? Or when a son of Korah says, [10] *this God is our God for ever and ever, He Himself* [9] *will be our guide over death* [10], what is death, but a mere point in our everlasting relation to Him, over which He Himself, like a tender Shepherd [11], leads us? Or when, in the sight of the fruitlessness of all worldly pursuits and aims, he asks God to teach him his end [12], what comfort was there to know his end, unless he saw therein what was beyond that end, even Him, of Whom in that same Psalm he says, *my longing is for Thee* [13]? David's words express our Christian hopes. We, whose hopes they express, cannot think that they meant less to David, whose hope they first fed.

. David knew also of a judgment of the world [14]. But since the inhabitants of this world are ever in one flux, some going, others replacing them, a judgment of the world implied a resurrection of the world, the great meeting of all before the judgment-seat of God.

David knew too of the second death, of a " Sheol," into which the wicked and *they who forget God* should be cast [15]. When then, under the sense of guilt, he says, [16] *In death there is no remembrance of Thee*, he speaks not of death only, but of the sentence after an evil death. At times, thirsting to advance the glory of God in this life, he desires life for the sake of *that*, for which the Chris-

[9] הוא.   [10] Ps. xlviii. 14.

[11] This is the simple meaning of ינהגנו על מות. Death cannot be the end of the guidance of a shepherd, (נהג Gen. xxxi. 18. Ex. iii. 1. Ps. lxxx. 2. Is. xi. 6. lxiii. 14.) nor would God be *our God for ever and ever*, if death were a break in that His relation to us. The most literal rendering is the truest. It is not *up to* (עד,) but *over* (על). So also in v. 11, the *praise* of God is not spoken of as reaching *to the ends* of the earth, exclusively of them, but overpassing them. So the Syr. renders " over death," and, in the same sense, Lxx. and St. Jer. " for ever;" as though it were an irregular plural, עלמות.

[12] Ib. xxxix. 4.   [13] See ab. p. 494.   [14] Ps. i. 5. ix. 8. xcvi. 13.
[15] Ib. ix. 18. (Heb.) lxiii. 9. comp. Ps. xlix. 21. lxxxviii. 10-12.   [16] Ps. vi. 5.

tian too desires it, because here is the scene of promoting that glory in others: whence Hezekiah says in the same contrast, [1] *The living, the living, shall praise Thee, as I do this day ; the fathers to the children shall make known Thy truth.*

The great passage in the book of Job is a confession intended for all times :

[2] O that my words were written, O that they were graven in a book, were cut with an iron pen and lead in the rock for ever !

Their most literal translation is ;

And I, I know that my Redeemer liveth ;
And that, the last, He shall arise upon the dust ;
And, after my skin[3], they have destroyed this *body,*
And from my flesh I shall behold God,
Whom I, I shall behold for myself,
And mine eyes shall behold, and not another [*lit.* a stranger ;]
My reins are consumed within me.

No doubtful meaning of any words can efface from the passage the doctrine of the resurrection of the flesh. Whether *the dust* mean *the surface of the earth* [4], or *the dust,* into which the human body *returns ;* whether *the consuming* of the *reins* be, (as elsewhere in Job [5],) their actual consumption, or whether it be an idiom, (although not occurring elsewhere [6],) expressing that his inmost self

---

[1] Is. xxxviii. 19. So Ps. xxx. 9. cxv. 17. cxviii. 17.　　[2] xix. 23-27.

[3] The two constructions, in which אֲחַר is taken as a conjunction, (1. *after they have destroyed my skin, this* shall be ; 2. *after my skin,* which *they have destroyed, this* shall be ;) interrupt the description, and would be very heavy and prosaic. The rendering, *And after they have destroyed this my skin,* joins a masc. and fem. עוֹרִי וְזֹאת.

[4] עָפָר occurs, 1) of the habitable surface of the earth, Job xli. 25. It is used also not merely of the dust, but of the solid earth, Job viii. 19. xiv. 8. Is. ii. 19. Elsewhere, the meaning of *dust,* friable earth, remains. 2) It is used of man's *returning to the dust,* Gen. iii. 19. Job x. 9. xxxiv. 15. Eccl. iii. 20. xx. 7. *to their dust,* Ps. civ. 29. *resting in the dust,* Job xvii. 16. *lying down in,* Job vii. 21. xx. 11. xxi. 26. *goers down to,* Ps. xxii. 30. *inhabiters of,* Is. xxvi. 19. *place in the dust of death.* Ps. xxii. 16. Man is spoken of as *dust,* Ps. xxx. 10. ciii. 14. Eccl. xii. 7 ; *dust and ashes,* עָפָר וָאֵפֶר. Gen. xviii. 27. But קוּם with עַל signifies to " arise against," not, " with power over."

[5] כָּלָה is used of actual " consuming away;" Job iv. 9, vii. 6, *a cloud which vanisheth away,* Ib. 9 ; *his flesh consumeth away,* xxxiii. 21 ; and so also כָּלָה, God *destroyeth,* ix. 22. and simply, *they pass away,* xxxvi. 1.

[6] The common expression, *his eyes shall consume,* (viz. with vain longing,)

was consumed with a longing for that day,—this remains, that Job looked forward to a manifestation of his Redeemer at the end, with power, whether on the earth, or over his own dust specially ; that he knew that he himself for himself should gaze upon his God ; and that, after the destruction of his body, he should, with the eyes of his flesh [7], behold Him.

The saying of Hosea, [8] *After two days He will quicken us ; in the third day He will raise us up and we shall live in His sight*, is a continuation of this connection of the Head and His members. " [9] The strictest application is the truest. The *two days* and *the third day* have nothing in history to correspond to them, except that, in which they were fulfilled, when Christ, ' [10] rising on the third day from the grave, raised with Him the whole human race.' "

Hosea and Isaiah carry on the triumph over death and the grave, in terms so large and so absolute, that St. Paul had no greater words wherewith to conclude his so-

---

occurs in Job xi. 20, xvii. 5, as in Ps. lxix. 4. cxix. 82. 123. Jer. xiv. 6. Lam. iv. 17, and in Piel, 1 Sam. ii. 33. Else, כָּלָה is joined, in the same sense, with the " soul," Ps. lxxxiv. 3. cxix. 81, and the " spirit," Ps. cxliii. 7 ; but does not, at least, happen to be used with " the reins."

[7] The rendering of מִבְּשָׂרִי " without my flesh," adopted by Davidson, ii. 227, from Ewald, &c. is unidiomatic and unnatural. מִן, can no more, of itself, mean " without," than our " from." Where we might render " without," the meaning is gained from the context. Job xi. 15, " thou shalt lift up thy face מִמּוּם, from spot," i. e. as we say, " above," or " removed from ; " Mic. iii. 6, " there shall be a night to you מֵחָזוֹן, from vision," i. e. hiding all vision from you. Jer. xlviii. 45, is best rendered as in E.V. " because of the force." (Gesenius' instances, Thes. p. 805.) Gen. xxvii. 39. is best rendered as in E. V. "Thy dwelling shall be of the fulness of the earth." Edom was rich once. Its desolation is prophesied. (See on Joel iii. 19. p. 144.) Obad. 9, also, (as in E.V.) " from slaughter," as the cause. (See Ib. p. 239.) Is. xxii. 3, (also as in E. V.) "bound by the bow," i. e. by the archers, as 3 verses before, xxi. 17. (These are all Ewald's instances, Ausf. Lehrb. § 217b p. 480. ed. 6. p. 551 ed. 7.) On the contrary, " I shall behold, מִבְּשָׂרִי, from my flesh," implies that he will be in the flesh, *from* which he shall *behold*, as he goes on to speak of the *eyes* of his flesh. Unless he had meant emphatically to assert, that he should *from his flesh behold God* after his body had been dissolved, the addition of מִבְּשָׂרִי had been not merely superfluous, but misleading. For the obvious meaning is "from out of my flesh," as the Versions shew.   [8] Hos. vi. 2.   [9] my Comm. Ib. p. 38.   [10] S. Jer.

lemn hymn of victory wherein he reverses, one by one, the temporary triumphs of the grave over our poor bodies, than the jubilant exultation of the two Prophets, [1]*Death is swallowed up in victory. O death, where is thy sting? O grave where is thy victory?* Hosea's words of triumph followed upon the most absolute declaration on the part of God, [2]*I will ransom them from the hand of the grave; I will redeem them from death.* The words of Isaiah go even beyond the resurrection. Death, the destroyer, is destroyed for ever.

All judgment is an earnest of *the* judgment to come; all deliverance, of *the* deliverance; and so Isaiah having, in previous chapters, pronounced God's judgments upon single nations, does, in the great prophecy, c. xxiv-xxvii, go beyond all particular judgments. The mention of the end of all earthly things fits in with the largeness of the other language. Three times in the prophecy he speaks of the end of all, 1) of that swallowing up of death; 2) of the resurrection of the body; 3) of judgment.

In the prophecy of the resurrection, his words too agree with those of Daniel.

[3] Thy dead men shall live; with my dead body (or, my dead bodies) shall they arise.

Awake and jubilate, ye inmates of the dust;
For Thy dew is like dew on herbs,
And earth shall cast out the dead [4].

Isaiah, like Daniel, foretold the resurrection of the good and bad [4]; only, that the good alone should rise to joy.

---

[1] 1 Cor. xv. 54, 5. from Is. xxv. 8. Hos. xiii. 14.   [2] Hos. xiii. 14. See my Comm. p. 86, 7.   [3] Is. xxvi. 19.

[4] רְפָאִים. "Refaim" is never used except of the evil dead. Primarily, it is the name of a giant-race, one of the early races in Palestine, (Gen. xiv. 5. xv. 20. Deut. iii. 11, 13. Josh. xii. 4. xiii. 12. xvii. 15.) who gave their name to "the valley of Refaim," South-West of Jerusalem, (Jos. xv. 8. xviii. 16. &c) and, then, (either from them or from the root, רפה, "height," common in Arabic,) "giants," generally; (Deut. ii. 11. 20.) as הָרָפָה (2 Sam. xxi. 16, 18, 20, 22.) הָרָפָא (1 Chr. xx. 4, 6, 8.) Thence, strength being so often abused to violence, it became the title of the ungodly dead; (Job. xxvi. 5. Pr. ii. 18. ix. 18. Is. xiv. 9.) whence it is said of them, that they shall not rise, i. e. to life, (Ps. lxxxviii. 11. Is. xxvi. 14.) and here, that they shall be cast forth.

As the dew quickens the vegetation which lies so parched and dead, so the life-giving power of God, which the Psalmist calls directly [5] *His Spirit,* should quicken those so long dead [6].

But, in one respect, Isaiah has more than Daniel. For he foretells the judgment, not only of all on the earth, but of those higher beings, who [7]*kept not their first estate.*

"[8] The LORD shall punish the host of the height in the height,
And the kings of the earth upon the earth;
And they shall be gathered in a gathering, prisoners down to the pit,
And shall be shut up in prison;
And after many days shall they be visited,
And the moon shall be ashamed and the sun confounded;
For the LORD of hosts reigneth on Mount Zion,
And before His ancients gloriously."

The "host of the height" is contrasted with "the kings of the earth," as, in Daniel, "[9] the army of heaven" with "the inhabitants of the earth." Each is to be punished in the place of their sin [10]. Both are to be kept in prison, until a visitation [11] after a long period, as St. Peter says, [12] *God spared not the angels that sinned, but cast them down to hell, and delivered them into chains of darkness to be reserved unto judgment.* Then, in the brightness of the Eternal Presence before which sun and moon shall pale, follows the blissful nearness of the righteous in glory. Isaiah mentions specifically *elders,* anticipating St. John [13].

And so we cannot doubt that the same is contained in the visitation of the crooked serpent and the dragon [14],

---

[5] Ps. civ. 30.

[6] Davidson says, (from Knobel Ies. p. 172,) "His, [the prophet's,] idiosyncrasy is deeply imprinted. Peculiar conceptions are, the life-giving influence of dew on the dead," &c. iii. 22. They obliterate the metaphor, in order to insult the prophet.   [7] S. Jude 6.   [8] Is. xxiv. 21-24.   [9] Dan. iv. 35. (32 Ch.)

[10] The E.V. supplies, "*that are* upon the earth," yet contrary to the parallelism.

[11] פָּקַד, "visited in punishment," as in Is. xxix. 6. Pr. xix. 23. comp. פָּקַד in the corresponding place Is. xxvii. 1.   [12] 2 Pet. ii. 4. add Jude 6. *He hath reserved in everlasting chains under darkness unto the judgment of the great Day.*   [13] Rev. iv. 4. 10. v. 6. 8. 11. 14. vii. 11. 13. xi. 16. xiv. 3. xix. 4.   [14] Is. xxvii. 1.

which, in the corresponding place, follows on the resurrection of the dead.

The prophecy in Daniel[1], *some shall awake to shame and everlasting contempt*, lies already in Isaiah, [2] *They shall go forth, and look upon the carcases of the men that have transgressed against Me: for their worm shall not die, neither shall their fire be quenched; and they shall be an abhorring unto all flesh.*

The great passage of Ezekiel[3],—with its vivid and thrilling minuteness of description of the bones, *exceeding many* and *exceeding dry*, which, at God's word, *came together, bone to his bone,* and were covered with *sinews, flesh, skin, and the breath came into them, and they lived and stood up upon their feet, an exceeding great army,*—implies the current belief of the resurrection of the flesh the more, because the application is figurative, and is made to strengthen a disheartened people. "Never," says St. Jerome[4], " would the likeness of the resurrection be used, in order to signify the restoration of the people of Israel, unless the resurrection itself stood firm and was believed as to be; for no one confirms things uncertain through things which are not."

We may make the case our own. To a Christian no future of the Church, (except whatever is involved in our Lord's promise of His own continual Presence with it, and that the gates of hell should not prevail against it,) is so certain as the Resurrection of the Flesh. To us, an assurance on God's part, that any future good condition of the Church would as surely be, as the Resurrection of the flesh, would be most reassuring, on the ground of our certain knowledge of that doctrine. So then to the Jews also.

On the first vague acquaintance with the writings of the Parsees, it became an axiom among rationalists, that all the fuller belief in the resurrection came from the

---

[1] Dan. xii. 2.   [2] lxvi. 24.   [3] xxxvii. 1-10.

[4] ad loc. "A figure could not be taken from the bones, unless the self-same reality were to come to pass as to the bones too." Tert. de res. carn. c. 30.

Zend writings. Those who disputed the antiquity of revelation, received with both hands any statements of the antiquity of Zoroastrism. Its books passed muster, *en masse*, with those who were dissecting every chapter of the prophets; any interpretation was accepted unhesitatingly, so that it presented a doctrine which might rival or eclipse revelation. The doctrine of the Zend books was preferred to the Old Testament by renegade Christians [5].

The statement, that the Zend books contained the doctrine of the Resurrection, was first rested on mistranslations. Anquetil had translated "until the resurrection [6]", a word which is now acknowledged to mean " for ever [7]," and on the strength of this mistranslation or from writings long after our era, it was received as infallible truth, that Isaiah and Daniel, or the writers who wrote under their names, borrowed the doctrine of the Resurrection

[5] Rhode, with whom the Bundehesh, (a book of the 7th century A.D.) was an authority earlier than Moses, said, "The Mosaic tradition and the Mosaic law gain more consistency and become more intelligible, if we consider them as offshoots of the older revealed doctrine, which is *preserved fuller in the Zend writings.*" (d. heil. Sage, p. 461.) "An impartial comparison of the relation [of the fall] in Genesis with that in the Zend, forces on us the conviction, that the older Zend tradition of the rebellion of Ahriman, of his strife with Ormuzd, of the position of man between those *two great beings* (!), and the consequent interest of Ahriman to draw man over to his side, is presupposed, and that one must of necessity refer to it, if the narrative of Moses is to become intelligible." (Ib. 393.) He maintained that the Pentateuch is dualistic, (p. 455,) and said, "One might in truth call the prayer of Jesus, [the Lord's prayer,] a brief extract from the prayers of the Zend writings." p. 416. Rhode's uncritical book, embodying Anquetil's necessarily faulty and unreliable translation of books of various dates, is still the source of the rationalist imputation of Parsism to Holy Scripture.

[6] "Of the resurrection of the dead, or the awakening of the dead at the end of the world, mention is often made in the Zend writings, and the expression which occurs so often, ' unto the resurrection of the dead,' always denotes the duration of the world which yet remains.'" Rhode heil. Sage p. 465. "The expression occurs in this sense countless times, e. g. Vendidad Farg. viii. p. 342." Ib. note.

[7] "In consequence of Burnouf's enquiries into the phrase *yavaécha yavatátaécha,* which had been translated by Anquetil, ' till resurrection,' but which means nothing but ' for ever,' the existence of such a doctrine in the Zend Avesta was lately doubted." Haug Essays on the Parsees p. 266.

from the Parsees[1]. Whether the doctrine was true or false, the school did not trouble itself; only it was to be borrowed. Probably it was supposed to be false, and its derivation from Zoroastrism was tacitly to prove its falsehood.

Another passage from the Vendidad, which had been so translated as directly to affirm the resurrection of the dead, and which used to be alleged as, beyond all question, containing that doctrine, now, in a more accurate version, plainly contains no such doctrine. It even shews that, at the date of the Vendidad in which it is contained, the doctrine of the resurrection, as it exists in the later Parsee books, was not known to them[2].

The statement, that the books of the earlier Parsism contained the doctrine of the Resurrection, being neces-

[1] e. g. Gesenius on Is. xxiv. 21 p. 772, 3. quoting Rhode. Herzfeld still derives the doctrine of the Resurrection in Ezek. Is. Dan. from Parsism, chiefly on the ground of the language of the very late Bundehesh. Gesch. Isr. ii. 307. früh. Gesch. 180, 1.

[2] Anquetil translated Vend. Farg. xix. thus, "Zoroaster consulted Ormusd, 'Ormusd, who knowest all, shall the pure man rise again, shall the pure woman rise again, the Darvands, the worshippers of the Dews who torment men, shall they rise again ? (shall one see) the running water, the corn which grows, go upon the earth given by Ormusd? Shall all these things go upon (the earth ?)' Ormusd answered, '(all) shall rise again, o pure Z.' ' How shall they be pure, how shall they walk pure, how shall they be pure, how shall they approach purely ; the men of the existing world, to whom the soul shall have been restored ? ' Ormusd answered, 'When the man is dead, when he is in this state, the Dew, master of the evil law, besieges the corpse behind and before during three nights,'" &c. Zend. Av. ii. p. 417, 8. Spiegel's translation is, "Shall I summon the holy man, shall I summon the holy woman, shall I summon the sinner among the evil, the Daeva-worshippers ? Shall they spread over the earth running-water, growing fruits, shall they spread other riches over it ? Ahuramazda answered, ' summon, o pure Zarathustra, !' ' Creator ! where are these judgments, where do these judgments take place, where are these judgments gathered, where do these judgments come together, which man discharges to the corporeal world for his soul ? '" Spiegel observes ; " The following passage is of moment and, taken together with § 26, is a proof, that the resurrection, at the time when the Vendidad was written, was not yet known to the Parsees. The pious here go at once on the 3rd day to paradise ; the bad to hell. Also the present passage exhibits the whole idea very simply, whereas the later Parsism in the Minokhired, Viraf-name, and a little fragment belonging to the older period (Anq. ZAv. i. 2. p. xiii. sqq.) variously deck it out." Av. i. p. 248, 9.

sarily abandoned, the germs of the doctrine, at least, were to be found in the Zend writings. One passage, whose meaning is confessedly extracted with great difficulty, has been found in what are claimed to be the older writings; "[3] We," [i. e. Zoroaster and his friends,] "will be they, who make this life lasting; and the living wise [a plural of Ahura mazda] are the supportings most moving and true; for the intelligent is wont to be, where prudence is at home." Granting the utmost which can be meant by this passage, of which all the important words have to be decyphered with difficulty, and from which any meaning certainly has not yet been decyphered, it contains, manifestly, no doctrine whatever of a resurrection. "A future life," after the death of the body, is the belief of mankind; a doctrine, which, like that of the Being of God, unless stifled, lives on, amid whatever debasements, in the human heart and consciousness. Not the immortality of the undying soul, but the restoration of this individual body, which is resolved into the dust whence it was taken, was, and is in part, the stumbling-block of intellect. The Zend phrase, "the perpetuation of life," is, by the force of the term, distinct from, and incompatible with, *resurrection* of the same substance. It expresses what Heathenism believed, the continued life of the soul; it had no bearing upon what God revealed in the Old and New Testament, the restoration of the body.

So this too has been eked out by a passage from one of those books, the Yashts[4], which the author, who quotes

[3] Gâthâ Ahunavaiti (Yaçna c. 30.) 4, 9. translated by Haug, d. Gâthâs d. Zarathr. i. 9. and Comm. p. 109-113. I have preferred the translation in his Latin and his Commentary, because his German translations are often a popular paraphrase, in which more or less is naturally added to the original. The uncertainty of the passage appears from the very different rendering of Spiegel, Avesta ii. 120; "May we belong to thee, we who seek to further this world. May the wise lords bring help through Asha. Whoso is here teachable, will there unite himself with wisdom."

[4] Haug translates the passage thus, "This splendour attached itself to the hero who is to arise out of the number of the prophets, (called Soshyanto,) and to his companions, in order to make the life everlasting, undecaying, imperishable, imputrescible, incorruptible, for ever existing, for ever vigorous, full

it, confesses to be of late date, calling it "[1] a literature, which grew up at a time, when the Zoroastrian religion had already very much degenerated[2]," itself largely "contributing towards that deterioration."

The modern Bundehesh has no claim to be considered a developement of Zoroastrism. It is written in a language, the basis of which is some form of Aramaic, (it is thought, Assyrian Aramaic[3].) According to the close of the book, it is later than Mohammed[4]. But, whatever of power, at the time when the dead will rise again, and imperishableness of life will exist, making the life lasting by itself. All the world will remain for eternity in the state of purity; the devil will disappear from all those places, whence he used to attack the religious men, in order to kill; and all his brood and creatures will be doomed to destruction." Zamyâd Yasht 19, 12. (90 West.) Spiegel translates it; "which attached itself to the victorious Çaoshyanç and his other friends, that he might make the world progressive, not aging, undying, not stinking, not putrid, ever-living, ever-benefitting, an empire according to wish, that the dead may arise, that deathlessness may come for the living, and the world advances itself according to wish. The worlds which teach purity will be undying, the Drukhs will disappear at that time. So soon as it comes to the pure to kill him and his hundred-fold seed, then is it for dying and fleeing away (ripe)." Avesta iii. p. 183, 4. 174.

[1] Haug Essays p. 223. "This kind of literature, [the Yashts,] grew up at a time, when the Zoroastrian religion had already very much degenerated, and its original monotheism [dualism] partially given way to the old gods, who had been stigmatised and banished by Zarathustra Spitama, but were afterwards transformed into Angels." "This kind of literature has, no doubt, largely contributed towards the deterioration of the religion founded by Z. Sp., and partially re-established what the prophet had endeavoured to destroy."

[2] The original purity of Zoroastrism is a theory of Haug's, contrary to the facts, in regard to Monotheism, since the Gâthâs are distinctly dualistic, and in regard to the inferior gods, since those borrowed from Vedism must always have belonged to it. Human nature would be to be pitied, if it could believe such trash as that Yasht to be the original of the doctrine of the Resurrection.   [3] Haug üb. d. Pehlewi Sprache u. d. Bundehesh, p. 28.

[4] "The grammatical and lexical peculiarities, which, to the philological enquirer, establish its late date, have been already mentioned in the preceding paragraphs. Lastly, the list of Emperors at the end of the book, often mentioned already, which brings us to the time after the destruction of the Empire of the Sassanidæ, is an undoubted mark of its late origin, and I can discover no mark which should justify criticism in considering these notices as appended later, as has often been maintained." Spiegel d. trad. literat. d. Parsen p. 94. Haug, who thinks the existing book to be probably a translation, supposes it to have "come into being in the first centuries of our era; the translation probably towards the end of the rule of the Sassanidæ; or, if the close of the book is genuine which speaks of the dominion of the Arabs, not until after the conquest of the Persian Empire by the Arabs." ib. p. 30.

its date, the writer has borrowed largely from Christian sources, as on other subjects, so here. The illustrations[5], by which it defends the resurrection of the body against objections to its possibility, are such as were current in Christian apologists[6], and were doubtless learned in the school of Edessa, where Persians also studied[7].

iii. The allegations, in regard to Daniel's teaching as to the Angels, also assume grave doctrinal error in the New Testament. For most of the points objected to are taught there also. Leaving this for the time, I will first remind you briefly, what is the doctrine as to Angels before Daniel; so we shall see the better, what accessions came through Daniel. The doctrine, as contained throughout the Old Testament previous to Daniel, is this; that there lives in the Presence of God a vast assembly[8],

[5] They are, in sum, that God, Who created, could restore what He created. He brought light out of darkness ; " created the seed of corn, which, after decaying in the earth, bursts forth anew, and multiplies countlessly." He created the sap in trees, the living fruit in the mother, &c. c. 31. p. 111, 12.

[6] " Thou sayest, how can matter, which hath been dissolved, be made to appear ? Consider thyself, O man, and thou wilt find how to believe this thing. Think what thou wast, before thou hadst a being ; simply nothing ; for hadst thou been anything, thou wouldest have remembered it. Thou therefore that wast nothing before thou didst exist, and that becomest also nothing, when thou ceasest to exist, why canst thou not begin to exist again from nothing by the will of that self-same Creator, Who hath willed that thou shouldest come into being, out of nothing ?—Declare, if thou canst, the manner in which thou wast made, and then seek to know how thou shalt be made. And yet surely thou shalt be more easily made that which thou once hast been, seeing thou wast made, equally without difficulty, that which thou never hadst at any time been. There will be a doubt, I suppose, as to the power of God, Who hath framed out of that which was not before, not less than out of a death-like void and nothingness, this vast body of the universe, animated by that Spirit which animateth all souls, stamped too by Himself as an emblem of the resurrection of man, for a testimony unto you. The light, which is extinct every day, shineth forth again, and the darkness in like manner departeth and succeedeth in its turn ;—the seasons, when they begin, end anew ; the fruits are consumed, and again return ; the seeds assuredly spring not up with new fruitfulness, except they be first corrupted and dissolved ; all things are by dying preserved ; all things are formed again after death." Tert. Apol. c. 48. p. 99, 100. Oxf. Tr. See other fathers, Greek and Latin, referred to ib. not. z. b. c.

[7] See ab. p. 146. n. 1.   [8] Ps. lxxxix. 5. 1 Kings xxii. 19. "all the host of heaven standing by Him on His right hand and His left."

myriads upon myriads[1] of spiritual beings[2], higher than we, but infinitely removed from God[3], [4]*mighty in strength, doers of His word, ever set*[5] *to hear the voice* of *His word;* who ceaselessly [6]bless and praise God; wise[7] also; *to whom* He *gives charge to guard* His own *in all their ways*[8]; *ascending and descending*[9] to and from heaven and earth, and who variously minister to men, most often invisibly[10]. But all, (it was declared,) are interested in us and our well-being.   For, when our earth was created, [11]*all the sons of God burst forth into jubilee,* in prospect of our birth, who were to be their care here, their fellow-citizens hereafter in bliss.   It was an anticipation of that which we know more fully, that *the angels desire to look into*[12] the mysteries of our salvation.   At the giving of the law on Mount Sinai, they were present[13] in myriads.   At that great manifestation of the goodness and condescension of God, how should not they be present, who rejoiced at the creation of our race?   Good beings must be interested in those capable of good, and in God's ways of forming them for Himself.   When God vouchsafed His Presence at Mount Zion, and the holy place became a new Sinai[14], *twice ten thousand angels, yea, thousands many times repeated,* were there.   They are present with God, witnessing the trials of our race.   On two occasions, when they *presented themselves*[15] before God, they heard of Job's spotlessness and of the great trial of his faith.   Job already, like the Apostles afterwards, was [16]*made a spectacle to Angels.*   This trial of Job was the proving of one outside

---

[1] Ps. lxviii. 18. (17 Eng.) lit. "twice ten thousand, yea thousands of repetition."   It is Daniel's "thousand thousands and ten thousand ten thousands." vii. 10.   [2] Ps. civ. 4.   [3] Ps. lxxxix. 6. Job iv. 18. תָּהֳלָה lit. "folly." Eng. V. from הלל. So Kim. AE. Saad. ap. Ges. Lex. p. 382. The Verss. render it as of a moral defect; σκολιόν τι, LXX; pravitatem, S. Jer.; iniquity, Ch.; in which case it would relate to the fallen angels.   [4] Ps. ciii. 20.   [5] לֵאמֹר
[6] Ps. lxxxix. 5. ciii. 20.   [7] 2 Sam. xiv. 17. 20.   [8] Ps. xci. 11.
[9] Gen. xxviii. 12, 13.   [10] as Gen. xxiv. 7. 40. Ex. xxiii. 20-23. xxxii. 34. xxxiii. 2. Num. xx. 16. Is. lxiii. 9. and note 7.
[11] Job xxxviii. 7.   [12] 1 Pet. i. 12.   [13] Deut. xxxii. 2. Ps. lxviii. 17.
[14] Ps. Ib.   [15] Job i. 6. ii. 1.   [16] 1 Cor. iv. 9.

of Israel; their joy at our creation related to the human race. They were again present[17], and learnt how Ahab's false prophets would, by the intervention of a lying spirit, have power to deceive to his destruction Ahab who wished to be deceived; Ahab and his prophets accomplishing, each of his own freewill, what was against their will. Their love for man shews itself, in that, when God commanded them to destroy the guilty in Jerusalem, the charge is given to them, [18]*let not your eye spare, neither have ye pity*, as though they would have pity, only that they must needs be of the same mind with God. It is in conformity with this, and an anticipation of the New Testament, that, in the prophecy of the Day of Judgment in Daniel, the myriads of the ministering spirits are exhibited as standing around the Throne. Their office there, it was reserved to our Lord, the Judge, to declare; Daniel only declared their interest in it. The Day of the judgment of our whole race must needs unfold, even to those blessed spirits, more of the wisdom and love and justice of the Creator of us all.

Some distinction among those heavenly hosts was revealed from the first. It would be out of harmony with the manifold beauty and gradations in the rest of God's creation, if those higher orders of intelligent beings were of one kind only. At the closed gates of Paradise were the Cherubim [19].

But chiefly there was one, designated as "*the* Angel of the Lord," in whom God accustomed His creatures to the thought of beholding Himself in human form. Whether it were God the Son, Who so manifested Himself beforehand [20], (His Godhead invisible, as in the days

[17] 1 Kings xxii. 19.   [18] Ez. ix. 5. comp. viii. 18. It is Herzfeld's observation. Gesch. Isr. ii. 277.   [19] Gen. iii. 24.

[20] This was the common belief of the earliest fathers. S. Augustine pointed out the mistake of inferring this from S. John i. 18, "No man hath seen God at any time," since the Divine Nature of the Son is as invisible as that of the Father. See references on Tertullian de Præscr. n. 12. p. 463. n. f. Oxf. Tr. ed. 2. S. Ath. de Conc. Arim. p. 120. n. q. O. T. S. Augustine's own summary is, "the modest and cautious consideration of the Divine mysteries per-

of His flesh,) or no, yet there was one, known as *the Angel of the Lord*, distinct from and above all the rest.   He
speaks with authority, as the Lord; therefore the Lord,
whether the Father or the Son or the Holy Ghost, was
present with him, and spake by him; he is called, not as
an epithet, but as a description of his being, *the Angel of
the Lord;* therefore it seems to me most probable, that he
was a created Angel[1].   It seems most probable, that the
word, *Angel,* describes his actual nature, not the higher
Nature, which spoke or was adored in him.   God spake
by *the Angel of the Lord* to Hagar[2], *I will multiply thy
seed exceedingly; and she called the Name of the Lord that*

suades us, I deem, not to pronounce rashly, *which* Person of the Trinity appeared to any one of the fathers or prophets in any body or likeness of a body,
except where the context supplies any probable indications." de Trin. L. ii.
fin.   "It is plain that all those objects which were seen by the fathers, when
God was represented to them according to His own manifestation, as befit-
ted those times, were wrought through the creature.   And if we cannot tell,
how He did them through the ministry of angels, yet that they were done by
angels, we say not of our own minds," but on "the authority of the Divine
Scriptures." iii. 11. n. 22.   "This Person [of God the Word] angelic nature
could aforetime figure, in order to fore-announce; it would not expropriate,
so as to be Itself." Ib. iv. 20. fin. n. 30.   "The Son Himself, Who is the Word
of God, not only in these last times, when He vouchsafed to appear in the
flesh, but aforetime too from the foundation of the world, announced as to the
Father to whom He willed, whether by speaking, or by appearing, either
by some angelic power or by any creature." c. Adimant. c. 9.   S. Irenæus
also speaks of "the shewing of God through the creature." iv. 20. 7.   And
S. Athanas. "But if, when an angel was seen, he who saw heard the voice
of God, as took place at the bush, for the Angel of the Lord was seen in the
flame of fire from the bush, and the Lord called Moses out of the bush, saying,
'I am the God of thy father, the God of Abraham, and the God of Isaac
and the God of Jacob,' and the Angel was not the God of Abraham, but it was
God who was speaking in the Angel, and he who appeared was an Angel, but
God spoke in him." Orat. 3. c. Arian. § 14. p. 421. Oxf. Tr.   So also Dionys.
de cæl. hierarch. c. 4. in Petav. de Trin. viii. 2.

[1] The fathers *mostly* applied the title of *the Angel* to God the Son on the
ground of the gloss of the LXX in Is. ix. 6. μεγάλης βουλῆς ἄγγελος, "magni
consilii Angelus."   But, although Malachi foretells our Lord's coming in the
Flesh, under the titles "the Lord," "the Angel," or Messenger, "of the Covenant," (iii. 1.) there is no proof that He is any where spoken of absolutely
as "the Angel," or that His Divine Nature is so entitled.

[2] Gen. xvi. 10. 13. add Ib. xxi. 17, 18. where *the Angel of God* says, *I will
make him a great nation.*

spake unto her, Thou, God, seest me. The Angel of the LORD arrested Abraham in doing that which God had bidden him to do, to offer Isaac his son. God in him accepted the obedience, as having been done to Himself. [3]*Now I know that thou fearest God, seeing thou hast not withheld thy son, thine only son, from Me.* Angels of *God's host met* Jacob [4]; but it was one, to whom *he made supplication,* and who *blessed him,* and who, Hosea says, was *the LORD of hosts,* of whom Jacob said, *I have seen God, face to face* [5]. The Angel of the Lord withstood Balaam, *because,* God says by him [6], *thy way is perverse before Me; the word that I shall speak unto thee, that thou shalt speak,* the self-same words which God had said to him in vision before [7]; those words, which were the turning-point of his next subsequent history [8]. Of this Angel God says, *My Name is in him* [9]; in him were manifested the Divine attributes; he was the minister of God's justice who would *not pardon* their transgressions; to him God required obedience to be paid. His speaking was God's speaking in him; for God says, [10]*If thou shalt indeed obey his voice and do all that I command you.* And since he was not present by any visible presence, there was no way of obeying *him,* except in obeying what God commanded to Moses. Since God was present in him, God uses as equivalent terms, the words, [11]*the Angel of His Presence,* or [12]*My Presence.* And when the time of fulfilment came, of which God had said, [13]*Mine Angel shall go before thee, and bring thee in unto the Amorites, &c, and I will cut them off,* it is still one Angel in human form, who says to Joshua, *As Captain of the LORD's host am I come,* in whom Joshua worshipped God, and by whom

---

[3] Ib. xxii. 11, 12. Dr. Stanley, (Jewish Church, p. 48. 50.,) avoiding the coarse language of Dr. Williams as to "the fierce ritual of Syria," in substance agrees with him, and represents that as "a stern logical consequence of the ancient view of sacrifice," "infirmity, exaggeration, excess," which, God says, was obedience to His voice. Gen. xxii. 18.   [4] Gen. xxxii. 1, 2.

[5] Ib. 24-30. Hos. xii. 2-5. See my Comm. p. 77.   [6] Num. xxii. 32-35.

[7] Ib. 20.   [8] Ib. xxiii. 12. 26. xxiv. 13.   [9] Ex. xxiii. 21.

[10] Ib. 22.   [11] Is. lxiii. 9.   [12] Ex. xxxiii. 14.   [13] Ib. xxiii. 23.

God required the same tokens of reverence as He had from Moses [1].

By *the Angel of the* Lord God upbraided Israel in the time of the Judges; [2]*I made you to go up out of Egypt, and have brought you unto the land which I sware unto your fathers, and I said, I will never break My covenant with you. Wherefore also I said, I will not drive them out from before you.* The Angel of the Lord pronounced the *curse* upon *Meroz* [3] for unfaithfulness; and it disappears from history. In the mission of Gideon, the titles, *the Angel of the* Lord, and *the* Lord, interchanged [4]. Yet both are evidently one. God promised by him what God only can promise [5], and accepted the sacrifice [6].

In the revelation to Manoah and his wife, the wife, ignorant, at first, who he was, yet speaks of the *Angel of the* Lord, as a being, known to them [7]. [8]*His countenance was like the countenance of the Angel of the* Lord, *very terrible.* To offer sacrifice unto the Lord and to the Angel of the Lord, was one [9]. His name was *wonderful* [10]. No mention having been made of *an Angel* previously, *the Angel* of the Lord is not, "*the* Angel," i.e. he who had been spoken of, but he who was known as "*the* Angel of the Lord."

Of this Angel, and of others with him, it seems to be said, [11]*The Angel of the* Lord *encampeth round about them that fear Him and delivereth them.* The word, *encampeth* [12], probably alludes to that appearance to Jacob on his return from Mesopotamia, when he saw *God's host* and from

[1] Josh. v. 13-15. and Ex. iii. 5.   [2] Judg. ii. 1, 3.   Dr. Stanley (J. Cb. p. 418.) following Ewald, makes him a human messenger, "an earlier Malachi," contrary to the uniform idiom, and the use of the 1st person, "I made you &c."   [3] Ib. v. 23.   [4] *the Angel of the* Lord, vi. 11. 12. 21. 22. *the angel of God,* 20. *the* Lord, 14. 16. 23.   [5] Ib. 16. 23.   [6] 21.

[7] as in 2 Sam. xxiv. 16. 1 Chron. xxi. 15.   [8] xiii. 6.

[9] The clause, *for Manoah knew not that he was the angel of the Lord,* explains the angel's injunction, *Thou must offer it unto the Lord.* Manoah and his wife wished to bring the kid, as ordinary food. He refuses it as ordinary food, and bids him, if he would offer it in sacrifice, to offer it to the Lord in him.   [10] פֶּלִא 18 as פֶּלֶא Is. ix. 5.   [11] Ps. xxxiv. 7.

[12] Hengst. on Ps. xxiv.

it called the name of the place, Mahanaim [13], "Two-camps," and, after that, saw the Angel of the LORD, who tried his strength and blessed him. The captain of a host is said to "encamp [14]," but he "encamps *around*," through the army of which he is the head. On account of this image, and the mention of "the chariots of God [15]," as a title for the angels present at His manifestations of Himself, it seems not improbable that the *horses of fire and chariots of fire* [16] round about Elisha, and those which carried up Elijah to heaven, were symbols of Angelic presence.

This same Angel, I think, was meant by Elihu, the *Angel-interpreter* [17], *one of a thousand, who sheweth unto man his righteousness,* i. e. how he may be righteous in God's sight, *and is gracious unto him, and saith, redeem him from going down to the pit, I have found a ransom.* For it is the office of no mere created Angel, but is anticipative of His Who came, at once to redeem and to justify; as S. Gregory says [18], "It is as though the Mediator of God and men said, 'since there hath been no man, who might appear a righteous intercessor for man, I made Myself man to make propitiation for man.'"

This then, in itself, involves a distinction among the heavenly beings, so far at least that, in the earliest books as well as in Daniel, we hear of one Angel, above those ordinarily spoken of.

In the Seraphim, (probably, *fiery* [19] spirits,) in Isaiah,

---

[13] Gen. xxxii. 1, 2. מַחֲנָיִם, from חָנָה "camped," the word used in the Psalm.

[14] 2 Sam. xii. 28. Hengst.　　[15] Ps. lxviii. 17.　　[16] 2 Kings vi. 17. ii. 11.

[17] Job xxxiii. 23. מֵלִיץ is unquestionably "interpreter," Gen. xlii. 23. "embassador," 2 Chr. xxxii. 13. In Is. xliii. 27, "thy interpreters have sinned against Me," it seems most natural to understand it of those who interpreted God's will to man. (comp. Mal. ii. 7.) "The Angel-interpreter," I think then, has more probably his name from an office from God to man, than from one for man with God, viz. intercessor. The office to man is explained, "to shew unto man his uprightness," i. e. how he should be upright with God.

[18] ad loc. L. xxiv. n. 6.

[19] So Kimchi and Abulwalid. The root שָׂרַף, "burned," is so common in Hebrew, (whence also שָׂרָף, like πρηστήρ, καῦσος, a poisonous serpent, whose bite was "inflaming,") that the Hebrew etymology is much safer than the Ara-

and the Cherubim[1], we have other orders of spirits in near relation to God. Of these, the Cherubim are not mentioned to have any office of ministry to man, but, having been placed, with symbols of terror, to forbid his return to Paradise, were objects of awe. The Seraphim are spoken of, as engaged in ceaseless praise in great nearness to God, yet as concerned also about us below; for part of their song was, [2] *the earth is full of His glory.* One of them also was sent to Isaiah with the symbolic burning coal, which was to cleanse his iniquity and fit him for the Seraphic mission of bringing good tidings to man.

In regard, then, to the greater dignity of some Angels above others, no addition is made in Daniel to what was known from the time of Abraham. It is even most probable that Michael is no other than that *Angel of the Lord*, by whom God manifested Himself of old. For *the Angel of the Lord* seems to be the same who declared himself to be *the prince of the host of the Lord*[3], a title given in Daniel to Michael, [4] *your prince*, [5] *one of the chief princes :* [6] *the great prince which standeth up for the children of thy people.*

We have, then, alike in Joshua and Daniel, the belief as to one spiritual being, to whom the charge and protection of the Jewish people was specially entrusted. In Daniel, there is the name only of Michael above what was known before, and the name and being of Gabriel[7], both, in common with the New Testament[8].

bic שׁר, "eminent." Gesenius' only objection is, that שׂרף signifies "burning," not "shining." But "burning" suits best with what the Church has thought to be the special character of the Seraphim, "burning love." All languages speak of "the *fire* of love," and the Holy Ghost, at the day of Pentecost, fell on the disciples, with the symbol of "cloven tongues, like as of fire." Acts ii. 3.

[1] The Semitic etymologies of כרוב are severally possible, yet no one is satisfactory enough to be adopted with confidence. The Persian etymology, in itself quite unsatisfactory, is also excluded by the early mention of the Cherubim.   [2] Is. vi. 3.

[3] Josh. v. 14. See ab. p. 517.   [4] Dan. x. 21.   [5] Ib. 13.   [6] Ib. xii. 1.
[7] Ib. viii. 16. ix. 21.   [8] Gabriel, S. Luke i. 19. 26 ; Michael, Jude 9. Rev. xii. 7. The statement in the Jerusalem Talmud, from R. Simeon ben La-

Such gradation then of heavenly beings, as is implied in Daniel, is in harmony with what had been revealed before. He sees one in great majesty [9], whom he describes in language of Ezekiel [10], probably that same Angel of the Lord, who had appeared to those before him. This Angel gives directions even to Gabriel [11]. It seems also that, among those exalted intelligences, some know more of the Divine purpose than others, and communicate that knowledge to others. Twice, in these visions, an Angel enquireth of that exalted Angel [12], (who yet himself is a creature, for he swears by the living God [13],) and receives an answer.

Both these relations of that one great Angel, his special office for the people and his superiority to other Angels, are mentioned in one of the prophets after the Captivity, Zechariah. There, other Angels, whom God had *sent to walk to and fro upon the earth,* give account of their mission to *the Angel of the Lord* [14], and he himself intercedes with the Lord [15]. He stands as judge, surrounded by Angels who fulfil his commands, hears the accusations of Satan, pronounces forgiveness to Joshua the high priest, and, in him, to the people whom he represents [16]. It is probably *"the* Angel of the Lord," certainly it is a superior Angel, who, in another vision, directs another Angel to instruct Zechariah [17]. Again, God speaks of *the Angel of the Lord,* as having a glory like His own [18].

chish, (in our 3rd century,) " The names of angels went up by the hand of Israel out of Babylon," plainly means no more than that the names of Angels first occur in Scripture written in Babylon. For so it continues ; "For, before, it was said, *Then flew one of the Seraphim unto me; before Him stood the Seraphim,* (Is. vi. 6. and 2.) but afterwards, *the man Gabriel,* (Dan. ix. 21.) and *Michael your prince.*" (Ib. x. 21.) But, although first given in Babylon, the names are opposed to the errors of Babylon. Michael is one of the oldest Hebrew names, a sort of watchword and challenge to all idolatry, " Who is like God ?" The name Gabriel also, " man of God," declares that Angels too are but agents of God.   [9] x. 5. xii. 6, 7.   [10] i. 7, 14, 16, 22.
    [11] viii. 16.   [12] xii. 6. viii. 13.   [13] xii. 7.
    [14] Zech. i. 10, 11.   [15] Ib. 12.   [16] Ib. iii. 1-5.
    [17] Ib. ii. 7, 8, Heb. 3, 4, Eng.   [18] Ib. xii. 8. *The house of David shall be as God, as the Angel of the Lord before Him.*

The one fact as to Angels, which is peculiar to Daniel, is in harmony with his position in God's revelation. As he was employed to disclose God's care and providence over Heathen nations, so through him it was disclosed, that, as God set one chief Angel as the deputed guardian of His people, so He set others over other nations. It is in harmony with all which we know about those blessed spirits. As we know that[1] *all* of them *are ministering spirits sent forth to minister for them who shall be heirs of salvation ;* as we know, from our Lord's words[2] and from the Apostolic belief[3], that each Christian at least is, from childhood, assigned to the care of his own guardian Angel; so Daniel, declaring that the heathen also were the objects of God's care, taught, in the case of two great nations, Persia and Græcia, that they were under the care of eminent Angels, *princes*[4] with God. For the Angels of Persia and Græcia were, manifestly, good Angels, since they desired the welfare of their people, and they contended with Gabriel and Michael before God, each, in submission to the Divine Will, desiring what seemed for the good of his people, which, since their apparent interests were diverse, seemed to be contrary. The interest of the heavenly beings in man had been revealed before. To Daniel it was made known as part of God's *mercy over all His works*, that "constituting the services of Angels and men in a wonderful order," He assigned to each nation one of those *ministering spirits*, to succour and defend them, and plead their cause with Himself, the Father of all.

In the dream, in which Nebuchadnezzar was warned of the insanity, which God was about to inflict on him unless he repented, there occur the remarkable words, [5]*The matter is the decree of the watchers*, the " ever wakeful[6] " ministers of God, *and the request is the word of the*

---

[1] Heb. i. 14.   [2] S. Matt. xviii. 10.   [3] Acts xii. 15.

[4] Dan. x. 20, 21.   [5] iv. 14, Ch. 17, Eng.

[6] עִיר. עוּר, (probably the same word as ἐγείρω or Sanscr. *gri*,) is used intrans. of "arousing one's self;" in Pi. Hif. of "arousing" others. It has not the meaning of שמר, " guard." In Job viii. 6, if it had had the sense of being " wakeful

holy ones [7]; for which Daniel, in his interpretation, substitutes, [8] *This is the decree of the Most High.* Daniel, using the self-same word [9], states that the decree was solely from God. There is no association of the creature with the Creator. The same decree is by Daniel called "the decree of the most High," and, if Nebuchadnezzar's memory was accurate [10], "the decree of the watchers," i. e. for," it would have had it, (as in Eng.) by force of the עַל, "over," not of the word itself. But there too the E.V. is best. " He would awake for thee," (as God is so often said to "awake" for His people, when He notices *that*, which He had before left unremedied, their "trouble" &c.). עִיר then (to judge from the Hebrew, for עִיר occurs in Daniel only, and in Syriac as ultimately derived from it,) is *watcher*, (i. e. one ever-aroused, unsleeping,) not *watchman*, which in Hebrew is שֹׁמֵר, in Ch. נָטַר, in Syr. נטר. In Aramaic, only Pal. Af. Ithpeh. seem to have been used, in the sense, "aroused, was aroused." This is the rendering of the Vulg. "vigil; " of Aq. Symm. ἐγρήγορος, and probably of the LXX, (whence the ἐγρήγοροι of the book of Enoch. See above p. 387, 8.) Theod. and the Pesh. retain the word, which, in Syriac, has the two senses which it has in the book of Enoch, and which doubtless are derived from it. There is absolutely no authority for the sense " custos."

[7] שְׁאֵלְתָּא is of course the Hebrew שְׁאֵלָה, which, in actual usage, signifies, "petition;" in 1 Sam. ii. 20. also ; for Hannah did not *lend* Samuel to God, but gave him back for life to Him, from Whom she had asked and obtained him. 1 Sam. i. 27, 8. In like way, שְׁאֵלְתָּא, in the instances of its use given by Buxtorf (col. 2300, 1,) from the Targums, signifies "petition." In itself, it might mean " interrogation," since שְׁאֵל, as well as שָׁאַל, signifies, 1) ask, i. e. to enquire ; 2) specifically, "ask " for a thing, request, beg. But this too comes no nearer to the sense which Gesenius would give it, " spec. *quæstio forensis*, (legal enquiry,) *causa forensis judicata*, inde *decretum*." No where in the Targums, any more than in Hebrew, does שְׁאֵלְתָּא mean a *decree ;* any more than our "suit" would mean " the judgment in a suit." Gesenius assigns this meaning, in order to make שְׁאֵלְתָּא identical with פִּתְגָּמָא. But פִּתְגָּם itself signifies "word," not "decree," which is טְעֵם, and from which it is distinguished in Ezr. vi. 11. The " word " of a king is with authority ; and if one with authority " sends *word*," (פִּתְגָּמָא שְׁלַח Ezr. iv. 17. v. 7,) that "word" is to be obeyed. But it does not follow that פִּתְגָּם means " decree," any more than our " word" does, which we use in precisely the same idiom. It is also one of those common abuses of Hebrew parallelism, to assume that each parallel word must mean the same thing.   [8] iv. 21, Ch. 24, Eng.

[9] גְּזֵרַת עִירִין 14, Ch. גְּזֵרַת עֲלָּאָה הִיא 21.

[10] Hengstenberg and others have held that the title of the " watchers" had reference to the θεοὶ βουλαῖοι of the Babylonians, and this, consistently with revelation, on the supposition that the revelation of God was amalgamated in Nebuchadnezzar's mind with his own belief, (Beitr. p. 161.) in which way Daniel's explanation would be a correction of it. But the θεοὶ βουλαῖοι of the Babylonians, (if Diodorus has represented them rightly ; there is probably an

of the holy Angels. This it might be, either as the decree of God, entrusted to them to execute, or, since the holy Angels must needs be of the same mind as God, it may be said to be *their* decree, in that they embraced His. This decree had been first their request. It appears from Daniel's advice to the king, that the sin, for which that aweful seven-years' insanity was inflicted upon him, was that common sin of conquerors, unmercifulness and op-

error as to the number,) are only stars, and have to do with astrology only. He says, " They say, that the most important calculation and motion is of the 5 stars called planets which they name 'interpreters,' and especially those of the star called by the Greeks Kronos [Saturn] but they call the clearest and the fore-signifier of the most and greatest things, El; but the other four they name as do our astrologers, Ares, Aphrodite, Hermes, Zeus, [Mars, Venus, Mercury, Jupiter,] wherefore they call them 'interpreters;' because, the other stars having their own fixed orbit, these alone, having an orbit of their own, shew what is about to happen, interpreting to men the good-will of the gods. For by their rising and setting, and partly by their colour, they say that they foreshew to those who choose to attend accurately. For sometimes they shew the vehemence of winds, sometimes excessive rain or drought. Sometimes also, the rising of comets, sometimes eclipses of sun and moon, earthquakes too, and altogether all the circumstances, resulting from the atmosphere, good as well as bad for nations and places, for kings too or private individuals. Beneath their orbit, they say that there are 30 [36] stars ordered, which they call 'gods of counsel,' and that half of these look to the places above the earth, and half under the earth, looking at once at the things which fall out among men and in heaven. And that, every 10 days, of those above to those below a messenger of the stars is sent, and of those under the earth to those above, in like manner, one. This orbit they have defined, established by an eternal circuit. But of the gods they say, that 12 are lords, to each of which they assign a month and one of the 12 signs of the Zodiac. Through these they say that the sun and moon and 5 planets have their orbit.—But after the Zodiac they separate off 24 stars, of which they say, half are set in the Northern parts, half in the Southern. Of these they assign those visible to the living, the invisible to the dead, which they call the judges of the universe. But the moon, they say, has its orbit below all these, &c." ii. 30. 1.

I doubt not that Gesenius combined rightly the 12 lords, of the gods, to whom the signs of the Zodiac were assigned, and the 24 extra-Zodiacal stars, which together make up these inferior "gods of counsel." The whole context is of astrology. In astrology, while the position of the planets in the heavens was held to be of chief import, yet, subordinately, so was the position which they occupied in the Zodiac at that time, two of the signs being the "houses" of each planet while the two remaining belonged to the sun and moon. (See in Ges. p. 354.) While then the 5 planets were the "interpreters," the fixed stars were so subordinately, and were called "gods of counsel." Among the Egyptians, the 12 signs of the zodiac were called "gods of counsel," the pla-

pression [1]. The word, " the request," gives another glimpse into the interest of the holy Angels in ourselves.   They too longed that the oppression should cease; and, joining in the cry which is ever going up from the oppressed to the Throne of mercy and judgment, prayed for that chastisement which was to relieve the oppressed and convert the oppressor.   But the statement, that it was a "request," precludes the supposition, that the holy Angels had any portion in the "decree;" for to "request" and to "decree" relate necessarily to different parties. One who can "decree" has no occasion to "request," nor does he.

All this, from the first book of the Old Testament to the last, is in harmony.   Throughout, it was revealed that there were different orders of the heavenly beings. This is as clear in Genesis, as in Daniel or Zechariah. Nor in all this is there any even seeming likeness to any thing Magian.   Had there been any likeness, it must have existed in the Pentateuch as much as in Daniel, since the doctrine in both is one.   An unbelieving Jewish writer, unable to escape the conviction of the oneness of the doctrine as to the holy Angels throughout the Old Testament, was, at least, consistent in laying down that it is ante-Biblical [2], and, (in regard to the evil angels,) in as-

nets, the "rabdophori;" (Schol. Apoll. Rhod. iv. 262. quoted by Wess. on Diod. l. c.) so that they occupied the same relative position.   It is only in relation then to the planets and in astrology, that certain stars were called " gods of counsel," either that by their astrological meaning they gave counsel, or that they were subordinate advisers to those which were reputed to be of primary significance.   [1] Dan. iv. 27, Eng. 24, Ch.

[2] " Through this belief in angels of such various sort and of such varied significance, there was gained for the ancient Hebrews an imaginative addition to the belief in One God which was as yet too spiritual and too bare for them, and the gulph which they saw between God and man, so long as God did not appear to them as indwelling in man, was filled up satisfactorily.   Yet evidently this belief was not created to satisfy that need, but was adopted from præ-Jahvist views, and only recast and developed in conformity with Jahvism, [God's revelation of Himself by Moses,] in which way it unquestionably did it good service." Ib. p. 278, 9.   It is true, of course, that the belief of other spiritual beings adds to our knowledge of the Creator of us all, yet not as "filling up a gulph;" for every creature is, of course, alike infinitely removed from the

serting the influence of Magism upon the religion of the Bible from the beginning, while he admits that such influence cannot be proved [1]. In one sense, the doctrine of the holy angels *was* ante-Biblical, since one portion is coeval with the closing of the entrance to Paradise. But then, of course, its existence in Daniel or any other book cannot be any proof of the late date of such books.

The harmony of the doctrine as to the Angels, from the first to the last, might have exempted us from any enquiry as to Magism. But since the imagination, that true religion, in both the Old and New Testament, is in some way indebted to Magism, is one of the " veteris vestigia fraudis," which still lingers on from times which knew little of Holy Scripture or of Magism, I would point out briefly, that, if any thing was borrowed, Magism must have been the borrower. And this, both from the character of the two religions and people, and also from the age of the books, in which the doctrines are contained.

In regard to the religions, the god of the Aryans, Ahura-mazda [2], is not the living God, such as He has revealed Himself [3], but a being, depending partly upon certain co-

Creator. There are no steps from the finite to the Infinite. Contrariwise, the conception of beings immeasurably above ourselves, yet, together with ourselves, infinitely below the Creator, helps us, like a long vista in created things, to conceive the more of His ever-communicated, never-exhausted, infinity of Goodness.

[1] " The inability to shew, in what way the Magian religion so early [as Genesis] gained this influence upon Israelite views, does not entitle us to deny that influence." Herzfeld, G. Isr. ii. 281, 2.

[2] Max Müller translates the name " wise spirit," Science of language, p. 208. Spiegel, " very wise Lord," Av. iii. p. 11; Haug, " living wise."

[3] Spiegel points out that Ahura-mazda is represented as corporeal, (" who has the best body," Yaçna I, 2. Farvardin Yast. 80, 81.) with a soul and *fravashi*, (Farv. Y. 81. Yaç. 26, 3. Vend. xix. 46, 7.) as human beings have their body, soul, and *fravashi*. Mention is even made of " Çpenta-armaiti and thy other wives," (Vispered iii. 21,) of " thy wives," (Yaç. 38, 2,) and of a daughter of this Çp. Armaiti and Ahura-mazda viz. Ashis-vaguhi, (Ashi-Yast n. 16. Av. iii. p. 164.) although Çp. Arm. is elsewhere daughter of Ahura-mazda. (Gâthâ Ust. 44, 4. Vd. xix. 45.) Av. iii. Einl. p. v. In Yaç. lxx, the praise of the body of Ahura-mazda intervenes between the praise of himself and that of the Amesha-çpentas ; " Ahura-mazda, the pure, lord of the pure, we praise. The

eternal existences [4], light, space, and time, which were also objects of worship [5], partly on the physical coopera- tion of what He is said to have created [6]. Time is not His creature, nor space His presence; they are conditions of His being, independent of Himself. In like way, those other beings, which were the objects of Zoroastrian wor-

whole body of Ahura-mazda we praise. All Amesha-çp. we praise." n. 10- 12. Av. ii. p. 203. Sp.

[4] Under the name Qadhâta, "self-created," or "self-governed," (Spiegel, Av. ii. 218. note) occur 1) "light without beginning," as contrasted with "created lights;" 2) thwâsha, (Spiegel thinks, "the boundless space of hea- ven" in contrast with Açman, "the firmament;") and 3) "Zrvâna akarana," "uncaused time." (Spiegel, Av. iii. xxxix. I have substituted "uncaused" for the common rendering "time without bounds," on the authority of Dr. Aufrecht.) Time, light, space, then, are coexistent with Ahuramazda. Plutarch speaks of the "light," as the original of Oromasdes, "Oromasdes sprang out of the purest light;" (de Is. et Osir. c. 46.) and later Parsism conceived "uncaused time" as his original, although this opinion was wrapped up in a myth. (Eznik of Armenia 5th. cent. A.D. "refutation of the false doctrine of the Persians," in Haug, Essays, p. 10, 11, and more concisely, but essentially the same, in the proclamation of a Persian general A.D. 450, in Elisæus Hist. of Vartan, trans- lated by Neumann, p. 11, 12.) There is no such opinion in the Zendavesta. The words rendered by Anquetil, "the boundless time has given thee," are now owned to mean, "Çpento-mainyus made, in the uncaused time." Herz- feld (translated by Davidson, iii. 177.) says, that "the 'time without bounds' of the Magian religion is an attribute of Ormusd," on the authority of the Hall. L.Z. 1845. n. 73. (früh. G. Isr. p. 460.) This is only the theory of a Parsee gen- tleman, Doshabai, one of the new school, who wishes to dress up Parsism as a respectable Deism. His language is strange enough, below any belief of any of the old heathen who were not Atheists. "Zervân is the name of time, and is an attribute of Ormusd, applied to him, because no one knew the be- ginning or end of that Lord, the Creator, or, in other words, when that Lord [the supreme God] *was created, or how long He will exist.*"

[5] "Praise the self-created firmament, the uncaused time, the air which ope- rates on high." Vend. xix. n. 44. "I praise the self-created firmament, &c." ib. n. 55. "I praise the brightly shining sky; I praise the unbegotten ["unbe- ginning" Sp.] lights, self-created." Vend. xix. 118, 19. Haug, Essays, p. 217. "I worship stars moon and sun, the unbeginning light, the set by itself, ["self- created" Sp.] and all the ["pure" Sp.] creatures of the holy spirit Ormusd." ["of Çpentomainyus, male and female, the lords of the pure." Sp.] Yaçna, i. 45. (Av. ii. p. 42, 3.) iii. 59. (Ib. p. 53.) "We praise the unbeginning lights, the unlimited." (Yç. xvii. 41. Av. ii. p. 92.) "All unbeginning lights we praise." (Yç. lxx. 45. Av. ii. p. 204.) Gâh Uzîran, 6 (Av. iii. 24.) "The un- beginning lights, which follow their own laws." Rashnu Yast, 35. (Av. iii. 111.) Siroza, 30. (Av. iii. 202.) See also Schlottm. Hiob. p. 145, 6.

[6] See below, p. 531. 535.

ship, are only a more refined form of creature-worship. They are connected with those elements, on whose harmony God has made the well-being of this order of things to depend [1]. Zoroastrism betrays its original, the Aryan creature-worship, to which has been added its characteristic Dualism.

The Zend religion is any thing but an original religion. It broke off, at some unknown time, from the religion of the Vedas in mutual and deadly hatred, which burst out into war, simultaneously with a change from the nomad to the agricultural life [2]. The adherents of the new religion continued to be fire-worshippers like the Vedists; they retained, with certain changes, much of the ancient worship [3], but they evinced their hatred of their antagonists, by employing the Vedic name for their gods generally, "*Devas,*" as the title for evil spirits [4], and making some of the gods themselves, Indra, Sarva [5], into devils. "They retained as gods, only some of the lesser deities [6]." There is no indication of any such changes on the part of the Brahmans [7]. But withal, the characteristic error

---

[1] See below, p. 530.   [2] Haug, Essays, p. 248, 9.

[3] Haug (Ib. p. 337-40.) points out "the identity of a good many terms relating to the priestly functions," "the Izeshne ceremony, as performed by the Parsee priests now," "the use of the juice of the Soma plant," "the Barsom, or bundle of twigs, used in reciting Izeshne," &c.

[4] "Deva, in all the Vedas and in the whole Brahmanic literature, is the name of the gods, who are the objects of worship among the Hindoos to the present day. In the Zend Avesta, from its earliest to its latest parts, *deva*, (modern Pers. *div*,) is the general name of an evil spirit. In the confession of faith, as recited to this day, the Zoroastrian religion is distinctly said to be vî daêvô, i. e. 'against the devas,' and one of their most sacred books is called vî-daêvô-dâta (now corrupted into Vendidâd,) i. e. 'what is given against, or for the removal of, the devas.' " Haug, Essays, p. 225, 6.   [5] Ib. p. 230.

[6] "The Devas that are not degraded to demons in the Zendavesta are mostly minor deities and personifications of nature, the natural meaning of which was not forgotten. They were not gods, but only bright poetical beings in the minds of those who took them over. Thus the Buddhists carry about the statues of Brahma, Vishnu, Siva and other gods; they tolerate them as ornaments, because they are not afraid of them." Prof. Max Müller, MS. letter to me.

[7] Prof. Max Müller kindly answered my enquiries, "I cannot agree with Haug in ascribing the later change of meaning in the Sanskrit *Asura* to a

of the Zend religion, its Dualism, was its blot from the
first. It is a mistake to represent Zarathustra as teaching "monotheism." Dualism is enunciated, in the most
distinct way, in what are held to be its oldest writings [8].

reacting influence of Zoroastrianism.—In the most sacred hymns of the Brahmans, *asura* constantly stands in the sense of 'god.' In the Brahmanas, a
new name of god springs up, *Sura*, from *suar*, 'heaven,' which has nothing
to do with *asu-ra* etymologically. But by a kind of irresistible etymological impulse, the Sanskrit language produced, in opposition to this *Sura*, a negative,
A-sura, " not-god," quite distinct in reality from the old *asu-ra*, though identical in sound. The Brahmanas are full of legends about Suras and Asuras,
but there is no trace of any Zoroastrian influence, nor do we ever meet with *one*
Asura, as in the hymns, but always with many." MS. letter.

[8] Two distinct passages occur in the Gâthâs, which are not affected by any
difference of translation.

1) " These two first-spirits, twins, are known to act of themselves,
In mind and word and act, these two, the good and the evil,
(Choose) between these two ; be doers of good and not of evil."
Gâthâ ahunavaiti, (Yaçna 30.) 3, 3. Haug, d. Gâthâs, i. p. 7. Spiegel renders ;
" These two heavenly beings, the twins, first allowed from themselves to perceive
Both, the good and the bad, in thoughts, words and works.
Rightly decided as to them the wise ; not so the unwise."

2) " So will I pronounce two first spirits of life ; Of which two the holier said
to the wicked, ["the white said to the black," Essays, p. 153]
'Do not thoughts, do not words, do not understandings, or doctrine ; do not
sayings, or ceremonies, ['actions' ib.] do not meditations, do not minds fol-
low (me)?'" Gâthâ Uçtavaiti, (Yaçna 45.) 10. 2. Haug, ii. p. 13. Spiegel ren-
ders ;
" Now will I announce the two heavenly from the world's beginning ;
Of the two the holy spake thus to the bad ;
Not our spirits, not our doctrines, not our understandings,
Not our wishes, not our speech, not our works,
Not the laws, not the souls will unite." Av. ii. p. 150.

The contrast of two primeval beings, one good, the other evil, remains in
both translations. Spiegel observes, " The term, ' twins,' applied to the two
heavenly beings, almost forces one to think of the myth as to the origin of the
two heavenly spirits, which is found among the Armenian writers, e. g. Eznik,
according to which Ahura-Mazda and Agra-mainyus are both thought of as
sons of time." (Avesta, ii. p. 119.) In Spiegel's translation, the Gâthâ Ahunav.
goes on to describe the creation by the "twins ; "

4) "As these two heavenly beings came together first to create
Life and perishableness, and how at last the world was to be ;
The Bad for the bad ; for the pure the best Spirit ;

5) "Of these two heavenly, the Bad chose the bad, (so) acting ;
The holiest Spirit (chose) the pure [neut.], and created the most firm heaven
And those who content Ahura with open acting, believing in Mazda."

A religion, starting, like this, in negatives, is not likely to have had truth unknown to other Heathenism.

Nor, in fact, is there anything peculiar in those inferior deities of the Persians, more than in those of the Vedic nature-worship of the Aryans from which some of them were taken, or those of any other polytheistic people. A genius of light[1], a genius who presides over marriage[2], a genius of the earth[3], a genius, identical with the morning wind[4], are no more like angels, than Apollo, or Juno, or Ceres, or Æolus. Yet these and the like were part of the original Zoroastrism; for, having been Vedic gods, they would not have been imported subsequently. In regard to those six beings, who, in the later books, are placed nearest to Ormusd, it is agreed that the common title, Amesha-çpentas, "holy immortals," does not occur in the oldest part of the Zendavesta[5], and that the names, whereby they are severally distinguished, occur there also as names of qualities or substances[6]. The names of three of them occur so frequently, that it is,

Haug renders these stanzas,

4) "And thence these two spirits meet together; they create the first, Existence and non-existence; and that the last should be; An evil life is to the liars, but to the truthful the best mind.

5) "Of these two spirits choose (one,) who (i. e. one of whom) is liar, doing things most wicked; (the other, doing) truth Spirit most holy. Whoso girdeth himself with very hard sling-stones (Haug, p. 103.) and they who venerate the Living-wise religiously by essential actions." Ib. p. 9.

[1] " Mithra, the Sanscrit form being Mitra." Haug, Ess. p. 230.

[2] "Aryaman, the genius Airyaman of the Zend-Avesta." ib. p. 231.

[3] " Aramati, a female genius in the Vedas, meaning 1) devotion, piety, 2) earth, is apparently identical with the archangel [!] Armaitii, which word has exactly the same two meanings in the Zend-Avesta." Ib. 231, 2.

[4] " The Vedic god Vâyu ('wind,' chiefly the morning wind) ' who first drinks the Soma at the morning sacrifice' is to be recognised in the genius Vayu of the Zend-Avesta, who is supposed to be roaming every where. (see the Râm Yasht, p. 194.)" Haug, p. 232. See Spiegel, Av. iii. xxxiv. 151 sqq.

[5] The Gâthâs. Haug noticed this, Essays, p. 220.

[6] Spiegel (Av. iii. Einl. p. viii.) owns this. Haug would make the names always appellative in the Gâthâs, except that of Armaiti; but he owns that it is most natural, in some places, to understand them to be the names of the genii. I cannot but think that he has been biassed by his wish to make out Zoroastrism to be a pure monotheism, and to gain an earlier date for the Gâthâs.

I suppose, certain that they are mentioned as living beings, although details depend upon interpretations, of which they, who have studied those poems most, are not yet agreed upon the first principles [7]. Yet taking these beings as what they became, a group of six invisible beings, they help to shew that Zóroastrism is no true Theism [8], but they do not approach to the nature or office of the holy Angels. Their character is below that of the holy Angels, as that of Ahura-mazda is below that of the Living God. They are but little removed from Ahura-mazda, are associated with him [9], and independent, in

[7] Spiegel rests chiefly on the traditional interpretation, (Av. T. iii. Vorr.;) Haug, on comparative philology.

[8] In the Behistun inscription, although Ahura-mazda is exclusively and repeatedly named, as he by whose help Darius conquered, it is twice added, "and the other gods which are." col. 4. par. 12. 4. par. 13. 2. revised in Rawl. Herod. ii. p. 612. Both Mithra and Anaitis were worshipped before this time. "Auramazda is not only called [in the inscriptions] ' the great God' (*baga*, as also in Yaçn. lxx. 1 ; and, in Yaçn. x. 10, *baghô* is certainly to be referred to Ahura,) but also ' the greatest of all gods,' (Darius inscr. H. Benfey, p. 52.) as of Mithra it is said, ' he is the most intelligent of the gods." (Mihr Y. 141.) For together with Auramazda other gods are mentioned, both generally (*uta aniyâ bagâha* Bis. iv. 61, 2.; *hadâ bagaibis* Xerxes A. 28, Ca 15, E. 18 ; *hadâ vithibis bagaibis*, Darius, H. 14, 22, 24, which signifies the patron-gods of the Achæmenidæ, the θεοὶ πατρῷοι of Xenophon,) and, in the inscriptions of Artaxerxes Mnemon, by name, Mithra and Anâhita ; whence, as has been shewn elsewhere, it cannot at all be inferred, that Artaxerxes introduced these worships, but only that he was especially devoted to them." Windischm. Zoroastr. Stud. p. 123.

[9] In the following list, I have omitted the passages which Spiegel owns to be difficult. In others, it will be recollected that almost every expression is disputed. Still any how the juxta-position remains. The references are to the sections of the Yaçna, in which the Gâthâs lie, in Spiegel's Avesta, T. ii. "*Mazda*, [i. e. Ahura-mazda, Ormusd,] *Vohumano*, *Asha* who furthereth the world, *Armaiti*, *Khshathra*," are appealed to together, Yaç. 33, 11; *Ahur. Voh. Asha, Arm.* and perhaps *Haurv.* Ib. 50, 4; *Ahur. Voh. Asha, Khsh.* are praised together, Ib. 49, 4. Else those chiefly named with *Ahura-mazda* are, *Vohumano, Asha,* and, (although less frequently,) *Armaiti.*

Vohumano is joined with *Ahuram.* 28, 1. prayed to with him and *Asha*, 34, 6. 48, 7, praised with them, 28, 3. 34, 15. 49, 7 ; the sight of them is the object of desire ; 28, 5. his *creatures* are spoken of, his works, " for those who labour with the driven cow," 34, 14. 28, 10. his goods, 31, 10. 34, 2, 45, 2. nurtured by him, 34, 3. his good dwelling, (joined with that of *Ahur.* and *Asha*,)30, 10. 32, 15. *Ahur.* has like dwelling with him and *Asha*, 43, 9. his kingdom, 33, 5. kingdoms, 45, 16, joined on to those of *Asha* and *Arm.* ib. (and perhaps 34, 11.)

great measure, of him; on the other hand, they have, each
his, or her, or its, own local office.

The six were, 1) Vohumano, (Bahman,) "the good mind,"
(neuter) which had the care of cattle; 2) Asha-vahista,
(Ardi-bihist) "the best purity," (neuter) which had the
charge of fire and what relates to it; 3) Khshathra-vai-
rya, (a neuter,) Shahrevar, which was in charge of metals
below the earth; 4) Çpenta-armaiti, a sort of female genius of the earth [1], and in charge of it; 5) Haurvatât, who
makes water to flow over the earth; 6) Ameretât, who
protected trees and fruits.   Both "are identified with the
things they protect [2]."   What have such beings as these,
mere genii, with their physical occupations, in common
with the Angels and Archangels of Holy Scripture?   So
connected are they with the things of which they are the
genii, that Spiegel says, "[3] it is a practice not unusual in

As to his personal being, *Khshathra* is said to *come* with him and *Asha*, 30, 7.
(see Haug, i. p. 105, 6.) and with him alone; 30, 8; he is said to be "given as
help" with *Asha* and *Khsh.* 29, 10.   A diligent agriculturist is said to be in the
service of *Vohum.* and *Asha*, 33, 3.

Asha invoked with *Ahura-mazda*, [in the plur.] 31, 4. with *Ahur.* [sing.]
34, 3, 4. 47, 9. 48, 6. 49, 5, with *Ahur.* and *Arm.* 50, 2. *Ahura-m.* has the same
will as *Asha*, 28, 8. 45, 18; created sacred poem in union with *Asha*, for the
cow, [earth] 29, 7.   *Zarathustra* desired of *us*, *Ahur.* and *Asha*, 29, 8. *Ahur.*
and *Asha* rule, 47, 9, are worshipped together, 28, 9. (comp. Haug) are thought
of together, 45, 17. *Asha* is joint-creator of the earth, 29, 2, has the " drujas,"
(evil genii, mostly female, Spiegel, Av. iii. p. l.) given into his hand, (30, 9.)
will slay them, 47, 1.   There is no protector save *Ahur.* and *Asha*, 49, 1. reward is asked from *Asha*, 28, 7. 47, 8. long life, 28, 6; to " obtain the cow from
Asha," 50, 4. (See also above with *Vohumano*.)

Khshathra is scarcely mentioned by himself.   See above with *Vohumano*.

Armaitis, female genius of the earth, is enthroned with *Asha*, where *Vohumano* reigns, and *Ahur.* dwells, 45, 16. she belonged to *Ahur.* (" in thee was
Armaitis, in thee was the former of the [cow] earth;" Haug, i. p. 11. 136.)
31, 9. "she gave strength to the body," (" created the body," Haug,) 30, 7. she
is invoked for "riches, blessing and the life of *Vohum.*" ("possession of a good
mind" Haug,) 42, 1. she, " the good agent, is the daughter of *Ahuram.*" 44,
11. (See also above with *Vohumano* and *Asha*.)

Haurvatât and *Ameretât*, who, elsewhere also, are almost always named together, are just named, "that *H.* and *A.* may be rulers, " 43, 17. "what *H.* and
A. have promised me;" 43, 18. " *Asha's* words" were created as help for *A.* as
a reward for *H.*" 33, 8. they come to the obedient. 44, 5.

[1] Burnouf sur le Yaçna, p. 157.   [2] Spiegel, Av. ii. p. 50.   [3] Ib. iii. p. viii.

the Zend-Avesta, that the name of the Amesha-çpenta is put for the thing entrusted to his care." "[4] Khsathra-vairya is directly called metal."

But, on the other hand, from a radical defect in heathen conception of God, they, like the gods of all heathenism, were too independent of Ahura-mazda, to have any bearing on our belief in Angels. Late books speak of them as his creatures [4], or again of him, as their father and lord, yet placing them at the same time on a level with him [5].

Any independence whatsoever of God is, of course, radically at variance with any true conception of God. God is All, His creatures nothing, save what, by His Will, they hold from Him. This truth is guarded throughout the Old Testament. The very name, "Angel," expresses, that they are "messengers" of God, a higher order of spirits, ministering, according to His Will, to the lower, man. Or, like the Seraphim, they are seen in adoring love, about His throne [6]. Whether or no all heavenly beings have, at times, any office for man, yet, no where

[4] Ib. p. x. " Khshathra we praise ; the metals we praise." Visp. n. 23. 1. Av. ii. 30. Hence the formula, " for Khsh., for the metal, for the compassion which nourishes the beggar." Sîroza, n. 4. Av. iii. 198. Yast, d. 7 Amsh. 16. p. 34. and 36. The name Kshathra vairya is even used for a "pointed metal-instrument," or "knife." Vend. ix. 21. Av. i. 164. and Spiegel's note 1. Vend. xvii. 17. Ib. 164 and note 1. So of Çpenta Armaiti (female genius of the earth,) "we praise thee, (our) dwelling, Çpenta Armaiti," Yaç. 17. 53. Av. ii. 92. So, Yaç. iii. 2. "Haurvatât and Ameretât with the well-made cow," stand for the things offered to Ahuramazda and the Amesha-çpentas. (See Spiegel, Av. ii. 50. note.) Again Haurvatât and Ameretât are identified with the things which they have in charge, in these formulæ; "For Haurvatât the lord, for the yearly good dwelling, for the years the lords of the pure, for Ameretât, the lord, for the fulness relating to the herds, for the corn for the horses ;" Yast, d. 7 Amsh. 3. Av. iii. 35. " Haurvatât the Amesha-çpenta we praise ; the yearly good dwelling we praise;" and so on, ib. p. 36. "Haurvatât and Ameretât conquer hunger and thirst." Zemyad Yast, n. 16. iii. 184. So as to Ardviçura, " I praise the water Ardviçura, the pure, the full-flowing," &c. Yaç. n. 64. Av. ii. 192. add Ormusd-Yast. n. 32. Av. iii. 32.

[5] Farv. Y. 83. " All which seven are of like mind, all seven of like speech, all seven like in acting. Like is their mind, like their word, like their action, like is their father and ruler, viz. the creator Ahuramazda." But Ahuram. is one of the " seven ;" so the words are self-contradictory as they now stand.

[6] Is. vi.

in Holy Scripture, does any, even the highest, so act, save as commissioned by God. They speak and act in His Name.

It is then a mere misnomer, that some have called the Amesha-çpentas, "Archangels," meaning to liken the Zoroastrian notion to the Christian belief[1]. They scarcely form a class by themselves; but, in any case, they are wanting in that one essential characteristic of every good creature, however exalted, that they are simply [2] *ministers* of God, *to do His pleasure.*

Then too they are, practically, not distinguishable from the other genii, who rank after them[3].

The six Amesha-çpentas have the precedence in the dry, insipid invocations of Parsism. They are invited to the sacrifice, next after Ahura-mazda[4]. They are invited before "[5] the body and soul of the" fabulous primeval "Cow," or "[6] the fire of Ahura-mazda, who comes *the readiest* of the Amesha-çpentas," &c. But practically, several of the other objects of worship or gods[6], the Izads, seem to have been thought more powerful. Of Mithra,

---

[1] "Archangel" is a title belonging to the New Testament, not to the Old. Another grave misstatement of the like sort, is the substitution of "guardian angels" for "Fravashis." The Fravashis are nothing less. They are a strange abstraction. For Ahura-mazda himself and the Amesha-çpentas also have their Fravashi. In the Vendidad, Ahura-mazda is made to say, "Praise my Fravashi, mine, Ahura-mazda's, (19. 46.) the greatest, best, most beautiful, &c. (47) whose soul is the holy word." (48) So, according to this paraphrase, the supreme god of Magism, and its "Archangels" would have their "guardian angels." This is stealing from Christianity to trick out Magism, with the view of reducing them to one level. [2] Ps. ciii. 21.

[3] "The word '*Yazata*' means properly, 'worthy of worship, worthy of sacrifice,' and must also often in the Avesta be still taken in its original meaning. The expression *bagha*, god, is probably nearly identical with it. There seems to be no very defined line of demarcation between the Amesha-çpentas and Yazatas, as, in fact, Ahuramazda himself is in some places called Yazata." Spiegel, Av. iii. Einl. xii. "*Yazatas* (now Izads) corresponds to the Vedic *Yajata*, i. e. 'a being who deserves worship'. The modern Persian *Yazdân*, 'God,' is the plural of this word Yazata." Haug, Essays, p. 175.

[4] Yaçna, i. 5. ii. iii. 3. vi. 2. vii. 1. In Yaçna, iv. 4. Çraosha is interposed before them, Av. iii. 54. In their Yast, after the two first there are interposed Airyama-ishya (the Vedic deity Aryaman, Haug, Essays, p. 221.) and Çaoka.

[5] Yaçna, i. 6.   [6] see p. 533. n. 9.

the god of light, "[7] possessor of wide plains, who has 1000 ears and 10,000 eyes," Ahura-mazda is made to say, "[8] I created him, as worthy of worship and praise as myself;" of Tistrya, the dog-star, he is made to add, "[9] as worthy to be satisfied, as upright as myself." Ahura-mazda is said to have sacrificed to Mithra[10], as also to Ardvî-çûra Anahita, too infamously celebrated as Anaitis[11], the genius of water, the fertiliser of the earth; of whom also "[12] he prayed the favour, 'grant me, O good, most beneficial Ardvî-çûra, spotless, that I may unite myself with the son of Pourashaspa, the pure Zarathustra, so that he thinks according to the law, speaks according to the law, acts according to the law.' Then Ardvî-çûra the spotless, granted to him [Ahuram.] this favour, to him who ever brings, gives, offers, sacrifices, who prayeth the givers [femin.] for a favour." Indeed, as man, in his wants, looks most to those from whom he expects most, one should think that those whose great gifts to the heroes of old who prayed to them are recited, Anaitis[13], Gosh[14] or the Cow, or Ashis-vaguhi[15], or, again, those who were held to give the gifts men which most desire, would probably be more worshipped than he, who was, in the abstract,

[7] his ordinary title. Av. iii. 79. &c. He is called "the first heavenly Yazata," Mihr Y. n. 13. iii. 81.

[8] Mihr Yast, n. l. Av. iii. 79. "to be of the same rank and dignity, (as far as worship is concerned) as I myself am." Haug, Ess. p. 183.

[9] Tistar-Yast, n. 50. Av. iii. 72.   [10] MihrY. n. 123. Av. iii. 99.

[11] Windischmann, üb. d. Pers. Anahita od. Anaitis. Munchen, 1846. 4.

[12] Aban Yast, n. 17. 18. Av. iii. 45, 6.   Spiegel says, "Here, as *often* in the Yasts, Ahura-mazda is represented as standing in need of the help of individual genii, which, taken accurately, is absurd, for they are his creatures and have received their strength from him." Ib. note.   The inconsistency could not have been, where there was any true conception of God, a real Theism.

[13] Ib. n. 21-83. 90. 97-90. 104-18. Ahura-mazda, and the old heroes and maidens sacrificed also to Ramaqâçtra (Râm Yast 2-21. Av. iii. 151-6.)   "To him sacrificed the Creator Ahura-mazda.—He begged of him this favour, Give me, O air thou that workest aloft, that I may slay among the creatures of Agramainyus, as one who to Çpentamainyus" (belongeth.) Ib. 2, 3. Spiegel says, "It almost seems as if the writer considered the air as a deity on a level with Ahuram. and so belonging to the Qadhâtas.   Otherwise, it were absurd that the creature grants his good-will to the Creator." p. 152. note.

[14] Gosh Yast, throughout, Av. iii. 74-9.   [15] Ashi Yast, n. 24-52. Av. iii. 165-8.

owned to be the supreme god.   Even Israel did so in the idolatries, into which it fell before the captivity; in Magism such idolatry was an essential part of the religion.

Accordingly we find a wide-spread worship of Anahita and Mithra, rooted in the countries of Parsism, and more popular, apparently, than that of Ahura-mazda.   In regard to Anaitis, Windischmann sums up, "[1] Anaitis had, in the midst of institutions plainly Zoroastrian and together with beings of the same religious system, a far-spread worship in Persia, Bactria, Media, Elymais, Cappadocia, Pontus, and Lydia; her temples are at Babylon, Susa, Ecbatana, Konkabar, Sardis, Hierocæsarea, and Hypæpa, in Damascus, Zela, Ariselene, an Armenian province.   Her worship was provided with priests and hieroduloi, and connected with mysteries, feasts, and unchaste ways.   The Persian Saciacs were connected with her, holy cows were dedicated to her.   Artaxerxes Mnemon first set up statues to her—thereby introducing image-worship into Persia.   The worship of an Aphrodite among the Persians, which Herodotus attests, allows us not to question its early date."   It lived on in Armenia, with that of Vahagn or Virathragna, until Armenia was converted by S. Gregory[2], and, while Ahuramazda was recognised as the creator, Anaitis was associated with him, as an equal source of the greatness of Armenia[3].

The worship of Mithra we hear of in Greek authors, from their first acquaintance with Persia.   Xenophon introduces Cyrus, swearing " by Mithra[4]."   Herodotus mentions a " Mitradates" ("given by Mitra[5]") and that,

---

[1] Windischmann, üb. Anahita, p. 19, 20.   [2] Wind. ib.

[3] "And those who are really ' makers,' thou insultest, and the great Artemis, [Anahita,] in whom the country of Armenia lives and hath life, and with her the most mighty Zeus, [Ahura-mazda,] the maker of heaven and earth, and, after him, the other gods thou hast called lifeless and speechless." Tiridates to S. Gregory, in Agathangelos Hist. of convers. of Armenia, c. 4. n. 28. Acta Sanctt. Sept. 30. T. viii. p. 335. quoted by Wind. Ib. p. 22.

[4] Cyrop. viii. 3. 53. Œcon. c. 4. n. 24.

[5] See Pott, Etym. Forsch. T. i. p. xlvii sqq. Rosen, in Journal of Education ix. p. 334. quoted by Smith, Biogr. Dict. ii. 1093.

a peasant, the herdsman of Astyages[6]; and a "Mitrobates," (probably the same name corrupted,) a Satrap under Cyrus or Cambyses[7]; a Mithridates was a trusted Eunuch under Xerxes[8]; a Mithridates accompanied Cyrus against Artaxerxes II.[9]; a Mithridates was the Satrap of Lycaonia and Cappadocia under Artaxerxes II.[10]; the ultimate founder of the kingdom of Pontus was a Mithridates, Satrap of Phrygia, under the same[11]. Then it became the name of the kings of Pontus; it occurs as the proper name in the line of the Arsacidæ, kings of Parthia[12]; a king of Media Atropatene, a king of Cappadocia, two kings of Commagene, bore the name[13]. But the corresponding title, Hormisdates, Hormisdas, "given by Ormusd," does not, I believe, occur until the revival of Magism under the Sassanidæ, when it became the name of some of their kings. One of the greatest Persian festivals, Mihragân[14], was in honor of Mithra; and while the Persian empire was still in being, "[15] the satrap of Armenia sent the king yearly 20,000 colts for the Mithriacs." Deceit against Mithra is a chief and most deadly sin. Morally, it relates to breach of promises or compacts, and is especially punished by law[16]. Yet Mi-

---

[6] Her. i. 110. Sir H. Rawl. thinks that *Atradates* in Nicol. Damasc. is the Median equivalent to it, "Atra" or "Adar" signifying the 'sun' or "fire." in Rawl. Her. i. p. 252.   [7] Her. iii. 120. 126.

[8] Diod. xi. 69.   [9] Xen. Anab. ii. 5. 9.   [10] Ib. vii. 8. pen.

[11] Ariobarzanes II. Satrap of Phrygia (Curt. ii. 6.) got possession of his *kingdom* after his death in 362. Diod. xv. 90. He himself betrayed his father Ariobarzanes. Xen. Cyrop. viii. 8. 4. See Clinton, F. H. ii. 431. ed. 2.

[12] See in Smith, Biogr. Dict. i. 354-6.

[13] See Smith, Ib. ii. 1094. *Mithrenes*, and *Mithrobarzanes* (first mentioned under Artaxerxes II. Diod. xi. 91, three others are mentioned;) *Rheomithras*, (under the same,) are other traces of the worship of Mithra. Pott also puts together, *Ithamitres*, (Her. viii. 130. ix. 102.) *Ithamatres*, (Ib. vii. 67.) *Siromitres*, (vii. 68. 79.) *Harmamithres*, (vii. 88.) *Mitraios*, (Xen. Hell. ii.1. 6.) *Mitragathes* (Æsch. Pers. 43.) *Mithraustes*. (Arr. iii. 8.9.)

[14] Hyde, De Rel. Vett. Pers. p. 245. Duris, (B.C. 320-281.) Hist. vii. (in Ath. x. 45. p. 434. Cas.) mentions the greatness of the festival. Windischm. Mithra, p. 57.   [15] Strabo, xi. 14. 9. p. 530. Cas. Wind. p. 58.

[16] The 4th Fargard of the Vendidad, which is on criminal law, assigns the punishments for "Mithra-deceit," at 300, 600, 700, 800, 900, 1000, stripes,

thra himself was held to punish it, especially in making "Mithra-deceivers," "Anti-mithras," powerless in war[1], so that the title seems very mainly to include foreign enemies, or non-Parsees[2].   Mithra is associated as the equal of Ahura-mazda[3].   "Ahura and Mithra, the two imperishable pure; and the stars, the creatures of Çpentomainyus." Not the name only of Mithra, but his relation to other gods is Indian[4], so that the mode of his worship, as well as his actual worship, must have bcén coeval with Parsism.

More remarkable still is the worship of Haoma, as identical with the Soma of the Vedas.   "[5]Soma is, in the Vedas, not only the holy sacrificial drink.   It is also itself a god.   So Haoma in the Zend-Avesta is not only a plant, but is also a mighty genius; in both, the ideas of the heavenly genius and the holy juice of the plant work marvellously into each other[6]."   Both are the causes of the birth of heroes[7]; their "gifts are immortality, firmness, health of body, long life, protection against un-

---

(Sp. Av. i. p. 93. n. 24-35.) "whereas 200 stripes are elsewhere a very great punishment, which is very seldom exceeded." Spiegel, Av. i. p. 89.

[1] Mihr, Yast n. 17. Av. iii. 83. Wind. n. 18 sqq. p. 3.

[2] Ib. 20, 21. 23. 24. 26-80.

[3] Yaç. i. 34. Av. ii. p. 40. Add Yç. ii. 44. iii. 48. "Come to our help, Mithra and Ahura, the great ones." Qarset-nyâyis. 9. (Av. iii. 2.) "M. and A. the two great, imperishable, pure, we praise." Mihr-nyâyis 3 (Av. iii. 12.) "Wherefore may these come to our help, M. and A. the great ones, yea M. and A. the great ones." Mihr Y. n. 113. (Av. iii. 97.)   [4] See Windischm. p. 54.

[5] Windischm. über d. Soma Cultus d. Arier, from Abhandl. d. K. Ak. d. Wiss. T. iv. P. 2. p. 132.

[6] W. proceeds; "The most important places on this personified Haoma are in the 9th and 10th Ha of the Yaçna, which are illustrated by striking analogies of the hymn of the Rig-Veda, hymn 91." "In early dawn came Haoma to Zarathustra, who was purifying his holy fire and repeating prayers. Z. asked him, 'What man art thou, whom, in the whole existing world, I see the noblest, on account of his immortal life?' Haoma the pure, the disease-removing, answered me; 'I am, O Z., Haoma, the pure, &c. Invoke me, holy one; drop me out to be tasted, praise me with praise, *as the pure have praised me before thee.*' Thereon said Z. 'Honor the Haoma.'" Ib.

[7] "Haoma was the cause of the birth of Jima and the blessings of his time; so Rig-veda to Soma, 'through thy guidance have our noble fathers, O glorious, obtained treasures from the gods.'" W. p. 134. "On the gifts of sons see Samoveda,(W. p. 135) Rig-veda." Ib. p. 137.

foreseen accidents[8]." "The worship is spoken of in the Avesta as præ-Zoroastrian[6]."

Yet these their gods, were in their turn, dependent on man. "It is known," says Spiegel[9], "that the genii of of the Parsees are just as much in need of men, as men of the genii. If these deities do not receive from men the prescribed sacrifices, they become powerless and unable to accomplish their duties, unless Ahura-mazda sees himself occasioned to help them in a supernatural and unusual manner. This idea occurs often enough in the Yasts[10]." And not only so, but, if the translation be correct, they needed it for themselves. Mithra's immortality depended on the sacrifices of man to him[11].

It is then a mere myth, to speak of the relative purity of early Magism, on the ground that, in five songs, consisting of not more than 404 lines of a longer and 494 of a shorter measure, which would occupy some 27 pages, there is no mention of the sacrificial rites, or of the generic names of the Amesha-çpentas or the Yazatas, when it is certain that those gods must have been always worshipped, and those offerings always made. And yet in those same songs there is the distinctest enunciation of dualism. Yet the god of dualism is, ipso facto, not less removed from the conception of the One Living God than Bel or Zeus or Jupiter or any other heathen god, with the overruling fate.

2) Then, also, in regard to the history of the two nations, however the Jewish people were seduced into the sensuality of idolatry, it is not even alleged that, in any

---

[8] "Its [the Haoma's] gifts are immortality, &c. all, traits which agree with those produced out of the Veda." W. p. 137. The parallel goes into even more detail, as of marvellous birds. Ib. p. 139.   [9] On Aban Yast, n. 9. Av. iii. p. 44.   [10] "See Yast, 8. 13 sqq. 10, 34 sqq. &c." Ib.

[11] "I am the beneficent protector of all creatures; I am the beneficent preserver of all creatures; and yet men do not sacrifice to me with named offerings, as they sacrifice to the other Yazatas with named offerings. For if men sacrificed to me with named offerings, as they do to the other Yazatas with named offerings, I should advance from the momentary, passing, limited, period, to the proper, lasting, undying, unlimited life." Mihir Yast, n. 54, 5. Wind. transl. p. 7. and n. 74. p. 9.

case before the Captivity, the sacred writers admitted any thing from profane sources. Contrariwise, on the approach of the captivity, Isaiah warned beforehand against the fundamental error of Parsism. It is in the prophecy of Cyrus by name, after the mention of the victory which God would give him, and of His call of him[1], that God immediately inculcates anew the fundamental truth, that there is no God but He Alone, and that He is the Creator of those which the Persians held to be primeval principles. [2] *I am the Lord, and there is none else ; I form the light, and create darkness ; I make peace, and create evil.* As we had no ground, from the original of Parsism, to look for any characteristic truth in it, so even beforehand we see the truth, (as it must be,) in direct antagonism to its error. The portion of Isaiah which bears upon the captivity and the deliverance from it, is full of challenges to all the objects of worship in heathenism. Jeremiah gives the Jews a Chaldee formula[3], wherewith to answer the heathen, who asked them why they did not worship their idols. Isaiah, Ezekiel, and Jeremiah denounced punishment for the worship of the heavenly influences[4]. Daniel's history is in harmony with this, that pious Jews were willing to give their lives, rather than deny God by worshipping any but Him.

I said "the sacred writers." But as to the Jewish people also, idolatries, not abstractions, were its temptations. The besetting sin of the Jews before the Captivity was idolatry. We have a long experience of their character in this, the experience of 900 years[5]. Nay we have the experience of every heathen nation. Whatever they took, they took wholly. Whether the Jews took the worship of Baal or Ashtoreth, or the Romans the Bacchanalia, or subsequently the worship of Mithra, they took the gods *as* gods. The temptation was to worship something nearer and more like themselves, from whom

[1] Is. xlv. 1-6.   [2] Ib. 6, 7.   [3] Jer. x. 11.   [4] Is. lxv. 11, 12. Jer. xliv. 15-28. Ezek. viii. 15, 16.   [5] From the Exodus to the captivity.

they hoped to gain the things of daily life, or to avoid evils, or for its sensuality. But the objects of Magian worship, under whatever name, whether Amesha-çpentas or Izeds, Anaitis or Mithra, were just as much objects of idolatry, as ever Baal or Ashtoreth had been; nay, they were the corresponding gods. The temptations to worship them were just the same. But it is not in human nature, certainly it was not in Jewish nature, to abstract the being from the object of worship. It *is* in human nature to worship an angel, if any one thought that he could obtain what he wanted, more easily than he could from God; it is *not* in human nature to form to himself, (if one so may speak,) an Angel out of a false god; to substitute a being to whom he should stand in no direct relation, from whom he had nothing to gain, for one from whom those, whom he is to have copied, thought that they gained the necessaries of life. But such, it is self-evident, is the characteristic of the Angels in the Old Testament as far as they have offices for us. Unless God made them in any case, the disclosers of His Will, or gave them an office *to* man, they were believed to be, in their offices *for* man, unknown, invisible, "ministering, spirits," doing whatsoever offices for man God willed, but not doing any thing at the request of man.

It is, again, in human nature, when it has come to see the falseness of its false worship, if it will not accept the truth, to trick out its fables anew, and form abstractions of its false gods. So did Alexandrian philosophy over-against the Gospel; so is neo-Parsism doing at this day. This it does in self-defence, over-against the truth, which it will not receive. It makes to itself as plausible a counterfeit as it can. It throws a veil over the grossness of its error, in presence of the light. But it is *not* in human nature, to adopt, in a refined form, the errors of others. Error has no intrinsic winningness for man, who was formed in the image of the Truth, Almighty God. To soften errors which he will not abandon, is a natural compromise with truth. Man's self-respect demands it of him; it is a tribute to the truth which he rejects, forced upon him by the yearnings of his nature which he stifles, and it is one of the subtlest snares of Satan.

The original error belonged to the coarser side of human nature, man's animal requirements or his passions. The refinement of his discovered error belongs to the sin of his intellectual nature, his pride. Both have their pleas. But there is no temptation to trick out or refine an error not its own. Least of all was this the character of the Jewish mind.

On the other hand, it is admitted that the Persians were, of all nations, the most impressible and the most imitative [1].   In the time of Cyrus, they had adopted religious symbols, originally Egyptian; in that of Darius, they had borrowed others from the Assyrians [2]. Herodotus says, "[3] they have learned *in addition*, to sacrifice to Urania, (i. e. Mylitta,) from the Arabians and Assyrians." Ammianus Marcellinus ascribes the Semitic admixture, which has been observed [4], to Zarathustra himself; "[5] he added many things from the secret lore of the Chaldæans." Artaxerxes II. brought in image-worship [6]. It would then be à priori probable, both from their known character and from other facts, that they would borrow from the Hebrews any thing which commended itself to them.

3) But the Zend books, which have any bearing on the revealed doctrines of the Old or New Testament, are acknowledged to be late. On the one hand, the tradition of the Parsees themselves is of a general destruction of their books under Alexander. This looks like an apology for the absence of ancient books, but is "[7] the unanimous belief of the Parsees up to this time." They give a list, moreover, of the literature, such as they allege it to have been collected in post-Christian times by the Sassanidæ, containing additions to what they suppose it to have con-

---

[1] See ab. Lect. iii. p. 129.   [2] See Sir H. Rawl. in Rawl. Herod. i. p. 270. n.
3. Layard's Nineveh, ii. c. 7.   [3] Herod. i. 131.   [4] in ZS. D. M. G.
v. 221 sqq. vi. 78 sqq.   [5] Amm. M. xxiii. 6.
   [6] S. Clem. Al. Exh. ad gentes, p. 43. Sylb.   [7] Haug, Essays, p. 124.

tained in the time of Alexander [8]. Out of twenty-one books, which they enumerate, two only have any bearing upon the books now extant [9]. They mention books on physics, law, medicine, panegyrics of men and angels, fabulous history [10], duties of their religion and morals ; but they make no mention of what is now accounted the oldest part of the Avesta [11], nor again of the modern [12], which has been mainly cited for approximations to the faith of Jews or Christians.

The question, moreover, does not depend on the date of Zoroaster, which those, who have most studied the subject, give up as a hopeless problem [13]; nor even on the age of some of the songs, or of the basis of the rules of purifying, or whether a fragment, here and there, can be recovered of ancient date. It is admitted that the books have come down by an unwritten tradition, and it is of the nature of that unchecked tradition in any human system to receive modifications, as it rolls onwards. "There are no facts," says Max Müller [14], "to prove that the text of the Avesta, in the shape in which the Parsees of Bombay and Yezd now possess it, was committed to writing, previous to the Sassanian Dynasty," which began "226, A.D." Spiegel says, " [15] Evidently very little in the writings of the Avesta, preserved to us, comes from Zarathustra himself; most comes from different and mostly late authors." " [16]The grounds for ascribing the authorship to Zarathustra are utterly untenable." Then, as to

[8] It is given by Haug, p. 125-7. It is taken from " two collections of decisions of Destoors," of which the earliest was made early in our 17th century, "about 250 years ago." Ib. 125. note.

[9] n. 20. the Vendidad, " on removal of uncleanness," and n. 1. their worship of the Yazatas or gods. [10] "11. Vishtasp Nosk, 60 ch. (in Alexander's time only 10.) " On the reign of king Gustasp and his conversion to the religion, and its propagation by him throughout the world. 13. Safand, miracles of Zoroaster, &c." [11] " The Yaçna (Izeshne) is not mentioned at all, or the Visparad." Haug, p. 128. The Yaçna contains the Gâthâs and the Yaçna Heptanhaiti, written in the oldest dialect. Ib. p. 161. [12] The Bundehesh. See above p. 512, 13. [13] As Lassen, " It will never be possible to fix his date." Ind. Alt. i. 754. [14] On the Veda and Zend-Avesta, p. 24.

[15] Avesta, p. i. 13. quoted by Hengst. Christ. iii. 2. p. 75. [16] Id. i. 54. ib.

its borrowing from others, Spiegel says; "[1] In this historical time, the Persians have certainly borrowed manifoldly from their more cultivated Semitic neighbours." He lays it down as a rule; "If we find any view in the later books, contradicting the clear letter of the earlier, we may unhesitatingly assume it to be later; if it clearly sounds like any foreign doctrine, we may mostly assume that it was borrowed." Burnouf also thought that "[2] the Zend fragments, which have reached us under the name of Zendavesta, are subsequent to the mixture of the Babylonian worship and of the ancient religion of the people of Aria, and that they were collected in a country where this mixture prevailed."

The analogy fails in every way. 1) There is no evidence, that the books, upon the extent of which Haug lays stress, ever existed. If they ever existed, many of them are on secular subjects and have no relation to Magism. 2) A tradition, resting on no written document, as to the titles, subjects, number of chapters of books, said to have existed some 2000 years before, more or less, would not be listened to, except to prop up a system. 3) The mere statement of the number of chapters, of which 21 books exist, does not necessarily involve the size of those books. The chapters, said by the Destoors to have existed before Alexander, amount to 626. The Hebrew Bible, as stated in the preface to our English Bibles (which counts the Psalms as so many chapters,) consists of 921 chapters; the New Testament, of 260: the Apocrypha, of 172. 4) The tradition contradicts that of the destruction of the books by Alexander, since this states, of four of the books, that some seven-ninths were added to them, after Alexander.

---

[1] Id. i. 374. ib.

[2] Yaçna, p. 351, referred to ib. Haug alone imagines them earlier, building on a fanciful analogy with " the sacred literature of the Jews," which, " to be dated from the earlier times of Moses (between 1300 and 1500, B. C.) down to the close of the Talmudic literature 960 A. D. [rather, about 500 A. D. See Wolf, Bibl Hebr. ii. p. 658 sqq.] comprises a space of about 2,400 years." (Essays, p. 129.) Had Haug known the Talmud, he could scarcely have placed it and the Old Testament together.

This relates to the facts. But in matter of principle,
5) There is neither developement nor corruption in the
Avesta, for all alike is corrupt; dualism, (which is inconsistent with the idea of God,) and the worship of inferior gods, tainted it from the first. 6) It has no history.
In the O. T. there is a continual history of the revelation for above 1000 years, during which revealed truth
was enlarged. But the length of time was no necessary
condition of the maturing of the revelation. When our
Lord came, fuller truth was revealed in less than four
years from the beginning of His Ministry to the Day of
Pentecost.

Amid this radical and essential difference between the
error and the truth, it is almost inconceivable that people
should have repeated so often and so long, that the Amesha-çpentas were the originals of the Archangels; and
that, on such grounds as these; 1) and chiefly, the number.
If the supreme god of Parsism is counted in with his
supposed creatures, the number seven is made out, (as it is
in some of the Yashts [3],) but only so. People have then
their choice, either to give up this point of the similarity
of numbers, or to own that the Persians made their supreme god, only first of a class, "primus inter pares."
And, in the book of Tobit, it is mentioned that there are
seven angels, (it is not said, "Archangels,") " [4] which present the prayers of the saints and which go in and out
before the Holy One[4]." To "present the prayers of the
saints" is no office of the Amesha-çpentas; nor will it be
readily believed that the number "seven" will identify a
system in which the creator is counted with his creatures, with one, in which the highest creatures appear as
servants in presence of their Lord.

2) In each there is to have been a "heavenly Council,"
in which God or Ahuramazda are to have deliberated
with creatures. There is no trace of any such council in
Parsism; in the Old Testament, it is rejected as a thing

<hr>

[3] Yasht 3, 26. Yasht 4, title.   [4] xii. 15.

abhorrent from faith. [1]*Who hath known the mind of the Lord? or who, being His counsellor, hath taught Him?*

3) They are to have had the common offices of "watching from the height over the soul[2]." In regard to the Amesha-çpentas, this is one of the exploded mistranslations of Anquetil. They have no moral office for the soul of man. In revelation, the Archangels have not this office assigned unto them, nor have any angels, in this sense, the title of "[3] Watchers."

Such being the sum of what is alleged as to doctrine, we may turn to morals.

v. The charges in regard to asceticism condemn prayer, fasting, the study of Holy Scripture, or any belief that alms, (given, of course, rightly,) are of any benefit to the soul of the giver. Of course, they condemn equally the Gospel and our Lord. It is however also contrary to facts, that these acts of religion belonged to later times only.

v. 1. Fasting, in the Pentateuch, is expressed by the words, "to afflict the soul." The great day of atonement was a sabbath of "affliction of the soul." Sin was not to be forgiven without sorrow for sin, as expressed by self-affliction. God commanded them to rest from work, and to afflict their souls by fasting. [4]*And it shall be a statute for ever unto you : in the seventh month, on the tenth of the month, ye shall afflict your souls and do no work at all :—for in that day he* [the high-priest] *shall make an atonement for you, to cleanse you ; that ye may be*

---

[1] Is. xl. 13.

[2] Lengerke, (p. 165, nearly translated by Dav. iii. 178,) says, " Who, by the holy watchers, is not reminded of the Amshaspands of the Zend-Avesta, whom, issuing from the seven planets, they honored as the first seven spirits or intelligences of heaven, to whom Ormuzd entrusted the oversight of the universe, [if they are seven, Ormuzd is one] who watch out of the height over the soul? " Kleuker's Zend-Avesta, ii. 257." " Hence the original is Parsism," adds Davidson. Anquetil's version, translated by Kleuker, is proverbially incorrect. It ran ; " O that they may watch out of the height over the soul, which strives after purity of heart, after purity of word, after purity of deed, which thinks of nothing but Garotman." "Yesht Farvardin, 23 Carde." In Spiegel's translations it is ; " Of which [the frawashis or spirits of the six Amesha-çpentas] the one sees the soul of the other, how it thinks on good thoughts," &c.

[3] See above p. 522.　　　　　　　　　　　　　　[4] Lev. xvi. 29-31.

clean from all your sins before the Lord. It is a sabbath of rest unto you, and ye shall afflict your souls, by a statute for ever. The self-affliction or fast, and the abstinence from work, were alike sanctioned by that solemn penalty[5]; *he shall be cut off from among his people; the same soul will I destroy from among his people.*

This fast alone was prescribed in the law; but it stood connected with the most solemn service of the whole year. Yet voluntary vows of self-affliction were so far regulated, that women's vows of such self-affliction might be annulled by their fathers before, or by their husbands after, marriage[6], when first they knew of the vow. Else, to prevent tampering with such vows, the penalty was annexed[7], *he shall bear her iniquity.* The vow of self-affliction, made by a man or a widow or one divorced[8], stood. We have accounts of such public and severe fastings before God from morning to evening, after the defeats at Ai[9] and at Gibeah[10], and in hope of deliverance from the Philistines, under Samuel at Mizpeh[11]; and in the mourning [12]*for Saul and Jonathan and the people of the Lord,* after the defeat at Gilboa. The men of Jabesh, when they buried the bones of Saul and his sons[13], *fasted seven days.* David fasted[14], in the hope that God might spare the child of his sin; Ahab fasted[15], and God deferred the temporal evil, for this temporary humiliation. Joel, as a pattern for all days of public calamity, bade, [16]*sanctify ye a fast.* [17]*Jehoshaphat proclaimed a fast throughout all Judah,* on the conspiracy of the neighbouring nations against it. Private, and that, severe fasting, is mentioned in the Psalms, as part of religious humiliation. [18]*I humbled my soul with fasting;* [19]*I wept and chastened my soul with fasting;* [20]*my knees are weak through fasting.* The repeated forty-days fasting of

---

[5] Ib. xxiii. 29, 30.　　[6] Num. xxx. 3-8. 13.　　[7] ver. 15.

[8] xxx. 2, 9.　　[9] Josh. vii. 6.　　[10] Judg. xx. 26.　　[11] 1 Sam. vii. 6.

[12] 2 Sam. i. 12.　　[13] 1 Sam. xxxi. 13.　　[14] 2 Sam. xii. 16—22.

[15] 1 Kings xxi. 27.　　[16] Joel i. 14. ii. 15.　　[17] 2 Chron. xx. 3.

[18] Ps. xxxv. 13.　　[19] Ib. lxix. 10.　　[20] Ib. cix. 24.

Moses [1] and that of Elijah [2], (images of that of our Lord,) were supernatural. A public fast was proclaimed probably in sorrowful memory of a conquest of Jerusalem by Nebuchadnezzar [3], even in the reign of the godless Jehoiakim. God accepted the fasting, humiliation, repentance of the Ninevites [4]. Ezra *proclaimed a fast* [5], in order to obtain a safe return for the people with him. Nehemiah *fasted and prayed before God* [6], when he desired to gain permission to restore Jerusalem. The ungodly had to pay this tribute to truth, masking their wickedness with a religious observance; as when they proclaimed a fast, to colour the conspiracy against Naboth [7], or fasted to *smite with the fist of wickedness* [8].

The very fact, that the prophets had to rebuke hypocritical fasting as well as hypocritical worship, shews how deep hold it had upon the people. Pharisaism is faith without love, and so is the product of human nature, not of one time only. It deludes itself and others with that which is in high repute. The prophets undervalue not (how should they?) even outward observances sanctioned by God. They condemn only the body without the soul of fasting: abstinence from food, in order to colour, either to the sinner himself or to others, indulgence in sin; fasting, which is " an image of famine."

But what is this amount of fasting, which is to be a characteristic of a later date? Literally this, that on two great public occasions,—the first, the approaching close of the 70 years of captivity, the 2nd, the hindrances to the rebuilding of the temple interposed by the councillors of Cyrus,—Daniel fasted, or abstained from pleasant food. On these occasions he did what Joel bade to be done, in times of trouble, what so many had done before him: he added outward expressions of sorrow, partly the natural, partly the prescribed accompaniments of grief. [9]*I set my face unto the Lord God, to seek by prayer and supplications, with fasting and sack-*

---

[1] Ex. xxxiv. 28. Deut. ix. 9, 18.   [2] 1 Kings xix. 8.   [3] Jer. xxxvi. 9. see ab. p. 399.   [4] Jon. iii. 5.   [5] Ezr. viii. 21, 23.   [6] Neh. i. 4.
[7] 1 Kings xxi. 9, 12.   [8] Is. lviii. 4.   [9] Dan. ix. 3.

cloth and ashes. On the second occasion, he was in sorrow for *three weeks*[10], lengthening out the period of the *bread of affliction*[11] of the Passover, which he could not celebrate, into three times its wonted length. For seventy years, he had longed for the promised restoration of his people from captivity. His life had been prolonged beyond man's ordinary term, that he might see it. And now, the rebuilding of the temple, the centre and condition of their public worship, the bond of their unity[12], was hindered[13]. Who, that had a heart, would not mourn? Daniel mourned in earnest. Like persons in deep grief, he did what would maintain life, but put away all pleasant things. *[14]I ate no pleasant bread, neither came flesh nor wine in my mouth, neither did I anoint myself at all.* A person must be very fond of good food, or not know what sorrow is, who counts *this* Pharisaism. God saw otherwise. He did not at once remove the hindrance; but He comforted Daniel and his people by foreshewing to them His Providence over them in future times of trouble. *[15]From the first day that thou didst set thine heart to understand, and to chasten thyself before thy God, thy words were heard, and I am come for thy words.* Daniel humbled himself before God; and God, as He did so often in the times of old, accepted the humiliation. What is in common with all times before Daniel, can be no proof that the book is later than Daniel.

v. 2. In like way as to prayer. Prayer being the voice of the creature to the Creator in its needs, something had to be found, characteristic of the prayer of Daniel. The prayers of Daniel are mentioned on four occasions 1) when his life was in peril, and God, on his prayer, made known to him Nebuchadnezzar's dream[16]; 2) that he persevered in praying to God, as aforetime, when forbidden by Darius, on which occasion it is mentioned that his habit was to pray three times in the day; and that 3, 4) he prayed earnestly, with fasting, on the two occasions

---

[10] Ib. x. 2.   [11] Deut. xvi. 3.   [12] Ps. cxxii. 3, 4.
[13] Ezr. iv. 5.   [14] Dan. x. 3.   [15] Ib. 12.   [16] Dan. ii. 19.

above mentioned.   On three of these occasions, the real objection is to the supernatural, that, "[1] upon his prayer revelations were made to him."   But Daniel did not ask for them, except on one occasion, to save his life and the lives of his companions.   Any how, this is nothing new, nothing late.   The whole attitude of prophets was that of watchers, men standing on their watch, as Habakkuk describes himself, [2] *I will stand upon my watch, and set me upon the tower, and will watch to see what He shall say unto me.—And the Lord answered me, and said, write the vision, and make it plain upon tables, &c.*   What occurs in Habakkuk cannot be a characteristic of a later date than that of Daniel.   Granted the supernatural in the abstract, that God does make revelations to His creatures, it is in harmony with the whole relation of the creature to the Creator, that the creature should ask for what the Creator gives.   God doubtless suggested to Daniel the prayer which He willed to grant.   Our Lord says of one sort of possession, [3] *This kind goeth not out, but by prayer and fasting.*   On earnest self-afflictive prayer alone, Jesus said that His Apostles should be able to free these sufferers by miraculous cure.   What is there incredible that God should reveal the future to Daniel on self-afflictive prayer, when He made self-afflictive prayer a condition of the exercise of miraculous powers?   It would of course, be presumption and fanaticism for man to ask for revelation or miraculous powers, without some secret inspiration of God.   But it is "begging the" whole "question," to assume that Daniel's prayer, that God would make known to him the dream which was to save his life, was not suggested by Him Who suggests all good thoughts, and Who, the history tells us, heard it.   *The* objection is to the supernatural in itself; one objection must not be made into two.   An objection to all revelation must not be made into a specific objection to the genuineness of the book of Daniel.   Prayer, such as Daniel's, belonged to the days of living faith, not to the life-

<hr>

[1] Leng. p. lxxii.   [2] Hab. ii. 1, 2.   [3] S. Matt. xvii. 21.

less routine of the later Pharisaism, which, content with its outward soulless round of observances, needed, as it thought, nothing of God, but [4] *thanked* Him, *that* it was *not as other men are.*

The next charge relating to Daniel's habit of prayer, which is to be of Parsee origin, I may just add that abstinence, such as Daniel, on two occasions, associated with prayer, is among the Parsees accounted a sin, contrary to the first principles of their dualism [5].

v. 3. Prayer "[6]three times a day, " however, is to "point to a time at which religious ideas had penetrated out of India into the neighbouring countries to the West." Nay, a learned Jewish rationalist held that, apart from that which is the point at issue, whether the minute prophecies in the book were of God or were forgeries after the event, "[7]of

---

[4] S. Luke xviii. 11.

[5] " Almsgiving too, [i. e. to the good, *not* to sinners,] is a pious duty of the Parsees: contrariwise, all self-affliction and fasting is forbidden, in strict contrast to the usages of the surrounding populations, Indians, Mendæans, Harranians,&c. This antagonism to self-affliction is very intelligible from the whole Parsee view of nature, according to which it could be as little meritorious to afflict *one's-self,* as any other being of the good creation." Spiegel, Av. ii. p. lviii.   " If you feed the hungry out of piety, you will gain great merit, if only they, who eat of thy food, be of good name, not sinners." Sadder, p. xxi. quoted ib. "You must beware of fasting ; for to eat nothing from morning to evening is not good in our religion. Our fast, each month and year, is, that we should not have even the least sin." Ib. p. xxv. ib.   [6] Herzfeld, (früh.) Gesch. Isr. 1827. Exc. 2. p. 295. translated by Dav. iii. 179.

[7] I see that Herzfeld unsaid this in his later history. He had said l. c. " Of other traces of a date so late, which people hold that they have found in these chapters, I regard one only as perfectly valid ; the prayer three times a day points to a time, &c." (as in text.)   In his later work, 1863, Gesch. Isr. ii. 191, he gives up this point altogether ; " I will not maintain, that Egyptian or Indian influence occasioned the Jews to pray three times a day ; but I conjecture that, in many places in the East and so in Judæa too, the custom of praying, by preference, at dawn, at midday, and at sunset, as being the most marked times in the day, originated in the mere aspect of nature ; as also, later, Julian recommends (Opp. p. 302) to pray three times a day, or, at least, morning and evening, according to which he took doubtless midday as the middle time of prayer, and so, according to Robinson, [ii. 282.] now too the Samaritans pray, morning, midday, and evening, on their sabbaths, festivals, and new-moons. Although then, even in the ante-Maccabee times, the morning and evening prayer had, more and more, in the soul of worshippers, grown into one with the morning and evening sacrifice, yet pious individuals still retained the custom to pray at midday also, and ' the men of the stations' (Maamad)

all the traces of such late date, which people will have it, that they have found in the chapters, this one alone altogether bears testing." Indeed? Prayer at morning and evening is the dictate of nature itself. To Israel these seasons were marked by the morning and evening sacrifice. Is it then necessary to have recourse to India, to suggest to the pious in Israel, the habit of praying to Him on Whom they knew that their being hung, Who had revealed Himself to them, as the Hearer of prayer[1], at some set time, a resting-place in all those long hours between morning and evening? Our proverbs tell us, "what may be done at any time, is done at no time." A fixed time of prayer is, as every one who has tried it knows by experience, a fresh centre from which other prayer ramifies. It would rather be a matter to be proved, that the pious in Israel did *not* use fixed prayers three times in the day, than that they did. They themselves say that they did. Rationalists, like other romancers, "ought to have good memories." Daniel's praying three times a day, is to be a proof that the writer had learned his duties to God from the Parsees.

From whom then did David learn them? Psalm lv. whose words typically prophesy of Judas in whom that treachery culminated, describes in the first instance the relation of Ahitophel to David. The Psalm is very individual. It was written in the midst of a secret conspiracy in Jerusalem against the subject of the Psalm; and in that conspiracy one was chief, his once smooth-tongued friend, with whom he had [2]*taken sweet counsel* and *walked unto the house of God as friends.* No situation in

adopted it for the weekdays." In another place, again, he leaves it open ; " Pious people especially prayed at that time a midday-prayer too. This custom comes either from without ; for both the Egyptian and the Indian religions prescribed the *worship of the* rising, culminating, setting *sun,* or it had its birth on Jewish soil out of the like (!) desire to distinguish by a pious employment, not only the sunrise and sunset, but also the next most marked time of the day." Ib. p. 136. So the custom, which was first to be clearly derived from India, and so of a date later than Daniel's, it is conceded, might be Egyptian, or, (which of course it was,) the worship of Jewish piety. In ii. 185, he speaks of the custom, as, "*certainly* much earlier." See p. 553. n. 9.

[1] Ps. lxv. 2, &c.   Ps. lv. 14.

the Old Testament agrees so well with this, as his, to whom the title ascribes the Psalm, David. It is a kindred Psalm to the xlist, also ascribed to David, written in like way in a period of conspiracy, in which alone, besides, is that trait of the once [3] *mine own familiar friend, in whom I trusted, which did eat of my bread, who magnified himself against me.* Both fall in with the conspiracy of Absalom; and Psalm xli, in that it speaks of David's sickness [4], fills up his history in Samuel, and explains how Absalom could charge his father with negligence, and so openly court the people who came to the king for judgment [5]. When he threw off the mask, he sent at once for Ahitophel [6], implying thereby the previous understanding between them. In that sickness the treacherous friend availed himself of his nearness and access, to spread evil reports as to David [7]. But since the Psalm, as we have reason to think, is David's, we have a trace of that expression of devotion, so natural to those who have devotion, prayer between morning and evening, and, according to the letter of the words, at that same time which became the fixed hour of prayer, halfway on the course from morning to evening, midday.

By a happy forgetfulness, some Rationalists, at least, did not remember the bearing of this Psalm upon the argument as to the book of Daniel; and so one [8] conjectured that Jeremiah wrote it; another [9], that it, with

[3] Ps. xli. 9. [4] Ib. 8. [5] 2 Sam. xv. 2-6. [6] Ib. 12. [7] Ps. xli. 7. [8] Hitzig.

[9] Ewald. Herzfeld's opinion as to the time "when the pious in Israel began to pray three times in the day," was changed apparently by this Psalm. In his last work, he says, " In Dan. vi. 11. prayer three times in each day is ascribed to Daniel. In itself indeed, this statement only proves that, at the time when it was written down, viz. at the beginning of the Maccabee times, pious individuals were wont to pray three times a day. Yet, on account of Ps. lv. 18, this custom seems certainly to have been much earlier. In like way Aristeas, about 80, B.C., relates, that the 70 translators went to their work of translating, ' after having washed their hands and prayed after the custom of all Jews.' The incidental character of this notice implies a very extensive use of the daily morning prayer. But if it is improbable, that even a single man should for years pray day by day at a fixed hour, without such prayer becoming, in consequence, fixed and formularised within a short time, it is simply impossible that prayers should be extemporised three times every day by many individuals and *perhaps for centuries.*" Gesch. Isr. 1863. ii. 185.

ten other Psalms, was written by some unknown author in the last ten years before the destruction of Jerusalem ; another [1] referred it to an early period in David's life ; and so on [2].

But what again are the prayers, what is that habit of praying, from which the Jews are to have learned to pray a third time in the day ?   Rationalists could, I hope, not make the charge, if they looked into the facts.   The Parsee-worship was a worship, not *at* only, but *of* the *five* portions into which they divided night and day.   It was part of that large worship of nature, which was the sin wherewith Israel was infected before the Captivity, for which it was punished, from which it was recovered. Time, in its grand course, containing within it all which receives being and passes away, the most spiritual of the unintelligent creatures of God, and, in its ceaseless flow, the nearest image of His own eternity, was, in all its parts, an object of Parsee-worship.

 "Uncaused time," (as they called it, asserting thereby an existence independent of God;) was too abstract a thought to enter much into the worship of a worshipper of nature.   The idolater worships chiefly what is, he supposes, useful to him, those operations or creatures of God, which touch his being most nearly.   "Uncaused time," then, was invoked but rarely.   More often, "time of the long periods," i. e. the time which envelopes the history of man and his future destiny in this world, the lifeless image of the all-embracing Providence of God, corresponding to the "fortune" or "fate" of more ab-

---

[1] Paullus, Colenso, Pent. ii. p. 285, 6. Davidson too does not count it post-Davidic, ii. 260.

[2] Hupfeld, (Ps. T. iii. p. 56, who seems to have no definite opinion as to its date,) will have it, that "evening, morning, and noonday, only describe the day in its most prominent turning-points," and so, that it means, "the whole day through."   But then, it means more than morning and evening, and it evinces, at least, a habit of praying more than twice in the day only.   It were an odd argument, that "evening, morning, noonday," do *not* mean the three periods of set prayer in the day, which the words describe, in the order of the Jewish day, beginning with the evening ; and that the less definite "three times in the day," does so precisely describe them, that people must have recourse to the Indian worship of the sun to explain it.

stract systems, according as they retained more or less
of the expression of the belief in God, the Ruler of all.
But nearer still to the agriculturist, to whom the cultivation of the earth was a central religious duty[3], were the
seasons and portions of the day, with their continual influences.   The portions of the day, five or four according
to the season of the year, each in union with its own set
of gods, celestial or terrestrial, among whom the operations in nature were mostly distributed, were daily objects
of Parsee-worship[4].   Strange and melancholy corpse of

[3] See e. g. in Haug, Essays, p. 141, 144, 146, 148, 154, 156, 7, espec. Vend.
Farg. iii. 24-33. "on the holiness of agriculture." Ib. p. 206-7.

[4] "Especially used is the invocation of the several portions of the day, and
of great importance in the daily worship. They are called Gâhs. There are five
of these, (in winter, four only.) 1) *Ushahina*, morning, from midnight till the
stars disappear; 2) *Hâwani*, from sunrise to midday; 3) *Rapithwina*, from
midday to the beginning of evening twilight; 4) *Uzayéirina*, from the beginning of the twilight till the stars become visible; 5) *Aiwiçrûthrema*,
from the time when the stars become visible, to midnight. The invocation
of the times of day are found especially in the first chapters of the Yaçna and
in the pieces, called Gâhs. In union with the times of day, commonly some
other deities are also invoked, which are accounted their helpers and protect-
ors: viz. a heavenly genius, and then two others, who, it appears, have to
work in the world, and are not further named. 1) In union with *Ushahina*,
Çraosha appears, as heavenly watcher; then Berejya and Nmânya, of whom
the first, according to later authorities, has to watch over the growth of corn;
while Nmânya, to judge from his name, must look to the growth of families." [Yç. i. 20-2. ii. 26-8. iii. 34-6. iv. 25-7. vi. 18-20. vii. 26-28. Qarsetnyâyis
n. 3. Av. iii. 10.   Rashnu and Arstat are, I suppose, to be added to the gods
presiding over this part of the day, because their names occur in each place at
this, which, in that order, is the last of the times of the day, and before the
invocations of the monthly festivals. i. 23. iii. 29, 30. iii. 37. iv. 28. vi. 21, 2. vii.
29.]   "2) The superintendent of the time *Hâvani* is Mithra; with him is united Çavaghi, the protector of the herds and Vîçya the protector of the clans,
[Yç. i. 7-9. ii. 13-15. iii. 21-3. iv. 13-5. vi. 4-6. vii. 13-5. lxv. 4-6.]   3) With
Rapithwina, Asha-vahista and the fire [son of Ahuramazda Yç. i. 12.] stand
in connection; of earthly deities, Frâdat-fshu, the multiplier of cattle, and
Zantuma, the protector of societies. [Yç. i. 10-12. ii. 16-18. iii. 24-6. iv. 16-8.
vi. 8-10. vii. 16-8.]   4) *Uzayéirina* has as his protector Apanmnapât, the na-
vel of the waters: (according to glosses, the mountain Arburj,) [or Alburg:]
co-operating in the world are Frâdat-vîra, the preserver of men, and Daqyuma,
the protector of districts. [Yç. i. 13-15. ii. 19-22. iii. 27, iv. 19-21. vi. 12-4. vii.
19-21.]   5) *Aiwiçrûthrema* is placed under the care of the Frawashis of the
pure; with them cooperate Verethraghna, 'victory' ["the Indian Vritahâ,"
Haug, Ess. p. 244.] and Vanainti, 'smiting,' from above; and of terrestrial
deities, Frâdat-viçpanm-hujyâitis," 'the complete good condition,' and Zara-

the living belief in the ever closely-present Omnipresence of God, Who, the Psalmist knew, [1]*hast known my sitting down and my uprising, hast understood my thought afar off. My path and my lying down hast Thou sifted, and all my ways Thou hast been acquainted with.* [2]*In whose hand is the soul of every living thing, and the breath of all mankind.*

A worship *of* the portions of the day has no connection with a worship *at* given seasons of the day. No one would venture to connect the morning and evening sacrifice, which, from the giving of the law, was part of the daily worship of Israel, with the worship of the sun, which that same law strictly forbade.

Granted that the worship of the god of fire, three times in the day, was, of old, a part of the Parsee, as it certainly was of Vedic idolatry [3]. The first mention of any such worship [4] among the Parsees occurs indeed in a book [5],

thrustrotema, the protector of priests." [Yç. i. 16-19. ii. 23-5. iii. 30-3. iv. 22-4. vi. 15-7. vii. 22-5.] Spiegel, Av. iii. p. xl, xli.

[1] Ps. cxxxix. 2, 3, &c.   [2] Job xii. 10.

[3] "The following hymn (in Rig-veda iii. 28. 1) to *Agni*, (fire,) was pointed out to me by Prof. Max Müller, as translated in his "history of ancient Sanskrit literature." (p. 492. ed. 1.) *Agni* was a *god*, created by Brahmah. (Ib. 452, 2.) I give the hymn in illustration of the character of the worship. "Agni, accept our offering, the cake, O Jâtavedas, at the *morning libation*, thou rich in prayer. The baked cake, O Agni, is prepared for thee alone indeed; accept it, O youngest of all the gods. Agni, eat the cake, offered to thee *when the day is over*, thou art the son of strength, stationed at the sacrifice. At the *midday libation*, O Jâtavedas, accept here the cake, O sage! Agni, the wise do not diminish at the sacrifices the share of thee, who art great. Agni, as thou lovest at *the third libation* the cake, O son of strength, that is offered to thee, therefore, moved by our praise, take this precious oblation to the immortal gods to rouse them. Agni, thou who art growing, accept, O Jâtavedas, the offering, the cake, at the *close of day.*"

[4] Haug introduces mention of the prayers, said five, or three, times in the day, into two neighbouring places of the Gâthâ Uçtavaiti. The first stands in his Essays, p. 151. In his text, as translated by himself, there is no mention of either. "What soul, (what guardian angel) may tell me good things, to perform five times (a day) the duties which are enjoined by thyself, thou Wise! and to recite those prayers, which are communicated for the welfare *of all beings* by the good mind? What good intended for the increase of life is to be had, that may come to me." The basis of this, in his own Latin translation which was meant exactly to represent the original, and in his German placed in the order of the Latin, is, "to remind me, what is thy doctrine, (ratio,) O Wise, and what the advancement promised (dicta) by the good

written after the revival of Magism by the Sassanidæ[6],
and so, long after our Lord.   Yet it is probable that this

mind, and what true things of life exist to possess them, what mind shews
(edicit) (good,) that it may approach." Die Gâthâs Yç. 44. n. 8. T. ii. p. 9. 43.

The place into which he introduces the prayer three times in the day, occurs
three stanzas earlier in the same poem.   His literal translation is, "Who
(created) what morning, noon-day, and night, which *are inventresses of
things*," ["*remind of his duties*" Germ. tr.] "to him who has a divine revelation." [Lat. Germ. "the priests." Essays, p. 150.] Die Gâthâs Yç. 44. n. 5.
T. ii. p. 9. 43.   In his notes, "inventresses of things to him who hath a divine
revelation," is expanded into, "which ever remind *the wise* of his duties;
i. e. which through their continued even changes define the different duties
and activities of the wise, i. e. of the priest, that he bring the offerings at the
right time, and at the right time sing praises to the honor of God." Ib. p. 41.
Granted, that "inventresses of things" could mean "reminding of duties,"
there is nothing to limit the expression to these any more than to other
duties of the day.   Spiegel renders the first,

> "This would I ask thee, tell me rightly, O Ahura.
> Who has, goodworking, made the light as the darkness?
> Who, goodworking, sleep and watching,
> Who the dawns, the middays, the nights,
> (Who) him who thinks on the measures of the law?"
> The second, "This would I ask, &c.
> Thy five fold doctrine, O Ahura,
> The prayers, for which thou art asked by Vohumano, (man)
> The purity, which in the world is perfectly to be known,
> How can my soul enjoy these goods, (and) obtain them?"

He observes, "what the fivefold things are, spoken of here, cannot be said."
Av. ii. 147.

[5] "The Mînôkhired prescribes to pray to the sun three times in the day, to the
moon and the fire Behrem and Adarô (Aderân?) at daybreak and midday.   The
more modern practice is commonly to pray the Nyâyish of the sun four times
in the day, and that of the moon thrice only in the month, when the moon
waxes, and in the middle of the month, and when it wanes." Spiegel, iii. li.

[6] "I account the Mînôkhired one of the most important works from the 2nd
period of Parsism." Spiegel, Tradit. Schr. d. Pars. p. 135. "On the ground
of language one must be inclined to assign it a comparatively higher age, under the rule of the Sassanidæ.   The book contains no historical points; yet
from some expressions I think myself justified in inferring that the book belongs to the rule of the Sassanidæ.   Kings are often mentioned in the work.
'It is most useful to kings to consult with intelligent persons.' 'A good
king takes care that the land is cultivated, the poor protected, right hereditary
custom preserved.   For the good mazdayaçn faith he gives his life, and if
any departs from the path of the Yazatas, he has him seized and brought back
to the right way.'   Such a picture seems to me to belong only to a ruler at a
time when the religion of Zarathustra was still supreme in Eran.—He mentions wheat as the chief corn, which a Parsee, living in India, certainly would

idolatry, having been part of the Vedic worship, was part of the original Zoroastrism, having, with the rest, been retained rather than subsequently adopted in it. The fact, however, that the Parsees, of old, did perform the libations thrice a day is denied by one who identifies the Parsee Homa ceremony with the *Soma libation*, or *Savana* of the Indian worship[1]. To us it is indifferent. For what has such idolatrous ritual to do with the private prayers of Daniel? The Parsee worshipped the creature; the Hebrew, the Creator; the old Vedic worship was a libation to the god of fire, in reference to the rising, meridian, and setting sun; Daniel's prayer was without ritual, without the Temple, amid suspended sacrifice, in his secret chamber, to the One Omnipresent, Invisible, God. His worship was as far removed from that of the Parsee, as God is above His unintelligent creation. Of simple *prayers* three times in the day, apart from ritual, no mention, I am informed, occurs in the Institute of Manu; the first mention of *these* prayers in Indian books is in a book whose earliest date is two centuries after our Lord[2].

v. 4. Lastly, Daniel's advice to Nebuchadnezzar is to

not have lighted on." Spiegel, Trad. Sch. p. 137. "Also the doctrine of the heavenly wisdom, so prominent in the book, and its contact with the ideas of Western Asia in the first centuries after Christ, speak for an early date of the book." Id. Ib.

[1] For the third, or evening oblation, there was no room in the Parsee ritual, because no sacrificial rites are allowed to be performed at evening or night time." Haug, Essays, p. 239.

[2] Dr. Aufrecht, with his wonted kindness, wrote for me the following statement on the times of prayer among the Hindus, (as distinct from the libations or Savanahs above mentioned.) "The term for *twilight* in Sanskrit is *sandhyá*. In this meaning it occurs already in Vedical books, and, as natural, very often in the Dual. As it was enjoined on every Hindu to say his private prayers before sunrise and sunset, *sandhyá* soon became the technical term for *the time of private devotions*, and ' to sit down to the sandhyâ,' is as much as to perform one's daily devotions. Manu knows only of two such periods, and, repeatedly, either uses the Dual (2, 78. 222.), or particularises them by saying *púrva* and *paschimá*, or *púrvá* and *apará sandhyá*, ' the former and latter time of prayer.' (2, 101. 4, 93.) *Yájnavalhya*, who avowedly is later than *Manu*, is the first who speaks of a *traikályasandhyá*, ' devotions performed three times a day,' (3, 308,) including the devotions at noon. But this third time of prayer has at no time become so obligatory as the two first." Stenzler,

have been wrong, and to ascribe a magical effect to alms, such as, it is assumed, could only belong to the decay of Judaism. "Magical" it certainly is not; for Daniel does not even venture to assure Nebuchadnezzar that it would avail. *This* future had not been revealed to him; so he ventures not to anticipate the judgment of God. He says only, *if it may be a lengthening of thy tranquillity.* But Daniel's advice is, to imitate those two great attributes of God, which are the theme of the whole Old Testament, justice and mercy. Oppression and injustice were, probably, almost inseparable from Heathen despotism. Any how, Daniel's advice implies that Nebuchadnezzar had fallen into them. His advice then is to those same two acts, which the Saviour of the world accepted in Zacchæus[3], reparation, and deeds of love. [4]*Redeem thy sins by righteousness and thine iniquities by shewing mercy to the poor, or afflicted.* If the Gospel has any other terms of forgiveness, than the breaking off of sin by its contrary, righteousness; if there is any other valid token of repentance than newness of life; or if mercy shall cease to have that prerogative with God, that [5]*the merciful shall obtain mercy*, then we may think that this advice belonged to a decayed Judaism. But, if the copying of those two great attributes of God is essential to the Christian, and, in the Great Day, [6]*mercy shall rejoice over judgment*, then we shall admire the great Prophet, who fearlessly admonished of his sins the conqueror of the world in the centre of his self-created magnificence, and exhorted him to a greater work than the conquest of the world, the conquest of himself, and to a greater glory than his stupendous works, to imitate that most glorious prerogative of the King of kings, the mercifulness of our God.

And now, by the mercy of my God, my task is done. I have pointed out to you that, place the book of Da-

---

who edited the work of *Yájnavalhya*, puts his earliest date in the 2nd cent. after our Lord. Vorr. p. xi.   [3] S. Luke xix. 8.

[4] Dan. iv. 27. Eng. 24. Ch.   [5] S. Matt. v. 7.   [6] S. James ii. 13.

niel where men will, it contains undeniable prophecy[1];
that its prophecy is at once vast and minute, relating both
to the natural events of God's Providence, and the supernatural order of His Grace[2]; that its minute prophecy
is in harmony with that of the rest of Holy Scripture[3]; so
that they who reject it, do, either nakedly or on the one
or other plea, reject all definite prophecy, leaving, of
Holy Scripture, only what they will; that, whereas the
minute prophecies of the book of Daniel exclude any date
between its real date, that of the close of the captivity,
and that which must have been its date, had it been a
human book, that of Antiochus Epiphanes, the later
date is precluded, both by the history of the closing
of the Canon[4], and by the references to the book of Daniel[4], as well in books of the Canon, Nehemiah and Zechariah, as also in other books, before, in, or soon after
the date of Epiphanes, and also by the character of its
first Greek translation; that neither its language[5], nor
its historical references[6], nor its doctrines[7], imply any
later date than that of Daniel himself; but that, contrariwise, the character of its Hebrew exactly fits with the
period of Daniel[5], that of its Chaldee excludes any later
period[5]; that the minute fearless touches, involving details of customs, state-institutions, history, belong to a
contemporary; and that what are, superficially, historical
difficulties, disappearing upon fuller knowledge, are indications of the accurate, familiar knowledge of one personally acquainted with customs or events[6]. I have
shewn too how its doctrines are in harmony with those
of other Scriptures, earlier and later[7].

Of the objections, I believe, that no one would have
been thought of, but for the necessity of getting rid of
the miracles and prophecies of Daniel, unless people
would believe them. Certainly, no one objection appears
to me even plausible. I have answered the objections.

---

[1] Lect. ii. and iii.   [2] Lect. iv.   [3] Lect. v.
[4] Lect. vi.   [5] Lect. l. and Note B and D at the end.
[6] Lect. vii.   [7] Lect. viii. and ix.

To convince, is the office not of man but of God.   Gibbon enunciated a larger truth than he was aware of, when, unable to see any escape from the contemporary evidence for a fact, or from its miraculousness, if it were true, he said, "[3] They all [all the witnesses of the fact] lived within the compass of a century; they all appeal to their personal knowledge or the public notoriety for the truth of a miracle which was repeated in several instances, displayed on the greatest theatre of the world, and submitted, during a series of years, to the calm examination of the senses.   But *the stubborn mind of an infidel is guarded by a secret incurable suspicion,"*— incurable save by God.

St. Paul had said the same before, *[4] the natural man receiveth not the things of the Spirit of God;* only, it is man's own fault, if, encompassed with the Gospel, he remain in, or apostatise into, a state of nature.   Yet to see, (as I believe,) a solid answer to those objections, although it cannot give faith to one who has lost faith, may aid in beating off unbelief or may predispose for faith.   It may put a person in the position, in which he will either not admit unbelief, or will seek for faith from Him Who gives it to all who seek Him.   It is not enquiry, but a non-enquiring acquiescence in doubt, which is the peril of this day.   It costs much to disbelieve; it requires submission to our God and His grace, to believe.   The temptation of this age is to try to find a middle path between faith and unbelief; to say that "there is much to be said on both sides;" to think that all things must be uncertain in themselves, because many of the persons around us are at sea as to all things, as if one thought all things to be in a whirl, because they seemed so to our neighbours who had dizzied themselves ; to be browbeaten out of belief; to shrink from avowing a steadfast adherence to that which must be old because it is eternal, and which must be unchangeable because it is truth; to pick something out of revelation, which, it thinks,

[3] Decline and Fall, c. 38. A.D. 530. "Persecution in Africa."
[4] 1 Cor. ii. 14.

will not be gainsaid, and to relegate all else to be matter of opinion ; an indolent, conceited, soft, weak, pains-hating, trifling with the truth of God.

It is not, for the present, a day of naked blasphemy. The age is mostly too soft for it. Voltaire's "écrasez l'infâme" shocks it. Yet I know not whether the open blasphemy of the 18th century is more offensive than the cold-blooded patronising ways of the 19th. Rebellion against God is not so degrading, nor so deceiving, as a condescending acknowledgement of His Being, while it denies His rights over us. Be not then imposed upon by smooth words. It is an age of counterfeits. Look not only at what is said, but look for what is suppressed and tacitly dropped out of the Creeds. The rationalism of this day will give you good words as far as they go, but will empty them of their meaning ; it will give as plausible a counterfeit as it can, but *the image and superscription*[1] is its own. It will gild its idols for you, if you will accept them for the Living God. It will give you sentiment instead of truth, but as the price at which you are to surrender truth. It will praise Jesus as, (God forgive it !) in fact, an enlightened Jew, a benefactor to mankind; and it will ask you in exchange to consent, not to say that He was God. It will extol His superiority to Judaism, and include under "Judaism" truths of God. It will praise His words as full of truth, and will call them, in a sense, divine truths, and will ask you in exchange, not to say that it is *the* infallible truth. It will say, in its sense, that "the Bible *contains* the word of God," and will ask of you to give up your belief that "it *is* the word of God." It will say, in *its* sense, that the prophets spake by the Holy Ghost, (i. e. as all which is good and true is spoken by inspiration of the Spirit of God,) and will ask of you, in exchange, to drop the words, or at least the meaning, of the Creed, that God the Holy Ghost "spake by the prophets." It will say to you, that the prophets were "elevated by a divine impulsion," and grant you "an intensified presentiment," but only in the sense common

[1] S. Matt. xxii. 20.

to the higher conditions of humanity, even unaided by the Grace of God[2]. It will acknowledge a fallible inspiration, fallible even as to matters of every-day-morality[3], and will ask of you to surrender the belief in the infallible. It will descant on the love of God, if you will surrender your belief in His aweful Holiness and Justice; it will speak with you of Heaven, if you, with it, will suppress the mention of Hell. It will retain the words of revelation, and substitute new meanings, if you will be content with the sound, and will part with the substance of the word of God[4].

The battle must be fought. It is half-won, when any one has firmly fixed in his mind the first principle, that God is All-Wise and All-Good, and that man's own wisdom, although from God, is no measure for the Wisdom of God, and cannot sound its depth. The criticism of rationalism is but a flimsy transparent veil, which hides from no eyes except its own, (if indeed it *does* hide it altogether from its own,) the real ground of its rebellion, its repugnance to receive a revelation to which it must submit, in order that it may see.

You must make your choice. Let it be a real one. But, before you choose, set before you that Day in which you shall see unveiled, all what you now see in part, and think what it will be to find, that they whom you adopted as teachers,—critics and criticism which has in no case survived its parents,—taught you to ignore or deny or disbelieve, or accuse in the Name of God, what is indeed the very truth of God. Even in this life, those mists which hurry along so vehemently, so darkly, so impetuously, like hosts disarrayed, in yon tumultuous, thronging and seemingly endless flight, part to the eye which watches well, and there opens to it the serene depth of heaven, in its own unchanging brightness, calm as ever beyond,

[2] " They shew that there is a preconscious region of the soul, with which the divine Spirit, evoking its latent phænomena, has sympathetic relation." Davidson, ii. 466. from Contributions to Mental Philosophy by I. M. Fichte, translated by Morell, c. 3, 4. [3] e. g. Dr. Stanley, Jewish Church, p. 329.

[4] Prof. Jowett, Epistles of St. Paul, ii. 589. Essay on the Atonement.

uneffaced, undimmed, uninjured, by the black earth-born clouds, which roll so far below.   Those glimpses, which, by the gift of God, come even in this world to the soul which resigns itself wholly to God, in prayer, in contemplation, in meditation, in devout study of His word, are earnests of the clearness of the Eternal Day.   The Christian is as certain of the truth of what rationalism impugns, as of his own existence.   For God, Who gave him his being, gave him also his faith.   God did not reveal Himself, that we should live in a twilight, seeing nothing of His truth distinctly, but only [1] *men, as trees, walking.* Twilight must brighten into full day, or darken into the heaviness of night.   To choose not to believe, is to disbelieve.   To halt between two divided ways [2], is to reject God-given truth.   *If the Lord be the God, follow Him; and if Baal, go after him.*

[1] S. Mark viii. 24.　　　　　[2] מצרים 2 Kings xviii. 21.

Thanks be to God.

NOTES.

Note A. on p. 38.

Explanation of the words in Daniel which are, or were supposed to be Aryan words, by Professor Max Muller.

One who is only a Semitic scholar cannot, of course, estimate the different explanations of the Aryan names in Daniel, except in so far as some are self-evidently bad. I applied therefore to one, who to his great Sanskrit knowledge adds a marvellous genius in comparative philology, Max Müller. With his wonted kindness, he has written down for me the following explanations of the words, upon which I consulted him. Words, which, as נְבִזְבָּה and מַדְּבְרִין, are clearly Semitic, or, as נֵבֶא, נְבִיא, are of simple etymology and became indigenous in other Semitic languages, needed no explanation, and on these I did not consult him.

"1) *Pathbag* is of Persian origin. *Path* corresponds to the Zend preposition *paiti*, and is the same as *pith* in *pithgam*. (No. 2.) This Zend preposition *paiti* corresponds to the Sanskrit preposition *prati*. (comp. προτί (Homer,) πορτί (Cretan,) ποτί, (Homer), and πρός.) This *paiti* in Zend expresses distribution, as *paiti asne*, day by day, (Sanskr. pratyaham.) It likewise conveys the notion of movement towards, whether in a friendly or hostile sense. (paity-ara, contrarius.) The second part of *pathbag* is the Persian *bág*, 'tribute,' the Sanskrit *bhága*, 'a portion.' It happens that the very compound *pratibhága* has been preserved in Sanskrit, where it is explained as ' A share of small articles, as fruit, flowers, &c. paid daily to the Rája for household expenditure.' This was pointed out by Gildemeister, Zeitschrift für Kunde des Morgenlandes, iv. p. 214.

" Scaliger (Animadversiones ad Euseb. Chron. p. 112,) speaking of the change of g into z, has the following remark: 'hanc commutationem G et Z nihil planius ostendere potest quam ποτίβαζις, quod dictum est pro ποτίβαγις vel πατίβαγις. Nomen est Assyriacum, *pathbag* Danielis, i, 8. Δείνων ἐν τρίτῳ Περσικῶν, citante Athenaeo,-ἐστι δὲ ποτίβαζις ἄρτος κρίθινος καὶ πύρινος ὀπτὸς, καὶ κυπαρίσσου στέφανος, καὶ οἶνος κεκραμένος ἐν ᾠῷ χρυσῷ, οὗ αὐτὸς βασιλεὶς πίνει. Itaque *pathbag* non solum cibum significat, ut interpretantur Iudaei, sed et omnia quae recensentur a Dinone, in quibus corona, quod ad superstitionem Chaldaicam pertinet.   Ideo Daniel et socii maluerunt abstinere quam iis uti.   Nam si solus πύρινος ἄρτος aut κρίθινος fuisset, non magis respuissent quam eorum legumina cocta.'

" 'The coincidence between Dinon's explanation of ποτίβαζις as vegetables, wreaths, &c. to be taken by the King, and the independent interpretation of *pratibhâga* by Sanskrit lexicographers is curious.

"2) In *pithgam*, the first portion is again the preposition *paiti*, in the sense of 'towards;' *gam* is to 'go' in Sanskrit, Zend, and the Cuneiform Inscriptions.   Hence *pratigama* might well have had the meaning of 'messenger,' though the compound does not occur in that sense in Sanskrit.   There is, however, a similar compound in Sansk., *pratisâsana*, which means ' sending a servant on a message,' from *prati*, 'towards,' and *sâsana*, 'commanding.'   That the compound *pratigama*, in the sense of ' messenger,' existed in Persian, is shown by the modern Persian *paiâm*, nuntius.   There is the intermediate form *paighâm*, and the Haft qulzum mentions an archaic form *paitâm*.   In Armenian too *patgam* exists, in the sense of 'message.'   *Paiti* sinks down to *pai* in modern Persian, as for instance, *paiker*, 'picture,' corresponding to a Sanskrit compound, *prati-kara*, literally *counterfeit*.   *Patikara* occurs in the Cuneiform Inscriptions."

· [The *i* in *paiti* was probably elided in Aramaic, (both *pathbag* and *pithgam* became indigenous in Syriac also,) on the principle of reducing the words to quadriliterals.]

3) "*Sagan* is very likely connected with the Modern Persian *shahneh*, a ' prefect,' but the etymology of the word is not clear.   The Sanskr. root *Kshi*, to rule, appears in the Cuneiform Inscriptions as *shi* in *shiyâti*, ' dominion ; ' once *shâyatâ*.   *Kshayathiya*, ' King,' in the Cuneif. Inscriptions, becomes *shdh* in Mod. Persian.

"4) *Pechah*.   Is this a foreign word, having a Semitic status constructus, and the plural *pachoth ?*   It could not be derived from Sansk. *paksha*, Prâkrit *pakkha*, which means, 'side,' ' wing ;' *pratipaksha*, ' enemy,' *sapaksha*, ' friend.'

[The Hebrew *Pechah* is remarkable from its early reception into Hebrew, having become a title of some "governors" in Solomon's outlying dominions.   For in that they are mentioned, both in 1 Kings x. 15. and 2 Chron. ix. 14, in union with " the kings of Arabia," as persons who supplied a yearly quantity of gold in addition to his regular revenue, and this, in connection with that derived from the merchants, it is in itself probable, that " the *Pachoth* of the land" were governors set over the outlying country beyond Judæa proper. And this is illustrated by the second place in which they are mentioned, (1 Kings xx. 24.) where Benhadad, after his first defeat, is advised to depose *the thirty-two* subordinate *kings who helped him*, (Ib. 16.) and to put *Pachoth* in their place. He substituted Syrian "governors" for the 32 tributary "kings." Then, still in that neighbourhood, and in part doubtless in the same country, they are in military command in Sennacherib's army, leading doubtless their own contingent of troops, in his multitudinous host. (2 Kings xviii. 24.) Sennacherib compares Hezekiah to one of the "governors" of the subjugated provinces, which he held subdued. (Comp. Is. x. 8, 9. 2 Kings xviii. 34.) Then, in each case joined with *Sagans, Pechah* is used of Babylonian, (Jer. li. 23, 57. Ez. xxiii. 6, 23.) and Median, (Jer. li. 28.) governors. Daniel, in recounting the Babylonian governors, places the *Pechahs* the third, after the *Satraps* and *Sagans*. (iii. 2. 3. 27.) Under Darius, they are not immediately united with the *Sagans*, but still are enumerated with these only, the *Satraps* and the *haddaberin*, " privy councillors." vi. 8. Somewhat later, (Esth. viii. 9. ix. 3,) the *Pechahs* are mentioned without the *Sagans*, but with the *Satraps* and the " princes of the provinces." In the times after the captivity there were several such *Pechahs*, westward of the Euphrates, between it and Judæa, (Ezr. viii. 36. Neh. ii. 7. 9,) probably the same locality, in regard to which the name was first used under Solomon. Specifically, Tatnai is entitled as " *Pechah* beyond the river," Ezr. v. 3. vi. 6, who, (although apparently he dwelt at Jerusalem, Neh. iii. 7,) is yet, in the same rescript of Darius, distinguished from " the *Pechah* of the Jews," (Ezr. vi. 7.) whom naturally there was most occasion to mention. (Hagg. i. 1. 14. ii. 2. 21. Mal. i. 8. Neh. v. 14. 18. xii. 26.)

It seems to me most probable, that Solomon adopted the title, as it already existed in the Syrian territories, for it is not said that he " placed *Pechahs*," but only that they paid him gold. Thus the name " Rajah" is continued in our Indian dominions.

On my replying that *Pechah* had no possible Semitic etymology, and enquiring whether it could be connected with *Pasha* or with *Beg*, Max Müller kindly gave me this further answer.]

" If *Pechâh* is connected with *Pashâh*, the history of the word would be very curious.

" 'The modern Persian *padshâh* is a compound; *pâd*, the Sansk. *pati*, ' lord,' (πόσις), Zend *paiti*. It does not occur in the Cuneiform Inscriptions. *Shâh*, ' King,' is what remains of the *Khshâyathiya*, the name for ' King ' is the Cuneiform Inscriptions ; Darius calling himself *Khsháyathíya Khsháyathiyánám*, just like the modern *Sháhinsháh.*   Hebrew does not tolerate, I believe, two such initial consonants as Kh + sh ; hence, in the name of *Xerxes*, the Cuneiform *Khshayárshá*, we get *Achashverush ;* instead of *Satrap*, the Cuneiform *Khshatrapává*, we get *Achashdarpením.*   In Persian, the guttural was afterwards dropt ; this gives *Satrap* instead of *Khshatrap.* In the same manner *Kksháyathiye* in Persian sank down to *sháyathiya,* and finally to *Sháh.*   Could the *cháh* in Chaldee be meant for this *sháh ?*   The guttural was there originally as much as the sibilant, but I find no trace of the sibilant being dropt in Persian and the guttural retained.

" As to *Beg* I can find nothing except that it is treated as a bonâ fide Turkish word, and would therefore be quite independent of Semitic or Aryan.

5) "*Gisbar*, a compound of *gis* and *bár.   Bár* is clearly Persian, meaning at the end of compounds, ' Keeper.'   *Gis* is most likely a contraction of *gins,* (comp. *ginsin,* ' treasures,') but it is doubtful whether *gins* is of Semitic or Aryan origin.   Dietrich thinks it can be explained as a Semitic formation and that it was borrowed by the Persians from their Semitic neighbours.   If on the contrary *gins* is, like *bár,* of Persian origin, it will have to be identified with the Mod. Pers. *genj,* ' treasure,' and the compound *gisbár* with *genjvár,* ' treasurer.'   *Genj* in Persian has been derived from Sansk. *ganja* ' treasure.'   But though *ganja* occurs in Sanskrit in that sense, and likewise *ganjavara,* ' treasurer,' they both occur in late Sanskrit only, and were probably transferred from Persian into Sanskrit. Other words for treasure in Sansk. are *kosa,* which has been suggested as an etymon of *gis ;* and *kánchana,* gold.

" The Old-Persian *gaitha* has been guessed by Dr. Haug as the origin of *genj* and *gins,* but none of these etymologies convey real conviction.   The Greek γάζα, ' royal treasure,' and γαζοφύλαξ, ' treasurer,' come from the same source as the Persian *genj,* but they throw no light on the original intention of the word."

[The Semitic etymology of גנז, "treasure," is, in itself, satisfactory; since, in Aramaic, it signifies, 1) " hidden," (as, in the unsettled state of the East, would be common as to "treasure,") then, "laid up."   In Syriac גניזא " the hidden," is a common title of God, the adv. גניזאית " in a veiled way " occurs in S. Ephr. i. 414. of one " lurking concealed," Barh. p. 490. l. 17. B.   A trace of the same meaning occurs in Arabic too, 1) " covered," 2) " collected." (See Ges. Thes. p. 296.)

And, since נג is used of a " chest" in which merchandise was " laid up" and conveyed, (Ez. xxxii. 24.) the name may have travelled with the thing ; and the word, which originally expressed the chest in which valuables were " stored up," may have been transferred to the stores themselves. The word having been naturalised in Persian, (see Max Müller above,) the difficulty of its etymology being half Semitic, half Persian, is removed. The naturalised Persian word was united with the old Persian, as we, in our familiar " stable-keeper," unite the Latin and Saxon, unconscious that they are such. The compound itself, *gidsabro*, "treasurer," occurs in the Peshito in Kings, Chron. Ezr. and also in Barh. Chr. p. 425. l. 6. 152. l. 7. and, (written אזגברא,) in a Nestorian Epistle, A.D. 1504, in Ass. B.O. iii. 594 (quoted by Ges. l. c.) as also the abstract, *gidsborutho*, "treasury." B. B. and B. A. The *gedabar* of Daniel is recognised as a variation, perhaps dialectic, of the *gidsbar* of Ezra and modern Syriac, the sibilant being dropped.]

" 6) *Dethabár* is clearly a Persian compound ; the second part *bár* is the same as in *gisbár* ; the first *deth* stands for the Mod. Pers. *dád*. It occurs also as *dath* in Daniel. The two roots *dá*, ' to give,' ($\delta i \delta \omega \mu \iota$) and *dhá*, ' to place' ($\tau i \theta \eta \mu \iota$) assume in Persian one and the same form. Hence *dád* means a ' gift,' (from *dá*,) and also 'law' and 'religion,' i. e. what is settled and established, (from *dhá*.) The Partic. past of *dá*, in the Cuneiform Inscr., is *data*."

" 7) *Tiphta* seems a Semitic word, though it occurs in Daniel only. The same Semitic root yields the Arabic Mufti."

[In answer to a subsequent enquiry, "whether Benfey's explanation of *Tifta* by *Atipaiti* was admissible?" Max Müller answered, "*atipati* is really no Sanskrit word at all;—at least, it never could mean 'Oberherr.' [Benfey's rendering.] *That* in Sanskrit would be *adhipat*. If it is objectionable to trace *Tifta* to the same root as *Mufti*, the word, *Tifta*, must be left for the present unexplained, without saying anything about such a mere guess as *atipati*." The Semitic etymology is perfectly satisfactory, *Tifta*, as well as *Mufti*, being the name of an office. I hesitated to adopt it, until Benfey's etymology should be disposed of, because, if *Atipaiti* had the meaning, which he assigned to it, it was a possible etymology, (although, as Fürst also observes, very vague,) and also because of the bearings of the etymology on the date of the book of Daniel. For, derived from the same root פתי, it involves this ; that the name of the office, in Daniel's time, was derived from a meaning of the root in Aramaic, which was subsequently wholly lost, although it survived in the corresponding title in Arabic. Its use in the Arabic verb is rather obscure. In conj. iv.

it signifies, " he taught another, by way of response, as to the truth
or law of a thing," (see in Freytag Lex.) whence the partic.
Mufti, " one who so taught."   Yet the words, *fatvai, fotvai*, the
" response" itself, indicate the existence of the simple root.   Probably it was connected with the Heb. root, חתפ, " was open," which, in
its stronger form, חתפ, signified, " laid open," which also in Arabic
is used of God's " laying open" by revelation, and of man's" dijudi-
cating."   See Freytag, sub v.]

" 8) *Sarbal*, like the Arabic *servál*, plur. *serável*, is of Persian origin.   Dozy (Dictionnaire des Noms des Vêtements, p. 204) shows
that Mohammed forbad pilgrims to wear *serável* on their pilgrimage
to Mekka.   The Persian word for *braccae* is *shalvár*, or more correctly *shulvár*.   *Shul* in Persian is femur, the Sanskrit *Kshura* or
Khura, hoof; Latin, crus, cruris.   The Greeks changed *Shulvar* into
σαράβαρα, (ἐσθὴς Περσική, Suidas), later, σαράβαλλα.   In *Sarbal*, the
r and l changed places.

"The Zend, *sdraváro*, [quoted by Gesenius Thes. p. 971,] is a different word, and means literally ' a cover of the head.'   From this
word *sdra*, 'head,' Sanskrit *siras*, the term

" 9) *Sarak* may be regularly derived, being an adjective in *ka*,
meaning 'head-man.'   In Sanskrit, *siras* is not used with reference to
persons, as little as the Greek κόρυς ; but *ser*, ' head,' is frequently applied to persons in modern Persian, in the sense of κορυφαῖος.

" 10) *Hamník*, derived from Sanskr. *mani*, a 'jewel,' with a secondary derivative, *ka, manika*.   The Latin *monile* is a cognate word."

"It is impossible to give any etymology of the proper names Mîshach,
Shadrach, &c. Mîshach may have been *mis*, 'friend,' *shdh*,'King,' but
in Persian this compound could only mean,'King of the friend.'   Mîshach may be 'lambkin,' Sanskr. *meshaka*, as Dietrich supposes; but
there can be nothing certain or even probable with regard to proper
names of which we know nothing but their sound.

"Κίθαρις cannot possibly be derived from the Persian *sitáreh*, a
three-stringed (not six-stringed) instrument.   Κίθαρις occurs in
Homer, and the numeral three, the Sanskr. *tri*, is still unchanged in
Zend, where it appears as *thri*.   *Si* is a much later corruption of this.

" *Partemím* is clearly the plural of a Persian word.   It is the
Sanskr. *prathama* ; Zend. *frathema* ; Cuneiform Inscriptions, *fra-
tama* ; Pehlevi, *pardom* ; πρῶτος.

"*Daryavesh* is a more accurate transcript of the name of the Persian king than Δαρεῖος.   Darius calls himself in his Inscriptions
Dáryavush, which means the 'holder' or 'supporter.' "

Note B. on p. 36.

On the Hebrew of the book of Daniel, and the argument alleged from it for the "lateness" of that Book.

The evidence for the "lateness" of the book of Daniel, to be derived from its six Hebrew chapters, was not a little eccentric. Of course, the book of Daniel was "late." According to its historical date, it was one of the "latest" books of the Canon. Eight books of the Canon only were later; the three prophets after the captivity, the Chronicles, (in which however earlier documents were used,) Ezra, Nehemiah, Esther. The date, however, required for the book of Daniel, if it was not to be his, was two centuries and a half later than the latest of these. In order then to prove that the style of the book of Daniel evinced that it was so much later than his date, it ought to have been shewn, that it was different in character from the books written soon after the captivity. On the contrary, the evidence chiefly alleged is, that it has certain words in common with them.

Thus, i. "Daniel, as well as Ezekiel and the author of the books of Chronicles, revived idioms out of the Pentateuch." (Leng. p. lxi.) This, at least, suits a date which lay between Ezekiel and the historian. Granted, that it shewed that Daniel wrote at a *late* date; yet it is not a date, later than that of the prophet himself.

ii. "There are agreements with Ezekiel, and the books of the latest period." (Leng. p. lx.) Again, correspondence with Ezekiel, who was older than Daniel, as a proof that Daniel was above four centuries younger!

iii. "He imitates Jeremiah, who, in the case of the genuineness [of the book,] was almost his contemporary." (Leng. followed by Dav. iii. 194.) But it is now acknowledged that the prophets did purposely use the words of those almost their contemporaries. (see ab. p. 308, 9.) The date, also, at which Daniel wrote the prophecies delivered through himself, was nearly 70 years after Jeremiah's prophecy of the captivity.

iv. "The prayer c. ix. contains verbal imitations of Nehemiah." (Leng. and from him De Wette and Dav.) The truth is the converse, that Nehemiah adopted a few words of address to God from Daniel's prayer. (See ab. p. 353-6.)

v. Daniel's expressions "are often careless, clumsy, or obscure."
Three such expressions are alleged out of his Chaldee; ii. 30. y. 4.
vi. 21.; four out of his Hebrew, i. 21. ix. 8. 26. xi. 6.   What, if there
had been obscurity ?   Is there none in Hosea, or in the hymn of Habakkuk, or in Ezekiel, or even here and there in Isaiah ?   This "obscurity, &c," however, is to be an indication, that he had not the full
grasp of the language, but wrote as one who had learned it. (Leng. Ib.)
Now, contrariwise, a writer, who has learned a language, avoids obscure expressions.   Obscurity arises from the use of words or idioms,
which, in course of time, become obsolete, or of allusions, which come
to be forgotten ; or in a pregnancy or conciseness of diction, which
a writer uses, in the full confidence that he shall be understood by
those to whom the language which he uses is as familiar as to himself.
Moreover, three out of the seven expressions are in his Aramaic, the
language which Daniel spoke, which, in a later style, the Jews continued to use.   Daniel's style in writing Aramaic is to be a proof of
his "clumsiness," &c. in writing Hebrew !   But after all, in three
out of the four Hebrew passages, there is no obscurity.   *a*) There
could not be a simpler sentence than that, Dan. i. 21. וַיְהִי דָנִיֵּאל עַד שְׁנַת
אַחַת לְכוֹרֶשׁ הַמֶּלֶךְ lit. "And Daniel was, [i. e. continued,] unto the year
one of Cyrus the king."   He states, in other words, that he continued
through the whole residue of the Babylonian empire.   "Unto," it
is well known, does not exclude the time beyond; it only reaches
quite up to the term.   This is an idiom of all Hebrew.   The expression is " unsuited to an author of the *Maccabee times.*" (Leng.)
Granted.   *b*) ix. 8. there is not even an alleged obscurity of style.
It is flowing Hebrew : אֲדֹנָי לָנוּ בֹּשֶׁת הַפָּנִים לִמְלָכֵינוּ לְשָׂרֵינוּ וְלַאֲבֹתֵינוּ אֲשֶׁר חָטָאנוּ לָךְ
" O Lord, to us confusion of face, to our kings, to our princes, and
to our fathers, us who have sinned against Thee."   What is alleged, is to be, not an obscurity, but an anachronism ; the mention of
their "kings" is not to suit either the time of Daniel or of the Maccabees ; the writer is to have " used places like Ezra ix. 7, forgetting
the contradiction that there were no kings in the exile."   But 1) the
shame of the Jewish kings must have been most keenly felt in Babylon, where Jehoiachin lived in his prison-garments for 37 years, during the whole reign of Nebuchadnezzar, and, when removed by
Evilmerodach above the other kings of Babylon, was still part of his
conqueror's show. (2 Kings xxv. 27-30.) There too, while he lived,
was the eyeless Zedekiah in chains. (Jer. xxxix. 7. 2 Kings xxv. 7.)
2) The mention of " our fathers," in the same sentence, shews that
Daniel was not thinking of his own generation only.   But his fathers

were kings. (Dan. i. 3.)   3) Of course, whatever explanation suited Ezra, who lived after the captivity, would have suited Daniel too, since at neither time were there kings reigning.   *c*) "Dan. ix. 26, וְאֵין לוֹ," is only too clear.   It *will* not mean, what these writers want it to mean, for their explanations. (See ab. p. 182. n. 11.)   *d*) Dan. xi. 6, requires attention; but the obscurity lies, not in the Hebrew words, but in the substance.   It is prophesied of the alliance between Antiochus Theos and Ptolemy Philadelphus, who married his daughter Berenice to Antiochus, *to make terms of agreement*, (the legitimate wife Laodice being dismissed,) that it should "not stand."   *She shall not retain the power of the arm, neither shall he stand nor his arm; but she shall be given up, and they that brought her, and he that begat her, and he that strengthened her, in the times.*   Out of all this, the one word, זְרֹעוֹ, "*his arm*," is selected as obscure, *neither he shall stand nor his arm*, i. e. according to the common Hebrew idiom, "neither he nor his helper," i. e. she who was to have strengthened him by her alliance, Berenice, (as Leng. himself explains it, p. 517, in seeming unconsciousness of any difficulty.)   I will add, In illustration of this criticism, that the Aramaic passages, against which Leng. excepts, are equally clear.

v. "He is unacquainted with vau conversive." (Leng. Dav. iii. 194.) This is a marvellous statement, since Daniel uses it continually.   It means, (as Leng. shews, p. 552,) that, in vivid prophetic description, Daniel used the abridged future with the simple "*and*."   But this occurs in books of the middle age, and even in the Pentateuch. (See below p. 587.)

vi. "He omits the article, where there can be no ambiguity." (Leng. translated by Dav.)   Why should he not?   He does so only in the more elevated prophetic descriptions, as do writers of the middle age of Hebrew. (See below p. 585.)

vii. "Other words only find their parallels in the Targums and the Rabbins.   Such are, זֵרֹעִים, [our "vegetables,"] only in Aramaic; מֵי עֹלָם 'everlasting life;' and זְהַר, in its original meaning 'shine,' only in the Targums (!); and a proverbial expression, (D. iv. 32.) which only occurs besides in the Targums and the Talmudists." (Leng. Dav.) This large language, (" the Targums and Talmudists,") really means, that Buxtorf noted one instance of the Aramaic expression, מָחֵא כִּידָא, in a late Targum, (Eccl. viii. 3.) and one in Sanh. 93. 1.   The expression would be remarkable, only if it had the meaning given to it by Gesenius, on the strength of an analogous Arabic idiom, "Who shall strike His hand?" Buxtorf, however, did not think that such was

its meaning, but rather, "restrain."   There is no trace of the physical meaning in the other idioms, given by Buxtorf, in which מחא, as
in this, signifies "restrain" or "prohibit."   In *them*, it cannot mean
"strike."   "It was in his power to hinder, and he hindered not," היה בידו
למחות ולא מיחה, Sanhedr. 103. 1. (in Buxt. c. 1186.)   " For My glory ye
did not avert it, (לא מיחתם) but for flesh and blood ye did avert it, (מיחתם)."
(Sanh. 10. 1. 103.2. Ib.) "He hindered them not." (ולא מחא בהן) Sanh.
93. 1. (Ib.)   " He who removes, takes away, his neighbour's wife."
דמחי ליה לאיתתא דחבריה Sanh. f. 109, 2. (Ib.)   מיחוי קרביו, "to remove its
intestines." Pesach. f. 65. (Ib.)   מחו ביד ולא מחו בכלי, "they remove
with the hand and do not remove with an instrument." Shabb. f. 440.
So then, probably, מחא בידו simply means " withhold his hand," as מחא בו
means " withhold him."   It would have been a remarkable expression, had Nebuchadnezzar used it of Almighty God.   Yet, in that case,
its occurring in Daniel's Aramaic could not indicate, even on the unbelieving hypothesis, a late date of the book ; for the character of the
Jewish mind (as seen in the Targums) was to efface or soften any
expressions, which speak of God after the manner of men.   But
after all, the critics must have forgotten that the expression occurs
in Daniel's *Aramaic*, not in his Hebrew.   For what an argument is
it, "We find a proverbial [Aramaic] expression, only found besides in
the Targums and Talmudists ! "   Where else should one find it, since
there was no occasion for it in Ezra, and there is no other Biblical Aramaic ?

But, in the Hebrew of Daniel, Aramaic as well as Aryan words
suit his real age.   On the other words, see below.

The result of the following arrangement of the marked words or
idioms in Daniel is, I think, to shew that his Hebrew is just what one
should expect at the age at which he lived.   The number of words
or idioms peculiar to himself suits the age of one who himself had
full mastery of the language.   The use of words, which have not
lived in the Aramaic which the Jews cultivated, (that which remains
in the Targums and the Gemara,) but which have lived on in the language of Western Syria, belongs to a date, when those dialects were
more allied than they came to be, or perhaps before they had yet separated.   The use of the Pentateuch, Jeremiah, and Ezekiel, is in
harmony with what we know of one who, when he had reached man's
threescore years and ten, was himself made the channel of prophecy,
but who, up to that time, had only had insight given to him as to the
meaning of the visions vouchsafed to Nebuchadnezzar, and who, he
himself tells us, had studied the previous Scriptures. (Dan. ix. 2.)

The proportion of the idioms, which he has in common with the middle age of Hebrew, to that of the books which are historically of a late period, shews that there is no marked preponderance of either, while there is not one word or idiom, which, in the slightest degree, betokens an age later than that of the prophet.

I have marked with a † the words or idioms, which Lengerke put together, De Wette copied, Stähelin selected mostly, and Davidson translated, in order to give a shew of proof for the "lateness" of the book of Daniel.

1) *Words or idioms peculiar to Daniel.*

עָמַר בְּהֵיכַל הַמֶּלֶךְ Dan. i. 4 ; else, לִפְנֵי.

מְנָה Dan. i. 5, 8, 13, 15. xi. 26. see Note A. p. 565, 6. and C. p. 595, 6.

יֵין מִשְׁתָּיו Dan. i. 5. 8. מִן מִשְׁתֵּיהֶם יֵין i. 16.

וַיָּשֶׂם לָהֶם שֵׁמוֹת, then, וַיָּשֶׂם with name, but omitting שֵׁם. Dan. i. 7.   The construction in the Chaldee of Daniel is that which is usual in Hebrew, שָׂם שְׁמָא with the name. Dan. v. 12. Judg. viii. 31. 2 Kings xvii. 34. Neh. ix. 7.

בִּקֵּשׁ מִן—אֲשֶׁר, "sought from—that," Dan. i. 8. comp. בְּעָא מִן—דִּי ii. 16. 23. Ch.

כְּגִילְכֶם †, " like (those of) your age," i. 10. (In Samaritan also נלה, גיל; and גיל, in the like idiom in Arabic, "with (those of) thine age." See Ges. p. 283.) from גול, as דּוֹר, "generation," from דאר.   In Talm. it survived in the one idiom, בֶּן גִּילוֹ, "his contemporary."   This then was to be Talmudic.   But did then Arabs and Samaritans get it from the Talmud ?

הַמֶּלְצַר, i. 11. 16.   The Hebrew article implies that a word, even if it becomes a proper name, retains its appellative meaning.   Hebrew writers do not add the art. to foreign proper names, when the etymology is lost. (See Ew. Gr. p. 569.)   The name *Melzar* must then have been an appellative or nearly so, in Daniel's time.   In the time of the earliest translations, it must have been lost; for all treat it as a proper name and corrupt it.   It has (Dr. Aufrecht tells me) a possible Persian etymology, (that of Bohlen,) *molsar*, "head of wine," i. e. "the chief cellarer," and this agrees with the context.   Only there is no proof that the compound existed in old Persian.   It has not survived.

הַזֵּרֹעִים, † i. 12. "herbs," lit. "things sown."   Also הַזֵּרֹעִנִים, † Dan. i. 16. (formed with Heb. ending, ן—) Syr. וַרְעָא, זֶרְעָא.   Isaiah has זֵרוּעִים, of "garden herbs," lxi. 11. and Moses has the sing. זֶרַע, Lev. xi. 37. The only other Hebrew words for *herbs* are, אֹרֹת, 2 Kgs. iv. 39. (poet. Is. xxvi. 19.) יָרָק, our *greens*, Deut. xi. 10. 1 Kgs. xxi. 2. Pr. xv. 17.

אַשָּׁפִים, † i. 20. ii. 2.   In Ch. אָשַׁף sing. Dan. ii. 10. plur. Dan. ii. 27.

iv. 4. v. 7. 11. 15. In Syriac, "ashoofo" was used by Bar Hebræus (Chron. p. 491,) so late as the end of the 13th cent., of a kind of enchanter; in the Targums or Talmud it does not apparently occur. (See Buxtorf.)

שְׁנָתוֹ נִהְיְתָה עָלָיו, "his sleep was away," lit. "upon him," (so that its absence was heavy on him,) ii. 1. like Ch. שַׁנְתֵּהּ נַדַּת עֲלוֹהִי "his sleep was fled, (so as to be oppressive,) upon him." Dan. vi. 19.

נִהְיְתָה, Ib. like נִהְיֵיתִי, viii. 27.

כַּשְׂדִּים, "The Chaldæans," i. e. the learned caste among them. Dan. ii. 2. 4. 5. 10. iv. 4. v. 7. 11.

נִרְאָה חָזוֹן אֵלַי, Dan. viii. 1. נִרְאָה is often used of God's "appearing," "allowing Himself to be seen," as man can see Him. Here only of a vision, shewn by Him.

נִרְאָה אֵלַי אֲנִי דָנִיֵּאל, viii. 1, (add 15,) an emphatic repetition of the pronoun, used throughout Hebrew, Gen. xxvii. 34. 1 Sam. xxv. 24. 2 Sam. xvii. 5. Ezek. xxxiv. 11. 20. (probably *not* in Ps. ix. 7. Hag. i. 4.) but the use of the noun after the pronoun so repeated is rare. לִי אֲנִי עַבְדְּךָ occurs in 1 Kings i. 26, the exact idiom only in the Chald. of Ezra, סְנֵי אֲנָא אַרְתַּחְשַׁסְתְּא vii. 21. and of Daniel, רוּחִי אֲנָה דָנִיֵּאל vii. 15.

אוּבָל or אֻבָל, "stream," Dan. viii. 2, 3, 6. The root occurs in יָבַל "stream." [plur.] Is. (ii.) יוּבַל, Id. (Jer.) and even מַבּוּל, "flood," and יַבֶּלֶת, (of diseased sheep) Lev. xxii. 22. Aquil. Theod. Syr. retain the word *Ubal;* lxx. render "gate;" Symm. "marsh."

קְרָנַיִם, Dan. viii. 3. [ii.] 6. 7. 20, after the analogy of וּדְרָכַיִם, Prov. xxviii. 6. See Ew. Ausf. Lehrb. § 186. g. p. 485. ed. 7.

וְאֵין נֹגֵעַ, viii. 5, more vividly than וְלֹא נָגַע; lit. "there was none touching the earth." In prose, אֵינֶנּוּ is used throughout Hebrew with the participle, as in Lev. xi. 4, Deut. xxi. 20, Judg. iii. 25, 1 Sam. xi. 7; and so with all the persons, אֵינֶנִּי נֹתֵן, Ex. v. 10, Deut. iv. 42; אֵינְךָ, Gen. xx. 7, xliii. 5, Ex. viii. 17; אֵינְכֶם, Deut. i. 32, iv. 12. See Fürst, Conc. p. 45, col. 3, 4. v. אֵינֶנִּי &c. The use of אֵין with the noun and the partic. following, occurs even in the Pent., probably to express more emphatically the utter absence of the act; as in Gen. xxxix. 23. אֵין שַׂר בֵּית־הַסֹּהַר רֹאֶה אֶת־כָּל־מְאוּמָה בְּיָדוֹ; "the keeper of the prison did not in any way regard anything whatever under his hand," (as we say, "wholly disregarded,") and in Ex. v. 16. וְתֶבֶן אֵין נִתָּן, "straw none is given;" as we might say, "there is no straw whatever given." In like way, אֵין כֶּסֶף נֶחְשָׁב, 2 Chron. ix. 20. add Ezr. iii. 13, Esth. iii. 4. The proper name occurs in the same construction in Esth. ii. 20. אֵין אֶסְתֵּר מַגֶּדֶת, and iii. 5. No other usage reaches the conciseness and energy of the idiom in Daniel.

חָזוּת, viii. 5, 8. of *conspicuous* beauty, as מַרְאֶה, 2 Sam. xxiii. 31.

בְּחֻסַּת לֹחוּ, viii. 6.

אֵצֶל, with verb of motion, viii. 7, 17.

יִתְמַרְמַר (Hithp.) Dan. viii. 7. xi. 11. comp. Arab. *marmara*, "was angry," Syr. *ethmarmar*, "was embittered."

לֹא הָיָה כֹחַ לָאַיִל מְיָדוֹ, viii. 7. לְ instead of אֶל, perhaps with the idea of "extending help to."

"And when it was strong, the great horn was broken," וַתַּעֲלֶינָה חָזוּת † אַרְבַּע, lit. "and there rose up, conspicuous beauty, four " (horns.) Dan. viii. 8. The idiom, קֶרֶן חָזוּת, " horn of conspicuous beauty," just before, (viii. 5.) which bears out the meaning, justified its exceeding boldness.

לְאַרְבַּע רוּחוֹת הַשָּׁמַיִם, the fuller form, Dan. viii. 8. xi. 4. comp. Dan. vii. 2. Ch. for לְאַרְבַּע רוּחוֹת, Ezek. xlii. 20.

מִצְּעִירָה " less than little," " very little," viii. 9 ; after the analogy of מִגּוֹאֵל " next to the גֹאֵל, nearest of kin," or מֵאָסֹר. See Ges. Thes. p. 801.

הַצְּבִי, lit. " the pleasantness," for, " the pleasant land," Dan. viii. 9. as Judæa is called, אֶרֶץ הַצְּבִי, " the land of pleasantness," Dan. xi. 16, 41. comp. צְבִי לְכָל-הָאֲרָצוֹת, " the glory of all lands," Ezek. xx. 6. 15. צְבִי אֶרֶץ, "the glory of the land," (Moab,) Ib. xxv. 9. צְבִי מַמְלָכוֹת, " the glory of kingdoms," (Babylonia,) Is. xiii. 19. אֶרֶץ הַצְּבִי is not an idiom sufficiently frequent, nor was the term צְבִי sufficiently appropriated to Judæa, that צְבִי should be a brief form for אֶרֶץ הַצְּבִי. Rather it is a bold use of the abstract, like מַשּׂאוֹת below, ix. 23.

With a like boldness, הַתָּמִיד,† " the continual," is used Dan. viii. 11, 12, 13. xi. 31. xii. 11. instead of the phrase in the law, עֹלַת הַתָּמִיד (in Numbers xvi times, also in Neh. x. 34.) " the perpetual sacrifice." Daniel may the rather have chosen this form, in order to include the whole continual worship of God, in which the shewbread is also called לֶחֶם הַתָּמִיד, Num. iv. 7. See Hengst. Christol. iii. p. 108, 9.

הֻרַם, with מִן of the person, viii. 11; of place, Is. lvii. 14; abs. Ezek. xxi. 31. Ewald would read the Khethib, הֵרִים, after the analogy of הֻנִּיחָה Zech. v. 11. and הֵקִים in Daniel's Chaldee, Dan. vii. 4. (Ausf. Lehrb. p. 343. ed. 7.) מִן, of the ultimate cause, as in Ps. xxxvii. 2. Eccl. xii. 13.

קָדוֹשׁ, (sing.) "holy," i. e. angel, viii. 13. as קַדִּישׁ Dan. iv. 10. Ch. The plur. הַקְּדֹשִׁים, "*the* holy ones," occurs in Job v. 1. (comp. iv. 18.) קְדֹשָׁיו, " His holy ones," Ib. xv. 15. סוֹד קְדֹשִׁים, קְהַל קְדֹשִׁים, " the congregation of holy ones," " the assembly of the holy ones," Ps. lxxxix. 6, 8. (the art. being omitted, as is usual in the poetical books ;) in these two places of the Heb. and Chald. of Daniel alone, it is used of a single " angel."

P p

חַפְּלֹנִי † viii. 13. See ab. p. 40, 1.

הֶחָזוֹן הַתָּמִיד וְהַפֶּשַׁע שֹׁמֵם, lit. "the vision, the continual sacrifice and the transgression, which maketh desolate." Dan. viii. 13.   The apposition is exceedingly bold ; the subject of the vision replacing the vision itself.   The ordinary cases, in which an explanatory word stands in apposition with the chief word in the sentence, are grammatically the same, (see ab. p. 472.) but have not the like emphasis.   The most like perhaps is Jer. xxv. 15. "take אֵת כּוֹס הַיַּיִן הַחֵמָה, the wine-cup, the wrath, from My hand."

שֹׁמֵם viii. 13. ix. 27. xii. 11, 12. for מְשׁוֹמֵם (Dan. ix. 27, xi. 31,) as עוֹלָל for מְעוֹלָל, (which occurs Is. xii. 12 ;) שַׂבֵּחַ, Eccl. iv. 2, for מְשַׁבֵּחַ.

וְנִצְדַּק קֹדֶשׁ Dan. viii. 14. "the sanctuary shall be cleansed," lit. "justified."

בִּינָה, abs. "understanding" of the vision. viii. 15. ix. 22. It is expressed more fully בִּינָה לוֹ בַּמַּרְאֶה, "he had understanding in the vision," x. 1. comp. the Imper. בִּין ix. 23. x. 1 ; הָבֵן, intrans. viii. 17. ix. 23. x. 11. trans. viii. 16. x. 14. אָבִין xii. 8. intrans.

כִּי לְמוֹעֵד קֵץ, Dan. viii. 19 ; כִּי לְיָמִים רַבִּים, Ib. 26 ; "For till the appointed end ; " "for till many days ; " "it is" being omitted, for energy.

יַעַמְדְנָה, viii. 22.   The form is not from the Chaldee, since the *whole* form is not Chaldee, and the ' is the Arabic præformant of the 3rd fem. fut. also, and תַּחְמְנָה occurs in Gen. xxx. 38, and תִּשְׂרְנָה in 1 Sam. vi. 2 ; the form also תִּקְרְאֶנָה is altogether rare, (Ges. Lehrg. p. 276.) תִּקְטְבוּ, יִקְטְבוּ, occurring for it.   (Ew. Krit. Gr. p. 643.) The regular form תַּעֲמֹדְנָה occurs in viii. 22.

כְּהָתֵם, "when they have filled up" i. e. their sin. viii. 23. Comp. the intrans. שָׁלֵם עָוֹן Gen. xv. 16. and כְּהָתִמְךָ שׁוֹדֵד Is. xxxiii. 1.

חִידוֹת, prob. *wiles*, from "twisting, intertwining," viii. 23. στροφαί. See Ges. Thes. v. ארב and חד.

עַל שִׂכְלוֹ, viii. 25, here only in a bad sense, "cunning."

בְּשַׁלְוָה, "in security," viii. 25 ; בָּא בְשַׁלְוָה "came when they were in security." xi. 21. 24. Comp. in Ch. שְׁלָא, "prosperity," "prosperous ease," Dan. iv. 24 ; שַׁלְוָה, Ps. cxxii. 7, Ez. xvi. 49. Plur. בְּשַׁלְוֺתֶיךָ "in thy prosperities," Jer. xxii. 21. "quietness," Prov. xvii. 1.

שַׂר שָׂרִים, of God, viii. 25, as in Ch. מָרֵא מַלְכִין ii. 47. ὁ βασιλεὺς τῶν βασιλευόντων καὶ κύριος τῶν κυριευόντων. 1 Tim. vi. 15. κύριος κυρίων καὶ βασιλεὺς βασιλέων. Rev. xvii. 14.

נֶאֱמַר, abs. "has been said," i. e. to thee. Dan. viii. 26. In Gen. x. 3. xxii. 14. "it is said," in proverbs ; in Num. xxi. 14. "it is said," in a book.

מָלַךְ Dan. ix. 1. See ab. p. 122, 3.

הַסְּפָרִים, "the books" of Scripture, ix. 2. Comp. מְגִלַּת סֵפֶר Ps. xl. 8. סֵפֶר Is. xxxiv. 16. " סֵפֶר Is. xxix. 18. Elsewhere, in the plur. "letters" or "letter."

לִמְלֹאות with ל r. ix. 2. The word is taken from Jer. xxix. 10, מְלֹאות לְבָבֶל שִׁבְעִים שָׁנָה comp. Jer. xxv. 12, בִּמְלֹאות שִׁבְעִים שָׁנָה

אֶתְּנָה אֶת פָּנַי, with אֶל p. (to God) and ל with infin. Ezekiel has שִׂים פָּנֶיךָ, with אֶל of the persons to whom he was to prophesy, xiii. 17. xxi. 7. xxv. 2. xxxviii. 2.

בָּעַ with cognate acc. abs., ix. 3. לְבַקֵּשׁ תְּפִלָּה וְתַחֲנוּנִים ix. 5. translated by the LXX, εὑρεῖν προσευχὴν καὶ ἔλεος.

חָטָאנוּ וְעָוִינוּ וְהִרְשַׁעְנוּ וּמָרָדְנוּ וְסוֹר. ix. 5. No instance of the use of the absolute inf. after finite verbs equals this in energy. After four words, in themselves containing a climax of their sin, *we have sinned*, &c. there follows in one word, "*and turning away*," וְסוֹר; as we should say, "it was all turning away." This was the root of all. See the converse, the finite verb after the accumulated infinitives, Hos. iv. 2, and my Comm. p. 26.

לְמַעַן אֲדֹנָי, ix. 17, "for the sake of my LORD." (The two words stand with great pathos at the end of the sentence.) לְמַעֲנֶךָ ix. 19; both single cases; elsewhere, שְׁמֶךָ or שֵׁם לְמַעַן הַצְּדִיק, לְמַעַן מִסְפָּר.

סָלְחָה שְׁמָעָה, סְלַח, only in Dan. ix. 19. as הַקְשִׁיבָה ix. 18. according to the analogy of שְׁאָלָה, Is. vii. 11, רְפָאָה, Ps. xli. 5. a very rare and emphatic form.

חֲמוּדוֹת, lit. "longednesses." (ix. 23.) It is not for אִישׁ חֲמוּדוֹת, "vir desideriorum," x. 11. 19, but an abstract, ("desiderium meum," Cat. or "mea desideria," Cic.) like עַמְּךָ נְדָבֹת "thy people are willingnesses," (i. e. all willing.) Ps. cx. 3.

נֶחְתַּךְ † Dan. ix. 24. "is decreed." The Nifal is not found elsewhere. Hithp. occurs in a late Targ. Esth. iv. 5, "*decided*." The physical sense, *cut*, survived in the Talmud. Buxt.

רְחֹב, "broad place, street of city," fem. Dan. ix. 25, according to the analogy of עִיר &c. The name, *Rechoboth*, Gen. x. 11, attests an early use of the fem. plur. Even this form רְחֹבוֹת עִיר is joined with the masc. verb, in Zech. viii. 5. Else the gender of רְחֹב is not marked.

מַשְׁחִית "corruption." *pass.* Dan. x. 8, like מָשְׁחַת, "a thing marred," Is. lii. 14. מַשְׁחִית is used *actively* of "wastefulness" (whereby a person destroys his *own* substance) Prov. xviii. 9. and in a double sense הַר הַמַּשְׁחִית "the mount of corruption" and so of "destruction" also, 2 Kgs. xxiii. 13. (of the scene of Solomon's idolatries, and thence Jer. li. 25;) and of "destructiveness" generally, 2 Chron. xx. 23. xxii. 4. Ezek. v. 16. ix. 6. xxi. 36. xxv. 15.

תַּרְגִּזֵנִי "set me trembling," Dan. x. 10.

כַּפּוֹת יָדָי, "palms of my hands," (Dan. x. 10.) after analogy of כַּפּוֹת רַגְלַיִם Josh. iii. 13. iv. 18. 1 Kings v. 17. Is. lx. 14. Ez. xliii. 7. Mal. iii. 21. of the statue of Dagon, 1 Sam. v. 4; of one dead, 2 Kings ix. 35; of hands amputated, 1 Sam. v. 4; handles, Cant. v. 5; "hollow vessels," and so, "spoons," Ex. xxv. 29, &c. כַּפַּיִם "hands," including the palm.

בָּאתִי בִּדְבָרֶיךָ, Dan. x. 12, "I am come at," or "through, thy words."

עָמַד לְנֶגְדִּי. Dan. viii. 5. x. 16, i. q. Syr. לקבל Ch. לָקֳבֵל. In a different sense, "stood opposed to," Dan. x. 13, as in Prov. xxi. 30. נֶגֶד .y Eccl. iv. 12.

רָשׁוּם, † "marked down as decreed." Dan. x. 21. In the Chaldee of Daniel, רְשַׁם is used of the sentence written against Belshazzar, v. 24, 25; of the king's subscribing the decree, vi. 9, 10, 11, 13, 14. (See ab. p. 40.) In the Targg. it corresponds to מְחֹקְקִים, "those who decree," Is. x. 1; הִתְוָה, "set a mark on," Ez. ix. 4. In Syriac, it is used, theologically, of the "seal" of Baptism and of predestination.

יָעִיר הַכֹּל אֵת "stir up all (in strife) with;" xi. 2, a single instance, as used of man. God is said הֵעִיר with acc. p. and עַל.

מִמְשָׁל, "dominion," Dan. xi. 3, 5. "dominions" i. e. princes. 1 Chron. xxvi. 6.

לַעֲשׂוֹת יְשָׁרִים Dan. xi. 6. (as, in familiar English, to 'set things straight.')

וְיֶחֱזַק מֶלֶךְ הַנֶּגֶב וּמִן שָׂרָיו "And the king of the South shall be strong and of his princes," i. e. one of them Dan. xi. 5. The idiom, "and there went of the people," (i. e. some of them,) is common. (See instances in Ges. Thes. p. 800.) Here only, the subject to be supplied is one person. In Dan. xi. 7. "and there shall stand up *from* the sucker of her roots," מִן most naturally expresses the extraction, i. e. from whom he should be born. In Mic. v. 1. מִן relates unquestionably to the birth-place.

כֹּחַ Dan. xi. 6, probably a trace of a fuller pronunciation. The Kri substitutes the common form, כֹּח, which Daniel too has 7 times, besides כֹחוֹ 4 times. This form of nouns, עֲע, occurs in middle as well as later Hebrew. אוֹן Ps. lxxii. 14. (in Ps. x. 7. lv. 12, אוֹן) רֹב Job xxxv. 9. (as well as Esth. x. 3.) תֹּם Prov. x. 9. עֹז, Ps. lxxxiv. 6. Prov. xxiv. 5. xxxi. 17. 25. עֻזְּמוֹ Ps. lxxxi. 2. שׁוֹד occurs only in Job v. 21. עֹל in Deut. xxi. 3. as well as in Jer. v. 3. The forms are too insulated in their several roots to argue from.

תָּבֹא אֶל, "shall come to," i. e. as a bride, ἅπ. Dan. xi. 6. abs. "came," of one actually married, Josh. xv. 18. Judg. i. 14. It corresponds with הֵבִיא with לְ p. "took a wife for" a son, Judg. xii. 9; here, קְבִיאִים.

עָמַר כַּנּוֹ "bestood his place," very boldly, Dan. xi. 7. i. q. עַל כַּנּוֹ Ib. 20. 21; עֹמֵד, "standing *up*," having the idea of motion.

יִתְגָּרוּ, abs. xi. 10. (ii.) "strive," lit. "stir themselves up." (comp. Syr. "they strove together," Barh. p. 219. in Ges. p. 301.) with לַמִּלְחָמָה added, Ib. 25.

עִמּוֹ עִם כָּלָה הַשָּׁטוֹן, Dan. xi. 11, probably an emphatic repetition of the preposition, retained by Daniel from the Aramaic. It occurs in the Chaldee both of Daniel, (v. 12. בֵּהּ בְּדָנִיֵּאל) and Ezra, (iv. 11. עֲלוֹהִי עַל אַרְתַּחְשַׁשְׁתְּא.) In Syriac, Rom. vi. 8. "'ameh 'am Meshicho," "with Him, even with Christ." (See Hofmann, Gram. Syr. p. 319.) The emphatic repetition of the preposition separates it from the cases of the so-called pleonastic pronoun. A similar emphasis, without a preposition, occurs in the earliest Hebrew, Ex. ii. 6, וַתִּרְאֵהוּ אֶת הַיֶּלֶד, "and she saw it, the child." In Prov. v. 22, xiv. 13, our Version retains the emphasis; in Jer. ix. 14, it is marked by the הִנֵּה following, "Lo, I am about to make them, this people, (אֶת הָעָם הַזֶּה) eat wormwood."

שָׁנִים, "years," determining לְקֵץ הָעִתִּים, "at the end of the times," Dan. xi. 13. as in x. 2. שְׁלֹשָׁה שָׁבֻעִים יָמִים "three weeks (of) days."

לְהַעֲמִיד חָזוֹן, "confirm the vision," lit. "make it stand," Dan. xi. 14. הֶעֱמִיד is used with abstracts, in the sense of "constituting a law to," with acc. and לְ p. Ps. cv. 10; with עַל p. "we constituted ordinances (as binding) on us." Neh. x. 33.

עִיר מִבְצָרוֹת Dan. xi. 15. fem. *ἅπ.* Jeremiah has עָרֵי מִבְצָרֶיךָ Jer. v. 17. Daniel has the form, מִבְצָרִים, "fortresses," xi. 24. 39.

זְרוֹעוֹת, with gen., "the arms of," i. e. "the might of," Dan. xi. 15, 22. זְרֹעִים, abs. xi. 31, according to the analogy of לֹא בְזְרוֹעַ גְּדוֹלָה וּבְעַם רָב Ez. xvii. 9. and Ch. בְּאֶדְרָע וְחַיִל Ezr. iv. 23; and the phrases, "I will break Pharaoh's arms;" "I will strengthen the arms of the king of Babylon;" (Ezek. xxx. 22, 24, 25.) although in these cases the metaphor is prominent.

עַם מִבְחָרָיו, "his people of choice," Dan. xi. 15. The pl. מִבְחָרִים occurs here only; the order is that of 2 Kings iii. 19, עִיר מִבְחוֹר; usually מִבְחַר stands first. (xi times.)

לֹא בְאַפַּיִם, "not in anger." Dan. xi. 20. אַפַּיִם, as "anger," occurs else only in the phrase אֶרֶךְ אַפַּיִם, and in the opposite, קְצַר אַפַּיִם, Pr. xiv. 17.

בַּחֲלַקְלַקּוֹת, "with flatteries," Dan. xi. 21. 34. בַּחֲלַקּוֹת, Dan. xi. 32, both once only; but we have שְׂפַת חֲלָקוֹת, שִׂפְתֵי חֲלָקוֹת, Ps. xii. 3, 4. חֲלַקְלַקּוֹת, "slippery places," Ps. xxxv. 6. Jer. xxiii. 12.

וּזְרֹעוֹת הַשֶּׁטֶף יִשָּׁטֵפוּ, xi. 22, lit. "the arms of the overflow shall be overflowed;" i. e. the tide of power which threatened to sweep away shall be swept back by a mightier tide. זְרֹעוֹת is construed with the masc., probably, from the idea of strength.

נְגִיד בְּרִית Ib. " a prince of a covenant,' after the analogy of אַנְשֵׁי בְרִית Obad. 7.

פָּנוּר xi. 24, only. Pi. only in Ps. lxviii. 31. In Ch. בדר, Pa., Dan. iv. 11. Aram. Samar. In Heb. פור, x times. Ps. (v.) Prov. Joel, Jer. (ii.) Esth.

אֹכְלֵי פַתְבָּגוֹ xi. 26, after the analogy of אוֹכֵל לַחְמִי, Ps. xli. 10.

לְהָרֵע, " for evil doing," Dan. xi. 27. subst. like סָבַב, Cant. i. 12.

בוא, with בּ p. " come *upon* him." Dan. xi. 30. Else, with acc. p. in poetry ; in prose, with עַל p. Yet there is ample analogy for this construction with ב, in that of עָצַר, כָּשַׁל, רָדָה, נִלְחַם, רִיב, with בּ p. (Ew. 606.)

צִיִּים " ships " (Ib.) as אִיִּים. In Num. xxiv. 24. Ez. xxx. 9. the plur. is צִים.

וּזְרֹעִים, fig. " arms," Dan. xi. 31. masc. with idea of strength, Gen. xlix. 24; of God, Is. li. 5; בֵּין זְרֹעָיו " between his arms," 2 Kings ix. 24. Else זְרוֹעוֹת (xix times in all, in Dan., ii.)

מַרְשִׁיעֵי בְרִית Dan. xi. 32. (peculiar idiom) " who acted wickedly as to the covenant."

† יַחֲנִיף Ib., " corrupt," i. e. seduce to defile themselves. This is trans. of חָנֵף Jer. xxiii. 11. " priests and prophets became polluted." Else, of the land, Kal Ps. cvi. 38. Is. xxiv. 5. Mic. iv. 11. Jer. iii. 1, 9. Hif. Jer. iii. 2. Num. xxxv. 33. In the Peshito, it is used as equivalent to the ἐθνικὸς of the N. T.; and Afel, of " apostatising," S. Ephr. de fide iii. 6. If it had this meaning in Daniel, it would be another instance of his language surviving in Syriac, while lost in the Chaldee of the Targg.

לְבָרֵר, " purify," Pi. only Dan. xi. 35.

הִלְבִּין trans. only ib.; יִתְחַלְּנוּ, " cleanse self," Ib. xii. 10. only.

אֵל אֵלִים, " God of gods," Dan. xi. 36. i. q. אֱלֹהֵי הָאֱלֹהִים Deut. x. 17. Josh. xxii. 22. Ps. cxxxvi. 2. אֱלָהּ אֱלָהִין, Dan. ii. 47. Ch. שַׂר שָׂרִים, of God, Dan. viii. 25.

יְדַבֵּר נִפְלָאוֹת " will speak marvellous," i. e. proud things, Dan. xi. 36. i. q. מְמַלֵּל רַבְרְבָן, " speaking great things," Dan. vii. 8. 28. Ch. and לָשׁוֹן מְדַבֶּרֶת גְּדֹלוֹת. Ps. xii. 4.

יִתְנַגַּח Hithp., only Dan. xi. 40; Piel, מְנַגֵּחַ, Dan. viii. 4. In the physical sense, " push with horns," Pi. Ex. xxi. [iii times ;] metaph. as here, Deut. (i.) Ps. (i.) 1 Kings (i.) Ez. (i.) Chr. (i.)

יִשְׂתָּעֵר Hithp. only Dan. xi. 40, " come as a whirlwind ;" comp. Job xxvii. 21, וִישָׂעֲרֵהוּ מִמְּקֹמוֹ.

הָיָה לִפְלֵיטָה Dan. xi. 42.

מִכְמַנִּים, † " hidden treasures," Dan. xi. 43. The root, כמן, must, in the time of Daniel, have had a meaning, " hide," which has survived in Arabic, but was lost both in Eastern and Western Aramaic. In the Targg. (see Buxtorf,) and where it occurs in the Peshito, as also in all the places noted by Bernstein and Quatremère, it has only the derived sense, which occurs in the Arabic also, " lay in wait for," i. e. *hid himself,* in order to fall on another.

בְּמִצְעָדָיו, lit. " at, in his steps," Dan. xi. 43; perhaps chosen, as more stately than בְּרַגְלָיו, the ordinary idiom in prose, Ex. xi. 8. Deut. xi. 6. Judg. iv. 10. viii. 5. 1 Sam. xxv. 27. 2 Sam. xv. 17. 1 Kings xx. 10, 2 Kings iii. 9. [viii times.]

חֵמָא, for חֵמָה, " anger." Dan. xi. 44.

אַפַּדְנוֹ, " his palace," xi. 45. See ab. p. 39, 40.

עָמַד with עַל p. " stood over," to protect. Dan. xii. 1. comp. 1 Sam. xxv. 16, חוֹמָה הָיוּ עָלֵינוּ, " they were a wall, protecting us;" Ez. xiii. 5. " Ye have not made up the fence, עַל בֵּית, for [protecting] the house of Israel;" and נִלְחַם with עַל p. " fight for." Neh. iv. 8.

כָּתוּב בַּסֵּפֶר " written in *the* book " (i. e. " the book of life " or " of God ") only in Dan. xii. 1. The idioms, " Thy book, My book," occur in Ex. xxxii. 22, 3; " Thy book," (of God) Ps. lvi. 8, cxxxvii. 16. " the book of life," Ps. lxix. 29. " every one written to life," כָּל הַכָּתוּב לַחַיִּים occurs in Is. iv. 3.

יְשֵׁנֵי אַדְמַת עָפָר יָקִיצוּ Dan. xii. 2. lit. " the sleepers of [in] the earth of dust shall awake ;" like Is. xxvi. 19. הָקִיצוּ שֹׁכְנֵי עָפָר lit. "awake, ye dwellers of [in] the dust." Comp. עָפָר Job vii. 21. xi. 11. Ps. xxii. 30. xxx. 10. and יִיקַץ Job xiv. 12. בְּהָקִיץ Ps. xvii. 15.

חַיֵּי עוֹלָם, lit. " life of eternity," Dan. xii. 2. חַיִּים, of " life," in itself, life unceasing, was fixed in the language by the title, עֵץ חַיִּים, " the tree of life," used metaphorically, without the art. Prov. iii. 18. xi. 30. xiii. 12. xv. 4. and חַיִּים absolutely in Ps. xxxvi. 10. "with Thee is מְקוֹר חַיִּים, the fountain of life ; " Prov. xi. 19, " as righteousness is לְחַיִּים, to life ; " so also in the idioms, דֶּרֶךְ חַיִּים, אֹרַח חַיִּים, " way of life." For the rest of the idiom, comp. שִׂמְחַת עוֹלָם, " perpetual joy," Is. xxxv. 10; דֶּרֶךְ עוֹלָם, "the way everlasting," i. e. which shall abide for ever, Ps. cxxxix. 24 ; and, of God, חַי הָעוֹלָם, " He Who liveth for ever," Dan. xii. 7. and חַי עָלְמָא Id. Dan. iv. 31. Ch.

דִּרְאוֹן עוֹלָם, Dan. xii. 2., drawn out from Is. lxvi. 24.

וְיַזְהִירוּ; lit. " give out brightness," " shine," only Dan. xii. 3. It is the original force of the word, which survived in Aramaic, and from which was derived the meaning, common to the earlier Hebrew, " teach," " warn." הֵאִיר, which Gesenius gives as its earlier equivalent, (p. 408) is used actively of " giving light to," " illumining," others, chiefly of God. Only in Ezek. xliii. 2, it is used of light reflected from God, " the earth shall shine from His glory," הָאִירָה מִכְּבֹדוֹ. Daniel, doubtless, revived the word in its primitive sense, in allusion to that, with which he joins it, וֹהַר רָקִיעַ, " brightness of the firmament," Dan. xii. 3. comp. כְּמַרְאֵה וֹהַר Ezek. viii. 2.

שׁוּט abs. Dan. xii. 4; with ל and inf. " go to and fro to seek," Am. viii. 12; with בּ of the place, Jer. v. 1. Zech. iv. 10. 2 Chron. xvi. 1.

הֵנָּה ל, הֵנָּה ל, " on this side of—on that side of," Dan. xii. 5. Else only הֵנָּה וָהֵנָּה, " hither and thither." Josh. viii. 20. 1 Kings xx. 40. 2 Kings ii. 8.

פְּלָאוֹת plur. only Dan. xii. 6.

מִי הָעוֹלָם Dan. xii. 6. see above xii. 3, commonly אֶל מִי, אֱלֹהִים חַיִּים.

ii. *Agreement with middle period of Hebrew.*

הִשְׂכִּיל with בּ, Dan. i. 4. ix. 25. Ps. ci. 2, מַשְׂכִּיל, noun, with בּ Dan. i. 7.

אֲשֶׁר אֵין בָּהֶם מְאוּם Dan. i. 4. viii. 7. [in xi. 15. בּ with pers. is omitted] also 1 Sam. xxx. 4. Is. l. 2. 2 Chron. xxv. 8. Ezr. x. 13. comp. Deut. viii. 18. כֹּחַ לַעֲשׂוֹת חָיִל

סֵפֶר *letters* Dan. i. 4, 17. Is. xxix. 11, 12.

מִכֵּן—יִנְצֹרֵהוּ—וּלְנֻדָלִם—וּמִקְצָתָם יַעֲשׂוּ Dan. i. 5. סַן Ps. lxi. 8.

שָׂם עַל לֵב Dan. i. 8. Is. xlvii. 7. lvii. 1, 11. Jer. xii. 11. with אֶל, 2 Sam. xix. 20. with בּ, Job xxii. 22. 1 Sam. xxi. 13.

וַיִּתֵּן אֶת דָּנִיֵּאל לְחֶסֶד וּלְרַחֲמִים לִפְנֵי Dan. i. 9. The same construction with acc. p., לְחֶסֶד וּלְרַחֲמִים and לִפְנֵי of p. occurs 1 Kings viii. 50. Ps. cvi. 46. Neh. i. 11.

אֲשֶׁר לָמָּה Dan. i. 10. i. q. שַׁלָּמָה Cant. i. 7. like Syr. דְּלָמָא.

חִיַּבְתֶּם Dan. i. 10. This intensive form occurs in nouns, פִּיד, Ex. xxx. 18; פִּיק, Am. v. 26; דַּיָּן, *judge*, 1 Sam. xxiv. 16. Ps. lxviii. 6; דִּיּג, Jer. xvi. 16. Keth. Ezek. xlvii. 10. In the verb, it occurs in קַם Ps. cxix. 28, 106. as well as in Ruth iv. 7. Ezek. xiii. 6. Esth. [vii time close together.]

שָׁמַע with ל p. and לִדְבַר חַזֶּה Dan. i. 14. 1 Sam. xxx. 24.

חָכְמַת בִּינָה Dan. i. 20. constr. as שָׂנֵא חָמָס Ps. xxv. 19.

מְדִינָה, " jurisdiction," (from דִּין ;) then, of some small " jurisdictions " in the kingdom of Israel, (1 Kings xx. 14, 15, 17, 19.) or of Solomon, (Eccl. v. 7.) [8. Eng.] or of petty tributary kingdoms, (Eccl. ii. 8 ;) then, in the general sense of " countries," (Lam. i. 1. Ezek. xix. 8. sing. Dan. xi. 24.) transferred to the " provinces " of the Babylonian and Persian Empires, in the Hebrew and Chaldee of Daniel, the Chaldee of Ezra, and the Hebrew of Esther, (Dan. viii. 2. and Ch. of Dan. ii. 48, 49. iii. 1, 2, 3, 12, 30. and of Ezra iv. 15. vi. 2. vii. 16. Esth. xxxix times) and to Judæa, after the return from the Captivity, as a Persian " province." Ezr. ii. 1. v. 8. Ch. Neh. i. 3. vii. 6. xi. 3. This sense is purely Hebrew ; in Aramaic and Arabic of old the word signifies simply " city," whence the name *Medina*. In Jon. it is retained from the Heb.; else it is " city."

יָתֵר יַגְבֵּל מַנְבֵּל (Syr. *yathir*) Dan. viii. 9. נֵרָל מָאוֹר, Gen. xxvi. 13. Job ii. 13. But Dan. has the common צַר מָאוֹר viii. 8. xi. 25. and Isaiah has יָתֵר מָאוֹר, lxvi. 12. and David עַל יָתֵר, Ps. xxxi. 24.

צְבָא fem. Dan. viii. 12. Is. xl. 2.

The use of וָ, וְ, "et, et," Dan. viii. 13. Ps. lxxvi. 7. Prov. xxvi. 10. Is. xiii. 9. Jer. xiii. 12. xxi. 6. xxxii. 14. Neh. i. 6. xii. 28 ; yet also once in the Pentat. Num. ix. 14. and Job xxxiv. 28. (The other instances in Nold. n. 64. are wrong or doubtful.)

† The omission of the article belongs to the elevated character of the prophetic style, as being essentially poetic. We could represent פֵּת וְקֹרֵשׁ וְצָבָא by "to give both sanctuary and host," so שַׂר שָׂרִים v. 25. See ab. p. 478. There is no characteristic omission of the article in Daniel, as Leng. would have it.

סַח—מִרְמָס, Dan. viii. 13. cp. לְמַרְמָס מִרְמָס, Is. x. 6. הָיָה לְמִרְמָס Is. v. 5. xxviii. 18. Mic. vii. 10. Else in two places with gen. after מִרְמָס, Is. vii. 25. Ezek. xxxiv. 19.

בֵּין, "between," used in regard to a whole. בֵּין אוּלָי, "between [the banks of] the Ulai," viii. 16. בֵּין הָרְחֹבוֹת "in the midst of the streets." Prov. xxvi. 13.

הַלָּז, without a subst., "*this* (man)," Dan. viii. 16. 1 Sam. xiv. 1. (as Arab. *allads* for *alladsi*) ; not in the Pent.; nor is the הַלָּזֶה of Pent. (iii) in later books.

הַבִין with לְ of pers. Dan. viii. 16. xi. 33. as in Job vi. 24. according to the analogy of other words, which signify "imparting instruction *to*." It is united with the personal affix, as an acc. Dan. x. 14.

צַר עֵת קֵץ כִּי עוֹד קֵץ לְמוֹעֵד, xi. 35, כִּי לְעֵת קֵץ הֶחָזוֹן, viii. 17, כִּי לְמוֹעֵד קֵץ, viii. 19, כִּי עוֹד קֵץ לַמּוֹעֵד xii. 4. עַד עֵת קֵץ, xi. 27, כִּי קֵץ מֶלְחָמָה ix. 26, refer back to the saying in Hab. ii. 3. כִּי עוֹד חָזוֹן לַמּוֹעֵד וְיָפֵחַ לַקֵּץ, that, though God's promises tarried, they did not tarry out. comp. Ps. cii. 14. כִּי עֵת לְחֶנְנָהּ כִּי בָא מוֹעֵד.

In like way, בְּאַחֲרִית הַזַּעַם, "at the end of the wrath," Dan. viii. 19, עַד כָּלָה זַעַם Dan. xi. 36. from Isaiah x. 25. וְכָלָה זַעַם xxvi. 20. עַד יַעֲבוֹר זַעַם of a fixed measure of God's chastening displeasure.

נִפְלָאוֹת adv. "marvellously," Dan. viii. 24, as in Job xxxvii. 5. The plural expresses "'manifold marvellous ways."

הִצְלִיחַ מִרְמָה בְּיָדוֹ, viii. 25, the reverse of חֵפֶץ יְהֹוָה בְּיָדוֹ יִצְלָח Is. liii. 10.

בְּאֶפֶס יָד, viii. 25. i. q. לֹא with noun, Job vii. 6. Prov. xiv. 28. xxvi. 20. Is. lii. 4. וְהֵסִיר אַבִּיר לֹא בְיָד Job xxxiv. 20.

הֵאִיר פָּנִים, of God, with aff. and prepos. of object ; viz. עַל Dan. ix. 17. Ps. xxxi. 17. אֶל Num. vi. 28. אֶת Ps. lxvii. 2. בְּ. Ps. cxix. 135. abs. Ps. lxxx. 4, 8, 20.

הַטֵּה אֱלֹהַי אָזְנְךָ וּֽשֲׁמָע פְּקַח עֵינֶיךָ וּרְאֵה Dan. ix. 18.
————————————————יהוה————————————פְּקַח "———2 Kings xix. 16.

אֲשֶׁר נִקְרָא שִׁמְךָ עָלָיו Dan. ix. 18 ; of God's house, בַּיִת Jer. vii. 10, 11.
14, 30. xxxii. 34. xxxiv. 15. ; of the city, עִיר Ib. xxv. 29.

אֶל תְּאַחַר, of God, Dan. ix. 19. only Ps. xl. 18. lxx. 6. לֹא יְאַחֵר, of the
vision, Hab. ii. 3. with לְשֹׂנְאוֹ, of God, "will not be slack to him that
hateth Him." Deut. vii. 10.

עוֹד הֵם מְדַבְּרִים וַאֲנִי עוֹד אֲנִי מְדַבֵּר—וּ Dan. ix. 20. 21. Is. lxv. 24.

כָּלָה וְנֶחֱרָצָה Dan. ix. 27. נֶחֱרָצָה ix. 26. נֶחֱרָצָה Dan. xi. 36. Is. x. 23.
xxviii. 22.

דָּבָר (abs.) " a word " revealed, (נִגְלָה, here) Dan. x. 1. Is. ix. 7. xlv.
23. l. 4. then Jer. xxxvii. 17. Ezek. iii. 17. xiii. 6. xxxiii. 7; of secret
inspiration, Job iv. 12.

סַרְבָּלוֹ Dan. x. 6. Ruth iii. 4, 7, 8, 14.

קוֹל הָמוֹן Dan. x. 6. Is. xxxiii. 3.

נָתַתִּי פְנֵי אַרְצָה Dan. x. 15. i. q. שׂוּם פָּנִים אַרְצָה 1 Kings ii. 15. 2 Kings xii. 8.
Ez. vi. 2.

נֶהְפְּכוּ צִירַי עָלָי Dan. x. 16. metaphoric use of the words of 1 Sam.
iv. 19.

חֲזַק וַחֲזָק, Dan. x. 19, חֲזַק וְנִתְחַזַּק 2 Sam. x. 12, thence 1 Chr. xix. 13.
חֲזַק וְנִתְחַזְּקָה. Generally, חֲזַק וֶאֱמָץ Deut. xxxi. 7. 23. Josh. i. 6, 7, 9, 18.
thence 1 Chron. xxii. 13. xxviii. 20. וְיַאֲמֵץ לִבֶּךָ Ps. xxvii. 14.

וּמֶשָׁרָה לֹא נִשְׁאֲרָה בִי Dan. x. 17. comp. לֹא הָיָה בָהּ עוֹד רוּחַ 1 Kings x. 5.

מֵנֵצֶר שָׁרָשֶׁיהָ Dan. xi. 7, as נֵצֶר מִשָּׁרָשָׁיו, Is. xi. 1. נֵצֶר only in these two
places and Is. xiv. 19. lx. 21, and שֹׁרֶשׁ of " sucker from root," only
in Is. xi. 10. liii. 2.

בִּלְתִּי, for בִּלְתִּי אֲשֶׁר, Dan. xi. 8. comp. Is. x. 4. and בִּלְתִּי אֲחִיכֶם אִתְּכֶם Gen.
xliii. 3.

וְשָׁטַף וְעָבַר Dan. xi. 10, 40. from Is. viii. 8.

הֶעֱמִיד הָמוֹן רַב, "*set*," in their place, "a great multitude," Dan. xi.
11. 13. הַעֲמֵד הַמְצַפֶּה "set the watch." Is. xxi. 6.   Else, of persons or
animate things, the place is expressed, as לִפְנֵי " with acc. of place,
Lev. xiv. 11. xvi. 7 ; or לִפְנֵי " alone, Num. v. 16, 18, 30, pass. Lev.
xvi. 10 ; or לִפְנֵי הַכֹּהֵן, Lev. xxvii. 8. 11. Num. iii. 6. viii. 13. xxvii. 19.
22; or, of a king, לִפְנֵי פַרְעֹה Gen. xlvii. 7 ; or with בְּ of place, 1 Kings
xii. 32. 1 Chron. xvii. 14. Neh. iv. 7. vii. 3 ; סְבִיבוֹת, Num. xi. 24 ; בֵּין,
Jud. xvi. 25 ; מִמַּתַּן, 2 Chron. xxiii. 10 ; לִימִין, Neh. xii. 31 ; עַל, of place,
implying watch, 2 Chron. xxiii. 19. xxxv. 2. Neh. xiii. 9.   The idiom
in which הֶעֱמִיד, c. acc. p. signifies " set up, constituted," is different,
and occurs in Exodus ix. 16. Neh. vi. 7. and with מְקוֹמָם, " in their
place," Job xxxiv. 24.   In Ps. cvii. 25, by a very bold image, it is
said, " God made the wind to stand."

בְּנֵי פָּרִיצֵי עַמְּךָ, "sons of the violent men of thy people," (seditious,) Dan. xi. 14. comp. בְּנֵי אֶבְיוֹן, "sons of poor," Ps. lxxii. 4. יַלְדֵי נָכְרִים, "children of strangers." Is. ii. 6.

שָׁפַךְ סֹלְלָה, "cast a mound," Dan. xi. 15. אֶל עִיר, 2 Sam. xx. 15. עַל עִיר, 2 Kings xix. 32. Is. xxxvii. 33. Jer. vi. 6. Ezek. iv. 2. xxvi. 8. abs. as here, Ezek. xvii. 17. xxi. 27.

וְיַעַשׂ Dan. xi. 16. וְיָשֵׂם, 17, וְיָשֵׁב, 10, 18, 19. וַיַּעַר 25, 28 וְיָכֶן 30. The condensation of this idiom, the use of the apocopated form, with the simple *and*, shews that there is great emphasis in it. Daniel used it besides in this chapter, v. 4. וַתֵּחָץ and viii. 12. וַתַּשְׁלֵךְ. But, (as noticed by Ewald, Ausf. Lehrb. § 343. c. p. 829, 30. ed. 7.) it occurs in Joel ii. 20, וַיַּעַל; Mic. iii. 4. וַיַּסְתֵּר, and even in Lev. xxvii. 43. וְתֵרָץ; and Lev. xv. 24. These cases in Daniel are the ground of Lengerke's strange assertion, that "he is not acquainted with the ו conv.," (" does not use vau conversive," Dav. iii. 194.) which he uses continually.

לֹא יַעֲמֹד וְלֹא לוֹ תִּהְיֶה, Dan. xi. 17. from Is. vii. 7. לֹא תָקוּם וְלֹא תִהְיֶה, comp. Is. xiv. 24.

הֶחֱזִיק, "laid hold of," with acc. instead of בְּ, Dan. xi. 21. 2 Sam. xv. 5. "terror seized hold of," c. acc. p. Mic. iv. 9. Jer. vi. 24. viii. 21. "trouble seized, &c." Jer. l. 43.

יָעִיר כֹּחוֹ וּלְבָבוֹ xi. 25. like לֹא יָעִיר כָּל חֲמָתוֹ Ps. lxxviii. 38. עִיר קִנְאָה; Is. xlii. 13.

נָפְלוּ חֲלָלִים רַבִּים, Dan. xi. 26. Judg. ix. 40. 1 Chron. v. 22.

כְּ וּכְ, lit. "as—and as," for כְּ כְּ Dan. xi. 29. as, Josh. xiv. 11. 1 Sam. xxx. 24. Ezek. xviii. 4.

נִכְאָה, "despond." Dan. xi. 30. נִכְאָה לֵבָב Ps. cix. 16.

רַבּוֹת יִכָּשְׁלוּ, "multitudes [fem.] shall stumble," [masc.] xi. 41. שְׁמֻעוֹת יְבַהֲלֻהוּ "rumours [fem.] shall terrify [masc.] him." xi. 44. These may be the use of the 3rd pers. masc. plur. as a common gender, including the fem., as in Job iii. 24. Cant. vi. 9. Prov. xvi. 3. Hos. xiv. 1, 7. and 2nd. person plur., Cant. ii. 7. viii. 4. Joel ii. 22. (Ew. Gr. p. 643.) Esth. i. 20; or they might be a very bold change of gender, in conformity with the image; since, as to the first, those who "stumble" must be persons; as to the second, the "terror" implies might; and Jeremiah has (xlix. 16.) תִּפְלַצְתְּךָ הִשִּׁיא אֹתָךְ, "thy terribleness [fem.] hath deceived (masc.) thee;" as חַטָּאת is construed as masc. from the image of a wild beast, "sin [fem.] coucheth [masc.] at the door." Gen. iv. 7.

הַדַּעַת with art. lit. "*the* [only] knowledge." Dan. xii. 4. Hos. iv. 6.

iii. *Words and idioms common to Daniel with later books.*

בִּשְׁנַת שָׁלוֹשׁ לְמַלְכוּת פ׳, "in the year three of the reign of," i. 1. ii. 1. viii. 1. 1 Chr. xxvi. 31. 2 Chr. iii. 2. xv. 10, 19. xvi. 1, 12. xxxv. 19.

Esth. ii. 16.   Moses has the fuller idiom בְּצֵאת שֵׁשׁ מֵאוֹת שָׁנָה לְחַיֵּי נֹחַ Gen. vii. 11. (followed in 1 Kings xvi. 8, 15, 23. [with the shorter form ver. 10.] 2 Kings viii. 25. xiii. 1, 10.) but also בְּצֵאת הָאֲרָצִים לְ without שָׁנָה Num. xxxiii. 38.   מַלְכֹה, however, only occurs in the Pentateuch in the mouth of Balaam (from Aram,) Num. xxiv. 7.; the form most used in the earlier books being מְמָלָכָה.

Daniel has also (i. 21. vii. 1. ix. 1. x. 1. xi. 1.) the shorter form, which is frequent in the Kings, with לְ simply prefixed to the name of the king, and בְּצֵאת אֶחָת לְמָלְכוֹ ix. 2, which occurs in Kings [ii.] Jeremiah [iii.] Chron. [v.] Esther [i.]

מִקְצָת [form מְנָת Ps. xvi. 5, &c.] "some," of things, Dan. i. 2. of persons, Neh. vii. 70. מִקְצֵה, Gen. xlvii. 2. (thence in Ezek. xxxiii. 2.) of time, Dan. i. 5, 15, 18. מִקֵּץ Gen. viii. 3, &c.

כְּלֵי בֵית הָאֱלֹהִים, Dan. i. 2. 2 Chron. xxviii. 24. (bis) xxxvi. 18. Neh. xiii. 9. בֵּית ״, Jer. xxvii. 16. xxviii. 3, 6. 2 Chron. xxxvi. 10. Ezr. i. 7; but כְּלֵי הַקֹּדֶשׁ, 1 Kings viii. 4. as Num. iii. 31. also 1 Chron. ix. 21. 2 Chron. v. 5.   The name יהוה occurs only in Daniel's own prayer, Dan. ix. 10. 13. 14. [ii.] and its immediate context ix. 2. 4. 20.

כְּלֵי חֲמֻדֹתָם Dan. xi. 8. comp. עַל כְּלֵי חֶמְדָּה 2 Chron. xxxii. 27. כְּלֵי חֶמְדָה בֵית ״ 2 Chron. xxxvi. 10. כִּי מַחְמַדֶּיהָ Ib. 19. but also Hos. xii. 10.

בֵּית אוֹצַר אֱלֹהָיו Dan. i. 2. ("the treasure-house of his gods," for the simple אוֹצָר,) בֵּית הָאוֹצָר, Mal. iii. 10. Neh. x. 39. in Jos. אוֹצַר ״, vi. 19. אוֹצַר בֵּית ״, Ib. 24. and so 1 Chron. xxix. 8. אֹצְרוֹת בֵּית ״ 1 Kings vii. 51. xv. 18. 2 Kings xii. 19. הָאֱלֹהִים א. ב., 2 Chron. v. 1.

אָמַר with לְ and inf. "commanded to," Dan. i. 3. 4. 18. ii. 2. (in Chald. of Dan. ii. 12. 46. iii. 13, 19, 20. iv. 23. vi. 24.) 1 Chron. xxi. 17. Esth. i. 17. iv. 13. ix. 14.   In 2 Sam. xxii. 16, (quoted by Ew. Lehrb. p. 818.) as in Ex. ii. 14, it signifies, "thought to." See Ges. Thes. p. 120.

מִזֶּרַע הַמְּלוּכָה Dan. i. 3. 2 Kings xxv. 25. Jer. xli. 1. Ez. xvii. 13.

פַּרְתְּמִים † "Nobles," Jewish, Dan. i. 3. Persian, Esth. i. 3. vi. 9. Aryan word. See Note A. p. 570.   The Hebrew title is אֵלֵי הָאָרֶץ Ez. xvii. 13. 2 Kings xxiv. 15. comp. Ezek. xv. 15. or חוֹרִים, see above p. 346, or generally אַדִּירִים, גְּדוֹלִים.

מַדָּע † knowledge, Dan. i. 4. 17. 2 Chron. i. 10, 11, 12. (מַנְדַּע Ch. Dan. ii. 21. iv. 31. 33. v. 12. Sam. מַדָּעָה) connected with contraction in the oldest Hebrew, מַדָּע for מַה־יָּדַע.

נִגְאָל, "was defiled," Dan. i. 8. Ezr. ii. 62. Mal. i. 7, 12. Neh. vii. 64. but also before Captivity, Is. lix. 3. lxiii. 3. Zeph. iii. 1. or at its beginning, Lam. iv. 14.

מֵבִין בְּכָל חָזוֹן, Dan. i. 17. חָשַׁב בִּרְאוֹת הָאֱלֹהִים, 2 Chron. xxvi. 5. and generally הָבִין with בְ ix. 23. (ii.) x. 11. 2 Chron. xxxiv. 12. Neh. viii. 8. xiii. 7.

גִּבְעָה, "castle," "tower," Dan. viii. 2. Chron. (ii.) Neh. (iii.) Esth. (x.)

עָשָׂה פְרָצוֹ Dan. viii. 4. xi. 3, 16. with plur. aff. Neh. ix. 24. Esth. xi. 5.

צְפִיר הָעִזִּים (i. q. שְׂעִיר עִזִּים of Pent.] Dan. viii. 5, 8. 2 Chron. xxix. 21. Ezr. vi. 17. Ch. הַצָּפִיר alone, Dan. viii. 5. Ezr. viii. 35 ; with הַשָּׂעִיר, Dan. viii. 21. (צְפִיר Ch. Sam. צְפַר Syr.)

סַלְקָיוֹת Dan. viii. 22. like מַצָּאוֹת Jer. xxxvii. 16.

ix. 6. accumulation like Jer. xliv. 17.

עָמַד c. עַל p. viii. 25. xi. 14. 1 Chron. xxi. 1. 2 Chron. xx. 23.

עָמְדִ, only with affix, "where I, he, stood," nearly = מָקוֹם, Dan. iii. 17, 18. x. 11. xi. 1. 2 Chron. (iii.) Neh. (iii.)

וָאֶעֱשֶׂה, Dan. viii. 27. only occurs in Ez. xx. 14 ; but וַיַּעַשׂ also, occurs only five times ; וַיַּעֲשֶׂה also occurs 1 Kings xvi. 25. 2 Kings iii. 2. xiii. 11. Ezek. xviii. 12.

בְּכָל הָאֲרָצוֹת אֲשֶׁר הִדַּחְתָּם שָׁם Dan. ix. 7. from Jer. xxiii. 3. 8. xxxii. 37.

בֹּשֶׁת פָּנִים, for בֹּשֶׁת only, Dan. ix. 7, 8. 2 Chron. xxxii. 21. with aff. בְּ. פָּנֵי Ps. xliv. 16. פְּנֵיהֶם בְּ. Jer. vii. 19.

לְאִישׁ יְהוּדָה וּלְיֹשְׁבֵי יְרוּשָׁלַם Dan. ix. 7. Jer. xxxv. 13. with the prep. אֶל and עַל, Jer. xi. 2. xviii. 11.

עַל אִישׁ יְהוּדָה וְיֹשְׁבֵי יְרוּשָׁלַם 2 Chron. xxxiv. 30.

עַל יְהוּדָה וְכָל ״י ״י Jer. xvii. 20. xxv. 2.

אֶל יְה׳ . וְאֶל כָּל ״י ״י Jer. xxxv. 17.

עַל כָּל עַם יה׳ וְאֶל ״י עַל ״י Jer. xxv. 2.

עַל יה׳ ר׳ ״י 2 Chron. xx. 15, 18. xxxii. 33.

יְהוּדָה ר׳ ״י 2 Chron. xx. 20. xxi. 13. xxxiii. 9.

הַקְּרֹבִים וְהָרְחֹקִים Dan. ix. 7. Jer. xxv. 26. Esth. ix. 20. from Deut. xiii. 8. הַקְּרֹבִים אֵלֶיךָ אוֹ הָרְחֹקִים כְּמָ.

מַעַל, verb and noun, revived from the Pentateuch in the later books; very little used in intervening books.

The verb occurs in the Pent. (vii times) Josh. (iv.) Prov. (i.) Dan. ix. 7. Ezek. (vii.) Ezr. (ii.) Chron. (xii.) Neh. (ii.); the noun, in Pent. (vii.) Josh. (v.) Job (i.) Ezek. (v.) Dan. ix. 7. Ezr. (iii.) Chron. (v.)

מָעַל מַעַל, with בְּיי, or pronoun relating to God, Lev. v. 21. xxvi. 40. Num. v. 6. Josh. xxii. 31. Ezek. xvii. 20. xx. 27. xxxix. 26. Dan. ix. 7. 1 Chron. x. 13. 2 Chron. xxviii. 19.

רַחֲמִים Dan. ix. 9. Jer. xvi. 5. "the mercies, compassions," רַחֲמֶיךָ הָרַבִּים Dan. ix. 18. "Thy mercies, the great," i. e. Thy great, well-known mercies.   Nehemiah has ברחי הר׳, מרח׳ הר׳, lit. "in, according to Thy mercies, the great."   Else, only רַחֲמֶיךָ רַבִּים, Ps. cxix. 156. "Thy mercies are great."   רַחֲמָיו רַבִּים, 2 Sam. xxiv. 14. 1 Chron. xxi. 13. כְּרֹב רַחֲמֶיךָ, "according to the multitude of," &c. Ps. li. 3. lxix. 17.

הַסְּלִיחוֹת Dan. ix. 9. הַסְּלִיחָה Ps. cxxx. 4. אֱלוֹהַ סְלִיחוֹת Neh. ix. 17.

וְלֹא שָׁמַעְנוּ בְּקוֹל יי אֱלֹהֵינוּ לָלֶכֶת בְּתוֹרֹתָיו Dan. ix. 10. from Jer. xliv. 23. לֹא שְׁמַעְתֶּם בְּקוֹל יְהֹוָה וּבְתֹרָתוֹ וּבְחֻקֹּתָיו וּבְעֵדְוֹתָיו לֹא הֲלַכְתֶּם

נִתַּךְ "poured out," of God's anger, Dan. ix. 11, 27. Nah. i. 6. Jer. vii. 20. xlii. 18. xliv. 6. 2 Chron. xii. 7. xxxiv. 17. 21. 25.

אֵת before Nominative, Dan. ix. 13. Jer. xxxvi. 22. Neh. ix. 19.

שָׁקַד with עַל of thg. Dan. ix. 14. Jer. i. 14. with עַל p. Jer. xxxi. 28. xxxiv. 27.

כִּי צַדִּיק יי עַל כָּל מַעֲשָׂיו Dan. ix. 14. וְאַתָּה צַדִּיק עַל כָּל הַבָּא עָלֵינוּ Neh. ix 33.

וַתַּעֲשֶׂה־לְּךָ שֵׁם כַּיּוֹם הַזֶּה Dan. ix. 15. verbatim from Jer. xxxii. 20. (only Jeremiah has the unabridged form, וַתַּעֲשֶׂה.) כַּיּוֹם הַזֶּה, like "hodie" for " adhuc " in good latin.

מַפִּיל תְּחִנָּתִי לִפְנֵי יי Dan. ix. 20. נֹפְלִים תְּחִנּוֹנֵינוּ לְפָנֶיךָ Dan. ix. 18. מַפִּיל אֲנִי תְחִנָּתִי לִפְנֵי הַמֶּלֶךְ Ib. xxxviii. 26. תְּחִנָּתָם לְפָנָיו Jer. xlii. 9. of God.

אוּזַל, Dan. x. 5. Jer. x. 9.

אֲבָל "nevertheless," "however," Dan. x. 7, 21. Ezr. x. 13. 2 Chr. i. 4. xix. 3. xxxiii. 17.   "nay but," Gen. xvii. 19. xlii. 21. 2 Sam. xiv. 5. 1 Kings i. 43. 2 Kings iv. 14.

עָצַר כֹּחַ Dan. x. 8, 16. xi. 6. 2 Chron. xiii. 20; with לְ 1 Chron. xxix. 14. 2 Chron. xxii. 9.

מַרְעִיד, † "trembling," of the human being, Dan. x. 11. Ezr. x. 9, after the analogy of מַעֲרִיץ Is. viii. 12. xxix. 24, and other words, expressive of emotion.   We say, "do not frighten yourselves."   The simple root, רָעַד, is used of the lifeless earth, Ps. civ. 33.   רַעַד, "trembling," occurs Ex. xv. 15. Ps. lv. 6.

נָתַן אֶת לִבּוֹ with לְ and inf. Dan. x. 12. Eccl. i. 13, 17. viii. 16. 1 Chr. xxii. 19. 2 Chron. xi. 16 ; with לְ of thing Eccl. vii. 21. viii. 9.

נָתַן

לְהִתְעַנּוֹת לִפְנֵי אֱלֹהֶיךָ Dan. x. 12. Ezr. viii. 21.

הֵיךְ † (for אֵיךְ) Dan. x. 17. 1 Chron. xiii. 12. Sam. הֵךְ, even in Sam. Pent. Gen. xxxiv. 21 ; Syr. אֵיךְ; Targ. has both אֵיכָא, הֵיכָא, "how ? " but אֵיךְ, הֵיךְ, are not interrogative, and the abstracts in late writers are formed, not from הֵיךְ but from אֵיךְ ; אֵיכוּת, "quality ; " מְתֻאָיָּ "endowed with qualities."

כְּתָב "writing," Dan. x. 21. 2 Chron. xxxv. 4. else "written characters," Ezr. Esth., "letter," 2 Chron. ii. 10 ; "writ," Esth. iii.

14. vii. 8, 13. iv. 8; God's "book" of the people, Ezek. xiii. 9, "register," Ezr. ii. 62. Neh. vii. 64; "book," Arab. Aram. Samarit. In Chald. "writing," Dan. v. 8, 15, 16, 24, 25.

עִמִּי כְּתֻמַּק Dan. x. 21. 1 Chron. xi. 10. 2 Chron. xvi. 9.

הִתְחַבֵּר Dan. xi. 6. with עַם p. 2 Chron. xx. 35, 37. הִתְחָבְּרוּת † Dan. xi. 23, verbal noun like הַמַּעֲשֶׂה, Ez. xxiv. 26.

עָשָׂה, with בְּ p. "do against," Dan. xi. 7; of God, Jer. xviii. 20.

הֲמוֹן חֲיָלִים, "forces," Dan. xi. 10. חֲיָלִים, chiefly of שָׂרֵי הַחֲיָלִים "the princes of the forces; (of Benhadad's 1 Kings xv. 20.) 2 Kings xxv. 23, 26. 2 Chron. xvi. 4. Jer. [ix times.] also גִּבּוֹרֵי חֲיָלִים 1 Chron. vii. 5, 7, 11, 40.

יָרוּם לְבָבוֹ Dan. xi. 12. Ez. xxxi. 10.

רְבָאוֹת, "10,000ᵃ," Dan. xi. 12. pointed in Ezr. ii. 69. רִבּוֹאת. On the sing. רִבּוֹ see on Jonah p. 250.

יָשֵׂם פָּנָיו לָבוֹא Dan. xi. 17. Jer. xlii. 15, 17. xliv. 12. שׂ פ׳ לַעֲלוֹת 2 Kings xii. 18.

גֶּקֶף, Dan. xi. 17. Esth. ix. 29. x. 2; Ch. Dan. ii. 37. iv. 27.

מַעֲבִיר נוֹגֵשׂ Dan. xi. 20, contrary prophecy of Israel, לֹא יַעֲבֹר עֲלֵיהֶם עוֹד נֹגֵשׂ Zech. ix. 8.

בִּזָּה † xi. 24, 33. fem. form of the ordinary, בַּז, (in Syr. fem. בֶּזְתָא, Sam. בזה.) "booty," Ezek. xxix. 19. Ezr. ix. 7. 2 Chron. (iii.) Neh. (i.) Esth. (iii. one phrase, ix. 10, 15, 16.)

חָשַׁב מַחֲשָׁבוֹת עַל Dan. xi. 24. Jer. xi. 19. xviii. 18. sing. Jer. xviii. 11. xlix. 30. Esth. viii. 3. plur. with אֶל Jer. xlix. 20. l. 45.

iv. *Words and idioms revived from the Pentateuch, in part in common with other of the later books of the O.T.*

אֶרֶץ שִׁנְעָר † Dan. i. 2. from Gen. x. 10; also adopted in Zech. v. 11. The name was still exstant in the time of Joshua, whether as derived from Genesis or as travelling with the article of merchandise, אַדֶּרֶת שִׁנְעָר "a garment of Shinar," i. e. of its tapestried manufacture. Josh. vii. 21. Isaiah used שִׁנְעָר, alone, xi. 11. The name, שִׁנְעָר, *Sen'ar*, was still the Syriac title for Babylon, in the time of Barhebræus, as distinct from Persia, Syria, Mesopotamia, Assyria, Chron. p. 9, 93, 169, 256, 274, 314, 529, 565, 578, in Tuch de Nino urbe, p. 9.

טוֹבֵי מַרְאֶה Dan. i. 4. Gen. xxiv. 16. xxvi. 7. 2 Sam. xi. 2. also in Esth. i. 11. ii. 2, 3, 7.

דְּבַר יוֹם בְּיוֹמוֹ Ex. (iii.) Lev. Num. Deut. Kings (ii.) Chron. (iii.) Ezr. (i.) Neh. (ii.) Jer. (i.)

זֹעֲפִים of the countenance, only Dan. i. 10. Gen. xl. 6.

בָּקַשׁ לְ, with gen. of abstract word, Dan. i. 20. from Ex. xxii. 8; also in 1 Chron. xxvii. 1.

עֲשֶׂר יָדוֹת, i. 20. from Gen. xliii. 34. חָמֵשׁ יָדוֹת; comp. Gen. xlvii. 24. אַרְבַּע הַיָּדֹת; this last in Neh. xi. 1.

חַרְטֻמִּים, ἱερογραμματεῖς, Dan. i. 20. ii. 2; in his Chaldee, ii. 10, 27. iv. 4, 6. v. 11.; a common name for a common office in Babylon and Egypt; Gen. xli. 8. 24. Ex. vii. 11. 22. viii. 3. 4. 15. ix. 11.

וַתִּפָּעֶם רוּחוֹ Dan. ii. 1, וַתִּפָּעֶם רוּחִי Ib. 3. from Gen. xli. 8. וַתִּפָּעֶם רוּחוֹ. פעם does not occur in Chald. except in the sense of the Heb. "times," nor in Syr. at all; in Arabic it only signifies "was full."

בַּתְּחִלָּה, "in the beginning," Dan. viii. 1. ix. 21. Gen. (iv) Jud. [iii]

וָאֶשָּׂא עֵינַי וָאֵרֶא וְהִנֵּה Dan. viii. 3, וָאֶשָּׂא אֶת עֵינַי וָאֵרֶא וְהִנֵּה Ib. x. 5; from Gen. xxxi. 10. וָאֶשָּׂא עֵינַי וָאֵרֶא בַּחֲלוֹם וְהִנֵּה.

יָמָּה וָקֵדְמָה וְצָפוֹנָה וָנֶגְבָּה † Dan. viii. 4. from Gen. xxviii. 14. The 4 points of the compass are given צָפֹנָה וָנֶגְבָּה וָקֵדְמָה יָמָּה Gen. xiii. 14. and in 1 Chron. ix. 24. It is not a mere imitation, since the East is omitted purposely. See ab. p. 86.

עֶרֶב בֹּקֶר † Dan. viii. 14. with art. הָעֶרֶב וְהַבֹּקֶר, referring to this, Ib. 26; from Gen. i. 5, sqq.

כְּמַרְאֵה גָבֶר Dan. viii. 15. "as the appearance of a man," (add x. 6, 18.) from Num. ix. 15, כְּמַרְאֵה אֵשׁ; thence Ezek. i. 13, 14, 26. (ii.) 27. (ii.) 28. viii. 2. (ii.) x. 1. xl. 3. xlii. 11. xliii. 3.

מַרְאֶה, "*vision*," viii. 16, from Ex. iii. 3, of the "burning bush;" then Ez. viii. 4. xi. 24. xliii. 3.

מַרְאֶה Id. Dan. x. 7. (ii.) 8. 16. Num. xii. 6. plur. Gen. xlvi. 2. Ezek. i. 1. viii. 3. xl. 2. sing. 1 Sam. iii. 15.

עַז פָּנִים Dan. viii. 23. from Deut. xxviii. 50. עַז פָּנִים Is. xix. 4.

הִתְוַדָּה, "confess," Lev. v. 5. xvi. 21. xxvi. 40. Num. v. 7. then Dan. ix. 4. 20, and Ezr. (i.) Chron. (i.) Neh. (iii.)

ix. 4. הָאֵל הַגָּדוֹל וְהַנּוֹרָא שֹׁמֵר הַבְּרִית וְהַחֶסֶד לְאֹהֲבָיו וּלְשֹׁמְרֵי מִצְוֺתָיו, verbatim from Deut. vii. 9, except that Dan. has substituted הַנּוֹרָא, *the aweful*, for הַנֶּאֱמָן, *the faithful*. Daniel has retained even the 3rd persons, מִצְוֺתָיו, אֹהֲבָיו. Nehemiah uses the verse, i. 5. and some of it in ix. 32. Solomon employed Moses' words שֹׁמֵר הַבְּרִית וְחֶסֶד in his prayer, 1 Kings viii. 23. 2 Chron. vi. 14. See ab. p. 356.

מָרַד, with בְּ, "rebelled against" God, Dan. ix. 9. Num. xiv. 9. Josh. xxii. 16, 18, 19, 29. Ezek. ii. 23. Neh. ix. 26.

רָבְצָה בוֹ עַל Dan. ix. 11. Deut. xxix. 19. הָאָלָה וְהַשְּׁבוּעָה אֲשֶׁר כְּתוּבָה בְּתוֹרַת מֹשֶׁה הָאָלָה הַכְּתוּבָה בַּסֵּפֶר הַזֶּה

פַּחַד כָּל־הָעַמִּים Dan. ix. 12. Gen. vii. 19. Deut. ii. 25. iv. 19. Job xxviii. 24. xxxvii. 3. xli. 3. [11. Eng.]

גְּוִיָּה of living body Dan. x. 6. Gen. xlvii. 18. thence Ez. i. 11, 23. Neh. ix. 27.

הַנָּהָר הַגָּדֹל x. 4. title given to the Euphrates (נְהַר פְּרָת) Gen. xv. 18. Deut. i. 7. then Jos. i. 4; here transferred to Tigris חִדָּקֶל.

חֲרָדָה גְדֹלָה Dan. x. 7. Gen. xxvii. 33.

נֹתַרְתִּי Dan. x. 13. as Gen. xxxii. 25.

נֶעֶשְׂתָה Dan. ix. 12. (ii.) Num. xv. 24. Deut. xiii. 14. xvii. 4. 2 Sam. (i.) Neh. (i.) Mal. (i.) נֶעֶשְׂתָה Dan. xi. 36. in pause.

† Dan. x. 14. אֵת אֲשֶׁר יִקְרָה לְעַמְּךָ בְּאַחֲרִית הַיָּמִים

——— ——— יִקְרָא אֹתָם ——— ———

In this place only, יִקְרָה is pointed like יִקְרָא for which it is substituted; and here only has ל p. not the acc.

מַלְכֻד Dan. xi. 4. Pent. (xxiv.) Jos. xvii. 49. 1 Kings x. 33. Ezr. (i.) Neh. (i.) Chron. (iii.)

מָשׂוֹת for מָשׂוֹת Dan. xi. 10, from old form in Pent. Gen. xlix. 11. [ii.] (changed by Kri once) Ex. xxii. 4. 26. xxxii. 17. Lev. xxiii. 13. thence 2 Kings xix. 23. xx. 13. Ezek. xlviii. 18. all corrected in Kri (Hiller Arc. Keth. p. 74. Ges. Lehrg. p. 212.)

רְכוּשׁ רַב Dan. xi. 13. from Gen. xiii. 6. xxxvi. 7. thence 2 Chron. xxxii. 29. רְכוּשׁ occurs in the Pent. xiii times; in Dan. iii; in Ezr. iv; in Chron. viii times.

עַל כֵּן Dan. xi. 20-21. 38, prob. from Gen. xl. 13. xli. 13.

יָמִים אֲחָדִים Dan. xi. 20, from Gen. xxvii. 44. xxix. 20.

מִשְׁמַנֵּי הָאָרֶץ "the rich (lit. *fat*) places of the land" Dan. xi. 24., from Gen. xxvii. 28. 39.

אֲבֹתָיו וַאֲבוֹת אֲבֹתָיו Ib. like Ex. x. 6. אֲבֹתֶיךָ וַאֲבוֹת אֲבֹתֶיךָ.

כָרִאשֹׁנָה וְכָאַחֲרוֹנָה Dan. xi. 29. כָרִאשֹׁנָה else only Deut. ix. 18.

נִלְוָה c. עַל p. "cleave (so as to lean) upon," Dan. xi. 34. from Num. xviii. 2. 4. but also Is. xiv. 1. and Esth. ix. 27. as to God; Is. lvi. 6.

שְׂפַת הַיְאֹר Dan. xii. 5; from Gen. xli. 3, לִיסוֹד הַיְאֹר, Dan. xii. 6, from Ex. vii. 24.

v. *Words or idioms taken from Ezekiel.*

סָתַם "shut up," of things obscure, Dan. viii. 26. xii. 4, 9. Ezek. xxviii. 3. "lo, thou art wiser than Daniel," כָּל סָתוּם לֹא עֲמָמוּךָ. It implies, not that the thing was not known, but that it was not understood; אֵין מֵבִין viii. 27. comp. Ps. li. 8. בַּסָּתֻם, "in the hidden part."

חַיָּבְתָּם, comp. חוֹב, *debt*, Ezek. xviii. 7.

בֶּן אָדָם "son of man," vocative, Dan. viii. 17. as Ezek. passim, comp. בַּר אֱנָשׁ Dan. vii. 13.

לָבוּשׁ בַּדִּים Dan. x. 5, from Ezek. ix. 2; and (referring to this) לְבוּשׁ הַבַּדִּים Dan. xii. 6. Ezek. ix. 11.

תַּרְשִׁישׁ Dan. x. 6. the word, not the idiom, from Ez. i. 16. x. 9.

כְּמַרְאֵה בָרָק Ez. i. 13. כְּמַרְאֵה הַלַּפִּידִים וּמִן תֵּאֵשׁ יוֹצֵא בָרָק Dan. x. 6. כְּלַפִּידֵי אֵשׁ, וּכְמַרְאֵה בָרָק
נְחֹשֶׁת קָלָל וְרַגְלֵיהֶם. Ib. Ezek. i. 7.

כִּי עוֹד חֲזוֹן לַיָּמִים "the vision is yet for those *(fixed)* days." Dan. x. 14.
Before, he said, undefined, כִּי לְיָמִים רַבִּים viii. 26.   Ezekiel says, בֵּית יִשְׂרָאֵל
אֹמְרִים הֶחָזוֹן אֲשֶׁר הוּא חֹזֶה לְיָמִים רַבִּים xii. 27.   If there be an allusion, it is a
remarkable adoption, as truth, of what was said scornfully.

Note C. on p. 38.

Of the Aryan or other rare words in Daniel relating to offices, dress,
musical instruments, most were lost in Aramaic, together with the
things themselves, several had become obsolete, when the book of
Daniel was translated.

The more common names of offices, *Achashdarpenin, sagan, pechah*, were understood and translated by the Peshito but had disappeared from the language.   The translation of these, and the retention of the names of the four next in order, in Dan. iii. 2, &c. makes
it probable that the meaning too of the four latter names of offices
was obliterated.   The original words can still be traced, being disguised only by the interchange of similar letters.   *Adargazeraiia*
lies hid under *agardoie ; gedaberaiia* under *gerabdoie*, (the *d* and *r*,
as differing only by the position of the dot, being transposed ;) *de-
thaberaiia* under *therabdoie*, (the *d* being again changed into *r* and
r into *d*, and *r*, so changed, being further transposed with *th* ;) *Tiftaiia*
under *Thibethoie* (the *f* being changed into *b* which it much resembles.)   The entire expiry of two of these words is the more remarkable, because they are pure Aramaic.   They perished with the offices
themselves.   A third was a variation of a word which lived on in
Syriac, which yet the translator did not recognise under the slight
disguise of *gedabar* for *gidsbar*.   The name *satrap* was revived, but
probably from the Greek, סטרפא (e. g. Barh. 159. 1.) whence was formed, with the Syriac ending, סטרפותא or סטרפאותא, "satrapy," (e. g. Barh.
162, 6.) *Hammelzar* was also retained, although without the Article.
It has now become *Meshizar* i. 11, *Menisar* in i. 16.   *Haddaberaiia*
(again an Aramaic word) is translated in Dan. iii. 24. iv. 33, as is also
Sarechin, Dan. vi. 3, &c.   *Partemim*, "nobles," was doubtless retained in what is now an unmeaning word, *partevoye*.   No trace of
any of these three words remains in Syriac.

Of the names of musical instruments, the Syriac name *mashrooki-tho* was naturally retained; as being Syriac, and remaining, although in a modified form, in the language. (See below Note D.) *Kithoro* also survived, being used in the Peshito, Gen. iv. 21, 1 Cor. xiv. 7, and Plur. Ps. lxxvi. 3; as was the Syrised *Kithooroodootho*, " music," Barh. p. 149. pen. p. 162. l. 6 ; *mekaithoro*, " minstrel ; " Nov. 149 ; *kithoroodo*, " minstrel;" F. *methkithar*, τό κιθαριζόμενον 1 Cor. xiv. 7. (Bernst.) It seems probable that, at the date of the Peshito, the Syrians had the instrument *symfoneyah* or *sifoneyah*, because the Peshito does not simply retain the word, but slightly inflects it, *ze-fooneyo*, (איפוני); yet there are no subsequent traces of it, and the learned lexicographers differ as to the nature of the instrument. (see Ges. de B. Ali, p. 26, 7.) It is even remarkable that there is no trace of the instrument *pesanterin* in Syriac, since it had become an Assyrian instrument in the time of Sennacherib, and continues in use to this day in Egypt, the trunk of its name, *santer, santur*, &c. still surviving. See ab. p. 32, 3.

Of the names of dress, the Peshito pronounces *sarbal, sharbolo*. This is designated as " a flowing garment " by Barhebræus, מלילא שרבלא p. 223. l. 16. and a verb is formed from it; " their dress was *me-sharbelin*," lit. " trousered." Barh. p. 80. l. 8. (The reading is undoubted, occurring in cod. Hunt. 1. also.) The defeat of the Persians is ascribed to this peculiarity of their dress, and their bows being relaxed by the humidity of the air.

The word *carbal*, the Peshito alone understood rightly. It is the more remarkable, that there is no trace of the word in Syriac, except as, " the *crest* of a cock." In Hebrew there occurs the derived verb מְכַרְבָּל 1 Chr. xv. 27.

Petsho was retained, is explained by the Syriac lexicographers, but no instance has been found of its use.

Hamnuca not only lived on in the form of the Kri, *hamnica*, as equivalent to *dsiro*, a " jewelled collar," but gave rise to a verb, *hamnec*, " girt," and a corrupted noun, *hamnisono*, " a girdle." See in Ges. de Bar Ali et B. B. ii. 10.

Pathbag had become a naturalised term in the Hebrew of Daniel, being used, not only of the royal food allotted to the three youths, (i. 5, 8, 13, 15, 16.) but also in the prophetic description of the treachery to Ptolemy Philometor, (xi. 26, not mentioned in exstant historians,) where " they who eat of his *pathbag* " replaces the " they who did eat of my bread " of the Psalmist. In the exstant Syriac, *pathbag*,

(מטבלא) occurs both in the more limited and in the wider sense. S. Ephrem uses it of the "royal dainties," which Barzillai declined, (i. 423,) but also of "the dainties of Egypt," which Israel pined after, (i. 260,) and of the food with which Abigail supplied David and his men. (Ib. 382.) Barhebræus uses it of something given by the Atabeg, which would keep for a year, unspoiled, in a cloth in the slave's bosom. Chron. p. 331.   The Syriac Lexica say, that *petboge* are " dates without rind ; " *patboge, pathbogotho*, "various sorts of strong soup ; " *pathbogo*, "a royal cook." Ges. on B. Ali. ii. 25.

Of the Hebrew of Daniel, we have, as is known, no Targum.   The Jewish tradition states that " Jonathan B. Uzziel was forbidden to write a Targum on the Hagiographa," "because in it," ("i. e. in Daniel," adds Rashi,) " is contained the term of the coming of the Messiah." (Megillah, f. 3. 1. in Schöttg. de Mess. p. 264.)

Of the titles of officers, which occur in the Hebrew or Chaldee of Daniel, the Targum of Esther substitutes a corrupt form of the Greek στρατηλάτης for אחשדרפנים in Esth. iii. 12. viii. 9. ix. 3.   (Buxtorf's reference to Esther x. 3. (Lex. p. 64.) must be an accidental erratum, since, there, אחשדרפנים occurs in the Hebrew, not in the Chaldee.)   *Sagan* was perpetuated in the Chaldee of the Targums and Gemara from the Hebrew ; yet so as to shew that the name was retained only in the generic sense of " prefect." (see Buxt. p. 1435.)   *Pechah*, although so common in Biblical Hebrew, was lost.   *Adargaderin*, although lost, was understood rightly by Saadiah.   Aben Ezra professes, not to understand it or the names which follow it.   Rashi thought it to be the name of a nation.   *Gedabar* Saadiah explains rightly by the *gidsbar* of Ezra ; but *dethabar* he explains wrongly by aid of the Hebrew *bar;* and *tiphtaie*, as though it were formed from *patach.* *Haddaberin* was lost, although Buxtorf gives a single instance of *medabbera* (מְדַבְּרָא) in the Targ. (Prov. xi. 4.) and of *medabberana*, (מְדַבְּרָנָא) in the Talmud, (Ketubh. f. 170, 1.) in the general sense, " ruler." *Partemim* is retained in one of the two places of Esther, in which it occurs besides Daniel, (i. 3,) as פַּרְתְּמַיָּא ; in Esth. vi. 9, it is replaced by אִסְטְרַטִיגִין i. e. στρατηγοί.

Of dress, *carbela* is used once (Berach. f. 20, 1.) of dress of a certain " gentile woman," and is explained in the gloss by reference to Dan. iii. 21. (Buxt. p. 1084.) *Sarbal*, like the Syriac *sharbal*, gave rise to a pass. part. מְסַרְבַּל or מְסֻרְבָּל. Buxt. 1544, 5.

Hamnuca survived in the form which the Kri substituted, *Hamnica*, (Prov. i. 9. Esth. ii. 9. Buxt. c. 1226,) or the more Greek form, *me-*

nica (Gen. xli. 42. Onk. xlix. 22. Targ. Jer. Esth. ii. 17. vii. 7. Buxt.)
or *moniak*, μανιάκης. (Buxt. c. 1228.)   *Pattish* was lost.   Of the musical instruments, the *Mashrokitha*, *Sabca*, *Pesanterin* were lost;
the *soomphonia* occurs in the Talmud twice, (Kelim c. 11 and 16)
and is explained wrongly "lyre." (Buxt. c. 1504.) *Kathros* occurs
wrongly in Jonathan Is. v. 12. for צלצל, i. e. timbrel and in Targ. Eccl.
ii. 8. (Buxt. c. 2164.) *Pathbag*, so common in Syriac, was lost.

Of the Greek-speaking Jews, the LXX translated in a general
way the names of *Offices*, shewing that they attached no definite meaning to them.   *Achashdarpenin* (Satraps) they rendered διοικηταὶ,
Esth. viii. 35; οἰκονόμος, Esth. viii. 9; σατράπης, in Dan. iii. 2. vi. 1. 4.
[2. 5.] where they were guided by the numbers; στρατηγοὶ in Esth.
iii. 1; τύραννοι in Esth. ix. 3, (where they render עַל שָׂרֵי הַמְּדִינוֹת "the
rulers of the Satraps," perhaps, " satrapies"); ὕπατοι, Dan. iii. 3, 27.
(94.)

Sagan, they render by ἄρχων (as they do many other words,) 4
times in Nehemiah and in Is. xli. 15; by στρατηγοὶ, 12 times, including Dan. iii. 27, (94); by ἡγούμενος, Dan. ii. 48, by τοπάρχαι, Ib.
iii. 27. (94.)

Pechah also they render in Nehemiah, twice by ἄρχων, as also twice
by βία, βίαι, and twice by ἔπαρχοι; in Ezra, by ἀφηγούμενος in vi. 7;
by ἔπαρχοι, 5 times; by θησαυροφύλαξ, v. 14.   They render it by ἡγεμών
Jer. li. 23; by ἡγούμενος, Jer. li. 28, and Ezek. xxiii. 6; by σατράπαι,
twice in Kings, once in Chron.; by τοπάρχης, in 2 Kings xviii. 24, Is.
xxxvi. 9, Dan. iii. 2, 3; by ἀρχιπατριῶται, iii. 27 (94); by ἐκ φυλῆς,
4 times in Haggai.

Of *adargadseriia, gedaberiia, dethaberiia, tiphtaiia*, the LXX rendering must be uncertain, since it has only six names for seven offices; and ὕπατοι, which occupies the first place in iii. 1, is now the
the fourth in iii. 2; but there is no one characteristic rendering.   In
Ezra the LXX retain *gisbar* in the form γαζβαρινός, i. 8.   In the
plural they render "treasures," instead of "treasurers," γάζαι. viii. 20.

Haddabere malca is rendered, "the king's friends," in Dan. iii. 27.
(94.) *haddaberohi*, " his friends," Ib. 24. The clause, in which it occurs, is omitted in iv. 33, and in vi. 8.   Theodotion renders it by
μεγιστᾶνες αὐτοῦ, iii. 24, δυνάσται τοῦ βασιλέως, iii. 27, οἱ τύραννοί μου,
iv. 33, and by ὕπατος in vi. 8.

Sarechin the LXX translated, vaguely, ἡγουμένους αὐτῶν, Dan. vi. 2,
omitted it in 4. 5. 6. 7. 8; Theodotion rendered τακτικοὶ in vi. 3. 4. 5.
6. 7. στρατηγοὶ in vi. 8.

The LXX were still acquainted with the musical instruments, and rendered *mashrokitha* rightly σύριγξ. Of the articles of dress, in Dan. iii. 21, they rendered *sarbalin* wrongly "sandals," and *pattishin*, "tiaras;" *carbelath* they omitted; but in iii. 27, (94.) they retained *sarbalin* in the form in which it had already been Grecised, (Antiphanes in Poll. x. 40.) σαράβαρα, yet they understood apparently neither the Chaldee nor the Greek word, since they mistranslated the Chaldee iii. 21'; *hamnic* they recognised by aid of the Greek μανιάκης. *Pathbag* they rendered by a general word "table," i. 5, or "feast," i. 8, 13, 15, where the context clearly guided them, but in xi. 26, they wholly missed the meaning, as did, subsequently, Theodotion. So also they were ignorant of the meaning of *Hammelzar*, of *gazerin*, a Babylonian class of soothsayers, which they retained with the Greek termination *Gazarenoi*, Dan. ii. 27, v. 7, repeating it v. 8, but omitting it altogether in iv. 4. v. 11. So also they omitted *Appadno*, in Dan. xi. 47, a well-known term in Babylonia, whose meaning was lost in their time in the West. They translated the proper name *Dura*, not knowing it to be such. In Daniel, as throughout the O.T., they rendered *rab-hattabbachim* or *sar-hattabbachim*, ἀρχιμάγειρος, except in Gen. xl. 4, where, determined by the context, they rendered, ἀρχιδεσμώτης, "captain of the prisoners." Nor did they understand מצפן, to which the later Chaldee did not guide them; nor אזל and other words of the date of Daniel. In a word, they knew the meaning of musical instruments still in use, but they were ignorant of the names of Babylonian officers, Babylonian dress, Babylonian soothsayers, a Babylonian castle. Naturally. For their fathers had quitted Babylon some centuries before. And yet, on the rationalist hypothesis, the writer of the book of Daniel is to have lived in Palestine, some 363 years after his people quitted Babylon, and yet to have been familiar with, and to have used rightly, all those non-Hebrew words, which, shortly after, his countrymen did not understand.

Note D on p. 49.

The chief characteristics, which sever the Chaldee of the Bible from that of the Targums, lie in those grammatical forms which run through the whole diction, a summary of which has already been given from the careful examination of the Rev. J. Mc Gill, p. 44-51.

It is only as very subsidiary to that decisive proof, that I have set down a certain number of words, which occur in the six chapters which Daniel wrote in Chaldee, and which do not apparently occur in the Targums or the Gemara, or either of them.   I say, " do not *apparently* occur," on the ground of the 30 years' labour of Buxtorf.

Even such a labour would leave many gleanings for those, who should make the subject either of the Targums or of the Gemara a special study, as he did.   They, who are not called to this, may rely with a certain degree of confidence on such a prolonged labour by one so accurate as Buxtorf; as, in fact, I have not observed in the Thesaurus of Gesenius a statement on the Chaldee of the Targums which is not taken from Buxtorf.   Meantime, while individual statements may have to be modified, the main fact of the difference between the Biblical Aramaic and that of the Targums, will only be established the more clearly.   Daniel was, of course, in early times a subject of study both to the Targumists and the writers in the Gemara.   Men do not infer that the Pentateuch is of the age of Daniel, on the ground that Daniel adopted some idioms from it.   So neither should they, that Daniel was of the age of or near the Targums, because the paraphrasts adopted idioms from Daniel.   Many words, doubtless, were retained in the later Chaldee, as the result of the study of Daniel.   On the other hand, Zündel has hinted at the converse of this argument, viz. the idioms of the Targums, which might naturally have occurred in Daniel, but for which Daniel uses his own equivalent expression. (Daniel, p. 246, 7.)   I have marked with a * those words only which Buxtorf did not know to exist in the Targums or the Gemara.

סְלָה in Dan. xxii times ; in Targg. less frequent, mostly מאמרא, or פתגמא.

אַוְדָא * probably from אוד i. q. אזל, (as Theod. Vulg.) Dan. ii. 5. 8. (d for l, as in קלחת from Arab. קרח; δάκρυον, *lacry*ma ; ἀδάμας, Arab. *al-más* &c.   In the Talm. it occurs only in the one phrase אורא אלתי למטמיה, " A. went after his own opinion." Ges. Thes. p. 58, from Saad.

הַדָּמִין תִּתְעַבְדוּן,* Dan. ii. 5. lit. "ye shall be made limbs," i. e. cut to pieces. Syriac, *hadom hadom*, "limb for limb."   It is the only version which translates right.

גְּלָו,* for גְּלָיְתּ, Dan. ii. 5. iii. 29. as גְּלָוִי* for גְּלוּת Ezr. vi. 11. Targ. has נגּל "foulness," Talm. מְגֻנָּל "defiled," of the יֵצֶר הָרָע, the "fomes peccati."   Buxt. p. 1317.   The word was understood by the Syr. only.

מטעי &c. Hafel, in Dan. ii. 6, 7, 9, 10, 16, 27. v. 15.   Pael is frequent in the Targg. Of Afel Buxt. gives 2 instances from the Talm., none from the Targg. But the infinitive noun, אַחֲוָה Dan. v. 12, occurs also in the Targg., so that Gesenius' inference from Buxt., "In Targg. hæc conjug. non usitata est," must be so far limited.

נְבִזְבָּה, Dan. ii. 6. v. 17. "large gifts," from נְבִזְבָּה with נ prefixed, Buxt. c. 281. "then, נבובה for נבובה, as Golgotha for Gulgoltha," &c. Ges. p. 842. In the Targ. Jer. xl. 5. (quoted Buxt. l. c.) the whole phrase, מתנן תבובן, was probably adopted from Daniel, as it is not the literal translation of Jeremiah. Else Buxt. quotes only the late Ps. Jon. Deut. xxxiii. 24.

לָהֵן,* "therefore," Dan. ii. 6, 9. iv. 24 ; in Heb. Ruth i. 13.

שְׁאַר,* שְׂאַר.* שׂ for ס. See ab. p. 51. n. 9.

מִן־יַצִּיב.*, like our, "of a certainty," Dan. ii. 8. as מִן־קְשֹׁט, Dan. ii. 47, our, "of a truth." comp. ἐξ ἀνάγκης, ἐκ περισσοῦ, ἐξ ἰσότητος, ἐξ ἐμφανοῦς, ἐξ ἴσου, ex æquo, ex integro."

עִדָּנָא—זָבְנִין,* "gaining [lit. buying] time." Dan. ii. 8.

וְחֶזְוֹן "sentence, [lit. "law"] for you." ii. 9. דָּת is always used from a superior to an inferior, law, religion. דָּת occurs viii times in the Ch. of Dan., vii times in that of Ezra ; not quoted from Targg. in Buxt.

סוּסָן * "settle." Ib. So Samar. often. Ges. In Targ., Af. only signifies "prepare," "invite," with ל p. Buxt. c. 677.

אֱזַל * Dan. ii. 10, 27. iv. 4. v. 7, 11, 15. i. q. Heb. and Syr. See ab. p. 40.

סְרִיחָהּ, ii. 11. חֲדַר only here ; else חֲדַר iv. 22. 29. מְדוֹר v. 21. as in Targg.

רַב טַבָּחַיָּא,* "chief of the executioners," (the "body-guard" having this office.) Dan. ii. 14. as רַב טַבָּחִים in Heb. In Targg. טַבָּח, "butcher," or "cook."

עַל, "went up," Dan. ii. 16. עַל is used ix times, in different conjugations, of "entrance" to the king, (in regard either to the dignity or the elevation of the palace,) once to Arioch, probably in the king's palace. ii. 24. No additional instance is given by Buxt.

נְהִירָא,* "light," as in Syr., Dan. ii. 22. The Kri changes it into the form used in the Targg., נְהוֹרָא. Dan. has again, in the spiritual sense, נְהִירוּ "illumination," (v. 11, 14.) abridged from the fuller Syriac form נְהִירוּתָא.

יְהוּד,* Judæa, Dan. ii. 25. v. 13. vi. 14. Ezr. vi. 8. vii. 14. In Syriac also.

יָכֵל * (part.) Dan. ii. 26. iv. 15. יָכְלִין * (part. plur.) Dan. v. 8. 15. i. q. Heb. יכל. It is probably i. q. יכל=כהל ; the ה, (as also in Æth.,) standing (as in some other cases) for the softer ו.

גָּזְרִין,* probably, "they who *define* the course of man's life," Dan.

ii. 27. iv. 4. v. 7, 11.   The root was in frequent use ; this meaning only in Daniel.

עַל דִּבְרַת דִּי,* "in order that," Dan. ii. 30 ; עַר דִּבְרַת דִּי Dan. iv. 14. (al. עַל) adopted from Heb. שֶׁ עַל דִּבְרַת Eccl. vii. 14, and, without שֶׁ, Eccl. iii. 18. viii. 2.

אֲלוּ * Dan. ii. 31. iv. 7, 10. vii. 8. bis. אֲרוּ,* Dan. vii. 2, 5, 6, 7, 13 ; in all cases, with the ו prefixed ; *and lo!* This may possibly be a mere exclamation, like one, sunk into vulgar use in English.   Or the original may be, רְאו, "see," and the ר may be softened into ל.   The Targg. have חֲרֵי.

צְלֵם חַד, "a certain image," Dan. ii. 31. אֶבֶן חֲדָה, "a certain stone," vi. 18. as in Ezr. iv. 8, אִגְּרָא חֲדָא, "a certain letter."   This is rare in Hebrew.   אִישׁ אֶחָד, "a certain man," 1 Sam. i. 1 ; רֹתֶם אֶחָד, "a certain broom," 1 Kings xix. 4 ; חֹר אֶחָד "a certain hole," Ez. viii. 7 ; עַם אֶחָד "a certain people." Esth. iii. 8.   This use of חר is common in Syriac ; it is not mentioned apparently by Buxt. c. 708.

חֲדִין, "breasts," Dan. ii. 32.   The Hebrew form, חָזֶה, used of animals, is the original, lit. "what may be seen," "the front, like פָּנִים.   In Dan. ii. 32, in Syriac, and in cod. Shabb. beg. (in Buxt. c. 710.) it is used of the human being.

עוּר,* "chaff," ii. 35.   In Syr. also.   Perhaps it is from עָרַר ; Ges. derives it from עִוֵּר, "blinded ;" which does not seem to me probable.

חֲשַׁל * i. q. Syr. "beat out with hammer," Dan. ii. 40.   In Talm. it occurs only in the derived sense "devised ;" as we say, "beat out ;" and perhaps in חִישְׁלָא "barley freed from its husk," "threshed."

נִצְבְּתָא, "firmness." Dan. ii. 41.   In Targg. it is only used for "planting."

הָא * (for הָאָ) Dan. ii. 43, perhaps retained from Gen. xlvi. 23. Ez. xvi. 43. In Syr. הא.

נִיחֹחִין * (lit. "acquiescences," "acceptablenesses,") is used in Dan. ii. 46, Ezr. vi. 10. absolutely, of "incense," not as in Heb. רֵיחַ נִיחֹחַ "smell of acceptableness."   In Heb. too, the plur. is only used Ezek. xx. 28.

בְּעָא with מִן pers. ii. 49. like בַּקֵּשׁ with מִן p. Dan. i. 8.

אֲדַרְגָּזְרַיָּא *, "noble judges," Dan. iii. 2. 3. from אֶדֶר, "magnificence," (comp. "his *Excellency*" &c. "his *Eminence*" &c) and גְּזַר, "decide." There is no other trace of the word.   Of the two halves of the word, אדר must have been old Aramaic, since it appears in the name of the idol of the Sepharvites of Mesopotamia, (2 Kings xvii. 31.,) אַדְרַמֶּלֶךְ, and, from it, of Sennacherib's parricide son, Is. xxxvii. 38. 2 Kings

xix. 37. (See Ges. Thes. p. 29.)   Yet this whole meaning of the root is entirely lost in Syriac. It occurs only, as a compound, in Persian names, mentioned in Syriac authors. (See Bernstein, Lex. p. 42 sqq.)

פֶּחְתָא * 1b. doubtless from the same root as the Arab. " Mufti ; " but there is no trace of the word elsewhere, the name having perished with the office. "The root פתא occurs in Syriac only in the sense 'latus fuit.' The Afel is very common in the sense of ' amplificavit.' " P. Smith from his own and Bernst. and Quatr's. collections. See above Note A. p. 569, 70.

עַמְמַיָּא אֻמַּיָּא וְלִשָּׁנַיָּא occur in this order, Dan. iii. 4, 7, 29. v. 19. vii. 14 ; אֻמָּה, Dan. iii. 29; שְׁאָר אֻמַּיָּא, Ezr. iv. 10.   In the Targg. אֻמִּין occurs apparently, only to represent the word in the Hebrew text; אֻמִּים in Ps. cxvii. 1, or אֻמּוֹת, Gen. xxv. 16, Num. xxv. 25, and by Ps. Jon., Jerus. Targ. in Gen. xxv. 3. in a wrong explanation of גְּאֻמִּים.

On the words of Aryan origin in this v. see Note A.

מַשְׁרוֹקִיתָא,* " pipe," Dan. iii. 5, 7, 10, 15.   שרק in Heb. Ch. Syr. Nasor. signifies "hiss."   In Heb. it is used of the sharp sound used in calling bees, and, seemingly, of the calls of shepherds to their flocks, שְׁרִיקוֹת Jud. v. 16.   In Syr. alone and the Ch. of Daniel it is used of a musical instrument. "*Mashrukitho*, except in the Syr. translation of Daniel, only occurs of ' hissing ' [as in the Carm. de Alex. Knōs Chr. p. 97.] or for συριγμοί, Judd. v. 16. Hexap. but *mashruko* is used of ' the pipe;' Bar-Ceph. Hem. 198. Bar-Salib. com. 174." P. Sm.   The exact gloss which Ges. quotes from Bar Ali of the Afel, " *ashrek*, shabbaba bilzaffâra," does not occur in the Oxford MSS, but there is abundant proof of the use of the Afel.   Bar Ali says that *mashrek* is chiefly used of the hissing of the serpent; (Hunt. 25. f. 184) but that it is used also of the *mashrukitho*, "played on the *Zaffárat* "(pipe) Ib. 12. v. and that *mashrukitho* is the *zaffárah*, and that *mashrekono* is used of " the player on the *zaffárah*." (f. 184.)   B. B. also says that *mashrekin* are " those who blow in the *ssur*." (a musical instrument.)   It is also used of those who suffer from *singing* in the ear. (B. B. Hunt. 157. f. 560.)   The *mashrukitho* is explained also as the instrument, *shebabah* (see Freyt. ii. 387.) and *ssur*, (Hunt. 170. f. 210.;) and those who play on it, *mashrekin*, are described by the verbs formed from those instruments, *ssaffara, shabbaba*. (in Hunt. 170. l. c.)   According to Bar Ali, Anton (i. e. Antonius Rhetor a learned Monophysite early in the 9th cent. Ass. B. O. ii. 345.) wrote the Afel, *ashreg*. Hunt. 25. f. 12. v.

סַבְּכָא* Dan. iii. 5. (written שַׂבְּכָא, Ib. 7. 10. 15,) a sort of harp, whence σαμβύκη, which the Greeks call a Syriac instrument. (See ab. p. 25, 6.) There is no other mention of the instrument. On the other instruments, see ab. p. 24–30.

בַּהּ שַׁעֲתָא, "in that hour," Dan. iii. 6. exactly as in Syr.

וְגֻבְרִין * plur. as from גְּבַר, Dan. iii. 8. It occurs in Dan. xv times; in Ezra, iii times. Else only Nasor. גוברא.

שָׂם טְעֵם, "made a decree," Dan. iii. 10. Ezr. iv. 21. v. 3, 9. 13. vi. 1. 3, 12. vii. 21. מִנִּי שִׂים טְעֵם, "a decree is made by me," Dan. iii. 29. iv. 3. Ezr. iv. 19. vi. 8, 11. vii. 13, and, in the same idiom, מִן קֳדָם שִׂים טְעֵם Ezr. v. 17. also שִׂים טְעֵם מִן קֳדָמַי, Dan. vi. 27.

שָׂם טְעֵם with עַל p. "take account of," (probably "set the mind on,") Dan. iii. 12. vi. 14.

צְדָא,* "of deliberate purpose," Dan. iii. 14. as in Heb. צָדָה Num. xxxv. 20. 22. יָצֹד Ex. xxi. 13. 1 Sam. xxiv. 12. and in Syr. In Targg. it only signifies "desolate," "mock;" Ethp. "intermingle." Buxt.

חַשַׁח * "need," (act.) Dan. iii. 16; is "needful," Ezr. vi. 9. חַשְׁחוּת, "need," Ezr. vii. 20. In Syr. "is useful, needful," a common word.

יַתִּיר שִׂבְעָה, "⅐," iii. 19.

חֲזָה, "it seemed good," "visum est." Dan. iii. 19. חֲזִי Targg.

פַּטִּישׁ,* "tunic," Dan. iii. 21. In the Targg. and Gem. the word survived in the meaning which it has in Heb. and Arab. but *not in Syriac*, "hammer." Of an article of dress it is retained in the Syriac out of Daniel, (see Note C. p. 595.) not in the Targg. or Gem. The case in which *in one MS.* פטיש occurs for שִׁיש, "shoe," is evidently wrong, and owing probably to a wrong explanation of Daniel. See Buxt. c. 1865.

כַּרְבְּלָא, "cloak," Dan. iii. 21. (In Heb. מַכְרֵלָל, i.q. חָגַר, "girded," 1 Chr. xv. 27.) In Berach. f. 20, 1. (Buxt. c. 1084.) probably taken from Daniel.

שְׁבִיבָא דִּי נוּרָא,* "flame of fire," Dan. iii. 22. שְׁבִיבִין דִּי נוּר Dan. vii. 9. In Syr. also. In Talm. בֵּי שַׁבְבֵי, explained in a gloss, "between the suns," "twilight," (Shabb. f. 109. 2. in Buxt. c. 2303) from Syr. שְׁבִיבֵי צַפְרָא "dawn."

הַדָּבְרִין,* "councillors," Dan. iii. 24, 27. iv. 33. vi. 8. doubtless (as Ges.) דַּבְּרִין, "leaders," with the art. It cannot be a compound with the Pers. "choda," because "choda," in compounds, retains its meaning "God," and is never used of a human "lord." Nor is the interchange of the strong Persian guttural with the weak ה probable. The name was lost with the office.

מַהְלְכִין * Af. Dan. iii. 25. iv. 34. Pa. iv. 26. In Targg. Pa. and Ethpa. only, in Buxt.

עִלָּיָא, as Syr. עֶלָּיָא, Dan. iii. 26, and ix other places in Daniel, "the most High." In Kri and Targg. always עִלָּאָה.

גְּשֵׁם, "body," Dan. iii. 27, 28. iv. 30. v. 21. vii. 11. In Targg. גּוּשְׁמָא.

שָׁלָה, "error," "any thing *amiss*," E.V. Dan. iii. 29. שָׁלוּ Kri, Dan. vi. 5. Ezr. iv. 22. as in Targg.

יִתְעֲבֵד, "shall be made," Dan. iii. 29. Pa. is common in this sense; Ethpa. not in Targg. in Buxt.

רַעֲנַן, "flourishing," Dan. iv. 1. In Job xv. 32, Buxtorf's only instance from the Targg., it is retained from the Hebrew.

הַרְהֹרִין * iv. 2. "imaginations." Syr. In Targ. "evil conceptions, evil thoughts of God, concupiscences."

אָחֳרֵין * עַד, "at last," iv. 5.

אֲנַס with לְ pers., "is oppressive to," i. e. too difficult for. Dan. iv. 6. In Targg. it is used of actual "oppression," and corresponds to Heb. עָשַׁק, גוּל, רָצַץ, Buxt.

עִיר,* "a watcher," iv. 10. עִירִין,* "watchers," iv. 14. see ab. p. 522, 3.

גְּדַד, "cut," Dan. iv. 11, 20, as in Arab., *jadda.* Only in Ber. Rab. c. 71. Buxt. In Targg. גְּזַז Buxt.

תְּחֹתוֹהִי, iv. 11. vii. 27. In Targg. לְתַחְתָּא Deut. xxviii. 13. else תְּחוֹת, and, with affixes, תְּחוֹתֹהִי &c see Buxt. col. 2586.

חֲלָק,* "portion." Dan. iv. 12. חֲלָקָא Syr. חוּלָק Targg.

אֲנַשָׁא,* Dan. iv. 13, 14. like Samarit. אֲנַשִׁיא. Kri conforms it to Targg. אֱנָשָׁא.

עִקַּר שָׁרְשׁוֹהִי, Dan. iv. 12, 20, 23. The Targg. use the one word עִקָּר, and, besides that they have not this idiom, they only retain the word שָׁרֵשׁ itself, in a few places out of the Hebrew text.

עִדָּנִין * שִׁבְעָה, "seven times," i. e. "years," iv. 13.

מָרְאִי, "my Lord," Dan. iv. 16, 21. Kri alters it to מָרִי as if it were from מָר, whence מָרַן, "our Lord." מָרָא, also, Dan. ii. 47. v. 23, is rare in Targg. even without affix. Buxt. only mentions מָרָא Prov. xxiii. 2, מָרִי frequently.

עֲבַד לְחֶם, "made bread," i. e. a feast, Dan. v. 1, as Heb. עָשָׂה לֶחֶם Eccl. x. 19. (a Chaldee idiom peculiar to Daniel.)

לָקֳבֵל אַלְפָּא חַמְרָא שָׁתֵה, "over against the thousand, wine he was drinking." v. 1. On the force of this idiom and its correspondence with Eastern customs see ab. p. 459.

אֲמַר לְהַיְתָיָה—וְיִשְׁאוֹן, Ib. transition from infinit. to finite verb as in i. 5.

בִּטְעֵם חַמְרָא, lit. "in the taste of the wine," v. 2. idiomatic for "exhilaration through the wine."

שְׁתָה with בְּ, of vessel, (as in Gen. xliv. 5. Am. vi. 6.) Dan. v. 2, 3, 23.

לְחֵנָתֵהּ * "his singing women " v. 2, 3, 23, according to the Babylonian and Persian customs.   Such was the original meaning of the Arab. לחן.   אלחאן "songs," Tochf. Ichw. in Freyt. Lex.; צנעת אלאחאן "the art of music;" thence it is used of the wrong pronunciation of vowels, making long short, short long, in singing. "Modulation" is a secondary, not, as Ges. says, the primary meaning.   In Targg. only "concubines."

נְתַל, wall, Dan. v. 5. Sam. כתלא i. q. כֹּתֶל Cant. ii. 9.   The form of the Targg. is כּוּתֶל, with which כְּתָלְא, Ezr. v. 8, with Heb. and Targg, agrees.

קִטְרֵי חַרְצֵהּ lit. "the bands of his loin," i. e. the vertebræ. Dan. v. 6. The idiom stands alone. קְמִרין, in a figurative sense, for "lineaments," occurs in Yelamm. and Vaiikra rabba in Buxt. c. 2024.   In Syriac, it is used of the "bands of the hand," i. e. wrist.

פַּלְתִּי:—שְׁלִט * lit. "he shall rule, third in the kingdom." Dan. v. 7. תַּפְלֶא—פַּלְתָּא * Ib. 16. פַּלְתָּא * שְׁלִיט, "third ruler," Ib. 29. i. e. next to the Vizier, and third, including the king as the first.

שַׂכְלְתָנוּ * for נְגַה— Syriac Dan. v. 11.

אַחֲיְדָן, with א prosth. Dan. v. 12.   In Targg., as in Syr., אַחֲמָתָא.

כָּרְסֵא, (Sam. כרסה,) "throne," Dan. v. 20.   In Targg. כּוּרְסִי. and so Syr.

שַׁוִּי, probably to be read שַׂוִּי, Peal, only in Dan. v. 21.

עֵלָּא with מִן Dan. vi. 3.   Targ. עֵלָּא.

יְהַב טְעֵם, "give account." Dan. vi. 3.

נֶזֶק, "suffer injury," only Dan. vi. 3.   In Targg. Peal is trans.; Buxt. quotes Ps. xci. 7. Pael is quoted once, Jer. xii. 14, else Afel is transitive, as is Haf. Ezr. iv. 13. 15. 22.

מִתְנַצַּח,* with עַל p., "was preferred above." Dan. vi. 4.   In Targg. and Syr. only of "victory."

עֲשִׁית * "was *minded*," Dan. vi. 4.   In Targg. only Ethp.

קְדָם lit. "on the *side* of the kingdom," i. e. in temporals. Dan. vi. 5. "[blasphemies] לְצַד against," so as to be "side by side" with God, contesting on equal terms, Dan. vii. 25. Buxt. quotes only one instance of לְצַד, "thou shalt not approach לְצַד of a woman," for אֶל Ex. xix. 15.

בְּאַשׁ with עַל p. vi. 15; as מְאַב with עַל p., vi. 24. and, in Hebrew חָרָה, with עַל Eccl. ii. 17.

אֱסָר, "an interdict," Dan. vi. 8. 9. 10. 13. 14. 16.   In Targg. Buxt. only gives the case in which the Heb. word אִסָּר, "obligation," (viz. to abstain from a thing,) has been retained in Num. xxx. 3. 4. 6. &c.

בְּרַךְ * "knelt" i.e. to God, Dan. vi. 11; as in Heb. Ps. xcv. 6, 2 Chron. vi. 13; more widely in Syr.

שָׂם * בְּל with עַל p. "set his heart upon," Dan. vi. 15; like שָׂם לֵב אֶל, 1 Sam. ix. 20. בל * for לֵב, is common Syriac, בללא, כאל Arab., but not Ch. or Talm.

כְּשִׂדַּר,* "laboured," Dan. vi. 15. יִשְׁדַּל, Targg. In the Targg. אִשְׁתַּדַּר signifies, "was sent," as in Syr.

שָׂמַח, Dan. vi. 18. "שׂם is rare in Targg. which generally have שׁוי." Buxt. c. 2349.

צְפַח, "hungered," Dan. vi. 19. (comp. the usage of the Arab. שׂי in Ges. ;) once in Talm. Berach. f. 55. 2. Buxt.

וּדְחָן,* Dan. vi. 19.   Uncertain, whether "musical instruments," "singing-women," or "concubines."

רֵאשׁ, "substance," much as we say "heads." Dan. vii. 1. (as in Heb. Ps. cxix. 160. and Lev. v. 24.)   No instance of this use of רֵישׁ in Buxt. from Targg.

אֲמַר, "said," (in writing)=wrote. Dan. vii. 1.

מְגִיחָן "bursting forth," of winds. Dan. vii. 2.   So in Heb. and Syr.; but in Targg. only of "going forth to war," whence commonly joined with קְרָב, Buxt. c. 402.   In Job xxxviii. 8, גיח, and in Jud. xx. 33, אֵיטַ, the word is retained in the Targ. from the Heb. text.

אָמְתָּנִי,* "strong," vii. 7.   The word, formed perhaps by Daniel, is from a root, exstant in Arabic only and in a derived word in Heb. מְתָנַיִם, not in any other Aramaic besides Daniel's, in any allied sense. See ab. p. 76. n. 2.

קַדְמָתְהִי יְקוּמוּן, vii. 10. i. q. יַעַמְדוּ לְפָנָי, i. 5.

דִּין יְתִיב, "judgment" (i. e. judges) "was set." Dan. vii. 26.

<h3 style="text-align:center">Note E. on p. 377.</h3>

The character of such a translation as that of the LXX is, with difficulty, exhibited by mere references or extracts, here and there.   I have therefore translated, throughout, what seemed to me characteristic renderings, and many which contain in them little which is characteristic.   The variation of the degrees of free translation or almost re-writing in different chapters is in itself remarkable.   Where there was little temptation to embellish or gloss, as in ch. viii, the prayer in ch. ix, and ch. x. there is very little variation.   But the adherence to the text in some parts makes it the more evident, that it was of set purpose, that the translator departed from his text, in other parts.   One who could so translate must have been removed by centuries from the prophet. The whole tone of mind is different, and not accounted for by the mere absence of inspiration in the translator.

i. 2. " The Lord delivered *it* (Jerusalem) into his hands *and* Joiakim," (stating the capture of Jerusalem.) Ib. "he carried them *to Babylon*," explaining *the land of Shinar* of the Hebrew. Ib. "*in his idol temple*," for, " in the treasure-house of his god." 3. " of the sons *of the nobles* of Israel," added. 7. "And to Daniel he gave understanding in every *word* and wisdom and dreams *and in all wisdom*." i. 10. (lest he should see) "your faces distressed *and weak* above the youths *of the aliens* who are nourished with you ; " (as though Daniel and his companions were the only Jews, and so no Jews had eaten forbidden food.) 11. " Daniel spake to Abiesdri who was appointed chief of the eunuchs," for, "*to Hammelzar* whom the chief &c. had appointed ; " probably not understanding *Hammelzar* (see ab. p. 575.) 20. "And the king glorified them, and made them rulers and declared them wise above all his, in affairs in all his land and in all his kingdom," added. 20. " the sophists and philosophers," for, " magicians and astrologers."

ii. 1. "*visions* and dreams." 2. " and sorcerers *of* the Chaldees," for " and," not understanding the Chaldees to be a distinct class. 3. "my spirit was troubled ; *I wish therefore* (added) to know my dream." ii. 5. " Unless ye shew me the vision *in truth*," added. 3. instead of, " ye shall be cut in pieces and your houses shall be made a dunghill," " ye shall be made an example and your property shall be taken into the royal." ii. 9. " ye shall die," for, " there is one decree for you." 8. " as I have commanded, so it shall be," added. 9. " and shew its interpretation," added ; " the word *which I have seen by night*," added, Ib. 11. " is rare *and glorious*," added. Ib. " except some angel," for, " except the gods," " wherefore it cannot be, as thou thinkest," added. 13. " Daniel and *all* who were with him, that they might perish *with*" (the wise men) as if they were a distinct class (τοῦ συναπολέσθαι)." 16. " Daniel went *quickly* to the king ;" " he would shew *all things*," for, " the interpretation." 18. for " that they would desire mercies from the God of Heaven," "and he *enjoined fasting* and supplication and *self-affliction* (lit. " revenge," τιμωρίαν, added) "to seek from the Lord the Most High, &c." " with the sophists of Bab.," for " with the rest of the wise men of B." separating Daniel from them. 19. " in a vision, in that same night," for, " in a night-vision." 23. " Thou hast made known unto

me what *I* desired, that I should make known to the king accordingly,"
for, " what *we* desired of Thee, for Thou hast made known unto *us.*"
25. " I have found a *wise* man."   26. " Daniel, who was surnamed *in
Chaldee* Belteshazzar."   34. " a stone was cut out *of a mountain,*"
added.   37. " gave them glory *in the whole world,*" added.   38. " the
fowls of heaven," he adds, " *and the fishes of the sea.*"   41. for " the
kingdom shall be divided," " there shall be *another* kingdom of two
parts in it" (διμερὴς), adapting the prophecy to the Seleucidæ and
Ptolemies.   43. " They shall be commingled for the generation of
men; but they shall not be of one mind nor well-minded to one
another."   44. " set up *another* kingdom," " and this kingdom shall
not *suffer* another nation," for, " shall not be left to."

iii. 1. " In the 18th year," King N. " governing cities and countries and all dwellers on the earth from India to Ethiopia," added,
this last probably from Esther i. 1.   " 2. in the plain of the circuit,"
not knowing *Dura,* as a proper name.   " N. the king *of kings and
ruling the whole world* sent to collect *all nations and tribes and
tongues* and satraps, &c. and all throughout the world."   12. " serve
not thy idol," for " thy gods," " and *thy* golden," &c. for " the, &c.
17. " For God is in heaven, our One Lord, whom we fear," for, " Our
God, whom we serve ; "   18. " And then it will be clear to thee,"
for, " And if not, be it known, &c. ; " " thy idol," for, " thy gods."
22. " And the men, who were appointed, having bound them and
bringing them to the furnace cast them into into it ; " added.   23.
" The men then who bound Azariah and his companions, the flame,
coming forth out of the furnace *burnt and* killed, *and these were
preserved,*" added.

The Greek has only " the height thereof [of the statue] six cubits," avoiding the statement of the want of proportion, but the Syriac Hexaplar agrees with the Heb.

After the prayer of Azarias, there follows an addition, 46. " And
they who cast them in, ministers of the king, ceased not heating the
furnace, and when they cast the three together into the furnace, and
the furnace was red-hot, sevenfold, according to its heat, and when
they cast them in, they who cast them were above them, but others
from below kindled under them naphtha, and tow, and pitch, and
faggots.   And the fire was poured forth above the furnace, 49
cubits.   And it went forth, and kindled those whom it found of the
Chaldæans around the furnace.   But the angel of the Lord descended
with Azariah and his companions into the furnace and struck out

the flame of fire from the furnace, and he made the midst of the furnace like a whistling wind of dew, and the fire touched them not at all, nor distressed them, nor troubled them." After the " hymn of the three children," 91. "And it came to pass when the king heard them hymning, and stood and saw them living," added (introductory to the mention of his surprise.) 92. (25. Ch.) " the form of the fourth is the likeness of an *angel of* God," for " the Son of God." 95. (28.) "yielded their bodies *to the burning*," added. 96. (29.) " shall be cut in pieces and his house shall be confiscated," for, " made a dunghill."

iv. 1. (4. Eng.) added, "*In the* 18*th year of the reign.* 3-6. (6-9,) omitted. 7. (10.) added, "and there was no other like to it, its branches *were in length as it were* 30 *furlongs*, its fruit was much *and good*," "*all* the beasts of the field, &c." 8. (11.) added, " and the trunk of it to the clouds, filling the space under heaven, the sun and the moon were in it; they dwelt and enlightened the whole earth." 10. (13.) " an Angel," for, " a watcher and a holy one." 11. " cut it down, and spoil it; for it is commanded by the Highest to uproot and make it useless." 12, 13. (14, 15.) " leave one root of it in the ground, that with the beasts of the earth *on the mountains* he may be fed with grass like an ox, and *by* the dew of heaven *his body may be changed*, and for 7 years he may be fed with them; " omitting the greater part of v. 14. 14. (17.) " until he know," for, " that the living may know; " " that the King of heaven hath power over all things in heaven and in earth, and what He wills to do He doth in them," omitting the characteristic language, " This matter is by decree, &c.—holy ones." 15. (18.) added, " In my presence it was cut down in one day, and its destruction was in one hour of the day, and its branches were given to every wind, and it was torn away and cast down, and he ate the grass of the field, and was given in charge, and was bound by them in fetters and handcuffs of brass. I wondered at these things exceedingly, and my sleep departed from my eyes, and, rising early from my bed, I called Daniel, chief of the sophists, and prefect of those who interpret dreams, and I related to him the dream, and he shewed me all its interpretation." 16. (19.) " and, affrighted, trembling seizing him, and, his aspect being changed, he, shaking his head, for one hour, much marvelled, having answered me with a mild voice," for, " The king said, let not the dream or the interpretation thereof trouble thee. Daniel answered." 17. (20.) abridged, " The tree which was planted in the earth, whose aspect was great, thou, O king, art it." 18. (21.) explained with omissions, " And all the birds of the heaven which nestled in it," " the might of the earth and of

the nations and of all tongues to the ends of the earth, and all countries shall serve thee."   19. (22.) The description of the tree is repeated from v. 8; " But that the tree was exalted, and reached to
the heaven, and its trunk touched the clouds;" then the comment is
added, " thou hast been lifted up above all men who are on the face
of all the earth ; thy heart has been lifted up with pride and might
over the things towards the Holy One and His angels; thy works
have been seen, according as thou hast utterly desolated the house
of the living God, for the sins of the sanctified people."   21. (24, 25.)
" This vision that thou hast seen, that an angel was sent in might from
the Lord, and that he said, ' Take away the tree and cut it down,' the
judgment of the great God cometh upon thee ; and the Highest and
His angels shall assail thee ; they shall lead thee away to prison, and
shall send thee to a desert place ;" 23. (26.) " And the root of the tree,
which was left that it was not uprooted, the place of thy throne shall
be kept for thee for a time and an hour.   Behold they are prepared
against thee, and shall scourge thee and bring all that is adjudged
against thee."   24. (27.) " Beseech Him for thy sins," for, " Wherefore—let my counsel be acceptable to thee : " " that gentle dealing
may be given thee, and thou mayest be for many days on the throne
of thy kingdom and He may not destroy thee," for, " thine iniquities—
tranquillity ;" 25. " Cherish these sayings ; for my word is accurate,
and thy time full.   And at the end of the words, Neb. when he
heard the interpretation of the vision, kept the sayings in his heart,"
instead of 28. Eng.   26. (29.) " the king was walking on the wall of
the city with all his glory and was going through upon its towers,"
for, " on the palace of the kingdom of Babylon."   28. (31.) added,
" at the end of his speech *he heard* a voice," and, " the kingdom *of
Babylon* is taken from thee, *and is given to another the most abject
man in thy house.* (suggested by iv. 17. [20])   It then adds, " Lo I set
him over thy kingdom, and he shall receive thy power and thy glory
and thy luxury, that thou mayest know, &c." (from 32.) Then, "to the
sunrising another king shall rejoice in thy house, and shall possess
thy glory and thy might and thy power." 29. (32.) " And the *Angels*
shall drive thee *for* seven *years, and thou shalt not be seen nor
shalt speak with any man ;* they shall feed thee with grass as an ox,
and of the tender grass of the field shall thy pasture be ; (from iv.
23.) then, " Lo ! for thy glory they shall bind thee, and the house
of thy luxury and of thy kingdom shall another have."   30. (33.)
" Till *the morning*, all these things shall be fulfilled upon thee, Nebuchadnezzar king of Babylon, and nothing of all these things shall be

wanting. I Nebuchadnezzar king of Babylon was bound with chains for seven years. They fed me with grass as an ox, and I ate of the herb of the earth." 31.(34.) "And after seven years I gave my soul unto prayer, and I entreated for my sins before the Lord God of heaven, and for my ignorances I besought the great God of gods." from 30,(33.) related by, not of, Nebuchadnezzar. " And my hairs became as eagle's wings, my nails *as a lion's*, my flesh and my heart was deranged. I walked naked with the beasts of the field." Then follows seemingly a hint that some of this passed in a dream, (which was perhaps hinted also by the "Till the morning" ἕως πρωΐ 36,) 32, " I saw a dream, and conjectures seized me and, during a time, much sleep seized me, and deep slumber fell upon me. And at the end of 7 years, the time of my redemption came, and my sins and my ignorances were filled up before the God of heaven, and I besought the great God of gods for my ignorances. And lo, an angel called me from heaven, saying, N., serve the Holy God of heaven, and give glory to the most Highest; the kingdom of thy nation is given back to thee." 34. (37) " The king of heaven," is explained " who created the heaven and the earth and the seas and the rivers and all things in them ;" then, instead of, " all Whose works are truth and His ways judgment," follows the addition, " because He is God of gods, and Lord of lords and King of kings; for He doth signs and wonders, and changes times and seasons, taking away the kingdom of kings, and setting others in their stead. Henceforth I will serve Him ; and from fear of Him trembling hath seized me, and I praise all His saints. For the gods of the heathen have not power in themselves to remove the kingdom of a king to another king, and to slay and make alive, and to do signs and wonders, great and terrible, and to change things exceeding great, as the God of heaven did in me, and changed great things upon me. I, all the days that I am king, will offer sacrifices to the Most High for my soul, a sweet savour unto the Lord, and will do what is pleasing in His sight, I and my people, my nation, and my countries which are in my power. And as many as have spoken against the God of heaven, or shall be found speaking anything, these will I condemn to death. King Nebuchadnezzar wrote an encyclical epistle to all the nations and countries, and all tongues which dwell in all the countries to generations and generations. Praise ye the Lord, the God of heaven, and offer to Him sacrifice and oblation gloriously. I, king of kings, confess to Him gloriously, because He dealt thus with me. In that same day He seated me on my throne, and my might and my kingdom; I prevailed in my people, and my greatness was restored to me.'   Nebuchadnezzar the king to all nations and to all countries and to all who dwell in them.   'Peace be multiplied to you at all times.   And now I will shew you the deeds, which the great God has done with me.   But it seemed good to me to shew you and your sophists, that there is a God and that His wonders are great; His kingdom is an everlasting kingdom, His power from generation to generation.'   And he sent letters concerning all things which befel him in his kingdom, to all the nations which were under his rule."

ch. v. Of ch. v. 1, 4, 5, there is a double translation, but neither quite complete.   In the one, the translator counts the thousand guests, twice mentioned, as 2000; says that the feast was "on the day of the dedication of his kingdoms," joins the beginning of v. 2. to v. 4, " Belshazzar elevated by the wine, and boasting, praised all the gods of the heathen, molten and graven, in his place," and adds from v. 23, " and to God most High he did not give praise."   In v. 5. the words written on the wall are added, from v. 25, and an interpretation, "*Mane*, it is numbered, *Phares*, it is taken away, *Thekel*, it is weighed."   The 2nd translation is closer.   But it omits the number of the guests in both places in v. 1. and the mention of " the wives and concubines," v. 3.   3, 4, are abridged; " And they (the vessels) were brought, and they drank out of them and praised their idols made with hands," and added to, "And the God of the world, who had power over their breath, they praised not."   5. " over against king Belshazzar," for, " the wall of the king's palace."   6. " the king then hastened and arose and saw that writing, and his companions around him boasted; " instead of " the joints—against another."   7, 8. " to tell the interpretation of the writing; and they (the wise men) entered to behold, to see the writing," added ; " and they could not explain to the king the interpretation of the writing," " and no one could explain the interpretation of the writing," is repeated.   " There shall be given him power *of the third part of the kingdom*," for, " shall be third ruler in, &c.   So also in v. 16. and 29.   9. " Then the king called the queen concerning this sign and shewed her that it was great, and that no man can shew the king the interpretation of the writing."   10. " Then the queen mentioned to him concerning Daniel who was of the captivity of Judæa." (instead of v. 10.)   11, 12. " There is a man of knowledge and wisdom, and surpassing all the wise of Babylon, and a holy spirit is in him, and, in the days of the king thy father, he shewed exceeding great interpretations to Nebuchadnezzar thy father." 13-16. "art thou that Daniel—canst dissolve doubts," omitted. The speech begins v. 16, "O Daniel, canst thou shew me the interpretation, &c. 17. "Then Daniel stood over against the writing, and read, and thus answered the king, 'this is the writing, it is numbered, it is completed, it is taken away,' and the hand which wrote, stayed; and this is its interpretation." Then he omits " Let thy gifts—to another," v. 17, and the account of God's dealings with Nebuchadnezzar, v. 18-22, and he substitutes for 22-28, the account, as he had given it before, " O king, thou madest a feast to thy friends, and drankest wine, and the vessels of the house of the living God were brought to thee, and ye drank wine, thou and thy nobles," [the "wives and concubines," again omitted] "and ye praised," [for " thou didst praise,"] all the idols of men made with hands, [for " the gods of silver—nor know;"] and the Living God— and He gave thee thy kingdom," (for, " whose are all thy ways,") thou didst not *bless nor* praise." 25-28. " This is the interpretation of the writing. *Is numbered*, the time of thy kingdom; thy kingdom ceaseth, is cut short, and accomplished; thy kingdom is *given to the Medes and Persians*." For 30, 31, " And this interpretation came upon king B. and the kingdom was taken from the Chaldees, and was given to the Medes and Persians. And Artaxerxes of the Medes received the kingdom, and Darius full of days and glorious in old age."

vi. 1. " an hundred and twenty *and seven* Satraps," from Esther. (repeated v. 4.) 2-9. "And Daniel was one of the three men, having power above all in the kingdom; and Daniel was clad in purple, and was great and glorious before Darius the king, because he was glorious and of knowledge and understanding, and a holy spirit was in him, and he was prosperous in the affairs of the king which he did. Then the king purposed to set over his whole kingdom Daniel, *and the two men* whom he set with him, and 127 Satraps. But when the king purposed to set Daniel over his whole kingdom, then *the two youths* counselled together saying, (because they found no sin or ignorance against Daniel for which to accuse him to the king,) and said, come let us make *a decree against ourselves*, that no man shall make a request, or pray a prayer of any god for 30 days, except of Darius the king; else, he shall die; that they might defeat Daniel before the king and he be cast into the den of lions. For they knew that Daniel prayed and besought the Lord his God thrice a day. Then these men came and said before the king; ' we have made a decree and a statute that any man, who shall pray a prayer or ask a request of any god for 30 days, save of Darius the king, shall be cast into the den of lions." ["And they persuaded the king to constitute this law, and not change it, because they knew that Daniel prayed thrice a day, that he might be made guilty before the king, and be cast into the den of lions." added in Syriac Tetrapl. p. 64, 5.] 10, 11. " But when Daniel knew the decree, which he made against him, he opened the windows in his hyperöon toward Jerusalem, and fell on his face thrice in the day, as he did before, and prayed. And they *observed* Daniel and found him praying three times a day every day." 13, 14. "And they said to him, [the king,] we adjure thee by the decrees of the Medes and Persians, that thou change not the command, nor accept persons, nor lessen ought thou hast said, but rather punish the man who abode not by this decree. And he said, I will do as ye say, and this stands with me. And they said, Behold we found Daniel *thy friend* praying and beseeching the face of his God thrice a day. And the king, grieved, said that Daniel should be cast into the lion's den according to the decree which he made against him. Then the king was greatly grieved for Daniel and succoured to deliver him, until sunset, *from the hand of the Satraps*, and he could not deliver him from them. Darius the king cried out and said to Daniel, thy God whom thou servest continually *thrice a day*, He will deliver thee *from the hand of the lions ; until morning, be of good courage.*" 17. " Then Daniel was cast into the den of lions, and a stone, &c.,—that Daniel might not be taken away of them, nor the king take him up out of the den," for, " that the purpose might not be changed concerning Daniel." 18. 17. "And he was grieved for Daniel," for "neither were instruments, &c.—sleep went from him." " Then the God of Daniel, having thought of him, shut the mouths of the lions and they troubled not Daniel," added. 19. Darius "took with him the Satraps," added. 20. " O Daniel, art thou then alive, and hath thy God [not, " is He able ? "] saved thee from the lions and they have not disabled thee ? " 21. " Then Daniel *shouted with a loud voice* and said, 22. O king, I am alive and God hath saved me from the lions" (" sent His angel" omitted)—" but thou hast listened to men who mislead kings, and hast cast me into the den of lions for destruction," added. 23. " Then all the authorities were collected and saw Daniel, that the lions had not troubled him." 24. " Then those two men, who witnessed against Daniel," &c. omitting " or ever they came to the bottom of the den." 26. omits, "and his kingdom—unto the end." 27. " I Darius will be a worshipper of Him, and serve Him all my days ; for the idols made with hands cannot save, as the God of Daniel has redeemed Daniel.

28. And king Darius was added to his race, and Daniel was set over the kingdom of Darius, and Cyrus the Persian received his kingdom."

vii. 7. " It had ten horns *and many counsels* in its horns."   8. "And three of the first horns were dried up by it."   "And it made war with the saints," added.   12. " And *those around* it He removed from their power."   13. "And as the Ancient of days was present, and they who stood by were present with Him."   17. "four kingdoms, which shall perish from the earth," for, " which shall arise."   24. " and he *in evils* shall be diverse above the first."   26. " and they shall destroy " [not " his "] " power, and *they shall will* to defile and destroy."

viii. 2. " at the gate Ælam," for, " at the river Ulai" (" gate" for " river" in 6 also).   3. " and the higher ascended, but after this," for, " went up last ; " missing the relation of the Persian to the Median empire.   9. " one *strong* horn" (for, "a little horn,") "and prevailed and smote ; " then, " and to the North" for " the pleasant land."   11. " Until the chief captain shall deliver the captivity, and for him the everlasting mountains were broken, and their place was taken away, and sacrifice ; and he set it down to the ground, upon the earth, and they prospered, and it was, and the holy place shall be desolated.   And the sins were in the sacrifice; and righteousness was cast to the ground." 16. It adds, "And the man crying aloud said, the vision is as to that commandment." 19. "at the end of the indignation *to the sons of thy people*," added ; "for it shall still abide unto the time, &c." 23. "And at the end of their kingdom, when *their* sins are fulfilled."   25. " And his purpose shall be against the saints," for "And his policy ; " " for the destruction of men and shall make a gathering of hand and shall repay," for, " against the Prince of princes, and he shall be broken without hand."

ix. 1. " Darius the son of Xerxes, of the Median race who reigned," [plural] &c.   10. " to obey Thy law, which Thou gavest before Moses and us through Thy servants the prophets," for, " to walk in His laws which He set before us by, &c."   12. " whatever Thou hast judged to bring," for, "that judged us."   17. " upon Thy holy mountain" for " Thy sanctuary."   19. " upon thy city *Sion* and thy people *Israel*." 21. " in my sleep" for " in the vision ; " " approached me," for " touched me."   On the grave alterations in the prophecy of the 70 weeks, see above p. 379, 80.

x. 1. " In the *first* year of Cyrus," for, " the third."   5. " and from the midst of him was light," for, " fine gold of Uphaz."   9. " And I heard *not* the voice of his speech."   13. " The General of the king of Persians," for, " the prince of the kingdom of Persia."   " And I left

him there with the General of the king of Persians," for, " And I
remained there with the kings of Persia." 16. " like the similitude of
the hand of man," for, " of the sons of men."   20. " to fight with the
General of the king of the Persians, and I went forth, and lo the
General of the Greeks came in."   21. " except Michael the Angel,"
· for, " your prince."

xi. 1. " And in the first year of Cyrus the king, he said to me, be
strong, and be of good courage, and now I have come to shew you,
&c." for, " And I, in the first year of Darius the Mede, I stood to
confirm and strengthen him, and now I will show you, &c." 2. "3 kings
have resisted," for, " are standing up ;" " he shall rise up against
every king of Greece," for, " stir up all against the kingdom of
Greece."   4. " not according to his strength," for, " not to his posterity ; " " and he shall *teach* to others these things," for, " and to
others besides these." מִלְפַּר for מִלְבַר 5. &c. " kingdom of Egypt " for,
" King of the South," " and he shall strengthen the kingdom of Egypt,"
for, " and the King of the South shall be strong."   6. " He shall bring
them, and the King of Egypt shall enter the kingdom of the North
to make treaties," for, " they shall associate themselves and *the
daughter* of the King of the South shall come to the King of the
North to make (i. e. produce) agreements ; " " and his arm shall be
paralysed and of those who go with him, and shall not prevail, for
his arm shall not establish strength and shall abide for a time," for,
"and *she* shall not retain the power of the arm, and he shall not stand,
nor his arm, and *she* shall be given up and those who brought *her*
and he that begat *her* and he that strengtheneth *her*, in the times."
7. " And the King of the North shall come to his power (army) in
his might and shall make *a tumult*," for, " and he shall come to his
army and shall enter the fortress of the King of the North and shall
do against them."   8. "And their gods *shall he overthrow* with their
molten images, and their crowds with their desirable vessels the silver and the gold, shall he lead into captivity to Egypt," for, " and
their gods also with their molten images, with their desirable, &c.
(missing the fact in which it was fulfilled ; see ab. p. 445.) " and there
shall be a year to the King of North," for, " and he shall stand years
more than the King of North."   9. " And the King of Egypt shall
enter a kingdom days," for, " And he shall enter the kingdom of the
King of the South and shall return to his land."   10. "And his son,
[i. e. the son of the King of the South, in both cases giving the victory
to Egypt,] and shall be irritated and shall gather a gathering of a great
multitude and shall enter with it sweeping, (So Syr. κατασύρων for the

κατὰ Σύρων of the Edd.) pass through and return and shall be exasperated greatly," for, "and his sons shall arouse themselves, and shall gather a multitude of many forces, and one coming shall come, and shall flood and pass through and return, &c. and they shall strive together even to his fortress." 12. "and shall trouble many and shall not fear," for, "and shall cast down ten thousands and shall not be *strong*." 13. "and shall gather a gathering *of a city*," added: "in the completion of the time of a year," for, "at the end of the times, years." 14. "Thoughts shall arise against the King of Egypt and *he shall rebuild what is fallen of thy nation*, and he shall arise to raise up the prophecy, and they shall stumble ; " for, "and in those times many shall stand against the King of the South, and the sons of the robbers of thy people shall lift themselves up to establish a vision, and shall stumble." 15. "and shall turn his spears," for, "and shall cast up a mount," "and take *the* [for " a "] strong city ; and the arms of the King of Egypt shall stand, with his princes, and he shall have no power to resist *him*," for, "and the arms of the South shall *not* stand, nor his chosen people, and there shall be no power to stand." 16. "And he shall stand in the land," omitting " of desire," which marks it to be Judæa ; "and all things which are in his hand shall be accomplished," for, "it shall be consumed by his hand." 17. "and shall not persuade and shall not be," for, "and she shall not stand and shall not be for him." 18. "and he shall turn his face to the *sea* and shall take many persons," for, "to the *islands* and shall take many ;" "and shall turn the anger of their reproach in an oath according to his reproach," for, "and a ruler shall make to cease his reproach to him, besides that he shall turn back his reproach to him." 20. "And there shall arise from his root, a plant of a kingdom for rising up, a man striking the glory of a king, and in the last days," for, "in some days " (אחרים for אֲחֵרִים, as though it had been בְּאַחֲרִית הַיָּמִים.) 21. "a king shall be strong in his lot," for, "obtain the kingdom by flatteries." 22. "And the arms, *which are broken*, he shall break before him," for, "And with the arms of a flood." 23. "And with the covenant and the people banded with him he shall do falsehood, and against a strong nation with a very small nation ;" for, " And also *a prince of* covenant ; and from the binding unto him he shall do treachery and shall go up and be strong with a small people." 24. "Suddenly he shall desolate a city," for, "in security and on the rich places of a province shall he enter ;" " and against *the* strong city shall he devise, and his thoughts shall be in vain," for, "and against fortresses shall he devise his devices, and even to the time."   26. "And his cares shall consume him, and they shall turn him away, and shall pass by and he shall hiss at, and many shall fall wounded," for, "And they who eat of his royal meat [pathbag] shall break him, and his army shall overflow and many, &c."   30. " And Romans shall come and shall expel him, and shall rebuke him angrily," [Popilius] for, "And ships of Chittim shall come against him, and he shall be grieved and return and shall be wroth ; " "and shall devise against them, because they have forsaken the covenant of the Holy One," for, "and shall observe those who forsake, &c." 31. "the holy place *of fear*," for, "the sanctuary, the fortress."   32. "And in sins of the covenant they shall defile in a hard nation and the people who knoweth these things," (אלה for אלהיו) &c. for, " And they who do wickedly against the covenant he shall corrupt with flatteries, and the people who knoweth their God, &c."   33. " and shall be worn away in it," for " and by the flame," (dividing בלחבה into ובלה בה but neglecting the plur.) " and in foray *of days they shall be defiled.*"   34. "and shall be gathered to them many in a city, and many as if appointed by lot," for, "and there shall cleave many to them in flatteries."   35. " And of those who understand, there shall *think* with view to purify themselves and to be elected," &c. for, "And of those who understand, there shall *stumble,* to purify among them and to cleanse, &c."   36. "for the end is towards him," for, " for that which is determined shall be done."   37. omits " nor regard any god." 38. " and mighty nations shall be subjected to him, to his place he shall move," for, " and the god of forces on his place he shall honour."   39. " And in the objects of desire of cities he shall do, and to a strong fortress he shall come with a strange god, whom when he shall recognise, he shall multiply glory and shall lord it over him much, and shall partition country as a gift," for, (38.) "and with things desired; (39,) and he shall do to the fortresses of strong [places] with a strange god whom he shall acknowledge, shall enlarge it with glory, and he shall make them rule over many, and shall divide land for a price."   40. " and shall come into the land of Egypt," for, "into the lands, and shall overflow and pass over."   41. "And he shall invade My land," for " the pleasant land."   43. " the place of gold and the place of silver," for, " the hidden treasures of gold and silver," rendering מכמנים as if מקום.   45. " he shall place his tent there, (as if it were אהלו and omitting ואפדנו,) between the seas and the mountain of the will (צבו for צבי) of the Holy One and the hour (עה for עת) of his end shall come."

    xii. 1. " Michael, the great angel," for, " prince ; " " all the peo-

ple shall be *exalted* who shall be found, &c." for, " shall be *delivered*."
2. " in the breadth," [for, " the dust,"] " of the earth shall arise, some
to everlasting life, and some to reproach and some to dispersion and
everlasting shame."   3. " they who confirm my words," for, " who
turn many to righteousness."   4. " until the many rave out their
madness, ἀπομανῶσιν," (" are mad " Syr.) " and the earth be filled
with iniquity," for, " many shall run to and fro, and knowledge shall
be increased."   6. " when shall be the end of the wonders, *which thou
hast spoken to me*, and the purifying of these ? " added.   7. " I heard
the man."   8. " I understood not *at that time*," added. " and whose
are these parables," added.   10. " and rise to thy glory," for, " stand
in thy lot."

Note F.

*On the secular predictions which Dr. Stanley parallels in regard
to exactness of fulfilment with those of the Old Testament.*

Dr. Stanley produces a certain number of alleged predictions in
secular history, as counterparts of " the predictions of the *political
events* of their own and the surrounding nations" in the Hebrew prophets, i. e. (in religious language) " of God's judgments upon both
for their sins against Himself and their fellow-men."   He says, " every
one knows instances, both in ancient and modern times, of predictions
which have been uttered and fulfilled in regard to events of this kind.
Sometimes such predictions have been the result of political foresight.
Many instances will occur to students of history.   Even within our
own memory the great catastrophe of the disruption of the United
States of America *was foretold, even with the exact date, several
years beforehand.*   Sometimes there has been an anticipation of
some future epoch in the pregnant sayings of eminent philosophers
or poets ; as, for example, the intimation of the discovery of America
by Seneca ; or of Shakspere by Plato, or the Reformation by Dante.
Sometimes the same result has been produced by the power of
divination, granted, in some inexplicable manner, to ordinary men.
Of such a kind were many of the ancient oracles, the fulfilment of
which, according to Cicero, could not be denied without a perversion
of all history.   Such was the foreshadowing of the twelve centuries
of Roman dominion by the legend of the apparition of the twelve
vultures to Romulus, which was so understood 400 years before its
actual accomplishment.   Such, but with less certainty, was the tra-

ditional prediction of the conquest of Constantinople by the Mussulmans; the alleged predictions by ABp. Malachi, whether composed in the 11th or the 16th century, of the series of Popes down to the present time; not to speak of the well-known instances which are recorded both in French and English history. But there are several points, which at once place the Prophetic predictions on a different level from any of these. *It is not, that they are more exact in particulars of time and place;* none can be more so than that of the twelve centuries of the Roman Empire; and our Lord Himself has excluded the precise knowledge of times and seasons from the widest and highest range of the prophetic vision." (Jewish Church, p. 463, 4. The Bible, its Form and Substance, p. 80-82.)

It might safely be admitted, that the outward prediction of time and place are of the body rather than of the soul of prophecy; yet, as indications that *He* revealed Himself, Who alone could know long before what He willed to bring to pass in His Providence, the predictions by the Hebrew prophets are not to be paralleled by any human history.

Definite predictions of the Hebrew prophets have been instanced above. Dr. Stanley's instances of secular fulfilment are unhappy.

1) Sterling, as quoted by Mr Spence, so far from predicting "the great catastrophe of the disruption of the United States" *at the end* of the four years, says, that no wise man would predict any thing even within those four years. " It appears to me, that amid so many elements of uncertainty as to the future, both from the excited state of men's minds in the States themselves, and the complication of surrounding circumstances, no wise man would venture to foretell the probable issue of American affairs *during* the next four years." (On the American Union, p. 14.) And this was written amid all the heavings, which preceded the bursting of the volcano. It followed, after statesmen had, one after another, seen the element of that disruption. The probability of the severance of the North and South has been a speculation to which the older of us have been long familiar. And now who would venture to predict the time of the close of that sad war?

2) The so-called prophecies of S. Malachi have long been recognised to be a forgery, unmeaning except for the immediate purpose, for which they were " forged by the partizans of the Card. Simoncelli, one of the candidates for the tiara, who was designated by the words 'de antiquitate orbis,' because he was of Orvietto, in Latin, ' urbs vetus.'" (Biogr. univ. v. Wion.) " Menestrier published ' a refutation of the pretended prophecies of S. Malachi,' Paris, 1689, written with much

solidity. Don Feijoo also refuted those pretended prophecies in his *Teatro critico.*" (Ib. v. Malachie.) The Nouveau Dictionnaire Historique by MM. Chaudon and Delandine speaks of "the errors and anachronisms with which this impertinent list swarms." "The forgetfulness of common sense makes itself felt in a few pages. Those who have set themselves to explain those too-noted insipidities, always find some allusion, forced or probable, in the country, name, arms, birth, talents of the Popes, the Cardinalate or dignities which they had borne; &c. e. g. the prophecy which related to Urban viii. was *Lilium et Rosæ.* ' It was fulfilled to the letter, (say these absurd interpreters,) for that Pope had, in his coat of arms, bees, which suck lilies and roses ?'" (art. Malachie and Wion.)

3) " In the Mosque of Sultan Mahommed II." says v. Hammer, " which was finished A.D. 874. (1469.) there stands, to the right of the main door, on a marble slab on azure field in gold raised characters the tradition of the prophet relating to Constantinople ; 'they *will conquer* Constantinople; and blessed the prince, blessed the army, which shall fulfil this ;'" (Constant. u. d. Bosporos, i. 393,) or (as he renders more exactly in Gesch. d. Osm. Reich. p. 523.), "the best prince is he who conquers it, and the best army, his army." This tradition being above 8 centuries after Mohammed, has, of course, no value. It reappears in a different form in Ockley, the conquest being presupposed rather than prophesied ; " Mahomet having said," says Ockley, ' The sins of the first army that takes the city of Cæsar are forgiven.' " (Hist. of Sarac. ii. 128.) Ockley referring only vaguely to Bokhari, who, early in the 3rd. cent. after Mohammed, selected 7000 traditions which he held to be genuine, only of some 267,000, I applied to my friend M. Reinaud, Prof. of Arabic at Paris, and Member of the Institute, &c., not doubting that with his large knowledge, he would be able to point out to me the passage in the *Sahih.* This, with his well-known kindness, which I have before experienced, he has done, amid his many labours. It puts an end to all question about prophecy. The passage is this ; " Omm-Heram has related to us that she heard the prophet say, ' the first army of my people which shall war by sea, will acquire merits (with God.') Omm-Heram said, ' I said, o apostle of God, I will be among them.' He said, ' thou shalt be among them.' Then the prophet said, ' The first army of my people which shall *attack* the city of Cæsar, their sins are forgiven them.' Then I said, ' I will be with them, o Apostle of God.' He said, ' no ! ' " Mr Reinaud adds, " There is no question but that Mahomet conceived the

idea of an invasion of the Roman empire and of the kingdom of Persia by his disciples. He himself, shortly before his death, tried his strength against the Roman forces in Syria. But the passage does not say what Ockley makes him say. It does not say that Constantinople would be taken. I will only add that in the *Sahih* what relates to the Jews and Turks, consists of some puerilities, and that nothing there resembles a prophecy. The passages cited by M. de Hammer in his history of the Ottoman empire are somewhat singular. I regret that I have been unable to read them in the works themselves, from which M. de Hammer has derived them. I explain them thus. The Seljucidæ, and subsequently the Ottoman Turks, subdued successively the whole of Asia Minor, and presented themselves before Constantinople. Afterwards the Ottomans invaded Thrace, and gradually the Greek empire found itself reduced to the Capital. It then became evident that, considering the political condition of Christian Europe, Constantinople would fall, like all the rest. Prophecies might be made without fear of failure.

" Ibn Khaldoun has given a paragraph of his prolegomena to the prophetic character of Mahomet. As he flourished before the end of the 14th cent. and so, more than 60 years before the capture of Constantinople, his testimony would have had some value; but he says not a word of it. (See his text in the Notices et Extraits, T. xvi. p. 160. and the French translation, Ib. xix. p. 205.)"

The two prophecies given by v. Hammer in his Gesch. d. Osmann. Reiches, L. xii. T. i. p. 522, 3, are, the one that already cited, and which seems to be a false colouring of the tradition given in the *Sahih ;* the other is indeed remarkable, in that it is stated to rest on undoubted authority, but is a fanatic prophecy, misapplied to the Ottoman capture.

"'Have you heard of a city, of which one side is land, the two others sea ? ' They said, ' Yea, o Apostle of God.' He said, ' The last hour will not come, without its being conquered by 70,000 sons of Isaac. When they come to it, they will not fight against it with weapons and engines of war, but with the word, There is no God but God, and God is great. Then will one side of the sea-walls fall; and at the second time, the second ; and at the third time, the wall on the land side; and they will enter in with gladness.' " The framer of this prophecy expected the walls of Constantinople to fall, like those of Jericho, which he must have had in his mind. He expected it to fall before Arabs, " sons of Isaac," not before Turks. Von Hammer says of it, " Ali and Edris guarantee the genuineness of this tradition through the first accreditors of the Hadith. The false application of it to the Ottomans has misled some historians, as the old Neshri, to derive the Turks from Esau, the son of Isaac, which however Ali (f. 7.) contradicts as a shameful error." (Ib. p. 668.) Yet, contrary to the expectation and the prophecy, it did fall before Turks, having been besieged seven times by the Arabs between A.D. 654, (Hejra 34.) and 798 (Hej. 182.); and, between A.D. 1396, (Hej. 797.) and A.D. 1422, (H. 826.) four times by the Turks, by whom it was taken A.D. 1453. (H. 857.) v. Hammer, Ib. p. 669. The Arabs are, in part, sons of Isaac through Esau. The framers of the prediction anticipated that the representatives of the followers of the prophet would be Arabs to some indefinite period, " near the last hour;" he expected a miraculous destruction of Constantinople; it was besieged 7 times by those, before whose war-cry he expected it miraculously to fall. It did not fall before those before whom he said that it would fall ; it fell in an ordinary way, not in that predicted ; it was besieged in the way in which he said that it would not be besieged ; lastly it fell, but its walls fell not. Every detail of the prediction is directly contrary to the fact. As for the mere capture, it befalls all great cities in turn ; so that a prediction of the capture of any city " before the end of the world" would be the safest of all prophecies. But the prediction did not anticipate, what is now certain, that, as soon as Christian jealousies permit, " before the end of the world," it will be wrested from its captors.

4) The " legend of the apparition of the 12 vultures to Romulus," is quoted by Censorinus (de Die Natali, c. 17. fin.) A.D. 238, from Varro who died 28, B.C. Varro stated (Antiq. L. xviii.) that " he had heard Vettius, no common augur, of great genius, in disputing a match with any the most learned, say, " *If it was so,* as the historians related, as to the auguries of the founding of the city of Romulus and the 12 vultures, *since* the Roman people had passed 120 years safe, *it would* reach 1200." A conjectural inference from a hypothetical fact! " If it was so as they relate." 1) The 12 vultures, if there were such, (and the vulture apparently was not then a bird of Italy) were to signify that the people should be safe during a period of years, which was to be a decuple of their own number, and this, since the event had shewn it to be more than 10, was to be 100. But 2) there is nothing as to Roman *dominion.* Varro speaks not of dominion, but of " safety." The vulture too is not a ravening, but a gentle bird, which preys only on carcases. 3) Then, as to time, while it was held as certain that Rome was founded 753, B.C., the ex-

tinction of the Western empire, A.D. 476, or 479, furnished a term, not much in excess of 1200 years from its supposed foundation.   But now, when, by common consent, it is agreed, that the early traditions as to Rome are uncertain ; that it was doubtless never " founded " at all, but gradually " grew ; " that, consequently, the era "ab Urbe condita,"" from the foundation of Rome," is a convenient measure of time, but is itself a fiction ; that, within this period, the 240 years, assigned to its 7 supposed kings, are an artificial calculation, based on the supposition that 3 generations went to a century, whence 7 kings would yield $233\frac{1}{3}$ years, which were probably rounded into 240, as the double of the 120 years, assigned to the consuls down to the burning of the city by the Gauls (Mommsen d. Rōm. Chronol. p. 133); it would be monstrous to speak of the 1200 years duration of "Roman empire," as the fulfilment of prophecy, since there is no certain date, within a century, from which to begin.   Whatever may have been the anticipations of a decaying people, amid a false chronology, as seen in Sidonius or Claudian, (who expected the destruction of Rome even be-before the 12 centuries had expired,) the conjectural interpretation was in no sense fulfilled ; 1200 years was not meant as any term of its duration.   Since it had survived for 120 years, it was to survive 1200 ; but, on that same principle, if it survived the 1200, it might be inferred that it would survive 12000.   There is no hint that it should perish *then*.   Had it perished *before*, Vettius' interpretation would have failed.   But Vettius did not anticipate any change at the end of the 1200 years.   Nor was there any real change as to Rome itself.   The change of dynasty did not worsen, it improved the condition of the people : Rome is still " the eternal city."   Even as to empire, its throne still remained set up in " New Rome " for nearly twice the 1200 years ; and now too the empire of Rome is diffused over many millions more than its temporal sway ever held controlled.

5) The one expression in Seneca's words, which has suggested the thought that they were a prophetic anticipation of the discovery of America is the mention of " annis seris."   People forgetting, or not knowing, that the words are in the mouth of supposed contemporaries of Medea (the Chorus,) and are ascribed to the fabulous times of Greece, have projected on those " late years" from the date of Seneca. In this way, the " late ages," which really fitted in with the times of Seneca himself, were thought marvellously to correspond with the 14 centuries between Seneca and Columbus.   Else, there is nothing remarkable in the words.   They do but express Seneca's belief of the

old traditions about the land beyond the seas.   Whatever be the source
of the story which Plato ascribes to the Egyptian priests, and which
he himself asserted to be "strange but altogether true," (Tim. p. 20.
D.) the description does correspond to the situation of America, a large
continent with intervening islands.   The words are; " the writings
state, how great a might, coming aggressively against all Europe and
Asia, invading from without from the Atlantic, your city checked.
For at that time the sea there was navigable.   For it had, before the
mouth which ye call the pillars of Hercules, an island, larger than
Africa and Asia together, from which there was access to the other
islands, and from the islands to the whole opposite continent, which
encircled that real ocean.   For all this, which is within that mouth
of which we speak, [the Mediterranean,] seems a harbour with a narrow entrance; but *that* may indeed be called ocean, and the land
which encircleth it may, correctly and in truth, be called a continent.
And in this island Atlantis there was a great and wondrous power of
kings which held the whole island and many other islands and parts
of the continent; and moreover they ruled these interior parts of
Africa, as far as Egypt, and Europe as far as Tyrrhenia."   (Ib. 24.
E—25. B.)   He further states that the island Atlantis, (not, the yet
further encircling continent,) "was submerged, so that the ocean there
was difficult to explore, on account of the shallowness and the mud
left when the island settled down."   Strabo says, that the account of
the submersion of Atlantis " admitted of not being a fiction," and that
it was thought probable by Posidonius (a Stoic as well as Seneca). ii.
p. 102. B.C.   Proclus also adduced from Marcellus, in his Æthiopica,
traditions of the existence of a " most exceeding large island Atlantis which was indeed there," among the inhabitants of an island, 125
miles in size, in the Atlantic. (on the Tim. p. 54. F.)   Ammianus
Marcellinus (xvii. 6. 13.) speaks of it, as not doubting of its truth;
Diodorus alludes to it. (iii. 54.)   Aristotle distinctly held it to be
probable, that there was such a continent and such islands.   " The
common account divides the world into continents and islands, not
knowing that the whole is one island, encircled by the Atlantic.   And
it is probable that afar there are many others, in the parts opposite
to these, some larger, some less; but all, save this, invisible to us.
For as our islands are to these seas, so is this our continent to the
Atlantic; and many other continents to the whole sea; for these too
are in a way large islands, washed on all sides by some great seas."
(de Mundo c. 3.)   Plutarch relates that Sertorius met some sailors,
who had recently come by sea from the Atlantic, the Fortunate

islands, 10,000 stadia,[1250 miles] from Libya.(vit. Sertorii, c. 8.) In the immediate context in Seneca the Chorus is speaking of bold navigations. " Every bound removed, and cities placed their walls in new lands.   The Indian drinks the cold Araxes ; the Persians the Elbe and the Rhine." What marvel then, that he should imagine that Plato's conception or tradition should be realised, and that the muddy sea, which must in his time have ceased to be believed, since Britain was laid open, yielding no hindrance, Plato's vast encircling continent, his own "ingens tellus," should be at length discovered ? When the spherical form of the earth was known, as it was in the days of Seneca, the existence of another Continent, corresponding to our's, became even more probable, than that all should be one expanse of sea.   It has been pointed out to me, that the Stoic philosophy, in other ways, carried men's minds beyond the Roman " world."   Horsley pointed out, in answer to Collins' taunt in regard to these words of Seneca, that there is nothing definite in his description. Seneca says not, across what sea the discovery would be made.   The anticipation is realised in Australasia, as much as in America ; and the only definite statement, that "Thule should not be the utmost land," if pressed, would be incorrect," as it points precisely to that quarter of the globe where discovery has ever been at a stand, where the ocean, to this hour, opposes his eternal barrier of impervious unnavigable ice." (Serm. 17 on 2 Pet. i. 20, 21.)   The argument, however, is superfluous, for Seneca's words relate only to an existing belief, that there was such a continent, and that this belief would prove true.   It is not, like prophecies of Holy Scripture, a foreannouncement of events, whose causes lay hid in the mind of God.

6) With regard to the heathen oracles, Cicero states the two sides in the two books on Divination; in the first book, in their favour, in the name of his brother Quintus ; in the second in his own, as one uncertain. (de Div. ii. 3.)   There he gives his opinion that the oracles of Apollo were " partly false ; partly true by accident, as happens very often in all language ; partly involved and obscure, partly ambiguous," as those stated by Herodotus and Ennius to have been given to Crœsus and Pyrrhus.   (Ib. 56.)   For myself, I see no evidence of any well-authenticated oracle, involving supernatural knowledge of the future.   If Herodotus' story be true, that the Pythian answered right, as to what Crœsus was at that moment doing, this related to the *present* not to the *future*, and is no more than mesmerists of this day claim. On the other hand, even according to the story, it alone of all

the oracles was right thus far, so that Crœsus pronounced it to be "the only oracle ; " (Herod. i. 48.) and it, with another oracle which he thought somehow to have spoken the truth, are related to have given him the well-known ambiguous answer about "destroying a mighty empire," encouraging his wishes, but providing an escape from the charge of falsehood in case of his failure. (Ib. 53.) And this in a prophecy as to the immediate future, and the issue of a war which they encouraged.

7, 8) Those best read in Dante and Plato are at a loss to find any trace·of a prediction either of the Reformation or of Shakspere. Dante, with his firm faith in all Roman doctrine, could not have imagined or anticipated such a disruption as Luther's. I can find nothing which bears a semblance to it.

In denying that there is any proof as to *these* prophecies or the genuineness of that set attributed to A Bp. Malachi, I do not, of course, deny *Christian* prophecy after the Apostolic age, such as I have myself pointed out, as having been vouchsafed to St. Cyprian, along the whole course of his Episcopate. (Pref. to S. Cyprian's Epist. p. xxi. See also references to other prophecies, S. Cypr. Ep. ix. p. 27, 8. n. k.) Prophecy, in the Christian Church, is but a fulfilment of the prophecy of Joel, vouchsafed or intermitted, as well as the gift of miracles, as God sees best. In both cases, the whole question is one of evidence.

ADDENDA et CORRIGENDA.
Addition to p. 481.

Among the characteristics of the King, who is the Object of Ps. lxxii, I should have mentioned His perpetual Intercession. The words, "And He shall pray for him continually," (Ps. lxxii. 15.) anticipate the revelation by St. Paul, "He ever liveth to make intercession for them." (Heb. vii. 26. add Rom. viii. 34.) The words, בַּעֲדוֹ יִתְפַּלֵּל, cannot be rendered, as in the P. B. version, "prayer shall be made ever *unto* Him ; " on the other hand, the idiom is used exclusively of the intercession of one nearer to God for one less near. It is used of Abraham, who as "a prophet" was to intercede for Abimelech, that he might live, Gen. xx. 7; of Moses, interceding for Aaron after the sin of the calf, Deut. ix. 20 ; of Samuel interceding for the people, on their putting away their idols, 1 Sam. vii. 5 ; of his intercession after the offence in asking for a king, asked for by them and owned by him as his perpetual office, Ib. xii. 19-23 ; of the prophet interceding for Jeroboam at his request, that the use of his hand might be restored to him, 1 Kgs. xiii. 6 ; of Zedekiah's request to Jeremiah, "intercede with the Lord our God for us," Jer. xxxvii. 3 ; of the like request of the

628 ADDENDA.

people to Jeremiah, Jer. xlii. 2. 20, and as forbidden by God, on the ground
that He would not remit the punishment, Jer. vii. 16. xi. 14. xiv. 11; of the
duty of the Jews in the captivity to intercede for the heathen, Ib. xxix. 7 ; of
Job, interceding for his friends that they might be forgiven, Job. xlii. 10. These
are all the cases in which the Concordances, at least, give the idiom. הִתְפַּלֵּל
is also used with עַל of the person for whom intercession is made, Job xlii. 8,
and with לְ 1 Sam. ii. 25.

Mr Filipowski, (known as the learned Editor of the Yuchasin of Zacut, of
the Lexicon of Menachem B. Merzuk, with the Teshuboth of Donash b. Librat
&c) who cast the Hebrew type for this work, has, by a thoughtful arrangement
of the "cases," which only a Hebrew probably could have lighted upon, made it
possible to use Hebrew type, in which the vowel-points are on the same "body"
as the letter. Those who have known the difficulty of combining pointed Hebrew with English type will appreciate the value of the discovery ; for such it
is. Mr F. has kindly corrected for me the " proofs " of the Hebrew of the last
sheets and has pointed out to me errata which, with ageing eyes, I had failed
to see in the proof. I have not noticed those which (like the omission of the
mute ,) could not perplex any one. Some pages I cancelled.

	read	for	
p. 24 pen.	סָבְכָא		סָבְכָא
28 note 1,	פְּסַנְתֵּרִין		פְּסַנ
53 ult.	יִשְׁאֶלֶנְכוֹן		כֵּן
54 n. 8.	בָּאֲרִין		רִין
58 note	סָד		סִיד
68 pen.	חֱיֵיתִי		תִי
75	Abbé		Abbe
179	חתם		תתם
185 four times	ס		ס
199 three times	ה		ה
313	בְּהִשְׁתַּחֲוָיתִי		ס
323 Not. 7. l. 3	ס		ס
324 n. 3. l. 2.	lix		xxxviii.
—n. 4. l. ult.	יִשְׁבִּיצַנִי סִפָּרִים		עֲנִי סָם
343 4 from bel.	ה		ח
345 note 9	סָלְכָת		נַּת
358 note 2	בְּרֻדִים		בְּרֻדִים
478 n. 1 ult.	סָלְכִי		יְ
483 n. 7. l. 3.	צֶדֶק		י
496 n. 8. l. 1.	יִפָּרֶה		י
506 l. 4. from bel.	ר		ר
520 note 3. l. 4. from bel.	ת		ה

Also in p. 250, n. 2. l. 11. the words should run, "and, in lieu of אִמְרֵי, אִמְרֵי
for אֲמִירֵי &c ; " i. e. Bochart, not seeing any explanation of the prophecy, coin-
ed a Hebrew plural, אֲמִירֵי, overlooking the ground why the Hebrews would not
use it.

THE END.